MILITARY WIVES'

NEW TESTAMENT

with Psalms & Proverbs

NEW INTERNATIONAL VERSION

MILITARY WIVES'
NEW TESTAMENT
with Psalms & Proverbs

90 DAYS *of* ENCOURAGEMENT *and* HOPE

ZONDERVAN®

TABLE OF CONTENTS

[FOREWORD]

Dear military wife,

Just as your husband is equipped with the proper armor and weaponry to do the job for which he has been trained, so you too need to be equipped for the battles you face daily on the home front — whether or not your spouse is currently deployed.

That's why I couldn't be more thrilled that you have picked up this Bible. If what you want — what you desperately crave — is a faith that shields you, a hope that sustains you, and a peace that defies the stress of your lifestyle, there is simply no substitute for the Word of God.

Ephesians 6 tells us to put on the armor of God: the belt of truth, the breastplate of righteousness, the gospel of peace, the shied of faith, the helmet of salvation, and the sword of the Spirit, which is the Word of God (see verses 14 – 17). Did you notice that our soul armor begins and ends with Scripture?

The Bible is powerful, living and active; it is sharper than any two-edged sword. And it is relevant to *you*. Amazingly, wonderfully and undeniably relevant.

I'm sure my own experience echoes yours when I say that not many people in my life could relate to what I went through once I married my husband and became a military wife. If I shared my struggles with those outside the military, I found they couldn't relate. And their advice, frankly, wasn't always applicable to my situation because of the deep chasm between civilian and military cultures. Eventually, many people ran out of things to say.

But God never did. And he never will. He has something to say to all of us, if we will only listen.

Do you feel alone due to a deployment, long work hours or emotional detachment from your husband? God says: "Never will I leave you; never will I forsake you" (Hebrews 13:5).

Does your heart ache from whatever separates you from your spouse, whether that separation is caused by distance or conflict? The Bible says we will never suffer any separation from our heavenly bridegroom: "Neither death nor life, neither angels or demons, neither the present nor the future, nor any powers, neither height nor depth, nor anything else in all creation, will be able to separate us from the love of God that is in Christ Jesus our Lord" (Romans 8:38 – 39).

Is your spirit burdened with unspeakable grief? "The Lord is close to the broken-hearted and saves those who are crushed in spirit" (Psalm 34:18).

Are you tempted to believe lies about yourself, about your life or about God? The Bible has the antidote for that too: "We demolish arguments and every pretension that sets itself up against the knowledge of God, and we take captive every thought to make it obedient to Christ" (2 Corinthians 10:5).

No matter what challenges you face in life right now, God always has something to say about it. I am amazed by that, and I want you to be amazed too. In more than 30 instances, the gospels tell us the people who heard Jesus speak were "amazed." If we spend time with Jesus by reading his Word and talking to him through prayer, we can't help but be amazed as well.

The Bible you hold in your hands contains 60 Reinforcements (devotions) written by military wives from all branches of service to illustrate how specific Scriptures speak into your life as a military wife. There are also 30 stories of Home Front Heroes from several American wars, including the Revolutionary War and the recent wars in Iraq and Afghanistan. In addition to a subject index and a biography of each contributor, a Basic Training section located in the back will guide you through a more in-depth study of 10 specific Bible passages. I hope these additional features will serve to encourage your heart and strengthen your spirit.

But, as in any devotional Bible, the most important aspect is the text of the Bible itself. Those of us who have contributed stories and devotions have strived to make sure our words are grounded in God's Word. But we are merely people. God, the author of life itself, is the author of the Bible. If you read only what we military wives have written, you may be encouraged. But if you also read the Bible text between the Reinforcements and Home Front Heroes stories, your life will be transformed.

As you read, pray for wisdom and understanding. Pray that you will interpret the Scriptures correctly and that the Lord will open your eyes to what he wants you to learn about him, about yourself and about what it means to "live a life worthy of the calling you have received" (Ephesians 4:1). Meditate on what you read. Write verses on note cards or sticky notes and place them around your house to help you focus your attention on God's Word throughout the day.

Just as surely as a physical enemy attacks our military, the enemy of your soul will attack you. The Bible is both your protection and your weapon. Read it, dwell in it, pray it, wield it. Be strong in the Lord and in his mighty power.

Together in Christ,
Jocelyn Green
General Editor

★ ★ ★

[HOW TO USE THIS BIBLE]

D o you ever feel like most of the people in your life don't quite understand the unique challenges you face as a military wife? Your husband's training, deployment and reintegration add an extra level of strain to everyday life. Frequent moves, unpredictable schedules and, in some cases, caregiving make stability an elusive reality.

We get it. More important, so does God. And he has something to say to you about exactly what you're going through.

The *NIV Military Wives' New Testament* was designed to guide military wives like you through Psalms, Proverbs and the New Testament by applying God's Word directly to the lives of heroes at home — military wives like you! It will help you align your focus to the unchanging character of God rather than the ever-changing circumstances of your life, and at the same time, it will provide hope, encouragement and spiritual maturity.

This Bible contains 90 reflective readings, all of them from veteran women of God who have walked where you walk as the wife of a military man. Each reading is firmly anchored to a relevant passage of Scripture, and each features a key verse, a devotional thought, an application question and a closing prayer. We encourage you to begin each time of meditation by first reading and reflecting on God's Word. Then we ask you to consider the devotions, applications and prayers in the illuminating glow of God's Word itself.

In the back of the Bible you will find additional materials to comfort and strengthen you on the journey.

Reinforcements

Throughout the text of Scripture you will find 60 devotions that focus on a specific passage with relevance to your life today. These passages, along with the reflection, will help you see your changing world in light of God's unchanging Word.

Read the devotions after you've pondered the recommended Scripture reading and the key verse. Then put them into practice with the "Debrief" feature, which will challenge you, and the "Report" feature, which will provide a model prayer that may give you the words you're looking for.

Home Front Heroes

The remaining 30 devotions found throughout the Scripture text feature 30 stories, each illustrating a key Bible principle, such as love, courage and perseverance, demonstrated by the lives of heroes on the American home front. Through these readings you will meet and be inspired by home front heroes who experienced both contemporary and historical military conflicts.

Hymns

At the back of the Bible you will find lyrics to ten enduring hymns of the faith that will provide you with words of encouragement, truth, valor and comfort. You will find the music to these all-time favorites online or in your favorite hymnbook.

Basic Training

Also at the back of the Bible you will find ten study features that will help guide you deeper into God's words for your life. Each one focuses on a specific Scripture passage and provides thoughts, questions and space to respond from your own heart and experience. This feature can serve as a model for how to study a Bible passage for yourself. We urge you to practice this method with the select pages in the back and then replicate the approach with any Bible passage you read in the future.

The Text Between

We hope these features will deepen your faith and enrich your personal relationship with Jesus Christ. But be sure to also read the text between the special features as part of your Bible reading plan. Rest assured, God has special blessings in store for those who read and meditate on his Word. Before and after you read, pray and ask the Holy Spirit to help you understand each passage. Watch for and seek out ways to apply what you've read to your own life.

[PREFACE]

The goal of the New International Version (NIV) is to enable English-speaking people from around the world to read and hear God's eternal Word in their own language. Our work as translators is motivated by our conviction that the Bible is God's Word in written form. We believe that the Bible contains the divine answer to the deepest needs of humanity, sheds unique light on our path in a dark world and sets forth the way to our eternal well-being. Out of these deep convictions, we have sought to recreate as far as possible the experience of the original audience — blending transparency to the original text with accessibility for the millions of English speakers around the world. We have prioritized accuracy, clarity and literary quality with the goal of creating a translation suitable for public and private reading, evangelism, teaching, preaching, memorizing and liturgical use. We have also sought to preserve a measure of continuity with the long tradition of translating the Scriptures into English.

The complete NIV Bible was first published in 1978. It was a completely new translation made by over a hundred scholars working directly from the best available Hebrew, Aramaic and Greek texts. The translators came from the United States, Great Britain, Canada, Australia and New Zealand, giving the translation an international scope. They were from many denominations and churches — including Anglican, Assemblies of God, Baptist, Brethren, Christian Reformed, Church of Christ, Evangelical Covenant, Evangelical Free, Lutheran, Mennonite, Methodist, Nazarene, Presbyterian, Wesleyan and others. This breadth of denominational and theological perspective helped to safeguard the translation from sectarian bias. For these reasons, and by the grace of God, the NIV has gained a wide readership in all parts of the English-speaking world.

The work of translating the Bible is never finished. As good as they are, English translations must be regularly updated so that they will continue to communicate accurately the meaning of God's Word. Updates are needed in order to reflect the latest developments in our understanding of the biblical world and its languages and to keep pace with changes in English usage. Recognizing, then, that the NIV would retain its ability to communicate God's Word accurately only if it were regularly updated, the original translators established The Committee on Bible Translation (CBT). The committee is a self-perpetuating group of biblical scholars charged with keeping abreast of advances in biblical scholarship and changes in English and issuing periodic updates to the NIV. CBT is an independent, self-governing body and has sole responsibility for the NIV text. The committee mirrors the original group of translators in its diverse international and denominational makeup and in its unifying commitment to the Bible as God's inspired Word.

In obedience to its mandate, the committee has issued periodic updates to the NIV. An initial revision was released in 1984. A more thorough revision process was completed in 2005, resulting in the separately published Today's New International Version (TNIV). The updated NIV you now have in your hands builds on both the original NIV and the TNIV and represents the latest effort of the committee to articulate God's unchanging Word in the way the original authors might have said it had they been speaking in English to the global English-speaking audience today.

The first concern of the translators has continued to be the accuracy of the translation and its faithfulness to the intended meaning of the biblical writers. This has moved the translators to go beyond a formal word-for-word rendering of the original texts. Because thought patterns and syntax differ from language to language, accurate communication of the meaning of the biblical authors demands constant regard for varied contextual uses of words and idioms and for frequent modifications in sentence structures.

As an aid to the reader, sectional headings have been inserted. They are not to be regarded as part of the biblical text and are not intended for oral reading. It is the committee's hope that these headings may prove more helpful to the reader than the traditional chapter divisions, which were introduced long after the Bible was written.

For the Old Testament the standard Hebrew text, the Masoretic Text as published in the latest edition of *Biblia Hebraica,* has been used throughout. The Masoretic Text tradition contains marginal notations that offer variant readings. These have sometimes been followed instead of the text itself. Because such instances involve variants within the Masoretic tradition, they have not been indicated in the textual notes. In a few cases, words in the basic consonantal text have been divided differently than in the Masoretic Text. Such cases are usually indicated in the textual footnotes. The Dead Sea Scrolls contain biblical texts that represent an earlier stage of the transmission of the Hebrew text. They have been consulted, as have been the Samaritan Pentateuch and the ancient scribal traditions concerning deliberate textual changes. The translators also consulted the more important early versions — the Greek Septuagint, Aquila, Symmachus and Theodotion, the Latin Vulgate, the Syriac Peshitta, the Aramaic Targums and, for the Psalms, the *Juxta Hebraica* of Jerome. Readings from these versions, the Dead Sea Scrolls and the scribal traditions were occasionally followed where the Masoretic Text seemed doubtful and where accepted principles of textual criticism showed that one or more of these textual witnesses appeared to provide the correct reading. In rare cases, the committee has emended the Hebrew text where it appears to have become corrupted at an even earlier stage of its transmission. These departures from the Masoretic Text are also indicated in the textual footnotes. Sometimes the vowel indicators (which are later additions to the basic consonantal text) found in the Masoretic Text did not, in the judgment of the committee, represent the correct vowels for the original text. Accordingly, some words have been read with a different set of vowels. These instances are usually not indicated in the footnotes.

The Greek text used in translating the New Testament is an eclectic one, based on the latest editions of the Nestle-Aland/United Bible Societies' Greek New Testament. The committee has made its choices among the variant readings in accordance with widely accepted principles of New Testament textual criticism. Footnotes call attention to places where uncertainty remains.

The New Testament authors, writing in Greek, often quote the Old Testament from its ancient Greek version, the Septuagint. This is one reason why some of the Old Testament quotations in the NIV New Testament are not identical to the corresponding passages in the NIV Old Testament. Such quotations in the New Testament are indicated with the footnote "(see Septuagint)."

Other footnotes in this version are of several kinds, most of which need no explanation. Those giving alternative translations begin with "Or" and generally introduce the alternative with the last word preceding it in the text, except when it is a single-word alternative. When poetry is quoted in a footnote, a slash mark indicates a line division.

It should be noted that references to diseases, minerals, flora and fauna, architectural details, clothing, jewelry, musical instruments and other articles cannot always be identified with precision. Also, linear measurements and measures of capacity can only be approximated (see the Table of Weights and Measures). Although *Selah*, used mainly in the Psalms, is probably a musical term, its meaning is uncertain. Since it may interrupt reading and distract the reader, this word has not been kept in the English text, but every occurrence has been signaled by a footnote.

One of the main reasons the task of Bible translation is never finished is the change in our own language, English. Although a basic core of the language remains relatively stable, many diverse and complex linguistic factors continue to bring about subtle shifts in the meanings and/or connotations of even old, well-established words and phrases. One of the shifts that creates particular challenges to writers and translators alike is the manner in which gender is presented. The original NIV (1978) was published in a time when "a man" would naturally be understood, in many contexts, to be referring to a person, whether male or female. But most English speakers today tend to hear a distinctly male connotation in this word. In recognition of this change in English, this edition of the NIV, along with almost all other recent English translations, substitutes other expressions when the original text intends to refer generically to men and women equally. Thus, for instance, the NIV (1984) rendering of 1 Corinthians 8:3, "But the man who loves God is known by God" becomes in this edition "But whoever loves God is known by God." On the other hand, "man" and "mankind," as ways of denoting the human race, are still widely used. This edition of the NIV therefore continues to use these words, along with other expressions, in this way.

A related shift in English creates a greater challenge for modern translations: the move away from using the third-person masculine singular pronouns — "he/him/his" — to refer to men and women equally. This usage does persist at a low level in some forms of English, and this revision therefore occasionally uses these pronouns in a generic sense.

But the tendency, recognized in day-to-day usage and confirmed by extensive research, is away from the generic use of "he," "him" and "his." In recognition of this shift in language and in an effort to translate into the "common" English that people are actually using, this revision of the NIV generally uses other constructions when the biblical text is plainly addressed to men and women equally. The reader will frequently encounter a "they," "them" or "their" to express a generic singular idea. Thus, for instance, Mark 8:36 reads: "What good is it for someone to gain the whole world, yet forfeit their soul?" This generic use of the "indefinite" or "singular" "they/them/their" has a venerable place in English idiom and has quickly become established as standard English, spoken and written, all over the world. Where an individual emphasis is deemed to be present, "anyone" or "everyone" or some other equivalent is generally used as the antecedent of such pronouns.

Sometimes the chapter and/or verse numbering in English translations of the Old Testament differs from that found in published Hebrew texts. This is particularly the case in the Psalms, where the traditional titles are often included in the Hebrew verse numbering. Such differences are indicated in the footnotes at the bottom of the page. In the New Testament, verse numbers that marked off portions of the traditional English text not supported by the best Greek manuscripts now appear in brackets, with a footnote indicating the text that has been omitted (see, for example, Matthew 17:[21]).

Mark 16:9–20 and John 7:53–8:11, although long accorded virtually equal status with the rest of the Gospels in which they stand, have a very questionable — and confused — standing in the textual history of the New Testament, as noted in the bracketed annotations with which they are set off. A different typeface has been chosen for these passages to indicate even more clearly their uncertain status.

Basic formatting of the text, such as lining the poetry, paragraphing (both prose and poetry), setting up of (administrative-like) lists, indenting letters and lengthy prayers within narratives and the insertion of sectional headings, has been the work of the committee. However, the choice between single-column and double-column formats has been left to the publishers. Also the issuing of "red-letter" editions is a publisher's choice — one the committee does not endorse.

The committee has again been reminded that every human effort is flawed — including this revision of the NIV. We trust, however, that many will find in it an improved representation of the Word of God, through which they hear his call to faith in our Lord Jesus Christ and to service in his kingdom. We offer this version of the Bible to him in whose name and for whose glory it has been made.

The Committee on Bible Translation
September 2010

The New Testament

Matthew

The Genealogy of Jesus the Messiah

1 This is the genealogy[a] of Jesus the Messiah[b] the son of David, the son of Abraham:

2 Abraham was the father of Isaac,
   Isaac the father of Jacob,
   Jacob the father of Judah and his brothers,
3 Judah the father of Perez and Zerah, whose mother was Tamar,
   Perez the father of Hezron,
   Hezron the father of Ram,
4 Ram the father of Amminadab,
   Amminadab the father of Nahshon,
   Nahshon the father of Salmon,
5 Salmon the father of Boaz, whose mother was Rahab,
   Boaz the father of Obed, whose mother was Ruth,
   Obed the father of Jesse,
6 and Jesse the father of King David.

David was the father of Solomon, whose mother had been Uriah's wife,
7 Solomon the father of Rehoboam,
   Rehoboam the father of Abijah,
   Abijah the father of Asa,
8 Asa the father of Jehoshaphat,
   Jehoshaphat the father of Jehoram,
   Jehoram the father of Uzziah,
9 Uzziah the father of Jotham,
   Jotham the father of Ahaz,
   Ahaz the father of Hezekiah,
10 Hezekiah the father of Manasseh,
   Manasseh the father of Amon,
   Amon the father of Josiah,
11 and Josiah the father of Jeconiah[c] and his brothers at the time of the exile to Babylon.

12 After the exile to Babylon:
   Jeconiah was the father of Shealtiel,
   Shealtiel the father of Zerubbabel,
13 Zerubbabel the father of Abihud,
   Abihud the father of Eliakim,
   Eliakim the father of Azor,
14 Azor the father of Zadok,
   Zadok the father of Akim,
   Akim the father of Elihud,
15 Elihud the father of Eleazar,
   Eleazar the father of Matthan,
   Matthan the father of Jacob,
16 and Jacob the father of Joseph, the husband of Mary, and Mary was the mother of Jesus who is called the Messiah.

17 Thus there were fourteen generations in all from Abraham to David, fourteen from David to the exile to Babylon, and fourteen from the exile to the Messiah.

Joseph Accepts Jesus as His Son

18 This is how the birth of Jesus the Messiah came about[d]: His mother Mary was pledged to be married to Joseph, but before they came together, she was found to be pregnant through the Holy Spirit. 19 Because Joseph her husband was faithful to the law, and yet[e] did not want to expose her to public disgrace, he had in mind to divorce her quietly.

20 But after he had considered this, an angel of the Lord appeared to him in a dream and said, "Joseph son of David, do not be afraid to take Mary home as your wife, because what is conceived in her is from the Holy Spirit. 21 She will give birth to a son, and you are to give him the name Jesus,[f] because he will save his people from their sins."

22 All this took place to fulfill what the Lord had said through the prophet: 23 "The virgin will conceive and give birth to a son, and they will call him Immanuel"[g] (which means "God with us").

24 When Joseph woke up, he did what the

---

[a] 1 Or *is an account of the origin*   [b] 1 Or *Jesus Christ. Messiah* (Hebrew) and *Christ* (Greek) both mean *Anointed One*; also in verse 18.   [c] 11 That is, Jehoiachin; also in verse 12   [d] 18 Or *The origin of Jesus the Messiah was like this*   [e] 19 Or *was a righteous man and*   [f] 21 *Jesus* is the Greek form of *Joshua*, which means *the* LORD *saves*.   [g] 23 Isaiah 7:14

angel of the Lord had commanded him and took Mary home as his wife. [25]But he did not consummate their marriage until she gave birth to a son. And he gave him the name Jesus.

The Magi Visit the Messiah

2 After Jesus was born in Bethlehem in Judea, during the time of King Herod, Magi[a] from the east came to Jerusalem [2]and asked, "Where is the one who has been born king of the Jews? We saw his star when it rose and have come to worship him."

[3]When King Herod heard this he was disturbed, and all Jerusalem with him. [4]When he had called together all the people's chief priests and teachers of the law, he asked them where the Messiah was to be born. [5]"In Bethlehem in Judea," they replied, "for this is what the prophet has written:

[6]" 'But you, Bethlehem, in the land of
        Judah,
    are by no means least among the rulers
        of Judah;
  for out of you will come a ruler
      who will shepherd my people Israel.'[b]"

[7]Then Herod called the Magi secretly and found out from them the exact time the star had appeared. [8]He sent them to Bethlehem and said, "Go and search carefully for the child. As soon as you find him, report to me, so that I too may go and worship him."

[9]After they had heard the king, they went on their way, and the star they had seen when it rose went ahead of them until it stopped over the place where the child was. [10]When they saw the star, they were overjoyed. [11]On coming to the house, they saw the child with his mother Mary, and they bowed down and worshiped him. Then they opened their treasures and presented him with gifts of gold, frankincense and myrrh. [12]And having been warned in a dream not to go back to Herod, they returned to their country by another route.

The Escape to Egypt

[13]When they had gone, an angel of the Lord appeared to Joseph in a dream. "Get up," he said, "take the child and his mother and escape to Egypt. Stay there until I tell you, for Herod is going to search for the child to kill him."

[14]So he got up, took the child and his mother during the night and left for Egypt, [15]where he stayed until the death of Herod. And so was fulfilled what the Lord had said through the prophet: "Out of Egypt I called my son."[c]

[16]When Herod realized that he had been outwitted by the Magi, he was furious, and he gave orders to kill all the boys in Bethlehem and its vicinity who were two years old and under, in accordance with the time he had learned from the Magi. [17]Then what was said through the prophet Jeremiah was fulfilled:

[18]"A voice is heard in Ramah,
    weeping and great mourning,
  Rachel weeping for her children
    and refusing to be comforted,
    because they are no more."[d]

The Return to Nazareth

[19]After Herod died, an angel of the Lord appeared in a dream to Joseph in Egypt [20]and said, "Get up, take the child and his mother and go to the land of Israel, for those who were trying to take the child's life are dead."

[21]So he got up, took the child and his mother and went to the land of Israel. [22]But when he heard that Archelaus was reigning in Judea in place of his father Herod, he was afraid to go there. Having been warned in a dream, he withdrew to the district of Galilee, [23]and he went and lived in a town called Nazareth. So was fulfilled what was said through the prophets, that he would be called a Nazarene.

John the Baptist Prepares the Way

3 In those days John the Baptist came, preaching in the wilderness of Judea [2]and saying, "Repent, for the kingdom of heaven has come near." [3]This is he who was spoken of through the prophet Isaiah:

"A voice of one calling in the wilderness,
  'Prepare the way for the Lord,
    make straight paths for him.' "[e]

[4]John's clothes were made of camel's hair, and he had a leather belt around his waist.

---

[a] 1 Traditionally *wise men*   [b] 6 Micah 5:2,4   [c] 15 Hosea 11:1   [d] 18 Jer. 31:15   [e] 3 Isaiah 40:3

His food was locusts and wild honey. [5]People went out to him from Jerusalem and all Judea and the whole region of the Jordan. [6]Confessing their sins, they were baptized by him in the Jordan River.

[7]But when he saw many of the Pharisees and Sadducees coming to where he was baptizing, he said to them: "You brood of vipers! Who warned you to flee from the coming wrath? [8]Produce fruit in keeping with repentance. [9]And do not think you can say to yourselves, 'We have Abraham as our father.' I tell you that out of these stones God can raise up children for Abraham. [10]The ax is already at the root of the trees, and every tree that does not produce good fruit will be cut down and thrown into the fire.

[11]"I baptize you with[a] water for repentance. But after me comes one who is more powerful than I, whose sandals I am not worthy to carry. He will baptize you with[a] the Holy Spirit and fire. [12]His winnowing fork is in his hand, and he will clear his threshing floor, gathering his wheat into the barn and burning up the chaff with unquenchable fire."

The Baptism of Jesus

[13]Then Jesus came from Galilee to the Jordan to be baptized by John. [14]But John tried to deter him, saying, "I need to be baptized by you, and do you come to me?"

[15]Jesus replied, "Let it be so now; it is proper for us to do this to fulfill all righteousness." Then John consented.

[16]As soon as Jesus was baptized, he went up out of the water. At that moment heaven was opened, and he saw the Spirit of God descending like a dove and alighting on him. [17]And a voice from heaven said, "This is my Son, whom I love; with him I am well pleased."

Jesus Is Tested in the Wilderness

4 Then Jesus was led by the Spirit into the wilderness to be tempted[b] by the devil. [2]After fasting forty days and forty nights, he was hungry. [3]The tempter came to him and said, "If you are the Son of God, tell these stones to become bread."

[4]Jesus answered, "It is written: 'Man shall not live on bread alone, but on every word that comes from the mouth of God.'[c]"

[5]Then the devil took him to the holy city and had him stand on the highest point of the temple. [6]"If you are the Son of God," he said, "throw yourself down. For it is written:

"'He will command his angels
        concerning you,
    and they will lift you up in their hands,
    so that you will not strike your foot
        against a stone.'[d]"

[7]Jesus answered him, "It is also written: 'Do not put the Lord your God to the test.'[e]"

[8]Again, the devil took him to a very high mountain and showed him all the kingdoms of the world and their splendor. [9]"All this I will give you," he said, "if you will bow down and worship me."

[10]Jesus said to him, "Away from me, Satan! For it is written: 'Worship the Lord your God, and serve him only.'[f]"

[11]Then the devil left him, and angels came and attended him.

Jesus Begins to Preach

[12]When Jesus heard that John had been put in prison, he withdrew to Galilee. [13]Leaving Nazareth, he went and lived in Capernaum, which was by the lake in the area of Zebulun and Naphtali— [14]to fulfill what was said through the prophet Isaiah:

[15]"Land of Zebulun and land of Naphtali,
        the Way of the Sea, beyond the Jordan,
        Galilee of the Gentiles—
[16]the people living in darkness
        have seen a great light;
    on those living in the land of the shadow
        of death
    a light has dawned."[g]

[17]From that time on Jesus began to preach, "Repent, for the kingdom of heaven has come near."

Jesus Calls His First Disciples

[18]As Jesus was walking beside the Sea of Galilee, he saw two brothers, Simon called Peter and his brother Andrew. They were casting a net into the lake, for they were fishermen. [19]"Come, follow me," Jesus said, "and

---

[a] 11 Or in   [b] 1 The Greek for tempted can also mean tested.   [c] 4 Deut. 8:3   [d] 6 Psalm 91:11,12
[e] 7 Deut. 6:16   [f] 10 Deut. 6:13   [g] 16 Isaiah 9:1,2

I will send you out to fish for people." [20]At once they left their nets and followed him.

[21]Going on from there, he saw two other brothers, James son of Zebedee and his brother John. They were in a boat with their father Zebedee, preparing their nets. Jesus called them, [22]and immediately they left the boat and their father and followed him.

Jesus Heals the Sick

[23]Jesus went throughout Galilee, teaching in their synagogues, proclaiming the good news of the kingdom, and healing every disease and sickness among the people. [24]News about him spread all over Syria, and people brought to him all who were ill with various diseases, those suffering severe pain, the demon-possessed, those having seizures, and the paralyzed; and he healed them. [25]Large crowds from Galilee, the Decapolis,[a] Jerusalem, Judea and the region across the Jordan followed him.

Introduction to the Sermon on the Mount

5 Now when Jesus saw the crowds, he went up on a mountainside and sat down. His disciples came to him, [2]and he began to teach them.

The Beatitudes

He said:

[3] "Blessed are the poor in spirit,
    for theirs is the kingdom of heaven.
[4] Blessed are those who mourn,
    for they will be comforted.
[5] Blessed are the meek,
    for they will inherit the earth.
[6] Blessed are those who hunger and thirst
        for righteousness,
    for they will be filled.
[7] Blessed are the merciful,
    for they will be shown mercy.
[8] Blessed are the pure in heart,
    for they will see God.
[9] Blessed are the peacemakers,
    for they will be called children of God.
[10] Blessed are those who are persecuted
      because of righteousness,
    for theirs is the kingdom of heaven.

[11] "Blessed are you when people insult you, persecute you and falsely say all kinds of evil against you because of me. [12]Rejoice and be glad, because great is your reward in heaven, for in the same way they persecuted the prophets who were before you.

Salt and Light

[13] "You are the salt of the earth. But if the salt loses its saltiness, how can it be made salty again? It is no longer good for anything, except to be thrown out and trampled underfoot.

[14] "You are the light of the world. A town built on a hill cannot be hidden. [15]Neither do people light a lamp and put it under a bowl. Instead they put it on its stand, and it gives light to everyone in the house. [16]In the same way, let your light shine before others, that they may see your good deeds and glorify your Father in heaven.

The Fulfillment of the Law

[17] "Do not think that I have come to abolish the Law or the Prophets; I have not come to abolish them but to fulfill them. [18]For truly I tell you, until heaven and earth disappear, not the smallest letter, not the least stroke of a pen, will by any means disappear from the Law until everything is accomplished. [19]Therefore anyone who sets aside one of the least of these commands and teaches others accordingly will be called least in the kingdom of heaven, but whoever practices and teaches these commands will be called great in the kingdom of heaven. [20]For I tell you that unless your righteousness surpasses that of the Pharisees and the teachers of the law, you will certainly not enter the kingdom of heaven.

Murder

[21] "You have heard that it was said to the people long ago, 'You shall not murder,[b] and anyone who murders will be subject to judgment.' [22]But I tell you that anyone who is angry with a brother or sister[c,d] will be subject to judgment. Again, anyone who says to a brother or sister, 'Raca,'[e] is answerable to the court. And anyone who says, 'You fool!' will be in danger of the fire of hell.

---

[a] 25 That is, the Ten Cities   [b] 21 Exodus 20:13   [c] 22 The Greek word for *brother or sister* (*adelphos*) refers here to a fellow disciple, whether man or woman; also in verse 23.   [d] 22 Some manuscripts *brother or sister without cause*   [e] 22 An Aramaic term of contempt

²³"Therefore, if you are offering your gift at the altar and there remember that your brother or sister has something against you, ²⁴leave your gift there in front of the altar. First go and be reconciled to them; then come and offer your gift.

²⁵"Settle matters quickly with your adversary who is taking you to court. Do it while you are still together on the way, or your adversary may hand you over to the judge, and the judge may hand you over to the officer, and you may be thrown into prison. ²⁶Truly I tell you, you will not get out until you have paid the last penny.

Adultery

²⁷"You have heard that it was said, 'You shall not commit adultery.'ᵃ ²⁸But I tell you that anyone who looks at a woman lustfully has already committed adultery with her in his heart. ²⁹If your right eye causes you to stumble, gouge it out and throw it away. It is better for you to lose one part of your body than for your whole body to be thrown into hell. ³⁰And if your right hand causes you to stumble, cut it off and throw it away. It is better for you to lose one part of your body than for your whole body to go into hell.

Divorce

³¹"It has been said, 'Anyone who divorces his wife must give her a certificate of divorce.'ᵇ ³²But I tell you that anyone who divorces his wife, except for sexual immorality, makes her the victim of adultery, and anyone who marries a divorced woman commits adultery.

Oaths

³³"Again, you have heard that it was said to the people long ago, 'Do not break your oath, but fulfill to the Lord the vows you have made.' ³⁴But I tell you, do not swear an oath at all: either by heaven, for it is God's throne; ³⁵or by the earth, for it is his footstool; or by Jerusalem, for it is the city of the Great King. ³⁶And do not swear by your head, for you cannot make even one hair white or black. ³⁷All you need to say is simply 'Yes' or 'No'; anything beyond this comes from the evil one.ᶜ

Eye for Eye

³⁸"You have heard that it was said, 'Eye for eye, and tooth for tooth.'ᵈ ³⁹But I tell you, do not resist an evil person. If anyone slaps you on the right cheek, turn to them the other cheek also. ⁴⁰And if anyone wants to sue you and take your shirt, hand over your coat as well. ⁴¹If anyone forces you to go one mile, go with them two miles. ⁴²Give to the one who asks you, and do not turn away from the one who wants to borrow from you.

Love for Enemies

⁴³"You have heard that it was said, 'Love your neighborᵉ and hate your enemy.' ⁴⁴But I tell you, love your enemies and pray for those who persecute you, ⁴⁵that you may be children of your Father in heaven. He causes his sun to rise on the evil and the good, and sends rain on the righteous and the unrighteous. ⁴⁶If you love those who love you, what reward will you get? Are not even the tax collectors doing that? ⁴⁷And if you greet only your own people, what are you doing more than others? Do not even pagans do that? ⁴⁸Be perfect, therefore, as your heavenly Father is perfect.

Giving to the Needy

6 "Be careful not to practice your righteousness in front of others to be seen by them. If you do, you will have no reward from your Father in heaven.

²"So when you give to the needy, do not announce it with trumpets, as the hypocrites do in the synagogues and on the streets, to be honored by others. Truly I tell you, they have received their reward in full. ³But when you give to the needy, do not let your left hand know what your right hand is doing, ⁴so that your giving may be in secret. Then your Father, who sees what is done in secret, will reward you.

Prayer

⁵"And when you pray, do not be like the hypocrites, for they love to pray standing in the synagogues and on the street corners to be seen by others. Truly I tell you, they have received their reward in full. ⁶But when you pray, go into your room, close the door and

ᵃ 27 Exodus 20:14   ᵇ 31 Deut. 24:1   ᶜ 37 Or from evil   ᵈ 38 Exodus 21:24; Lev. 24:20; Deut. 19:21
ᵉ 43 Lev. 19:18

Protecting Your Marriage

By Linda Montgomery

READ: Matthew 5:27–32

In 1941, Eugene and Louise got married two days before he shipped out for combat in Europe during World War II. Louise, also on active duty, reported for duty in Indonesia. They were apart for three and a half years.

Realizing the temptations of this long-term separation, Eugene and Louise were careful. As Christians they wanted to please the Lord and stay true to their marriage vows. If they had yielded to a flirtatious look, a seductive picture or a suggestive conversation, their legacy of a 50-year marriage would have begun badly.

God's Word is strong on this account. Jesus gave a clear warning in the Sermon on the Mount: "You have heard that it was said, 'You shall not commit adultery.' But I tell you that anyone who looks at a woman lustfully has already committed adultery with her in his heart" (Matthew 5:27–28). In Matthew 19:6 Jesus said, "So they are no longer two, but one flesh. Therefore what God has joined together, let no one separate."

Here are ways that you as a wife can guard your eyes, ears, mind, body and steps:

1. *Be careful what you read or watch.* What you see on TV, the Internet and social media can lead to unrealistic expectations. Psalm 119:37 says, "Turn my eyes away from worthless things; preserve my life according to your word."

2. *Be careful what and who you listen to.* Christian praise music can turn a weary heart into a joy-filled heart. And Christian friends will be careful to guard your relationship with your husband — not turn your heart to discontentment.

3. *Be careful what you think about.* Guarding your devotional time with the Lord each day will ensure that you think on things that are true, noble, right, pure, lovely and admirable (see Philippians 4:8).

4. *Be careful to keep your body pure.* The apostle Paul reminds us, "It is God's will that you should be sanctified: that you should avoid sexual immorality; that each of you should learn to control your own body in a way that is holy and honorable" (1 Thessalonians 4:3–4).

5. *Be careful where you go.* Do not seek a friendship with someone of the opposite sex. Growing in oneness with your husband means keeping yourself only for him.

A marriage is worth guarding — at all costs. Even when you are absent from each other due to military service, it can grow stronger. Eugene and Louise would agree!

> "You have heard that it was said, 'You shall not commit adultery.' But I tell you that anyone who looks at a woman lustfully has already committed adultery with her in his heart."
> MATTHEW 5:27–28

DEBRIEF
- Regarding my marriage, am I careful to guard myself from unholy influences?
- How can I make my marriage stronger? What practical steps can I take to make this happen?

REPORT
Lord, you warn us that our marital relationship should be guarded from temptations. Please keep me close to my husband, even when we are miles apart. In Jesus' name I pray. Amen.

pray to your Father, who is unseen. Then your Father, who sees what is done in secret, will reward you. [7]And when you pray, do not keep on babbling like pagans, for they think they will be heard because of their many words. [8]Do not be like them, for your Father knows what you need before you ask him.

[9]"This, then, is how you should pray:

"'Our Father in heaven,
    hallowed be your name,
[10]your kingdom come,
    your will be done,
        on earth as it is in heaven.
[11]Give us today our daily bread.
[12]And forgive us our debts,
    as we also have forgiven our debtors.
[13]And lead us not into temptation,[a]
    but deliver us from the evil one.[b]'

[14]For if you forgive other people when they sin against you, your heavenly Father will also forgive you. [15]But if you do not forgive others their sins, your Father will not forgive your sins.

Fasting

[16]"When you fast, do not look somber as the hypocrites do, for they disfigure their faces to show others they are fasting. Truly I tell you, they have received their reward in full. [17]But when you fast, put oil on your head and wash your face, [18]so that it will not be obvious to others that you are fasting, but only to your Father, who is unseen; and your Father, who sees what is done in secret, will reward you.

Treasures in Heaven

[19]"Do not store up for yourselves treasures on earth, where moths and vermin destroy, and where thieves break in and steal. [20]But store up for yourselves treasures in heaven, where moths and vermin do not destroy, and where thieves do not break in and steal. [21]For where your treasure is, there your heart will be also.

[22]"The eye is the lamp of the body. If your eyes are healthy,[c] your whole body will be full of light. [23]But if your eyes are unhealthy,[d] your whole body will be full of darkness. If

then the light within you is darkness, how great is that darkness!

[24]"No one can serve two masters. Either you will hate the one and love the other, or you will be devoted to the one and despise the other. You cannot serve both God and money.

Do Not Worry

[25]"Therefore I tell you, do not worry about your life, what you will eat or drink; or about your body, what you will wear. Is not life more than food, and the body more than clothes? [26]Look at the birds of the air; they do not sow or reap or store away in barns, and yet your heavenly Father feeds them. Are you not much more valuable than they? [27]Can any one of you by worrying add a single hour to your life[e]?

[28]"And why do you worry about clothes? See how the flowers of the field grow. They do not labor or spin. [29]Yet I tell you that not even Solomon in all his splendor was dressed like one of these. [30]If that is how God clothes the grass of the field, which is here today and tomorrow is thrown into the fire, will he not much more clothe you—you of little faith? [31]So do not worry, saying, 'What shall we eat?' or 'What shall we drink?' or 'What shall we wear?' [32]For the pagans run after all these things, and your heavenly Father knows that you need them. [33]But seek first his kingdom and his righteousness, and all these things will be given to you as well. [34]Therefore do not worry about tomorrow, for tomorrow will worry about itself. Each day has enough trouble of its own.

Judging Others

7 "Do not judge, or you too will be judged. [2]For in the same way you judge others, you will be judged, and with the measure you use, it will be measured to you.

[3]"Why do you look at the speck of sawdust in your brother's eye and pay no attention to the plank in your own eye? [4]How can you say to your brother, 'Let me take the speck out of your eye,' when all the time there is a plank in your own eye? [5]You hypocrite, first take the plank out of your own eye, and then

---

[a] 13 The Greek for *temptation* can also mean *testing*. *yours is the kingdom and the power and the glory forever. Amen.* *generous.*   [d] 23 The Greek for *unhealthy* here implies *stingy*.   [b] 13 Or *from evil*; some late manuscripts *one, / for*   [c] 22 The Greek for *healthy* here implies   [e] 27 Or *single cubit to your height*

you will see clearly to remove the speck from your brother's eye.

⁶ "Do not give dogs what is sacred; do not throw your pearls to pigs. If you do, they may trample them under their feet, and turn and tear you to pieces.

Ask, Seek, Knock

⁷ "Ask and it will be given to you; seek and you will find; knock and the door will be opened to you. ⁸ For everyone who asks receives; the one who seeks finds; and to the one who knocks, the door will be opened.

⁹ "Which of you, if your son asks for bread, will give him a stone? ¹⁰ Or if he asks for a fish, will give him a snake? ¹¹ If you, then, though you are evil, know how to give good gifts to your children, how much more will your Father in heaven give good gifts to those who ask him! ¹² So in everything, do to others what you would have them do to you, for this sums up the Law and the Prophets.

The Narrow and Wide Gates

¹³ "Enter through the narrow gate. For wide is the gate and broad is the road that leads to destruction, and many enter through it. ¹⁴ But small is the gate and narrow the road that leads to life, and only a few find it.

True and False Prophets

¹⁵ "Watch out for false prophets. They come to you in sheep's clothing, but inwardly they are ferocious wolves. ¹⁶ By their fruit you will recognize them. Do people pick grapes from thornbushes, or figs from thistles? ¹⁷ Likewise, every good tree bears good fruit, but a bad tree bears bad fruit. ¹⁸ A good tree cannot bear bad fruit, and a bad tree cannot bear good fruit. ¹⁹ Every tree that does not bear good fruit is cut down and thrown into the fire. ²⁰ Thus, by their fruit you will recognize them.

True and False Disciples

²¹ "Not everyone who says to me, 'Lord, Lord,' will enter the kingdom of heaven, but only the one who does the will of my Father who is in heaven. ²² Many will say to me on that day, 'Lord, Lord, did we not prophesy in your name and in your name drive out de-

mons and in your name perform many miracles?' ²³ Then I will tell them plainly, 'I never knew you. Away from me, you evildoers!'

The Wise and Foolish Builders

²⁴ "Therefore everyone who hears these words of mine and puts them into practice is like a wise man who built his house on the rock. ²⁵ The rain came down, the streams rose, and the winds blew and beat against that house; yet it did not fall, because it had its foundation on the rock. ²⁶ But everyone who hears these words of mine and does not put them into practice is like a foolish man who built his house on sand. ²⁷ The rain came down, the streams rose, and the winds blew and beat against that house, and it fell with a great crash."

²⁸ When Jesus had finished saying these things, the crowds were amazed at his teaching, ²⁹ because he taught as one who had authority, and not as their teachers of the law.

Jesus Heals a Man With Leprosy

8 When Jesus came down from the mountainside, large crowds followed him. ² A man with leprosy*ᵃ* came and knelt before him and said, "Lord, if you are willing, you can make me clean."

³ Jesus reached out his hand and touched the man. "I am willing," he said. "Be clean!" Immediately he was cleansed of his leprosy. ⁴ Then Jesus said to him, "See that you don't tell anyone. But go, show yourself to the priest and offer the gift Moses commanded, as a testimony to them."

The Faith of the Centurion

⁵ When Jesus had entered Capernaum, a centurion came to him, asking for help. ⁶ "Lord," he said, "my servant lies at home paralyzed, suffering terribly."

⁷ Jesus said to him, "Shall I come and heal him?"

⁸ The centurion replied, "Lord, I do not deserve to have you come under my roof. But just say the word, and my servant will be healed. ⁹ For I myself am a man under authority, with soldiers under me. I tell this one, 'Go,' and he goes; and that one, 'Come,' and he comes. I say to my servant, 'Do this,' and he does it."

ᵃ *2* The Greek word traditionally translated *leprosy* was used for various diseases affecting the skin.

Wise or Foolish?

By Sarah Ball

READ: Matthew 7:24–27

Foundations matter. If you've ever lived in a house with a flawed foundation, you know that even a small crack can have big consequences.

At the conclusion of the Sermon on the Mount (see Matthew 5 – 7), Jesus told a parable about foundations. The wise man of the parable built his house on a solid foundation of rock. The foolish man chose sand. Both houses stood until stormy weather arrived. When the rain, floods and wind beat on the houses, the one with the weaker foundation collapsed.

I love illustrating this story for children. The wise man gets a block house stacked on large rocks. The foolish man has an identical block house, but I use jiggly squares of Jell-O for the foundation. When the "stormy weather" hits, the foolish man's house collapses.

After the shrieks of laughter and flying Jell-O bits, the children are ready to hear the parable's simple, profound truths. We are all building houses as we live and make choices. If we hear and obey God's Word, we will have solid foundations for our lives. If we hear God's Word but choose to ignore it, we will have flawed foundations. Difficult times come in every life, and these storms test the strength of each foundation.

I've noticed a funny thing about this lesson. Every time I teach it, the children always want to eat the leftover Jell-O. Even after it's dirty and smashed into bits, the Jell-O still holds strong appeal. Isn't that the way we view many things? We know the truth of God's Word, but other truths seem prettier and more palatable. Sometimes we begin building on God's Word, only to realize later that we have mixed in a few blocks of Jell-O. We pick up things from everywhere — TV, magazines, online forums, the actions of our friends and family. We rationalize our decisions because they keep us comfortable and in step with our peers.

Our mixtures of God's truth and popular culture may seem adequate until difficulty comes and life's problems expose the cracks in our foundations. Often, the challenges we face are simply consequences of the choices we've made that ignored God's Word. Storms in our relationships, children's behaviors or finances become opportunities to check our foundations.

Are you ready to inspect your foundation? Begin by reading prayerfully through the Sermon on the Mount. Hear the words of Jesus and then put them into practice. Choose Scriptural bedrock for your life — no Jell-O allowed.

> **"Therefore everyone who hears these words of mine and puts them into practice is like a wise man who built his house on the rock."**
>
> MATTHEW 7:24

DEBRIEF
- Is my life built on the solid foundation of God's Word?
- What influences from my culture am I tempted to mix into my foundation?

REPORT
Lord, thank you for the gift of your Word, given to me as a solid foundation for life. Help me to hear and practice your truth in every part of my life. In Jesus' name I pray. Amen.

for your next devotional reading, go to page 15

¹⁰When Jesus heard this, he was amazed and said to those following him, "Truly I tell you, I have not found anyone in Israel with such great faith. ¹¹I say to you that many will come from the east and the west, and will take their places at the feast with Abraham, Isaac and Jacob in the kingdom of heaven. ¹²But the subjects of the kingdom will be thrown outside, into the darkness, where there will be weeping and gnashing of teeth."

¹³Then Jesus said to the centurion, "Go! Let it be done just as you believed it would." And his servant was healed at that moment.

Jesus Heals Many

¹⁴When Jesus came into Peter's house, he saw Peter's mother-in-law lying in bed with a fever. ¹⁵He touched her hand and the fever left her, and she got up and began to wait on him.

¹⁶When evening came, many who were demon-possessed were brought to him, and he drove out the spirits with a word and healed all the sick. ¹⁷This was to fulfill what was spoken through the prophet Isaiah:

"He took up our infirmities
and bore our diseases."ᵃ

The Cost of Following Jesus

¹⁸When Jesus saw the crowd around him, he gave orders to cross to the other side of the lake. ¹⁹Then a teacher of the law came to him and said, "Teacher, I will follow you wherever you go."

²⁰Jesus replied, "Foxes have dens and birds have nests, but the Son of Man has no place to lay his head."

²¹Another disciple said to him, "Lord, first let me go and bury my father."

²²But Jesus told him, "Follow me, and let the dead bury their own dead."

Jesus Calms the Storm

²³Then he got into the boat and his disciples followed him. ²⁴Suddenly a furious storm came up on the lake, so that the waves swept over the boat. But Jesus was sleeping. ²⁵The disciples went and woke him, saying, "Lord, save us! We're going to drown!"

²⁶He replied, "You of little faith, why are you so afraid?" Then he got up and rebuked the winds and the waves, and it was completely calm.

²⁷The men were amazed and asked, "What kind of man is this? Even the winds and the waves obey him!"

Jesus Restores Two Demon-Possessed Men

²⁸When he arrived at the other side in the region of the Gadarenes,ᵇ two demon-possessed men coming from the tombs met him. They were so violent that no one could pass that way. ²⁹"What do you want with us, Son of God?" they shouted. "Have you come here to torture us before the appointed time?"

³⁰Some distance from them a large herd of pigs was feeding. ³¹The demons begged Jesus, "If you drive us out, send us into the herd of pigs."

³²He said to them, "Go!" So they came out and went into the pigs, and the whole herd rushed down the steep bank into the lake and died in the water. ³³Those tending the pigs ran off, went into the town and reported all this, including what had happened to the demon-possessed men. ³⁴Then the whole town went out to meet Jesus. And when they saw him, they pleaded with him to leave their region.

Jesus Forgives and Heals a Paralyzed Man

9 Jesus stepped into a boat, crossed over and came to his own town. ²Some men brought to him a paralyzed man, lying on a mat. When Jesus saw their faith, he said to the man, "Take heart, son; your sins are forgiven."

³At this, some of the teachers of the law said to themselves, "This fellow is blaspheming!"

⁴Knowing their thoughts, Jesus said, "Why do you entertain evil thoughts in your hearts? ⁵Which is easier: to say, 'Your sins are forgiven,' or to say, 'Get up and walk'? ⁶But I want you to know that the Son of Man has authority on earth to forgive sins." So he said to the paralyzed man, "Get up, take your mat and go home." ⁷Then the man got up and went home. ⁸When the crowd saw this, they were filled with awe; and they praised God, who had given such authority to man.

ᵃ 17 Isaiah 53:4 (see Septuagint)   ᵇ 28 Some manuscripts Gergesenes; other manuscripts Gerasenes

The Calling of Matthew

⁹As Jesus went on from there, he saw a man named Matthew sitting at the tax collector's booth. "Follow me," he told him, and Matthew got up and followed him.

¹⁰While Jesus was having dinner at Matthew's house, many tax collectors and sinners came and ate with him and his disciples. ¹¹When the Pharisees saw this, they asked his disciples, "Why does your teacher eat with tax collectors and sinners?"

¹²On hearing this, Jesus said, "It is not the healthy who need a doctor, but the sick. ¹³But go and learn what this means: 'I desire mercy, not sacrifice.'ᵃ For I have not come to call the righteous, but sinners."

Jesus Questioned About Fasting

¹⁴Then John's disciples came and asked him, "How is it that we and the Pharisees fast often, but your disciples do not fast?"

¹⁵Jesus answered, "How can the guests of the bridegroom mourn while he is with them? The time will come when the bridegroom will be taken from them; then they will fast.

¹⁶"No one sews a patch of unshrunk cloth on an old garment, for the patch will pull away from the garment, making the tear worse. ¹⁷Neither do people pour new wine into old wineskins. If they do, the skins will burst; the wine will run out and the wineskins will be ruined. No, they pour new wine into new wineskins, and both are preserved."

Jesus Raises a Dead Girl and Heals a Sick Woman

¹⁸While he was saying this, a synagogue leader came and knelt before him and said, "My daughter has just died. But come and put your hand on her, and she will live." ¹⁹Jesus got up and went with him, and so did his disciples.

²⁰Just then a woman who had been subject to bleeding for twelve years came up behind him and touched the edge of his cloak. ²¹She said to herself, "If I only touch his cloak, I will be healed."

²²Jesus turned and saw her. "Take heart, daughter," he said, "your faith has healed you." And the woman was healed at that moment.

²³When Jesus entered the synagogue leader's house and saw the noisy crowd and people playing pipes, ²⁴he said, "Go away. The girl is not dead but asleep." But they laughed at him. ²⁵After the crowd had been put outside, he went in and took the girl by the hand, and she got up. ²⁶News of this spread through all that region.

Jesus Heals the Blind and the Mute

²⁷As Jesus went on from there, two blind men followed him, calling out, "Have mercy on us, Son of David!"

²⁸When he had gone indoors, the blind men came to him, and he asked them, "Do you believe that I am able to do this?"

"Yes, Lord," they replied.

²⁹Then he touched their eyes and said, "According to your faith let it be done to you"; ³⁰and their sight was restored. Jesus warned them sternly, "See that no one knows about this." ³¹But they went out and spread the news about him all over that region.

³²While they were going out, a man who was demon-possessed and could not talk was brought to Jesus. ³³And when the demon was driven out, the man who had been mute spoke. The crowd was amazed and said, "Nothing like this has ever been seen in Israel."

³⁴But the Pharisees said, "It is by the prince of demons that he drives out demons."

The Workers Are Few

³⁵Jesus went through all the towns and villages, teaching in their synagogues, proclaiming the good news of the kingdom and healing every disease and sickness. ³⁶When he saw the crowds, he had compassion on them, because they were harassed and helpless, like sheep without a shepherd. ³⁷Then he said to his disciples, "The harvest is plentiful but the workers are few. ³⁸Ask the Lord of the harvest, therefore, to send out workers into his harvest field."

Jesus Sends Out the Twelve

10 Jesus called his twelve disciples to him and gave them authority to drive out impure spirits and to heal every disease and sickness.

²These are the names of the twelve apostles: first, Simon (who is called Peter) and

ᵃ 13 Hosea 6:6

his brother Andrew; James son of Zebedee, and his brother John; ³Philip and Bartholomew; Thomas and Matthew the tax collector; James son of Alphaeus, and Thaddaeus; ⁴Simon the Zealot and Judas Iscariot, who betrayed him.

⁵These twelve Jesus sent out with the following instructions: "Do not go among the Gentiles or enter any town of the Samaritans. ⁶Go rather to the lost sheep of Israel. ⁷As you go, proclaim this message: 'The kingdom of heaven has come near.' ⁸Heal the sick, raise the dead, cleanse those who have leprosy,ᵃ drive out demons. Freely you have received; freely give.

⁹"Do not get any gold or silver or copper to take with you in your belts — ¹⁰no bag for the journey or extra shirt or sandals or a staff, for the worker is worth his keep. ¹¹Whatever town or village you enter, search there for some worthy person and stay at their house until you leave. ¹²As you enter the home, give it your greeting. ¹³If the home is deserving, let your peace rest on it; if it is not, let your peace return to you. ¹⁴If anyone will not welcome you or listen to your words, leave that home or town and shake the dust off your feet. ¹⁵Truly I tell you, it will be more bearable for Sodom and Gomorrah on the day of judgment than for that town.

¹⁶"I am sending you out like sheep among wolves. Therefore be as shrewd as snakes and as innocent as doves. ¹⁷Be on your guard; you will be handed over to the local councils and be flogged in the synagogues. ¹⁸On my account you will be brought before governors and kings as witnesses to them and to the Gentiles. ¹⁹But when they arrest you, do not worry about what to say or how to say it. At that time you will be given what to say, ²⁰for it will not be you speaking, but the Spirit of your Father speaking through you.

²¹"Brother will betray brother to death, and a father his child; children will rebel against their parents and have them put to death. ²²You will be hated by everyone because of me, but the one who stands firm to the end will be saved. ²³When you are persecuted in one place, flee to another. Truly I tell you, you will not finish going through the towns of Israel before the Son of Man comes.

²⁴"The student is not above the teacher, nor a servant above his master. ²⁵It is enough for students to be like their teachers, and servants like their masters. If the head of the house has been called Beelzebul, how much more the members of his household!

²⁶"So do not be afraid of them, for there is nothing concealed that will not be disclosed, or hidden that will not be made known. ²⁷What I tell you in the dark, speak in the daylight; what is whispered in your ear, proclaim from the roofs. ²⁸Do not be afraid of those who kill the body but cannot kill the soul. Rather, be afraid of the One who can destroy both soul and body in hell. ²⁹Are not two sparrows sold for a penny? Yet not one of them will fall to the ground outside your Father's care.ᵇ ³⁰And even the very hairs of your head are all numbered. ³¹So don't be afraid; you are worth more than many sparrows.

³²"Whoever acknowledges me before others, I will also acknowledge before my Father in heaven. ³³But whoever disowns me before others, I will disown before my Father in heaven.

³⁴"Do not suppose that I have come to bring peace to the earth. I did not come to bring peace, but a sword. ³⁵For I have come to turn

" 'a man against his father,
    a daughter against her mother,
  a daughter-in-law against her mother-
    in-law —
³⁶ a man's enemies will be the members
    of his own household.'ᶜ

³⁷"Anyone who loves their father or mother more than me is not worthy of me; anyone who loves their son or daughter more than me is not worthy of me. ³⁸Whoever does not take up their cross and follow me is not worthy of me. ³⁹Whoever finds their life will lose it, and whoever loses their life for my sake will find it.

⁴⁰"Anyone who welcomes you welcomes me, and anyone who welcomes me welcomes the one who sent me. ⁴¹Whoever welcomes a prophet as a prophet will receive a prophet's reward, and whoever welcomes a righteous person as a righteous person will receive a righteous person's reward. ⁴²And if

---

ᵃ 8 The Greek word traditionally translated *leprosy* was used for various diseases affecting the skin.   ᵇ 29 Or *will*; or *knowledge*   ᶜ 36 Micah 7:6

Pray for the One Who Is Sent

By Marshéle Carter Waddell

READ: Matthew 10

In Matthew 10, Jesus called his 12 disciples for one last briefing before "deploying" them to the countryside and towns of Galilee. Warning them of the dangers ahead, he stated, "I am sending you out like sheep among wolves. Therefore be as shrewd as snakes and as innocent as doves" (Matthew 10:16).

When my Navy SEAL husband deployed to Operation Iraqi Freedom the first time, I didn't think of him as a sheep among wolves. Mark had already spent the last two decades deploying around the world. I viewed the pending deployment, our seventh as a family, as no big deal. Though I prayed for my husband's physical safety many times a day, I never knew to pray for his mind. But the war came home with him, lodged in his spirit as an invisible wound.

Once our family experienced how war affects the mind and soul of the warrior, I began to intercede for my husband, and later for our son, with more authority, urgency, faith and conviction than ever before. As you pray for your loved ones who are deployed, here are some important guidelines:

1. *Pray according to the Word of God.* As you read Scripture, literally pray the words, phrases and verses back to your Father in heaven on behalf of your loved one. God's Word reveals God's will; and when we pray according to God's will, we can be sure that he hears us (see 1 John 5:14).

2. *Pray with authority and confidence.* Pray in the name of the Lord Jesus Christ (see John 14:13 – 14).

3. *Ask the Holy Spirit to pray through you.* When you don't know how to pray, the Holy Spirit will intercede for you (see Romans 8:26 – 27).

4. *Refuse to live in fear and doubt.* Release your loved one to God and choose to believe and not doubt (see James 1:6 – 7).

5. *Believe God.* Once you have prayed in this way, focus on your own walk with Jesus, your own character and accomplishing the good works God has prepared in advance for you to do during this time of separation from your loved one (see Ephesians 2:10).

Also study the prayers that our Lord Jesus prayed for us that are recorded in John 17. Learn from seasoned prayer warriors in your church and women's ministry. Learn from trustworthy authors, like Stormie Omartian and her *The Power of a Praying...* series.

Pray for the one being sent. Pray for your warrior's body, mind and soul. Fear nothing but God (see Proverbs 9:10).

"Do not be afraid of those who kill the body but cannot kill the soul. Rather, be afraid of the One who can destroy both soul and body in hell."

MATTHEW 10:28

DEBRIEF
- Do my prayers focus only on my warrior's physical safety? Am I also praying for his mental and spiritual health?
- How can I pray with more urgency, faith and conviction?

REPORT
Lord, I want to pray more effectively for the one I love as he is sent. Teach me to do so through your Word and your people. Help me to pray and to live in the authority you have given me and to overcome all the power of the enemy. In Jesus' name I pray. Amen.

---

for your next devotional reading, go to page 25

anyone gives even a cup of cold water to one of these little ones who is my disciple, truly I tell you, that person will certainly not lose their reward."

Jesus and John the Baptist

11 After Jesus had finished instructing his twelve disciples, he went on from there to teach and preach in the towns of Galilee.[a]

²When John, who was in prison, heard about the deeds of the Messiah, he sent his disciples ³to ask him, "Are you the one who is to come, or should we expect someone else?"

⁴Jesus replied, "Go back and report to John what you hear and see: ⁵The blind receive sight, the lame walk, those who have leprosy[b] are cleansed, the deaf hear, the dead are raised, and the good news is proclaimed to the poor. ⁶Blessed is anyone who does not stumble on account of me."

⁷As John's disciples were leaving, Jesus began to speak to the crowd about John: "What did you go out into the wilderness to see? A reed swayed by the wind? ⁸If not, what did you go out to see? A man dressed in fine clothes? No, those who wear fine clothes are in kings' palaces. ⁹Then what did you go out to see? A prophet? Yes, I tell you, and more than a prophet. ¹⁰This is the one about whom it is written:

" 'I will send my messenger ahead
    of you,
who will prepare your way
    before you.'[c]

¹¹Truly I tell you, among those born of women there has not risen anyone greater than John the Baptist; yet whoever is least in the kingdom of heaven is greater than he. ¹²From the days of John the Baptist until now, the kingdom of heaven has been subjected to violence,[d] and violent people have been raiding it. ¹³For all the Prophets and the Law prophesied until John. ¹⁴And if you are willing to accept it, he is the Elijah who was to come. ¹⁵Whoever has ears, let them hear.

¹⁶"To what can I compare this generation? They are like children sitting in the marketplaces and calling out to others:

¹⁷" 'We played the pipe for you,
    and you did not dance;

we sang a dirge,
    and you did not mourn.'

¹⁸For John came neither eating nor drinking, and they say, 'He has a demon.' ¹⁹The Son of Man came eating and drinking, and they say, 'Here is a glutton and a drunkard, a friend of tax collectors and sinners.' But wisdom is proved right by her deeds."

Woe on Unrepentant Towns

²⁰Then Jesus began to denounce the towns in which most of his miracles had been performed, because they did not repent. ²¹"Woe to you, Chorazin! Woe to you, Bethsaida! For if the miracles that were performed in you had been performed in Tyre and Sidon, they would have repented long ago in sackcloth and ashes. ²²But I tell you, it will be more bearable for Tyre and Sidon on the day of judgment than for you. ²³And you, Capernaum, will you be lifted to the heavens? No, you will go down to Hades.[e] For if the miracles that were performed in you had been performed in Sodom, it would have remained to this day. ²⁴But I tell you that it will be more bearable for Sodom on the day of judgment than for you."

The Father Revealed in the Son

²⁵At that time Jesus said, "I praise you, Father, Lord of heaven and earth, because you have hidden these things from the wise and learned, and revealed them to little children. ²⁶Yes, Father, for this is what you were pleased to do.

²⁷"All things have been committed to me by my Father. No one knows the Son except the Father, and no one knows the Father except the Son and those to whom the Son chooses to reveal him.

²⁸"Come to me, all you who are weary and burdened, and I will give you rest. ²⁹Take my yoke upon you and learn from me, for I am gentle and humble in heart, and you will find rest for your souls. ³⁰For my yoke is easy and my burden is light."

Jesus Is Lord of the Sabbath

12 At that time Jesus went through the grainfields on the Sabbath. His disciples were hungry and began to pick some heads of grain and eat them. ²When the

---

[a] 1 Greek in their towns   [b] 5 The Greek word traditionally translated leprosy was used for various diseases affecting the skin.   [c] 10 Mal. 3:1   [d] 12 Or been forcefully advancing   [e] 23 That is, the realm of the dead

Pharisees saw this, they said to him, "Look! Your disciples are doing what is unlawful on the Sabbath."

³He answered, "Haven't you read what David did when he and his companions were hungry? ⁴He entered the house of God, and he and his companions ate the consecrated bread—which was not lawful for them to do, but only for the priests. ⁵Or haven't you read in the Law that the priests on Sabbath duty in the temple desecrate the Sabbath and yet are innocent? ⁶I tell you that something greater than the temple is here. ⁷If you had known what these words mean, 'I desire mercy, not sacrifice,'ᵃ you would not have condemned the innocent. ⁸For the Son of Man is Lord of the Sabbath."

⁹Going on from that place, he went into their synagogue, ¹⁰and a man with a shriveled hand was there. Looking for a reason to bring charges against Jesus, they asked him, "Is it lawful to heal on the Sabbath?"

¹¹He said to them, "If any of you has a sheep and it falls into a pit on the Sabbath, will you not take hold of it and lift it out? ¹²How much more valuable is a person than a sheep! Therefore it is lawful to do good on the Sabbath."

¹³Then he said to the man, "Stretch out your hand." So he stretched it out and it was completely restored, just as sound as the other. ¹⁴But the Pharisees went out and plotted how they might kill Jesus.

God's Chosen Servant

¹⁵Aware of this, Jesus withdrew from that place. A large crowd followed him, and he healed all who were ill. ¹⁶He warned them not to tell others about him. ¹⁷This was to fulfill what was spoken through the prophet Isaiah:

¹⁸ "Here is my servant whom I have chosen,
the one I love, in whom I delight;
I will put my Spirit on him,
and he will proclaim justice to the nations.
¹⁹ He will not quarrel or cry out;
no one will hear his voice in the streets.
²⁰ A bruised reed he will not break,
and a smoldering wick he will not snuff out,
till he has brought justice through to victory.
²¹ In his name the nations will put their hope."ᵇ

Jesus and Beelzebul

²²Then they brought him a demon-possessed man who was blind and mute, and Jesus healed him, so that he could both talk and see. ²³All the people were astonished and said, "Could this be the Son of David?"

²⁴But when the Pharisees heard this, they said, "It is only by Beelzebul, the prince of demons, that this fellow drives out demons."

²⁵Jesus knew their thoughts and said to them, "Every kingdom divided against itself will be ruined, and every city or household divided against itself will not stand. ²⁶If Satan drives out Satan, he is divided against himself. How then can his kingdom stand? ²⁷And if I drive out demons by Beelzebul, by whom do your people drive them out? So then, they will be your judges. ²⁸But if it is by the Spirit of God that I drive out demons, then the kingdom of God has come upon you.

²⁹"Or again, how can anyone enter a strong man's house and carry off his possessions unless he first ties up the strong man? Then he can plunder his house.

³⁰"Whoever is not with me is against me, and whoever does not gather with me scatters. ³¹And so I tell you, every kind of sin and slander can be forgiven, but blasphemy against the Spirit will not be forgiven. ³²Anyone who speaks a word against the Son of Man will be forgiven, but anyone who speaks against the Holy Spirit will not be forgiven, either in this age or in the age to come.

³³"Make a tree good and its fruit will be good, or make a tree bad and its fruit will be bad, for a tree is recognized by its fruit. ³⁴You brood of vipers, how can you who are evil say anything good? For the mouth speaks what the heart is full of. ³⁵A good man brings good things out of the good stored up in him, and an evil man brings evil things out of the evil stored up in him. ³⁶But I tell you that everyone will have to give account on the day of judgment for every empty word they have spoken. ³⁷For by your words you will

ᵃ 7 Hosea 6:6   ᵇ 21 Isaiah 42:1-4

be acquitted, and by your words you will be condemned."

The Sign of Jonah

[38] Then some of the Pharisees and teachers of the law said to him, "Teacher, we want to see a sign from you."

[39] He answered, "A wicked and adulterous generation asks for a sign! But none will be given it except the sign of the prophet Jonah. [40] For as Jonah was three days and three nights in the belly of a huge fish, so the Son of Man will be three days and three nights in the heart of the earth. [41] The men of Nineveh will stand up at the judgment with this generation and condemn it; for they repented at the preaching of Jonah, and now something greater than Jonah is here. [42] The Queen of the South will rise at the judgment with this generation and condemn it; for she came from the ends of the earth to listen to Solomon's wisdom, and now something greater than Solomon is here.

[43] "When an impure spirit comes out of a person, it goes through arid places seeking rest and does not find it. [44] Then it says, 'I will return to the house I left.' When it arrives, it finds the house unoccupied, swept clean and put in order. [45] Then it goes and takes with it seven other spirits more wicked than itself, and they go in and live there. And the final condition of that person is worse than the first. That is how it will be with this wicked generation."

Jesus' Mother and Brothers

[46] While Jesus was still talking to the crowd, his mother and brothers stood outside, wanting to speak to him. [47] Someone told him, "Your mother and brothers are standing outside, wanting to speak to you."

[48] He replied to him, "Who is my mother, and who are my brothers?" [49] Pointing to his disciples, he said, "Here are my mother and my brothers. [50] For whoever does the will of my Father in heaven is my brother and sister and mother."

The Parable of the Sower

13 That same day Jesus went out of the house and sat by the lake. [2] Such large crowds gathered around him that he got into a boat and sat in it, while all the people stood on the shore. [3] Then he told them many things in parables, saying: "A farmer went out to sow his seed. [4] As he was scattering the seed, some fell along the path, and the birds came and ate it up. [5] Some fell on rocky places, where it did not have much soil. It sprang up quickly, because the soil was shallow. [6] But when the sun came up, the plants were scorched, and they withered because they had no root. [7] Other seed fell among thorns, which grew up and choked the plants. [8] Still other seed fell on good soil, where it produced a crop — a hundred, sixty or thirty times what was sown. [9] Whoever has ears, let them hear."

[10] The disciples came to him and asked, "Why do you speak to the people in parables?"

[11] He replied, "Because the knowledge of the secrets of the kingdom of heaven has been given to you, but not to them. [12] Whoever has will be given more, and they will have an abundance. Whoever does not have, even what they have will be taken from them. [13] This is why I speak to them in parables:

"Though seeing, they do not see;
    though hearing, they do not hear or
        understand.

[14] In them is fulfilled the prophecy of Isaiah:

" 'You will be ever hearing but never
        understanding;
    you will be ever seeing but never
        perceiving.
[15] For this people's heart has become
        calloused;
    they hardly hear with their ears,
    and they have closed their eyes.
Otherwise they might see with their eyes,
    hear with their ears,
    understand with their hearts
    and turn, and I would heal them.'[a]

[16] But blessed are your eyes because they see, and your ears because they hear. [17] For truly I tell you, many prophets and righteous people longed to see what you see but did not see it, and to hear what you hear but did not hear it.

----

[a] 15 Isaiah 6:9,10 (see Septuagint)

[18] "Listen then to what the parable of the sower means: [19] When anyone hears the message about the kingdom and does not understand it, the evil one comes and snatches away what was sown in their heart. This is the seed sown along the path. [20] The seed falling on rocky ground refers to someone who hears the word and at once receives it with joy. [21] But since they have no root, they last only a short time. When trouble or persecution comes because of the word, they quickly fall away. [22] The seed falling among the thorns refers to someone who hears the word, but the worries of this life and the deceitfulness of wealth choke the word, making it unfruitful. [23] But the seed falling on good soil refers to someone who hears the word and understands it. This is the one who produces a crop, yielding a hundred, sixty or thirty times what was sown."

The Parable of the Weeds

[24] Jesus told them another parable: "The kingdom of heaven is like a man who sowed good seed in his field. [25] But while everyone was sleeping, his enemy came and sowed weeds among the wheat, and went away. [26] When the wheat sprouted and formed heads, then the weeds also appeared.

[27] "The owner's servants came to him and said, 'Sir, didn't you sow good seed in your field? Where then did the weeds come from?'

[28] " 'An enemy did this,' he replied.

"The servants asked him, 'Do you want us to go and pull them up?'

[29] " 'No,' he answered, 'because while you are pulling the weeds, you may uproot the wheat with them. [30] Let both grow together until the harvest. At that time I will tell the harvesters: First collect the weeds and tie them in bundles to be burned; then gather the wheat and bring it into my barn.' "

The Parables of the Mustard Seed and the Yeast

[31] He told them another parable: "The kingdom of heaven is like a mustard seed, which a man took and planted in his field. [32] Though it is the smallest of all seeds, yet when it grows, it is the largest of garden plants and becomes a tree, so that the birds come and perch in its branches."

[33] He told them still another parable: "The kingdom of heaven is like yeast that a woman took and mixed into about sixty pounds[a] of flour until it worked all through the dough."

[34] Jesus spoke all these things to the crowd in parables; he did not say anything to them without using a parable. [35] So was fulfilled what was spoken through the prophet:

"I will open my mouth in parables,
    I will utter things hidden since the
        creation of the world."[b]

The Parable of the Weeds Explained

[36] Then he left the crowd and went into the house. His disciples came to him and said, "Explain to us the parable of the weeds in the field."

[37] He answered, "The one who sowed the good seed is the Son of Man. [38] The field is the world, and the good seed stands for the people of the kingdom. The weeds are the people of the evil one, [39] and the enemy who sows them is the devil. The harvest is the end of the age, and the harvesters are angels.

[40] "As the weeds are pulled up and burned in the fire, so it will be at the end of the age. [41] The Son of Man will send out his angels, and they will weed out of his kingdom everything that causes sin and all who do evil. [42] They will throw them into the blazing furnace, where there will be weeping and gnashing of teeth. [43] Then the righteous will shine like the sun in the kingdom of their Father. Whoever has ears, let them hear.

The Parables of the Hidden Treasure and the Pearl

[44] "The kingdom of heaven is like treasure hidden in a field. When a man found it, he hid it again, and then in his joy went and sold all he had and bought that field.

[45] "Again, the kingdom of heaven is like a merchant looking for fine pearls. [46] When he found one of great value, he went away and sold everything he had and bought it.

The Parable of the Net

[47] "Once again, the kingdom of heaven is like a net that was let down into the lake and caught all kinds of fish. [48] When it was full, the fishermen pulled it up on the shore. Then they sat down and collected the good

---

[a] 33 Or about 27 kilograms   [b] 35 Psalm 78:2

fish in baskets, but threw the bad away.
⁴⁹This is how it will be at the end of the age.
The angels will come and separate the wicked from the righteous ⁵⁰and throw them into the blazing furnace, where there will be weeping and gnashing of teeth.

⁵¹"Have you understood all these things?" Jesus asked.

"Yes," they replied.

⁵²He said to them, "Therefore every teacher of the law who has become a disciple in the kingdom of heaven is like the owner of a house who brings out of his storeroom new treasures as well as old."

A Prophet Without Honor

⁵³When Jesus had finished these parables, he moved on from there. ⁵⁴Coming to his hometown, he began teaching the people in their synagogue, and they were amazed. "Where did this man get this wisdom and these miraculous powers?" they asked. ⁵⁵"Isn't this the carpenter's son? Isn't his mother's name Mary, and aren't his brothers James, Joseph, Simon and Judas? ⁵⁶Aren't all his sisters with us? Where then did this man get all these things?" ⁵⁷And they took offense at him.

But Jesus said to them, "A prophet is not without honor except in his own town and in his own home."

⁵⁸And he did not do many miracles there because of their lack of faith.

John the Baptist Beheaded

14 At that time Herod the tetrarch heard the reports about Jesus, ²and he said to his attendants, "This is John the Baptist; he has risen from the dead! That is why miraculous powers are at work in him."

³Now Herod had arrested John and bound him and put him in prison because of Herodias, his brother Philip's wife, ⁴for John had been saying to him: "It is not lawful for you to have her." ⁵Herod wanted to kill John, but he was afraid of the people, because they considered John a prophet.

⁶On Herod's birthday the daughter of Herodias danced for the guests and pleased Herod so much ⁷that he promised with an oath to give her whatever she asked. ⁸Prompted by her mother, she said, "Give me here on a platter the head of John the Baptist." ⁹The king was distressed, but because

of his oaths and his dinner guests, he ordered that her request be granted ¹⁰and had John beheaded in the prison. ¹¹His head was brought in on a platter and given to the girl, who carried it to her mother. ¹²John's disciples came and took his body and buried it. Then they went and told Jesus.

Jesus Feeds the Five Thousand

¹³When Jesus heard what had happened, he withdrew by boat privately to a solitary place. Hearing of this, the crowds followed him on foot from the towns. ¹⁴When Jesus landed and saw a large crowd, he had compassion on them and healed their sick.

¹⁵As evening approached, the disciples came to him and said, "This is a remote place, and it's already getting late. Send the crowds away, so they can go to the villages and buy themselves some food."

¹⁶Jesus replied, "They do not need to go away. You give them something to eat."

¹⁷"We have here only five loaves of bread and two fish," they answered.

¹⁸"Bring them here to me," he said. ¹⁹And he directed the people to sit down on the grass. Taking the five loaves and the two fish and looking up to heaven, he gave thanks and broke the loaves. Then he gave them to the disciples, and the disciples gave them to the people. ²⁰They all ate and were satisfied, and the disciples picked up twelve basketfuls of broken pieces that were left over. ²¹The number of those who ate was about five thousand men, besides women and children.

Jesus Walks on the Water

²²Immediately Jesus made the disciples get into the boat and go on ahead of him to the other side, while he dismissed the crowd. ²³After he had dismissed them, he went up on a mountainside by himself to pray. Later that night, he was there alone, ²⁴and the boat was already a considerable distance from land, buffeted by the waves because the wind was against it.

²⁵Shortly before dawn Jesus went out to them, walking on the lake. ²⁶When the disciples saw him walking on the lake, they were terrified. "It's a ghost," they said, and cried out in fear.

²⁷But Jesus immediately said to them: "Take courage! It is I. Don't be afraid."

²⁸"Lord, if it's you," Peter replied, "tell me to come to you on the water."

²⁹"Come," he said.

Then Peter got down out of the boat, walked on the water and came toward Jesus. ³⁰But when he saw the wind, he was afraid and, beginning to sink, cried out, "Lord, save me!"

³¹Immediately Jesus reached out his hand and caught him. "You of little faith," he said, "why did you doubt?"

³²And when they climbed into the boat, the wind died down. ³³Then those who were in the boat worshiped him, saying, "Truly you are the Son of God."

³⁴When they had crossed over, they landed at Gennesaret. ³⁵And when the men of that place recognized Jesus, they sent word to all the surrounding country. People brought all their sick to him ³⁶and begged him to let the sick just touch the edge of his cloak, and all who touched it were healed.

That Which Defiles

15 Then some Pharisees and teachers of the law came to Jesus from Jerusalem and asked, ²"Why do your disciples break the tradition of the elders? They don't wash their hands before they eat!"

³Jesus replied, "And why do you break the command of God for the sake of your tradition? ⁴For God said, 'Honor your father and mother'ᵃ and 'Anyone who curses their father or mother is to be put to death.'ᵇ ⁵But you say that if anyone declares that what might have been used to help their father or mother is 'devoted to God,' ⁶they are not to 'honor their father or mother' with it. Thus you nullify the word of God for the sake of your tradition. ⁷You hypocrites! Isaiah was right when he prophesied about you:

⁸ " 'These people honor me with their
    lips,
  but their hearts are far from me.
⁹They worship me in vain;
  their teachings are merely human
    rules.'ᶜ"

¹⁰Jesus called the crowd to him and said, "Listen and understand. ¹¹What goes into someone's mouth does not defile them, but what comes out of their mouth, that is what defiles them."

¹²Then the disciples came to him and asked, "Do you know that the Pharisees were offended when they heard this?"

¹³He replied, "Every plant that my heavenly Father has not planted will be pulled up by the roots. ¹⁴Leave them; they are blind guides.ᵈ If the blind lead the blind, both will fall into a pit."

¹⁵Peter said, "Explain the parable to us."

¹⁶"Are you still so dull?" Jesus asked them. ¹⁷"Don't you see that whatever enters the mouth goes into the stomach and then out of the body? ¹⁸But the things that come out of a person's mouth come from the heart, and these defile them. ¹⁹For out of the heart come evil thoughts—murder, adultery, sexual immorality, theft, false testimony, slander. ²⁰These are what defile a person; but eating with unwashed hands does not defile them."

The Faith of a Canaanite Woman

²¹Leaving that place, Jesus withdrew to the region of Tyre and Sidon. ²²A Canaanite woman from that vicinity came to him, crying out, "Lord, Son of David, have mercy on me! My daughter is demon-possessed and suffering terribly."

²³Jesus did not answer a word. So his disciples came to him and urged him, "Send her away, for she keeps crying out after us."

²⁴He answered, "I was sent only to the lost sheep of Israel."

²⁵The woman came and knelt before him. "Lord, help me!" she said.

²⁶He replied, "It is not right to take the children's bread and toss it to the dogs."

²⁷"Yes it is, Lord," she said. "Even the dogs eat the crumbs that fall from their master's table."

²⁸Then Jesus said to her, "Woman, you have great faith! Your request is granted." And her daughter was healed at that moment.

Jesus Feeds the Four Thousand

²⁹Jesus left there and went along the Sea of Galilee. Then he went up on a mountainside and sat down. ³⁰Great crowds came to

ᵃ 4 Exodus 20:12; Deut. 5:16   ᵇ 4 Exodus 21:17; Lev. 20:9   ᶜ 9 Isaiah 29:13   ᵈ 14 Some manuscripts blind guides of the blind

him, bringing the lame, the blind, the crippled, the mute and many others, and laid them at his feet; and he healed them. [31]The people were amazed when they saw the mute speaking, the crippled made well, the lame walking and the blind seeing. And they praised the God of Israel.

[32]Jesus called his disciples to him and said, "I have compassion for these people; they have already been with me three days and have nothing to eat. I do not want to send them away hungry, or they may collapse on the way."

[33]His disciples answered, "Where could we get enough bread in this remote place to feed such a crowd?"

[34]"How many loaves do you have?" Jesus asked.

"Seven," they replied, "and a few small fish."

[35]He told the crowd to sit down on the ground. [36]Then he took the seven loaves and the fish, and when he had given thanks, he broke them and gave them to the disciples, and they in turn to the people. [37]They all ate and were satisfied. Afterward the disciples picked up seven basketfuls of broken pieces that were left over. [38]The number of those who ate was four thousand men, besides women and children. [39]After Jesus had sent the crowd away, he got into the boat and went to the vicinity of Magadan.

The Demand for a Sign

16 The Pharisees and Sadducees came to Jesus and tested him by asking him to show them a sign from heaven.

[2]He replied, "When evening comes, you say, 'It will be fair weather, for the sky is red,' [3]and in the morning, 'Today it will be stormy, for the sky is red and overcast.' You know how to interpret the appearance of the sky, but you cannot interpret the signs of the times.[a] [4]A wicked and adulterous generation looks for a sign, but none will be given it except the sign of Jonah." Jesus then left them and went away.

The Yeast of the Pharisees and Sadducees

[5]When they went across the lake, the disciples forgot to take bread. [6]"Be careful," Jesus said to them. "Be on your guard against the yeast of the Pharisees and Sadducees."

[7]They discussed this among themselves and said, "It is because we didn't bring any bread."

[8]Aware of their discussion, Jesus asked, "You of little faith, why are you talking among yourselves about having no bread? [9]Do you still not understand? Don't you remember the five loaves for the five thousand, and how many basketfuls you gathered? [10]Or the seven loaves for the four thousand, and how many basketfuls you gathered? [11]How is it you don't understand that I was not talking to you about bread? But be on your guard against the yeast of the Pharisees and Sadducees." [12]Then they understood that he was not telling them to guard against the yeast used in bread, but against the teaching of the Pharisees and Sadducees.

Peter Declares That Jesus Is the Messiah

[13]When Jesus came to the region of Caesarea Philippi, he asked his disciples, "Who do people say the Son of Man is?"

[14]They replied, "Some say John the Baptist; others say Elijah; and still others, Jeremiah or one of the prophets."

[15]"But what about you?" he asked. "Who do you say I am?"

[16]Simon Peter answered, "You are the Messiah, the Son of the living God."

[17]Jesus replied, "Blessed are you, Simon son of Jonah, for this was not revealed to you by flesh and blood, but by my Father in heaven. [18]And I tell you that you are Peter,[b] and on this rock I will build my church, and the gates of Hades[c] will not overcome it. [19]I will give you the keys of the kingdom of heaven; whatever you bind on earth will be[d] bound in heaven, and whatever you loose on earth will be[d] loosed in heaven." [20]Then he ordered his disciples not to tell anyone that he was the Messiah.

Jesus Predicts His Death

[21]From that time on Jesus began to explain to his disciples that he must go to Jerusalem and suffer many things at the hands of the elders, the chief priests and the teachers

[a] 2,3 Some early manuscripts do not have When evening comes . . . of the times.   [b] 18 The Greek word for Peter means rock.   [c] 18 That is, the realm of the dead   [d] 19 Or will have been

of the law, and that he must be killed and on the third day be raised to life.

²²Peter took him aside and began to rebuke him. "Never, Lord!" he said. "This shall never happen to you!"

²³Jesus turned and said to Peter, "Get behind me, Satan! You are a stumbling block to me; you do not have in mind the concerns of God, but merely human concerns."

²⁴Then Jesus said to his disciples, "Whoever wants to be my disciple must deny themselves and take up their cross and follow me. ²⁵For whoever wants to save their life*a* will lose it, but whoever loses their life for me will find it. ²⁶What good will it be for someone to gain the whole world, yet forfeit their soul? Or what can anyone give in exchange for their soul? ²⁷For the Son of Man is going to come in his Father's glory with his angels, and then he will reward each person according to what they have done.

²⁸"Truly I tell you, some who are standing here will not taste death before they see the Son of Man coming in his kingdom."

The Transfiguration

17 After six days Jesus took with him Peter, James and John the brother of James, and led them up a high mountain by themselves. ²There he was transfigured before them. His face shone like the sun, and his clothes became as white as the light. ³Just then there appeared before them Moses and Elijah, talking with Jesus.

⁴Peter said to Jesus, "Lord, it is good for us to be here. If you wish, I will put up three shelters — one for you, one for Moses and one for Elijah."

⁵While he was still speaking, a bright cloud covered them, and a voice from the cloud said, "This is my Son, whom I love; with him I am well pleased. Listen to him!"

⁶When the disciples heard this, they fell facedown to the ground, terrified. ⁷But Jesus came and touched them. "Get up," he said. "Don't be afraid." ⁸When they looked up, they saw no one except Jesus.

⁹As they were coming down the mountain, Jesus instructed them, "Don't tell anyone what you have seen, until the Son of Man has been raised from the dead."

¹⁰The disciples asked him, "Why then do the teachers of the law say that Elijah must come first?"

¹¹Jesus replied, "To be sure, Elijah comes and will restore all things. ¹²But I tell you, Elijah has already come, and they did not recognize him, but have done to him everything they wished. In the same way the Son of Man is going to suffer at their hands." ¹³Then the disciples understood that he was talking to them about John the Baptist.

Jesus Heals a Demon-Possessed Boy

¹⁴When they came to the crowd, a man approached Jesus and knelt before him. ¹⁵"Lord, have mercy on my son," he said. "He has seizures and is suffering greatly. He often falls into the fire or into the water. ¹⁶I brought him to your disciples, but they could not heal him."

¹⁷"You unbelieving and perverse generation," Jesus replied, "how long shall I stay with you? How long shall I put up with you? Bring the boy here to me." ¹⁸Jesus rebuked the demon, and it came out of the boy, and he was healed at that moment.

¹⁹Then the disciples came to Jesus in private and asked, "Why couldn't we drive it out?"

²⁰He replied, "Because you have so little faith. Truly I tell you, if you have faith as small as a mustard seed, you can say to this mountain, 'Move from here to there,' and it will move. Nothing will be impossible for you." [21] *b*

Jesus Predicts His Death a Second Time

²²When they came together in Galilee, he said to them, "The Son of Man is going to be delivered into the hands of men. ²³They will kill him, and on the third day he will be raised to life." And the disciples were filled with grief.

The Temple Tax

²⁴After Jesus and his disciples arrived in Capernaum, the collectors of the two-drachma temple tax came to Peter and asked, "Doesn't your teacher pay the temple tax?"

²⁵"Yes, he does," he replied.

---

a 25 The Greek word means either *life* or *soul*; also in verse 26.   *b* 21 Some manuscripts include here words similar to Mark 9:29.

When Peter came into the house, Jesus was the first to speak. "What do you think, Simon?" he asked. "From whom do the kings of the earth collect duty and taxes — from their own children or from others?"

26 "From others," Peter answered.

"Then the children are exempt," Jesus said to him. 27 "But so that we may not cause offense, go to the lake and throw out your line. Take the first fish you catch; open its mouth and you will find a four-drachma coin. Take it and give it to them for my tax and yours."

The Greatest in the Kingdom of Heaven

18 At that time the disciples came to Jesus and asked, "Who, then, is the greatest in the kingdom of heaven?" 2 He called a little child to him, and placed the child among them. 3 And he said: "Truly I tell you, unless you change and become like little children, you will never enter the kingdom of heaven. 4 Therefore, whoever takes the lowly position of this child is the greatest in the kingdom of heaven. 5 And whoever welcomes one such child in my name welcomes me.

Causing to Stumble

6 "If anyone causes one of these little ones — those who believe in me — to stumble, it would be better for them to have a large millstone hung around their neck and to be drowned in the depths of the sea. 7 Woe to the world because of the things that cause people to stumble! Such things must come, but woe to the person through whom they come! 8 If your hand or your foot causes you to stumble, cut it off and throw it away. It is better for you to enter life maimed or crippled than to have two hands or two feet and be thrown into eternal fire. 9 And if your eye causes you to stumble, gouge it out and throw it away. It is better for you to enter life with one eye than to have two eyes and be thrown into the fire of hell.

The Parable of the Wandering Sheep

10 "See that you do not despise one of these little ones. For I tell you that their angels in heaven always see the face of my Father in heaven. [11]a

12 "What do you think? If a man owns a hundred sheep, and one of them wanders away, will he not leave the ninety-nine on the hills and go to look for the one that wandered off? 13 And if he finds it, truly I tell you, he is happier about that one sheep than about the ninety-nine that did not wander off. 14 In the same way your Father in heaven is not willing that any of these little ones should perish.

Dealing With Sin in the Church

15 "If your brother or sisterb sins,c go and point out their fault, just between the two of you. If they listen to you, you have won them over. 16 But if they will not listen, take one or two others along, so that 'every matter may be established by the testimony of two or three witnesses.'d 17 If they still refuse to listen, tell it to the church; and if they refuse to listen even to the church, treat them as you would a pagan or a tax collector.

18 "Truly I tell you, whatever you bind on earth will bee bound in heaven, and whatever you loose on earth will bee loosed in heaven.

19 "Again, truly I tell you that if two of you on earth agree about anything they ask for, it will be done for them by my Father in heaven. 20 For where two or three gather in my name, there am I with them."

The Parable of the Unmerciful Servant

21 Then Peter came to Jesus and asked, "Lord, how many times shall I forgive my brother or sister who sins against me? Up to seven times?"

22 Jesus answered, "I tell you, not seven times, but seventy-seven times.f

23 "Therefore, the kingdom of heaven is like a king who wanted to settle accounts with his servants. 24 As he began the settlement, a man who owed him ten thousand bags of goldg was brought to him. 25 Since he was not able to pay, the master ordered that he and his wife and his children and all that he had be sold to repay the debt.

---

a 11 Some manuscripts include here the words of Luke 19:10.   b 15 The Greek word for *brother or sister* (*adelphos*) refers here to a fellow disciple, whether man or woman; also in verses 21 and 35.   c 15 Some manuscripts *sins against you*   d 16 Deut. 19:15   e 18 Or *will have been*   f 22 Or *seventy times seven*   g 24 Greek *ten thousand talents*; a talent was worth about 20 years of a day laborer's wages.

Freedom Through Forgiveness

By Rebekah Benimoff

READ: Matthew 18:21–35

Military wives face many challenges, including dealing with disappointments and wounds. When we are hurt by someone else, we can choose how to respond. Jesus told us to forgive (see Matthew 18:22). Forgiving may take time and a willingness to look within ourselves, but doing so opens the path to healing.

The first response to a wound is pain, followed by anger. Anger is an indication that an issue needs to be dealt with. The first stirrings of anger, the recognition that harm has been done, is akin to what Jesus felt when he defended the oppressed and chased the money changers out of God's holy temple (see Matthew 21:12–13). However, holding on to our anger or attempting to use it as power over those who've hurt us only causes more trouble. Emotional scarring deepens as we chew on anger, turning it over and over in our minds until bitterness has permeated our souls.

Such behavior and withholding forgiveness leaves us shackled to the one who wounded us. Forgiving frees us. Forgiveness is not excusing the offense — as in "she couldn't help it." Nor is it pretending we are not angry about the hurt we feel. Forgiveness is a gift already bought with the blood of our Savior. Because God chose to forgive us, through his grace we can also forgive others.

We have a choice: We can be like Jesus — loving, compassionate and freely offering forgiveness. Or we can be like those who crucified him — angry, sullen, sin-sick and holding on to hate. On the cross — not after he rose again, but in the midst of his agony — Jesus forgave his tormentors. I am washed in awe at human flesh mangled into a bloody mess, yet crying out, "Father, forgive them, for they do not know what they are doing" (Luke 23:34). When we connect with gratitude for all that Jesus is releasing us from (it's a continuing process), we choose to extend that same forgiveness to others.

Healing the hurts in hidden places is worth the work. Hurt may be buried deep and, like tangled string, may require a lot of patience to undo. But our healer tenderly unearths each strand, unwinding what has knotted our soul. Soothing, covering, restoring. His hands are firm but gentle, rebuilding what was broken and breathing newness and life into our soul. He sets the order, the how and the why and the when. He works with us, not against us, for our own wellness, asking us to forgive, so that we do not remain broken.

Then Peter came to Jesus and asked, "Lord, how many times shall I forgive my brother or sister who sins against me? Up to seven times?" Jesus answered, "I tell you, not seven times, but seventy-seven times."
MATTHEW 18:21–22

DEBRIEF
- For what specific wound in my life do I need to offer forgiveness to someone as a first step toward healing?
- How can I ensure that I remain free from the chains of anger, bitterness and unforgiveness?

REPORT
Jesus, I thank you for choosing to accept the nails of the cross and bear my mark, my shame, my loss. You took the weight of all my sin, my every imperfection. You held steadfast in the place of anguish so I could have release. Show me those places where you want to bring me healing and freedom. Show me how to do the work of forgiveness, step by step. I speak my choice. I submit to my cleansing. I choose forgiveness. I choose to walk in freedom. Amen.

for your next devotional reading, go to page 34

26 "At this the servant fell on his knees before him. 'Be patient with me,' he begged, 'and I will pay back everything.' 27 The servant's master took pity on him, canceled the debt and let him go.

28 "But when that servant went out, he found one of his fellow servants who owed him a hundred silver coins.[a] He grabbed him and began to choke him. 'Pay back what you owe me!' he demanded.

29 "His fellow servant fell to his knees and begged him, 'Be patient with me, and I will pay it back.'

30 "But he refused. Instead, he went off and had the man thrown into prison until he could pay the debt. 31 When the other servants saw what had happened, they were outraged and went and told their master everything that had happened.

32 "Then the master called the servant in. 'You wicked servant,' he said, 'I canceled all that debt of yours because you begged me to. 33 Shouldn't you have had mercy on your fellow servant just as I had on you?' 34 In anger his master handed him over to the jailers to be tortured, until he should pay back all he owed.

35 "This is how my heavenly Father will treat each of you unless you forgive your brother or sister from your heart."

Divorce

19 When Jesus had finished saying these things, he left Galilee and went into the region of Judea to the other side of the Jordan. 2 Large crowds followed him, and he healed them there.

3 Some Pharisees came to him to test him. They asked, "Is it lawful for a man to divorce his wife for any and every reason?"

4 "Haven't you read," he replied, "that at the beginning the Creator 'made them male and female,'[b] 5 and said, 'For this reason a man will leave his father and mother and be united to his wife, and the two will become one flesh'[c]? 6 So they are no longer two, but one flesh. Therefore what God has joined together, let no one separate."

7 "Why then," they asked, "did Moses command that a man give his wife a certificate of divorce and send her away?"

8 Jesus replied, "Moses permitted you to divorce your wives because your hearts were hard. But it was not this way from the beginning. 9 I tell you that anyone who divorces his wife, except for sexual immorality, and marries another woman commits adultery."

10 The disciples said to him, "If this is the situation between a husband and wife, it is better not to marry."

11 Jesus replied, "Not everyone can accept this word, but only those to whom it has been given. 12 For there are eunuchs who were born that way, and there are eunuchs who have been made eunuchs by others — and there are those who choose to live like eunuchs for the sake of the kingdom of heaven. The one who can accept this should accept it."

The Little Children and Jesus

13 Then people brought little children to Jesus for him to place his hands on them and pray for them. But the disciples rebuked them.

14 Jesus said, "Let the little children come to me, and do not hinder them, for the kingdom of heaven belongs to such as these." 15 When he had placed his hands on them, he went on from there.

The Rich and the Kingdom of God

16 Just then a man came up to Jesus and asked, "Teacher, what good thing must I do to get eternal life?"

17 "Why do you ask me about what is good?" Jesus replied. "There is only One who is good. If you want to enter life, keep the commandments."

18 "Which ones?" he inquired.

Jesus replied, "'You shall not murder, you shall not commit adultery, you shall not steal, you shall not give false testimony, 19 honor your father and mother,'[d] and 'love your neighbor as yourself.'[e]"

20 "All these I have kept," the young man said. "What do I still lack?"

21 Jesus answered, "If you want to be perfect, go, sell your possessions and give to the poor, and you will have treasure in heaven. Then come, follow me."

22 When the young man heard this, he went away sad, because he had great wealth.

---

[a] 28 Greek *a hundred denarii*; a denarius was the usual daily wage of a day laborer (see 20:2).
[b] 4 Gen. 1:27   [c] 5 Gen. 2:24   [d] 19 Exodus 20:12-16; Deut. 5:16-20   [e] 19 Lev. 19:18

²³Then Jesus said to his disciples, "Truly I tell you, it is hard for someone who is rich to enter the kingdom of heaven. ²⁴Again I tell you, it is easier for a camel to go through the eye of a needle than for someone who is rich to enter the kingdom of God."

²⁵When the disciples heard this, they were greatly astonished and asked, "Who then can be saved?"

²⁶Jesus looked at them and said, "With man this is impossible, but with God all things are possible."

²⁷Peter answered him, "We have left everything to follow you! What then will there be for us?"

²⁸Jesus said to them, "Truly I tell you, at the renewal of all things, when the Son of Man sits on his glorious throne, you who have followed me will also sit on twelve thrones, judging the twelve tribes of Israel. ²⁹And everyone who has left houses or brothers or sisters or father or mother or wife[a] or children or fields for my sake will receive a hundred times as much and will inherit eternal life. ³⁰But many who are first will be last, and many who are last will be first.

The Parable of the Workers in the Vineyard

20 "For the kingdom of heaven is like a landowner who went out early in the morning to hire workers for his vineyard. ²He agreed to pay them a denarius[b] for the day and sent them into his vineyard.

³"About nine in the morning he went out and saw others standing in the marketplace doing nothing. ⁴He told them, 'You also go and work in my vineyard, and I will pay you whatever is right.' ⁵So they went.

"He went out again about noon and about three in the afternoon and did the same thing. ⁶About five in the afternoon he went out and found still others standing around. He asked them, 'Why have you been standing here all day long doing nothing?'

⁷"'Because no one has hired us,' they answered.

"He said to them, 'You also go and work in my vineyard.'

⁸"When evening came, the owner of the vineyard said to his foreman, 'Call the workers and pay them their wages, beginning with the last ones hired and going on to the first.'

⁹"The workers who were hired about five in the afternoon came and each received a denarius. ¹⁰So when those came who were hired first, they expected to receive more. But each one of them also received a denarius. ¹¹When they received it, they began to grumble against the landowner. ¹²'These who were hired last worked only one hour,' they said, 'and you have made them equal to us who have borne the burden of the work and the heat of the day.'

¹³"But he answered one of them, 'I am not being unfair to you, friend. Didn't you agree to work for a denarius? ¹⁴Take your pay and go. I want to give the one who was hired last the same as I gave you. ¹⁵Don't I have the right to do what I want with my own money? Or are you envious because I am generous?'

¹⁶"So the last will be first, and the first will be last."

Jesus Predicts His Death a Third Time

¹⁷Now Jesus was going up to Jerusalem. On the way, he took the Twelve aside and said to them, ¹⁸"We are going up to Jerusalem, and the Son of Man will be delivered over to the chief priests and the teachers of the law. They will condemn him to death ¹⁹and will hand him over to the Gentiles to be mocked and flogged and crucified. On the third day he will be raised to life!"

A Mother's Request

²⁰Then the mother of Zebedee's sons came to Jesus with her sons and, kneeling down, asked a favor of him.

²¹"What is it you want?" he asked.

She said, "Grant that one of these two sons of mine may sit at your right and the other at your left in your kingdom."

²²"You don't know what you are asking," Jesus said to them. "Can you drink the cup I am going to drink?"

"We can," they answered.

²³Jesus said to them, "You will indeed drink from my cup, but to sit at my right or left is not for me to grant. These places belong to those for whom they have been prepared by my Father."

[a] 29 Some manuscripts do not have or wife.   [b] 2 A denarius was the usual daily wage of a day laborer.

²⁴When the ten heard about this, they were indignant with the two brothers. ²⁵Jesus called them together and said, "You know that the rulers of the Gentiles lord it over them, and their high officials exercise authority over them. ²⁶Not so with you. Instead, whoever wants to become great among you must be your servant, ²⁷and whoever wants to be first must be your slave— ²⁸just as the Son of Man did not come to be served, but to serve, and to give his life as a ransom for many."

Two Blind Men Receive Sight

²⁹As Jesus and his disciples were leaving Jericho, a large crowd followed him. ³⁰Two blind men were sitting by the roadside, and when they heard that Jesus was going by, they shouted, "Lord, Son of David, have mercy on us!"

³¹The crowd rebuked them and told them to be quiet, but they shouted all the louder, "Lord, Son of David, have mercy on us!"

³²Jesus stopped and called them. "What do you want me to do for you?" he asked.

³³"Lord," they answered, "we want our sight."

³⁴Jesus had compassion on them and touched their eyes. Immediately they received their sight and followed him.

Jesus Comes to Jerusalem as King

21 As they approached Jerusalem and came to Bethphage on the Mount of Olives, Jesus sent two disciples, ²saying to them, "Go to the village ahead of you, and at once you will find a donkey tied there, with her colt by her. Untie them and bring them to me. ³If anyone says anything to you, say that the Lord needs them, and he will send them right away."

⁴This took place to fulfill what was spoken through the prophet:

⁵ "Say to Daughter Zion,
    'See, your king comes to you,
    gentle and riding on a donkey,
    and on a colt, the foal of
        a donkey.' " ᵃ

⁶The disciples went and did as Jesus had instructed them. ⁷They brought the donkey and the colt and placed their cloaks on them for Jesus to sit on. ⁸A very large crowd spread their cloaks on the road, while others cut branches from the trees and spread them on the road. ⁹The crowds that went ahead of him and those that followed shouted,

"Hosannaᵇ to the Son of David!"

"Blessed is he who comes in the name of
    the Lord!"ᶜ

"Hosannaᵇ in the highest heaven!"

¹⁰When Jesus entered Jerusalem, the whole city was stirred and asked, "Who is this?"

¹¹The crowds answered, "This is Jesus, the prophet from Nazareth in Galilee."

Jesus at the Temple

¹²Jesus entered the temple courts and drove out all who were buying and selling there. He overturned the tables of the money changers and the benches of those selling doves. ¹³"It is written," he said to them, " 'My house will be called a house of prayer,'ᵈ but you are making it 'a den of robbers.'ᵉ"

¹⁴The blind and the lame came to him at the temple, and he healed them. ¹⁵But when the chief priests and the teachers of the law saw the wonderful things he did and the children shouting in the temple courts, "Hosanna to the Son of David," they were indignant.

¹⁶"Do you hear what these children are saying?" they asked him.

"Yes," replied Jesus, "have you never read,

" 'From the lips of children and infants
    you, Lord, have called forth your
        praise'ᶠ?"

¹⁷And he left them and went out of the city to Bethany, where he spent the night.

Jesus Curses a Fig Tree

¹⁸Early in the morning, as Jesus was on his way back to the city, he was hungry. ¹⁹Seeing a fig tree by the road, he went up to it but found nothing on it except leaves. Then he said to it, "May you never bear fruit again!" Immediately the tree withered.

²⁰When the disciples saw this, they were amazed. "How did the fig tree wither so quickly?" they asked.

ᵃ 5 Zech. 9:9   ᵇ 9 A Hebrew expression meaning "Save!" which became an exclamation of praise; also in verse 15   ᶜ 9 Psalm 118:25,26   ᵈ 13 Isaiah 56:7   ᵉ 13 Jer. 7:11   ᶠ 16 Psalm 8:2 (see Septuagint)

²¹Jesus replied, "Truly I tell you, if you have faith and do not doubt, not only can you do what was done to the fig tree, but also you can say to this mountain, 'Go, throw yourself into the sea,' and it will be done. ²²If you believe, you will receive whatever you ask for in prayer."

The Authority of Jesus Questioned

²³Jesus entered the temple courts, and, while he was teaching, the chief priests and the elders of the people came to him. "By what authority are you doing these things?" they asked. "And who gave you this authority?"

²⁴Jesus replied, "I will also ask you one question. If you answer me, I will tell you by what authority I am doing these things. ²⁵John's baptism—where did it come from? Was it from heaven, or of human origin?"

They discussed it among themselves and said, "If we say, 'From heaven,' he will ask, 'Then why didn't you believe him?' ²⁶But if we say, 'Of human origin'—we are afraid of the people, for they all hold that John was a prophet."

²⁷So they answered Jesus, "We don't know."

Then he said, "Neither will I tell you by what authority I am doing these things.

The Parable of the Two Sons

²⁸"What do you think? There was a man who had two sons. He went to the first and said, 'Son, go and work today in the vineyard.'

²⁹"'I will not,' he answered, but later he changed his mind and went.

³⁰"Then the father went to the other son and said the same thing. He answered, 'I will, sir,' but he did not go.

³¹"Which of the two did what his father wanted?"

"The first," they answered.

Jesus said to them, "Truly I tell you, the tax collectors and the prostitutes are entering the kingdom of God ahead of you. ³²For John came to you to show you the way of righteousness, and you did not believe him, but the tax collectors and the prostitutes did. And even after you saw this, you did not repent and believe him.

The Parable of the Tenants

³³"Listen to another parable: There was a landowner who planted a vineyard. He put a wall around it, dug a winepress in it and built a watchtower. Then he rented the vineyard to some farmers and moved to another place. ³⁴When the harvest time approached, he sent his servants to the tenants to collect his fruit.

³⁵"The tenants seized his servants; they beat one, killed another, and stoned a third. ³⁶Then he sent other servants to them, more than the first time, and the tenants treated them the same way. ³⁷Last of all, he sent his son to them. 'They will respect my son,' he said.

³⁸"But when the tenants saw the son, they said to each other, 'This is the heir. Come, let's kill him and take his inheritance.' ³⁹So they took him and threw him out of the vineyard and killed him.

⁴⁰"Therefore, when the owner of the vineyard comes, what will he do to those tenants?"

⁴¹"He will bring those wretches to a wretched end," they replied, "and he will rent the vineyard to other tenants, who will give him his share of the crop at harvest time."

⁴²Jesus said to them, "Have you never read in the Scriptures:

"'The stone the builders rejected
has become the cornerstone;
the Lord has done this,
and it is marvelous in our eyes'ᵃ?

⁴³"Therefore I tell you that the kingdom of God will be taken away from you and given to a people who will produce its fruit. ⁴⁴Anyone who falls on this stone will be broken to pieces; anyone on whom it falls will be crushed."ᵇ

⁴⁵When the chief priests and the Pharisees heard Jesus' parables, they knew he was talking about them. ⁴⁶They looked for a way to arrest him, but they were afraid of the crowd because the people held that he was a prophet.

The Parable of the Wedding Banquet

22 Jesus spoke to them again in parables, saying: ²"The kingdom of heaven is like a king who prepared a wedding banquet for his son. ³He sent his servants to those who had been invited to the banquet to tell them to come, but they refused to come.

ᵃ 42 Psalm 118:22,23   ᵇ 44 Some manuscripts do not have verse 44.

4 "Then he sent some more servants and said, 'Tell those who have been invited that I have prepared my dinner: My oxen and fattened cattle have been butchered, and everything is ready. Come to the wedding banquet.'

5 "But they paid no attention and went off—one to his field, another to his business. 6 The rest seized his servants, mistreated them and killed them. 7 The king was enraged. He sent his army and destroyed those murderers and burned their city.

8 "Then he said to his servants, 'The wedding banquet is ready, but those I invited did not deserve to come. 9 So go to the street corners and invite to the banquet anyone you find.' 10 So the servants went out into the streets and gathered all the people they could find, the bad as well as the good, and the wedding hall was filled with guests.

11 "But when the king came in to see the guests, he noticed a man there who was not wearing wedding clothes. 12 He asked, 'How did you get in here without wedding clothes, friend?' The man was speechless.

13 "Then the king told the attendants, 'Tie him hand and foot, and throw him outside, into the darkness, where there will be weeping and gnashing of teeth.'

14 "For many are invited, but few are chosen."

Paying the Imperial Tax to Caesar

15 Then the Pharisees went out and laid plans to trap him in his words. 16 They sent their disciples to him along with the Herodians. "Teacher," they said, "we know that you are a man of integrity and that you teach the way of God in accordance with the truth. You aren't swayed by others, because you pay no attention to who they are. 17 Tell us then, what is your opinion? Is it right to pay the imperial tax[a] to Caesar or not?"

18 But Jesus, knowing their evil intent, said, "You hypocrites, why are you trying to trap me? 19 Show me the coin used for paying the tax." They brought him a denarius, 20 and he asked them, "Whose image is this? And whose inscription?"

21 "Caesar's," they replied.

Then he said to them, "So give back to Caesar what is Caesar's, and to God what is God's."

22 When they heard this, they were amazed. So they left him and went away.

Marriage at the Resurrection

23 That same day the Sadducees, who say there is no resurrection, came to him with a question. 24 "Teacher," they said, "Moses told us that if a man dies without having children, his brother must marry the widow and raise up offspring for him. 25 Now there were seven brothers among us. The first one married and died, and since he had no children, he left his wife to his brother. 26 The same thing happened to the second and third brother, right on down to the seventh. 27 Finally, the woman died. 28 Now then, at the resurrection, whose wife will she be of the seven, since all of them were married to her?"

29 Jesus replied, "You are in error because you do not know the Scriptures or the power of God. 30 At the resurrection people will neither marry nor be given in marriage; they will be like the angels in heaven. 31 But about the resurrection of the dead—have you not read what God said to you, 32 'I am the God of Abraham, the God of Isaac, and the God of Jacob'[b]? He is not the God of the dead but of the living."

33 When the crowds heard this, they were astonished at his teaching.

The Greatest Commandment

34 Hearing that Jesus had silenced the Sadducees, the Pharisees got together. 35 One of them, an expert in the law, tested him with this question: 36 "Teacher, which is the greatest commandment in the Law?"

37 Jesus replied: " 'Love the Lord your God with all your heart and with all your soul and with all your mind.'[c] 38 This is the first and greatest commandment. 39 And the second is like it: 'Love your neighbor as yourself.'[d] 40 All the Law and the Prophets hang on these two commandments."

Whose Son Is the Messiah?

41 While the Pharisees were gathered together, Jesus asked them, 42 "What do you think about the Messiah? Whose son is he?"

"The son of David," they replied.

43 He said to them, "How is it then that

---

[a] 17 A special tax levied on subject peoples, not on Roman citizens   [b] 32 Exodus 3:6   [c] 37 Deut. 6:5
[d] 39 Lev. 19:18

David, speaking by the Spirit, calls him 'Lord'? For he says,

44 " 'The Lord said to my Lord:
    "Sit at my right hand
    until I put your enemies
    under your feet." ' [a]

45 If then David calls him 'Lord,' how can he be his son?" 46 No one could say a word in reply, and from that day on no one dared to ask him any more questions.

A Warning Against Hypocrisy

23 Then Jesus said to the crowds and to his disciples: 2 "The teachers of the law and the Pharisees sit in Moses' seat. 3 So you must be careful to do everything they tell you. But do not do what they do, for they do not practice what they preach. 4 They tie up heavy, cumbersome loads and put them on other people's shoulders, but they themselves are not willing to lift a finger to move them.

5 "Everything they do is done for people to see: They make their phylacteries [b] wide and the tassels on their garments long; 6 they love the place of honor at banquets and the most important seats in the synagogues; 7 they love to be greeted with respect in the marketplaces and to be called 'Rabbi' by others.

8 "But you are not to be called 'Rabbi,' for you have one Teacher, and you are all brothers. 9 And do not call anyone on earth 'father,' for you have one Father, and he is in heaven. 10 Nor are you to be called instructors, for you have one Instructor, the Messiah. 11 The greatest among you will be your servant. 12 For those who exalt themselves will be humbled, and those who humble themselves will be exalted.

Seven Woes on the Teachers of the Law and the Pharisees

13 "Woe to you, teachers of the law and Pharisees, you hypocrites! You shut the door of the kingdom of heaven in people's faces. You yourselves do not enter, nor will you let those enter who are trying to. [14] [c]

15 "Woe to you, teachers of the law and Pharisees, you hypocrites! You travel over land and sea to win a single convert, and when you have succeeded, you make them twice as much a child of hell as you are.

16 "Woe to you, blind guides! You say, 'If anyone swears by the temple, it means nothing; but anyone who swears by the gold of the temple is bound by that oath.' 17 You blind fools! Which is greater: the gold, or the temple that makes the gold sacred? 18 You also say, 'If anyone swears by the altar, it means nothing; but anyone who swears by the gift on the altar is bound by that oath.' 19 You blind men! Which is greater: the gift, or the altar that makes the gift sacred? 20 Therefore, anyone who swears by the altar swears by it and by everything on it. 21 And anyone who swears by the temple swears by it and by the one who dwells in it. 22 And anyone who swears by heaven swears by God's throne and by the one who sits on it.

23 "Woe to you, teachers of the law and Pharisees, you hypocrites! You give a tenth of your spices — mint, dill and cumin. But you have neglected the more important matters of the law — justice, mercy and faithfulness. You should have practiced the latter, without neglecting the former. 24 You blind guides! You strain out a gnat but swallow a camel.

25 "Woe to you, teachers of the law and Pharisees, you hypocrites! You clean the outside of the cup and dish, but inside they are full of greed and self-indulgence. 26 Blind Pharisee! First clean the inside of the cup and dish, and then the outside also will be clean.

27 "Woe to you, teachers of the law and Pharisees, you hypocrites! You are like whitewashed tombs, which look beautiful on the outside but on the inside are full of the bones of the dead and everything unclean. 28 In the same way, on the outside you appear to people as righteous but on the inside you are full of hypocrisy and wickedness.

29 "Woe to you, teachers of the law and Pharisees, you hypocrites! You build tombs for the prophets and decorate the graves of the righteous. 30 And you say, 'If we had lived in the days of our ancestors, we would not have taken part with them in shedding the blood of the prophets.' 31 So you testify

---

[a] 44 Psalm 110:1   [b] 5 That is, boxes containing Scripture verses, worn on forehead and arm
[c] 14 Some manuscripts include here words similar to Mark 12:40 and Luke 20:47.

against yourselves that you are the descendants of those who murdered the prophets. [32]Go ahead, then, and complete what your ancestors started!

[33]"You snakes! You brood of vipers! How will you escape being condemned to hell? [34]Therefore I am sending you prophets and sages and teachers. Some of them you will kill and crucify; others you will flog in your synagogues and pursue from town to town. [35]And so upon you will come all the righteous blood that has been shed on earth, from the blood of righteous Abel to the blood of Zechariah son of Berekiah, whom you murdered between the temple and the altar. [36]Truly I tell you, all this will come on this generation.

[37]"Jerusalem, Jerusalem, you who kill the prophets and stone those sent to you, how often I have longed to gather your children together, as a hen gathers her chicks under her wings, and you were not willing. [38]Look, your house is left to you desolate. [39]For I tell you, you will not see me again until you say, 'Blessed is he who comes in the name of the Lord.'[a]"

The Destruction of the Temple and Signs of the End Times

24 Jesus left the temple and was walking away when his disciples came up to him to call his attention to its buildings. [2]"Do you see all these things?" he asked. "Truly I tell you, not one stone here will be left on another; every one will be thrown down."

[3]As Jesus was sitting on the Mount of Olives, the disciples came to him privately. "Tell us," they said, "when will this happen, and what will be the sign of your coming and of the end of the age?"

[4]Jesus answered: "Watch out that no one deceives you. [5]For many will come in my name, claiming, 'I am the Messiah,' and will deceive many. [6]You will hear of wars and rumors of wars, but see to it that you are not alarmed. Such things must happen, but the end is still to come. [7]Nation will rise against nation, and kingdom against kingdom. There will be famines and earthquakes in various places. [8]All these are the beginning of birth pains.

[9]"Then you will be handed over to be persecuted and put to death, and you will be hated by all nations because of me. [10]At that time many will turn away from the faith and will betray and hate each other, [11]and many false prophets will appear and deceive many people. [12]Because of the increase of wickedness, the love of most will grow cold, [13]but the one who stands firm to the end will be saved. [14]And this gospel of the kingdom will be preached in the whole world as a testimony to all nations, and then the end will come.

[15]"So when you see standing in the holy place 'the abomination that causes desolation,'[b] spoken of through the prophet Daniel—let the reader understand— [16]then let those who are in Judea flee to the mountains. [17]Let no one on the housetop go down to take anything out of the house. [18]Let no one in the field go back to get their cloak. [19]How dreadful it will be in those days for pregnant women and nursing mothers! [20]Pray that your flight will not take place in winter or on the Sabbath. [21]For then there will be great distress, unequaled from the beginning of the world until now—and never to be equaled again.

[22]"If those days had not been cut short, no one would survive, but for the sake of the elect those days will be shortened. [23]At that time if anyone says to you, 'Look, here is the Messiah!' or, 'There he is!' do not believe it. [24]For false messiahs and false prophets will appear and perform great signs and wonders to deceive, if possible, even the elect. [25]See, I have told you ahead of time.

[26]"So if anyone tells you, 'There he is, out in the wilderness,' do not go out; or, 'Here he is, in the inner rooms,' do not believe it. [27]For as lightning that comes from the east is visible even in the west, so will be the coming of the Son of Man. [28]Wherever there is a carcass, there the vultures will gather.

[29]"Immediately after the distress of those days

"'the sun will be darkened,
    and the moon will not give
        its light;
the stars will fall from the sky,
    and the heavenly bodies will be
        shaken.'[c]

---

[a] 39 Psalm 118:26   [b] 15 Daniel 9:27; 11:31; 12:11   [c] 29 Isaiah 13:10; 34:4

[30] "Then will appear the sign of the Son of Man in heaven. And then all the peoples of the earth[a] will mourn when they see the Son of Man coming on the clouds of heaven, with power and great glory.[b] [31] And he will send his angels with a loud trumpet call, and they will gather his elect from the four winds, from one end of the heavens to the other.

[32] "Now learn this lesson from the fig tree: As soon as its twigs get tender and its leaves come out, you know that summer is near. [33] Even so, when you see all these things, you know that it[c] is near, right at the door. [34] Truly I tell you, this generation will certainly not pass away until all these things have happened. [35] Heaven and earth will pass away, but my words will never pass away.

The Day and Hour Unknown

[36] "But about that day or hour no one knows, not even the angels in heaven, nor the Son,[d] but only the Father. [37] As it was in the days of Noah, so it will be at the coming of the Son of Man. [38] For in the days before the flood, people were eating and drinking, marrying and giving in marriage, up to the day Noah entered the ark; [39] and they knew nothing about what would happen until the flood came and took them all away. That is how it will be at the coming of the Son of Man. [40] Two men will be in the field; one will be taken and the other left. [41] Two women will be grinding with a hand mill; one will be taken and the other left.

[42] "Therefore keep watch, because you do not know on what day your Lord will come. [43] But understand this: If the owner of the house had known at what time of night the thief was coming, he would have kept watch and would not have let his house be broken into. [44] So you also must be ready, because the Son of Man will come at an hour when you do not expect him.

[45] "Who then is the faithful and wise servant, whom the master has put in charge of the servants in his household to give them their food at the proper time? [46] It will be good for that servant whose master finds him doing so when he returns. [47] Truly I tell you, he will put him in charge of all his possessions. [48] But suppose that servant is wicked and says to himself, 'My master is staying away a long time,' [49] and he then begins to beat his fellow servants and to eat and drink with drunkards. [50] The master of that servant will come on a day when he does not expect him and at an hour he is not aware of. [51] He will cut him to pieces and assign him a place with the hypocrites, where there will be weeping and gnashing of teeth.

The Parable of the Ten Virgins

25 "At that time the kingdom of heaven will be like ten virgins who took their lamps and went out to meet the bridegroom. [2] Five of them were foolish and five were wise. [3] The foolish ones took their lamps but did not take any oil with them. [4] The wise ones, however, took oil in jars along with their lamps. [5] The bridegroom was a long time in coming, and they all became drowsy and fell asleep.

[6] "At midnight the cry rang out: 'Here's the bridegroom! Come out to meet him!'

[7] "Then all the virgins woke up and trimmed their lamps. [8] The foolish ones said to the wise, 'Give us some of your oil; our lamps are going out.'

[9] " 'No,' they replied, 'there may not be enough for both us and you. Instead, go to those who sell oil and buy some for yourselves.'

[10] "But while they were on their way to buy the oil, the bridegroom arrived. The virgins who were ready went in with him to the wedding banquet. And the door was shut.

[11] "Later the others also came. 'Lord, Lord,' they said, 'open the door for us!'

[12] "But he replied, 'Truly I tell you, I don't know you.'

[13] "Therefore keep watch, because you do not know the day or the hour.

The Parable of the Bags of Gold

[14] "Again, it will be like a man going on a journey, who called his servants and entrusted his wealth to them. [15] To one he gave five bags of gold, to another two bags, and to another one bag,[e] each according to his ability. Then he went on his journey. [16] The man who had received five bags of gold went at once and put his money to work and gained five

---

[a] 30 Or *the tribes of the land*   [b] 30 See Daniel 7:13-14.   [c] 33 Or *he*   [d] 36 Some manuscripts do not have *nor the Son*.   [e] 15 Greek *five talents . . . two talents . . . one talent*; also throughout this parable; a talent was worth about 20 years of a day laborer's wage.

The Game of Risk

By Catherine Fitzgerald

READ: Matthew 25:14–30

The parable of the bags of gold (see Matthew 25:14 – 30) speaks directly to our lives as military wives. A "bag of gold" was a "talent" in Greek; and a talent, first used for a unit of weight and then for a unit of coinage, was worth about 20 years of a laborer's wages. God gives us gifts, time and other resources, and he expects us to invest them wisely. But so often we feel as though we have to shelve them to accommodate the demands of military life.

One day a woman sat at my table looking into her cup of tea as tears welled in her eyes. "I feel so alone and depressed, like I have no purpose here," she said.

Her story was one I had heard many times. In fact, it had once been mine. Every military wife struggles to find her mission within a lifestyle that revolves around the career of the man she loves. The woman told me about her love for music and singing and about her desire to help others and serve the Lord. I explained that I had been in her shoes a few years before, asking God what he wanted me to do in the midst of constant moves, deployments and changes. It was then that he called me to a life of ministry: using my organizational skills to gather women around me for fellowship and using my teaching degree to explain God's Word and its application to our lives. Quickly, her eyes lit up and she knew what had to be done. Within weeks she was singing on stage at the church and using her spiritual gifts within our military ministry.

Too often we become like the wicked, lazy servant as we hide what God has given us. But when we use our gifts and talents, we are like the faithful servants who earned praise from their master (see Matthew 25:21,23). The two servants who heard, "Well done, good and faithful servant," were willing to *risk* and *invest*.

Fear, excuses and doubt can keep us from the return God longs for in our lives. We can blame the military. We can blame our husband's schedule or deployment. Yet when we risk possible failure or even losing the resources God has given us, God's strength is shown in our weakness.

Our God longs to produce fruit from the gifts he has entrusted to us. We need to get creative and find new ways to use our abilities right where we are. Are you up for the challenge? God has uniquely gifted each one of us with a set of talents, gifts, education and experiences so that we can take the risk of using those things for his glory. He expects his investment to come back with bountiful fruit.

> "His master replied, 'Well done, good and faithful servant! You have been faithful with a few things; I will put you in charge of many things. Come and share your master's happiness!'"
>
> MATTHEW 25:23

DEBRIEF

- What talents and other assets has God given me?
- How can I use these gifts in this season of my life?

REPORT

Lord, give me the boldness to risk using the gifts you have entrusted to me. Reveal to me the opportunities to invest in the lives around me. Show me the way to those words my heart longs to hear: "Well done, good and faithful servant." In your Son's precious name I pray. Amen.

bags more. [17] So also, the one with two bags of gold gained two more. [18] But the man who had received one bag went off, dug a hole in the ground and hid his master's money.

[19] "After a long time the master of those servants returned and settled accounts with them. [20] The man who had received five bags of gold brought the other five. 'Master,' he said, 'you entrusted me with five bags of gold. See, I have gained five more.'

[21] "His master replied, 'Well done, good and faithful servant! You have been faithful with a few things; I will put you in charge of many things. Come and share your master's happiness!'

[22] "The man with two bags of gold also came. 'Master,' he said, 'you entrusted me with two bags of gold; see, I have gained two more.'

[23] "His master replied, 'Well done, good and faithful servant! You have been faithful with a few things; I will put you in charge of many things. Come and share your master's happiness!'

[24] "Then the man who had received one bag of gold came. 'Master,' he said, 'I knew that you are a hard man, harvesting where you have not sown and gathering where you have not scattered seed. [25] So I was afraid and went out and hid your gold in the ground. See, here is what belongs to you.'

[26] "His master replied, 'You wicked, lazy servant! So you knew that I harvest where I have not sown and gather where I have not scattered seed? [27] Well then, you should have put my money on deposit with the bankers, so that when I returned I would have received it back with interest.

[28] " 'So take the bag of gold from him and give it to the one who has ten bags. [29] For whoever has will be given more, and they will have an abundance. Whoever does not have, even what they have will be taken from them. [30] And throw that worthless servant outside, into the darkness, where there will be weeping and gnashing of teeth.'

The Sheep and the Goats

[31] "When the Son of Man comes in his glory, and all the angels with him, he will sit on his glorious throne. [32] All the nations will be gathered before him, and he will separate the people one from another as a shepherd separates the sheep from the goats. [33] He will put the sheep on his right and the goats on his left.

[34] "Then the King will say to those on his right, 'Come, you who are blessed by my Father; take your inheritance, the kingdom prepared for you since the creation of the world. [35] For I was hungry and you gave me something to eat, I was thirsty and you gave me something to drink, I was a stranger and you invited me in, [36] I needed clothes and you clothed me, I was sick and you looked after me, I was in prison and you came to visit me.'

[37] "Then the righteous will answer him, 'Lord, when did we see you hungry and feed you, or thirsty and give you something to drink? [38] When did we see you a stranger and invite you in, or needing clothes and clothe you? [39] When did we see you sick or in prison and go to visit you?'

[40] "The King will reply, 'Truly I tell you, whatever you did for one of the least of these brothers and sisters of mine, you did for me.'

[41] "Then he will say to those on his left, 'Depart from me, you who are cursed, into the eternal fire prepared for the devil and his angels. [42] For I was hungry and you gave me nothing to eat, I was thirsty and you gave me nothing to drink, [43] I was a stranger and you did not invite me in, I needed clothes and you did not clothe me, I was sick and in prison and you did not look after me.'

[44] "They also will answer, 'Lord, when did we see you hungry or thirsty or a stranger or needing clothes or sick or in prison, and did not help you?'

[45] "He will reply, 'Truly I tell you, whatever you did not do for one of the least of these, you did not do for me.'

[46] "Then they will go away to eternal punishment, but the righteous to eternal life."

The Plot Against Jesus

26 When Jesus had finished saying all these things, he said to his disciples, [2] "As you know, the Passover is two days away — and the Son of Man will be handed over to be crucified."

[3] Then the chief priests and the elders of the people assembled in the palace of the high priest, whose name was Caiaphas, [4] and they schemed to arrest Jesus secretly and kill him. [5] "But not during the festival," they said, "or there may be a riot among the people."

Jesus Anointed at Bethany

[6]While Jesus was in Bethany in the home of Simon the Leper, [a]a woman came to him with an alabaster jar of very expensive perfume, which she poured on his head as he was reclining at the table.

[8]When the disciples saw this, they were indignant. "Why this waste?" they asked. [9]"This perfume could have been sold at a high price and the money given to the poor."

[10]Aware of this, Jesus said to them, "Why are you bothering this woman? She has done a beautiful thing to me. [11]The poor you will always have with you,[a] but you will not always have me. [12]When she poured this perfume on my body, she did it to prepare me for burial. [13]Truly I tell you, wherever this gospel is preached throughout the world, what she has done will also be told, in memory of her."

Judas Agrees to Betray Jesus

[14]Then one of the Twelve—the one called Judas Iscariot—went to the chief priests [15]and asked, "What are you willing to give me if I deliver him over to you?" So they counted out for him thirty pieces of silver. [16]From then on Judas watched for an opportunity to hand him over.

The Last Supper

[17]On the first day of the Festival of Unleavened Bread, the disciples came to Jesus and asked, "Where do you want us to make preparations for you to eat the Passover?"

[18]He replied, "Go into the city to a certain man and tell him, 'The Teacher says: My appointed time is near. I am going to celebrate the Passover with my disciples at your house.'" [19]So the disciples did as Jesus had directed them and prepared the Passover.

[20]When evening came, Jesus was reclining at the table with the Twelve. [21]And while they were eating, he said, "Truly I tell you, one of you will betray me."

[22]They were very sad and began to say to him one after the other, "Surely you don't mean me, Lord?"

[23]Jesus replied, "The one who has dipped his hand into the bowl with me will betray me. [24]The Son of Man will go just as it is written about him. But woe to that man who be-trays the Son of Man! It would be better for him if he had not been born."

[25]Then Judas, the one who would betray him, said, "Surely you don't mean me, Rabbi?"

Jesus answered, "You have said so."

[26]While they were eating, Jesus took bread, and when he had given thanks, he broke it and gave it to his disciples, saying, "Take and eat; this is my body."

[27]Then he took a cup, and when he had given thanks, he gave it to them, saying, "Drink from it, all of you. [28]This is my blood of the[b] covenant, which is poured out for many for the forgiveness of sins. [29]I tell you, I will not drink from this fruit of the vine from now on until that day when I drink it new with you in my Father's kingdom."

[30]When they had sung a hymn, they went out to the Mount of Olives.

Jesus Predicts Peter's Denial

[31]Then Jesus told them, "This very night you will all fall away on account of me, for it is written:

"'I will strike the shepherd,
    and the sheep of the flock will be
        scattered.'[c]

[32]But after I have risen, I will go ahead of you into Galilee."

[33]Peter replied, "Even if all fall away on account of you, I never will."

[34]"Truly I tell you," Jesus answered, "this very night, before the rooster crows, you will disown me three times."

[35]But Peter declared, "Even if I have to die with you, I will never disown you." And all the other disciples said the same.

Gethsemane

[36]Then Jesus went with his disciples to a place called Gethsemane, and he said to them, "Sit here while I go over there and pray." [37]He took Peter and the two sons of Zebedee along with him, and he began to be sorrowful and troubled. [38]Then he said to them, "My soul is overwhelmed with sorrow to the point of death. Stay here and keep watch with me."

[39]Going a little farther, he fell with his face to the ground and prayed, "My Father, if it is

---

[a] 11 See Deut. 15:11.   [b] 28 Some manuscripts the new   [c] 31 Zech. 13:7

possible, may this cup be taken from me. Yet not as I will, but as you will."

⁴⁰Then he returned to his disciples and found them sleeping. "Couldn't you men keep watch with me for one hour?" he asked Peter. ⁴¹"Watch and pray so that you will not fall into temptation. The spirit is willing, but the flesh is weak."

⁴²He went away a second time and prayed, "My Father, if it is not possible for this cup to be taken away unless I drink it, may your will be done."

⁴³When he came back, he again found them sleeping, because their eyes were heavy. ⁴⁴So he left them and went away once more and prayed the third time, saying the same thing.

⁴⁵Then he returned to the disciples and said to them, "Are you still sleeping and resting? Look, the hour has come, and the Son of Man is delivered into the hands of sinners. ⁴⁶Rise! Let us go! Here comes my betrayer!"

Jesus Arrested

⁴⁷While he was still speaking, Judas, one of the Twelve, arrived. With him was a large crowd armed with swords and clubs, sent from the chief priests and the elders of the people. ⁴⁸Now the betrayer had arranged a signal with them: "The one I kiss is the man; arrest him." ⁴⁹Going at once to Jesus, Judas said, "Greetings, Rabbi!" and kissed him.

⁵⁰Jesus replied, "Do what you came for, friend."[a]

Then the men stepped forward, seized Jesus and arrested him. ⁵¹With that, one of Jesus' companions reached for his sword, drew it out and struck the servant of the high priest, cutting off his ear.

⁵²"Put your sword back in its place," Jesus said to him, "for all who draw the sword will die by the sword. ⁵³Do you think I cannot call on my Father, and he will at once put at my disposal more than twelve legions of angels? ⁵⁴But how then would the Scriptures be fulfilled that say it must happen in this way?"

⁵⁵In that hour Jesus said to the crowd, "Am I leading a rebellion, that you have come out with swords and clubs to capture me? Every day I sat in the temple courts teaching, and you did not arrest me. ⁵⁶But this has all taken place that the writings of the prophets might be fulfilled." Then all the disciples deserted him and fled.

Jesus Before the Sanhedrin

⁵⁷Those who had arrested Jesus took him to Caiaphas the high priest, where the teachers of the law and the elders had assembled. ⁵⁸But Peter followed him at a distance, right up to the courtyard of the high priest. He entered and sat down with the guards to see the outcome.

⁵⁹The chief priests and the whole Sanhedrin were looking for false evidence against Jesus so that they could put him to death. ⁶⁰But they did not find any, though many false witnesses came forward.

Finally two came forward ⁶¹and declared, "This fellow said, 'I am able to destroy the temple of God and rebuild it in three days.'"

⁶²Then the high priest stood up and said to Jesus, "Are you not going to answer? What is this testimony that these men are bringing against you?" ⁶³But Jesus remained silent.

The high priest said to him, "I charge you under oath by the living God: Tell us if you are the Messiah, the Son of God."

⁶⁴"You have said so," Jesus replied. "But I say to all of you: From now on you will see the Son of Man sitting at the right hand of the Mighty One and coming on the clouds of heaven."[b]

⁶⁵Then the high priest tore his clothes and said, "He has spoken blasphemy! Why do we need any more witnesses? Look, now you have heard the blasphemy. ⁶⁶What do you think?"

"He is worthy of death," they answered.

⁶⁷Then they spit in his face and struck him with their fists. Others slapped him ⁶⁸and said, "Prophesy to us, Messiah. Who hit you?"

Peter Disowns Jesus

⁶⁹Now Peter was sitting out in the courtyard, and a servant girl came to him. "You also were with Jesus of Galilee," she said.

⁷⁰But he denied it before them all. "I don't know what you're talking about," he said.

⁷¹Then he went out to the gateway, where another servant girl saw him and said to the people there, "This fellow was with Jesus of Nazareth."

[a] 50 Or "Why have you come, friend?"   [b] 64 See Psalm 110:1; Daniel 7:13.

⁷²He denied it again, with an oath: "I don't know the man!"

⁷³After a little while, those standing there went up to Peter and said, "Surely you are one of them; your accent gives you away."

⁷⁴Then he began to call down curses, and he swore to them, "I don't know the man!"

Immediately a rooster crowed. ⁷⁵Then Peter remembered the word Jesus had spoken: "Before the rooster crows, you will disown me three times." And he went outside and wept bitterly.

Judas Hangs Himself

27 Early in the morning, all the chief priests and the elders of the people made their plans how to have Jesus executed. ²So they bound him, led him away and handed him over to Pilate the governor.

³When Judas, who had betrayed him, saw that Jesus was condemned, he was seized with remorse and returned the thirty pieces of silver to the chief priests and the elders. ⁴"I have sinned," he said, "for I have betrayed innocent blood."

"What is that to us?" they replied. "That's your responsibility."

⁵So Judas threw the money into the temple and left. Then he went away and hanged himself.

⁶The chief priests picked up the coins and said, "It is against the law to put this into the treasury, since it is blood money." ⁷So they decided to use the money to buy the potter's field as a burial place for foreigners. ⁸That is why it has been called the Field of Blood to this day. ⁹Then what was spoken by Jeremiah the prophet was fulfilled: "They took the thirty pieces of silver, the price set on him by the people of Israel, ¹⁰and they used them to buy the potter's field, as the Lord commanded me."ᵃ

Jesus Before Pilate

¹¹Meanwhile Jesus stood before the governor, and the governor asked him, "Are you the king of the Jews?"

"You have said so," Jesus replied.

¹²When he was accused by the chief priests and the elders, he gave no answer. ¹³Then Pilate asked him, "Don't you hear the testimony they are bringing against you?"

¹⁴But Jesus made no reply, not even to a single charge — to the great amazement of the governor.

¹⁵Now it was the governor's custom at the festival to release a prisoner chosen by the crowd. ¹⁶At that time they had a well-known prisoner whose name was Jesusᵇ Barabbas. ¹⁷So when the crowd had gathered, Pilate asked them, "Which one do you want me to release to you: Jesus Barabbas, or Jesus who is called the Messiah?" ¹⁸For he knew it was out of self-interest that they had handed Jesus over to him.

¹⁹While Pilate was sitting on the judge's seat, his wife sent him this message: "Don't have anything to do with that innocent man, for I have suffered a great deal today in a dream because of him."

²⁰But the chief priests and the elders persuaded the crowd to ask for Barabbas and to have Jesus executed.

²¹"Which of the two do you want me to release to you?" asked the governor.

"Barabbas," they answered.

²²"What shall I do, then, with Jesus who is called the Messiah?" Pilate asked.

They all answered, "Crucify him!"

²³"Why? What crime has he committed?" asked Pilate.

But they shouted all the louder, "Crucify him!"

²⁴When Pilate saw that he was getting nowhere, but that instead an uproar was starting, he took water and washed his hands in front of the crowd. "I am innocent of this man's blood," he said. "It is your responsibility!"

²⁵All the people answered, "His blood is on us and on our children!"

²⁶Then he released Barabbas to them. But he had Jesus flogged, and handed him over to be crucified.

The Soldiers Mock Jesus

²⁷Then the governor's soldiers took Jesus into the Praetorium and gathered the whole company of soldiers around him. ²⁸They stripped him and put a scarlet robe on him, ²⁹and then twisted together a crown of thorns and set it on his head. They put a staff in his right hand. Then they knelt in front of him and mocked him. "Hail, king of the Jews!" they said. ³⁰They spit on him, and

---

ᵃ 10 See Zech. 11:12,13; Jer. 19:1-13; 32:6-9.   ᵇ 16 Many manuscripts do not have *Jesus*; also in verse 17.

took the staff and struck him on the head again and again. [31] After they had mocked him, they took off the robe and put his own clothes on him. Then they led him away to crucify him.

The Crucifixion of Jesus

[32] As they were going out, they met a man from Cyrene, named Simon, and they forced him to carry the cross. [33] They came to a place called Golgotha (which means "the place of the skull"). [34] There they offered Jesus wine to drink, mixed with gall; but after tasting it, he refused to drink it. [35] When they had crucified him, they divided up his clothes by casting lots. [36] And sitting down, they kept watch over him there. [37] Above his head they placed the written charge against him: THIS IS JESUS, THE KING OF THE JEWS.

[38] Two rebels were crucified with him, one on his right and one on his left. [39] Those who passed by hurled insults at him, shaking their heads [40] and saying, "You who are going to destroy the temple and build it in three days, save yourself! Come down from the cross, if you are the Son of God!" [41] In the same way the chief priests, the teachers of the law and the elders mocked him. [42] "He saved others," they said, "but he can't save himself! He's the king of Israel! Let him come down now from the cross, and we will believe in him. [43] He trusts in God. Let God rescue him now if he wants him, for he said, 'I am the Son of God.'" [44] In the same way the rebels who were crucified with him also heaped insults on him.

The Death of Jesus

[45] From noon until three in the afternoon darkness came over all the land. [46] About three in the afternoon Jesus cried out in a loud voice, *"Eli, Eli,[a] lema sabachthani?"* (which means "My God, my God, why have you forsaken me?").[b]

[47] When some of those standing there heard this, they said, "He's calling Elijah."

[48] Immediately one of them ran and got a sponge. He filled it with wine vinegar, put it on a staff, and offered it to Jesus to drink. [49] The rest said, "Now leave him alone. Let's see if Elijah comes to save him."

[50] And when Jesus had cried out again in a loud voice, he gave up his spirit.

[51] At that moment the curtain of the temple was torn in two from top to bottom. The earth shook, the rocks split [52] and the tombs broke open. The bodies of many holy people who had died were raised to life. [53] They came out of the tombs after Jesus' resurrection and[c] went into the holy city and appeared to many people.

[54] When the centurion and those with him who were guarding Jesus saw the earthquake and all that had happened, they were terrified, and exclaimed, "Surely he was the Son of God!"

[55] Many women were there, watching from a distance. They had followed Jesus from Galilee to care for his needs. [56] Among them were Mary Magdalene, Mary the mother of James and Joseph,[d] and the mother of Zebedee's sons.

The Burial of Jesus

[57] As evening approached, there came a rich man from Arimathea, named Joseph, who had himself become a disciple of Jesus. [58] Going to Pilate, he asked for Jesus' body, and Pilate ordered that it be given to him. [59] Joseph took the body, wrapped it in a clean linen cloth, [60] and placed it in his own new tomb that he had cut out of the rock. He rolled a big stone in front of the entrance to the tomb and went away. [61] Mary Magdalene and the other Mary were sitting there opposite the tomb.

The Guard at the Tomb

[62] The next day, the one after Preparation Day, the chief priests and the Pharisees went to Pilate. [63] "Sir," they said, "we remember that while he was still alive that deceiver said, 'After three days I will rise again.' [64] So give the order for the tomb to be made secure until the third day. Otherwise, his disciples may come and steal the body and tell the people that he has been raised from the dead. This last deception will be worse than the first."

[65] "Take a guard," Pilate answered. "Go, make the tomb as secure as you know how." [66] So they went and made the tomb secure by

---

[a] 46 Some manuscripts *Eloi, Eloi*   [b] 46 Psalm 22:1   [c] 53 Or *tombs, and after Jesus' resurrection they*
[d] 56 Greek *Joses*, a variant of *Joseph*

Being in the Minority Doesn't Mean You're Outnumbered

By Marshéle Carter Waddell

READ: Matthew 28:16–20

J esus sent out the 11 disciples to "make disciples of all nations" (see Matthew 28:19). When their commission eventually took them outside of Israel, they were most decidedly in the minority wherever they went — religiously, ethnically, culturally, probably even economically.

Can you relate to how they must have felt? As an American living in a foreign country, I recognized I was in the minority. My strength didn't lie in numbers any longer. Being stationed overseas meant the next-door neighbors, the store owners I did business with, and the children my kids played with were of different background, race, customs and language. We were the oddity. Every conversation and every transaction was a draining cultural and linguistic exercise. Frustrations mounted. Loneliness crept into many of my days.

The same thing happens to Christians who are brave enough to live and work *in* the world yet not be *of* the world. We are tempted to think we are alone. We tend to think, "I'm the only one left who loves God and lives to serve him." At a very low point in the prophet Elijah's life, he felt very alone. "I am the only [true prophet] left," he told God (1 Kings 19:14). But Elijah was not truly alone because God was standing right there with him and had great news for him: "I reserve seven thousand in Israel — all whose knees have not bowed down to Baal and whose mouths have not kissed him" (1 Kings 19:18).

God has promised that even as the minority we will never be alone. Jesus said, "And surely I am with you always, to the very end of the age" (Matthew 28:20). We are mistaken when we conclude there is no one else who is devoted to God. God always preserves a group of believers, a remnant. He knows we need people of like mind and like faith. He knows we need the encouragement and refreshment that come from relationships with other Christians.

I've made an awesome discovery: These remnants are in every nation of the world. Whether we are at home or overseas, we can pray to connect with other believers. God will orchestrate it in his perfect measure of time. Interestingly, it was right after Elijah's lowest, loneliest moment that God brought Elisha, the man who would become Elijah's successor, into Elijah's life. As long as God is present, our lowest, loneliest points can be the prelude to a great big blessing.

"**Therefore go and make disciples of all nations, baptizing them in the name of the Father and of the Son and of the Holy Spirit, and teaching them to obey everything I have commanded you. And surely I am with you always, to the very end of the age.**"

MATTHEW 28:19–20

DEBRIEF

- What makes me feel alone or outnumbered?
- How do Matthew 28:20 and the story from 1 King 19 affect my perspective?

REPORT

Heavenly Father, thank you for your great and precious promises, the best of which is that you will never leave me. Nothing can separate me from your love. Thank you for preserving a remnant, a group of believers, in every nation. In your timing and perfect ways, please connect me with those who love you. In Jesus' name I pray. Amen.

putting a seal on the stone and posting the guard.

Jesus Has Risen

28 After the Sabbath, at dawn on the first day of the week, Mary Magdalene and the other Mary went to look at the tomb. ²There was a violent earthquake, for an angel of the Lord came down from heaven and, going to the tomb, rolled back the stone and sat on it. ³His appearance was like lightning, and his clothes were white as snow. ⁴The guards were so afraid of him that they shook and became like dead men.

⁵The angel said to the women, "Do not be afraid, for I know that you are looking for Jesus, who was crucified. ⁶He is not here; he has risen, just as he said. Come and see the place where he lay. ⁷Then go quickly and tell his disciples: 'He has risen from the dead and is going ahead of you into Galilee. There you will see him.' Now I have told you."

⁸So the women hurried away from the tomb, afraid yet filled with joy, and ran to tell his disciples. ⁹Suddenly Jesus met them. "Greetings," he said. They came to him, clasped his feet and worshiped him. ¹⁰Then Jesus said to them, "Do not be afraid. Go and tell my brothers to go to Galilee; there they will see me."

The Guards' Report

¹¹While the women were on their way, some of the guards went into the city and reported to the chief priests everything that had happened. ¹²When the chief priests had met with the elders and devised a plan, they gave the soldiers a large sum of money, ¹³telling them, "You are to say, 'His disciples came during the night and stole him away while we were asleep.' ¹⁴If this report gets to the governor, we will satisfy him and keep you out of trouble." ¹⁵So the soldiers took the money and did as they were instructed. And this story has been widely circulated among the Jews to this very day.

The Great Commission

¹⁶Then the eleven disciples went to Galilee, to the mountain where Jesus had told them to go. ¹⁷When they saw him, they worshiped him; but some doubted. ¹⁸Then Jesus came to them and said, "All authority in heaven and on earth has been given to me. ¹⁹Therefore go and make disciples of all nations, baptizing them in the name of the Father and of the Son and of the Holy Spirit, ²⁰and teaching them to obey everything I have commanded you. And surely I am with you always, to the very end of the age."

Mark

John the Baptist Prepares the Way

1 The beginning of the good news about Jesus the Messiah,[a] the Son of God,[b] [2] as it is written in Isaiah the prophet:

"I will send my messenger ahead of you,
who will prepare your way"[c] —
[3] "a voice of one calling in the wilderness,
'Prepare the way for the Lord,
make straight paths for him.' "[d]

[4] And so John the Baptist appeared in the wilderness, preaching a baptism of repentance for the forgiveness of sins. [5] The whole Judean countryside and all the people of Jerusalem went out to him. Confessing their sins, they were baptized by him in the Jordan River. [6] John wore clothing made of camel's hair, with a leather belt around his waist, and he ate locusts and wild honey. [7] And this was his message: "After me comes the one more powerful than I, the straps of whose sandals I am not worthy to stoop down and untie. [8] I baptize you with[e] water, but he will baptize you with[e] the Holy Spirit."

The Baptism and Testing of Jesus

[9] At that time Jesus came from Nazareth in Galilee and was baptized by John in the Jordan. [10] Just as Jesus was coming up out of the water, he saw heaven being torn open and the Spirit descending on him like a dove. [11] And a voice came from heaven: "You are my Son, whom I love; with you I am well pleased."

[12] At once the Spirit sent him out into the wilderness, [13] and he was in the wilderness forty days, being tempted[f] by Satan. He was with the wild animals, and angels attended him.

Jesus Announces the Good News

[14] After John was put in prison, Jesus went into Galilee, proclaiming the good news of God. [15] "The time has come," he said. "The kingdom of God has come near. Repent and believe the good news!"

Jesus Calls His First Disciples

[16] As Jesus walked beside the Sea of Galilee, he saw Simon and his brother Andrew casting a net into the lake, for they were fishermen. [17] "Come, follow me," Jesus said, "and I will send you out to fish for people." [18] At once they left their nets and followed him.

[19] When he had gone a little farther, he saw James son of Zebedee and his brother John in a boat, preparing their nets. [20] Without delay he called them, and they left their father Zebedee in the boat with the hired men and followed him.

Jesus Drives Out an Impure Spirit

[21] They went to Capernaum, and when the Sabbath came, Jesus went into the synagogue and began to teach. [22] The people were amazed at his teaching, because he taught them as one who had authority, not as the teachers of the law. [23] Just then a man in their synagogue who was possessed by an impure spirit cried out, [24] "What do you want with us, Jesus of Nazareth? Have you come to destroy us? I know who you are — the Holy One of God!"

[25] "Be quiet!" said Jesus sternly. "Come out of him!" [26] The impure spirit shook the man violently and came out of him with a shriek.

[27] The people were all so amazed that they asked each other, "What is this? A new teaching — and with authority! He even gives orders to impure spirits and they obey him." [28] News about him spread quickly over the whole region of Galilee.

Jesus Heals Many

[29] As soon as they left the synagogue, they went with James and John to the home of

---

[a] 1 Or *Jesus Christ.* Messiah (Hebrew) and *Christ* (Greek) both mean *Anointed One.*   [b] 1 Some manuscripts do not have *the Son of God.*   [c] 2 Mal. 3:1   [d] 3 Isaiah 40:3   [e] 8 Or *in*   [f] 13 The Greek for *tempted* can also mean *tested.*

Simon and Andrew. [30] Simon's mother-in-law was in bed with a fever, and they immediately told Jesus about her. [31] So he went to her, took her hand and helped her up. The fever left her and she began to wait on them.

[32] That evening after sunset the people brought to Jesus all the sick and demon-possessed. [33] The whole town gathered at the door, [34] and Jesus healed many who had various diseases. He also drove out many demons, but he would not let the demons speak because they knew who he was.

Jesus Prays in a Solitary Place

[35] Very early in the morning, while it was still dark, Jesus got up, left the house and went off to a solitary place, where he prayed. [36] Simon and his companions went to look for him, [37] and when they found him, they exclaimed: "Everyone is looking for you!"

[38] Jesus replied, "Let us go somewhere else — to the nearby villages — so I can preach there also. That is why I have come." [39] So he traveled throughout Galilee, preaching in their synagogues and driving out demons.

Jesus Heals a Man With Leprosy

[40] A man with leprosy[a] came to him and begged him on his knees, "If you are willing, you can make me clean."

[41] Jesus was indignant.[b] He reached out his hand and touched the man. "I am willing," he said. "Be clean!" [42] Immediately the leprosy left him and he was cleansed.

[43] Jesus sent him away at once with a strong warning: [44] "See that you don't tell this to anyone. But go, show yourself to the priest and offer the sacrifices that Moses commanded for your cleansing, as a testimony to them." [45] Instead he went out and began to talk freely, spreading the news. As a result, Jesus could no longer enter a town openly but stayed outside in lonely places. Yet the people still came to him from everywhere.

Jesus Forgives and Heals a Paralyzed Man

2 A few days later, when Jesus again entered Capernaum, the people heard that he had come home. [2] They gathered in such large numbers that there was no room left, not even outside the door, and he preached the word to them. [3] Some men came, bringing to him a paralyzed man, carried by four of them. [4] Since they could not get him to Jesus because of the crowd, they made an opening in the roof above Jesus by digging through it and then lowered the mat the man was lying on. [5] When Jesus saw their faith, he said to the paralyzed man, "Son, your sins are forgiven."

[6] Now some teachers of the law were sitting there, thinking to themselves, [7] "Why does this fellow talk like that? He's blaspheming! Who can forgive sins but God alone?"

[8] Immediately Jesus knew in his spirit that this was what they were thinking in their hearts, and he said to them, "Why are you thinking these things? [9] Which is easier: to say to this paralyzed man, 'Your sins are forgiven,' or to say, 'Get up, take your mat and walk'? [10] But I want you to know that the Son of Man has authority on earth to forgive sins." So he said to the man, [11] "I tell you, get up, take your mat and go home." [12] He got up, took his mat and walked out in full view of them all. This amazed everyone and they praised God, saying, "We have never seen anything like this!"

Jesus Calls Levi and Eats With Sinners

[13] Once again Jesus went out beside the lake. A large crowd came to him, and he began to teach them. [14] As he walked along, he saw Levi son of Alphaeus sitting at the tax collector's booth. "Follow me," Jesus told him, and Levi got up and followed him.

[15] While Jesus was having dinner at Levi's house, many tax collectors and sinners were eating with him and his disciples, for there were many who followed him. [16] When the teachers of the law who were Pharisees saw him eating with the sinners and tax collectors, they asked his disciples: "Why does he eat with tax collectors and sinners?"

[17] On hearing this, Jesus said to them, "It is not the healthy who need a doctor, but the sick. I have not come to call the righteous, but sinners."

[a] 40 The Greek word traditionally translated leprosy was used for various diseases affecting the skin.
[b] 41 Many manuscripts Jesus was filled with compassion

Silence and Solitude

By Ronda Sturgill

READ: Mark 1:35–39

I love the word picture Mark 1:35 conjures up in my mind. Before the break of dawn, Jesus slipped into his sandals and silently headed to a remote place in the hills. Was this a special place he often visited when he felt like he needed to be alone? Although we may not know exactly where he was headed, we do know that he was intentional about getting there. He deliberately sought out a time of solitude.

I recently led a workshop on silence and solitude at a retreat for military wives. For one hour, we individually went off to a solitary place. Some prayed, some worshiped, some listened, but we all attended to God. In our hour of stillness, each of us heard and saw God in unexpected ways.

In *Emotionally Healthy Spirituality*, Peter Scazzero writes, "Silence and solitude are the most challenging and least practiced disciplines among Christians today." Most of us tend to feel guilty if we spend time doing nothing, and if we were to be completely honest, few of us like the idea of being still and quiet for long periods of time. But as Dallas Willard states in *The Great Omission: Reclaiming Jesus' Essential Teachings on Discipleship*, the truth is that "no time is more profitably spent than that used to heighten the quality of an intimate walk with God."

Time alone with God allows us to center ourselves, set aside our long to-do lists and frenzied schedules, and be still. Silent. Quiet. Moving into his presence we can open our heart as we attend to God. What is he telling us through the events of the day? In what ways might God be challenging us to rethink old habits and behaviors and take on new thoughts, attitudes and actions?

The time alone that Jesus spent in prayer allowed him to reevaluate his work. Notice that when the disciples found Jesus, he immediately left that location and moved on to another place so he could preach somewhere else (see Mark 1:38–39). Through his time alone with God, Jesus was able to hear and discern the will of the Father. How can we expect to hear and discern the will of the Father if we're being bombarded with noise all day long?

Just as Jesus was determined to find solitude, so must we. Dallas Willard wrote that "time is made, not found." Start out with small amounts of time and gradually build up to longer periods. God waits lovingly and longingly for us to enter into his presence. Will we deliberately make time to meet him there?

> **Very early in the morning, while it was still dark, Jesus got up, left the house and went off to a solitary place, where he prayed.**
>
> MARK 1:35

DEBRIEF

- As I look at my schedule for the coming week, where can I spend 10 minutes in silence and solitude each day?
- What might happen if I did this faithfully?

REPORT

Dear heavenly Father, I want to spend time with you in silence and solitude. Help me to find a few minutes each day to set aside my busy schedule and enter into your presence. As I attend to you, speak to me. I am listening and waiting expectantly. Amen.

Jesus Questioned About Fasting

[18] Now John's disciples and the Pharisees were fasting. Some people came and asked Jesus, "How is it that John's disciples and the disciples of the Pharisees are fasting, but yours are not?"

[19] Jesus answered, "How can the guests of the bridegroom fast while he is with them? They cannot, so long as they have him with them. [20] But the time will come when the bridegroom will be taken from them, and on that day they will fast.

[21] "No one sews a patch of unshrunk cloth on an old garment. Otherwise, the new piece will pull away from the old, making the tear worse. [22] And no one pours new wine into old wineskins. Otherwise, the wine will burst the skins, and both the wine and the wineskins will be ruined. No, they pour new wine into new wineskins."

Jesus Is Lord of the Sabbath

[23] One Sabbath Jesus was going through the grainfields, and as his disciples walked along, they began to pick some heads of grain. [24] The Pharisees said to him, "Look, why are they doing what is unlawful on the Sabbath?"

[25] He answered, "Have you never read what David did when he and his companions were hungry and in need? [26] In the days of Abiathar the high priest, he entered the house of God and ate the consecrated bread, which is lawful only for priests to eat. And he also gave some to his companions."

[27] Then he said to them, "The Sabbath was made for man, not man for the Sabbath. [28] So the Son of Man is Lord even of the Sabbath."

Jesus Heals on the Sabbath

3 Another time Jesus went into the synagogue, and a man with a shriveled hand was there. [2] Some of them were looking for a reason to accuse Jesus, so they watched him closely to see if he would heal him on the Sabbath. [3] Jesus said to the man with the shriveled hand, "Stand up in front of everyone."

[4] Then Jesus asked them, "Which is lawful on the Sabbath: to do good or to do evil, to save life or to kill?" But they remained silent.

[5] He looked around at them in anger and, deeply distressed at their stubborn hearts, said to the man, "Stretch out your hand." He stretched it out, and his hand was completely restored. [6] Then the Pharisees went out and began to plot with the Herodians how they might kill Jesus.

Crowds Follow Jesus

[7] Jesus withdrew with his disciples to the lake, and a large crowd from Galilee followed. [8] When they heard about all he was doing, many people came to him from Judea, Jerusalem, Idumea, and the regions across the Jordan and around Tyre and Sidon. [9] Because of the crowd he told his disciples to have a small boat ready for him, to keep the people from crowding him. [10] For he had healed many, so that those with diseases were pushing forward to touch him. [11] Whenever the impure spirits saw him, they fell down before him and cried out, "You are the Son of God." [12] But he gave them strict orders not to tell others about him.

Jesus Appoints the Twelve

[13] Jesus went up on a mountainside and called to him those he wanted, and they came to him. [14] He appointed twelve[a] that they might be with him and that he might send them out to preach [15] and to have authority to drive out demons. [16] These are the twelve he appointed: Simon (to whom he gave the name Peter), [17] James son of Zebedee and his brother John (to them he gave the name Boanerges, which means "sons of thunder"), [18] Andrew, Philip, Bartholomew, Matthew, Thomas, James son of Alphaeus, Thaddaeus, Simon the Zealot [19] and Judas Iscariot, who betrayed him.

Jesus Accused by His Family and by Teachers of the Law

[20] Then Jesus entered a house, and again a crowd gathered, so that he and his disciples were not even able to eat. [21] When his family[b] heard about this, they went to take charge of him, for they said, "He is out of his mind."

[22] And the teachers of the law who came down from Jerusalem said, "He is possessed by Beelzebul! By the prince of demons he is driving out demons."

[23] So Jesus called them over to him and

---

[a] 14 Some manuscripts *twelve—designating them apostles* —   [b] 21 Or *his associates*

began to speak to them in parables: "How can Satan drive out Satan? [24]If a kingdom is divided against itself, that kingdom cannot stand. [25]If a house is divided against itself, that house cannot stand. [26]And if Satan opposes himself and is divided, he cannot stand; his end has come. [27]In fact, no one can enter a strong man's house without first tying him up. Then he can plunder the strong man's house. [28]Truly I tell you, people can be forgiven all their sins and every slander they utter, [29]but whoever blasphemes against the Holy Spirit will never be forgiven; they are guilty of an eternal sin."

[30]He said this because they were saying, "He has an impure spirit."

[31]Then Jesus' mother and brothers arrived. Standing outside, they sent someone in to call him. [32]A crowd was sitting around him, and they told him, "Your mother and brothers are outside looking for you."

[33]"Who are my mother and my brothers?" he asked.

[34]Then he looked at those seated in a circle around him and said, "Here are my mother and my brothers! [35]Whoever does God's will is my brother and sister and mother."

The Parable of the Sower

4 Again Jesus began to teach by the lake. The crowd that gathered around him was so large that he got into a boat and sat in it out on the lake, while all the people were along the shore at the water's edge. [2]He taught them many things by parables, and in his teaching said: [3]"Listen! A farmer went out to sow his seed. [4]As he was scattering the seed, some fell along the path, and the birds came and ate it up. [5]Some fell on rocky places, where it did not have much soil. It sprang up quickly, because the soil was shallow. [6]But when the sun came up, the plants were scorched, and they withered because they had no root. [7]Other seed fell among thorns, which grew up and choked the plants, so that they did not bear grain. [8]Still other seed fell on good soil. It came up, grew and produced a crop, some multiplying thirty, some sixty, some a hundred times."

[9]Then Jesus said, "Whoever has ears to hear, let them hear."

[10]When he was alone, the Twelve and the others around him asked him about the parables. [11]He told them, "The secret of the kingdom of God has been given to you. But to those on the outside everything is said in parables [12]so that,

" 'they may be ever seeing but never
        perceiving,
    and ever hearing but never
        understanding;
otherwise they might turn and be
        forgiven!'[a]"

[13]Then Jesus said to them, "Don't you understand this parable? How then will you understand any parable? [14]The farmer sows the word. [15]Some people are like seed along the path, where the word is sown. As soon as they hear it, Satan comes and takes away the word that was sown in them. [16]Others, like seed sown on rocky places, hear the word and at once receive it with joy. [17]But since they have no root, they last only a short time. When trouble or persecution comes because of the word, they quickly fall away. [18]Still others, like seed sown among thorns, hear the word; [19]but the worries of this life, the deceitfulness of wealth and the desires for other things come in and choke the word, making it unfruitful. [20]Others, like seed sown on good soil, hear the word, accept it, and produce a crop—some thirty, some sixty, some a hundred times what was sown."

A Lamp on a Stand

[21]He said to them, "Do you bring in a lamp to put it under a bowl or a bed? Instead, don't you put it on its stand? [22]For whatever is hidden is meant to be disclosed, and whatever is concealed is meant to be brought out into the open. [23]If anyone has ears to hear, let them hear."

[24]"Consider carefully what you hear," he continued. "With the measure you use, it will be measured to you—and even more. [25]Whoever has will be given more; whoever does not have, even what they have will be taken from them."

The Parable of the Growing Seed

[26]He also said, "This is what the kingdom of God is like. A man scatters seed on the ground. [27]Night and day, whether he sleeps

[a] 12 Isaiah 6:9,10

Quiet! Be Still!

By Rosie Williams

READ: Mark 4

I can't do this anymore!" Marcia's husband blurted out. Thinking he just needed encouragement to finish the culminating exercise for his three years of Special Forces training, she responded, "I'm sure you can do it!" But he spouted back, "You don't understand. I can't do this anymore. I'm past the breaking point. I want out!"

Marcia realized it was more than the training course he wanted out of … it was his very life. The trauma he experienced as a medic during multiple tours of duty consumed him. Suddenly, the tidal wave that had overwhelmed Marcia's husband now hit her. Feelings of helplessness and despair flooded in.

The disciples had a similar experience on the Sea of Galilee (see Mark 4:35 – 41). They were hit with a violent and unexpected storm that threatened to sink the boat, and they feared they would drown. As Jesus slept, the disciples panicked.

All day they had listened to Jesus teach. In Mark 4:17, Jesus said, "But since they have no root, they last only a short time. When trouble or persecution comes because of the word, they quickly fall away." Little did they know that this furious squall was a test of faith — faith that was rocking right along with the boat. When they cried out to Jesus for help, they watched in amazement as he spoke three terse words that completely calmed the storm: "Quiet! Be still!" (verse 39). Then Jesus asked them a sobering question: "Why are you so afraid? Do you still have no faith?" (verse 40). Jesus understood they knew him as a teacher and had heard his parables, but they did not truly believe that their teacher had the power to save them from spiritual death as well as physical death.

The description of waves nearly swamping the boat is comparable to the many ways military wives sometimes feel swamped by financial problems, household maintenance, isolation, parenting and the combat trauma their spouses have experienced. Consider how Jesus showed the disciples he really did care.

1. *When they cried out to Jesus, he completely calmed the storm.* There is comfort in knowing God can and will restore inner calm when we cry out to him.

2. *It was okay for them to be honest with Jesus about their concerns.* Express your honest prayers to God and watch him gently care for you.

3. *Jesus helped them deal with their fear.* When you are afraid, remember God's past care and be strong in faith.

A furious squall came up, and the waves broke over the boat, so that it was nearly swamped. Jesus was in the stern, sleeping on a cushion. The disciples woke him and said to him, "Teacher, don't you care if we drown?"
MARK 4:37 – 38

DEBRIEF

• Am I placing my faith in my own efforts to save me from the storms of life? Where should I be placing my faith instead?

• When was the last time I was quiet and still in the midst of a stressful circumstance, trusting completely in the Lord?

REPORT

Dear Lord, please take my small mustard seed of faith and make it grow strong for your kingdom. Help my husband seek you and receive healing for his emotional and physical wounds. Give me times of quietness and stillness in your presence. In Jesus' name I pray. Amen.

---

for your next devotional reading, go to page 49

or gets up, the seed sprouts and grows, though he does not know how. [28]All by itself the soil produces grain—first the stalk, then the head, then the full kernel in the head. [29]As soon as the grain is ripe, he puts the sickle to it, because the harvest has come."

The Parable of the Mustard Seed

[30]Again he said, "What shall we say the kingdom of God is like, or what parable shall we use to describe it? [31]It is like a mustard seed, which is the smallest of all seeds on earth. [32]Yet when planted, it grows and becomes the largest of all garden plants, with such big branches that the birds can perch in its shade."

[33]With many similar parables Jesus spoke the word to them, as much as they could understand. [34]He did not say anything to them without using a parable. But when he was alone with his own disciples, he explained everything.

Jesus Calms the Storm

[35]That day when evening came, he said to his disciples, "Let us go over to the other side." [36]Leaving the crowd behind, they took him along, just as he was, in the boat. There were also other boats with him. [37]A furious squall came up, and the waves broke over the boat, so that it was nearly swamped. [38]Jesus was in the stern, sleeping on a cushion. The disciples woke him and said to him, "Teacher, don't you care if we drown?"

[39]He got up, rebuked the wind and said to the waves, "Quiet! Be still!" Then the wind died down and it was completely calm.

[40]He said to his disciples, "Why are you so afraid? Do you still have no faith?"

[41]They were terrified and asked each other, "Who is this? Even the wind and the waves obey him!"

Jesus Restores a Demon-Possessed Man

5 They went across the lake to the region of the Gerasenes.[a] [2]When Jesus got out of the boat, a man with an impure spirit came from the tombs to meet him. [3]This man lived in the tombs, and no one could bind him anymore, not even with a chain. [4]For he had often been chained hand and

foot, but he tore the chains apart and broke the irons on his feet. No one was strong enough to subdue him. [5]Night and day among the tombs and in the hills he would cry out and cut himself with stones.

[6]When he saw Jesus from a distance, he ran and fell on his knees in front of him. [7]He shouted at the top of his voice, "What do you want with me, Jesus, Son of the Most High God? In God's name don't torture me!" [8]For Jesus had said to him, "Come out of this man, you impure spirit!"

[9]Then Jesus asked him, "What is your name?"

"My name is Legion," he replied, "for we are many." [10]And he begged Jesus again and again not to send them out of the area.

[11]A large herd of pigs was feeding on the nearby hillside. [12]The demons begged Jesus, "Send us among the pigs; allow us to go into them." [13]He gave them permission, and the impure spirits came out and went into the pigs. The herd, about two thousand in number, rushed down the steep bank into the lake and were drowned.

[14]Those tending the pigs ran off and reported this in the town and countryside, and the people went out to see what had happened. [15]When they came to Jesus, they saw the man who had been possessed by the legion of demons, sitting there, dressed and in his right mind; and they were afraid. [16]Those who had seen it told the people what had happened to the demon-possessed man— and told about the pigs as well. [17]Then the people began to plead with Jesus to leave their region.

[18]As Jesus was getting into the boat, the man who had been demon-possessed begged to go with him. [19]Jesus did not let him, but said, "Go home to your own people and tell them how much the Lord has done for you, and how he has had mercy on you." [20]So the man went away and began to tell in the Decapolis[b] how much Jesus had done for him. And all the people were amazed.

Jesus Raises a Dead Girl and Heals a Sick Woman

[21]When Jesus had again crossed over by boat to the other side of the lake, a large crowd gathered around him while he was by

---

[a] 1 Some manuscripts *Gadarenes*; other manuscripts *Gergesenes*   [b] 20 That is, the Ten Cities

From Exile to Belonging

By Leeana Tankersley

READ: Mark 5:21–34

Given the transient lifestyle of the military, it's easy to feel like we don't really belong. This feeling of isolation can be very shaming. Sometimes we cover up our shame in all the wrong ways — trying to be someone we're not or projecting an image of who we are that isn't really true — thus creating more isolation and shame. Like a cycle of bleeding.

The woman in Mark 5 knew all about this. Literally. She had been bleeding for 12 years, which meant she was required by the Law of Moses to live in exile. Talk about shame! Excommunicated. Isolated. And bleeding. In her desperation, she fought her way to Jesus through a sea of people, reached out to him and touched his clothes. Immediately, she knew she had been healed.

The story could have ended there. An amazing miracle — 12 years of bleeding stopped! But there's more. Scripture says, "At once Jesus realized that power had gone out from him. He turned around in the crowd and asked, 'Who touched my clothes?'" (Mark 5:30). It wasn't that he didn't already know. Jesus, because of his love for this woman, wanted to bring attention to what had just happened. Not because her body needed anything more. But because her soul did. Jesus wasn't just healing her bleeding. He was healing her shame.

Jesus' actions sent the message that she was worthy of healing. She didn't just slip by and steal something from him. Her healing wasn't an accident or some kind of clandestine leaking of power. She was worthy. Jesus said to her, as he says to you and to me today, "Daughter, your faith has healed you. Go in peace and be freed from your suffering" (verse 34).

The Greek word translated "suffering" in verses 29 and 34 is *mastix*, which literally refers to the lashes delivered by a whip. It wasn't much more than a year later that Jesus suffered — took the lashes — on behalf of this woman and on behalf of you and me, so that we could go in peace and be free. Through Jesus, we are no longer required to live in shame — exiled and isolated. We are made whole and freed from our suffering.

As Tim Keller wrote in *The Prodigal God: Recovering the Heart of the Christian Faith*, "[Jesus] took upon himself the full curse of human rebellion, cosmic homelessness, so that we could be welcomed into our true home."

Once we were not a people. Once we had no name. Once we were subject to shame. Now we are his daughters. Now we are free. Now we belong.

He said to her, "Daughter, your faith has healed you. Go in peace and be freed from your suffering."

MARK 5:34

DEBRIEF

- How are my issues of shame keeping me exiled and isolated?
- How can I reach out and touch Jesus today?

REPORT

God, I want to experience true belonging. Heal my shame. Bring me out of exile and suffering and into your grace and love. Amen.

for your next devotional reading, go to page 52

the lake. [22]Then one of the synagogue leaders, named Jairus, came, and when he saw Jesus, he fell at his feet. [23]He pleaded earnestly with him, "My little daughter is dying. Please come and put your hands on her so that she will be healed and live." [24]So Jesus went with him.

A large crowd followed and pressed around him. [25]And a woman was there who had been subject to bleeding for twelve years. [26]She had suffered a great deal under the care of many doctors and had spent all she had, yet instead of getting better she grew worse. [27]When she heard about Jesus, she came up behind him in the crowd and touched his cloak, [28]because she thought, "If I just touch his clothes, I will be healed." [29]Immediately her bleeding stopped and she felt in her body that she was freed from her suffering.

[30]At once Jesus realized that power had gone out from him. He turned around in the crowd and asked, "Who touched my clothes?"

[31]"You see the people crowding against you," his disciples answered, "and yet you can ask, 'Who touched me?'"

[32]But Jesus kept looking around to see who had done it. [33]Then the woman, knowing what had happened to her, came and fell at his feet and, trembling with fear, told him the whole truth. [34]He said to her, "Daughter, your faith has healed you. Go in peace and be freed from your suffering."

[35]While Jesus was still speaking, some people came from the house of Jairus, the synagogue leader. "Your daughter is dead," they said. "Why bother the teacher anymore?"

[36]Overhearing[a] what they said, Jesus told him, "Don't be afraid; just believe."

[37]He did not let anyone follow him except Peter, James and John the brother of James. [38]When they came to the home of the synagogue leader, Jesus saw a commotion, with people crying and wailing loudly. [39]He went in and said to them, "Why all this commotion and wailing? The child is not dead but asleep." [40]But they laughed at him.

After he put them all out, he took the child's father and mother and the disciples who were with him, and went in where the child was. [41]He took her by the hand and said

to her, "Talitha koum!" (which means "Little girl, I say to you, get up!"). [42]Immediately the girl stood up and began to walk around (she was twelve years old). At this they were completely astonished. [43]He gave strict orders not to let anyone know about this, and told them to give her something to eat.

A Prophet Without Honor

6 Jesus left there and went to his hometown, accompanied by his disciples. [2]When the Sabbath came, he began to teach in the synagogue, and many who heard him were amazed.

"Where did this man get these things?" they asked. "What's this wisdom that has been given him? What are these remarkable miracles he is performing? [3]Isn't this the carpenter? Isn't this Mary's son and the brother of James, Joseph,[b] Judas and Simon? Aren't his sisters here with us?" And they took offense at him.

[4]Jesus said to them, "A prophet is not without honor except in his own town, among his relatives and in his own home." [5]He could not do any miracles there, except lay his hands on a few sick people and heal them. [6]He was amazed at their lack of faith.

Jesus Sends Out the Twelve

Then Jesus went around teaching from village to village. [7]Calling the Twelve to him, he began to send them out two by two and gave them authority over impure spirits.

[8]These were his instructions: "Take nothing for the journey except a staff—no bread, no bag, no money in your belts. [9]Wear sandals but not an extra shirt. [10]Whenever you enter a house, stay there until you leave that town. [11]And if any place will not welcome you or listen to you, leave that place and shake the dust off your feet as a testimony against them."

[12]They went out and preached that people should repent. [13]They drove out many demons and anointed many sick people with oil and healed them.

John the Baptist Beheaded

[14]King Herod heard about this, for Jesus' name had become well known. Some were saying,[c] "John the Baptist has been raised

---

[a] 36 Or *Ignoring*   [b] 3 Greek *Joses*, a variant of *Joseph*   [c] 14 Some early manuscripts *He was saying*

from the dead, and that is why miraculous powers are at work in him."

[15] Others said, "He is Elijah."

And still others claimed, "He is a prophet, like one of the prophets of long ago."

[16] But when Herod heard this, he said, "John, whom I beheaded, has been raised from the dead!"

[17] For Herod himself had given orders to have John arrested, and he had him bound and put in prison. He did this because of Herodias, his brother Philip's wife, whom he had married. [18] For John had been saying to Herod, "It is not lawful for you to have your brother's wife." [19] So Herodias nursed a grudge against John and wanted to kill him. But she was not able to, [20] because Herod feared John and protected him, knowing him to be a righteous and holy man. When Herod heard John, he was greatly puzzled[a]; yet he liked to listen to him.

[21] Finally the opportune time came. On his birthday Herod gave a banquet for his high officials and military commanders and the leading men of Galilee. [22] When the daughter of[b] Herodias came in and danced, she pleased Herod and his dinner guests.

The king said to the girl, "Ask me for anything you want, and I'll give it to you." [23] And he promised her with an oath, "Whatever you ask I will give you, up to half my kingdom."

[24] She went out and said to her mother, "What shall I ask for?"

"The head of John the Baptist," she answered.

[25] At once the girl hurried in to the king with the request: "I want you to give me right now the head of John the Baptist on a platter."

[26] The king was greatly distressed, but because of his oaths and his dinner guests, he did not want to refuse her. [27] So he immediately sent an executioner with orders to bring John's head. The man went, beheaded John in the prison, [28] and brought back his head on a platter. He presented it to the girl, and she gave it to her mother. [29] On hearing of this, John's disciples came and took his body and laid it in a tomb.

Jesus Feeds the Five Thousand

[30] The apostles gathered around Jesus and reported to him all they had done and taught. [31] Then, because so many people were coming and going that they did not even have a chance to eat, he said to them, "Come with me by yourselves to a quiet place and get some rest."

[32] So they went away by themselves in a boat to a solitary place. [33] But many who saw them leaving recognized them and ran on foot from all the towns and got there ahead of them. [34] When Jesus landed and saw a large crowd, he had compassion on them, because they were like sheep without a shepherd. So he began teaching them many things.

[35] By this time it was late in the day, so his disciples came to him. "This is a remote place," they said, "and it's already very late. [36] Send the people away so that they can go to the surrounding countryside and villages and buy themselves something to eat."

[37] But he answered, "You give them something to eat."

They said to him, "That would take more than half a year's wages[c]! Are we to go and spend that much on bread and give it to them to eat?"

[38] "How many loaves do you have?" he asked. "Go and see."

When they found out, they said, "Five— and two fish."

[39] Then Jesus directed them to have all the people sit down in groups on the green grass. [40] So they sat down in groups of hundreds and fifties. [41] Taking the five loaves and the two fish and looking up to heaven, he gave thanks and broke the loaves. Then he gave them to his disciples to distribute to the people. He also divided the two fish among them all. [42] They all ate and were satisfied, [43] and the disciples picked up twelve basketfuls of broken pieces of bread and fish. [44] The number of the men who had eaten was five thousand.

Jesus Walks on the Water

[45] Immediately Jesus made his disciples get into the boat and go on ahead of him to Bethsaida, while he dismissed the crowd. [46] After leaving them, he went up on a mountainside to pray.

[47] Later that night, the boat was in the middle of the lake, and he was alone on land. [48] He saw the disciples straining at the oars,

a 20 Some early manuscripts *he did many things*   *b 22* Some early manuscripts *When his daughter*
c 37 Greek *take two hundred denarii*

Self-Care Isn't Selfish

By Jocelyn Green

READ: Mark 6:30–44

Military wives are the backbones of their families, famous for their service and quiet support of others. But when it comes to taking care of ourselves, we could use a little prompting — like the disciples received from Jesus in Mark 6:30–31.

I'll never forget what one woman said at a retreat I attended. When someone asked what they could do to support military wives during deployments, she quietly said, "Take me out for lunch. I don't have kids to cook for, so when my husband isn't home, I don't really eat."

I can relate. When my husband is gone, I skimp on sleep and settle for snacks. But when I let that go on for too long, I have a much harder time coping with life, let alone serving others with a godly attitude.

What we all need to recognize is that self-care isn't selfish. Yes, we need to spend time reading the Bible, praying, working, worshiping, serving … But neglecting our physical needs is not a spiritual discipline! If we want to function at full capacity, taking good care of our bodies is not optional — it's mission critical. Jesus said, "It is written: 'Man shall not live on bread *alone*, but on every word that comes from the mouth of God'" (Matthew 4:4, emphasis added). We need the bread of life *and* our daily bread.

Look again at Mark 6:30–44. Jesus wanted his disciples to get some rest (see also Psalm 23:2 and Psalm 127:2). As military wives, I'm sure we would welcome a quiet break in our own lives! Not only did Jesus show concern for his disciples' physical needs, but he also performed a miracle to feed the 5,000 people who interrupted their day off. Jesus could have assumed these people were content to skip a meal in order to hear him teach. But Jesus was concerned for them. He fed their souls — and then he also fed their bodies.

"God made us a unity of body and soul, and one influences the other," Donald S. Whitney wrote in *Simplify Your Spiritual Life: Spiritual Disciplines for the Overwhelmed*. "When your body is exhausted, it tends to dampen the zeal of your soul. In fact, fatigue often weakens our resolve against temptation, and provides excuses for anger, lust, and other sins."

If you feel guilty for meeting your own physical needs, remember this: Jesus told his disciples to eat and rest, and if you are his follower, that applies to you too! When you take care of yourself, you'll be able to take better care of others.

Then, because so many people were coming and going that they did not even have a chance to eat, he said to them, "Come with me by yourselves to a quiet place and get some rest." So they went away by themselves in a boat to a solitary place.

MARK 6:31–32

DEBRIEF
- In what area(s) of my life could I take better care of myself?
- How would my ability to serve improve if I took better care of myself?

REPORT
Lord, please nourish my soul with your Word, and help me take proper care of the body you have given me. I value all the gifts you have given me and promise to work to protect them. Amen.

because the wind was against them. Shortly before dawn he went out to them, walking on the lake. He was about to pass by them, [49] but when they saw him walking on the lake, they thought he was a ghost. They cried out, [50] because they all saw him and were terrified.

Immediately he spoke to them and said, "Take courage! It is I. Don't be afraid." [51] Then he climbed into the boat with them, and the wind died down. They were completely amazed, [52] for they had not understood about the loaves; their hearts were hardened.

[53] When they had crossed over, they landed at Gennesaret and anchored there. [54] As soon as they got out of the boat, people recognized Jesus. [55] They ran throughout that whole region and carried the sick on mats to wherever they heard he was. [56] And wherever he went — into villages, towns or countryside — they placed the sick in the marketplaces. They begged him to let them touch even the edge of his cloak, and all who touched it were healed.

That Which Defiles

7 The Pharisees and some of the teachers of the law who had come from Jerusalem gathered around Jesus [2] and saw some of his disciples eating food with hands that were defiled, that is, unwashed. [3] (The Pharisees and all the Jews do not eat unless they give their hands a ceremonial washing, holding to the tradition of the elders. [4] When they come from the marketplace they do not eat unless they wash. And they observe many other traditions, such as the washing of cups, pitchers and kettles.[a])

[5] So the Pharisees and teachers of the law asked Jesus, "Why don't your disciples live according to the tradition of the elders instead of eating their food with defiled hands?"

[6] He replied, "Isaiah was right when he prophesied about you hypocrites; as it is written:

" 'These people honor me with their lips,
    but their hearts are far from me.
[7] They worship me in vain;
    their teachings are merely human
        rules.'[b]

[8] You have let go of the commands of God and are holding on to human traditions."

[9] And he continued, "You have a fine way of setting aside the commands of God in order to observe[c] your own traditions! [10] For Moses said, 'Honor your father and mother,'[d] and, 'Anyone who curses their father or mother is to be put to death.'[e] [11] But you say that if anyone declares that what might have been used to help their father or mother is Corban (that is, devoted to God) — [12] then you no longer let them do anything for their father or mother. [13] Thus you nullify the word of God by your tradition that you have handed down. And you do many things like that."

[14] Again Jesus called the crowd to him and said, "Listen to me, everyone, and understand this. [15] Nothing outside a person can defile them by going into them. Rather, it is what comes out of a person that defiles them." [16]f

[17] After he had left the crowd and entered the house, his disciples asked him about this parable. [18] "Are you so dull?" he asked. "Don't you see that nothing that enters a person from the outside can defile them? [19] For it doesn't go into their heart but into their stomach, and then out of the body." (In saying this, Jesus declared all foods clean.)

[20] He went on: "What comes out of a person is what defiles them. [21] For it is from within, out of a person's heart, that evil thoughts come — sexual immorality, theft, murder, [22] adultery, greed, malice, deceit, lewdness, envy, slander, arrogance and folly. [23] All these evils come from inside and defile a person."

Jesus Honors a Syrophoenician Woman's Faith

[24] Jesus left that place and went to the vicinity of Tyre.[g] He entered a house and did not want anyone to know it; yet he could not keep his presence secret. [25] In fact, as soon as she heard about him, a woman whose little daughter was possessed by an impure spirit came and fell at his feet. [26] The woman was a Greek, born in Syrian Phoenicia. She begged Jesus to drive the demon out of her daughter.

[27] "First let the children eat all they want,"

---

[a] 4 Some early manuscripts *pitchers, kettles and dining couches*   [b] 6,7 Isaiah 29:13   [c] 9 Some manuscripts *set up*   [d] 10 Exodus 20:12; Deut. 5:16   [e] 10 Exodus 21:17; Lev. 20:9   [f] 16 Some manuscripts include here the words of 4:23.   [g] 24 Many early manuscripts *Tyre and Sidon*

he told her, "for it is not right to take the children's bread and toss it to the dogs."

28 "Lord," she replied, "even the dogs under the table eat the children's crumbs."

29 Then he told her, "For such a reply, you may go; the demon has left your daughter."

30 She went home and found her child lying on the bed, and the demon gone.

Jesus Heals a Deaf and Mute Man

31 Then Jesus left the vicinity of Tyre and went through Sidon, down to the Sea of Galilee and into the region of the Decapolis.[a] 32 There some people brought to him a man who was deaf and could hardly talk, and they begged Jesus to place his hand on him.

33 After he took him aside, away from the crowd, Jesus put his fingers into the man's ears. Then he spit and touched the man's tongue. 34 He looked up to heaven and with a deep sigh said to him, *"Ephphatha!"* (which means "Be opened!"). 35 At this, the man's ears were opened, his tongue was loosened and he began to speak plainly.

36 Jesus commanded them not to tell anyone. But the more he did so, the more they kept talking about it. 37 People were overwhelmed with amazement. "He has done everything well," they said. "He even makes the deaf hear and the mute speak."

Jesus Feeds the Four Thousand

8 During those days another large crowd gathered. Since they had nothing to eat, Jesus called his disciples to him and said, 2 "I have compassion for these people; they have already been with me three days and have nothing to eat. 3 If I send them home hungry, they will collapse on the way, because some of them have come a long distance."

4 His disciples answered, "But where in this remote place can anyone get enough bread to feed them?"

5 "How many loaves do you have?" Jesus asked.

"Seven," they replied.

6 He told the crowd to sit down on the ground. When he had taken the seven loaves and given thanks, he broke them and gave them to his disciples to distribute to the people, and they did so. 7 They had a few small fish as well; he gave thanks for them also and

told the disciples to distribute them. 8 The people ate and were satisfied. Afterward the disciples picked up seven basketfuls of broken pieces that were left over. 9 About four thousand were present. After he had sent them away, 10 he got into the boat with his disciples and went to the region of Dalmanutha.

11 The Pharisees came and began to question Jesus. To test him, they asked him for a sign from heaven. 12 He sighed deeply and said, "Why does this generation ask for a sign? Truly I tell you, no sign will be given to it." 13 Then he left them, got back into the boat and crossed to the other side.

The Yeast of the Pharisees and Herod

14 The disciples had forgotten to bring bread, except for one loaf they had with them in the boat. 15 "Be careful," Jesus warned them. "Watch out for the yeast of the Pharisees and that of Herod."

16 They discussed this with one another and said, "It is because we have no bread."

17 Aware of their discussion, Jesus asked them: "Why are you talking about having no bread? Do you still not see or understand? Are your hearts hardened? 18 Do you have eyes but fail to see, and ears but fail to hear? And don't you remember? 19 When I broke the five loaves for the five thousand, how many basketfuls of pieces did you pick up?"

"Twelve," they replied.

20 "And when I broke the seven loaves for the four thousand, how many basketfuls of pieces did you pick up?"

They answered, "Seven."

21 He said to them, "Do you still not understand?"

Jesus Heals a Blind Man at Bethsaida

22 They came to Bethsaida, and some people brought a blind man and begged Jesus to touch him. 23 He took the blind man by the hand and led him outside the village. When he had spit on the man's eyes and put his hands on him, Jesus asked, "Do you see anything?"

24 He looked up and said, "I see people; they look like trees walking around."

25 Once more Jesus put his hands on the man's eyes. Then his eyes were opened, his

---

a 31 That is, the Ten Cities

sight was restored, and he saw everything clearly. ²⁶Jesus sent him home, saying, "Don't even go into^a the village."

Peter Declares That Jesus Is the Messiah

²⁷Jesus and his disciples went on to the villages around Caesarea Philippi. On the way he asked them, "Who do people say I am?"

²⁸They replied, "Some say John the Baptist; others say Elijah; and still others, one of the prophets."

²⁹"But what about you?" he asked. "Who do you say I am?"

Peter answered, "You are the Messiah."

³⁰Jesus warned them not to tell anyone about him.

Jesus Predicts His Death

³¹He then began to teach them that the Son of Man must suffer many things and be rejected by the elders, the chief priests and the teachers of the law, and that he must be killed and after three days rise again. ³²He spoke plainly about this, and Peter took him aside and began to rebuke him.

³³But when Jesus turned and looked at his disciples, he rebuked Peter. "Get behind me, Satan!" he said. "You do not have in mind the concerns of God, but merely human concerns."

The Way of the Cross

³⁴Then he called the crowd to him along with his disciples and said: "Whoever wants to be my disciple must deny themselves and take up their cross and follow me. ³⁵For whoever wants to save their life^b will lose it, but whoever loses their life for me and for the gospel will save it. ³⁶What good is it for someone to gain the whole world, yet forfeit their soul? ³⁷Or what can anyone give in exchange for their soul? ³⁸If anyone is ashamed of me and my words in this adulterous and sinful generation, the Son of Man will be ashamed of them when he comes in his Father's glory with the holy angels."

9 And he said to them, "Truly I tell you, some who are standing here will not taste death before they see that the kingdom of God has come with power."

The Transfiguration

²After six days Jesus took Peter, James and John with him and led them up a high mountain, where they were all alone. There he was transfigured before them. ³His clothes became dazzling white, whiter than anyone in the world could bleach them. ⁴And there appeared before them Elijah and Moses, who were talking with Jesus.

⁵Peter said to Jesus, "Rabbi, it is good for us to be here. Let us put up three shelters—one for you, one for Moses and one for Elijah." ⁶(He did not know what to say, they were so frightened.)

⁷Then a cloud appeared and covered them, and a voice came from the cloud: "This is my Son, whom I love. Listen to him!"

⁸Suddenly, when they looked around, they no longer saw anyone with them except Jesus.

⁹As they were coming down the mountain, Jesus gave them orders not to tell anyone what they had seen until the Son of Man had risen from the dead. ¹⁰They kept the matter to themselves, discussing what "rising from the dead" meant.

¹¹And they asked him, "Why do the teachers of the law say that Elijah must come first?"

¹²Jesus replied, "To be sure, Elijah does come first, and restores all things. Why then is it written that the Son of Man must suffer much and be rejected? ¹³But I tell you, Elijah has come, and they have done to him everything they wished, just as it is written about him."

Jesus Heals a Boy Possessed by an Impure Spirit

¹⁴When they came to the other disciples, they saw a large crowd around them and the teachers of the law arguing with them. ¹⁵As soon as all the people saw Jesus, they were overwhelmed with wonder and ran to greet him.

¹⁶"What are you arguing with them about?" he asked.

¹⁷A man in the crowd answered, "Teacher, I brought you my son, who is possessed by a spirit that has robbed him of speech. ¹⁸Whenever it seizes him, it throws him to the ground.

^a 26 Some manuscripts *go and tell anyone in* verses 36 and 37.   ^b 35 The Greek word means either *life* or *soul*; also in

He foams at the mouth, gnashes his teeth and becomes rigid. I asked your disciples to drive out the spirit, but they could not."

¹⁹"You unbelieving generation," Jesus replied, "how long shall I stay with you? How long shall I put up with you? Bring the boy to me."

²⁰So they brought him. When the spirit saw Jesus, it immediately threw the boy into a convulsion. He fell to the ground and rolled around, foaming at the mouth.

²¹Jesus asked the boy's father, "How long has he been like this?"

"From childhood," he answered. ²²"It has often thrown him into fire or water to kill him. But if you can do anything, take pity on us and help us."

²³" 'If you can'?" said Jesus. "Everything is possible for one who believes."

²⁴Immediately the boy's father exclaimed, "I do believe; help me overcome my unbelief!"

²⁵When Jesus saw that a crowd was running to the scene, he rebuked the impure spirit. "You deaf and mute spirit," he said, "I command you, come out of him and never enter him again."

²⁶The spirit shrieked, convulsed him violently and came out. The boy looked so much like a corpse that many said, "He's dead." ²⁷But Jesus took him by the hand and lifted him to his feet, and he stood up.

²⁸After Jesus had gone indoors, his disciples asked him privately, "Why couldn't we drive it out?"

²⁹He replied, "This kind can come out only by prayer.ᵃ"

Jesus Predicts His Death a Second Time

³⁰They left that place and passed through Galilee. Jesus did not want anyone to know where they were, ³¹because he was teaching his disciples. He said to them, "The Son of Man is going to be delivered into the hands of men. They will kill him, and after three days he will rise." ³²But they did not understand what he meant and were afraid to ask him about it.

³³They came to Capernaum. When he was in the house, he asked them, "What were you arguing about on the road?" ³⁴But they kept quiet because on the way they had argued about who was the greatest.

³⁵Sitting down, Jesus called the Twelve and said, "Anyone who wants to be first must be the very last, and the servant of all."

³⁶He took a little child whom he placed among them. Taking the child in his arms, he said to them, ³⁷"Whoever welcomes one of these little children in my name welcomes me; and whoever welcomes me does not welcome me but the one who sent me."

Whoever Is Not Against Us Is for Us

³⁸"Teacher," said John, "we saw someone driving out demons in your name and we told him to stop, because he was not one of us."

³⁹"Do not stop him," Jesus said. "For no one who does a miracle in my name can in the next moment say anything bad about me, ⁴⁰for whoever is not against us is for us. ⁴¹Truly I tell you, anyone who gives you a cup of water in my name because you belong to the Messiah will certainly not lose their reward.

Causing to Stumble

⁴²"If anyone causes one of these little ones — those who believe in me — to stumble, it would be better for them if a large millstone were hung around their neck and they were thrown into the sea. ⁴³If your hand causes you to stumble, cut it off. It is better for you to enter life maimed than with two hands to go into hell, where the fire never goes out. [⁴⁴]ᵇ ⁴⁵And if your foot causes you to stumble, cut it off. It is better for you to enter life crippled than to have two feet and be thrown into hell. [⁴⁶]ᵇ ⁴⁷And if your eye causes you to stumble, pluck it out. It is better for you to enter the kingdom of God with one eye than to have two eyes and be thrown into hell, ⁴⁸where

" 'the worms that eat them do not die,
      and the fire is not quenched.'ᶜ

⁴⁹Everyone will be salted with fire.

⁵⁰"Salt is good, but if it loses its saltiness, how can you make it salty again? Have salt among yourselves, and be at peace with each other."

Divorce

10 Jesus then left that place and went into the region of Judea and across the Jordan. Again crowds of people came to him, and as was his custom, he taught them.

[2] Some Pharisees came and tested him by asking, "Is it lawful for a man to divorce his wife?"

[3] "What did Moses command you?" he replied.

[4] They said, "Moses permitted a man to write a certificate of divorce and send her away."

[5] "It was because your hearts were hard that Moses wrote you this law," Jesus replied. [6] "But at the beginning of creation God 'made them male and female.'[a] [7] 'For this reason a man will leave his father and mother and be united to his wife,[b] [8] and the two will become one flesh.'[c] So they are no longer two, but one flesh. [9] Therefore what God has joined together, let no one separate."

[10] When they were in the house again, the disciples asked Jesus about this. [11] He answered, "Anyone who divorces his wife and marries another woman commits adultery against her. [12] And if she divorces her husband and marries another man, she commits adultery."

The Little Children and Jesus

[13] People were bringing little children to Jesus for him to place his hands on them, but the disciples rebuked them. [14] When Jesus saw this, he was indignant. He said to them, "Let the little children come to me, and do not hinder them, for the kingdom of God belongs to such as these. [15] Truly I tell you, anyone who will not receive the kingdom of God like a little child will never enter it." [16] And he took the children in his arms, placed his hands on them and blessed them.

The Rich and the Kingdom of God

[17] As Jesus started on his way, a man ran up to him and fell on his knees before him. "Good teacher," he asked, "what must I do to inherit eternal life?"

[18] "Why do you call me good?" Jesus answered. "No one is good — except God alone. [19] You know the commandments: 'You shall not murder, you shall not commit adultery, you shall not steal, you shall not give false

testimony, you shall not defraud, honor your father and mother.'[d]"

[20] "Teacher," he declared, "all these I have kept since I was a boy."

[21] Jesus looked at him and loved him. "One thing you lack," he said. "Go, sell everything you have and give to the poor, and you will have treasure in heaven. Then come, follow me."

[22] At this the man's face fell. He went away sad, because he had great wealth.

[23] Jesus looked around and said to his disciples, "How hard it is for the rich to enter the kingdom of God!"

[24] The disciples were amazed at his words. But Jesus said again, "Children, how hard it is[e] to enter the kingdom of God! [25] It is easier for a camel to go through the eye of a needle than for someone who is rich to enter the kingdom of God."

[26] The disciples were even more amazed, and said to each other, "Who then can be saved?"

[27] Jesus looked at them and said, "With man this is impossible, but not with God; all things are possible with God."

[28] Then Peter spoke up, "We have left everything to follow you!"

[29] "Truly I tell you," Jesus replied, "no one who has left home or brothers or sisters or mother or father or children or fields for me and the gospel [30] will fail to receive a hundred times as much in this present age: homes, brothers, sisters, mothers, children and fields — along with persecutions — and in the age to come eternal life. [31] But many who are first will be last, and the last first."

Jesus Predicts His Death a Third Time

[32] They were on their way up to Jerusalem, with Jesus leading the way, and the disciples were astonished, while those who followed were afraid. Again he took the Twelve aside and told them what was going to happen to him. [33] "We are going up to Jerusalem," he said, "and the Son of Man will be delivered over to the chief priests and the teachers of the law. They will condemn him to death and will hand him over to the Gentiles, [34] who will mock him and spit on him, flog him and kill him. Three days later he will rise."

---

[a] 6 Gen. 1:27   [b] 7 Some early manuscripts do not have *and be united to his wife.*   [c] 8 Gen. 2:24
[d] 19 Exodus 20:12-16; Deut. 5:16-20   [e] 24 Some manuscripts *is for those who trust in riches*

The Request of James and John

35 Then James and John, the sons of Zebedee, came to him. "Teacher," they said, "we want you to do for us whatever we ask."
36 "What do you want me to do for you?" he asked.
37 They replied, "Let one of us sit at your right and the other at your left in your glory."
38 "You don't know what you are asking," Jesus said. "Can you drink the cup I drink or be baptized with the baptism I am baptized with?"
39 "We can," they answered.
Jesus said to them, "You will drink the cup I drink and be baptized with the baptism I am baptized with, 40 but to sit at my right or left is not for me to grant. These places belong to those for whom they have been prepared."
41 When the ten heard about this, they became indignant with James and John. 42 Jesus called them together and said, "You know that those who are regarded as rulers of the Gentiles lord it over them, and their high officials exercise authority over them. 43 Not so with you. Instead, whoever wants to become great among you must be your servant, 44 and whoever wants to be first must be slave of all. 45 For even the Son of Man did not come to be served, but to serve, and to give his life as a ransom for many."

Blind Bartimaeus Receives His Sight

46 Then they came to Jericho. As Jesus and his disciples, together with a large crowd, were leaving the city, a blind man, Bartimaeus (which means "son of Timaeus"), was sitting by the roadside begging. 47 When he heard that it was Jesus of Nazareth, he began to shout, "Jesus, Son of David, have mercy on me!"
48 Many rebuked him and told him to be quiet, but he shouted all the more, "Son of David, have mercy on me!"
49 Jesus stopped and said, "Call him."
So they called to the blind man, "Cheer up! On your feet! He's calling you." 50 Throwing his cloak aside, he jumped to his feet and came to Jesus.
51 "What do you want me to do for you?" Jesus asked him.
The blind man said, "Rabbi, I want to see."

52 "Go," said Jesus, "your faith has healed you." Immediately he received his sight and followed Jesus along the road.

Jesus Comes to Jerusalem as King

11 As they approached Jerusalem and came to Bethphage and Bethany at the Mount of Olives, Jesus sent two of his disciples, 2 saying to them, "Go to the village ahead of you, and just as you enter it, you will find a colt tied there, which no one has ever ridden. Untie it and bring it here. 3 If anyone asks you, 'Why are you doing this?' say, 'The Lord needs it and will send it back here shortly.'"
4 They went and found a colt outside in the street, tied at a doorway. As they untied it, 5 some people standing there asked, "What are you doing, untying that colt?" 6 They answered as Jesus had told them to, and the people let them go. 7 When they brought the colt to Jesus and threw their cloaks over it, he sat on it. 8 Many people spread their cloaks on the road, while others spread branches they had cut in the fields. 9 Those who went ahead and those who followed shouted,

"Hosanna!"[a]

"Blessed is he who comes in the name of the Lord!"[b]

10 "Blessed is the coming kingdom of our father David!"

"Hosanna in the highest heaven!"

11 Jesus entered Jerusalem and went into the temple courts. He looked around at everything, but since it was already late, he went out to Bethany with the Twelve.

Jesus Curses a Fig Tree and Clears the Temple Courts

12 The next day as they were leaving Bethany, Jesus was hungry. 13 Seeing in the distance a fig tree in leaf, he went to find out if it had any fruit. When he reached it, he found nothing but leaves, because it was not the season for figs. 14 Then he said to the tree, "May no one ever eat fruit from you again." And his disciples heard him say it.
15 On reaching Jerusalem, Jesus entered the temple courts and began driving out

a 9 A Hebrew expression meaning "Save!" which became an exclamation of praise; also in verse 10
b 9 Psalm 118:25,26

those who were buying and selling there. He overturned the tables of the money changers and the benches of those selling doves, [16] and would not allow anyone to carry merchandise through the temple courts. [17] And as he taught them, he said, "Is it not written:

'My house will be called a house of prayer for all nations'[a]? But you have made it 'a den of robbers.'[b]"

[18] The chief priests and the teachers of the law heard this and began looking for a way to kill him, for they feared him, because the whole crowd was amazed at his teaching.

[19] When evening came, Jesus and his disciples[c] went out of the city.

[20] In the morning, as they went along, they saw the fig tree withered from the roots. [21] Peter remembered and said to Jesus, "Rabbi, look! The fig tree you cursed has withered!"

[22] "Have faith in God," Jesus answered. [23] "Truly[d] I tell you, if anyone says to this mountain, 'Go, throw yourself into the sea,' and does not doubt in their heart but believes that what they say will happen, it will be done for them. [24] Therefore I tell you, whatever you ask for in prayer, believe that you have received it, and it will be yours. [25] And when you stand praying, if you hold anything against anyone, forgive them, so that your Father in heaven may forgive you your sins." [26][e]

The Authority of Jesus Questioned

[27] They arrived again in Jerusalem, and while Jesus was walking in the temple courts, the chief priests, the teachers of the law and the elders came to him. [28] "By what authority are you doing these things?" they asked. "And who gave you authority to do this?"

[29] Jesus replied, "I will ask you one question. Answer me, and I will tell you by what authority I am doing these things. [30] John's baptism—was it from heaven, or of human origin? Tell me!"

[31] They discussed it among themselves and said, "If we say, 'From heaven,' he will ask, 'Then why didn't you believe him?' [32] But if we say, 'Of human origin' . . ." (They feared the people, for everyone held that John really was a prophet.)

[33] So they answered Jesus, "We don't know."

Jesus said, "Neither will I tell you by what authority I am doing these things."

The Parable of the Tenants

12 Jesus then began to speak to them in parables: "A man planted a vineyard. He put a wall around it, dug a pit for the winepress and built a watchtower. Then he rented the vineyard to some farmers and moved to another place. [2] At harvest time he sent a servant to the tenants to collect from them some of the fruit of the vineyard. [3] But they seized him, beat him and sent him away empty-handed. [4] Then he sent another servant to them; they struck this man on the head and treated him shamefully. [5] He sent still another, and that one they killed. He sent many others; some of them they beat, others they killed.

[6] "He had one left to send, a son, whom he loved. He sent him last of all, saying, 'They will respect my son.'

[7] "But the tenants said to one another, 'This is the heir. Come, let's kill him, and the inheritance will be ours.' [8] So they took him and killed him, and threw him out of the vineyard.

[9] "What then will the owner of the vineyard do? He will come and kill those tenants and give the vineyard to others. [10] Haven't you read this passage of Scripture:

" 'The stone the builders rejected
   has become the cornerstone;
[11] the Lord has done this,
   and it is marvelous in our eyes'[f]?"

[12] Then the chief priests, the teachers of the law and the elders looked for a way to arrest him because they knew he had spoken the parable against them. But they were afraid of the crowd; so they left him and went away.

Paying the Imperial Tax to Caesar

[13] Later they sent some of the Pharisees and Herodians to Jesus to catch him in his words. [14] They came to him and said, "Teacher, we know that you are a man of integrity. You aren't swayed by others, because you pay

---

[a] 17 Isaiah 56:7   [b] 17 Jer. 7:11   [c] 19 Some early manuscripts came, Jesus   [d] 22,23 Some early manuscripts "If you have faith in God," Jesus answered, [23] "truly   [e] 26 Some manuscripts include here words similar to Matt. 6:15.   [f] 11 Psalm 118:22,23

no attention to who they are; but you teach the way of God in accordance with the truth. Is it right to pay the imperial tax*a* to Caesar or not? ¹⁵Should we pay or shouldn't we?"

But Jesus knew their hypocrisy. "Why are you trying to trap me?" he asked. "Bring me a denarius and let me look at it." ¹⁶They brought the coin, and he asked them, "Whose image is this? And whose inscription?"

"Caesar's," they replied.

¹⁷Then Jesus said to them, "Give back to Caesar what is Caesar's and to God what is God's."

And they were amazed at him.

Marriage at the Resurrection

¹⁸Then the Sadducees, who say there is no resurrection, came to him with a question. ¹⁹"Teacher," they said, "Moses wrote for us that if a man's brother dies and leaves a wife but no children, the man must marry the widow and raise up offspring for his brother. ²⁰Now there were seven brothers. The first one married and died without leaving any children. ²¹The second one married the widow, but he also died, leaving no child. It was the same with the third. ²²In fact, none of the seven left any children. Last of all, the woman died too. ²³At the resurrection*b* whose wife will she be, since the seven were married to her?"

²⁴Jesus replied, "Are you not in error because you do not know the Scriptures or the power of God? ²⁵When the dead rise, they will neither marry nor be given in marriage; they will be like the angels in heaven. ²⁶Now about the dead rising—have you not read in the Book of Moses, in the account of the burning bush, how God said to him, 'I am the God of Abraham, the God of Isaac, and the God of Jacob'*c*? ²⁷He is not the God of the dead, but of the living. You are badly mistaken!"

The Greatest Commandment

²⁸One of the teachers of the law came and heard them debating. Noticing that Jesus had given them a good answer, he asked him, "Of all the commandments, which is the most important?"

²⁹"The most important one," answered Jesus, "is this: 'Hear, O Israel: The Lord our God, the Lord is one.*d* ³⁰Love the Lord your God with all your heart and with all your soul and with all your mind and with all your strength.'*e* ³¹The second is this: 'Love your neighbor as yourself.'*f* There is no commandment greater than these."

³²"Well said, teacher," the man replied. "You are right in saying that God is one and there is no other but him. ³³To love him with all your heart, with all your understanding and with all your strength, and to love your neighbor as yourself is more important than all burnt offerings and sacrifices."

³⁴When Jesus saw that he had answered wisely, he said to him, "You are not far from the kingdom of God." And from then on no one dared ask him any more questions.

Whose Son Is the Messiah?

³⁵While Jesus was teaching in the temple courts, he asked, "Why do the teachers of the law say that the Messiah is the son of David? ³⁶David himself, speaking by the Holy Spirit, declared:

" 'The Lord said to my Lord:
    "Sit at my right hand
until I put your enemies
    under your feet." '*g*

³⁷David himself calls him 'Lord.' How then can he be his son?"

The large crowd listened to him with delight.

Warning Against the Teachers of the Law

³⁸As he taught, Jesus said, "Watch out for the teachers of the law. They like to walk around in flowing robes and be greeted with respect in the marketplaces, ³⁹and have the most important seats in the synagogues and the places of honor at banquets. ⁴⁰They devour widows' houses and for a show make lengthy prayers. These men will be punished most severely."

The Widow's Offering

⁴¹Jesus sat down opposite the place where the offerings were put and watched the crowd putting their money into the temple treasury. Many rich people threw in large

---

a 14 A special tax levied on subject peoples, not on Roman citizens   *b 23* Some manuscripts *resurrection, when people rise from the dead,*   *c 26* Exodus 3:6   *d 29* Or *The Lord our God is one Lord*   *e 30* Deut. 6:4,5   *f 31* Lev. 19:18   *g 36* Psalm 110:1

amounts. [42]But a poor widow came and put in two very small copper coins, worth only a few cents.

[43]Calling his disciples to him, Jesus said, "Truly I tell you, this poor widow has put more into the treasury than all the others. [44]They all gave out of their wealth; but she, out of her poverty, put in everything—all she had to live on."

The Destruction of the Temple and Signs of the End Times

13 As Jesus was leaving the temple, one of his disciples said to him, "Look, Teacher! What massive stones! What magnificent buildings!"

[2]"Do you see all these great buildings?" replied Jesus. "Not one stone here will be left on another; every one will be thrown down."

[3]As Jesus was sitting on the Mount of Olives opposite the temple, Peter, James, John and Andrew asked him privately, [4]"Tell us, when will these things happen? And what will be the sign that they are all about to be fulfilled?"

[5]Jesus said to them: "Watch out that no one deceives you. [6]Many will come in my name, claiming, 'I am he,' and will deceive many. [7]When you hear of wars and rumors of wars, do not be alarmed. Such things must happen, but the end is still to come. [8]Nation will rise against nation, and kingdom against kingdom. There will be earthquakes in various places, and famines. These are the beginning of birth pains.

[9]"You must be on your guard. You will be handed over to the local councils and flogged in the synagogues. On account of me you will stand before governors and kings as witnesses to them. [10]And the gospel must first be preached to all nations. [11]Whenever you are arrested and brought to trial, do not worry beforehand about what to say. Just say whatever is given you at the time, for it is not you speaking, but the Holy Spirit.

[12]"Brother will betray brother to death, and a father his child. Children will rebel against their parents and have them put to death. [13]Everyone will hate you because of me, but the one who stands firm to the end will be saved.

[14]"When you see 'the abomination that causes desolation'[a] standing where it[b] does not belong—let the reader understand—then let those who are in Judea flee to the mountains. [15]Let no one on the housetop go down or enter the house to take anything out. [16]Let no one in the field go back to get their cloak. [17]How dreadful it will be in those days for pregnant women and nursing mothers! [18]Pray that this will not take place in winter, [19]because those will be days of distress unequaled from the beginning, when God created the world, until now—and never to be equaled again.

[20]"If the Lord had not cut short those days, no one would survive. But for the sake of the elect, whom he has chosen, he has shortened them. [21]At that time if anyone says to you, 'Look, here is the Messiah!' or, 'Look, there he is!' do not believe it. [22]For false messiahs and false prophets will appear and perform signs and wonders to deceive, if possible, even the elect. [23]So be on your guard; I have told you everything ahead of time.

[24]"But in those days, following that distress,

"'the sun will be darkened,
    and the moon will not give its light;
[25]the stars will fall from the sky,
    and the heavenly bodies will be shaken.'[c]

[26]"At that time people will see the Son of Man coming in clouds with great power and glory. [27]And he will send his angels and gather his elect from the four winds, from the ends of the earth to the ends of the heavens.

[28]"Now learn this lesson from the fig tree: As soon as its twigs get tender and its leaves come out, you know that summer is near. [29]Even so, when you see these things happening, you know that it[b] is near, right at the door. [30]Truly I tell you, this generation will certainly not pass away until all these things have happened. [31]Heaven and earth will pass away, but my words will never pass away.

The Day and Hour Unknown

[32]"But about that day or hour no one knows, not even the angels in heaven, nor the Son, but only the Father. [33]Be on guard!

Be alert[a]! You do not know when that time will come. [34]It's like a man going away: He leaves his house and puts his servants in charge, each with their assigned task, and tells the one at the door to keep watch.

[35]"Therefore keep watch because you do not know when the owner of the house will come back—whether in the evening, or at midnight, or when the rooster crows, or at dawn. [36]If he comes suddenly, do not let him find you sleeping. [37]What I say to you, I say to everyone: 'Watch!'"

Jesus Anointed at Bethany

14 Now the Passover and the Festival of Unleavened Bread were only two days away, and the chief priests and the teachers of the law were scheming to arrest Jesus secretly and kill him. [2]"But not during the festival," they said, "or the people may riot."

[3]While he was in Bethany, reclining at the table in the home of Simon the Leper, a woman came with an alabaster jar of very expensive perfume, made of pure nard. She broke the jar and poured the perfume on his head.

[4]Some of those present were saying indignantly to one another, "Why this waste of perfume? [5]It could have been sold for more than a year's wages[b] and the money given to the poor." And they rebuked her harshly.

[6]"Leave her alone," said Jesus. "Why are you bothering her? She has done a beautiful thing to me. [7]The poor you will always have with you,[c] and you can help them any time you want. But you will not always have me. [8]She did what she could. She poured perfume on my body beforehand to prepare for my burial. [9]Truly I tell you, wherever the gospel is preached throughout the world, what she has done will also be told, in memory of her."

[10]Then Judas Iscariot, one of the Twelve, went to the chief priests to betray Jesus to them. [11]They were delighted to hear this and promised to give him money. So he watched for an opportunity to hand him over.

The Last Supper

[12]On the first day of the Festival of Unleavened Bread, when it was customary to sacrifice the Passover lamb, Jesus' disciples asked him, "Where do you want us to go and make preparations for you to eat the Passover?"

[13]So he sent two of his disciples, telling them, "Go into the city, and a man carrying a jar of water will meet you. Follow him. [14]Say to the owner of the house he enters, 'The Teacher asks: Where is my guest room, where I may eat the Passover with my disciples?' [15]He will show you a large room upstairs, furnished and ready. Make preparations for us there."

[16]The disciples left, went into the city and found things just as Jesus had told them. So they prepared the Passover.

[17]When evening came, Jesus arrived with the Twelve. [18]While they were reclining at the table eating, he said, "Truly I tell you, one of you will betray me—one who is eating with me."

[19]They were saddened, and one by one they said to him, "Surely you don't mean me?"

[20]"It is one of the Twelve," he replied, "one who dips bread into the bowl with me. [21]The Son of Man will go just as it is written about him. But woe to that man who betrays the Son of Man! It would be better for him if he had not been born."

[22]While they were eating, Jesus took bread, and when he had given thanks, he broke it and gave it to his disciples, saying, "Take it; this is my body."

[23]Then he took a cup, and when he had given thanks, he gave it to them, and they all drank from it.

[24]"This is my blood of the[d] covenant, which is poured out for many," he said to them. [25]"Truly I tell you, I will not drink again from the fruit of the vine until that day when I drink it new in the kingdom of God."

[26]When they had sung a hymn, they went out to the Mount of Olives.

Jesus Predicts Peter's Denial

[27]"You will all fall away," Jesus told them, "for it is written:

" 'I will strike the shepherd,
    and the sheep will be scattered.'[e]

[28]But after I have risen, I will go ahead of you into Galilee."

[a]33 Some manuscripts *alert and pray*   [b]5 Greek *than three hundred denarii*   [c]7 See Deut. 15:11.
[d]24 Some manuscripts *the new*   [e]27 Zech. 13:7

²⁹Peter declared, "Even if all fall away, I will not."

³⁰"Truly I tell you," Jesus answered, "today — yes, tonight — before the rooster crows twice[a] you yourself will disown me three times."

³¹But Peter insisted emphatically, "Even if I have to die with you, I will never disown you." And all the others said the same.

Gethsemane

³²They went to a place called Gethsemane, and Jesus said to his disciples, "Sit here while I pray." ³³He took Peter, James and John along with him, and he began to be deeply distressed and troubled. ³⁴"My soul is overwhelmed with sorrow to the point of death," he said to them. "Stay here and keep watch."

³⁵Going a little farther, he fell to the ground and prayed that if possible the hour might pass from him. ³⁶"Abba,[b] Father," he said, "everything is possible for you. Take this cup from me. Yet not what I will, but what you will."

³⁷Then he returned to his disciples and found them sleeping. "Simon," he said to Peter, "are you asleep? Couldn't you keep watch for one hour? ³⁸Watch and pray so that you will not fall into temptation. The spirit is willing, but the flesh is weak."

³⁹Once more he went away and prayed the same thing. ⁴⁰When he came back, he again found them sleeping, because their eyes were heavy. They did not know what to say to him.

⁴¹Returning the third time, he said to them, "Are you still sleeping and resting? Enough! The hour has come. Look, the Son of Man is delivered into the hands of sinners. ⁴²Rise! Let us go! Here comes my betrayer!"

Jesus Arrested

⁴³Just as he was speaking, Judas, one of the Twelve, appeared. With him was a crowd armed with swords and clubs, sent from the chief priests, the teachers of the law, and the elders. ⁴⁴Now the betrayer had arranged a signal with them: "The one I kiss is the man; arrest him and lead him away under guard." ⁴⁵Going at once to Jesus, Judas said, "Rabbi!" and

kissed him. ⁴⁶The men seized Jesus and arrested him. ⁴⁷Then one of those standing near drew his sword and struck the servant of the high priest, cutting off his ear.

⁴⁸"Am I leading a rebellion," said Jesus, "that you have come out with swords and clubs to capture me? ⁴⁹Every day I was with you, teaching in the temple courts, and you did not arrest me. But the Scriptures must be fulfilled." ⁵⁰Then everyone deserted him and fled.

⁵¹A young man, wearing nothing but a linen garment, was following Jesus. When they seized him, ⁵²he fled naked, leaving his garment behind.

Jesus Before the Sanhedrin

⁵³They took Jesus to the high priest, and all the chief priests, the elders and the teachers of the law came together. ⁵⁴Peter followed him at a distance, right into the courtyard of the high priest. There he sat with the guards and warmed himself at the fire.

⁵⁵The chief priests and the whole Sanhedrin were looking for evidence against Jesus so that they could put him to death, but they did not find any. ⁵⁶Many testified falsely against him, but their statements did not agree.

⁵⁷Then some stood up and gave this false testimony against him: ⁵⁸"We heard him say, 'I will destroy this temple made with human hands and in three days will build another, not made with hands.' " ⁵⁹Yet even then their testimony did not agree.

⁶⁰Then the high priest stood up before them and asked Jesus, "Are you not going to answer? What is this testimony that these men are bringing against you?" ⁶¹But Jesus remained silent and gave no answer.

Again the high priest asked him, "Are you the Messiah, the Son of the Blessed One?"

⁶²"I am," said Jesus. "And you will see the Son of Man sitting at the right hand of the Mighty One and coming on the clouds of heaven."

⁶³The high priest tore his clothes. "Why do we need any more witnesses?" he asked. ⁶⁴"You have heard the blasphemy. What do you think?"

They all condemned him as worthy of death. ⁶⁵Then some began to spit at him;

---

[a] 30 Some early manuscripts do not have twice.   [b] 36 Aramaic for father

they blindfolded him, struck him with their fists, and said, "Prophesy!" And the guards took him and beat him.

Peter Disowns Jesus

⁶⁶While Peter was below in the courtyard, one of the servant girls of the high priest came by. ⁶⁷When she saw Peter warming himself, she looked closely at him.

"You also were with that Nazarene, Jesus," she said.

⁶⁸But he denied it. "I don't know or understand what you're talking about," he said, and went out into the entryway.ᵃ

⁶⁹When the servant girl saw him there, she said again to those standing around, "This fellow is one of them." ⁷⁰Again he denied it.

After a little while, those standing near said to Peter, "Surely you are one of them, for you are a Galilean."

⁷¹He began to call down curses, and he swore to them, "I don't know this man you're talking about."

⁷²Immediately the rooster crowed the second time.ᵇ Then Peter remembered the word Jesus had spoken to him: "Before the rooster crows twiceᶜ you will disown me three times." And he broke down and wept.

Jesus Before Pilate

15 Very early in the morning, the chief priests, with the elders, the teachers of the law and the whole Sanhedrin, made their plans. So they bound Jesus, led him away and handed him over to Pilate.

²"Are you the king of the Jews?" asked Pilate.

"You have said so," Jesus replied.

³The chief priests accused him of many things. ⁴So again Pilate asked him, "Aren't you going to answer? See how many things they are accusing you of."

⁵But Jesus still made no reply, and Pilate was amazed.

⁶Now it was the custom at the festival to release a prisoner whom the people requested. ⁷A man called Barabbas was in prison with the insurrectionists who had committed murder in the uprising. ⁸The crowd came up and asked Pilate to do for them what he usually did.

⁹"Do you want me to release to you the king of the Jews?" asked Pilate, ¹⁰knowing it was out of self-interest that the chief priests had handed Jesus over to him. ¹¹But the chief priests stirred up the crowd to have Pilate release Barabbas instead.

¹²"What shall I do, then, with the one you call the king of the Jews?" Pilate asked them.

¹³"Crucify him!" they shouted.

¹⁴"Why? What crime has he committed?" asked Pilate.

But they shouted all the louder, "Crucify him!"

¹⁵Wanting to satisfy the crowd, Pilate released Barabbas to them. He had Jesus flogged, and handed him over to be crucified.

The Soldiers Mock Jesus

¹⁶The soldiers led Jesus away into the palace (that is, the Praetorium) and called together the whole company of soldiers. ¹⁷They put a purple robe on him, then twisted together a crown of thorns and set it on him. ¹⁸And they began to call out to him, "Hail, king of the Jews!" ¹⁹Again and again they struck him on the head with a staff and spit on him. Falling on their knees, they paid homage to him. ²⁰And when they had mocked him, they took off the purple robe and put his own clothes on him. Then they led him out to crucify him.

The Crucifixion of Jesus

²¹A certain man from Cyrene, Simon, the father of Alexander and Rufus, was passing by on his way in from the country, and they forced him to carry the cross. ²²They brought Jesus to the place called Golgotha (which means "the place of the skull"). ²³Then they offered him wine mixed with myrrh, but he did not take it. ²⁴And they crucified him. Dividing up his clothes, they cast lots to see what each would get.

²⁵It was nine in the morning when they crucified him. ²⁶The written notice of the charge against him read: THE KING OF THE JEWS.

²⁷They crucified two rebels with him, one on his right and one on his left. [28]ᵈ ²⁹Those who passed by hurled insults at him, shaking

---

ᵃ 68 Some early manuscripts *entryway and the rooster crowed*   ᵇ 72 Some early manuscripts do not have *the second time.*   ᶜ 72 Some early manuscripts do not have *twice.*   ᵈ 28 Some manuscripts include here words similar to Luke 22:37.

their heads and saying, "So! You who are going to destroy the temple and build it in three days, [30]come down from the cross and save yourself!" [31]In the same way the chief priests and the teachers of the law mocked him among themselves. "He saved others," they said, "but he can't save himself! [32]Let this Messiah, this king of Israel, come down now from the cross, that we may see and believe." Those crucified with him also heaped insults on him.

The Death of Jesus

[33]At noon, darkness came over the whole land until three in the afternoon. [34]And at three in the afternoon Jesus cried out in a loud voice, *"Eloi, Eloi, lema sabachthani?"* (which means "My God, my God, why have you forsaken me?").[a]

[35]When some of those standing near heard this, they said, "Listen, he's calling Elijah."

[36]Someone ran, filled a sponge with wine vinegar, put it on a staff, and offered it to Jesus to drink. "Now leave him alone. Let's see if Elijah comes to take him down," he said.

[37]With a loud cry, Jesus breathed his last.

[38]The curtain of the temple was torn in two from top to bottom. [39]And when the centurion, who stood there in front of Jesus, saw how he died,[b] he said, "Surely this man was the Son of God!"

[40]Some women were watching from a distance. Among them were Mary Magdalene, Mary the mother of James the younger and of Joseph,[c] and Salome. [41]In Galilee these women had followed him and cared for his needs. Many other women who had come up with him to Jerusalem were also there.

The Burial of Jesus

[42]It was Preparation Day (that is, the day before the Sabbath). So as evening approached, [43]Joseph of Arimathea, a prominent member of the Council, who was himself waiting for the kingdom of God, went boldly to Pilate and asked for Jesus' body. [44]Pilate was surprised to hear that he was

already dead. Summoning the centurion, he asked him if Jesus had already died. [45]When he learned from the centurion that it was so, he gave the body to Joseph. [46]So Joseph bought some linen cloth, took down the body, wrapped it in the linen, and placed it in a tomb cut out of rock. Then he rolled a stone against the entrance of the tomb. [47]Mary Magdalene and Mary the mother of Joseph saw where he was laid.

Jesus Has Risen

16 When the Sabbath was over, Mary Magdalene, Mary the mother of James, and Salome bought spices so that they might go to anoint Jesus' body. [2]Very early on the first day of the week, just after sunrise, they were on their way to the tomb [3]and they asked each other, "Who will roll the stone away from the entrance of the tomb?"

[4]But when they looked up, they saw that the stone, which was very large, had been rolled away. [5]As they entered the tomb, they saw a young man dressed in a white robe sitting on the right side, and they were alarmed.

[6]"Don't be alarmed," he said. "You are looking for Jesus the Nazarene, who was crucified. He has risen! He is not here. See the place where they laid him. [7]But go, tell his disciples and Peter, 'He is going ahead of you into Galilee. There you will see him, just as he told you.'"

[8]Trembling and bewildered, the women went out and fled from the tomb. They said nothing to anyone, because they were afraid.[d]

[The earliest manuscripts and some other ancient witnesses do not have verses 9 – 20.]

[9]*When Jesus rose early on the first day of the week, he appeared first to Mary Magdalene, out of whom he had driven seven demons. [10]She went and told those who had been with him and who were mourning and weeping. [11]When they heard that Jesus was alive and that she had seen him, they did not believe it.*

---

[a] 34 Psalm 22:1   [b] 39 Some manuscripts *saw that he died with such a cry*   [c] 40 Greek *Joses*, a variant of *Joseph*; also in verse 47   [d] 8 Some manuscripts have the following ending between verses 8 and 9, and one manuscript has it after verse 8 (omitting verses 9-20): *Then they quickly reported all these instructions to those around Peter. After this, Jesus himself also sent out through them from east to west the sacred and imperishable proclamation of eternal salvation. Amen.*

[12] Afterward Jesus appeared in a different form to two of them while they were walking in the country. [13] These returned and reported it to the rest; but they did not believe them either.

[14] Later Jesus appeared to the Eleven as they were eating; he rebuked them for their lack of faith and their stubborn refusal to believe those who had seen him after he had risen.

[15] He said to them, "Go into all the world and preach the gospel to all creation. [16] Whoever believes and is baptized will be saved, but whoever does not believe will be condemned. [17] And these signs will accompany those who believe: In my name they will drive out demons; they will speak in new tongues; [18] they will pick up snakes with their hands; and when they drink deadly poison, it will not hurt them at all; they will place their hands on sick people, and they will get well."

[19] After the Lord Jesus had spoken to them, he was taken up into heaven and he sat at the right hand of God. [20] Then the disciples went out and preached everywhere, and the Lord worked with them and confirmed his word by the signs that accompanied it.

Luke

Introduction

1 Many have undertaken to draw up an account of the things that have been fulfilled[a] among us, [2]just as they were handed down to us by those who from the first were eyewitnesses and servants of the word. [3]With this in mind, since I myself have carefully investigated everything from the beginning, I too decided to write an orderly account for you, most excellent Theophilus, [4]so that you may know the certainty of the things you have been taught.

The Birth of John the Baptist Foretold

[5]In the time of Herod king of Judea there was a priest named Zechariah, who belonged to the priestly division of Abijah; his wife Elizabeth was also a descendant of Aaron. [6]Both of them were righteous in the sight of God, observing all the Lord's commands and decrees blamelessly. [7]But they were childless because Elizabeth was not able to conceive, and they were both very old.

[8]Once when Zechariah's division was on duty and he was serving as priest before God, [9]he was chosen by lot, according to the custom of the priesthood, to go into the temple of the Lord and burn incense. [10]And when the time for the burning of incense came, all the assembled worshipers were praying outside.

[11]Then an angel of the Lord appeared to him, standing at the right side of the altar of incense. [12]When Zechariah saw him, he was startled and was gripped with fear. [13]But the angel said to him: "Do not be afraid, Zechariah; your prayer has been heard. Your wife Elizabeth will bear you a son, and you are to call him John. [14]He will be a joy and delight to you, and many will rejoice because of his birth, [15]for he will be great in the sight of the Lord. He is never to take wine or other fermented drink, and he will be filled with the Holy Spirit even before he is born. [16]He will bring back many of the people of Israel to the Lord their God. [17]And he will go on before the Lord, in the spirit and power of Elijah, to turn the hearts of the parents to their children and the disobedient to the wisdom of the righteous—to make ready a people prepared for the Lord."

[18]Zechariah asked the angel, "How can I be sure of this? I am an old man and my wife is well along in years."

[19]The angel said to him, "I am Gabriel. I stand in the presence of God, and I have been sent to speak to you and to tell you this good news. [20]And now you will be silent and not able to speak until the day this happens, because you did not believe my words, which will come true at their appointed time."

[21]Meanwhile, the people were waiting for Zechariah and wondering why he stayed so long in the temple. [22]When he came out, he could not speak to them. They realized he had seen a vision in the temple, for he kept making signs to them but remained unable to speak.

[23]When his time of service was completed, he returned home. [24]After this his wife Elizabeth became pregnant and for five months remained in seclusion. [25]"The Lord has done this for me," she said. "In these days he has shown his favor and taken away my disgrace among the people."

The Birth of Jesus Foretold

[26]In the sixth month of Elizabeth's pregnancy, God sent the angel Gabriel to Nazareth, a town in Galilee, [27]to a virgin pledged to be married to a man named Joseph, a descendant of David. The virgin's name was Mary. [28]The angel went to her and said, "Greetings, you who are highly favored! The Lord is with you."

[29]Mary was greatly troubled at his words and wondered what kind of greeting this might be. [30]But the angel said to her, "Do not be afraid, Mary; you have found favor with God. [31]You will conceive and give birth

---

[a] 1 Or *been surely believed*

to a son, and you are to call him Jesus. ³²He will be great and will be called the Son of the Most High. The Lord God will give him the throne of his father David, ³³and he will reign over Jacob's descendants forever; his kingdom will never end."

³⁴"How will this be," Mary asked the angel, "since I am a virgin?"

³⁵The angel answered, "The Holy Spirit will come on you, and the power of the Most High will overshadow you. So the holy one to be born will be called* the Son of God. ³⁶Even Elizabeth your relative is going to have a child in her old age, and she who was said to be unable to conceive is in her sixth month. ³⁷For no word from God will ever fail."

³⁸"I am the Lord's servant," Mary answered. "May your word to me be fulfilled." Then the angel left her.

Mary Visits Elizabeth

³⁹At that time Mary got ready and hurried to a town in the hill country of Judea, ⁴⁰where she entered Zechariah's home and greeted Elizabeth. ⁴¹When Elizabeth heard Mary's greeting, the baby leaped in her womb, and Elizabeth was filled with the Holy Spirit. ⁴²In a loud voice she exclaimed: "Blessed are you among women, and blessed is the child you will bear! ⁴³But why am I so favored, that the mother of my Lord should come to me? ⁴⁴As soon as the sound of your greeting reached my ears, the baby in my womb leaped for joy. ⁴⁵Blessed is she who has believed that the Lord would fulfill his promises to her!"

Mary's Song

⁴⁶And Mary said:

"My soul glorifies the Lord
⁴⁷   and my spirit rejoices in God my
        Savior,
⁴⁸for he has been mindful
    of the humble state of his servant.
From now on all generations will call
        me blessed,
⁴⁹   for the Mighty One has done great
        things for me —
    holy is his name.
⁵⁰His mercy extends to those who
        fear him,
    from generation to generation.

⁵¹He has performed mighty deeds with
        his arm;
    he has scattered those who are proud
        in their inmost thoughts.
⁵²He has brought down rulers from their
        thrones
    but has lifted up the humble.
⁵³He has filled the hungry with good things
    but has sent the rich away empty.
⁵⁴He has helped his servant Israel,
    remembering to be merciful
⁵⁵to Abraham and his descendants forever,
    just as he promised our ancestors."

⁵⁶Mary stayed with Elizabeth for about three months and then returned home.

The Birth of John the Baptist

⁵⁷When it was time for Elizabeth to have her baby, she gave birth to a son. ⁵⁸Her neighbors and relatives heard that the Lord had shown her great mercy, and they shared her joy.

⁵⁹On the eighth day they came to circumcise the child, and they were going to name him after his father Zechariah, ⁶⁰but his mother spoke up and said, "No! He is to be called John."

⁶¹They said to her, "There is no one among your relatives who has that name."

⁶²Then they made signs to his father, to find out what he would like to name the child. ⁶³He asked for a writing tablet, and to everyone's astonishment he wrote, "His name is John." ⁶⁴Immediately his mouth was opened and his tongue set free, and he began to speak, praising God. ⁶⁵All the neighbors were filled with awe, and throughout the hill country of Judea people were talking about all these things. ⁶⁶Everyone who heard this wondered about it, asking, "What then is this child going to be?" For the Lord's hand was with him.

Zechariah's Song

⁶⁷His father Zechariah was filled with the Holy Spirit and prophesied:

⁶⁸"Praise be to the Lord, the God of Israel,
    because he has come to his people and
        redeemed them.
⁶⁹He has raised up a horn* of salvation
    for us
    in the house of his servant David

---

a 35 Or *So the child to be born will be called holy,*   *b 69 Horn* here symbolizes a strong king.

Didn't Sign Up for This!

By Bettina Dowell

READ: Luke 1:26—2:20

Mary was never asked if she wanted to be Jesus' mother. Though Mary was initially "greatly troubled" by the angel's presence and greeting (Luke 1:29), she accepted Gabriel's message (see verse 38). Military wives are often given troubling orders too — only they don't come from an angel of the Lord!

As wife of a deployed Navy officer and a mother of two boys, Tricia Grippin was not overjoyed with her latest "assignment." As her family transferred to San Diego and her husband deployed, she found herself scheduled to chaperone a fifth-grade bike trip across California. Thinking about a week without her spouse that included camping, not showering and extended time with a relatively unknown group of adults, Tricia found her attitude was one of simple endurance. As Luke 2:19 describes Mary processing all the changes in her life, Tricia also found herself pondering many things in her heart. She was anticipating the end of the trip and nothing else, though she did not let on her feelings to her sons or the other chaperones.

As the trip grew closer, Tricia realized she didn't want to just survive it — she wanted to thrive and enjoy the experience. She began to pray, asking God for help.

How often as military wives do we find ourselves in Tricia's position? Whether we complain loudly or harbor our resentment quietly inside our hearts, most of us have shared the same feeling at times. We think, "I didn't sign up for this!" PCS moves, deployments, managing household chores alone, single parenting or any number of military-life dilemmas can cause stress. How often do we beg God to change our circumstances instead of our hearts?

Look again at Luke 1. In verse 29 Mary was bewildered and evidently afraid. But by verse 46 she was singing praises to the Lord. We don't know how much time passed between verses 29 and 46, but we do know God gave Mary a change of heart.

God answered Tricia's prayers for a new attitude too. Her days of driving across the desert became times of blessing. She describes those days as being times of just "her and God," noting that "you hear God a lot clearer" when the distractions of life are removed. Tricia says the memories of that trip are ones she and her sons now cherish.

So what might God be willing to do if you started asking him to change your heart? There might be cherished memories in store for you — right in the place you didn't sign up to be.

But Mary treasured up all these things and pondered them in her heart.

LUKE 2:19

DEBRIEF

- Where in my life am I crying, "I didn't sign up for this!"?
- How can I give the ponderings of my heart to God in exchange for a new attitude?

REPORT

Dear Lord, sometimes life as a military spouse is challenging. Help me understand that you see where I am and know the ponderings of my heart. Please change my attitude so I can see your blessings in this place and be a blessing to others. In Jesus' name I pray. Amen.

for your next devotional reading, go to page 84

[70] (as he said through his holy prophets
of long ago),
[71] salvation from our enemies
and from the hand of all who
hate us —
[72] to show mercy to our ancestors
and to remember his holy covenant,
[73]   the oath he swore to our father
Abraham:
[74] to rescue us from the hand of our
enemies,
and to enable us to serve him without
fear
[75]   in holiness and righteousness before
him all our days.

[76] And you, my child, will be called a
prophet of the Most High;
for you will go on before the Lord to
prepare the way for him,
[77] to give his people the knowledge of
salvation
through the forgiveness of their sins,
[78] because of the tender mercy of our God,
by which the rising sun will come to
us from heaven
[79] to shine on those living in darkness
and in the shadow of death,
to guide our feet into the path
of peace."

[80] And the child grew and became strong
in spirit[a]; and he lived in the wilderness until he appeared publicly to Israel.

The Birth of Jesus

2 In those days Caesar Augustus issued a
decree that a census should be taken of
the entire Roman world. [2](This was the first
census that took place while[b] Quirinius was
governor of Syria.) [3]And everyone went to
their own town to register.
[4]So Joseph also went up from the town of
Nazareth in Galilee to Judea, to Bethlehem
the town of David, because he belonged to
the house and line of David. [5]He went there
to register with Mary, who was pledged to be
married to him and was expecting a child.
[6]While they were there, the time came for
the baby to be born, [7]and she gave birth to
her firstborn, a son. She wrapped him in
cloths and placed him in a manger, because
there was no guest room available for them.

[8] And there were shepherds living out in
the fields nearby, keeping watch over their
flocks at night. [9]An angel of the Lord appeared to them, and the glory of the Lord
shone around them, and they were terrified. [10]But the angel said to them, "Do not be
afraid. I bring you good news that will cause
great joy for all the people. [11]Today in the
town of David a Savior has been born to you;
he is the Messiah, the Lord. [12]This will be a
sign to you: You will find a baby wrapped in
cloths and lying in a manger."
[13]Suddenly a great company of the heavenly host appeared with the angel, praising
God and saying,

[14] "Glory to God in the highest heaven,
and on earth peace to those on whom
his favor rests."

[15]When the angels had left them and gone
into heaven, the shepherds said to one another, "Let's go to Bethlehem and see this
thing that has happened, which the Lord has
told us about."
[16]So they hurried off and found Mary
and Joseph, and the baby, who was lying
in the manger. [17]When they had seen him,
they spread the word concerning what had
been told them about this child, [18]and all
who heard it were amazed at what the shepherds said to them. [19]But Mary treasured up
all these things and pondered them in her
heart. [20]The shepherds returned, glorifying
and praising God for all the things they had
heard and seen, which were just as they had
been told.
[21]On the eighth day, when it was time to
circumcise the child, he was named Jesus,
the name the angel had given him before he
was conceived.

Jesus Presented in the Temple

[22]When the time came for the purification rites required by the Law of Moses, Joseph and Mary took him to Jerusalem to present him to the Lord [23](as it is written in the
Law of the Lord, "Every firstborn male is to
be consecrated to the Lord"[c]), [24]and to offer a sacrifice in keeping with what is said in
the Law of the Lord: "a pair of doves or two
young pigeons."[d]
[25]Now there was a man in Jerusalem called

---

[a] 80 Or in the Spirit   [b] 2 Or This census took place before   [c] 23 Exodus 13:2,12   [d] 24 Lev. 12:8

Simeon, who was righteous and devout. He was waiting for the consolation of Israel, and the Holy Spirit was on him. [26] It had been revealed to him by the Holy Spirit that he would not die before he had seen the Lord's Messiah. [27] Moved by the Spirit, he went into the temple courts. When the parents brought in the child Jesus to do for him what the custom of the Law required, [28] Simeon took him in his arms and praised God, saying:

[29] "Sovereign Lord, as you have promised,
    you may now dismiss[a] your servant
        in peace.
[30] For my eyes have seen your salvation,
[31]   which you have prepared in the
        sight of all nations:
[32] a light for revelation to the Gentiles,
    and the glory of your people
        Israel."

[33] The child's father and mother marveled at what was said about him. [34] Then Simeon blessed them and said to Mary, his mother: "This child is destined to cause the falling and rising of many in Israel, and to be a sign that will be spoken against, [35] so that the thoughts of many hearts will be revealed. And a sword will pierce your own soul too."

[36] There was also a prophet, Anna, the daughter of Penuel, of the tribe of Asher. She was very old; she had lived with her husband seven years after her marriage, [37] and then was a widow until she was eighty-four.[b] She never left the temple but worshiped night and day, fasting and praying. [38] Coming up to them at that very moment, she gave thanks to God and spoke about the child to all who were looking forward to the redemption of Jerusalem.

[39] When Joseph and Mary had done everything required by the Law of the Lord, they returned to Galilee to their own town of Nazareth. [40] And the child grew and became strong; he was filled with wisdom, and the grace of God was on him.

The Boy Jesus at the Temple

[41] Every year Jesus' parents went to Jerusalem for the Festival of the Passover. [42] When he was twelve years old, they went up to the festival, according to the custom. [43] After the festival was over, while his parents were returning home, the boy Jesus stayed behind in Jerusalem, but they were unaware of it. [44] Thinking he was in their company, they traveled on for a day. Then they began looking for him among their relatives and friends. [45] When they did not find him, they went back to Jerusalem to look for him. [46] After three days they found him in the temple courts, sitting among the teachers, listening to them and asking them questions. [47] Everyone who heard him was amazed at his understanding and his answers. [48] When his parents saw him, they were astonished. His mother said to him, "Son, why have you treated us like this? Your father and I have been anxiously searching for you."

[49] "Why were you searching for me?" he asked. "Didn't you know I had to be in my Father's house?"[c] [50] But they did not understand what he was saying to them.

[51] Then he went down to Nazareth with them and was obedient to them. But his mother treasured all these things in her heart. [52] And Jesus grew in wisdom and stature, and in favor with God and man.

John the Baptist Prepares the Way

3 In the fifteenth year of the reign of Tiberius Caesar — when Pontius Pilate was governor of Judea, Herod tetrarch of Galilee, his brother Philip tetrarch of Iturea and Traconitis, and Lysanias tetrarch of Abilene — [2] during the high-priesthood of Annas and Caiaphas, the word of God came to John son of Zechariah in the wilderness. [3] He went into all the country around the Jordan, preaching a baptism of repentance for the forgiveness of sins. [4] As it is written in the book of the words of Isaiah the prophet:

"A voice of one calling in the
    wilderness,
'Prepare the way for the Lord,
    make straight paths for him.
[5] Every valley shall be filled in,
    every mountain and hill made low.
The crooked roads shall become
    straight,
    the rough ways smooth.
[6] And all people will see God's
    salvation.'"[d]

---

[a] 29 Or promised, / now dismiss   [b] 37 Or then had been a widow for eighty-four years.   [c] 49 Or be about my Father's business   [d] 6 Isaiah 40:3-5

[7]John said to the crowds coming out to be baptized by him, "You brood of vipers! Who warned you to flee from the coming wrath? [8]Produce fruit in keeping with repentance. And do not begin to say to yourselves, 'We have Abraham as our father.' For I tell you that out of these stones God can raise up children for Abraham. [9]The ax is already at the root of the trees, and every tree that does not produce good fruit will be cut down and thrown into the fire."

[10]"What should we do then?" the crowd asked.

[11]John answered, "Anyone who has two shirts should share with the one who has none, and anyone who has food should do the same."

[12]Even tax collectors came to be baptized. "Teacher," they asked, "what should we do?"

[13]"Don't collect any more than you are required to," he told them.

[14]Then some soldiers asked him, "And what should we do?"

He replied, "Don't extort money and don't accuse people falsely — be content with your pay."

[15]The people were waiting expectantly and were all wondering in their hearts if John might possibly be the Messiah. [16]John answered them all, "I baptize you with[a] water. But one who is more powerful than I will come, the straps of whose sandals I am not worthy to untie. He will baptize you with[a] the Holy Spirit and fire. [17]His winnowing fork is in his hand to clear his threshing floor and to gather the wheat into his barn, but he will burn up the chaff with unquenchable fire." [18]And with many other words John exhorted the people and proclaimed the good news to them.

[19]But when John rebuked Herod the tetrarch because of his marriage to Herodias, his brother's wife, and all the other evil things he had done, [20]Herod added this to them all: He locked John up in prison.

The Baptism and Genealogy of Jesus

[21]When all the people were being baptized, Jesus was baptized too. And as he was praying, heaven was opened [22]and the Holy Spirit descended on him in bodily form like a dove. And a voice came from heaven: "You are my Son, whom I love; with you I am well pleased."

[23]Now Jesus himself was about thirty years old when he began his ministry. He was the son, so it was thought, of Joseph,

the son of Heli, [24]the son of Matthat,
the son of Levi, the son of Melki,
the son of Jannai, the son of Joseph,
[25]the son of Mattathias, the son of Amos,
the son of Nahum, the son of Esli,
the son of Naggai, [26]the son of Maath,
the son of Mattathias, the son of Semein,
the son of Josek, the son of Joda,
[27]the son of Joanan, the son of Rhesa,
the son of Zerubbabel, the son of Shealtiel,
the son of Neri, [28]the son of Melki,
the son of Addi, the son of Cosam,
the son of Elmadam, the son of Er,
[29]the son of Joshua, the son of Eliezer,
the son of Jorim, the son of Matthat,
the son of Levi, [30]the son of Simeon,
the son of Judah, the son of Joseph,
the son of Jonam, the son of Eliakim,
[31]the son of Melea, the son of Menna,
the son of Mattatha, the son of Nathan,
the son of David, [32]the son of Jesse,
the son of Obed, the son of Boaz,
the son of Salmon,[b] the son of Nahshon,
[33]the son of Amminadab, the son of Ram,[c]
the son of Hezron, the son of Perez,
the son of Judah, [34]the son of Jacob,
the son of Isaac, the son of Abraham,
the son of Terah, the son of Nahor,
[35]the son of Serug, the son of Reu,
the son of Peleg, the son of Eber,
the son of Shelah, [36]the son of Cainan,
the son of Arphaxad, the son of Shem,
the son of Noah, the son of Lamech,
[37]the son of Methuselah, the son of Enoch,
the son of Jared, the son of Mahalalel,
the son of Kenan, [38]the son of Enosh,
the son of Seth, the son of Adam,
the son of God.

Jesus Is Tested in the Wilderness

4 Jesus, full of the Holy Spirit, left the Jordan and was led by the Spirit into the wilderness, [2]where for forty days he was tempted[d] by the devil. He ate nothing during

---

[a] 16 Or in   [b] 32 Some early manuscripts Sala   [c] 33 Some manuscripts Amminadab, the son of Admin, the son of Arni; other manuscripts vary widely.   [d] 2 The Greek for tempted can also mean tested.

those days, and at the end of them he was hungry.

³The devil said to him, "If you are the Son of God, tell this stone to become bread."

⁴Jesus answered, "It is written: 'Man shall not live on bread alone.'ᵃ"

⁵The devil led him up to a high place and showed him in an instant all the kingdoms of the world. ⁶And he said to him, "I will give you all their authority and splendor; it has been given to me, and I can give it to anyone I want to. ⁷If you worship me, it will all be yours."

⁸Jesus answered, "It is written: 'Worship the Lord your God and serve him only.'ᵇ"

⁹The devil led him to Jerusalem and had him stand on the highest point of the temple. "If you are the Son of God," he said, "throw yourself down from here. ¹⁰For it is written:

"'He will command his angels
    concerning you
    to guard you carefully;
¹¹ they will lift you up in their hands,
    so that you will not strike your foot
    against a stone.'ᶜ"

¹²Jesus answered, "It is said: 'Do not put the Lord your God to the test.'ᵈ"

¹³When the devil had finished all this tempting, he left him until an opportune time.

Jesus Rejected at Nazareth

¹⁴Jesus returned to Galilee in the power of the Spirit, and news about him spread through the whole countryside. ¹⁵He was teaching in their synagogues, and everyone praised him.

¹⁶He went to Nazareth, where he had been brought up, and on the Sabbath day he went into the synagogue, as was his custom. He stood up to read, ¹⁷and the scroll of the prophet Isaiah was handed to him. Unrolling it, he found the place where it is written:

¹⁸"The Spirit of the Lord is on me,
    because he has anointed me
    to proclaim good news to the poor.
He has sent me to proclaim freedom for
    the prisoners

and recovery of sight for the blind,
    to set the oppressed free,
¹⁹   to proclaim the year of the Lord's
        favor."ᵉ

²⁰Then he rolled up the scroll, gave it back to the attendant and sat down. The eyes of everyone in the synagogue were fastened on him. ²¹He began by saying to them, "Today this scripture is fulfilled in your hearing."

²²All spoke well of him and were amazed at the gracious words that came from his lips. "Isn't this Joseph's son?" they asked.

²³Jesus said to them, "Surely you will quote this proverb to me: 'Physician, heal yourself!' And you will tell me, 'Do here in your hometown what we have heard that you did in Capernaum.'"

²⁴"Truly I tell you," he continued, "no prophet is accepted in his hometown. ²⁵I assure you that there were many widows in Israel in Elijah's time, when the sky was shut for three and a half years and there was a severe famine throughout the land. ²⁶Yet Elijah was not sent to any of them, but to a widow in Zarephath in the region of Sidon. ²⁷And there were many in Israel with leprosyᶠ in the time of Elisha the prophet, yet not one of them was cleansed—only Naaman the Syrian."

²⁸All the people in the synagogue were furious when they heard this. ²⁹They got up, drove him out of the town, and took him to the brow of the hill on which the town was built, in order to throw him off the cliff. ³⁰But he walked right through the crowd and went on his way.

Jesus Drives Out an Impure Spirit

³¹Then he went down to Capernaum, a town in Galilee, and on the Sabbath he taught the people. ³²They were amazed at his teaching, because his words had authority.

³³In the synagogue there was a man possessed by a demon, an impure spirit. He cried out at the top of his voice, ³⁴"Go away! What do you want with us, Jesus of Nazareth? Have you come to destroy us? I know who you are—the Holy One of God!"

³⁵"Be quiet!" Jesus said sternly. "Come

ᵃ 4 Deut. 8:3   ᵇ 8 Deut. 6:13   ᶜ 11 Psalm 91:11,12   ᵈ 12 Deut. 6:16   ᵉ 19 Isaiah 61:1,2 (see Septuagint); Isaiah 58:6   ᶠ 27 The Greek word traditionally translated leprosy was used for various diseases affecting the skin.

out of him!" Then the demon threw the man down before them all and came out without injuring him.

[36] All the people were amazed and said to each other, "What words these are! With authority and power he gives orders to impure spirits and they come out!" [37] And the news about him spread throughout the surrounding area.

Jesus Heals Many

[38] Jesus left the synagogue and went to the home of Simon. Now Simon's mother-in-law was suffering from a high fever, and they asked Jesus to help her. [39] So he bent over her and rebuked the fever, and it left her. She got up at once and began to wait on them.

[40] At sunset, the people brought to Jesus all who had various kinds of sickness, and laying his hands on each one, he healed them. [41] Moreover, demons came out of many people, shouting, "You are the Son of God!" But he rebuked them and would not allow them to speak, because they knew he was the Messiah.

[42] At daybreak, Jesus went out to a solitary place. The people were looking for him and when they came to where he was, they tried to keep him from leaving them. [43] But he said, "I must proclaim the good news of the kingdom of God to the other towns also, because that is why I was sent." [44] And he kept on preaching in the synagogues of Judea.

Jesus Calls His First Disciples

5 One day as Jesus was standing by the Lake of Gennesaret,[a] the people were crowding around him and listening to the word of God. [2] He saw at the water's edge two boats, left there by the fishermen, who were washing their nets. [3] He got into one of the boats, the one belonging to Simon, and asked him to put out a little from shore. Then he sat down and taught the people from the boat.

[4] When he had finished speaking, he said to Simon, "Put out into deep water, and let down the nets for a catch."

[5] Simon answered, "Master, we've worked hard all night and haven't caught anything. But because you say so, I will let down the nets."

[6] When they had done so, they caught such a large number of fish that their nets began to break. [7] So they signaled their partners in the other boat to come and help them, and they came and filled both boats so full that they began to sink.

[8] When Simon Peter saw this, he fell at Jesus' knees and said, "Go away from me, Lord; I am a sinful man!" [9] For he and all his companions were astonished at the catch of fish they had taken, [10] and so were James and John, the sons of Zebedee, Simon's partners.

Then Jesus said to Simon, "Don't be afraid; from now on you will fish for people." [11] So they pulled their boats up on shore, left everything and followed him.

Jesus Heals a Man With Leprosy

[12] While Jesus was in one of the towns, a man came along who was covered with leprosy.[b] When he saw Jesus, he fell with his face to the ground and begged him, "Lord, if you are willing, you can make me clean."

[13] Jesus reached out his hand and touched the man. "I am willing," he said. "Be clean!" And immediately the leprosy left him.

[14] Then Jesus ordered him, "Don't tell anyone, but go, show yourself to the priest and offer the sacrifices that Moses commanded for your cleansing, as a testimony to them."

[15] Yet the news about him spread all the more, so that crowds of people came to hear him and to be healed of their sicknesses. [16] But Jesus often withdrew to lonely places and prayed.

Jesus Forgives and Heals a Paralyzed Man

[17] One day Jesus was teaching, and Pharisees and teachers of the law were sitting there. They had come from every village of Galilee and from Judea and Jerusalem. And the power of the Lord was with Jesus to heal the sick. [18] Some men came carrying a paralyzed man on a mat and tried to take him into the house to lay him before Jesus. [19] When they could not find a way to do this because of the crowd, they went up on the roof and lowered him on his mat through the tiles into the middle of the crowd, right in front of Jesus.

---

[a] 1 That is, the Sea of Galilee   [b] 12 The Greek word traditionally translated leprosy was used for various diseases affecting the skin.

²⁰When Jesus saw their faith, he said, "Friend, your sins are forgiven."

²¹The Pharisees and the teachers of the law began thinking to themselves, "Who is this fellow who speaks blasphemy? Who can forgive sins but God alone?"

²²Jesus knew what they were thinking and asked, "Why are you thinking these things in your hearts? ²³Which is easier: to say, 'Your sins are forgiven,' or to say, 'Get up and walk'? ²⁴But I want you to know that the Son of Man has authority on earth to forgive sins." So he said to the paralyzed man, "I tell you, get up, take your mat and go home." ²⁵Immediately he stood up in front of them, took what he had been lying on and went home praising God. ²⁶Everyone was amazed and gave praise to God. They were filled with awe and said, "We have seen remarkable things today."

Jesus Calls Levi and Eats With Sinners

²⁷After this, Jesus went out and saw a tax collector by the name of Levi sitting at his tax booth. "Follow me," Jesus said to him, ²⁸and Levi got up, left everything and followed him.

²⁹Then Levi held a great banquet for Jesus at his house, and a large crowd of tax collectors and others were eating with them. ³⁰But the Pharisees and the teachers of the law who belonged to their sect complained to his disciples, "Why do you eat and drink with tax collectors and sinners?"

³¹Jesus answered them, "It is not the healthy who need a doctor, but the sick. ³²I have not come to call the righteous, but sinners to repentance."

Jesus Questioned About Fasting

³³They said to him, "John's disciples often fast and pray, and so do the disciples of the Pharisees, but yours go on eating and drinking."

³⁴Jesus answered, "Can you make the friends of the bridegroom fast while he is with them? ³⁵But the time will come when the bridegroom will be taken from them; in those days they will fast."

³⁶He told them this parable: "No one tears a piece out of a new garment to patch an old one. Otherwise, they will have torn the new garment, and the patch from the new will not match the old. ³⁷And no one pours new wine into old wineskins. Otherwise, the new wine will burst the skins; the wine will run out and the wineskins will be ruined. ³⁸No, new wine must be poured into new wineskins. ³⁹And no one after drinking old wine wants the new, for they say, 'The old is better.'"

Jesus Is Lord of the Sabbath

6 One Sabbath Jesus was going through the grainfields, and his disciples began to pick some heads of grain, rub them in their hands and eat the kernels. ²Some of the Pharisees asked, "Why are you doing what is unlawful on the Sabbath?"

³Jesus answered them, "Have you never read what David did when he and his companions were hungry? ⁴He entered the house of God, and taking the consecrated bread, he ate what is lawful only for priests to eat. And he also gave some to his companions." ⁵Then Jesus said to them, "The Son of Man is Lord of the Sabbath."

⁶On another Sabbath he went into the synagogue and was teaching, and a man was there whose right hand was shriveled. ⁷The Pharisees and the teachers of the law were looking for a reason to accuse Jesus, so they watched him closely to see if he would heal on the Sabbath. ⁸But Jesus knew what they were thinking and said to the man with the shriveled hand, "Get up and stand in front of everyone." So he got up and stood there.

⁹Then Jesus said to them, "I ask you, which is lawful on the Sabbath: to do good or to do evil, to save life or to destroy it?"

¹⁰He looked around at them all, and then said to the man, "Stretch out your hand." He did so, and his hand was completely restored. ¹¹But the Pharisees and the teachers of the law were furious and began to discuss with one another what they might do to Jesus.

The Twelve Apostles

¹²One of those days Jesus went out to a mountainside to pray, and spent the night praying to God. ¹³When morning came, he called his disciples to him and chose twelve of them, whom he also designated apostles: ¹⁴Simon (whom he named Peter), his brother Andrew, James, John, Philip, Bartholomew, ¹⁵Matthew, Thomas, James son of Alphaeus, Simon who was called the Zealot, ¹⁶Judas

son of James, and Judas Iscariot, who became a traitor.

Blessings and Woes

[17] He went down with them and stood on a level place. A large crowd of his disciples was there and a great number of people from all over Judea, from Jerusalem, and from the coastal region around Tyre and Sidon, [18] who had come to hear him and to be healed of their diseases. Those troubled by impure spirits were cured, [19] and the people all tried to touch him, because power was coming from him and healing them all.

[20] Looking at his disciples, he said:

"Blessed are you who are poor,
    for yours is the kingdom of God.
[21] Blessed are you who hunger now,
    for you will be satisfied.
Blessed are you who weep now,
    for you will laugh.
[22] Blessed are you when people hate you,
    when they exclude you and insult you
    and reject your name as evil,
        because of the Son of Man.

[23] "Rejoice in that day and leap for joy, because great is your reward in heaven. For that is how their ancestors treated the prophets.

[24] "But woe to you who are rich,
    for you have already received your
        comfort.
[25] Woe to you who are well fed now,
    for you will go hungry.
Woe to you who laugh now,
    for you will mourn and weep.
[26] Woe to you when everyone speaks well
        of you,
    for that is how their ancestors treated
        the false prophets.

Love for Enemies

[27] "But to you who are listening I say: Love your enemies, do good to those who hate you, [28] bless those who curse you, pray for those who mistreat you. [29] If someone slaps you on one cheek, turn to them the other also. If someone takes your coat, do not withhold your shirt from them. [30] Give to everyone who asks you, and if anyone takes what belongs to you, do not demand it back. [31] Do to others as you would have them do to you.

[32] "If you love those who love you, what credit is that to you? Even sinners love those who love them. [33] And if you do good to those who are good to you, what credit is that to you? Even sinners do that. [34] And if you lend to those from whom you expect repayment, what credit is that to you? Even sinners lend to sinners, expecting to be repaid in full. [35] But love your enemies, do good to them, and lend to them without expecting to get anything back. Then your reward will be great, and you will be children of the Most High, because he is kind to the ungrateful and wicked. [36] Be merciful, just as your Father is merciful.

Judging Others

[37] "Do not judge, and you will not be judged. Do not condemn, and you will not be condemned. Forgive, and you will be forgiven. [38] Give, and it will be given to you. A good measure, pressed down, shaken together and running over, will be poured into your lap. For with the measure you use, it will be measured to you."

[39] He also told them this parable: "Can the blind lead the blind? Will they not both fall into a pit? [40] The student is not above the teacher, but everyone who is fully trained will be like their teacher.

[41] "Why do you look at the speck of sawdust in your brother's eye and pay no attention to the plank in your own eye? [42] How can you say to your brother, 'Brother, let me take the speck out of your eye,' when you yourself fail to see the plank in your own eye? You hypocrite, first take the plank out of your eye, and then you will see clearly to remove the speck from your brother's eye.

A Tree and Its Fruit

[43] "No good tree bears bad fruit, nor does a bad tree bear good fruit. [44] Each tree is recognized by its own fruit. People do not pick figs from thornbushes, or grapes from briers. [45] A good man brings good things out of the good stored up in his heart, and an evil man brings evil things out of the evil stored up in his heart. For the mouth speaks what the heart is full of.

The Wise and Foolish Builders

[46] "Why do you call me, 'Lord, Lord,' and do not do what I say? [47] As for everyone who

comes to me and hears my words and puts them into practice, I will show you what they are like. [48]They are like a man building a house, who dug down deep and laid the foundation on rock. When a flood came, the torrent struck that house but could not shake it, because it was well built. [49]But the one who hears my words and does not put them into practice is like a man who built a house on the ground without a foundation. The moment the torrent struck that house, it collapsed and its destruction was complete."

The Faith of the Centurion

7 When Jesus had finished saying all this to the people who were listening, he entered Capernaum. [2]There a centurion's servant, whom his master valued highly, was sick and about to die. [3]The centurion heard of Jesus and sent some elders of the Jews to him, asking him to come and heal his servant. [4]When they came to Jesus, they pleaded earnestly with him, "This man deserves to have you do this, [5]because he loves our nation and has built our synagogue." [6]So Jesus went with them.

He was not far from the house when the centurion sent friends to say to him: "Lord, don't trouble yourself, for I do not deserve to have you come under my roof. [7]That is why I did not even consider myself worthy to come to you. But say the word, and my servant will be healed. [8]For I myself am a man under authority, with soldiers under me. I tell this one, 'Go,' and he goes; and that one, 'Come,' and he comes. I say to my servant, 'Do this,' and he does it."

[9]When Jesus heard this, he was amazed at him, and turning to the crowd following him, he said, "I tell you, I have not found such great faith even in Israel." [10]Then the men who had been sent returned to the house and found the servant well.

Jesus Raises a Widow's Son

[11]Soon afterward, Jesus went to a town called Nain, and his disciples and a large crowd went along with him. [12]As he approached the town gate, a dead person was being carried out — the only son of his mother, and she was a widow. And a large crowd from the town was with her. [13]When the Lord saw her, his heart went out to her and he said, "Don't cry."

[14]Then he went up and touched the bier they were carrying him on, and the bearers stood still. He said, "Young man, I say to you, get up!" [15]The dead man sat up and began to talk, and Jesus gave him back to his mother.

[16]They were all filled with awe and praised God. "A great prophet has appeared among us," they said. "God has come to help his people." [17]This news about Jesus spread throughout Judea and the surrounding country.

Jesus and John the Baptist

[18]John's disciples told him about all these things. Calling two of them, [19]he sent them to the Lord to ask, "Are you the one who is to come, or should we expect someone else?"

[20]When the men came to Jesus, they said, "John the Baptist sent us to you to ask, 'Are you the one who is to come, or should we expect someone else?'"

[21]At that very time Jesus cured many who had diseases, sicknesses and evil spirits, and gave sight to many who were blind. [22]So he replied to the messengers, "Go back and report to John what you have seen and heard: The blind receive sight, the lame walk, those who have leprosy[a] are cleansed, the deaf hear, the dead are raised, and the good news is proclaimed to the poor. [23]Blessed is anyone who does not stumble on account of me."

[24]After John's messengers left, Jesus began to speak to the crowd about John: "What did you go out into the wilderness to see? A reed swayed by the wind? [25]If not, what did you go out to see? A man dressed in fine clothes? No, those who wear expensive clothes and indulge in luxury are in palaces. [26]But what did you go out to see? A prophet? Yes, I tell you, and more than a prophet. [27]This is the one about whom it is written:

"'I will send my messenger ahead of you, who will prepare your way before you.'[b]

[28]I tell you, among those born of women there is no one greater than John; yet the one who is least in the kingdom of God is greater than he."

---

[a] 22 The Greek word traditionally translated *leprosy* was used for various diseases affecting the skin.
[b] 27 Mal. 3:1

[29](All the people, even the tax collectors, when they heard Jesus' words, acknowledged that God's way was right, because they had been baptized by John. [30]But the Pharisees and the experts in the law rejected God's purpose for themselves, because they had not been baptized by John.)

[31]Jesus went on to say, "To what, then, can I compare the people of this generation? What are they like? [32]They are like children sitting in the marketplace and calling out to each other:

" 'We played the pipe for you,
    and you did not dance;
we sang a dirge,
    and you did not cry.'

[33]For John the Baptist came neither eating bread nor drinking wine, and you say, 'He has a demon.' [34]The Son of Man came eating and drinking, and you say, 'Here is a glutton and a drunkard, a friend of tax collectors and sinners.' [35]But wisdom is proved right by all her children."

Jesus Anointed by a Sinful Woman

[36]When one of the Pharisees invited Jesus to have dinner with him, he went to the Pharisee's house and reclined at the table. [37]A woman in that town who lived a sinful life learned that Jesus was eating at the Pharisee's house, so she came there with an alabaster jar of perfume. [38]As she stood behind him at his feet weeping, she began to wet his feet with her tears. Then she wiped them with her hair, kissed them and poured perfume on them.

[39]When the Pharisee who had invited him saw this, he said to himself, "If this man were a prophet, he would know who is touching him and what kind of woman she is—that she is a sinner."

[40]Jesus answered him, "Simon, I have something to tell you."

"Tell me, teacher," he said.

[41]"Two people owed money to a certain moneylender. One owed him five hundred denarii,[a] and the other fifty. [42]Neither of them had the money to pay him back, so he forgave the debts of both. Now which of them will love him more?"

[43]Simon replied, "I suppose the one who had the bigger debt forgiven."

"You have judged correctly," Jesus said.

[44]Then he turned toward the woman and said to Simon, "Do you see this woman? I came into your house. You did not give me any water for my feet, but she wet my feet with her tears and wiped them with her hair. [45]You did not give me a kiss, but this woman, from the time I entered, has not stopped kissing my feet. [46]You did not put oil on my head, but she has poured perfume on my feet. [47]Therefore, I tell you, her many sins have been forgiven—as her great love has shown. But whoever has been forgiven little loves little."

[48]Then Jesus said to her, "Your sins are forgiven."

[49]The other guests began to say among themselves, "Who is this who even forgives sins?"

[50]Jesus said to the woman, "Your faith has saved you; go in peace."

The Parable of the Sower

8 After this, Jesus traveled about from one town and village to another, proclaiming the good news of the kingdom of God. The Twelve were with him, [2]and also some women who had been cured of evil spirits and diseases: Mary (called Magdalene) from whom seven demons had come out; [3]Joanna the wife of Chuza, the manager of Herod's household; Susanna; and many others. These women were helping to support them out of their own means.

[4]While a large crowd was gathering and people were coming to Jesus from town after town, he told this parable: [5]"A farmer went out to sow his seed. As he was scattering the seed, some fell along the path; it was trampled on, and the birds ate it up. [6]Some fell on rocky ground, and when it came up, the plants withered because they had no moisture. [7]Other seed fell among thorns, which grew up with it and choked the plants. [8]Still other seed fell on good soil. It came up and yielded a crop, a hundred times more than was sown."

When he said this, he called out, "Whoever has ears to hear, let them hear."

[9]His disciples asked him what this parable meant. [10]He said, "The knowledge of the secrets of the kingdom of God has been given

---

[a] 41 A denarius was the usual daily wage of a day laborer (see Matt. 20:2).

to you, but to others I speak in parables, so that,

> " 'though seeing, they may not see;
>   though hearing, they may not
>   understand.'*a*

[11] "This is the meaning of the parable: The seed is the word of God. [12] Those along the path are the ones who hear, and then the devil comes and takes away the word from their hearts, so that they may not believe and be saved. [13] Those on the rocky ground are the ones who receive the word with joy when they hear it, but they have no root. They believe for a while, but in the time of testing they fall away. [14] The seed that fell among thorns stands for those who hear, but as they go on their way they are choked by life's worries, riches and pleasures, and they do not mature. [15] But the seed on good soil stands for those with a noble and good heart, who hear the word, retain it, and by persevering produce a crop.

A Lamp on a Stand

[16] "No one lights a lamp and hides it in a clay jar or puts it under a bed. Instead, they put it on a stand, so that those who come in can see the light. [17] For there is nothing hidden that will not be disclosed, and nothing concealed that will not be known or brought out into the open. [18] Therefore consider carefully how you listen. Whoever has will be given more; whoever does not have, even what they think they have will be taken from them."

Jesus' Mother and Brothers

[19] Now Jesus' mother and brothers came to see him, but they were not able to get near him because of the crowd. [20] Someone told him, "Your mother and brothers are standing outside, wanting to see you."

[21] He replied, "My mother and brothers are those who hear God's word and put it into practice."

Jesus Calms the Storm

[22] One day Jesus said to his disciples, "Let us go over to the other side of the lake." So they got into a boat and set out. [23] As they sailed, he fell asleep. A squall came down on the lake, so that the boat was being swamped, and they were in great danger.

[24] The disciples went and woke him, saying, "Master, Master, we're going to drown!"

He got up and rebuked the wind and the raging waters; the storm subsided, and all was calm. [25] "Where is your faith?" he asked his disciples.

In fear and amazement they asked one another, "Who is this? He commands even the winds and the water, and they obey him."

Jesus Restores a Demon-Possessed Man

[26] They sailed to the region of the Gerasenes,*b* which is across the lake from Galilee. [27] When Jesus stepped ashore, he was met by a demon-possessed man from the town. For a long time this man had not worn clothes or lived in a house, but had lived in the tombs. [28] When he saw Jesus, he cried out and fell at his feet, shouting at the top of his voice, "What do you want with me, Jesus, Son of the Most High God? I beg you, don't torture me!" [29] For Jesus had commanded the impure spirit to come out of the man. Many times it had seized him, and though he was chained hand and foot and kept under guard, he had broken his chains and had been driven by the demon into solitary places.

[30] Jesus asked him, "What is your name?"

"Legion," he replied, because many demons had gone into him. [31] And they begged Jesus repeatedly not to order them to go into the Abyss.

[32] A large herd of pigs was feeding there on the hillside. The demons begged Jesus to let them go into the pigs, and he gave them permission. [33] When the demons came out of the man, they went into the pigs, and the herd rushed down the steep bank into the lake and was drowned.

[34] When those tending the pigs saw what had happened, they ran off and reported this in the town and countryside, [35] and the people went out to see what had happened. When they came to Jesus, they found the man from whom the demons had gone out, sitting at Jesus' feet, dressed and in his right mind; and they were afraid. [36] Those who had seen it told the people how the demon-possessed

---

a 10 Isaiah 6:9   *b* 26 Some manuscripts *Gadarenes*; other manuscripts *Gergesenes*; also in verse 37

man had been cured. [37]Then all the people of the region of the Gerasenes asked Jesus to leave them, because they were overcome with fear. So he got into the boat and left.

[38]The man from whom the demons had gone out begged to go with him, but Jesus sent him away, saying, [39]"Return home and tell how much God has done for you." So the man went away and told all over town how much Jesus had done for him.

Jesus Raises a Dead Girl and Heals a Sick Woman

[40]Now when Jesus returned, a crowd welcomed him, for they were all expecting him. [41]Then a man named Jairus, a synagogue leader, came and fell at Jesus' feet, pleading with him to come to his house [42]because his only daughter, a girl of about twelve, was dying.

As Jesus was on his way, the crowds almost crushed him. [43]And a woman was there who had been subject to bleeding for twelve years,[a] but no one could heal her. [44]She came up behind him and touched the edge of his cloak, and immediately her bleeding stopped.

[45]"Who touched me?" Jesus asked.

When they all denied it, Peter said, "Master, the people are crowding and pressing against you."

[46]But Jesus said, "Someone touched me; I know that power has gone out from me."

[47]Then the woman, seeing that she could not go unnoticed, came trembling and fell at his feet. In the presence of all the people, she told why she had touched him and how she had been instantly healed. [48]Then he said to her, "Daughter, your faith has healed you. Go in peace."

[49]While Jesus was still speaking, someone came from the house of Jairus, the synagogue leader. "Your daughter is dead," he said. "Don't bother the teacher anymore."

[50]Hearing this, Jesus said to Jairus, "Don't be afraid; just believe, and she will be healed."

[51]When he arrived at the house of Jairus, he did not let anyone go in with him except Peter, John and James, and the child's father and mother. [52]Meanwhile, all the people were wailing and mourning for her. "Stop wailing," Jesus said. "She is not dead but asleep."

[53]They laughed at him, knowing that she was dead. [54]But he took her by the hand and said, "My child, get up!" [55]Her spirit returned, and at once she stood up. Then Jesus told them to give her something to eat. [56]Her parents were astonished, but he ordered them not to tell anyone what had happened.

Jesus Sends Out the Twelve

9 When Jesus had called the Twelve together, he gave them power and authority to drive out all demons and to cure diseases, [2]and he sent them out to proclaim the kingdom of God and to heal the sick. [3]He told them: "Take nothing for the journey— no staff, no bag, no bread, no money, no extra shirt. [4]Whatever house you enter, stay there until you leave that town. [5]If people do not welcome you, leave their town and shake the dust off your feet as a testimony against them." [6]So they set out and went from village to village, proclaiming the good news and healing people everywhere.

[7]Now Herod the tetrarch heard about all that was going on. And he was perplexed because some were saying that John had been raised from the dead, [8]others that Elijah had appeared, and still others that one of the prophets of long ago had come back to life. [9]But Herod said, "I beheaded John. Who, then, is this I hear such things about?" And he tried to see him.

Jesus Feeds the Five Thousand

[10]When the apostles returned, they reported to Jesus what they had done. Then he took them with him and they withdrew by themselves to a town called Bethsaida, [11]but the crowds learned about it and followed him. He welcomed them and spoke to them about the kingdom of God, and healed those who needed healing.

[12]Late in the afternoon the Twelve came to him and said, "Send the crowd away so they can go to the surrounding villages and countryside and find food and lodging, because we are in a remote place here."

[13]He replied, "You give them something to eat."

They answered, "We have only five loaves

---

[a] 43 Many manuscripts *years, and she had spent all she had on doctors*

of bread and two fish — unless we go and buy food for all this crowd." [14](About five thousand men were there.)

But he said to his disciples, "Have them sit down in groups of about fifty each." [15]The disciples did so, and everyone sat down. [16]Taking the five loaves and the two fish and looking up to heaven, he gave thanks and broke them. Then he gave them to the disciples to distribute to the people. [17]They all ate and were satisfied, and the disciples picked up twelve basketfuls of broken pieces that were left over.

Peter Declares That Jesus Is the Messiah

[18]Once when Jesus was praying in private and his disciples were with him, he asked them, "Who do the crowds say I am?"

[19]They replied, "Some say John the Baptist; others say Elijah; and still others, that one of the prophets of long ago has come back to life."

[20]"But what about you?" he asked. "Who do you say I am?"

Peter answered, "God's Messiah."

Jesus Predicts His Death

[21]Jesus strictly warned them not to tell this to anyone. [22]And he said, "The Son of Man must suffer many things and be rejected by the elders, the chief priests and the teachers of the law, and he must be killed and on the third day be raised to life."

[23]Then he said to them all: "Whoever wants to be my disciple must deny themselves and take up their cross daily and follow me. [24]For whoever wants to save their life will lose it, but whoever loses their life for me will save it. [25]What good is it for someone to gain the whole world, and yet lose or forfeit their very self? [26]Whoever is ashamed of me and my words, the Son of Man will be ashamed of them when he comes in his glory and in the glory of the Father and of the holy angels.

[27]"Truly I tell you, some who are standing here will not taste death before they see the kingdom of God."

The Transfiguration

[28]About eight days after Jesus said this, he took Peter, John and James with him and went up onto a mountain to pray. [29]As he was praying, the appearance of his face changed, and his clothes became as bright as a flash of lightning. [30]Two men, Moses and Elijah, appeared in glorious splendor, talking with Jesus. [31]They spoke about his departure,[a] which he was about to bring to fulfillment at Jerusalem. [32]Peter and his companions were very sleepy, but when they became fully awake, they saw his glory and the two men standing with him. [33]As the men were leaving Jesus, Peter said to him, "Master, it is good for us to be here. Let us put up three shelters — one for you, one for Moses and one for Elijah." (He did not know what he was saying.)

[34]While he was speaking, a cloud appeared and covered them, and they were afraid as they entered the cloud. [35]A voice came from the cloud, saying, "This is my Son, whom I have chosen; listen to him." [36]When the voice had spoken, they found that Jesus was alone. The disciples kept this to themselves and did not tell anyone at that time what they had seen.

Jesus Heals a Demon-Possessed Boy

[37]The next day, when they came down from the mountain, a large crowd met him. [38]A man in the crowd called out, "Teacher, I beg you to look at my son, for he is my only child. [39]A spirit seizes him and he suddenly screams; it throws him into convulsions so that he foams at the mouth. It scarcely ever leaves him and is destroying him. [40]I begged your disciples to drive it out, but they could not."

[41]"You unbelieving and perverse generation," Jesus replied, "how long shall I stay with you and put up with you? Bring your son here."

[42]Even while the boy was coming, the demon threw him to the ground in a convulsion. But Jesus rebuked the impure spirit, healed the boy and gave him back to his father. [43]And they were all amazed at the greatness of God.

Jesus Predicts His Death a Second Time

While everyone was marveling at all that Jesus did, he said to his disciples, [44]"Listen carefully to what I am about to tell you: The Son of Man is going to be delivered into the

[a] 31 Greek exodos

hands of men." [45]But they did not understand what this meant. It was hidden from them, so that they did not grasp it, and they were afraid to ask him about it.

[46]An argument started among the disciples as to which of them would be the greatest. [47]Jesus, knowing their thoughts, took a little child and had him stand beside him. [48]Then he said to them, "Whoever welcomes this little child in my name welcomes me; and whoever welcomes me welcomes the one who sent me. For it is the one who is least among you all who is the greatest."

[49]"Master," said John, "we saw someone driving out demons in your name and we tried to stop him, because he is not one of us."

[50]"Do not stop him," Jesus said, "for whoever is not against you is for you."

Samaritan Opposition

[51]As the time approached for him to be taken up to heaven, Jesus resolutely set out for Jerusalem. [52]And he sent messengers on ahead, who went into a Samaritan village to get things ready for him; [53]but the people there did not welcome him, because he was heading for Jerusalem. [54]When the disciples James and John saw this, they asked, "Lord, do you want us to call fire down from heaven to destroy them[a]?" [55]But Jesus turned and rebuked them. [56]Then he and his disciples went to another village.

The Cost of Following Jesus

[57]As they were walking along the road, a man said to him, "I will follow you wherever you go."

[58]Jesus replied, "Foxes have dens and birds have nests, but the Son of Man has no place to lay his head."

[59]He said to another man, "Follow me."

But he replied, "Lord, first let me go and bury my father."

[60]Jesus said to him, "Let the dead bury their own dead, but you go and proclaim the kingdom of God."

[61]Still another said, "I will follow you, Lord; but first let me go back and say goodbye to my family."

[62]Jesus replied, "No one who puts a hand to the plow and looks back is fit for service in the kingdom of God."

Jesus Sends Out the Seventy-Two

10 After this the Lord appointed seventy-two[b] others and sent them two by two ahead of him to every town and place where he was about to go. [2]He told them, "The harvest is plentiful, but the workers are few. Ask the Lord of the harvest, therefore, to send out workers into his harvest field. [3]Go! I am sending you out like lambs among wolves. [4]Do not take a purse or bag or sandals; and do not greet anyone on the road.

[5]"When you enter a house, first say, 'Peace to this house.' [6]If someone who promotes peace is there, your peace will rest on them; if not, it will return to you. [7]Stay there, eating and drinking whatever they give you, for the worker deserves his wages. Do not move around from house to house.

[8]"When you enter a town and are welcomed, eat what is offered to you. [9]Heal the sick who are there and tell them, 'The kingdom of God has come near to you.' [10]But when you enter a town and are not welcomed, go into its streets and say, [11]'Even the dust of your town we wipe from our feet as a warning to you. Yet be sure of this: The kingdom of God has come near.' [12]I tell you, it will be more bearable on that day for Sodom than for that town.

[13]"Woe to you, Chorazin! Woe to you, Bethsaida! For if the miracles that were performed in you had been performed in Tyre and Sidon, they would have repented long ago, sitting in sackcloth and ashes. [14]But it will be more bearable for Tyre and Sidon at the judgment than for you. [15]And you, Capernaum, will you be lifted to the heavens? No, you will go down to Hades.[c]

[16]"Whoever listens to you listens to me; whoever rejects you rejects me; but whoever rejects me rejects him who sent me."

[17]The seventy-two returned with joy and said, "Lord, even the demons submit to us in your name."

[18]He replied, "I saw Satan fall like lightning from heaven. [19]I have given you authority to trample on snakes and scorpions and to overcome all the power of the enemy; nothing will harm you. [20]However, do not

---

[a] 54 Some manuscripts *them, just as Elijah did*   [b] 1 Some manuscripts *seventy*; also in verse 17
[c] 15 That is, the realm of the dead

rejoice that the spirits submit to you, but rejoice that your names are written in heaven."

²¹ At that time Jesus, full of joy through the Holy Spirit, said, "I praise you, Father, Lord of heaven and earth, because you have hidden these things from the wise and learned, and revealed them to little children. Yes, Father, for this is what you were pleased to do.

²² "All things have been committed to me by my Father. No one knows who the Son is except the Father, and no one knows who the Father is except the Son and those to whom the Son chooses to reveal him."

²³ Then he turned to his disciples and said privately, "Blessed are the eyes that see what you see. ²⁴ For I tell you that many prophets and kings wanted to see what you see but did not see it, and to hear what you hear but did not hear it."

The Parable of the Good Samaritan

²⁵ On one occasion an expert in the law stood up to test Jesus. "Teacher," he asked, "what must I do to inherit eternal life?"

²⁶ "What is written in the Law?" he replied. "How do you read it?"

²⁷ He answered, " 'Love the Lord your God with all your heart and with all your soul and with all your strength and with all your mind'ᵃ; and, 'Love your neighbor as yourself.'ᵇ"

²⁸ "You have answered correctly," Jesus replied. "Do this and you will live."

²⁹ But he wanted to justify himself, so he asked Jesus, "And who is my neighbor?"

³⁰ In reply Jesus said: "A man was going down from Jerusalem to Jericho, when he was attacked by robbers. They stripped him of his clothes, beat him and went away, leaving him half dead. ³¹ A priest happened to be going down the same road, and when he saw the man, he passed by on the other side. ³² So too, a Levite, when he came to the place and saw him, passed by on the other side. ³³ But a Samaritan, as he traveled, came where the man was; and when he saw him, he took pity on him. ³⁴ He went to him and bandaged his wounds, pouring on oil and wine. Then he put the man on his own donkey, brought him to an inn and took care of him. ³⁵ The next

day he took out two denariiᶜ and gave them to the innkeeper. 'Look after him,' he said, 'and when I return, I will reimburse you for any extra expense you may have.'

³⁶ "Which of these three do you think was a neighbor to the man who fell into the hands of robbers?"

³⁷ The expert in the law replied, "The one who had mercy on him."

Jesus told him, "Go and do likewise."

At the Home of Martha and Mary

³⁸ As Jesus and his disciples were on their way, he came to a village where a woman named Martha opened her home to him. ³⁹ She had a sister called Mary, who sat at the Lord's feet listening to what he said. ⁴⁰ But Martha was distracted by all the preparations that had to be made. She came to him and asked, "Lord, don't you care that my sister has left me to do the work by myself? Tell her to help me!"

⁴¹ "Martha, Martha," the Lord answered, "you are worried and upset about many things, ⁴² but few things are needed — or indeed only one.ᵈ Mary has chosen what is better, and it will not be taken away from her."

Jesus' Teaching on Prayer

11 One day Jesus was praying in a certain place. When he finished, one of his disciples said to him, "Lord, teach us to pray, just as John taught his disciples."

² He said to them, "When you pray, say:

" 'Father,ᵉ
hallowed be your name,
  your kingdom come.ᶠ
³ Give us each day our daily bread.
⁴ Forgive us our sins,
    for we also forgive everyone who sins
        against us.ᵍ
And lead us not into temptation.ʰ' "

⁵ Then Jesus said to them, "Suppose you have a friend, and you go to him at midnight and say, 'Friend, lend me three loaves of bread; ⁶ a friend of mine on a journey has come to me, and I have no food to offer him.'

ᵃ 27 Deut. 6:5   ᵇ 27 Lev. 19:18   ᶜ 35 A denarius was the usual daily wage of a day laborer (see Matt. 20:2).   ᵈ 42 Some manuscripts *but only one thing is needed*   ᵉ 2 Some manuscripts *Our Father in heaven*   ᶠ 2 Some manuscripts *come. May your will be done on earth as it is in heaven.*   ᵍ 4 Greek *everyone who is indebted to us*   ʰ 4 Some manuscripts *temptation, but deliver us from the evil one*

The One Thing We Need

By Sheryl Shearer

READ: Luke 10:38–42

Nobody does multitasking like the military spouse, especially during a deployment. Work, kids, pets, meal preparation, housekeeping, church activities, fitness, FRG meetings, connecting with our spouse … the scope of our responsibilities can be overwhelming. Many activities are necessary, but how often do they take over our lives and cause us to leapfrog over the important issues?

In the story of Mary and Martha in Luke 10:38 – 42, we watch busyness trump what is truly important. Martha models a discipleship of serving, but she lost sight of why. "Her fault was not that she served," Charles Spurgeon wrote. "The condition of a servant well becomes every Christian. Her fault was that she grew 'cumbered with much serving,' so that she forgot him and only remembered the service." Service to God is admirable, but not if the act takes priority over worship.

The common advice given to military wives when their husbands deploy is: stay busy. Yes, a certain amount of activity is healthy. But there is also danger in a jam-packed calendar: In our efforts to crowd out loneliness by filling all the gaps and spaces in our lives, we can also crowd out relationships — with Jesus and with those in our community.

The "one thing" Martha needed was fellowship with Jesus (see verse 42). The same is true for us: No matter how busy we are, no matter our responsibilities, especially during deployment, we still desperately need to spend time with the One who made us, the One who has everything under control.

If you're feeling more like Martha than Mary, now may be a good time for reflection. Jesus rebuked Martha not for her service but for her focus. Martha called Jesus "Lord," but she also got swallowed up in self-absorption, which is evident in her words: "me," "by myself," and "help me!" (verse 40).

When we feel more frazzled than tranquil, we would be wise to pause and examine our words and thought patterns. Ask yourself some important questions. Do I often demand my way? Do I think of myself first and Jesus second? If so, then follow the example of Mary: Spend time with Jesus.

Jesus affirmed Mary's choice, saying, "It will not be taken away from her" (verse 42). The cares of the world and the responsibilities of life will always be with us. As you go about your day and plan for days ahead, may you remember the one thing to put at the top of your list: fellowship with the Lord.

"Martha, Martha," the Lord answered, **"you are worried and upset about many things, but few things are needed — or indeed only one. Mary has chosen what is better, and it will not be taken away from her."**
LUKE 10:41 – 42

DEBRIEF

- Are my activities distracting me from fellowship with Jesus?
- What needs to change in order to maintain balance in my life and keep the important issues and relationships (specifically with God) in life my top priority?

REPORT

Lord, help me, like Mary, to sit at your feet with a humble, teachable heart. I desire to be your disciple and learn from you the rest of my days. Amen.

for your next devotional reading, go to page 88

[7] And suppose the one inside answers, 'Don't bother me. The door is already locked, and my children and I are in bed. I can't get up and give you anything.' [8] I tell you, even though he will not get up and give you the bread because of friendship, yet because of your shameless audacity[a] he will surely get up and give you as much as you need.

[9] "So I say to you: Ask and it will be given to you; seek and you will find; knock and the door will be opened to you. [10] For everyone who asks receives; the one who seeks finds; and to the one who knocks, the door will be opened.

[11] "Which of you fathers, if your son asks for[b] a fish, will give him a snake instead? [12] Or if he asks for an egg, will give him a scorpion? [13] If you then, though you are evil, know how to give good gifts to your children, how much more will your Father in heaven give the Holy Spirit to those who ask him!"

Jesus and Beelzebul

[14] Jesus was driving out a demon that was mute. When the demon left, the man who had been mute spoke, and the crowd was amazed. [15] But some of them said, "By Beelzebul, the prince of demons, he is driving out demons." [16] Others tested him by asking for a sign from heaven.

[17] Jesus knew their thoughts and said to them: "Any kingdom divided against itself will be ruined, and a house divided against itself will fall. [18] If Satan is divided against himself, how can his kingdom stand? I say this because you claim that I drive out demons by Beelzebul. [19] Now if I drive out demons by Beelzebul, by whom do your followers drive them out? So then, they will be your judges. [20] But if I drive out demons by the finger of God, then the kingdom of God has come upon you.

[21] "When a strong man, fully armed, guards his own house, his possessions are safe. [22] But when someone stronger attacks and overpowers him, he takes away the armor in which the man trusted and divides up his plunder.

[23] "Whoever is not with me is against me, and whoever does not gather with me scatters.

[24] "When an impure spirit comes out of a person, it goes through arid places seeking rest and does not find it. Then it says, 'I will return to the house I left.' [25] When it arrives, it finds the house swept clean and put in order. [26] Then it goes and takes seven other spirits more wicked than itself, and they go in and live there. And the final condition of that person is worse than the first."

[27] As Jesus was saying these things, a woman in the crowd called out, "Blessed is the mother who gave you birth and nursed you."

[28] He replied, "Blessed rather are those who hear the word of God and obey it."

The Sign of Jonah

[29] As the crowds increased, Jesus said, "This is a wicked generation. It asks for a sign, but none will be given it except the sign of Jonah. [30] For as Jonah was a sign to the Ninevites, so also will the Son of Man be to this generation. [31] The Queen of the South will rise at the judgment with the people of this generation and condemn them, for she came from the ends of the earth to listen to Solomon's wisdom; and now something greater than Solomon is here. [32] The men of Nineveh will stand up at the judgment with this generation and condemn it, for they repented at the preaching of Jonah; and now something greater than Jonah is here.

The Lamp of the Body

[33] "No one lights a lamp and puts it in a place where it will be hidden, or under a bowl. Instead they put it on its stand, so that those who come in may see the light. [34] Your eye is the lamp of your body. When your eyes are healthy,[c] your whole body also is full of light. But when they are unhealthy,[d] your body also is full of darkness. [35] See to it, then, that the light within you is not darkness. [36] Therefore, if your whole body is full of light, and no part of it dark, it will be just as full of light as when a lamp shines its light on you."

Woes on the Pharisees and the Experts in the Law

[37] When Jesus had finished speaking, a Pharisee invited him to eat with him; so he went in and reclined at the table. [38] But the Pharisee was surprised when he noticed that Jesus did not first wash before the meal.

[a] 8 Or yet to preserve his good name   [b] 11 Some manuscripts for bread, will give him a stone? Or if he asks for   [c] 34 The Greek for healthy here implies generous.   [d] 34 The Greek for unhealthy here implies stingy.

³⁹Then the Lord said to him, "Now then, you Pharisees clean the outside of the cup and dish, but inside you are full of greed and wickedness. ⁴⁰You foolish people! Did not the one who made the outside make the inside also? ⁴¹But now as for what is inside you — be generous to the poor, and everything will be clean for you.

⁴²"Woe to you Pharisees, because you give God a tenth of your mint, rue and all other kinds of garden herbs, but you neglect justice and the love of God. You should have practiced the latter without leaving the former undone.

⁴³"Woe to you Pharisees, because you love the most important seats in the synagogues and respectful greetings in the marketplaces.

⁴⁴"Woe to you, because you are like unmarked graves, which people walk over without knowing it."

⁴⁵One of the experts in the law answered him, "Teacher, when you say these things, you insult us also."

⁴⁶Jesus replied, "And you experts in the law, woe to you, because you load people down with burdens they can hardly carry, and you yourselves will not lift one finger to help them.

⁴⁷"Woe to you, because you build tombs for the prophets, and it was your ancestors who killed them. ⁴⁸So you testify that you approve of what your ancestors did; they killed the prophets, and you build their tombs. ⁴⁹Because of this, God in his wisdom said, 'I will send them prophets and apostles, some of whom they will kill and others they will persecute.' ⁵⁰Therefore this generation will be held responsible for the blood of all the prophets that has been shed since the beginning of the world, ⁵¹from the blood of Abel to the blood of Zechariah, who was killed between the altar and the sanctuary. Yes, I tell you, this generation will be held responsible for it all.

⁵²"Woe to you experts in the law, because you have taken away the key to knowledge. You yourselves have not entered, and you have hindered those who were entering."

⁵³When Jesus went outside, the Pharisees and the teachers of the law began to oppose him fiercely and to besiege him with questions, ⁵⁴waiting to catch him in something he might say.

Warnings and Encouragements

12 Meanwhile, when a crowd of many thousands had gathered, so that they were trampling on one another, Jesus began to speak first to his disciples, saying: "Be[a] on your guard against the yeast of the Pharisees, which is hypocrisy. ²There is nothing concealed that will not be disclosed, or hidden that will not be made known. ³What you have said in the dark will be heard in the daylight, and what you have whispered in the ear in the inner rooms will be proclaimed from the roofs.

⁴"I tell you, my friends, do not be afraid of those who kill the body and after that can do no more. ⁵But I will show you whom you should fear: Fear him who, after your body has been killed, has authority to throw you into hell. Yes, I tell you, fear him. ⁶Are not five sparrows sold for two pennies? Yet not one of them is forgotten by God. ⁷Indeed, the very hairs of your head are all numbered. Don't be afraid; you are worth more than many sparrows.

⁸"I tell you, whoever publicly acknowledges me before others, the Son of Man will also acknowledge before the angels of God. ⁹But whoever disowns me before others will be disowned before the angels of God. ¹⁰And everyone who speaks a word against the Son of Man will be forgiven, but anyone who blasphemes against the Holy Spirit will not be forgiven.

¹¹"When you are brought before synagogues, rulers and authorities, do not worry about how you will defend yourselves or what you will say, ¹²for the Holy Spirit will teach you at that time what you should say."

The Parable of the Rich Fool

¹³Someone in the crowd said to him, "Teacher, tell my brother to divide the inheritance with me."

¹⁴Jesus replied, "Man, who appointed me a judge or an arbiter between you?" ¹⁵Then he said to them, "Watch out! Be on your guard against all kinds of greed; life does not consist in an abundance of possessions."

¹⁶And he told them this parable: "The ground of a certain rich man yielded an abundant harvest. ¹⁷He thought to himself, 'What shall I do? I have no place to store my crops.'

---

a 1 Or *speak to his disciples, saying: "First of all, be*

¹⁸"Then he said, 'This is what I'll do. I will tear down my barns and build bigger ones, and there I will store my surplus grain. ¹⁹And I'll say to myself, "You have plenty of grain laid up for many years. Take life easy; eat, drink and be merry."'

²⁰"But God said to him, 'You fool! This very night your life will be demanded from you. Then who will get what you have prepared for yourself?'

²¹"This is how it will be with whoever stores up things for themselves but is not rich toward God."

Do Not Worry

²²Then Jesus said to his disciples: "Therefore I tell you, do not worry about your life, what you will eat; or about your body, what you will wear. ²³For life is more than food, and the body more than clothes. ²⁴Consider the ravens: They do not sow or reap, they have no storeroom or barn; yet God feeds them. And how much more valuable you are than birds! ²⁵Who of you by worrying can add a single hour to your life[a]? ²⁶Since you cannot do this very little thing, why do you worry about the rest?

²⁷"Consider how the wild flowers grow. They do not labor or spin. Yet I tell you, not even Solomon in all his splendor was dressed like one of these. ²⁸If that is how God clothes the grass of the field, which is here today, and tomorrow is thrown into the fire, how much more will he clothe you — you of little faith! ²⁹And do not set your heart on what you will eat or drink; do not worry about it. ³⁰For the pagan world runs after all such things, and your Father knows that you need them. ³¹But seek his kingdom, and these things will be given to you as well.

³²"Do not be afraid, little flock, for your Father has been pleased to give you the kingdom. ³³Sell your possessions and give to the poor. Provide purses for yourselves that will not wear out, a treasure in heaven that will never fail, where no thief comes near and no moth destroys. ³⁴For where your treasure is, there your heart will be also.

Watchfulness

³⁵"Be dressed ready for service and keep your lamps burning, ³⁶like servants waiting for their master to return from a wedding banquet, so that when he comes and knocks they can immediately open the door for him. ³⁷It will be good for those servants whose master finds them watching when he comes. Truly I tell you, he will dress himself to serve, will have them recline at the table and will come and wait on them. ³⁸It will be good for those servants whose master finds them ready, even if he comes in the middle of the night or toward daybreak. ³⁹But understand this: If the owner of the house had known at what hour the thief was coming, he would not have let his house be broken into. ⁴⁰You also must be ready, because the Son of Man will come at an hour when you do not expect him."

⁴¹Peter asked, "Lord, are you telling this parable to us, or to everyone?"

⁴²The Lord answered, "Who then is the faithful and wise manager, whom the master puts in charge of his servants to give them their food allowance at the proper time? ⁴³It will be good for that servant whom the master finds doing so when he returns. ⁴⁴Truly I tell you, he will put him in charge of all his possessions. ⁴⁵But suppose the servant says to himself, 'My master is taking a long time in coming,' and he then begins to beat the other servants, both men and women, and to eat and drink and get drunk. ⁴⁶The master of that servant will come on a day when he does not expect him and at an hour he is not aware of. He will cut him to pieces and assign him a place with the unbelievers.

⁴⁷"The servant who knows the master's will and does not get ready or does not do what the master wants will be beaten with many blows. ⁴⁸But the one who does not know and does things deserving punishment will be beaten with few blows. From everyone who has been given much, much will be demanded; and from the one who has been entrusted with much, much more will be asked.

Not Peace but Division

⁴⁹"I have come to bring fire on the earth, and how I wish it were already kindled! ⁵⁰But I have a baptism to undergo, and what constraint I am under until it is completed! ⁵¹Do you think I came to bring peace on

---

[a] 25 Or *single cubit to your height*

Be Ready

By Sarah Ball

READ: Luke 12:35–48

How can I "be ready" if I do not know when to expect someone (see Luke 12:40)? Life as a military spouse has certainly given me opportunities to practice waiting. My husband's last deployment ended with the usual checklist: "Welcome Home" banner hung, house cleaned, favorite goodies baked, patriotic outfits for the kids purchased. My in-laws arrived to attend the welcome home ceremony with us, and we were completely ready.

Unfortunately, the Eyjafjallajökull volcano in Iceland was also ready. Its eruption threw a massive cloud of volcanic ash into the air, shutting down air traffic across much of Europe. My husband's unit waited days for their plane. Then after reaching U.S. airspace, their plane lost an engine and conducted an emergency landing. The homecoming ceremony was postponed again, and we continued waiting.

God understands the challenges of waiting. He knew it would be hard for Jesus' followers to see Jesus leave the earth, especially since they didn't know when he would return. He knew that centuries of time would pass before Jesus' return to earth and that believers would struggle to wait for him.

To explain our need for readiness, Jesus used the metaphor of servants waiting for their master's return — servants who were ready to throw open the door and welcome him. He instructed, "Be dressed ready for service and keep your lamps burning" (verse 35). At the same time, Jesus warned that they would never know when he might appear, "because the Son of Man will come at an hour when you do not expect him" (verse 40).

Our instructions are clear: Be ready. Watchful. Vigilant. Be always thinking about the return of the Son of Man. Do not let his return come at a time when you have grown forgetful or indifferent. Without careful vigilance, our daily priorities begin to mirror those of the world.

Take a look at Jesus' challenging words in Luke 12:22 – 34: "Therefore I tell you, do not worry about your life, what you will eat; or about your body, what you will wear" (verse 22). If God clothes the grass of the field, he can certainly care for us (see verses 27 – 28)! "But seek his kingdom, and these things will be given to you as well" (verse 31). Jesus then tells us to live generously, thereby storing up eternal treasure in heaven (see verses 33 – 34).

Each day we spend waiting for Jesus' return is an opportunity to build his kingdom. Our lives and possessions are finite, but the things we do in service of God's kingdom are eternal.

"You also must be ready, because the Son of Man will come at an hour when you do not expect him."

LUKE 12:40

DEBRIEF

• Am I living in daily anticipation of Christ's return?

• How do my plans for today seek to build the kingdom of God?

REPORT

Lord, thank you for the promise that you will return to the earth. During this time of waiting, help me to remain watchful and to seek your kingdom. In Jesus' name I pray. Amen.

earth? No, I tell you, but division. ⁵²From now on there will be five in one family divided against each other, three against two and two against three. ⁵³They will be divided, father against son and son against father, mother against daughter and daughter against mother, mother-in-law against daughter-in-law and daughter-in-law against mother-in-law."

Interpreting the Times

⁵⁴He said to the crowd: "When you see a cloud rising in the west, immediately you say, 'It's going to rain,' and it does. ⁵⁵And when the south wind blows, you say, 'It's going to be hot,' and it is. ⁵⁶Hypocrites! You know how to interpret the appearance of the earth and the sky. How is it that you don't know how to interpret this present time?

⁵⁷"Why don't you judge for yourselves what is right? ⁵⁸As you are going with your adversary to the magistrate, try hard to be reconciled on the way, or your adversary may drag you off to the judge, and the judge turn you over to the officer, and the officer throw you into prison. ⁵⁹I tell you, you will not get out until you have paid the last penny."

Repent or Perish

13 Now there were some present at that time who told Jesus about the Galileans whose blood Pilate had mixed with their sacrifices. ²Jesus answered, "Do you think that these Galileans were worse sinners than all the other Galileans because they suffered this way? ³I tell you, no! But unless you repent, you too will all perish. ⁴Or those eighteen who died when the tower in Siloam fell on them—do you think they were more guilty than all the others living in Jerusalem? ⁵I tell you, no! But unless you repent, you too will all perish."

⁶Then he told this parable: "A man had a fig tree growing in his vineyard, and he went to look for fruit on it but did not find any. ⁷So he said to the man who took care of the vineyard, 'For three years now I've been coming to look for fruit on this fig tree and haven't found any. Cut it down! Why should it use up the soil?'

⁸"'Sir,' the man replied, 'leave it alone for one more year, and I'll dig around it and fertilize it. ⁹If it bears fruit next year, fine! If not, then cut it down.'"

Jesus Heals a Crippled Woman on the Sabbath

¹⁰On a Sabbath Jesus was teaching in one of the synagogues, ¹¹and a woman was there who had been crippled by a spirit for eighteen years. She was bent over and could not straighten up at all. ¹²When Jesus saw her, he called her forward and said to her, "Woman, you are set free from your infirmity." ¹³Then he put his hands on her, and immediately she straightened up and praised God.

¹⁴Indignant because Jesus had healed on the Sabbath, the synagogue leader said to the people, "There are six days for work. So come and be healed on those days, not on the Sabbath."

¹⁵The Lord answered him, "You hypocrites! Doesn't each of you on the Sabbath untie your ox or donkey from the stall and lead it out to give it water? ¹⁶Then should not this woman, a daughter of Abraham, whom Satan has kept bound for eighteen long years, be set free on the Sabbath day from what bound her?"

¹⁷When he said this, all his opponents were humiliated, but the people were delighted with all the wonderful things he was doing.

The Parables of the Mustard Seed and the Yeast

¹⁸Then Jesus asked, "What is the kingdom of God like? What shall I compare it to? ¹⁹It is like a mustard seed, which a man took and planted in his garden. It grew and became a tree, and the birds perched in its branches."

²⁰Again he asked, "What shall I compare the kingdom of God to? ²¹It is like yeast that a woman took and mixed into about sixty pounds*a* of flour until it worked all through the dough."

The Narrow Door

²²Then Jesus went through the towns and villages, teaching as he made his way to Jerusalem. ²³Someone asked him, "Lord, are only a few people going to be saved?"

He said to them, ²⁴"Make every effort to enter through the narrow door, because

a 21 Or about 27 kilograms

many, I tell you, will try to enter and will not be able to. ²⁵Once the owner of the house gets up and closes the door, you will stand outside knocking and pleading, 'Sir, open the door for us.'

"But he will answer, 'I don't know you or where you come from.'

²⁶"Then you will say, 'We ate and drank with you, and you taught in our streets.'

²⁷"But he will reply, 'I don't know you or where you come from. Away from me, all you evildoers!'

²⁸"There will be weeping there, and gnashing of teeth, when you see Abraham, Isaac and Jacob and all the prophets in the kingdom of God, but you yourselves thrown out. ²⁹People will come from east and west and north and south, and will take their places at the feast in the kingdom of God. ³⁰Indeed there are those who are last who will be first, and first who will be last."

Jesus' Sorrow for Jerusalem

³¹At that time some Pharisees came to Jesus and said to him, "Leave this place and go somewhere else. Herod wants to kill you."

³²He replied, "Go tell that fox, 'I will keep on driving out demons and healing people today and tomorrow, and on the third day I will reach my goal.' ³³In any case, I must press on today and tomorrow and the next day—for surely no prophet can die outside Jerusalem!

³⁴"Jerusalem, Jerusalem, you who kill the prophets and stone those sent to you, how often I have longed to gather your children together, as a hen gathers her chicks under her wings, and you were not willing. ³⁵Look, your house is left to you desolate. I tell you, you will not see me again until you say, 'Blessed is he who comes in the name of the Lord.'^a"

Jesus at a Pharisee's House

14 One Sabbath, when Jesus went to eat in the house of a prominent Pharisee, he was being carefully watched. ²There in front of him was a man suffering from abnormal swelling of his body. ³Jesus asked the Pharisees and experts in the law, "Is it lawful to heal on the Sabbath or not?" ⁴But they remained silent. So taking hold of the man, he healed him and sent him on his way.

⁵Then he asked them, "If one of you has a child^b or an ox that falls into a well on the Sabbath day, will you not immediately pull it out?" ⁶And they had nothing to say.

⁷When he noticed how the guests picked the places of honor at the table, he told them this parable: ⁸"When someone invites you to a wedding feast, do not take the place of honor, for a person more distinguished than you may have been invited. ⁹If so, the host who invited both of you will come and say to you, 'Give this person your seat.' Then, humiliated, you will have to take the least important place. ¹⁰But when you are invited, take the lowest place, so that when your host comes, he will say to you, 'Friend, move up to a better place.' Then you will be honored in the presence of all the other guests. ¹¹For all those who exalt themselves will be humbled, and those who humble themselves will be exalted."

¹²Then Jesus said to his host, "When you give a luncheon or dinner, do not invite your friends, your brothers or sisters, your relatives, or your rich neighbors; if you do, they may invite you back and so you will be repaid. ¹³But when you give a banquet, invite the poor, the crippled, the lame, the blind, ¹⁴and you will be blessed. Although they cannot repay you, you will be repaid at the resurrection of the righteous."

The Parable of the Great Banquet

¹⁵When one of those at the table with him heard this, he said to Jesus, "Blessed is the one who will eat at the feast in the kingdom of God."

¹⁶Jesus replied: "A certain man was preparing a great banquet and invited many guests. ¹⁷At the time of the banquet he sent his servant to tell those who had been invited, 'Come, for everything is now ready.'

¹⁸"But they all alike began to make excuses. The first said, 'I have just bought a field, and I must go and see it. Please excuse me.'

¹⁹"Another said, 'I have just bought five yoke of oxen, and I'm on my way to try them out. Please excuse me.'

²⁰"Still another said, 'I just got married, so I can't come.'

²¹"The servant came back and reported this to his master. Then the owner of the

^a 35 Psalm 118:26   ^b 5 Some manuscripts *donkey*

house became angry and ordered his servant, 'Go out quickly into the streets and alleys of the town and bring in the poor, the crippled, the blind and the lame.'

²²"'Sir,' the servant said, 'what you ordered has been done, but there is still room.'

²³"Then the master told his servant, 'Go out to the roads and country lanes and compel them to come in, so that my house will be full. ²⁴I tell you, not one of those who were invited will get a taste of my banquet.'"

The Cost of Being a Disciple

²⁵Large crowds were traveling with Jesus, and turning to them he said: ²⁶"If anyone comes to me and does not hate father and mother, wife and children, brothers and sisters — yes, even their own life — such a person cannot be my disciple. ²⁷And whoever does not carry their cross and follow me cannot be my disciple.

²⁸"Suppose one of you wants to build a tower. Won't you first sit down and estimate the cost to see if you have enough money to complete it? ²⁹For if you lay the foundation and are not able to finish it, everyone who sees it will ridicule you, ³⁰saying, 'This person began to build and wasn't able to finish.'

³¹"Or suppose a king is about to go to war against another king. Won't he first sit down and consider whether he is able with ten thousand men to oppose the one coming against him with twenty thousand? ³²If he is not able, he will send a delegation while the other is still a long way off and will ask for terms of peace. ³³In the same way, those of you who do not give up everything you have cannot be my disciples.

³⁴"Salt is good, but if it loses its saltiness, how can it be made salty again? ³⁵It is fit neither for the soil nor for the manure pile; it is thrown out.

"Whoever has ears to hear, let them hear."

The Parable of the Lost Sheep

15 Now the tax collectors and sinners were all gathering around to hear Jesus. ²But the Pharisees and the teachers of the law muttered, "This man welcomes sinners and eats with them."

³Then Jesus told them this parable: ⁴"Suppose one of you has a hundred sheep and loses one of them. Doesn't he leave the ninety-nine in the open country and go after the lost sheep until he finds it? ⁵And when he finds it, he joyfully puts it on his shoulders ⁶and goes home. Then he calls his friends and neighbors together and says, 'Rejoice with me; I have found my lost sheep.' ⁷I tell you that in the same way there will be more rejoicing in heaven over one sinner who repents than over ninety-nine righteous persons who do not need to repent.

The Parable of the Lost Coin

⁸"Or suppose a woman has ten silver coins*ᵃ* and loses one. Doesn't she light a lamp, sweep the house and search carefully until she finds it? ⁹And when she finds it, she calls her friends and neighbors together and says, 'Rejoice with me; I have found my lost coin.' ¹⁰In the same way, I tell you, there is rejoicing in the presence of the angels of God over one sinner who repents."

The Parable of the Lost Son

¹¹Jesus continued: "There was a man who had two sons. ¹²The younger one said to his father, 'Father, give me my share of the estate.' So he divided his property between them.

¹³"Not long after that, the younger son got together all he had, set off for a distant country and there squandered his wealth in wild living. ¹⁴After he had spent everything, there was a severe famine in that whole country, and he began to be in need. ¹⁵So he went and hired himself out to a citizen of that country, who sent him to his fields to feed pigs. ¹⁶He longed to fill his stomach with the pods that the pigs were eating, but no one gave him anything.

¹⁷"When he came to his senses, he said, 'How many of my father's hired servants have food to spare, and here I am starving to death! ¹⁸I will set out and go back to my father and say to him: Father, I have sinned against heaven and against you. ¹⁹I am no longer worthy to be called your son; make me like one of your hired servants.' ²⁰So he got up and went to his father.

"But while he was still a long way off, his father saw him and was filled with compassion for him; he ran to his son, threw his arms around him and kissed him.

ᵃ 8 Greek ten drachmas, each worth about a day's wages

²¹"The son said to him, 'Father, I have sinned against heaven and against you. I am no longer worthy to be called your son.'

²²"But the father said to his servants, 'Quick! Bring the best robe and put it on him. Put a ring on his finger and sandals on his feet. ²³Bring the fattened calf and kill it. Let's have a feast and celebrate. ²⁴For this son of mine was dead and is alive again; he was lost and is found.' So they began to celebrate.

²⁵"Meanwhile, the older son was in the field. When he came near the house, he heard music and dancing. ²⁶So he called one of the servants and asked him what was going on. ²⁷'Your brother has come,' he replied, 'and your father has killed the fattened calf because he has him back safe and sound.'

²⁸"The older brother became angry and refused to go in. So his father went out and pleaded with him. ²⁹But he answered his father, 'Look! All these years I've been slaving for you and never disobeyed your orders. Yet you never gave me even a young goat so I could celebrate with my friends. ³⁰But when this son of yours who has squandered your property with prostitutes comes home, you kill the fattened calf for him!'

³¹" 'My son,' the father said, 'you are always with me, and everything I have is yours. ³²But we had to celebrate and be glad, because this brother of yours was dead and is alive again; he was lost and is found.' "

The Parable of the Shrewd Manager

16 Jesus told his disciples: "There was a rich man whose manager was accused of wasting his possessions. ²So he called him in and asked him, 'What is this I hear about you? Give an account of your management, because you cannot be manager any longer.'

³"The manager said to himself, 'What shall I do now? My master is taking away my job. I'm not strong enough to dig, and I'm ashamed to beg— ⁴I know what I'll do so that, when I lose my job here, people will welcome me into their houses.'

⁵"So he called in each one of his master's debtors. He asked the first, 'How much do you owe my master?'

⁶" 'Nine hundred gallons*a* of olive oil,' he replied.

"The manager told him, 'Take your bill, sit down quickly, and make it four hundred and fifty.'

⁷"Then he asked the second, 'And how much do you owe?'

" 'A thousand bushels*b* of wheat,' he replied.

"He told him, 'Take your bill and make it eight hundred.'

⁸"The master commended the dishonest manager because he had acted shrewdly. For the people of this world are more shrewd in dealing with their own kind than are the people of the light. ⁹I tell you, use worldly wealth to gain friends for yourselves, so that when it is gone, you will be welcomed into eternal dwellings.

¹⁰"Whoever can be trusted with very little can also be trusted with much, and whoever is dishonest with very little will also be dishonest with much. ¹¹So if you have not been trustworthy in handling worldly wealth, who will trust you with true riches? ¹²And if you have not been trustworthy with someone else's property, who will give you property of your own?

¹³"No one can serve two masters. Either you will hate the one and love the other, or you will be devoted to the one and despise the other. You cannot serve both God and money."

¹⁴The Pharisees, who loved money, heard all this and were sneering at Jesus. ¹⁵He said to them, "You are the ones who justify yourselves in the eyes of others, but God knows your hearts. What people value highly is detestable in God's sight.

Additional Teachings

¹⁶"The Law and the Prophets were proclaimed until John. Since that time, the good news of the kingdom of God is being preached, and everyone is forcing their way into it. ¹⁷It is easier for heaven and earth to disappear than for the least stroke of a pen to drop out of the Law.

¹⁸"Anyone who divorces his wife and marries another woman commits adultery, and the man who marries a divorced woman commits adultery.

The Rich Man and Lazarus

¹⁹"There was a rich man who was dressed in purple and fine linen and lived in luxury

---

a 6 Or about 3,000 liters   *b* 7 Or about 30 tons

every day. [20]At his gate was laid a beggar named Lazarus, covered with sores [21]and longing to eat what fell from the rich man's table. Even the dogs came and licked his sores.

[22]"The time came when the beggar died and the angels carried him to Abraham's side. The rich man also died and was buried. [23]In Hades, where he was in torment, he looked up and saw Abraham far away, with Lazarus by his side. [24]So he called to him, 'Father Abraham, have pity on me and send Lazarus to dip the tip of his finger in water and cool my tongue, because I am in agony in this fire.'

[25]"But Abraham replied, 'Son, remember that in your lifetime you received your good things, while Lazarus received bad things, but now he is comforted here and you are in agony. [26]And besides all this, between us and you a great chasm has been set in place, so that those who want to go from here to you cannot, nor can anyone cross over from there to us.'

[27]"He answered, 'Then I beg you, father, send Lazarus to my family, [28]for I have five brothers. Let him warn them, so that they will not also come to this place of torment.'

[29]"Abraham replied, 'They have Moses and the Prophets; let them listen to them.'

[30]"'No, father Abraham,' he said, 'but if someone from the dead goes to them, they will repent.'

[31]"He said to him, 'If they do not listen to Moses and the Prophets, they will not be convinced even if someone rises from the dead.'"

Sin, Faith, Duty

17 Jesus said to his disciples: "Things that cause people to stumble are bound to come, but woe to anyone through whom they come. [2]It would be better for them to be thrown into the sea with a millstone tied around their neck than to cause one of these little ones to stumble. [3]So watch yourselves.

"If your brother or sister[a] sins against you, rebuke them; and if they repent, forgive them. [4]Even if they sin against you seven times in a day and seven times come back to you saying 'I repent,' you must forgive them."

[5]The apostles said to the Lord, "Increase our faith!"

[6]He replied, "If you have faith as small as a mustard seed, you can say to this mulberry tree, 'Be uprooted and planted in the sea,' and it will obey you.

[7]"Suppose one of you has a servant plowing or looking after the sheep. Will he say to the servant when he comes in from the field, 'Come along now and sit down to eat'? [8]Won't he rather say, 'Prepare my supper, get yourself ready and wait on me while I eat and drink; after that you may eat and drink'? [9]Will he thank the servant because he did what he was told to do? [10]So you also, when you have done everything you were told to do, should say, 'We are unworthy servants; we have only done our duty.'"

Jesus Heals Ten Men With Leprosy

[11]Now on his way to Jerusalem, Jesus traveled along the border between Samaria and Galilee. [12]As he was going into a village, ten men who had leprosy[b] met him. They stood at a distance [13]and called out in a loud voice, "Jesus, Master, have pity on us!"

[14]When he saw them, he said, "Go, show yourselves to the priests." And as they went, they were cleansed.

[15]One of them, when he saw he was healed, came back, praising God in a loud voice. [16]He threw himself at Jesus' feet and thanked him — and he was a Samaritan.

[17]Jesus asked, "Were not all ten cleansed? Where are the other nine? [18]Has no one returned to give praise to God except this foreigner?" [19]Then he said to him, "Rise and go; your faith has made you well."

The Coming of the Kingdom of God

[20]Once, on being asked by the Pharisees when the kingdom of God would come, Jesus replied, "The coming of the kingdom of God is not something that can be observed, [21]nor will people say, 'Here it is,' or 'There it is,' because the kingdom of God is in your midst."[c]

[22]Then he said to his disciples, "The time is coming when you will long to see one of the days of the Son of Man, but you will not see it. [23]People will tell you, 'There he is!'

---

[a] 3 The Greek word for *brother or sister* (*adelphos*) refers here to a fellow disciple, whether man or woman.
[b] 12 The Greek word traditionally translated *leprosy* was used for various diseases affecting the skin.
[c] 21 Or *is within you*

Grasping Gratitude

By Rebekah Benimoff

READ: Luke 17:11–19

When my husband was diagnosed with post-traumatic stress disorder (PTSD) after returning from Iraq, our marriage was plunged into a battle-field. Roger learned his triggers and how to navigate the difficulties of PTSD, and I sought help too. Through counseling, forgiveness and prayer, God began to heal my heart. Yet lies from the enemy still attack me when Roger withdraws. As I practice thankfulness, I wield the greatest weapon in the fight.

In Luke 17:15 – 16, the Samaritan thanked Jesus for healing him of leprosy. It was only after this that Jesus said his faith had made him well (see v. 19). The Greek word for "made you well" is *sozo*, which literally means "to save." "Our very saving is associated with gratitude," wrote Ann Voskamp in *One Thousand Gifts: A Dare to Live Fully Right Where You Are*. "And the leper's faith was a faith that said thank you … Jesus counts thanksgiving as integral in a faith that saves."

True thanksgiving is specific. As the old hymn says, "Count your blessings, name them one by one." When I find myself grieving over how PTSD has changed our lives, that is the moment to let go of the past and grasp gratitude. I am thankful my husband survived his deployments. I am thankful he is healing. And I am thankful he is still here with our family. Roger, unlike some with PTSD, did not take his life even in his deepest suffering.

The truth is that *this moment* is a gift, and my very saving from despair is hinged on gratitude. So I make the conscious effort to punctuate the moment with thanksgiving — even when my plans are erased to the point that the page itself is no longer there. When all that is left is a tearing in the parchment of my life, I will trust that God will write my story on a new page. When I give thanks even in the tearing, the Author can pen another Once Upon A Time — one in which my wholeness is the theme.

Sometimes we see only brokenness, but when we look through the lens of gratitude, our story is infused with light. Even in mundane daily living. Even in living past a loss. When is life made whole? When we lay down our disappointments and show gratitude instead, for then the miracle can begin.

My own new narrative began with two words: Thank you. Remember, only when the Samaritan returned with thanksgiving did Jesus say, "Your faith has made you well" (verse 19). Healing begins with gratitude.

Jesus asked, **"Were not all ten cleansed? Where are the other nine? Has no one returned to give praise to God except this foreigner?"** Then he said to him, **"Rise and go; your faith has made you well."**

LUKE 17:17 – 19

DEBRIEF

- Am I willing to let go of any expectations and disappointments that are causing me stress?
- I will read the words to "Count Your Blessings" on page 494.

REPORT

Father God, teach me to turn the whys and the wonderings over to you and focus on living fully today. I am thankful for the way you love me so deeply, drawing me in and holding me close. I am thankful for your patience with me. And I am thankful for the many blessings you have placed in my life. I list them out now, that you will write hope and healing on my heart. Thank you, Lord. Amen.

for your next devotional reading, go to page 104

or 'Here he is!' Do not go running off after them. [24] For the Son of Man in his day[a] will be like the lightning, which flashes and lights up the sky from one end to the other. [25] But first he must suffer many things and be rejected by this generation.

[26] "Just as it was in the days of Noah, so also will it be in the days of the Son of Man. [27] People were eating, drinking, marrying and being given in marriage up to the day Noah entered the ark. Then the flood came and destroyed them all.

[28] "It was the same in the days of Lot. People were eating and drinking, buying and selling, planting and building. [29] But the day Lot left Sodom, fire and sulfur rained down from heaven and destroyed them all.

[30] "It will be just like this on the day the Son of Man is revealed. [31] On that day no one who is on the housetop, with possessions inside, should go down to get them. Likewise, no one in the field should go back for anything. [32] Remember Lot's wife! [33] Whoever tries to keep their life will lose it, and whoever loses their life will preserve it. [34] I tell you, on that night two people will be in one bed; one will be taken and the other left. [35] Two women will be grinding grain together; one will be taken and the other left." [36][b]

[37] "Where, Lord?" they asked.

He replied, "Where there is a dead body, there the vultures will gather."

The Parable of the Persistent Widow

18 Then Jesus told his disciples a parable to show them that they should always pray and not give up. [2] He said: "In a certain town there was a judge who neither feared God nor cared what people thought. [3] And there was a widow in that town who kept coming to him with the plea, 'Grant me justice against my adversary.'

[4] "For some time he refused. But finally he said to himself, 'Even though I don't fear God or care what people think, [5] yet because this widow keeps bothering me, I will see that she gets justice, so that she won't eventually come and attack me!' "

[6] And the Lord said, "Listen to what the unjust judge says. [7] And will not God bring about justice for his chosen ones, who cry out to him day and night? Will he keep putting them off? [8] I tell you, he will see that they get justice, and quickly. However, when the Son of Man comes, will he find faith on the earth?"

The Parable of the Pharisee and the Tax Collector

[9] To some who were confident of their own righteousness and looked down on everyone else, Jesus told this parable: [10] "Two men went up to the temple to pray, one a Pharisee and the other a tax collector. [11] The Pharisee stood by himself and prayed: 'God, I thank you that I am not like other people—robbers, evildoers, adulterers—or even like this tax collector. [12] I fast twice a week and give a tenth of all I get.'

[13] "But the tax collector stood at a distance. He would not even look up to heaven, but beat his breast and said, 'God, have mercy on me, a sinner.'

[14] "I tell you that this man, rather than the other, went home justified before God. For all those who exalt themselves will be humbled, and those who humble themselves will be exalted."

The Little Children and Jesus

[15] People were also bringing babies to Jesus for him to place his hands on them. When the disciples saw this, they rebuked them. [16] But Jesus called the children to him and said, "Let the little children come to me, and do not hinder them, for the kingdom of God belongs to such as these. [17] Truly I tell you, anyone who will not receive the kingdom of God like a little child will never enter it."

The Rich and the Kingdom of God

[18] A certain ruler asked him, "Good teacher, what must I do to inherit eternal life?"

[19] "Why do you call me good?" Jesus answered. "No one is good—except God alone. [20] You know the commandments: 'You shall not commit adultery, you shall not murder, you shall not steal, you shall not give false testimony, honor your father and mother.'[c]"

[21] "All these I have kept since I was a boy," he said.

---

[a] 24 Some manuscripts do not have *in his day*.   [b] 36 Some manuscripts include here words similar to Matt. 24:40.   [c] 20 Exodus 20:12-16; Deut. 5:16-20

22When Jesus heard this, he said to him, "You still lack one thing. Sell everything you have and give to the poor, and you will have treasure in heaven. Then come, follow me."

23When he heard this, he became very sad, because he was very wealthy. 24Jesus looked at him and said, "How hard it is for the rich to enter the kingdom of God! 25Indeed, it is easier for a camel to go through the eye of a needle than for someone who is rich to enter the kingdom of God."

26Those who heard this asked, "Who then can be saved?"

27Jesus replied, "What is impossible with man is possible with God."

28Peter said to him, "We have left all we had to follow you!"

29"Truly I tell you," Jesus said to them, "no one who has left home or wife or brothers or sisters or parents or children for the sake of the kingdom of God 30will fail to receive many times as much in this age, and in the age to come eternal life."

Jesus Predicts His Death a Third Time

31Jesus took the Twelve aside and told them, "We are going up to Jerusalem, and everything that is written by the prophets about the Son of Man will be fulfilled. 32He will be delivered over to the Gentiles. They will mock him, insult him and spit on him; 33they will flog him and kill him. On the third day he will rise again."

34The disciples did not understand any of this. Its meaning was hidden from them, and they did not know what he was talking about.

A Blind Beggar Receives His Sight

35As Jesus approached Jericho, a blind man was sitting by the roadside begging. 36When he heard the crowd going by, he asked what was happening. 37They told him, "Jesus of Nazareth is passing by."

38He called out, "Jesus, Son of David, have mercy on me!"

39Those who led the way rebuked him and told him to be quiet, but he shouted all the more, "Son of David, have mercy on me!"

40Jesus stopped and ordered the man to be brought to him. When he came near, Jesus asked him, 41"What do you want me to do for you?"

"Lord, I want to see," he replied.

42Jesus said to him, "Receive your sight; your faith has healed you." 43Immediately he received his sight and followed Jesus, praising God. When all the people saw it, they also praised God.

Zacchaeus the Tax Collector

19 Jesus entered Jericho and was passing through. 2A man was there by the name of Zacchaeus; he was a chief tax collector and was wealthy. 3He wanted to see who Jesus was, but because he was short he could not see over the crowd. 4So he ran ahead and climbed a sycamore-fig tree to see him, since Jesus was coming that way.

5When Jesus reached the spot, he looked up and said to him, "Zacchaeus, come down immediately. I must stay at your house today." 6So he came down at once and welcomed him gladly.

7All the people saw this and began to mutter, "He has gone to be the guest of a sinner."

8But Zacchaeus stood up and said to the Lord, "Look, Lord! Here and now I give half of my possessions to the poor, and if I have cheated anybody out of anything, I will pay back four times the amount."

9Jesus said to him, "Today salvation has come to this house, because this man, too, is a son of Abraham. 10For the Son of Man came to seek and to save the lost."

The Parable of the Ten Minas

11While they were listening to this, he went on to tell them a parable, because he was near Jerusalem and the people thought that the kingdom of God was going to appear at once. 12He said: "A man of noble birth went to a distant country to have himself appointed king and then to return. 13So he called ten of his servants and gave them ten minas.a 'Put this money to work,' he said, 'until I come back.'

14"But his subjects hated him and sent a delegation after him to say, 'We don't want this man to be our king.'

15"He was made king, however, and returned home. Then he sent for the servants to whom he had given the money, in order to find out what they had gained with it.

16"The first one came and said, 'Sir, your mina has earned ten more.'

a 13 A mina was about three months' wages.

¹⁷ "'Well done, my good servant!' his master replied. 'Because you have been trustworthy in a very small matter, take charge of ten cities.'

¹⁸ "The second came and said, 'Sir, your mina has earned five more.'

¹⁹ "His master answered, 'You take charge of five cities.'

²⁰ "Then another servant came and said, 'Sir, here is your mina; I have kept it laid away in a piece of cloth. ²¹ I was afraid of you, because you are a hard man. You take out what you did not put in and reap what you did not sow.'

²² "His master replied, 'I will judge you by your own words, you wicked servant! You knew, did you, that I am a hard man, taking out what I did not put in, and reaping what I did not sow? ²³ Why then didn't you put my money on deposit, so that when I came back, I could have collected it with interest?'

²⁴ "Then he said to those standing by, 'Take his mina away from him and give it to the one who has ten minas.'

²⁵ "'Sir,' they said, 'he already has ten!'

²⁶ "He replied, 'I tell you that to everyone who has, more will be given, but as for the one who has nothing, even what they have will be taken away. ²⁷ But those enemies of mine who did not want me to be king over them — bring them here and kill them in front of me.'"

Jesus Comes to Jerusalem as King

²⁸ After Jesus had said this, he went on ahead, going up to Jerusalem. ²⁹ As he approached Bethphage and Bethany at the hill called the Mount of Olives, he sent two of his disciples, saying to them, ³⁰ "Go to the village ahead of you, and as you enter it, you will find a colt tied there, which no one has ever ridden. Untie it and bring it here. ³¹ If anyone asks you, 'Why are you untying it?' say, 'The Lord needs it.'"

³² Those who were sent ahead went and found it just as he had told them. ³³ As they were untying the colt, its owners asked them, "Why are you untying the colt?"

³⁴ They replied, "The Lord needs it."

³⁵ They brought it to Jesus, threw their cloaks on the colt and put Jesus on it. ³⁶ As he went along, people spread their cloaks on the road.

³⁷ When he came near the place where the road goes down the Mount of Olives, the whole crowd of disciples began joyfully to praise God in loud voices for all the miracles they had seen:

³⁸ "Blessed is the king who comes in the
　　name of the Lord!"ᵃ

"Peace in heaven and glory in the highest!"

³⁹ Some of the Pharisees in the crowd said to Jesus, "Teacher, rebuke your disciples!"

⁴⁰ "I tell you," he replied, "if they keep quiet, the stones will cry out."

⁴¹ As he approached Jerusalem and saw the city, he wept over it ⁴² and said, "If you, even you, had only known on this day what would bring you peace — but now it is hidden from your eyes. ⁴³ The days will come upon you when your enemies will build an embankment against you and encircle you and hem you in on every side. ⁴⁴ They will dash you to the ground, you and the children within your walls. They will not leave one stone on another, because you did not recognize the time of God's coming to you."

Jesus at the Temple

⁴⁵ When Jesus entered the temple courts, he began to drive out those who were selling. ⁴⁶ "It is written," he said to them, "'My house will be a house of prayer'ᵇ; but you have made it 'a den of robbers.'ᶜ"

⁴⁷ Every day he was teaching at the temple. But the chief priests, the teachers of the law and the leaders among the people were trying to kill him. ⁴⁸ Yet they could not find any way to do it, because all the people hung on his words.

The Authority of Jesus Questioned

20 One day as Jesus was teaching the people in the temple courts and proclaiming the good news, the chief priests and the teachers of the law, together with the elders, came up to him. ² "Tell us by what authority you are doing these things," they said. "Who gave you this authority?"

³ He replied, "I will also ask you a question. Tell me: ⁴ John's baptism — was it from heaven, or of human origin?"

⁵ They discussed it among themselves and said, "If we say, 'From heaven,' he will ask,

---

ᵃ 38 Psalm 118:26　　ᵇ 46 Isaiah 56:7　　ᶜ 46 Jer. 7:11

'Why didn't you believe him?' [6]But if we say, 'Of human origin,' all the people will stone us, because they are persuaded that John was a prophet."

[7]So they answered, "We don't know where it was from."

[8]Jesus said, "Neither will I tell you by what authority I am doing these things."

The Parable of the Tenants

[9]He went on to tell the people this parable: "A man planted a vineyard, rented it to some farmers and went away for a long time. [10]At harvest time he sent a servant to the tenants so they would give him some of the fruit of the vineyard. But the tenants beat him and sent him away empty-handed. [11]He sent another servant, but that one also they beat and treated shamefully and sent away empty-handed. [12]He sent still a third, and they wounded him and threw him out.

[13]"Then the owner of the vineyard said, 'What shall I do? I will send my son, whom I love; perhaps they will respect him.'

[14]"But when the tenants saw him, they talked the matter over. 'This is the heir,' they said. 'Let's kill him, and the inheritance will be ours.' [15]So they threw him out of the vineyard and killed him.

"What then will the owner of the vineyard do to them? [16]He will come and kill those tenants and give the vineyard to others."

When the people heard this, they said, "God forbid!"

[17]Jesus looked directly at them and asked, "Then what is the meaning of that which is written:

" 'The stone the builders rejected
has become the cornerstone'[a]?

[18]Everyone who falls on that stone will be broken to pieces; anyone on whom it falls will be crushed."

[19]The teachers of the law and the chief priests looked for a way to arrest him immediately, because they knew he had spoken this parable against them. But they were afraid of the people.

Paying Taxes to Caesar

[20]Keeping a close watch on him, they sent spies, who pretended to be sincere. They hoped to catch Jesus in something he said, so that they might hand him over to the power and authority of the governor. [21]So the spies questioned him: "Teacher, we know that you speak and teach what is right, and that you do not show partiality but teach the way of God in accordance with the truth. [22]Is it right for us to pay taxes to Caesar or not?"

[23]He saw through their duplicity and said to them, [24]"Show me a denarius. Whose image and inscription are on it?"

"Caesar's," they replied.

[25]He said to them, "Then give back to Caesar what is Caesar's, and to God what is God's."

[26]They were unable to trap him in what he had said there in public. And astonished by his answer, they became silent.

The Resurrection and Marriage

[27]Some of the Sadducees, who say there is no resurrection, came to Jesus with a question. [28]"Teacher," they said, "Moses wrote for us that if a man's brother dies and leaves a wife but no children, the man must marry the widow and raise up offspring for his brother. [29]Now there were seven brothers. The first one married a woman and died childless. [30]The second [31]and then the third married her, and in the same way the seven died, leaving no children. [32]Finally, the woman died too. [33]Now then, at the resurrection whose wife will she be, since the seven were married to her?"

[34]Jesus replied, "The people of this age marry and are given in marriage. [35]But those who are considered worthy of taking part in the age to come and in the resurrection from the dead will neither marry nor be given in marriage, [36]and they can no longer die; for they are like the angels. They are God's children, since they are children of the resurrection. [37]But in the account of the burning bush, even Moses showed that the dead rise, for he calls the Lord 'the God of Abraham, and the God of Isaac, and the God of Jacob.'[b] [38]He is not the God of the dead, but of the living, for to him all are alive."

[39]Some of the teachers of the law responded, "Well said, teacher!" [40]And no one dared to ask him any more questions.

[a] 17 Psalm 118:22   [b] 37 Exodus 3:6

Whose Son Is the Messiah?

⁴¹Then Jesus said to them, "Why is it said that the Messiah is the son of David? ⁴²David himself declares in the Book of Psalms:

" 'The Lord said to my Lord:
  "Sit at my right hand
⁴³until I make your enemies
  a footstool for your feet." ' ᵃ

⁴⁴David calls him 'Lord.' How then can he be his son?"

Warning Against the Teachers of the Law

⁴⁵While all the people were listening, Jesus said to his disciples, ⁴⁶"Beware of the teachers of the law. They like to walk around in flowing robes and love to be greeted with respect in the marketplaces and have the most important seats in the synagogues and the places of honor at banquets. ⁴⁷They devour widows' houses and for a show make lengthy prayers. These men will be punished most severely."

The Widow's Offering

21 As Jesus looked up, he saw the rich putting their gifts into the temple treasury. ²He also saw a poor widow put in two very small copper coins. ³"Truly I tell you," he said, "this poor widow has put in more than all the others. ⁴All these people gave their gifts out of their wealth; but she out of her poverty put in all she had to live on."

The Destruction of the Temple and Signs of the End Times

⁵Some of his disciples were remarking about how the temple was adorned with beautiful stones and with gifts dedicated to God. But Jesus said, ⁶"As for what you see here, the time will come when not one stone will be left on another; every one of them will be thrown down."

⁷"Teacher," they asked, "when will these things happen? And what will be the sign that they are about to take place?"

⁸He replied: "Watch out that you are not deceived. For many will come in my name, claiming, 'I am he,' and, 'The time is near.'

Do not follow them. ⁹When you hear of wars and uprisings, do not be frightened. These things must happen first, but the end will not come right away."

¹⁰Then he said to them: "Nation will rise against nation, and kingdom against kingdom. ¹¹There will be great earthquakes, famines and pestilences in various places, and fearful events and great signs from heaven.

¹²"But before all this, they will seize you and persecute you. They will hand you over to synagogues and put you in prison, and you will be brought before kings and governors, and all on account of my name. ¹³And so you will bear testimony to me. ¹⁴But make up your mind not to worry beforehand how you will defend yourselves. ¹⁵For I will give you words and wisdom that none of your adversaries will be able to resist or contradict. ¹⁶You will be betrayed even by parents, brothers and sisters, relatives and friends, and they will put some of you to death. ¹⁷Everyone will hate you because of me. ¹⁸But not a hair of your head will perish. ¹⁹Stand firm, and you will win life.

²⁰"When you see Jerusalem being surrounded by armies, you will know that its desolation is near. ²¹Then let those who are in Judea flee to the mountains, let those in the city get out, and let those in the country not enter the city. ²²For this is the time of punishment in fulfillment of all that has been written. ²³How dreadful it will be in those days for pregnant women and nursing mothers! There will be great distress in the land and wrath against this people. ²⁴They will fall by the sword and will be taken as prisoners to all the nations. Jerusalem will be trampled on by the Gentiles until the times of the Gentiles are fulfilled.

²⁵"There will be signs in the sun, moon and stars. On the earth, nations will be in anguish and perplexity at the roaring and tossing of the sea. ²⁶People will faint from terror, apprehensive of what is coming on the world, for the heavenly bodies will be shaken. ²⁷At that time they will see the Son of Man coming in a cloud with power and great glory. ²⁸When these things begin to take place, stand up and lift up your heads, because your redemption is drawing near."

ᵃ 43 Psalm 110:1

[29] He told them this parable: "Look at the fig tree and all the trees. [30] When they sprout leaves, you can see for yourselves and know that summer is near. [31] Even so, when you see these things happening, you know that the kingdom of God is near.

[32] "Truly I tell you, this generation will certainly not pass away until all these things have happened. [33] Heaven and earth will pass away, but my words will never pass away.

[34] "Be careful, or your hearts will be weighed down with carousing, drunkenness and the anxieties of life, and that day will close on you suddenly like a trap. [35] For it will come on all those who live on the face of the whole earth. [36] Be always on the watch, and pray that you may be able to escape all that is about to happen, and that you may be able to stand before the Son of Man."

[37] Each day Jesus was teaching at the temple, and each evening he went out to spend the night on the hill called the Mount of Olives, [38] and all the people came early in the morning to hear him at the temple.

Judas Agrees to Betray Jesus

22 Now the Festival of Unleavened Bread, called the Passover, was approaching, [2] and the chief priests and the teachers of the law were looking for some way to get rid of Jesus, for they were afraid of the people. [3] Then Satan entered Judas, called Iscariot, one of the Twelve. [4] And Judas went to the chief priests and the officers of the temple guard and discussed with them how he might betray Jesus. [5] They were delighted and agreed to give him money. [6] He consented, and watched for an opportunity to hand Jesus over to them when no crowd was present.

The Last Supper

[7] Then came the day of Unleavened Bread on which the Passover lamb had to be sacrificed. [8] Jesus sent Peter and John, saying, "Go and make preparations for us to eat the Passover."

[9] "Where do you want us to prepare for it?" they asked.

[10] He replied, "As you enter the city, a man carrying a jar of water will meet you. Follow him to the house that he enters, [11] and say to the owner of the house, 'The Teacher asks: Where is the guest room, where I may eat the Passover with my disciples?' [12] He will show you a large room upstairs, all furnished. Make preparations there."

[13] They left and found things just as Jesus had told them. So they prepared the Passover.

[14] When the hour came, Jesus and his apostles reclined at the table. [15] And he said to them, "I have eagerly desired to eat this Passover with you before I suffer. [16] For I tell you, I will not eat it again until it finds fulfillment in the kingdom of God."

[17] After taking the cup, he gave thanks and said, "Take this and divide it among you. [18] For I tell you I will not drink again from the fruit of the vine until the kingdom of God comes."

[19] And he took bread, gave thanks and broke it, and gave it to them, saying, "This is my body given for you; do this in remembrance of me."

[20] In the same way, after the supper he took the cup, saying, "This cup is the new covenant in my blood, which is poured out for you.[a] [21] But the hand of him who is going to betray me is with mine on the table. [22] The Son of Man will go as it has been decreed. But woe to that man who betrays him!" [23] They began to question among themselves which of them it might be who would do this.

[24] A dispute also arose among them as to which of them was considered to be greatest. [25] Jesus said to them, "The kings of the Gentiles lord it over them; and those who exercise authority over them call themselves Benefactors. [26] But you are not to be like that. Instead, the greatest among you should be like the youngest, and the one who rules like the one who serves. [27] For who is greater, the one who is at the table or the one who serves? Is it not the one who is at the table? But I am among you as one who serves. [28] You are those who have stood by me in my trials. [29] And I confer on you a kingdom, just as my Father conferred one on me, [30] so that you may eat and drink at my table in my kingdom and sit on thrones, judging the twelve tribes of Israel.

---

[a] 19,20 Some manuscripts do not have *given for you . . . poured out for you.*

[31] "Simon, Simon, Satan has asked to sift all of you as wheat. [32] But I have prayed for you, Simon, that your faith may not fail. And when you have turned back, strengthen your brothers."

[33] But he replied, "Lord, I am ready to go with you to prison and to death."

[34] Jesus answered, "I tell you, Peter, before the rooster crows today, you will deny three times that you know me."

[35] Then Jesus asked them, "When I sent you without purse, bag or sandals, did you lack anything?"

"Nothing," they answered.

[36] He said to them, "But now if you have a purse, take it, and also a bag; and if you don't have a sword, sell your cloak and buy one. [37] It is written: 'And he was numbered with the transgressors'[a]; and I tell you that this must be fulfilled in me. Yes, what is written about me is reaching its fulfillment."

[38] The disciples said, "See, Lord, here are two swords."

"That's enough!" he replied.

Jesus Prays on the Mount of Olives

[39] Jesus went out as usual to the Mount of Olives, and his disciples followed him. [40] On reaching the place, he said to them, "Pray that you will not fall into temptation." [41] He withdrew about a stone's throw beyond them, knelt down and prayed, [42] "Father, if you are willing, take this cup from me; yet not my will, but yours be done." [43] An angel from heaven appeared to him and strengthened him. [44] And being in anguish, he prayed more earnestly, and his sweat was like drops of blood falling to the ground.[b]

[45] When he rose from prayer and went back to the disciples, he found them asleep, exhausted from sorrow. [46] "Why are you sleeping?" he asked them. "Get up and pray so that you will not fall into temptation."

Jesus Arrested

[47] While he was still speaking a crowd came up, and the man who was called Judas, one of the Twelve, was leading them. He approached Jesus to kiss him, [48] but Jesus asked him, "Judas, are you betraying the Son of Man with a kiss?"

[49] When Jesus' followers saw what was going to happen, they said, "Lord, should we

strike with our swords?" [50] And one of them struck the servant of the high priest, cutting off his right ear.

[51] But Jesus answered, "No more of this!" And he touched the man's ear and healed him.

[52] Then Jesus said to the chief priests, the officers of the temple guard, and the elders, who had come for him, "Am I leading a rebellion, that you have come with swords and clubs? [53] Every day I was with you in the temple courts, and you did not lay a hand on me. But this is your hour — when darkness reigns."

Peter Disowns Jesus

[54] Then seizing him, they led him away and took him into the house of the high priest. Peter followed at a distance. [55] And when some there had kindled a fire in the middle of the courtyard and had sat down together, Peter sat down with them. [56] A servant girl saw him seated there in the firelight. She looked closely at him and said, "This man was with him."

[57] But he denied it. "Woman, I don't know him," he said.

[58] A little later someone else saw him and said, "You also are one of them."

"Man, I am not!" Peter replied.

[59] About an hour later another asserted, "Certainly this fellow was with him, for he is a Galilean."

[60] Peter replied, "Man, I don't know what you're talking about!" Just as he was speaking, the rooster crowed. [61] The Lord turned and looked straight at Peter. Then Peter remembered the word the Lord had spoken to him: "Before the rooster crows today, you will disown me three times." [62] And he went outside and wept bitterly.

The Guards Mock Jesus

[63] The men who were guarding Jesus began mocking and beating him. [64] They blindfolded him and demanded, "Prophesy! Who hit you?" [65] And they said many other insulting things to him.

Jesus Before Pilate and Herod

[66] At daybreak the council of the elders of the people, both the chief priests and the

[a] 37 Isaiah 53:12   [b] 43,44 Many early manuscripts do not have verses 43 and 44.

teachers of the law, met together, and Jesus was led before them. [67] "If you are the Messiah," they said, "tell us."

Jesus answered, "If I tell you, you will not believe me, [68] and if I asked you, you would not answer. [69] But from now on, the Son of Man will be seated at the right hand of the mighty God."

[70] They all asked, "Are you then the Son of God?"

He replied, "You say that I am."

[71] Then they said, "Why do we need any more testimony? We have heard it from his own lips."

23 Then the whole assembly rose and led him off to Pilate. [2] And they began to accuse him, saying, "We have found this man subverting our nation. He opposes payment of taxes to Caesar and claims to be Messiah, a king."

[3] So Pilate asked Jesus, "Are you the king of the Jews?"

"You have said so," Jesus replied.

[4] Then Pilate announced to the chief priests and the crowd, "I find no basis for a charge against this man."

[5] But they insisted, "He stirs up the people all over Judea by his teaching. He started in Galilee and has come all the way here."

[6] On hearing this, Pilate asked if the man was a Galilean. [7] When he learned that Jesus was under Herod's jurisdiction, he sent him to Herod, who was also in Jerusalem at that time.

[8] When Herod saw Jesus, he was greatly pleased, because for a long time he had been wanting to see him. From what he had heard about him, he hoped to see him perform a sign of some sort. [9] He plied him with many questions, but Jesus gave him no answer. [10] The chief priests and the teachers of the law were standing there, vehemently accusing him. [11] Then Herod and his soldiers ridiculed and mocked him. Dressing him in an elegant robe, they sent him back to Pilate. [12] That day Herod and Pilate became friends — before this they had been enemies.

[13] Pilate called together the chief priests, the rulers and the people, [14] and said to them, "You brought me this man as one who was inciting the people to rebellion. I have examined him in your presence and have found no basis for your charges against him. [15] Neither has Herod, for he sent him back to us; as you can see, he has done nothing to deserve death. [16] Therefore, I will punish him and then release him." [17] [a]

[18] But the whole crowd shouted, "Away with this man! Release Barabbas to us!" [19] (Barabbas had been thrown into prison for an insurrection in the city, and for murder.)

[20] Wanting to release Jesus, Pilate appealed to them again. [21] But they kept shouting, "Crucify him! Crucify him!"

[22] For the third time he spoke to them: "Why? What crime has this man committed? I have found in him no grounds for the death penalty. Therefore I will have him punished and then release him."

[23] But with loud shouts they insistently demanded that he be crucified, and their shouts prevailed. [24] So Pilate decided to grant their demand. [25] He released the man who had been thrown into prison for insurrection and murder, the one they asked for, and surrendered Jesus to their will.

The Crucifixion of Jesus

[26] As the soldiers led him away, they seized Simon from Cyrene, who was on his way in from the country, and put the cross on him and made him carry it behind Jesus. [27] A large number of people followed him, including women who mourned and wailed for him. [28] Jesus turned and said to them, "Daughters of Jerusalem, do not weep for me; weep for yourselves and for your children. [29] For the time will come when you will say, 'Blessed are the childless women, the wombs that never bore and the breasts that never nursed!' [30] Then

" 'they will say to the mountains, "Fall on us!"
and to the hills, "Cover us!" ' [b]

[31] For if people do these things when the tree is green, what will happen when it is dry?"

[32] Two other men, both criminals, were also led out with him to be executed. [33] When they came to the place called the Skull, they crucified him there, along with the criminals — one on his right, the other on his left. [34] Jesus said, "Father, forgive

---

[a] 17 Some manuscripts include here words similar to Matt. 27:15 and Mark 15:6.   [b] 30 Hosea 10:8

them, for they do not know what they are doing."[a] And they divided up his clothes by casting lots.

[35] The people stood watching, and the rulers even sneered at him. They said, "He saved others; let him save himself if he is God's Messiah, the Chosen One."

[36] The soldiers also came up and mocked him. They offered him wine vinegar [37] and said, "If you are the king of the Jews, save yourself."

[38] There was a written notice above him, which read: THIS IS THE KING OF THE JEWS.

[39] One of the criminals who hung there hurled insults at him: "Aren't you the Messiah? Save yourself and us!"

[40] But the other criminal rebuked him. "Don't you fear God," he said, "since you are under the same sentence? [41] We are punished justly, for we are getting what our deeds deserve. But this man has done nothing wrong."

[42] Then he said, "Jesus, remember me when you come into your kingdom.[b]"

[43] Jesus answered him, "Truly I tell you, today you will be with me in paradise."

The Death of Jesus

[44] It was now about noon, and darkness came over the whole land until three in the afternoon, [45] for the sun stopped shining. And the curtain of the temple was torn in two. [46] Jesus called out with a loud voice, "Father, into your hands I commit my spirit."[c] When he had said this, he breathed his last.

[47] The centurion, seeing what had happened, praised God and said, "Surely this was a righteous man." [48] When all the people who had gathered to witness this sight saw what took place, they beat their breasts and went away. [49] But all those who knew him, including the women who had followed him from Galilee, stood at a distance, watching these things.

The Burial of Jesus

[50] Now there was a man named Joseph, a member of the Council, a good and upright man, [51] who had not consented to their decision and action. He came from the Jude-

an town of Arimathea, and he himself was waiting for the kingdom of God. [52] Going to Pilate, he asked for Jesus' body. [53] Then he took it down, wrapped it in linen cloth and placed it in a tomb cut in the rock, one in which no one had yet been laid. [54] It was Preparation Day, and the Sabbath was about to begin.

[55] The women who had come with Jesus from Galilee followed Joseph and saw the tomb and how his body was laid in it. [56] Then they went home and prepared spices and perfumes. But they rested on the Sabbath in obedience to the commandment.

Jesus Has Risen

24 On the first day of the week, very early in the morning, the women took the spices they had prepared and went to the tomb. [2] They found the stone rolled away from the tomb, [3] but when they entered, they did not find the body of the Lord Jesus. [4] While they were wondering about this, suddenly two men in clothes that gleamed like lightning stood beside them. [5] In their fright the women bowed down with their faces to the ground, but the men said to them, "Why do you look for the living among the dead? [6] He is not here; he has risen! Remember how he told you, while he was still with you in Galilee: [7] 'The Son of Man must be delivered over to the hands of sinners, be crucified and on the third day be raised again.' " [8] Then they remembered his words.

[9] When they came back from the tomb, they told all these things to the Eleven and to all the others. [10] It was Mary Magdalene, Joanna, Mary the mother of James, and the others with them who told this to the apostles. [11] But they did not believe the women, because their words seemed to them like nonsense. [12] Peter, however, got up and ran to the tomb. Bending over, he saw the strips of linen lying by themselves, and he went away, wondering to himself what had happened.

On the Road to Emmaus

[13] Now that same day two of them were going to a village called Emmaus, about seven miles[d] from Jerusalem. [14] They were talking

---

[a] 34 Some early manuscripts do not have this sentence.   [b] 42 Some manuscripts *come with your kingly power*   [c] 46 Psalm 31:5   [d] 13 Or about 11 kilometers

Finding Jesus

By Marshéle Carter Waddell

READ: Luke 24:13–35

The whirlwind weekend of overdue laughter, new insights, renewed hope and heartfelt worship at the annual women's retreat had filled my soul to the brim. I didn't want to leave this mountaintop. I felt closer to God here, more aware of his presence and calling on my life. The thought of descending from this glorious peak of spiritual safety and returning to sea-level life on the Navy base made my heart heavy.

My long drive dropped me several thousand feet down until I arrived at sunset at my address: 100 Reality Lane. I took a deep breath before I reentered the lower atmosphere of cluttered countertops, dirty laundry piles and kids' homework sinkholes that awaited me. I was surprised to find a semi-sparkly kitchen eagerly presented by only slightly smudged kids and a harried, grateful-to-see-me husband.

That evening I reflected on the retreat's theme — The Road to Emmaus: An Intersection of Heaven and Heartache. Two disciples were on their way to the village of Emmaus, likely their home, after what should have been a special weekend on the mountaintop of Jerusalem. They had expected this particular Passover celebration to be the pinnacle of the people's long wait for the Messiah. Instead, their long-awaited King had been crucified and buried.

As they walked the seven miles from Jerusalem to Emmaus, an unexpected travel companion joined them on the trek. He walked and talked with them for the rest of the journey and even had a sunset supper with them. The risen Jesus had met them on the road. Until those last sacred seconds, when Jesus allowed them to recognize him, they hadn't known that heaven had intersected their heartbreak. At the perfect time, Jesus made it clear that the Most High was present at their lowest point. Then he vanished from sight, going ahead of them back to Jerusalem. Suddenly, their hearts were light and their feet swift. The undeniable presence of their living Lord had renewed their faith.

The lesson of this story is inspiring. Mountaintop experiences can fortify our faith and strengthen our spirits. We can meet with God there. But most of life is lived at lower elevations, down in the trenches, where the air is thicker and the shadows longer. Here too Jesus appears to us, in our everyday realities. He doesn't come with fanfare, so we may not recognize him at first. But our Lord is present at our highest highs and our lowest lows.

As they talked and discussed these things with each other, Jesus himself came up and walked along with them; but they were kept from recognizing him.

LUKE 24:15 – 16

DEBRIEF

- From what mountaintop experience am I currently descending?

- I promise to invite Jesus to walk with me and to share my heartache with him. I'll listen as he speaks to my heart.

REPORT

Lord, you have promised to never leave me. Whether my path leads upward or downward today, help me recognize you and hear your voice along the way. In Jesus' name I pray. Amen.

with each other about everything that had happened. [15] As they talked and discussed these things with each other, Jesus himself came up and walked along with them; [16] but they were kept from recognizing him.

[17] He asked them, "What are you discussing together as you walk along?"

They stood still, their faces downcast. [18] One of them, named Cleopas, asked him, "Are you the only one visiting Jerusalem who does not know the things that have happened there in these days?"

[19] "What things?" he asked.

"About Jesus of Nazareth," they replied. "He was a prophet, powerful in word and deed before God and all the people. [20] The chief priests and our rulers handed him over to be sentenced to death, and they crucified him; [21] but we had hoped that he was the one who was going to redeem Israel. And what is more, it is the third day since all this took place. [22] In addition, some of our women amazed us. They went to the tomb early this morning [23] but didn't find his body. They came and told us that they had seen a vision of angels, who said he was alive. [24] Then some of our companions went to the tomb and found it just as the women had said, but they did not see Jesus."

[25] He said to them, "How foolish you are, and how slow to believe all that the prophets have spoken! [26] Did not the Messiah have to suffer these things and then enter his glory?" [27] And beginning with Moses and all the Prophets, he explained to them what was said in all the Scriptures concerning himself.

[28] As they approached the village to which they were going, Jesus continued on as if he were going farther. [29] But they urged him strongly, "Stay with us, for it is nearly evening; the day is almost over." So he went in to stay with them.

[30] When he was at the table with them, he took bread, gave thanks, broke it and began to give it to them. [31] Then their eyes were opened and they recognized him, and he disappeared from their sight. [32] They asked each other, "Were not our hearts burning within us while he talked with us on the road and opened the Scriptures to us?"

[33] They got up and returned at once to Jerusalem. There they found the Eleven and those with them, assembled together [34] and saying, "It is true! The Lord has risen and has appeared to Simon." [35] Then the two told what had happened on the way, and how Jesus was recognized by them when he broke the bread.

Jesus Appears to the Disciples

[36] While they were still talking about this, Jesus himself stood among them and said to them, "Peace be with you."

[37] They were startled and frightened, thinking they saw a ghost. [38] He said to them, "Why are you troubled, and why do doubts rise in your minds? [39] Look at my hands and my feet. It is I myself! Touch me and see; a ghost does not have flesh and bones, as you see I have."

[40] When he had said this, he showed them his hands and feet. [41] And while they still did not believe it because of joy and amazement, he asked them, "Do you have anything here to eat?" [42] They gave him a piece of broiled fish, [43] and he took it and ate it in their presence.

[44] He said to them, "This is what I told you while I was still with you: Everything must be fulfilled that is written about me in the Law of Moses, the Prophets and the Psalms."

[45] Then he opened their minds so they could understand the Scriptures. [46] He told them, "This is what is written: The Messiah will suffer and rise from the dead on the third day, [47] and repentance for the forgiveness of sins will be preached in his name to all nations, beginning at Jerusalem. [48] You are witnesses of these things. [49] I am going to send you what my Father has promised; but stay in the city until you have been clothed with power from on high."

The Ascension of Jesus

[50] When he had led them out to the vicinity of Bethany, he lifted up his hands and blessed them. [51] While he was blessing them, he left them and was taken up into heaven. [52] Then they worshiped him and returned to Jerusalem with great joy. [53] And they stayed continually at the temple, praising God.

John

The Word Became Flesh

1 In the beginning was the Word, and the Word was with God, and the Word was God. ²He was with God in the beginning. ³Through him all things were made; without him nothing was made that has been made. ⁴In him was life, and that life was the light of all mankind. ⁵The light shines in the darkness, and the darkness has not overcome[a] it.

⁶There was a man sent from God whose name was John. ⁷He came as a witness to testify concerning that light, so that through him all might believe. ⁸He himself was not the light; he came only as a witness to the light.

⁹The true light that gives light to everyone was coming into the world. ¹⁰He was in the world, and though the world was made through him, the world did not recognize him. ¹¹He came to that which was his own, but his own did not receive him. ¹²Yet to all who did receive him, to those who believed in his name, he gave the right to become children of God — ¹³children born not of natural descent, nor of human decision or a husband's will, but born of God.

¹⁴The Word became flesh and made his dwelling among us. We have seen his glory, the glory of the one and only Son, who came from the Father, full of grace and truth.

¹⁵(John testified concerning him. He cried out, saying, "This is the one I spoke about when I said, 'He who comes after me has surpassed me because he was before me.'") ¹⁶Out of his fullness we have all received grace in place of grace already given. ¹⁷For the law was given through Moses; grace and truth came through Jesus Christ. ¹⁸No one has ever seen God, but the one and only Son, who is himself God and[b] is in closest relationship with the Father, has made him known.

John the Baptist Denies Being the Messiah

¹⁹Now this was John's testimony when the Jewish leaders[c] in Jerusalem sent priests and Levites to ask him who he was. ²⁰He did not fail to confess, but confessed freely, "I am not the Messiah."

²¹They asked him, "Then who are you? Are you Elijah?"

He said, "I am not."

"Are you the Prophet?"

He answered, "No."

²²Finally they said, "Who are you? Give us an answer to take back to those who sent us. What do you say about yourself?"

²³John replied in the words of Isaiah the prophet, "I am the voice of one calling in the wilderness, 'Make straight the way for the Lord.'"[d]

²⁴Now the Pharisees who had been sent ²⁵questioned him, "Why then do you baptize if you are not the Messiah, nor Elijah, nor the Prophet?"

²⁶"I baptize with[e] water," John replied, "but among you stands one you do not know. ²⁷He is the one who comes after me, the straps of whose sandals I am not worthy to untie."

²⁸This all happened at Bethany on the other side of the Jordan, where John was baptizing.

John Testifies About Jesus

²⁹The next day John saw Jesus coming toward him and said, "Look, the Lamb of God, who takes away the sin of the world! ³⁰This is the one I meant when I said, 'A man who comes after me has surpassed me because he was before me.' ³¹I myself did not know him, but the reason I came baptizing with water was that he might be revealed to Israel."

³²Then John gave this testimony: "I saw

---

[a] 5 Or *understood*   [b] 18 Some manuscripts *but the only Son, who*   [c] 19 The Greek term traditionally translated *the Jews* (*hoi Ioudaioi*) refers here and elsewhere in John's Gospel to those Jewish leaders who opposed Jesus; also in 5:10, 15, 16; 7:1, 11, 13; 9:22; 18:14, 28, 36; 19:7, 12, 31, 38; 20:19.   [d] 23 Isaiah 40:3   [e] 26 Or *in*; also in verses 31 and 33 (twice)

the Spirit come down from heaven as a dove and remain on him. ³³And I myself did not know him, but the one who sent me to baptize with water told me, 'The man on whom you see the Spirit come down and remain is the one who will baptize with the Holy Spirit.' ³⁴I have seen and I testify that this is God's Chosen One."ᵃ

John's Disciples Follow Jesus

³⁵The next day John was there again with two of his disciples. ³⁶When he saw Jesus passing by, he said, "Look, the Lamb of God!"

³⁷When the two disciples heard him say this, they followed Jesus. ³⁸Turning around, Jesus saw them following and asked, "What do you want?"

They said, "Rabbi" (which means "Teacher"), "where are you staying?"

³⁹"Come," he replied, "and you will see."

So they went and saw where he was staying, and they spent that day with him. It was about four in the afternoon.

⁴⁰Andrew, Simon Peter's brother, was one of the two who heard what John had said and who had followed Jesus. ⁴¹The first thing Andrew did was to find his brother Simon and tell him, "We have found the Messiah" (that is, the Christ). ⁴²And he brought him to Jesus.

Jesus looked at him and said, "You are Simon son of John. You will be called Cephas" (which, when translated, is Peterᵇ).

Jesus Calls Philip and Nathanael

⁴³The next day Jesus decided to leave for Galilee. Finding Philip, he said to him, "Follow me."

⁴⁴Philip, like Andrew and Peter, was from the town of Bethsaida. ⁴⁵Philip found Nathanael and told him, "We have found the one Moses wrote about in the Law, and about whom the prophets also wrote—Jesus of Nazareth, the son of Joseph."

⁴⁶"Nazareth! Can anything good come from there?" Nathanael asked.

"Come and see," said Philip.

⁴⁷When Jesus saw Nathanael approaching, he said of him, "Here truly is an Israelite in whom there is no deceit."

⁴⁸"How do you know me?" Nathanael asked.

Jesus answered, "I saw you while you were still under the fig tree before Philip called you."

⁴⁹Then Nathanael declared, "Rabbi, you are the Son of God; you are the king of Israel."

⁵⁰Jesus said, "You believeᶜ because I told you I saw you under the fig tree. You will see greater things than that." ⁵¹He then added, "Very truly I tell you,ᵈ youᵈ will see 'heaven open, and the angels of God ascending and descending on'ᵉ the Son of Man."

Jesus Changes Water Into Wine

2 On the third day a wedding took place at Cana in Galilee. Jesus' mother was there, ²and Jesus and his disciples had also been invited to the wedding. ³When the wine was gone, Jesus' mother said to him, "They have no more wine."

⁴"Woman,ᶠ why do you involve me?" Jesus replied. "My hour has not yet come."

⁵His mother said to the servants, "Do whatever he tells you."

⁶Nearby stood six stone water jars, the kind used by the Jews for ceremonial washing, each holding from twenty to thirty gallons.ᵍ

⁷Jesus said to the servants, "Fill the jars with water"; so they filled them to the brim.

⁸Then he told them, "Now draw some out and take it to the master of the banquet."

They did so, ⁹and the master of the banquet tasted the water that had been turned into wine. He did not realize where it had come from, though the servants who had drawn the water knew. Then he called the bridegroom aside ¹⁰and said, "Everyone brings out the choice wine first and then the cheaper wine after the guests have had too much to drink; but you have saved the best till now."

¹¹What Jesus did here in Cana of Galilee was the first of the signs through which he revealed his glory; and his disciples believed in him.

¹²After this he went down to Capernaum with his mother and brothers and his disciples. There they stayed for a few days.

ᵃ 34 See Isaiah 42:1; many manuscripts is the Son of God.   ᵇ 42 Cephas (Aramaic) and Peter (Greek) both mean rock.   ᶜ 50 Or Do you believe...?   ᵈ 51 The Greek is plural.   ᵉ 51 Gen. 28:12   ᶠ 4 The Greek for Woman does not denote any disrespect.   ᵍ 6 Or from about 75 to about 115 liters

Jesus Clears the Temple Courts

[13]When it was almost time for the Jewish Passover, Jesus went up to Jerusalem. [14]In the temple courts he found people selling cattle, sheep and doves, and others sitting at tables exchanging money. [15]So he made a whip out of cords, and drove all from the temple courts, both sheep and cattle; he scattered the coins of the money changers and overturned their tables. [16]To those who sold doves he said, "Get these out of here! Stop turning my Father's house into a market!" [17]His disciples remembered that it is written: "Zeal for your house will consume me."[a]

[18]The Jews then responded to him, "What sign can you show us to prove your authority to do all this?"

[19]Jesus answered them, "Destroy this temple, and I will raise it again in three days."

[20]They replied, "It has taken forty-six years to build this temple, and you are going to raise it in three days?" [21]But the temple he had spoken of was his body. [22]After he was raised from the dead, his disciples recalled what he had said. Then they believed the scripture and the words that Jesus had spoken.

[23]Now while he was in Jerusalem at the Passover Festival, many people saw the signs he was performing and believed in his name.[b] [24]But Jesus would not entrust himself to them, for he knew all people. [25]He did not need any testimony about mankind, for he knew what was in each person.

Jesus Teaches Nicodemus

3 Now there was a Pharisee, a man named Nicodemus who was a member of the Jewish ruling council. [2]He came to Jesus at night and said, "Rabbi, we know that you are a teacher who has come from God. For no one could perform the signs you are doing if God were not with him."

[3]Jesus replied, "Very truly I tell you, no one can see the kingdom of God unless they are born again.[c]"

[4]"How can someone be born when they are old?" Nicodemus asked. "Surely they cannot enter a second time into their mother's womb to be born!"

[5]Jesus answered, "Very truly I tell you, no one can enter the kingdom of God unless they are born of water and the Spirit. [6]Flesh gives birth to flesh, but the Spirit[d] gives birth to spirit. [7]You should not be surprised at my saying, 'You[e] must be born again.' [8]The wind blows wherever it pleases. You hear its sound, but you cannot tell where it comes from or where it is going. So it is with everyone born of the Spirit."[f]

[9]"How can this be?" Nicodemus asked.

[10]"You are Israel's teacher," said Jesus, "and do you not understand these things? [11]Very truly I tell you, we speak of what we know, and we testify to what we have seen, but still you people do not accept our testimony. [12]I have spoken to you of earthly things and you do not believe; how then will you believe if I speak of heavenly things? [13]No one has ever gone into heaven except the one who came from heaven—the Son of Man.[g] [14]Just as Moses lifted up the snake in the wilderness, so the Son of Man must be lifted up,[h] [15]that everyone who believes may have eternal life in him."[i]

[16]For God so loved the world that he gave his one and only Son, that whoever believes in him shall not perish but have eternal life. [17]For God did not send his Son into the world to condemn the world, but to save the world through him. [18]Whoever believes in him is not condemned, but whoever does not believe stands condemned already because they have not believed in the name of God's one and only Son. [19]This is the verdict: Light has come into the world, but people loved darkness instead of light because their deeds were evil. [20]Everyone who does evil hates the light, and will not come into the light for fear that their deeds will be exposed. [21]But whoever lives by the truth comes into the light, so that it may be seen plainly that what they have done has been done in the sight of God.

John Testifies Again About Jesus

[22]After this, Jesus and his disciples went out into the Judean countryside, where he

[a] 17 Psalm 69:9   [b] 23 Or in him   [c] 3 The Greek for again also means from above; also in verse 7.
[d] 6 Or but spirit   [e] 7 The Greek is plural.   [f] 8 The Greek for Spirit is the same as that for wind.
[g] 13 Some manuscripts Man, who is in heaven   [h] 14 The Greek for lifted up also means exalted.
[i] 15 Some interpreters end the quotation with verse 21.

spent some time with them, and baptized. ²³Now John also was baptizing at Aenon near Salim, because there was plenty of water, and people were coming and being baptized. ²⁴(This was before John was put in prison.) ²⁵An argument developed between some of John's disciples and a certain Jew over the matter of ceremonial washing. ²⁶They came to John and said to him, "Rabbi, that man who was with you on the other side of the Jordan — the one you testified about — look, he is baptizing, and everyone is going to him."

²⁷To this John replied, "A person can receive only what is given them from heaven. ²⁸You yourselves can testify that I said, 'I am not the Messiah but am sent ahead of him.' ²⁹The bride belongs to the bridegroom. The friend who attends the bridegroom waits and listens for him, and is full of joy when he hears the bridegroom's voice. That joy is mine, and it is now complete. ³⁰He must become greater; I must become less."ᵃ

³¹The one who comes from above is above all; the one who is from the earth belongs to the earth, and speaks as one from the earth. The one who comes from heaven is above all. ³²He testifies to what he has seen and heard, but no one accepts his testimony. ³³Whoever has accepted it has certified that God is truthful. ³⁴For the one whom God has sent speaks the words of God, for Godᵇ gives the Spirit without limit. ³⁵The Father loves the Son and has placed everything in his hands. ³⁶Whoever believes in the Son has eternal life, but whoever rejects the Son will not see life, for God's wrath remains on them.

Jesus Talks With a Samaritan Woman

4 Now Jesus learned that the Pharisees had heard that he was gaining and baptizing more disciples than John — ²although in fact it was not Jesus who baptized, but his disciples. ³So he left Judea and went back once more to Galilee.

⁴Now he had to go through Samaria. ⁵So he came to a town in Samaria called Sychar, near the plot of ground Jacob had given to his son Joseph. ⁶Jacob's well was there, and Jesus, tired as he was from the journey, sat down by the well. It was about noon.

⁷When a Samaritan woman came to draw water, Jesus said to her, "Will you give me a drink?" ⁸(His disciples had gone into the town to buy food.)

⁹The Samaritan woman said to him, "You are a Jew and I am a Samaritan woman. How can you ask me for a drink?" (For Jews do not associate with Samaritans.ᶜ)

¹⁰Jesus answered her, "If you knew the gift of God and who it is that asks you for a drink, you would have asked him and he would have given you living water."

¹¹"Sir," the woman said, "you have nothing to draw with and the well is deep. Where can you get this living water? ¹²Are you greater than our father Jacob, who gave us the well and drank from it himself, as did also his sons and his livestock?"

¹³Jesus answered, "Everyone who drinks this water will be thirsty again, ¹⁴but whoever drinks the water I give them will never thirst. Indeed, the water I give them will become in them a spring of water welling up to eternal life."

¹⁵The woman said to him, "Sir, give me this water so that I won't get thirsty and have to keep coming here to draw water."

¹⁶He told her, "Go, call your husband and come back."

¹⁷"I have no husband," she replied.

Jesus said to her, "You are right when you say you have no husband. ¹⁸The fact is, you have had five husbands, and the man you now have is not your husband. What you have just said is quite true."

¹⁹"Sir," the woman said, "I can see that you are a prophet. ²⁰Our ancestors worshiped on this mountain, but you Jews claim that the place where we must worship is in Jerusalem."

²¹"Woman," Jesus replied, "believe me, a time is coming when you will worship the Father neither on this mountain nor in Jerusalem. ²²You Samaritans worship what you do not know; we worship what we do know, for salvation is from the Jews. ²³Yet a time is coming and has now come when the true worshipers will worship the Father in the Spirit and in truth, for they are the kind of worshipers the Father seeks. ²⁴God is spirit, and his worshipers must worship in the Spirit and in truth."

ᵃ 30 Some interpreters end the quotation with verse 36.   ᵇ 34 Greek *he*   ᶜ 9 Or *do not use dishes Samaritans have used*

²⁵The woman said, "I know that Messiah" (called Christ) "is coming. When he comes, he will explain everything to us."

²⁶Then Jesus declared, "I, the one speaking to you—I am he."

The Disciples Rejoin Jesus

²⁷Just then his disciples returned and were surprised to find him talking with a woman. But no one asked, "What do you want?" or "Why are you talking with her?"

²⁸Then, leaving her water jar, the woman went back to the town and said to the people, ²⁹"Come, see a man who told me everything I ever did. Could this be the Messiah?" ³⁰They came out of the town and made their way toward him.

³¹Meanwhile his disciples urged him, "Rabbi, eat something."

³²But he said to them, "I have food to eat that you know nothing about."

³³Then his disciples said to each other, "Could someone have brought him food?"

³⁴"My food," said Jesus, "is to do the will of him who sent me and to finish his work. ³⁵Don't you have a saying, 'It's still four months until harvest'? I tell you, open your eyes and look at the fields! They are ripe for harvest. ³⁶Even now the one who reaps draws a wage and harvests a crop for eternal life, so that the sower and the reaper may be glad together. ³⁷Thus the saying 'One sows and another reaps' is true. ³⁸I sent you to reap what you have not worked for. Others have done the hard work, and you have reaped the benefits of their labor."

Many Samaritans Believe

³⁹Many of the Samaritans from that town believed in him because of the woman's testimony, "He told me everything I ever did." ⁴⁰So when the Samaritans came to him, they urged him to stay with them, and he stayed two days. ⁴¹And because of his words many more became believers.

⁴²They said to the woman, "We no longer believe just because of what you said; now we have heard for ourselves, and we know that this man really is the Savior of the world."

Jesus Heals an Official's Son

⁴³After the two days he left for Galilee. ⁴⁴(Now Jesus himself had pointed out that a prophet has no honor in his own country.) ⁴⁵When he arrived in Galilee, the Galileans welcomed him. They had seen all that he had done in Jerusalem at the Passover Festival, for they also had been there.

⁴⁶Once more he visited Cana in Galilee, where he had turned the water into wine. And there was a certain royal official whose son lay sick at Capernaum. ⁴⁷When this man heard that Jesus had arrived in Galilee from Judea, he went to him and begged him to come and heal his son, who was close to death.

⁴⁸"Unless you people see signs and wonders," Jesus told him, "you will never believe."

⁴⁹The royal official said, "Sir, come down before my child dies."

⁵⁰"Go," Jesus replied, "your son will live."

The man took Jesus at his word and departed. ⁵¹While he was still on the way, his servants met him with the news that his boy was living. ⁵²When he inquired as to the time when his son got better, they said to him, "Yesterday, at one in the afternoon, the fever left him."

⁵³Then the father realized that this was the exact time at which Jesus had said to him, "Your son will live." So he and his whole household believed.

⁵⁴This was the second sign Jesus performed after coming from Judea to Galilee.

The Healing at the Pool

5 Some time later, Jesus went up to Jerusalem for one of the Jewish festivals. ²Now there is in Jerusalem near the Sheep Gate a pool, which in Aramaic is called Bethesda*a* and which is surrounded by five covered colonnades. ³Here a great number of disabled people used to lie—the blind, the lame, the paralyzed. [4]*b* 5One who was there had been an invalid for thirty-eight years. ⁶When Jesus saw him lying there and learned that he had been in this condition for a long time, he asked him, "Do you want to get well?"

---

a 2 Some manuscripts *Bethzatha*; other manuscripts *Bethsaida*   *b* 3,4 Some manuscripts include here, wholly or in part, *paralyzed—and they waited for the moving of the waters.* ⁴*From time to time an angel of the Lord would come down and stir up the waters. The first one into the pool after each such disturbance would be cured of whatever disease they had.*

Soul Food

By Marshéle Carter Waddell

READ: John 4:27–38

We believers from the South consider our favorite Southern dishes to be good for the soul. I get my favorite soul food fix these days from Mama Dips, an unassuming house-turned-restaurant on a quiet corner in Carrboro, North Carolina. There are times when only stewed okra and tomatoes, black-eyed peas, collard greens with vinegar, salt-cured country ham, a sweet-potato biscuit and sweet tea will do. I put that first bite in my mouth, close my eyes, and I am instantly transported back in time to my grandmother's kitchen — a place I loved to be, a place I called home.

God's Word tells us that there is another, more important form of soul food. Jesus mentioned his preference for it in John 4. After an unconventional conversation with a Samaritan woman, Jesus made an unexpected culinary comment. When his disciples came back from the Samaritan town and said, "Rabbi, eat something," Jesus passed on it.

"'I have food to eat that you know nothing about … My food,' said Jesus, 'is to do the will of him who sent me and to finish his work'" (John 4:32,34). Jesus was fueled by his focus on God's purpose for his life. Sure, he needed olives, hummus and pita bread to maintain his physical health and endurance; however, he knew pursuing God's plan preempts all other appetites.

Christ Jesus our Lord came to tear down everything that separates us, an unholy people, from the holy God and to tear down everything that divides us as people groups (see Ephesians 3:6,10 – 12). Jesus reconciled us to God *and* to one another so that God's wisdom should be made known to the rulers and authorities in the heavenly realms. And the Scriptures make it clear that God accomplished this in Christ Jesus our Lord.

Just as our Father had a defined purpose for his Son's life, he has a specific reason for creating you, his daughter. His purpose for your life, the food that fuels your personal faith and work, is far more important than your grocery list and meal preparations. While God's plan and purpose can feel like a mystery, he has provided more than enough insight in his Word about his will for your life. The best news is that he has promised to share those details with you as you make following and loving him daily the only food your soul craves.

"My food," said Jesus, "is to do the will of him who sent me and to finish his work."
JOHN 4:34

DEBRIEF
- Do I hunger only for the things the world offers me?
- Am I living the plan and purpose God designed uniquely for me?

REPORT
Father, thank you for the one-of-a-kind plan you have for my life here on earth. Thank you that I can know your plan for my life more fully as I consume truth and strength from your Word each day. You have said that we are not designed to live on bread alone, but on every word that comes from your mouth. Lord, help me to more fully rely on your Word and trust your plan for my life. Thank you for true soul food. In Jesus' name I pray. Amen.

for your next devotional reading, go to page 117

[7] "Sir," the invalid replied, "I have no one to help me into the pool when the water is stirred. While I am trying to get in, someone else goes down ahead of me."

[8] Then Jesus said to him, "Get up! Pick up your mat and walk." [9] At once the man was cured; he picked up his mat and walked.

The day on which this took place was a Sabbath, [10] and so the Jewish leaders said to the man who had been healed, "It is the Sabbath; the law forbids you to carry your mat."

[11] But he replied, "The man who made me well said to me, 'Pick up your mat and walk.'"

[12] So they asked him, "Who is this fellow who told you to pick it up and walk?"

[13] The man who was healed had no idea who it was, for Jesus had slipped away into the crowd that was there.

[14] Later Jesus found him at the temple and said to him, "See, you are well again. Stop sinning or something worse may happen to you." [15] The man went away and told the Jewish leaders that it was Jesus who had made him well.

The Authority of the Son

[16] So, because Jesus was doing these things on the Sabbath, the Jewish leaders began to persecute him. [17] In his defense Jesus said to them, "My Father is always at his work to this very day, and I too am working." [18] For this reason they tried all the more to kill him; not only was he breaking the Sabbath, but he was even calling God his own Father, making himself equal with God.

[19] Jesus gave them this answer: "Very truly I tell you, the Son can do nothing by himself; he can do only what he sees his Father doing, because whatever the Father does the Son also does. [20] For the Father loves the Son and shows him all he does. Yes, and he will show him even greater works than these, so that you will be amazed. [21] For just as the Father raises the dead and gives them life, even so the Son gives life to whom he is pleased to give it. [22] Moreover, the Father judges no one, but has entrusted all judgment to the Son, [23] that all may honor the Son just as they honor the Father. Whoever does not honor the Son does not honor the Father, who sent him.

[24] "Very truly I tell you, whoever hears my word and believes him who sent me has eternal life and will not be judged but has crossed over from death to life. [25] Very truly I tell you, a time is coming and has now come when the dead will hear the voice of the Son of God and those who hear will live. [26] For as the Father has life in himself, so he has granted the Son also to have life in himself. [27] And he has given him authority to judge because he is the Son of Man.

[28] "Do not be amazed at this, for a time is coming when all who are in their graves will hear his voice [29] and come out — those who have done what is good will rise to live, and those who have done what is evil will rise to be condemned. [30] By myself I can do nothing; I judge only as I hear, and my judgment is just, for I seek not to please myself but him who sent me.

Testimonies About Jesus

[31] "If I testify about myself, my testimony is not true. [32] There is another who testifies in my favor, and I know that his testimony about me is true.

[33] "You have sent to John and he has testified to the truth. [34] Not that I accept human testimony; but I mention it that you may be saved. [35] John was a lamp that burned and gave light, and you chose for a time to enjoy his light.

[36] "I have testimony weightier than that of John. For the works that the Father has given me to finish — the very works that I am doing — testify that the Father has sent me. [37] And the Father who sent me has himself testified concerning me. You have never heard his voice nor seen his form, [38] nor does his word dwell in you, for you do not believe the one he sent. [39] You study[a] the Scriptures diligently because you think that in them you have eternal life. These are the very Scriptures that testify about me, [40] yet you refuse to come to me to have life.

[41] "I do not accept glory from human beings, [42] but I know you. I know that you do not have the love of God in your hearts. [43] I have come in my Father's name, and you do not accept me; but if someone else comes in his own name, you will accept him. [44] How can you believe since you accept glory from one

[a] 39 Or [39]Study

another but do not seek the glory that comes from the only God[a]?

⁴⁵ "But do not think I will accuse you before the Father. Your accuser is Moses, on whom your hopes are set. ⁴⁶ If you believed Moses, you would believe me, for he wrote about me. ⁴⁷ But since you do not believe what he wrote, how are you going to believe what I say?"

Jesus Feeds the Five Thousand

6 Some time after this, Jesus crossed to the far shore of the Sea of Galilee (that is, the Sea of Tiberias), ² and a great crowd of people followed him because they saw the signs he had performed by healing the sick. ³ Then Jesus went up on a mountainside and sat down with his disciples. ⁴ The Jewish Passover Festival was near.

⁵ When Jesus looked up and saw a great crowd coming toward him, he said to Philip, "Where shall we buy bread for these people to eat?" ⁶ He asked this only to test him, for he already had in mind what he was going to do.

⁷ Philip answered him, "It would take more than half a year's wages[b] to buy enough bread for each one to have a bite!"

⁸ Another of his disciples, Andrew, Simon Peter's brother, spoke up, ⁹ "Here is a boy with five small barley loaves and two small fish, but how far will they go among so many?"

¹⁰ Jesus said, "Have the people sit down." There was plenty of grass in that place, and they sat down (about five thousand men were there). ¹¹ Jesus then took the loaves, gave thanks, and distributed to those who were seated as much as they wanted. He did the same with the fish.

¹² When they had all had enough to eat, he said to his disciples, "Gather the pieces that are left over. Let nothing be wasted." ¹³ So they gathered them and filled twelve baskets with the pieces of the five barley loaves left over by those who had eaten.

¹⁴ After the people saw the sign Jesus performed, they began to say, "Surely this is the Prophet who is to come into the world." ¹⁵ Jesus, knowing that they intended to come and make him king by force, withdrew again to a mountain by himself.

Jesus Walks on the Water

¹⁶ When evening came, his disciples went down to the lake, ¹⁷ where they got into a boat and set off across the lake for Capernaum. By now it was dark, and Jesus had not yet joined them. ¹⁸ A strong wind was blowing and the waters grew rough. ¹⁹ When they had rowed about three or four miles,[c] they saw Jesus approaching the boat, walking on the water; and they were frightened. ²⁰ But he said to them, "It is I; don't be afraid." ²¹ Then they were willing to take him into the boat, and immediately the boat reached the shore where they were heading.

²² The next day the crowd that had stayed on the opposite shore of the lake realized that only one boat had been there, and that Jesus had not entered it with his disciples, but that they had gone away alone. ²³ Then some boats from Tiberias landed near the place where the people had eaten the bread after the Lord had given thanks. ²⁴ Once the crowd realized that neither Jesus nor his disciples were there, they got into the boats and went to Capernaum in search of Jesus.

Jesus the Bread of Life

²⁵ When they found him on the other side of the lake, they asked him, "Rabbi, when did you get here?"

²⁶ Jesus answered, "Very truly I tell you, you are looking for me, not because you saw the signs I performed but because you ate the loaves and had your fill. ²⁷ Do not work for food that spoils, but for food that endures to eternal life, which the Son of Man will give you. For on him God the Father has placed his seal of approval."

²⁸ Then they asked him, "What must we do to do the works God requires?"

²⁹ Jesus answered, "The work of God is this: to believe in the one he has sent."

³⁰ So they asked him, "What sign then will you give that we may see it and believe you? What will you do? ³¹ Our ancestors ate the manna in the wilderness; as it is written: 'He gave them bread from heaven to eat.'[d]"

³² Jesus said to them, "Very truly I tell you, it is not Moses who has given you the bread from heaven, but it is my Father who gives you the true bread from heaven. ³³ For the

---

[a] 44 Some early manuscripts *the Only One*   [b] 7 Greek *take two hundred denarii*   [c] 19 Or about 5 or 6 kilometers   [d] 31 Exodus 16:4; Neh. 9:15; Psalm 78:24,25

bread of God is the bread that comes down from heaven and gives life to the world."

³⁴"Sir," they said, "always give us this bread."

³⁵Then Jesus declared, "I am the bread of life. Whoever comes to me will never go hungry, and whoever believes in me will never be thirsty. ³⁶But as I told you, you have seen me and still you do not believe. ³⁷All those the Father gives me will come to me, and whoever comes to me I will never drive away. ³⁸For I have come down from heaven not to do my will but to do the will of him who sent me. ³⁹And this is the will of him who sent me, that I shall lose none of all those he has given me, but raise them up at the last day. ⁴⁰For my Father's will is that everyone who looks to the Son and believes in him shall have eternal life, and I will raise them up at the last day."

⁴¹At this the Jews there began to grumble about him because he said, "I am the bread that came down from heaven." ⁴²They said, "Is this not Jesus, the son of Joseph, whose father and mother we know? How can he now say, 'I came down from heaven'?"

⁴³"Stop grumbling among yourselves," Jesus answered. ⁴⁴"No one can come to me unless the Father who sent me draws them, and I will raise them up at the last day. ⁴⁵It is written in the Prophets: 'They will all be taught by God.'ᵃ Everyone who has heard the Father and learned from him comes to me. ⁴⁶No one has seen the Father except the one who is from God; only he has seen the Father. ⁴⁷Very truly I tell you, the one who believes has eternal life. ⁴⁸I am the bread of life. ⁴⁹Your ancestors ate the manna in the wilderness, yet they died. ⁵⁰But here is the bread that comes down from heaven, which anyone may eat and not die. ⁵¹I am the living bread that came down from heaven. Whoever eats this bread will live forever. This bread is my flesh, which I will give for the life of the world."

⁵²Then the Jews began to argue sharply among themselves, "How can this man give us his flesh to eat?"

⁵³Jesus said to them, "Very truly I tell you, unless you eat the flesh of the Son of Man and drink his blood, you have no life in you. ⁵⁴Whoever eats my flesh and drinks my blood has eternal life, and I will raise them up at the last day. ⁵⁵For my flesh is real food and my blood is real drink. ⁵⁶Whoever eats my flesh and drinks my blood remains in me, and I in them. ⁵⁷Just as the living Father sent me and I live because of the Father, so the one who feeds on me will live because of me. ⁵⁸This is the bread that came down from heaven. Your ancestors ate manna and died, but whoever feeds on this bread will live forever." ⁵⁹He said this while teaching in the synagogue in Capernaum.

Many Disciples Desert Jesus

⁶⁰On hearing it, many of his disciples said, "This is a hard teaching. Who can accept it?"

⁶¹Aware that his disciples were grumbling about this, Jesus said to them, "Does this offend you? ⁶²Then what if you see the Son of Man ascend to where he was before! ⁶³The Spirit gives life; the flesh counts for nothing. The words I have spoken to you — they are full of the Spiritᵇ and life. ⁶⁴Yet there are some of you who do not believe." For Jesus had known from the beginning which of them did not believe and who would betray him. ⁶⁵He went on to say, "This is why I told you that no one can come to me unless the Father has enabled them."

⁶⁶From this time many of his disciples turned back and no longer followed him.

⁶⁷"You do not want to leave too, do you?" Jesus asked the Twelve.

⁶⁸Simon Peter answered him, "Lord, to whom shall we go? You have the words of eternal life. ⁶⁹We have come to believe and to know that you are the Holy One of God."

⁷⁰Then Jesus replied, "Have I not chosen you, the Twelve? Yet one of you is a devil!" ⁷¹(He meant Judas, the son of Simon Iscariot, who, though one of the Twelve, was later to betray him.)

Jesus Goes to the Festival of Tabernacles

7 After this, Jesus went around in Galilee. He did not wantᶜ to go about in Judea because the Jewish leaders there were looking for a way to kill him. ²But when the Jewish Festival of Tabernacles was near, ³Jesus' brothers said to him, "Leave Galilee and go to Judea, so that your disciples there may see

---

ᵃ 45 Isaiah 54:13   ᵇ 63 Or *are Spirit*; or *are spirit*   ᶜ 1 Some manuscripts *not have authority*

the works you do. [4]No one who wants to become a public figure acts in secret. Since you are doing these things, show yourself to the world." [5]For even his own brothers did not believe in him.

[6]Therefore Jesus told them, "My time is not yet here; for you any time will do. [7]The world cannot hate you, but it hates me because I testify that its works are evil. [8]You go to the festival. I am not[a] going up to this festival, because my time has not yet fully come." [9]After he had said this, he stayed in Galilee.

[10]However, after his brothers had left for the festival, he went also, not publicly, but in secret. [11]Now at the festival the Jewish leaders were watching for Jesus and asking, "Where is he?"

[12]Among the crowds there was widespread whispering about him. Some said, "He is a good man."

Others replied, "No, he deceives the people." [13]But no one would say anything publicly about him for fear of the leaders.

Jesus Teaches at the Festival

[14]Not until halfway through the festival did Jesus go up to the temple courts and begin to teach. [15]The Jews there were amazed and asked, "How did this man get such learning without having been taught?"

[16]Jesus answered, "My teaching is not my own. It comes from the one who sent me. [17]Anyone who chooses to do the will of God will find out whether my teaching comes from God or whether I speak on my own. [18]Whoever speaks on their own does so to gain personal glory, but he who seeks the glory of the one who sent him is a man of truth; there is nothing false about him. [19]Has not Moses given you the law? Yet not one of you keeps the law. Why are you trying to kill me?"

[20]"You are demon-possessed," the crowd answered. "Who is trying to kill you?"

[21]Jesus said to them, "I did one miracle, and you are all amazed. [22]Yet, because Moses gave you circumcision (though actually it did not come from Moses, but from the patriarchs), you circumcise a boy on the Sabbath. [23]Now if a boy can be circumcised on the Sabbath so that the law of Moses may not be broken, why are you angry with me for healing a man's whole body on the Sabbath? [24]Stop judging by mere appearances, but instead judge correctly."

Division Over Who Jesus Is

[25]At that point some of the people of Jerusalem began to ask, "Isn't this the man they are trying to kill? [26]Here he is, speaking publicly, and they are not saying a word to him. Have the authorities really concluded that he is the Messiah? [27]But we know where this man is from; when the Messiah comes, no one will know where he is from."

[28]Then Jesus, still teaching in the temple courts, cried out, "Yes, you know me, and you know where I am from. I am not here on my own authority, but he who sent me is true. You do not know him, [29]but I know him because I am from him and he sent me."

[30]At this they tried to seize him, but no one laid a hand on him, because his hour had not yet come. [31]Still, many in the crowd believed in him. They said, "When the Messiah comes, will he perform more signs than this man?"

[32]The Pharisees heard the crowd whispering such things about him. Then the chief priests and the Pharisees sent temple guards to arrest him.

[33]Jesus said, "I am with you for only a short time, and then I am going to the one who sent me. [34]You will look for me, but you will not find me; and where I am, you cannot come."

[35]The Jews said to one another, "Where does this man intend to go that we cannot find him? Will he go where our people live scattered among the Greeks, and teach the Greeks? [36]What did he mean when he said, 'You will look for me, but you will not find me,' and 'Where I am, you cannot come'?"

[37]On the last and greatest day of the festival, Jesus stood and said in a loud voice, "Let anyone who is thirsty come to me and drink. [38]Whoever believes in me, as Scripture has said, rivers of living water will flow from within them."[b] [39]By this he meant the Spirit, whom those who believed in him were later to receive. Up to that time the Spirit had

---

[a] 8 Some manuscripts *not yet*   [b] 37,38 Or *me. And let anyone drink* [38]*who believes in me." As Scripture has said, "Out of him* (or *them*) *will flow rivers of living water."*

not been given, since Jesus had not yet been glorified.

[40] On hearing his words, some of the people said, "Surely this man is the Prophet."

[41] Others said, "He is the Messiah."

Still others asked, "How can the Messiah come from Galilee? [42] Does not Scripture say that the Messiah will come from David's descendants and from Bethlehem, the town where David lived?" [43] Thus the people were divided because of Jesus. [44] Some wanted to seize him, but no one laid a hand on him.

Unbelief of the Jewish Leaders

[45] Finally the temple guards went back to the chief priests and the Pharisees, who asked them, "Why didn't you bring him in?"

[46] "No one ever spoke the way this man does," the guards replied.

[47] "You mean he has deceived you also?" the Pharisees retorted. [48] "Have any of the rulers or of the Pharisees believed in him? [49] No! But this mob that knows nothing of the law — there is a curse on them."

[50] Nicodemus, who had gone to Jesus earlier and who was one of their own number, asked, [51] "Does our law condemn a man without first hearing him to find out what he has been doing?"

[52] They replied, "Are you from Galilee, too? Look into it, and you will find that a prophet does not come out of Galilee."

[The earliest manuscripts and many other ancient witnesses do not have John 7:53 — 8:11.
A few manuscripts include these verses, wholly or in part, after John 7:36, John 21:25, Luke 21:38 or Luke 24:53.]

8 [53] Then they all went home, [1] but Jesus went to the Mount of Olives.

[2] At dawn he appeared again in the temple courts, where all the people gathered around him, and he sat down to teach them. [3] The teachers of the law and the Pharisees brought in a woman caught in adultery. They made her stand before the group [4] and said to Jesus, "Teacher, this woman was caught in the act of adultery. [5] In the Law Moses commanded us to stone such women. Now what do you say?" [6] They were using this question as a trap, in order to have a basis for accusing him.

But Jesus bent down and started to write on the ground with his finger. [7] When they kept on questioning him, he straightened up and said to them,

"Let any one of you who is without sin be the first to throw a stone at her." [8] Again he stooped down and wrote on the ground.

[9] At this, those who heard began to go away one at a time, the older ones first, until only Jesus was left, with the woman still standing there. [10] Jesus straightened up and asked her, "Woman, where are they? Has no one condemned you?"

[11] "No one, sir," she said.

"Then neither do I condemn you," Jesus declared. "Go now and leave your life of sin."

Dispute Over Jesus' Testimony

[12] When Jesus spoke again to the people, he said, "I am the light of the world. Whoever follows me will never walk in darkness, but will have the light of life."

[13] The Pharisees challenged him, "Here you are, appearing as your own witness; your testimony is not valid."

[14] Jesus answered, "Even if I testify on my own behalf, my testimony is valid, for I know where I came from and where I am going. But you have no idea where I come from or where I am going. [15] You judge by human standards; I pass judgment on no one. [16] But if I do judge, my decisions are true, because I am not alone. I stand with the Father, who sent me. [17] In your own Law it is written that the testimony of two witnesses is true. [18] I am one who testifies for myself; my other witness is the Father, who sent me."

[19] Then they asked him, "Where is your father?"

"You do not know me or my Father," Jesus replied. "If you knew me, you would know my Father also." [20] He spoke these words while teaching in the temple courts near the place where the offerings were put. Yet no one seized him, because his hour had not yet come.

Dispute Over Who Jesus Is

[21] Once more Jesus said to them, "I am going away, and you will look for me, and you will die in your sin. Where I go, you cannot come."

[22] This made the Jews ask, "Will he kill himself? Is that why he says, 'Where I go, you cannot come'?"

[23] But he continued, "You are from below; I am from above. You are of this world; I am not of this world. [24] I told you that you would

Passing Through Someplace Dark

By Marshéle Carter Waddell

READ: John 8:12–20

Even as followers of Jesus, "the light of the world" (John 8:12), our family's journey through combat-related PTSD and a traumatic brain injury (TBI) has been full of dark days. We wandered for years in a maze of emotional pain before medical professionals finally provided the diagnoses.

One of the first lessons God taught us is that PTSD can become something much different when we rely on his promises. PTSD can become "**P**assing **T**hrough **S**omeplace **D**ark." What a tremendous relief to view PTSD as only a dark stretch of life through which we are traveling, not a place where we will establish our permanent address.

Adopting this perspective gave me much hope; however, there are still days so difficult and dark that I am tempted to doubt we will ever reach a place of wholeness again. When those days come, I have two options: I can let the darkness paralyze me or I can inch my way forward even though the path is black as midnight. Every time I have chosen to keep pressing ahead, God has been perfect in his timing to shine just enough light for the next step.

Verdell Davis Krisher wrote in her book, *Let Me Grieve but Not Forever: A Journey Out of the Darkness of Loss,* about the monks of ancient Europe who walked the dark hallways of the monasteries with candles secured to the toes of their shoes, giving light only for the next step. Walking by candlelight required a slower, more deliberate pace. Though small and awkward, the flames that danced on top of their toes carpeted the cold stone floors with a soft, warm spotlight, one step at a time. As the monks placed each foot into the flickering golden glow, they reached their destination without any drama. If the monks took their eyes off the stepping-stones of candlelight or tried to sprint to the prayer meeting, the result was always a bruised brother tangled in a wad of robe, sandals and hot wax.

I'm thankful that I don't have to mess with wicks and wax when I need light for my path. Light is a person, and his name is Jesus. The monks attached candles to their shoes. The Bible is a lamp for our feet and a light on our path (see Psalm 119:105). We who follow Jesus are "children of the light and children of the day" (1 Thessalonians 5:5) and citizens of the kingdom of light (see Colossians 1:12). Jesus is the light we desperately need for those dark nights of the soul. He is the light for the next step.

> When Jesus spoke again to the people, he said, "I am the light of the world. Whoever follows me will never walk in darkness, but will have the light of life."
>
> JOHN 8:12

DEBRIEF

- Am I dwelling in the dark or following the light?
- Where is God throwing a little bit of light on my path today?

REPORT

Lord, you see the end from the beginning, the present in light of the future, the past in perspective of the bigger picture. We are bound by time and space, hopes and dreams, joys and sorrows. Let us not so desire the brilliance of the sun that we miss the glow of your candles. Amen.

for your next devotional reading, go to page 120

die in your sins; if you do not believe that I am he, you will indeed die in your sins."

²⁵ "Who are you?" they asked.

"Just what I have been telling you from the beginning," Jesus replied. ²⁶ "I have much to say in judgment of you. But he who sent me is trustworthy, and what I have heard from him I tell the world."

²⁷ They did not understand that he was telling them about his Father. ²⁸ So Jesus said, "When you have lifted up*a* the Son of Man, then you will know that I am he and that I do nothing on my own but speak just what the Father has taught me. ²⁹ The one who sent me is with me; he has not left me alone, for I always do what pleases him." ³⁰ Even as he spoke, many believed in him.

Dispute Over Whose Children Jesus' Opponents Are

³¹ To the Jews who had believed him, Jesus said, "If you hold to my teaching, you are really my disciples. ³² Then you will know the truth, and the truth will set you free."

³³ They answered him, "We are Abraham's descendants and have never been slaves of anyone. How can you say that we shall be set free?"

³⁴ Jesus replied, "Very truly I tell you, everyone who sins is a slave to sin. ³⁵ Now a slave has no permanent place in the family, but a son belongs to it forever. ³⁶ So if the Son sets you free, you will be free indeed. ³⁷ I know that you are Abraham's descendants. Yet you are looking for a way to kill me, because you have no room for my word. ³⁸ I am telling you what I have seen in the Father's presence, and you are doing what you have heard from your father.*b*"

³⁹ "Abraham is our father," they answered.

"If you were Abraham's children," said Jesus, "then you would*c* do what Abraham did. ⁴⁰ As it is, you are looking for a way to kill me, a man who has told you the truth that I heard from God. Abraham did not do such things. ⁴¹ You are doing the works of your own father."

"We are not illegitimate children," they protested. "The only Father we have is God himself."

⁴² Jesus said to them, "If God were your Father, you would love me, for I have come here from God. I have not come on my own; God sent me. ⁴³ Why is my language not clear to you? Because you are unable to hear what I say. ⁴⁴ You belong to your father, the devil, and you want to carry out your father's desires. He was a murderer from the beginning, not holding to the truth, for there is no truth in him. When he lies, he speaks his native language, for he is a liar and the father of lies. ⁴⁵ Yet because I tell the truth, you do not believe me! ⁴⁶ Can any of you prove me guilty of sin? If I am telling the truth, why don't you believe me? ⁴⁷ Whoever belongs to God hears what God says. The reason you do not hear is that you do not belong to God."

Jesus' Claims About Himself

⁴⁸ The Jews answered him, "Aren't we right in saying that you are a Samaritan and demon-possessed?"

⁴⁹ "I am not possessed by a demon," said Jesus, "but I honor my Father and you dishonor me. ⁵⁰ I am not seeking glory for myself; but there is one who seeks it, and he is the judge. ⁵¹ Very truly I tell you, whoever obeys my word will never see death."

⁵² At this they exclaimed, "Now we know that you are demon-possessed! Abraham died and so did the prophets, yet you say that whoever obeys your word will never taste death. ⁵³ Are you greater than our father Abraham? He died, and so did the prophets. Who do you think you are?"

⁵⁴ Jesus replied, "If I glorify myself, my glory means nothing. My Father, whom you claim as your God, is the one who glorifies me. ⁵⁵ Though you do not know him, I know him. If I said I did not, I would be a liar like you, but I do know him and obey his word. ⁵⁶ Your father Abraham rejoiced at the thought of seeing my day; he saw it and was glad."

⁵⁷ "You are not yet fifty years old," they said to him, "and you have seen Abraham!"

⁵⁸ "Very truly I tell you," Jesus answered, "before Abraham was born, I am!" ⁵⁹ At this, they picked up stones to stone him, but Jesus hid himself, slipping away from the temple grounds.

Jesus Heals a Man Born Blind

9 As he went along, he saw a man blind from birth. ²His disciples asked him,

---

a 28 The Greek for *lifted up* also means *exalted.*   *b 38* Or *presence. Therefore do what you have heard from the Father.*   *c 39* Some early manuscripts *"If you are Abraham's children," said Jesus, "then*

"Rabbi, who sinned, this man or his parents, that he was born blind?"

3 "Neither this man nor his parents sinned," said Jesus, "but this happened so that the works of God might be displayed in him. 4 As long as it is day, we must do the works of him who sent me. Night is coming, when no one can work. 5 While I am in the world, I am the light of the world."

6 After saying this, he spit on the ground, made some mud with the saliva, and put it on the man's eyes. 7 "Go," he told him, "wash in the Pool of Siloam" (this word means "Sent"). So the man went and washed, and came home seeing.

8 His neighbors and those who had formerly seen him begging asked, "Isn't this the same man who used to sit and beg?" 9 Some claimed that he was.

Others said, "No, he only looks like him." But he himself insisted, "I am the man."

10 "How then were your eyes opened?" they asked.

11 He replied, "The man they call Jesus made some mud and put it on my eyes. He told me to go to Siloam and wash. So I went and washed, and then I could see."

12 "Where is this man?" they asked him.

"I don't know," he said.

The Pharisees Investigate the Healing

13 They brought to the Pharisees the man who had been blind. 14 Now the day on which Jesus had made the mud and opened the man's eyes was a Sabbath. 15 Therefore the Pharisees also asked him how he had received his sight. "He put mud on my eyes," the man replied, "and I washed, and now I see."

16 Some of the Pharisees said, "This man is not from God, for he does not keep the Sabbath."

But others asked, "How can a sinner perform such signs?" So they were divided.

17 Then they turned again to the blind man, "What have you to say about him? It was your eyes he opened."

The man replied, "He is a prophet."

18 They still did not believe that he had been blind and had received his sight until they sent for the man's parents. 19 "Is this your son?" they asked. "Is this the one you say was born blind? How is it that now he can see?"

20 "We know he is our son," the parents answered, "and we know he was born blind. 21 But how he can see now, or who opened his eyes, we don't know. Ask him. He is of age; he will speak for himself." 22 His parents said this because they were afraid of the Jewish leaders, who already had decided that anyone who acknowledged that Jesus was the Messiah would be put out of the synagogue. 23 That was why his parents said, "He is of age; ask him."

24 A second time they summoned the man who had been blind. "Give glory to God by telling the truth," they said. "We know this man is a sinner."

25 He replied, "Whether he is a sinner or not, I don't know. One thing I do know. I was blind but now I see!"

26 Then they asked him, "What did he do to you? How did he open your eyes?"

27 He answered, "I have told you already and you did not listen. Why do you want to hear it again? Do you want to become his disciples too?"

28 Then they hurled insults at him and said, "You are this fellow's disciple! We are disciples of Moses! 29 We know that God spoke to Moses, but as for this fellow, we don't even know where he comes from."

30 The man answered, "Now that is remarkable! You don't know where he comes from, yet he opened my eyes. 31 We know that God does not listen to sinners. He listens to the godly person who does his will. 32 Nobody has ever heard of opening the eyes of a man born blind. 33 If this man were not from God, he could do nothing."

34 To this they replied, "You were steeped in sin at birth; how dare you lecture us!" And they threw him out.

Spiritual Blindness

35 Jesus heard that they had thrown him out, and when he found him, he said, "Do you believe in the Son of Man?"

36 "Who is he, sir?" the man asked. "Tell me so that I may believe in him."

37 Jesus said, "You have now seen him; in fact, he is the one speaking with you."

38 Then the man said, "Lord, I believe," and he worshiped him.

39 Jesus said, [a] "For judgment I have come into this world, so that the blind will see and those who see will become blind."

[a] 38,39 Some early manuscripts do not have Then the man said . . . 39 Jesus said.

SURVIVING SULLIVANS CARRY ON

By Jocelyn Green

A knock at the door early one January morning in 1943 brought Thomas Sullivan face to face with three men in naval dress uniforms. "Which one?" Thomas asked.

"I'm sorry," replied one of them. "All five."

George, Francis, Joseph, Madison and Albert Sullivan had enlisted in the Navy after a friend was killed at Pearl Harbor. The one condition of their service was that they be allowed to serve on the same ship. Their request was granted, and all five served on the U.S.S. *Juneau*. And now the Navy had declared all five missing in action in the South Pacific after a torpedo sunk their ship on November 13, 1942.

Grief hung thickly in the air — and yet the clock ticked on. Thomas was due at the Illinois Central Railroad, where he worked as a freight conductor. Turning to his wife, Alleta, he asked, "Shall I go?"

"I knew the train was carrying war freight," Alleta wrote in an article for *The American Magazine*. "If the freight didn't reach the battle fronts in time, it might mean … other boys would die; that other mothers might have to face such grief needlessly, so I said, 'There isn't anything you can do at home. You might as well go.'" So he did.

The following week a letter arrived and was reprinted in the *Waterloo Courier*. It read:

All hope is gone for your boys being found alive. George got off the ship, as his battle station was on a depth charger, but he died on a life raft I was on. The other four boys went down with the ship, and were killed immediately, so they did not suffer … I know you will carry on in the fine Navy spirit.

The surviving Sullivans did carry on. The brothers' sister Genevieve joined the Navy Women Accepted for Volunteer Emergency Service (WAVES) on June 14, 1943, and by 1944, Thomas and Alleta Sullivan had spoken to more than a million workers in war-production plants in 65 cities, urging them to maximize production so the war might end sooner.

"I knew that it had been God's will that my boys should die, and I felt that it must be his will that we should, in some way, carry on the work that they had begun," Alleta wrote. " … I met some mothers and wives who were working on those plants. Some of them had boys who were killed in the same battle which had seen the loss of my sons. These mothers … were in much better spirits than those who grieved and worked alone."

The Sullivans were carrying on for the cause for which their sons had given their lives. In the same way, we as believers must carry on for the cause for which Jesus gave his life. Jesus died so that we might be truly free, not just from other human beings, but from sin itself. Our job is to share the Good News, helping to save the lives of many.

Prayer: Lord, help me to carry on your kingdom work.

"We must do the works of him who sent me."
JOHN 9:4

40 Some Pharisees who were with him heard him say this and asked, "What? Are we blind too?"

41 Jesus said, "If you were blind, you would not be guilty of sin; but now that you claim you can see, your guilt remains.

The Good Shepherd and His Sheep

10 "Very truly I tell you Pharisees, anyone who does not enter the sheep pen by the gate, but climbs in by some other way, is a thief and a robber. 2 The one who enters by the gate is the shepherd of the sheep. 3 The gatekeeper opens the gate for him, and the sheep listen to his voice. He calls his own sheep by name and leads them out. 4 When he has brought out all his own, he goes on ahead of them, and his sheep follow him because they know his voice. 5 But they will never follow a stranger; in fact, they will run away from him because they do not recognize a stranger's voice." 6 Jesus used this figure of speech, but the Pharisees did not understand what he was telling them.

7 Therefore Jesus said again, "Very truly I tell you, I am the gate for the sheep. 8 All who have come before me are thieves and robbers, but the sheep have not listened to them. 9 I am the gate; whoever enters through me will be saved.[a] They will come in and go out, and find pasture. 10 The thief comes only to steal and kill and destroy; I have come that they may have life, and have it to the full.

11 "I am the good shepherd. The good shepherd lays down his life for the sheep. 12 The hired hand is not the shepherd and does not own the sheep. So when he sees the wolf coming, he abandons the sheep and runs away. Then the wolf attacks the flock and scatters it. 13 The man runs away because he is a hired hand and cares nothing for the sheep.

14 "I am the good shepherd; I know my sheep and my sheep know me — 15 just as the Father knows me and I know the Father — and I lay down my life for the sheep. 16 I have other sheep that are not of this sheep pen. I must bring them also. They too will listen to my voice, and there shall be one flock and one shepherd. 17 The reason my Father loves me is that I lay down my life — only to take

it up again. 18 No one takes it from me, but I lay it down of my own accord. I have authority to lay it down and authority to take it up again. This command I received from my Father."

19 The Jews who heard these words were again divided. 20 Many of them said, "He is demon-possessed and raving mad. Why listen to him?"

21 But others said, "These are not the sayings of a man possessed by a demon. Can a demon open the eyes of the blind?"

Further Conflict Over Jesus' Claims

22 Then came the Festival of Dedication[b] at Jerusalem. It was winter, 23 and Jesus was in the temple courts walking in Solomon's Colonnade. 24 The Jews who were there gathered around him, saying, "How long will you keep us in suspense? If you are the Messiah, tell us plainly."

25 Jesus answered, "I did tell you, but you do not believe. The works I do in my Father's name testify about me, 26 but you do not believe because you are not my sheep. 27 My sheep listen to my voice; I know them, and they follow me. 28 I give them eternal life, and they shall never perish; no one will snatch them out of my hand. 29 My Father, who has given them to me, is greater than all[c]; no one can snatch them out of my Father's hand. 30 I and the Father are one."

31 Again his Jewish opponents picked up stones to stone him, 32 but Jesus said to them, "I have shown you many good works from the Father. For which of these do you stone me?"

33 "We are not stoning you for any good work," they replied, "but for blasphemy, because you, a mere man, claim to be God."

34 Jesus answered them, "Is it not written in your Law, 'I have said you are "gods"'[d]? 35 If he called them 'gods,' to whom the word of God came — and Scripture cannot be set aside — 36 what about the one whom the Father set apart as his very own and sent into the world? Why then do you accuse me of blasphemy because I said, 'I am God's Son'? 37 Do not believe me unless I do the works of my Father. 38 But if I do them, even though you do not believe me, believe the works,

---

[a] 9 Or *kept safe*   [b] 22 That is, Hanukkah   [c] 29 Many early manuscripts *What my Father has given me is greater than all*   [d] 34 Psalm 82:6

that you may know and understand that the Father is in me, and I in the Father." [39]Again they tried to seize him, but he escaped their grasp.

[40]Then Jesus went back across the Jordan to the place where John had been baptizing in the early days. There he stayed, [41]and many people came to him. They said, "Though John never performed a sign, all that John said about this man was true." [42]And in that place many believed in Jesus.

The Death of Lazarus

11 Now a man named Lazarus was sick. He was from Bethany, the village of Mary and her sister Martha. [2](This Mary, whose brother Lazarus now lay sick, was the same one who poured perfume on the Lord and wiped his feet with her hair.) [3]So the sisters sent word to Jesus, "Lord, the one you love is sick."

[4]When he heard this, Jesus said, "This sickness will not end in death. No, it is for God's glory so that God's Son may be glorified through it." [5]Now Jesus loved Martha and her sister and Lazarus. [6]So when he heard that Lazarus was sick, he stayed where he was two more days, [7]and then he said to his disciples, "Let us go back to Judea."

[8]"But Rabbi," they said, "a short while ago the Jews there tried to stone you, and yet you are going back?"

[9]Jesus answered, "Are there not twelve hours of daylight? Anyone who walks in the daytime will not stumble, for they see by this world's light. [10]It is when a person walks at night that they stumble, for they have no light."

[11]After he had said this, he went on to tell them, "Our friend Lazarus has fallen asleep; but I am going there to wake him up."

[12]His disciples replied, "Lord, if he sleeps, he will get better." [13]Jesus had been speaking of his death, but his disciples thought he meant natural sleep.

[14]So then he told them plainly, "Lazarus is dead, [15]and for your sake I am glad I was not there, so that you may believe. But let us go to him."

[16]Then Thomas (also known as Didymus[a]) said to the rest of the disciples, "Let us also go, that we may die with him."

Jesus Comforts the Sisters of Lazarus

[17]On his arrival, Jesus found that Lazarus had already been in the tomb for four days. [18]Now Bethany was less than two miles[b] from Jerusalem, [19]and many Jews had come to Martha and Mary to comfort them in the loss of their brother. [20]When Martha heard that Jesus was coming, she went out to meet him, but Mary stayed at home.

[21]"Lord," Martha said to Jesus, "if you had been here, my brother would not have died. [22]But I know that even now God will give you whatever you ask."

[23]Jesus said to her, "Your brother will rise again."

[24]Martha answered, "I know he will rise again in the resurrection at the last day."

[25]Jesus said to her, "I am the resurrection and the life. The one who believes in me will live, even though they die; [26]and whoever lives by believing in me will never die. Do you believe this?"

[27]"Yes, Lord," she replied, "I believe that you are the Messiah, the Son of God, who is to come into the world."

[28]After she had said this, she went back and called her sister Mary aside. "The Teacher is here," she said, "and is asking for you." [29]When Mary heard this, she got up quickly and went to him. [30]Now Jesus had not yet entered the village, but was still at the place where Martha had met him. [31]When the Jews who had been with Mary in the house, comforting her, noticed how quickly she got up and went out, they followed her, supposing she was going to the tomb to mourn there.

[32]When Mary reached the place where Jesus was and saw him, she fell at his feet and said, "Lord, if you had been here, my brother would not have died."

[33]When Jesus saw her weeping, and the Jews who had come along with her also weeping, he was deeply moved in spirit and troubled. [34]"Where have you laid him?" he asked.

"Come and see, Lord," they replied.

[35]Jesus wept.

[36]Then the Jews said, "See how he loved him!"

[37]But some of them said, "Could not he who opened the eyes of the blind man have kept this man from dying?"

---

[a] 16 *Thomas* (Aramaic) and *Didymus* (Greek) both mean *twin*.   [b] 18 Or about 3 kilometers

Dealing With Loss

By Rebekah Benimoff

READ: John 11:1–44

Humans have a need to work through grief rather than push it down and simply survive. Jesus himself was quite familiar with grief, including the time when his good friend Lazarus died. Notice that Jesus took time to grieve this loss, even though he had power over death and the grave.

Jesus surely knows the pull military families feel when tragedy occurs and they cannot retreat into the comfort of shared loss. When word came that Lazarus was ill, Jesus stayed where he was for two more days so the disciples' faith would later increase. Jesus never said it was easy to stay, but he knew God had a purpose. Waiting to travel until after Lazarus died allowed Jesus to fully experience what we go through as we face grief. And what did Jesus do in his grief? "Jesus wept" (John 11:35).

But why did Jesus *weep* when he knew God had given him authority to raise the dead? He was undoubtedly moved by the grief of others who loved Lazarus. And remember, everything he did in his ministry was for a purpose — to glorify God and show us God's way. In a culture where we pride ourselves on being strong, we must remember that Jesus' strength was also expressed through tears. He was strong enough to face grief rather than hide from it. Jesus not only knows but also completely understands grief. And he purposely set the example of healthy grieving.

It's also important to remember that not every loss involves death. There are many kinds of losses: loss of a job, loss of a relationship, and when moving to a faraway place, loss of community. There's also loss of a dream or loss of our expectations for the future. Grief and stress cause toxins to build up in our bodies, and tears are God's gift to us. They bring cleansing and relief. As we cry, toxins flow out of our bodies and healing can begin. Tears are a literal cleansing of the wound. The truth is that when we hold in our grief, we cannot heal. It takes courage to find release, but know you are not alone. There is one who heals, and he stands ready to hold you, to comfort you and to help you through.

As with Lazarus, Jesus has the power to bring new life in places that have only known death and loss. Isaiah 61:3 tells us that God provides for those who grieve. Matthew 5:4 says, "Blessed are those who mourn, for they will be comforted." We can hold God at arm's length and struggle on, or we can allow him to draw near and cover us with his love. Rest assured, healing is worth the work.

Jesus wept.
JOHN 11:35

DEBRIEF
- What losses do I need to grieve?
- Will I invite my Healer into the grieving process?

REPORT
Lord, I know you love me perfectly, as no one else can. You are my safe place. Thank you that I can cry out to you. Teach me how to remain in your embrace and grieve fully, so I can be whole. Amen.

for your next devotional reading, go to page 128

Jesus Raises Lazarus From the Dead

[38]Jesus, once more deeply moved, came to the tomb. It was a cave with a stone laid across the entrance. [39]"Take away the stone," he said.

"But, Lord," said Martha, the sister of the dead man, "by this time there is a bad odor, for he has been there four days."

[40]Then Jesus said, "Did I not tell you that if you believe, you will see the glory of God?"

[41]So they took away the stone. Then Jesus looked up and said, "Father, I thank you that you have heard me. [42]I knew that you always hear me, but I said this for the benefit of the people standing here, that they may believe that you sent me."

[43]When he had said this, Jesus called in a loud voice, "Lazarus, come out!" [44]The dead man came out, his hands and feet wrapped with strips of linen, and a cloth around his face.

Jesus said to them, "Take off the grave clothes and let him go."

The Plot to Kill Jesus

[45]Therefore many of the Jews who had come to visit Mary, and had seen what Jesus did, believed in him. [46]But some of them went to the Pharisees and told them what Jesus had done. [47]Then the chief priests and the Pharisees called a meeting of the Sanhedrin.

"What are we accomplishing?" they asked. "Here is this man performing many signs. [48]If we let him go on like this, everyone will believe in him, and then the Romans will come and take away both our temple and our nation."

[49]Then one of them, named Caiaphas, who was high priest that year, spoke up, "You know nothing at all! [50]You do not realize that it is better for you that one man die for the people than that the whole nation perish."

[51]He did not say this on his own, but as high priest that year he prophesied that Jesus would die for the Jewish nation, [52]and not only for that nation but also for the scattered children of God, to bring them together and make them one. [53]So from that day on they plotted to take his life.

[54]Therefore Jesus no longer moved about publicly among the people of Judea. Instead he withdrew to a region near the wilderness, to a village called Ephraim, where he stayed with his disciples.

[55]When it was almost time for the Jewish Passover, many went up from the country to Jerusalem for their ceremonial cleansing before the Passover. [56]They kept looking for Jesus, and as they stood in the temple courts they asked one another, "What do you think? Isn't he coming to the festival at all?" [57]But the chief priests and the Pharisees had given orders that anyone who found out where Jesus was should report it so that they might arrest him.

Jesus Anointed at Bethany

12 Six days before the Passover, Jesus came to Bethany, where Lazarus lived, whom Jesus had raised from the dead. [2]Here a dinner was given in Jesus' honor. Martha served, while Lazarus was among those reclining at the table with him. [3]Then Mary took about a pint[a] of pure nard, an expensive perfume; she poured it on Jesus' feet and wiped his feet with her hair. And the house was filled with the fragrance of the perfume.

[4]But one of his disciples, Judas Iscariot, who was later to betray him, objected, [5]"Why wasn't this perfume sold and the money given to the poor? It was worth a year's wages.[b]" [6]He did not say this because he cared about the poor but because he was a thief; as keeper of the money bag, he used to help himself to what was put into it.

[7]"Leave her alone," Jesus replied. "It was intended that she should save this perfume for the day of my burial. [8]You will always have the poor among you,[c] but you will not always have me."

[9]Meanwhile a large crowd of Jews found out that Jesus was there and came, not only because of him but also to see Lazarus, whom he had raised from the dead. [10]So the chief priests made plans to kill Lazarus as well, [11]for on account of him many of the Jews were going over to Jesus and believing in him.

Jesus Comes to Jerusalem as King

[12]The next day the great crowd that had come for the festival heard that Jesus was on his way to Jerusalem. [13]They took palm branches and went out to meet him, shouting,

---

[a] 3 Or about 0.5 liter   [b] 5 Greek *three hundred denarii*   [c] 8 See Deut. 15:11.

"Hosanna![a]"

"Blessed is he who comes in the name
of the Lord!"[b]

"Blessed is the king of Israel!"

[14] Jesus found a young donkey and sat on it,
as it is written:

[15] "Do not be afraid, Daughter Zion;
    see, your king is coming,
        seated on a donkey's colt."[c]

[16] At first his disciples did not understand all this. Only after Jesus was glorified
did they realize that these things had been
written about him and that these things had
been done to him.

[17] Now the crowd that was with him when
he called Lazarus from the tomb and raised
him from the dead continued to spread the
word. [18] Many people, because they had
heard that he had performed this sign, went
out to meet him. [19] So the Pharisees said to
one another, "See, this is getting us nowhere.
Look how the whole world has gone after
him!"

Jesus Predicts His Death

[20] Now there were some Greeks among
those who went up to worship at the festival.
[21] They came to Philip, who was from Bethsaida in Galilee, with a request. "Sir," they
said, "we would like to see Jesus." [22] Philip
went to tell Andrew; Andrew and Philip in
turn told Jesus.

[23] Jesus replied, "The hour has come for
the Son of Man to be glorified. [24] Very truly I tell you, unless a kernel of wheat falls
to the ground and dies, it remains only a
single seed. But if it dies, it produces many
seeds. [25] Anyone who loves their life will lose
it, while anyone who hates their life in this
world will keep it for eternal life. [26] Whoever
serves me must follow me; and where I am,
my servant also will be. My Father will honor
the one who serves me.

[27] "Now my soul is troubled, and what
shall I say? 'Father, save me from this hour'?
No, it was for this very reason I came to this
hour. [28] Father, glorify your name!"

Then a voice came from heaven, "I have
glorified it, and will glorify it again." [29] The
crowd that was there and heard it said it had
thundered; others said an angel had spoken
to him.

[30] Jesus said, "This voice was for your benefit, not mine. [31] Now is the time for judgment on this world; now the prince of this
world will be driven out. [32] And I, when I am
lifted up[d] from the earth, will draw all people to myself." [33] He said this to show the
kind of death he was going to die.

[34] The crowd spoke up, "We have heard
from the Law that the Messiah will remain
forever, so how can you say, 'The Son of Man
must be lifted up'? Who is this 'Son of Man'?"

[35] Then Jesus told them, "You are going to
have the light just a little while longer. Walk
while you have the light, before darkness
overtakes you. Whoever walks in the dark
does not know where they are going. [36] Believe in the light while you have the light,
so that you may become children of light."
When he had finished speaking, Jesus left
and hid himself from them.

Belief and Unbelief Among the Jews

[37] Even after Jesus had performed so many
signs in their presence, they still would not
believe in him. [38] This was to fulfill the word
of Isaiah the prophet:

"Lord, who has believed our message
    and to whom has the arm of the Lord
        been revealed?"[e]

[39] For this reason they could not believe,
because, as Isaiah says elsewhere:

[40] "He has blinded their eyes
    and hardened their hearts,
so they can neither see with their eyes,
    nor understand with their hearts,
    nor turn—and I would heal them."[f]

[41] Isaiah said this because he saw Jesus' glory
and spoke about him.

[42] Yet at the same time many even among
the leaders believed in him. But because
of the Pharisees they would not openly acknowledge their faith for fear they would be
put out of the synagogue; [43] for they loved
human praise more than praise from God.

[44] Then Jesus cried out, "Whoever believes

---

[a] 13 A Hebrew expression meaning "Save!" which became an exclamation of praise   [b] 13 Psalm 118:25,26
[c] 15 Zech. 9:9   [d] 32 The Greek for *lifted up* also means *exalted.*   [e] 38 Isaiah 53:1   [f] 40 Isaiah 6:10

in me does not believe in me only, but in the one who sent me. ⁴⁵The one who looks at me is seeing the one who sent me. ⁴⁶I have come into the world as a light, so that no one who believes in me should stay in darkness.

⁴⁷"If anyone hears my words but does not keep them, I do not judge that person. For I did not come to judge the world, but to save the world. ⁴⁸There is a judge for the one who rejects me and does not accept my words; the very words I have spoken will condemn them at the last day. ⁴⁹For I did not speak on my own, but the Father who sent me commanded me to say all that I have spoken. ⁵⁰I know that his command leads to eternal life. So whatever I say is just what the Father has told me to say."

Jesus Washes His Disciples' Feet

13 It was just before the Passover Festival. Jesus knew that the hour had come for him to leave this world and go to the Father. Having loved his own who were in the world, he loved them to the end.

²The evening meal was in progress, and the devil had already prompted Judas, the son of Simon Iscariot, to betray Jesus. ³Jesus knew that the Father had put all things under his power, and that he had come from God and was returning to God; ⁴so he got up from the meal, took off his outer clothing, and wrapped a towel around his waist. ⁵After that, he poured water into a basin and began to wash his disciples' feet, drying them with the towel that was wrapped around him.

⁶He came to Simon Peter, who said to him, "Lord, are you going to wash my feet?"

⁷Jesus replied, "You do not realize now what I am doing, but later you will understand."

⁸"No," said Peter, "you shall never wash my feet."

Jesus answered, "Unless I wash you, you have no part with me."

⁹"Then, Lord," Simon Peter replied, "not just my feet but my hands and my head as well!"

¹⁰Jesus answered, "Those who have had a bath need only to wash their feet; their whole body is clean. And you are clean, though not every one of you." ¹¹For he knew who was go-

ing to betray him, and that was why he said not every one was clean.

¹²When he had finished washing their feet, he put on his clothes and returned to his place. "Do you understand what I have done for you?" he asked them. ¹³"You call me 'Teacher' and 'Lord,' and rightly so, for that is what I am. ¹⁴Now that I, your Lord and Teacher, have washed your feet, you also should wash one another's feet. ¹⁵I have set you an example that you should do as I have done for you. ¹⁶Very truly I tell you, no servant is greater than his master, nor is a messenger greater than the one who sent him. ¹⁷Now that you know these things, you will be blessed if you do them.

Jesus Predicts His Betrayal

¹⁸"I am not referring to all of you; I know those I have chosen. But this is to fulfill this passage of Scripture: 'He who shared my bread has turned[a] against me.'[b]

¹⁹"I am telling you now before it happens, so that when it does happen you will believe that I am who I am. ²⁰Very truly I tell you, whoever accepts anyone I send accepts me; and whoever accepts me accepts the one who sent me."

²¹After he had said this, Jesus was troubled in spirit and testified, "Very truly I tell you, one of you is going to betray me."

²²His disciples stared at one another, at a loss to know which of them he meant. ²³One of them, the disciple whom Jesus loved, was reclining next to him. ²⁴Simon Peter motioned to this disciple and said, "Ask him which one he means."

²⁵Leaning back against Jesus, he asked him, "Lord, who is it?"

²⁶Jesus answered, "It is the one to whom I will give this piece of bread when I have dipped it in the dish." Then, dipping the piece of bread, he gave it to Judas, the son of Simon Iscariot. ²⁷As soon as Judas took the bread, Satan entered into him.

So Jesus told him, "What you are about to do, do quickly." ²⁸But no one at the meal understood why Jesus said this to him. ²⁹Since Judas had charge of the money, some thought Jesus was telling him to buy what was needed for the festival, or to give something to the poor. ³⁰As soon as Judas

---

[a] 18 Greek *has lifted up his heel*   [b] 18 Psalm 41:9

had taken the bread, he went out. And it was night.

Jesus Predicts Peter's Denial

[31] When he was gone, Jesus said, "Now the Son of Man is glorified and God is glorified in him. [32] If God is glorified in him,[a] God will glorify the Son in himself, and will glorify him at once.

[33] "My children, I will be with you only a little longer. You will look for me, and just as I told the Jews, so I tell you now: Where I am going, you cannot come.

[34] "A new command I give you: Love one another. As I have loved you, so you must love one another. [35] By this everyone will know that you are my disciples, if you love one another."

[36] Simon Peter asked him, "Lord, where are you going?"

Jesus replied, "Where I am going, you cannot follow now, but you will follow later."

[37] Peter asked, "Lord, why can't I follow you now? I will lay down my life for you."

[38] Then Jesus answered, "Will you really lay down your life for me? Very truly I tell you, before the rooster crows, you will disown me three times!

Jesus Comforts His Disciples

14 "Do not let your hearts be troubled. You believe in God[b]; believe also in me. [2] My Father's house has many rooms; if that were not so, would I have told you that I am going there to prepare a place for you? [3] And if I go and prepare a place for you, I will come back and take you to be with me that you also may be where I am. [4] You know the way to the place where I am going."

Jesus the Way to the Father

[5] Thomas said to him, "Lord, we don't know where you are going, so how can we know the way?"

[6] Jesus answered, "I am the way and the truth and the life. No one comes to the Father except through me. [7] If you really know me, you will know[c] my Father as well. From now on, you do know him and have seen him."

[8] Philip said, "Lord, show us the Father and that will be enough for us."

[9] Jesus answered: "Don't you know me, Philip, even after I have been among you such a long time? Anyone who has seen me has seen the Father. How can you say, 'Show us the Father'? [10] Don't you believe that I am in the Father, and that the Father is in me? The words I say to you I do not speak on my own authority. Rather, it is the Father, living in me, who is doing his work. [11] Believe me when I say that I am in the Father and the Father is in me; or at least believe on the evidence of the works themselves. [12] Very truly I tell you, whoever believes in me will do the works I have been doing, and they will do even greater things than these, because I am going to the Father. [13] And I will do whatever you ask in my name, so that the Father may be glorified in the Son. [14] You may ask me for anything in my name, and I will do it.

Jesus Promises the Holy Spirit

[15] "If you love me, keep my commands. [16] And I will ask the Father, and he will give you another advocate to help you and be with you forever— [17] the Spirit of truth. The world cannot accept him, because it neither sees him nor knows him. But you know him, for he lives with you and will be[d] in you. [18] I will not leave you as orphans; I will come to you. [19] Before long, the world will not see me anymore, but you will see me. Because I live, you also will live. [20] On that day you will realize that I am in my Father, and you are in me, and I am in you. [21] Whoever has my commands and keeps them is the one who loves me. The one who loves me will be loved by my Father, and I too will love them and show myself to them."

[22] Then Judas (not Judas Iscariot) said, "But, Lord, why do you intend to show yourself to us and not to the world?"

[23] Jesus replied, "Anyone who loves me will obey my teaching. My Father will love them, and we will come to them and make our home with them. [24] Anyone who does not love me will not obey my teaching. These words you hear are not my own; they belong to the Father who sent me.

[25] "All this I have spoken while still with you. [26] But the Advocate, the Holy Spirit, whom the Father will send in my name, will teach you all things and will remind you of

---

[a] 32 Many early manuscripts do not have *If God is glorified in him.*   [b] 1 Or *Believe in God*   [c] 7 Some manuscripts *If you really knew me, you would know*   [d] 17 Some early manuscripts *and is*

Peace in Trying Circumstances

By Sheryl Shearer

READ: John 14:15–31

For the past year, peace has been a slippery thing to grasp because of health issues. After a series of tests, the potential diagnosis petrified me. I lost my father to cancer a few years ago and continually wondered if this was my time. The results always came back negative, yet the health problems remained — and so did my troubled heart.

Jesus promised us peace that is beyond peace of mind and beyond a truce with our enemies. This "peace" (Greek, *eirçnç*) is equivalent to the Old Testament concept of *shalom* (Hebrew). We see this in the priestly blessing: "The LORD bless you and keep you ... the LORD turn his face toward you and give you peace [*shalom*]" (Numbers 6:24,26). The Hebrew understanding of *shalom* embraced a holistic view, that is, a view of the entire person — spirit, soul, body.

Our fallen nature and fractured world present challenges to experiencing this peace. We must examine ourselves from God's perspective. After nine months of sickness, I discerned that my physical issues resulted from a spiritual cancer that infected my soul: unforgiveness. God reached me through the story of Corrie ten Boom.

During World War II, a man betrayed the Ten Boom family, who had helped many Jews escape the Nazi Holocaust, and the family was sent to concentration camps. Corrie was eventually released, but Corrie's father and sister, Betsie, died while imprisoned.

While imprisoned, Betsie forgave their betrayer and the Nazis. The peace of Christ controlled Betsie's heart and shaped her perspective, so that even while imprisoned, she lived in *shalom*. Corrie, however, struggled to forgive the betrayer. Consequently, her spirit became as captive as her body until she finally relented and forgave. Then peace and joy filled her heart anew.

Like Corrie, unforgiveness impeded Christ's peace in my life and began to affect my physical being. When I confessed my sin of unforgiveness, the burden lifted and the darkness left. God's peace flooded my heart. At my next doctor's appointment, the nurse said, "Everything's gone." Whether the news had been dire or all clear, I had acknowledged my sin and knew that Christ's peace reigned in my heart and governed my life.

God's shalom peace doesn't always change our circumstances. But it changes us. If you desire the peace that Jesus gives, pray Psalm 139:23–24. Cleanse your heart, through the power of the Holy Spirit, and let Jesus give you inner rest.

"Peace I leave with you; my peace I give you. I do not give to you as the world gives. Do not let your hearts be troubled and do not be afraid."
JOHN 14:27

DEBRIEF
- Am I honest with myself and with God about my sin?
- Is there anything in my life hindering me from enjoying *shalom*?

REPORT
Lord, cleanse my heart from all sin, and allow me to experience the peace that only you can give. Amen.

everything I have said to you. [27]Peace I leave with you; my peace I give you. I do not give to you as the world gives. Do not let your hearts be troubled and do not be afraid.

[28]"You heard me say, 'I am going away and I am coming back to you.' If you loved me, you would be glad that I am going to the Father, for the Father is greater than I. [29]I have told you now before it happens, so that when it does happen you will believe. [30]I will not say much more to you, for the prince of this world is coming. He has no hold over me, [31]but he comes so that the world may learn that I love the Father and do exactly what my Father has commanded me.

"Come now; let us leave.

The Vine and the Branches

15 "I am the true vine, and my Father is the gardener. [2]He cuts off every branch in me that bears no fruit, while every branch that does bear fruit he prunes[a] so that it will be even more fruitful. [3]You are already clean because of the word I have spoken to you. [4]Remain in me, as I also remain in you. No branch can bear fruit by itself; it must remain in the vine. Neither can you bear fruit unless you remain in me.

[5]"I am the vine; you are the branches. If you remain in me and I in you, you will bear much fruit; apart from me you can do nothing. [6]If you do not remain in me, you are like a branch that is thrown away and withers; such branches are picked up, thrown into the fire and burned. [7]If you remain in me and my words remain in you, ask whatever you wish, and it will be done for you. [8]This is to my Father's glory, that you bear much fruit, showing yourselves to be my disciples.

[9]"As the Father has loved me, so have I loved you. Now remain in my love. [10]If you keep my commands, you will remain in my love, just as I have kept my Father's commands and remain in his love. [11]I have told you this so that my joy may be in you and that your joy may be complete. [12]My command is this: Love each other as I have loved you. [13]Greater love has no one than this: to lay down one's life for one's friends. [14]You are my friends if you do what I command. [15]I no longer call you servants, because a servant does not know his master's business.

Instead, I have called you friends, for everything that I learned from my Father I have made known to you. [16]You did not choose me, but I chose you and appointed you so that you might go and bear fruit — fruit that will last — and so that whatever you ask in my name the Father will give you. [17]This is my command: Love each other.

The World Hates the Disciples

[18]"If the world hates you, keep in mind that it hated me first. [19]If you belonged to the world, it would love you as its own. As it is, you do not belong to the world, but I have chosen you out of the world. That is why the world hates you. [20]Remember what I told you: 'A servant is not greater than his master.'[b] If they persecuted me, they will persecute you also. If they obeyed my teaching, they will obey yours also. [21]They will treat you this way because of my name, for they do not know the one who sent me. [22]If I had not come and spoken to them, they would not be guilty of sin; but now they have no excuse for their sin. [23]Whoever hates me hates my Father as well. [24]If I had not done among them the works no one else did, they would not be guilty of sin. As it is, they have seen, and yet they have hated both me and my Father. [25]But this is to fulfill what is written in their Law: 'They hated me without reason.'[c]

The Work of the Holy Spirit

[26]"When the Advocate comes, whom I will send to you from the Father — the Spirit of truth who goes out from the Father — he will testify about me. [27]And you also must testify, for you have been with me from the beginning.

16 "All this I have told you so that you will not fall away. [2]They will put you out of the synagogue; in fact, the time is coming when anyone who kills you will think they are offering a service to God. [3]They will do such things because they have not known the Father or me. [4]I have told you this, so that when their time comes you will remember that I warned you about them. I did not tell you this from the beginning because I was with you, [5]but now I am going to him who sent me. None of you asks me, 'Where are you going?' [6]Rather, you are filled with grief

---

[a] 2 The Greek for *he prunes* also means *he cleans.*   [b] 20 John 13:16   [c] 25 Psalms 35:19; 69:4

because I have said these things. ⁷But very truly I tell you, it is for your good that I am going away. Unless I go away, the Advocate will not come to you; but if I go, I will send him to you. ⁸When he comes, he will prove the world to be in the wrong about sin and righteousness and judgment: ⁹about sin, because people do not believe in me; ¹⁰about righteousness, because I am going to the Father, where you can see me no longer; ¹¹and about judgment, because the prince of this world now stands condemned.

¹²"I have much more to say to you, more than you can now bear. ¹³But when he, the Spirit of truth, comes, he will guide you into all the truth. He will not speak on his own; he will speak only what he hears, and he will tell you what is yet to come. ¹⁴He will glorify me because it is from me that he will receive what he will make known to you. ¹⁵All that belongs to the Father is mine. That is why I said the Spirit will receive from me what he will make known to you."

The Disciples' Grief Will Turn to Joy

¹⁶Jesus went on to say, "In a little while you will see me no more, and then after a little while you will see me."

¹⁷At this, some of his disciples said to one another, "What does he mean by saying, 'In a little while you will see me no more, and then after a little while you will see me,' and 'Because I am going to the Father'?" ¹⁸They kept asking, "What does he mean by 'a little while'? We don't understand what he is saying."

¹⁹Jesus saw that they wanted to ask him about this, so he said to them, "Are you asking one another what I meant when I said, 'In a little while you will see me no more, and then after a little while you will see me'? ²⁰Very truly I tell you, you will weep and mourn while the world rejoices. You will grieve, but your grief will turn to joy. ²¹A woman giving birth to a child has pain because her time has come; but when her baby is born she forgets the anguish because of her joy that a child is born into the world. ²²So with you: Now is your time of grief, but I will see you again and you will rejoice, and no one will take away your joy. ²³In that day you will no longer ask me anything. Very truly I tell you, my Father will give you whatever you ask in my name. ²⁴Until now you have not asked for anything in my name. Ask and you will receive, and your joy will be complete.

²⁵"Though I have been speaking figuratively, a time is coming when I will no longer use this kind of language but will tell you plainly about my Father. ²⁶In that day you will ask in my name. I am not saying that I will ask the Father on your behalf. ²⁷No, the Father himself loves you because you have loved me and have believed that I came from God. ²⁸I came from the Father and entered the world; now I am leaving the world and going back to the Father."

²⁹Then Jesus' disciples said, "Now you are speaking clearly and without figures of speech. ³⁰Now we can see that you know all things and that you do not even need to have anyone ask you questions. This makes us believe that you came from God."

³¹"Do you now believe?" Jesus replied. ³²"A time is coming and in fact has come when you will be scattered, each to your own home. You will leave me all alone. Yet I am not alone, for my Father is with me.

³³"I have told you these things, so that in me you may have peace. In this world you will have trouble. But take heart! I have overcome the world."

Jesus Prays to Be Glorified

17 After Jesus said this, he looked toward heaven and prayed:

"Father, the hour has come. Glorify your Son, that your Son may glorify you. ²For you granted him authority over all people that he might give eternal life to all those you have given him. ³Now this is eternal life: that they know you, the only true God, and Jesus Christ, whom you have sent. ⁴I have brought you glory on earth by finishing the work you gave me to do. ⁵And now, Father, glorify me in your presence with the glory I had with you before the world began.

Jesus Prays for His Disciples

⁶"I have revealed you*ᵃ* to those whom you gave me out of the world. They were yours; you gave them to

ᵃ 6 Greek *your name*

me and they have obeyed your word. ⁷Now they know that everything you have given me comes from you. ⁸For I gave them the words you gave me and they accepted them. They knew with certainty that I came from you, and they believed that you sent me. ⁹I pray for them. I am not praying for the world, but for those you have given me, for they are yours. ¹⁰All I have is yours, and all you have is mine. And glory has come to me through them. ¹¹I will remain in the world no longer, but they are still in the world, and I am coming to you. Holy Father, protect them by the power of ᵃ your name, the name you gave me, so that they may be one as we are one. ¹²While I was with them, I protected them and kept them safe by ᵇ that name you gave me. None has been lost except the one doomed to destruction so that Scripture would be fulfilled.

¹³"I am coming to you now, but I say these things while I am still in the world, so that they may have the full measure of my joy within them. ¹⁴I have given them your word and the world has hated them, for they are not of the world any more than I am of the world. ¹⁵My prayer is not that you take them out of the world but that you protect them from the evil one. ¹⁶They are not of the world, even as I am not of it. ¹⁷Sanctify them by ᶜ the truth; your word is truth. ¹⁸As you sent me into the world, I have sent them into the world. ¹⁹For them I sanctify myself, that they too may be truly sanctified.

Jesus Prays for All Believers

²⁰"My prayer is not for them alone. I pray also for those who will believe in me through their message, ²¹that all of them may be one, Father, just as you are in me and I am in you. May they also be in us so that the world may believe that you have sent me. ²²I have given them the glory that you gave me, that they may be one as we are one— ²³I in them and you in me—so that they may be brought to complete unity. Then

the world will know that you sent me and have loved them even as you have loved me.

²⁴"Father, I want those you have given me to be with me where I am, and to see my glory, the glory you have given me because you loved me before the creation of the world.

²⁵"Righteous Father, though the world does not know you, I know you, and they know that you have sent me. ²⁶I have made you ᵈ known to them, and will continue to make you known in order that the love you have for me may be in them and that I myself may be in them."

Jesus Arrested

18 When he had finished praying, Jesus left with his disciples and crossed the Kidron Valley. On the other side there was a garden, and he and his disciples went into it.

²Now Judas, who betrayed him, knew the place, because Jesus had often met there with his disciples. ³So Judas came to the garden, guiding a detachment of soldiers and some officials from the chief priests and the Pharisees. They were carrying torches, lanterns and weapons.

⁴Jesus, knowing all that was going to happen to him, went out and asked them, "Who is it you want?"

⁵"Jesus of Nazareth," they replied.

"I am he," Jesus said. (And Judas the traitor was standing there with them.) ⁶When Jesus said, "I am he," they drew back and fell to the ground.

⁷Again he asked them, "Who is it you want?"

"Jesus of Nazareth," they said.

⁸Jesus answered, "I told you that I am he. If you are looking for me, then let these men go." ⁹This happened so that the words he had spoken would be fulfilled: "I have not lost one of those you gave me." ᵉ

¹⁰Then Simon Peter, who had a sword, drew it and struck the high priest's servant, cutting off his right ear. (The servant's name was Malchus.)

¹¹Jesus commanded Peter, "Put your sword away! Shall I not drink the cup the Father has given me?"

ᵃ 11 Or Father, keep them faithful to   ᵇ 12 Or kept them faithful to   ᶜ 17 Or them to live in accordance with   ᵈ 26 Greek your name   ᵉ 9 John 6:39

[12]Then the detachment of soldiers with its commander and the Jewish officials arrested Jesus. They bound him [13]and brought him first to Annas, who was the father-in-law of Caiaphas, the high priest that year. [14]Caiaphas was the one who had advised the Jewish leaders that it would be good if one man died for the people.

Peter's First Denial

[15]Simon Peter and another disciple were following Jesus. Because this disciple was known to the high priest, he went with Jesus into the high priest's courtyard, [16]but Peter had to wait outside at the door. The other disciple, who was known to the high priest, came back, spoke to the servant girl on duty there and brought Peter in.

[17]"You aren't one of this man's disciples too, are you?" she asked Peter.

He replied, "I am not."

[18]It was cold, and the servants and officials stood around a fire they had made to keep warm. Peter also was standing with them, warming himself.

The High Priest Questions Jesus

[19]Meanwhile, the high priest questioned Jesus about his disciples and his teaching.

[20]"I have spoken openly to the world," Jesus replied. "I always taught in synagogues or at the temple, where all the Jews come together. I said nothing in secret. [21]Why question me? Ask those who heard me. Surely they know what I said."

[22]When Jesus said this, one of the officials nearby slapped him in the face. "Is this the way you answer the high priest?" he demanded.

[23]"If I said something wrong," Jesus replied, "testify as to what is wrong. But if I spoke the truth, why did you strike me?" [24]Then Annas sent him bound to Caiaphas the high priest.

Peter's Second and Third Denials

[25]Meanwhile, Simon Peter was still standing there warming himself. So they asked him, "You aren't one of his disciples too, are you?"

He denied it, saying, "I am not."

[26]One of the high priest's servants, a relative of the man whose ear Peter had cut off, challenged him, "Didn't I see you with him

in the garden?" [27]Again Peter denied it, and at that moment a rooster began to crow.

Jesus Before Pilate

[28]Then the Jewish leaders took Jesus from Caiaphas to the palace of the Roman governor. By now it was early morning, and to avoid ceremonial uncleanness they did not enter the palace, because they wanted to be able to eat the Passover. [29]So Pilate came out to them and asked, "What charges are you bringing against this man?"

[30]"If he were not a criminal," they replied, "we would not have handed him over to you."

[31]Pilate said, "Take him yourselves and judge him by your own law."

"But we have no right to execute anyone," they objected. [32]This took place to fulfill what Jesus had said about the kind of death he was going to die.

[33]Pilate then went back inside the palace, summoned Jesus and asked him, "Are you the king of the Jews?"

[34]"Is that your own idea," Jesus asked, "or did others talk to you about me?"

[35]"Am I a Jew?" Pilate replied. "Your own people and chief priests handed you over to me. What is it you have done?"

[36]Jesus said, "My kingdom is not of this world. If it were, my servants would fight to prevent my arrest by the Jewish leaders. But now my kingdom is from another place."

[37]"You are a king, then!" said Pilate.

Jesus answered, "You say that I am a king. In fact, the reason I was born and came into the world is to testify to the truth. Everyone on the side of truth listens to me."

[38]"What is truth?" retorted Pilate. With this he went out again to the Jews gathered there and said, "I find no basis for a charge against him. [39]But it is your custom for me to release to you one prisoner at the time of the Passover. Do you want me to release 'the king of the Jews'?"

[40]They shouted back, "No, not him! Give us Barabbas!" Now Barabbas had taken part in an uprising.

Jesus Sentenced to Be Crucified

19 Then Pilate took Jesus and had him flogged. [2]The soldiers twisted together a crown of thorns and put it on his head. They clothed him in a purple robe [3]and went

up to him again and again, saying, "Hail, king of the Jews!" And they slapped him in the face.

[4] Once more Pilate came out and said to the Jews gathered there, "Look, I am bringing him out to you to let you know that I find no basis for a charge against him." [5] When Jesus came out wearing the crown of thorns and the purple robe, Pilate said to them, "Here is the man!"

[6] As soon as the chief priests and their officials saw him, they shouted, "Crucify! Crucify!"

But Pilate answered, "You take him and crucify him. As for me, I find no basis for a charge against him."

[7] The Jewish leaders insisted, "We have a law, and according to that law he must die, because he claimed to be the Son of God."

[8] When Pilate heard this, he was even more afraid, [9] and he went back inside the palace. "Where do you come from?" he asked Jesus, but Jesus gave him no answer. [10] "Do you refuse to speak to me?" Pilate said. "Don't you realize I have power either to free you or to crucify you?"

[11] Jesus answered, "You would have no power over me if it were not given to you from above. Therefore the one who handed me over to you is guilty of a greater sin."

[12] From then on, Pilate tried to set Jesus free, but the Jewish leaders kept shouting, "If you let this man go, you are no friend of Caesar. Anyone who claims to be a king opposes Caesar."

[13] When Pilate heard this, he brought Jesus out and sat down on the judge's seat at a place known as the Stone Pavement (which in Aramaic is Gabbatha). [14] It was the day of Preparation of the Passover; it was about noon.

"Here is your king," Pilate said to the Jews.

[15] But they shouted, "Take him away! Take him away! Crucify him!"

"Shall I crucify your king?" Pilate asked.

"We have no king but Caesar," the chief priests answered.

[16] Finally Pilate handed him over to them to be crucified.

The Crucifixion of Jesus

So the soldiers took charge of Jesus. [17] Carrying his own cross, he went out to the place of the Skull (which in Aramaic is called Golgotha). [18] There they crucified him, and with him two others — one on each side and Jesus in the middle.

[19] Pilate had a notice prepared and fastened to the cross. It read: JESUS OF NAZARETH, THE KING OF THE JEWS. [20] Many of the Jews read this sign, for the place where Jesus was crucified was near the city, and the sign was written in Aramaic, Latin and Greek. [21] The chief priests of the Jews protested to Pilate, "Do not write 'The King of the Jews,' but that this man claimed to be king of the Jews."

[22] Pilate answered, "What I have written, I have written."

[23] When the soldiers crucified Jesus, they took his clothes, dividing them into four shares, one for each of them, with the undergarment remaining. This garment was seamless, woven in one piece from top to bottom.

[24] "Let's not tear it," they said to one another. "Let's decide by lot who will get it."

This happened that the scripture might be fulfilled that said,

"They divided my clothes among them
    and cast lots for my garment."[a]

So this is what the soldiers did.

[25] Near the cross of Jesus stood his mother, his mother's sister, Mary the wife of Clopas, and Mary Magdalene. [26] When Jesus saw his mother there, and the disciple whom he loved standing nearby, he said to her, "Woman,[b] here is your son," [27] and to the disciple, "Here is your mother." From that time on, this disciple took her into his home.

The Death of Jesus

[28] Later, knowing that everything had now been finished, and so that Scripture would be fulfilled, Jesus said, "I am thirsty." [29] A jar of wine vinegar was there, so they soaked a sponge in it, put the sponge on a stalk of the hyssop plant, and lifted it to Jesus' lips. [30] When he had received the drink, Jesus said, "It is finished." With that, he bowed his head and gave up his spirit.

[31] Now it was the day of Preparation, and the next day was to be a special Sabbath. Because the Jewish leaders did not want the

---

[a] 24 Psalm 22:18   [b] 26 The Greek for *Woman* does not denote any disrespect.

bodies left on the crosses during the Sabbath, they asked Pilate to have the legs broken and the bodies taken down. [32] The soldiers therefore came and broke the legs of the first man who had been crucified with Jesus, and then those of the other. [33] But when they came to Jesus and found that he was already dead, they did not break his legs. [34] Instead, one of the soldiers pierced Jesus' side with a spear, bringing a sudden flow of blood and water. [35] The man who saw it has given testimony, and his testimony is true. He knows that he tells the truth, and he testifies so that you also may believe. [36] These things happened so that the scripture would be fulfilled: "Not one of his bones will be broken,"[a] [37] and, as another scripture says, "They will look on the one they have pierced."[b]

The Burial of Jesus

[38] Later, Joseph of Arimathea asked Pilate for the body of Jesus. Now Joseph was a disciple of Jesus, but secretly because he feared the Jewish leaders. With Pilate's permission, he came and took the body away. [39] He was accompanied by Nicodemus, the man who earlier had visited Jesus at night. Nicodemus brought a mixture of myrrh and aloes, about seventy-five pounds.[c] [40] Taking Jesus' body, the two of them wrapped it, with the spices, in strips of linen. This was in accordance with Jewish burial customs. [41] At the place where Jesus was crucified, there was a garden, and in the garden a new tomb, in which no one had ever been laid. [42] Because it was the Jewish day of Preparation and since the tomb was nearby, they laid Jesus there.

The Empty Tomb

20 Early on the first day of the week, while it was still dark, Mary Magdalene went to the tomb and saw that the stone had been removed from the entrance. [2] So she came running to Simon Peter and the other disciple, the one Jesus loved, and said, "They have taken the Lord out of the tomb, and we don't know where they have put him!"

[3] So Peter and the other disciple started for the tomb. [4] Both were running, but the other disciple outran Peter and reached the tomb first. [5] He bent over and looked in at the strips of linen lying there but did not go in. [6] Then Simon Peter came along behind him and went straight into the tomb. He saw the strips of linen lying there, [7] as well as the cloth that had been wrapped around Jesus' head. The cloth was still lying in its place, separate from the linen. [8] Finally the other disciple, who had reached the tomb first, also went inside. He saw and believed. [9] (They still did not understand from Scripture that Jesus had to rise from the dead.) [10] Then the disciples went back to where they were staying.

Jesus Appears to Mary Magdalene

[11] Now Mary stood outside the tomb crying. As she wept, she bent over to look into the tomb [12] and saw two angels in white, seated where Jesus' body had been, one at the head and the other at the foot.

[13] They asked her, "Woman, why are you crying?"

"They have taken my Lord away," she said, "and I don't know where they have put him." [14] At this, she turned around and saw Jesus standing there, but she did not realize that it was Jesus.

[15] He asked her, "Woman, why are you crying? Who is it you are looking for?"

Thinking he was the gardener, she said, "Sir, if you have carried him away, tell me where you have put him, and I will get him."

[16] Jesus said to her, "Mary."

She turned toward him and cried out in Aramaic, "Rabboni!" (which means "Teacher").

[17] Jesus said, "Do not hold on to me, for I have not yet ascended to the Father. Go instead to my brothers and tell them, 'I am ascending to my Father and your Father, to my God and your God.'"

[18] Mary Magdalene went to the disciples with the news: "I have seen the Lord!" And she told them that he had said these things to her.

Jesus Appears to His Disciples

[19] On the evening of that first day of the week, when the disciples were together, with the doors locked for fear of the Jewish leaders, Jesus came and stood among them and said, "Peace be with you!" [20] After he said

---

[a] 36 Exodus 12:46; Num. 9:12; Psalm 34:20   [b] 37 Zech. 12:10   [c] 39 Or about 34 kilograms

Do We Dare Believe?

By Leeana Tankersley

READ: John 20:19–29

Sometimes God feels far away. Through work-ups, deployments, redeployments and knowing few specifics about my husband's job, I've too often asked God where he might be. My latest search for him is in the experiences of mothering small children in the midst of military life.

I've got a wild-eyed set of boy-girl twin toddlers, a precious itty-bitty baby girl, a regrettably unspiritual internal monologue, and subpar personal hygiene. Recently, I saw a fresh-looking 20-something walking down the street. She had on enviable boots, her hair was pulled back into a messy-on-purpose chignon, and she was carrying a *venti* Starbucks and an I've-got-things-together sort of handbag. She was clean, newly washed, and I was the furthest thing from such ease. I started crying right there at the red light as I watched her float down the street, while I felt like nothing more than a big barnacle.

These are critical moments for me — moments when I will either torment myself with self-loathing and despair or allow God to be near me. The voices in my head beat me down: "The other Navy wives can handle life, why can't you?" Where is God in the ugly toxicity of my inner thoughts? Or when I'm doing time on the living room floor, crazed and unshowered?

The answer, of course, is: God is here. Right here. With me. In the middle of all the crazy yuck. But do I believe it? Do *you* believe he's with *you*?

When the disciples first heard, on the third day after Jesus' death on the cross, that Jesus was alive, they didn't believe it (see Luke 24:11). That evening, Jesus suddenly appeared inside the locked room where the disciples were hiding out, and they had no choice but to believe (see John 20:19–20). But since Thomas happened to be gone at the time, he declared that he simply couldn't believe it was true (see John 20:24–25). Even though Jesus had previously predicted his death and resurrection (see Mark 8:31; 9:31), Thomas simply didn't believe the good news because it just seemed too good to be true.

As easy as it is to condemn Thomas and the other disciples, how many of us do the same thing? Because we don't see him, we don't think he's present. But we need to remember that although Jesus isn't physically present, his spirit is. When we *feel* like God is not with us, we need to remember these comforting words: "Surely I am with you always, to the very end of the age" (Matthew 28:20). When we find ourselves relying on our own perspective rather than on the truth of God's Word, may we pray like the man in Mark 9:24, "I do believe; help me overcome my unbelief!"

> Now Thomas (also known as Didymus), one of the Twelve, was not with the disciples when Jesus came. So the other disciples told him, "We have seen the Lord!" But he said to them, "Unless I see the nail marks in his hands and put my finger where the nails were, and put my hand into his side, I will not believe."
>
> JOHN 20:24–25

DEBRIEF

- What am I having trouble believing, even though the Bible says it's true?
- Which verses can I memorize to reinforce the truth?

REPORT

God, give me the faith to believe that you are alive and that you are with me always. I pray this in your Son's name. Amen.

for your next devotional reading, go to page 139

this, he showed them his hands and side. The disciples were overjoyed when they saw the Lord.

²¹ Again Jesus said, "Peace be with you! As the Father has sent me, I am sending you." ²² And with that he breathed on them and said, "Receive the Holy Spirit. ²³ If you forgive anyone's sins, their sins are forgiven; if you do not forgive them, they are not forgiven."

Jesus Appears to Thomas

²⁴ Now Thomas (also known as Didymus*ᵃ*), one of the Twelve, was not with the disciples when Jesus came. ²⁵ So the other disciples told him, "We have seen the Lord!"

But he said to them, "Unless I see the nail marks in his hands and put my finger where the nails were, and put my hand into his side, I will not believe."

²⁶ A week later his disciples were in the house again, and Thomas was with them. Though the doors were locked, Jesus came and stood among them and said, "Peace be with you!" ²⁷ Then he said to Thomas, "Put your finger here; see my hands. Reach out your hand and put it into my side. Stop doubting and believe."

²⁸ Thomas said to him, "My Lord and my God!"

²⁹ Then Jesus told him, "Because you have seen me, you have believed; blessed are those who have not seen and yet have believed."

The Purpose of John's Gospel

³⁰ Jesus performed many other signs in the presence of his disciples, which are not recorded in this book. ³¹ But these are written that you may believe*ᵇ* that Jesus is the Messiah, the Son of God, and that by believing you may have life in his name.

Jesus and the Miraculous Catch of Fish

21 Afterward Jesus appeared again to his disciples, by the Sea of Galilee.*ᶜ* It happened this way: ² Simon Peter, Thomas (also known as Didymus*ᵃ*), Nathanael from Cana in Galilee, the sons of Zebedee, and two other disciples were together. ³ "I'm going out to fish," Simon Peter told them, and they said, "We'll go with you." So they went

out and got into the boat, but that night they caught nothing.

⁴ Early in the morning, Jesus stood on the shore, but the disciples did not realize that it was Jesus.

⁵ He called out to them, "Friends, haven't you any fish?"

"No," they answered.

⁶ He said, "Throw your net on the right side of the boat and you will find some." When they did, they were unable to haul the net in because of the large number of fish.

⁷ Then the disciple whom Jesus loved said to Peter, "It is the Lord!" As soon as Simon Peter heard him say, "It is the Lord," he wrapped his outer garment around him (for he had taken it off) and jumped into the water. ⁸ The other disciples followed in the boat, towing the net full of fish, for they were not far from shore, about a hundred yards.*ᵈ* ⁹ When they landed, they saw a fire of burning coals there with fish on it, and some bread.

¹⁰ Jesus said to them, "Bring some of the fish you have just caught." ¹¹ So Simon Peter climbed back into the boat and dragged the net ashore. It was full of large fish, 153, but even with so many the net was not torn. ¹² Jesus said to them, "Come and have breakfast." None of the disciples dared ask him, "Who are you?" They knew it was the Lord. ¹³ Jesus came, took the bread and gave it to them, and did the same with the fish. ¹⁴ This was now the third time Jesus appeared to his disciples after he was raised from the dead.

Jesus Reinstates Peter

¹⁵ When they had finished eating, Jesus said to Simon Peter, "Simon son of John, do you love me more than these?"

"Yes, Lord," he said, "you know that I love you."

Jesus said, "Feed my lambs."

¹⁶ Again Jesus said, "Simon son of John, do you love me?"

He answered, "Yes, Lord, you know that I love you."

Jesus said, "Take care of my sheep."

¹⁷ The third time he said to him, "Simon son of John, do you love me?"

ᵃ 24,2 Thomas (Aramaic) and Didymus (Greek) both mean *twin.*   *ᵇ 31* Or *may continue to believe*
ᶜ 1 Greek *Tiberias*   *ᵈ 8* Or about 90 meters

Peter was hurt because Jesus asked him the third time, "Do you love me?" He said, "Lord, you know all things; you know that I love you."

Jesus said, "Feed my sheep. [18]Very truly I tell you, when you were younger you dressed yourself and went where you wanted; but when you are old you will stretch out your hands, and someone else will dress you and lead you where you do not want to go." [19]Jesus said this to indicate the kind of death by which Peter would glorify God. Then he said to him, "Follow me!"

[20]Peter turned and saw that the disciple whom Jesus loved was following them. (This was the one who had leaned back against Jesus at the supper and had said, "Lord, who is going to betray you?") [21]When Peter saw him, he asked, "Lord, what about him?"

[22]Jesus answered, "If I want him to remain alive until I return, what is that to you? You must follow me." [23]Because of this, the rumor spread among the believers that this disciple would not die. But Jesus did not say that he would not die; he only said, "If I want him to remain alive until I return, what is that to you?"

[24]This is the disciple who testifies to these things and who wrote them down. We know that his testimony is true.

[25]Jesus did many other things as well. If every one of them were written down, I suppose that even the whole world would not have room for the books that would be written.

Acts

Jesus Taken Up Into Heaven

1 In my former book, Theophilus, I wrote about all that Jesus began to do and to teach ²until the day he was taken up to heaven, after giving instructions through the Holy Spirit to the apostles he had chosen. ³After his suffering, he presented himself to them and gave many convincing proofs that he was alive. He appeared to them over a period of forty days and spoke about the kingdom of God. ⁴On one occasion, while he was eating with them, he gave them this command: "Do not leave Jerusalem, but wait for the gift my Father promised, which you have heard me speak about. ⁵For John baptized with*ᵃ* water, but in a few days you will be baptized with*ᵃ* the Holy Spirit."

⁶Then they gathered around him and asked him, "Lord, are you at this time going to restore the kingdom to Israel?"

⁷He said to them: "It is not for you to know the times or dates the Father has set by his own authority. ⁸But you will receive power when the Holy Spirit comes on you; and you will be my witnesses in Jerusalem, and in all Judea and Samaria, and to the ends of the earth."

⁹After he said this, he was taken up before their very eyes, and a cloud hid him from their sight.

¹⁰They were looking intently up into the sky as he was going, when suddenly two men dressed in white stood beside them. ¹¹"Men of Galilee," they said, "why do you stand here looking into the sky? This same Jesus, who has been taken from you into heaven, will come back in the same way you have seen him go into heaven."

Matthias Chosen to Replace Judas

¹²Then the apostles returned to Jerusalem from the hill called the Mount of Olives, a Sabbath day's walk*ᵇ* from the city. ¹³When they arrived, they went upstairs to the room where they were staying. Those present were Peter, John, James and Andrew; Philip and Thomas, Bartholomew and Matthew; James son of Alphaeus and Simon the Zealot, and Judas son of James. ¹⁴They all joined together constantly in prayer, along with the women and Mary the mother of Jesus, and with his brothers.

¹⁵In those days Peter stood up among the believers (a group numbering about a hundred and twenty) ¹⁶and said, "Brothers and sisters,*ᶜ* the Scripture had to be fulfilled in which the Holy Spirit spoke long ago through David concerning Judas, who served as guide for those who arrested Jesus. ¹⁷He was one of our number and shared in our ministry."

¹⁸(With the payment he received for his wickedness, Judas bought a field; there he fell headlong, his body burst open and all his intestines spilled out. ¹⁹Everyone in Jerusalem heard about this, so they called that field in their language Akeldama, that is, Field of Blood.)

²⁰"For," said Peter, "it is written in the Book of Psalms:

"'May his place be deserted;
    let there be no one to dwell in it,'*ᵈ*

and,

"'May another take his place of
    leadership.'*ᵉ*

²¹Therefore it is necessary to choose one of the men who have been with us the whole time the Lord Jesus was living among us, ²²beginning from John's baptism to the time when Jesus was taken up from us. For one of these must become a witness with us of his resurrection."

²³So they nominated two men: Joseph called Barsabbas (also known as Justus)

ᵃ 5 Or *in*   *ᵇ 12* That is, about 5/8 mile or about 1 kilometer   *ᶜ 16* The Greek word for *brothers and sisters (adelphoi)* refers here to believers, both men and women, as part of God's family; also in 6:3; 11:29; 12:17; 16:40; 18:18, 27; 21:7, 17; 28:14, 15.   *ᵈ 20* Psalm 69:25   *ᵉ 20* Psalm 109:8

God of the Assignment System

By Ronda Sturgill

READ: Acts 1:1–11

Have you ever considered that your journey relocating around the country or world as a military family may be similar to the missionary journeys of the apostles in the early church? For one thing, we don't choose our own assignments. In Acts 1:8, Jesus clued the apostles in about the progression of places where they would be going, and throughout the New Testament we see them responding to the leading of the Holy Spirit. Today, the government tells military families where to move, but isn't God still sovereign over those orders?

It doesn't always feel that way. I remember the day we were told to report to Davis-Monthan Air Force Base in Tucson, Arizona. We hadn't even listed Arizona on our dream sheet. In spite of leaving Virginia mad and sad, our time in Arizona turned out to be one of our favorite assignments. God had specific work for us to do there and filled us with the power of the Holy Spirit for the task, just as the apostles were filled for their journeys. As we were witnesses for the Lord, we witnessed him doing incredible work in the lives of those we served.

God's plan has always been for the earth to be "filled with the knowledge of the glory of the LORD" (Habakkuk 2:14), and he has always used people to accomplish this plan. We can trace the spread of the gospel through the early missionary journeys of Barnabas and Paul, who were sent out by the Holy Spirit (see Acts 13:2–4). They encountered hardship and persecution, but they also met a great number of people who became believers.

God was always in charge of the apostles' itinerary. Although they made plans to go to one place, God often redirected them to another. God was not only watching out for their safety and protection but also directing them to the people whose hearts were already open to receive the message of salvation.

Being a member of today's military gives us the unique opportunity to live in and experience a variety of countries and cultures all over the world. As God fills us with the power of the Holy Spirit, we too can be his witnesses "to the ends of the earth" (Acts 1:8)!

The next time you fill out your dream sheet, let the military know where you'd prefer to live. But know that in the end, God controls the assignment system and will send you where he wants you to go, filling you with the power of the Holy Spirit to spread the Good News to those you meet.

> **"You will receive power when the Holy Spirit comes on you; and you will be my witnesses in Jerusalem, and in all Judea and Samaria, and to the ends of the earth."**
>
> ACTS 1:8

DEBRIEF
- Which point in this devotion is the most significant to me? Why?
- What might be my response the next time we receive a new duty assignment?

REPORT
Dear heavenly Father, you are Lord over all. As you send us to new duty assignments all over your great earth, give us wisdom and discernment to see what your purposes are for us in each specific location. Protect us and fill us with the power of your Holy Spirit, so that we may embrace this work and be fully equipped to accomplish it. Amen.

for your next devotional reading, go to page 149

and Matthias. [24] Then they prayed, "Lord, you know everyone's heart. Show us which of these two you have chosen [25] to take over this apostolic ministry, which Judas left to go where he belongs." [26] Then they cast lots, and the lot fell to Matthias; so he was added to the eleven apostles.

The Holy Spirit Comes at Pentecost

2 When the day of Pentecost came, they were all together in one place. [2] Suddenly a sound like the blowing of a violent wind came from heaven and filled the whole house where they were sitting. [3] They saw what seemed to be tongues of fire that separated and came to rest on each of them. [4] All of them were filled with the Holy Spirit and began to speak in other tongues[a] as the Spirit enabled them.

[5] Now there were staying in Jerusalem God-fearing Jews from every nation under heaven. [6] When they heard this sound, a crowd came together in bewilderment, because each one heard their own language being spoken. [7] Utterly amazed, they asked: "Aren't all these who are speaking Galileans? [8] Then how is it that each of us hears them in our native language? [9] Parthians, Medes and Elamites; residents of Mesopotamia, Judea and Cappadocia, Pontus and Asia,[b] [10] Phrygia and Pamphylia, Egypt and the parts of Libya near Cyrene; visitors from Rome [11] (both Jews and converts to Judaism); Cretans and Arabs—we hear them declaring the wonders of God in our own tongues!" [12] Amazed and perplexed, they asked one another, "What does this mean?"

[13] Some, however, made fun of them and said, "They have had too much wine."

Peter Addresses the Crowd

[14] Then Peter stood up with the Eleven, raised his voice and addressed the crowd: "Fellow Jews and all of you who live in Jerusalem, let me explain this to you; listen carefully to what I say. [15] These people are not drunk, as you suppose. It's only nine in the morning! [16] No, this is what was spoken by the prophet Joel:

[17] " 'In the last days, God says,
    I will pour out my Spirit on all people.

Your sons and daughters will prophesy,
    your young men will see visions,
    your old men will dream dreams.
[18] Even on my servants, both men and
        women,
    I will pour out my Spirit in those days,
    and they will prophesy.
[19] I will show wonders in the heavens above
    and signs on the earth below,
    blood and fire and billows of smoke.
[20] The sun will be turned to darkness
    and the moon to blood
    before the coming of the great and
        glorious day of the Lord.
[21] And everyone who calls
    on the name of the Lord will be saved.'[c]

[22] "Fellow Israelites, listen to this: Jesus of Nazareth was a man accredited by God to you by miracles, wonders and signs, which God did among you through him, as you yourselves know. [23] This man was handed over to you by God's deliberate plan and foreknowledge; and you, with the help of wicked men,[d] put him to death by nailing him to the cross. [24] But God raised him from the dead, freeing him from the agony of death, because it was impossible for death to keep its hold on him. [25] David said about him:

" 'I saw the Lord always before me.
    Because he is at my right hand,
    I will not be shaken.
[26] Therefore my heart is glad and my
        tongue rejoices;
    my body also will rest in hope,
[27] because you will not abandon me to the
        realm of the dead,
    you will not let your holy one see
        decay.
[28] You have made known to me the paths
        of life;
    you will fill me with joy in your
        presence.'[e]

[29] "Fellow Israelites, I can tell you confidently that the patriarch David died and was buried, and his tomb is here to this day. [30] But he was a prophet and knew that God had promised him on oath that he would place one of his descendants on his throne. [31] Seeing what was to come, he spoke of the resurrection of the Messiah, that he was not

---

[a] 4 Or *languages*; also in verse 11   [b] 9 That is, the Roman province by that name   [c] 21 Joel 2:28-32
[d] 23 Or *of those not having the law* (that is, Gentiles)   [e] 28 Psalm 16:8-11 (see Septuagint)

abandoned to the realm of the dead, nor did his body see decay. ³²God has raised this Jesus to life, and we are all witnesses of it. ³³Exalted to the right hand of God, he has received from the Father the promised Holy Spirit and has poured out what you now see and hear. ³⁴For David did not ascend to heaven, and yet he said,

" 'The Lord said to my Lord:
    "Sit at my right hand
³⁵ until I make your enemies
    a footstool for your feet." ' ᵃ

³⁶"Therefore let all Israel be assured of this: God has made this Jesus, whom you crucified, both Lord and Messiah."

³⁷When the people heard this, they were cut to the heart and said to Peter and the other apostles, "Brothers, what shall we do?"

³⁸Peter replied, "Repent and be baptized, every one of you, in the name of Jesus Christ for the forgiveness of your sins. And you will receive the gift of the Holy Spirit. ³⁹The promise is for you and your children and for all who are far off—for all whom the Lord our God will call."

⁴⁰With many other words he warned them; and he pleaded with them, "Save yourselves from this corrupt generation." ⁴¹Those who accepted his message were baptized, and about three thousand were added to their number that day.

The Fellowship of the Believers

⁴²They devoted themselves to the apostles' teaching and to fellowship, to the breaking of bread and to prayer. ⁴³Everyone was filled with awe at the many wonders and signs performed by the apostles. ⁴⁴All the believers were together and had everything in common. ⁴⁵They sold property and possessions to give to anyone who had need. ⁴⁶Every day they continued to meet together in the temple courts. They broke bread in their homes and ate together with glad and sincere hearts, ⁴⁷praising God and enjoying the favor of all the people. And the Lord added to their number daily those who were being saved.

Peter Heals a Lame Beggar

3 One day Peter and John were going up to the temple at the time of prayer—at three in the afternoon. ²Now a man who was lame from birth was being carried to the temple gate called Beautiful, where he was put every day to beg from those going into the temple courts. ³When he saw Peter and John about to enter, he asked them for money. ⁴Peter looked straight at him, as did John. Then Peter said, "Look at us!" ⁵So the man gave them his attention, expecting to get something from them.

⁶Then Peter said, "Silver or gold I do not have, but what I do have I give you. In the name of Jesus Christ of Nazareth, walk." ⁷Taking him by the right hand, he helped him up, and instantly the man's feet and ankles became strong. ⁸He jumped to his feet and began to walk. Then he went with them into the temple courts, walking and jumping, and praising God. ⁹When all the people saw him walking and praising God, ¹⁰they recognized him as the same man who used to sit begging at the temple gate called Beautiful, and they were filled with wonder and amazement at what had happened to him.

Peter Speaks to the Onlookers

¹¹While the man held on to Peter and John, all the people were astonished and came running to them in the place called Solomon's Colonnade. ¹²When Peter saw this, he said to them: "Fellow Israelites, why does this surprise you? Why do you stare at us as if by our own power or godliness we had made this man walk? ¹³The God of Abraham, Isaac and Jacob, the God of our fathers, has glorified his servant Jesus. You handed him over to be killed, and you disowned him before Pilate, though he had decided to let him go. ¹⁴You disowned the Holy and Righteous One and asked that a murderer be released to you. ¹⁵You killed the author of life, but God raised him from the dead. We are witnesses of this. ¹⁶By faith in the name of Jesus, this man whom you see and know was made strong. It is Jesus' name and the faith that comes through him that has completely healed him, as you can all see.

¹⁷"Now, fellow Israelites, I know that you acted in ignorance, as did your leaders. ¹⁸But this is how God fulfilled what he had foretold through all the prophets, saying that his

ᵃ 35 Psalm 110:1

Messiah would suffer. ¹⁹Repent, then, and turn to God, so that your sins may be wiped out, that times of refreshing may come from the Lord, ²⁰and that he may send the Messiah, who has been appointed for you — even Jesus. ²¹Heaven must receive him until the time comes for God to restore everything, as he promised long ago through his holy prophets. ²²For Moses said, 'The Lord your God will raise up for you a prophet like me from among your own people; you must listen to everything he tells you. ²³Anyone who does not listen to him will be completely cut off from their people.'ᵃ

²⁴"Indeed, beginning with Samuel, all the prophets who have spoken have foretold these days. ²⁵And you are heirs of the prophets and of the covenant God made with your fathers. He said to Abraham, 'Through your offspring all peoples on earth will be blessed.'ᵇ ²⁶When God raised up his servant, he sent him first to you to bless you by turning each of you from your wicked ways."

Peter and John Before the Sanhedrin

4 The priests and the captain of the temple guard and the Sadducees came up to Peter and John while they were speaking to the people. ²They were greatly disturbed because the apostles were teaching the people, proclaiming in Jesus the resurrection of the dead. ³They seized Peter and John and, because it was evening, they put them in jail until the next day. ⁴But many who heard the message believed; so the number of men who believed grew to about five thousand.

⁵The next day the rulers, the elders and the teachers of the law met in Jerusalem. ⁶Annas the high priest was there, and so were Caiaphas, John, Alexander and others of the high priest's family. ⁷They had Peter and John brought before them and began to question them: "By what power or what name did you do this?"

⁸Then Peter, filled with the Holy Spirit, said to them: "Rulers and elders of the people! ⁹If we are being called to account today for an act of kindness shown to a man who was lame and are being asked how he was healed, ¹⁰then know this, you and all the people of Israel: It is by the name of Jesus Christ of Nazareth, whom you crucified but

whom God raised from the dead, that this man stands before you healed. ¹¹Jesus is

" 'the stone you builders rejected,
    which has become the
        cornerstone.'ᶜ

¹²Salvation is found in no one else, for there is no other name under heaven given to mankind by which we must be saved."

¹³When they saw the courage of Peter and John and realized that they were unschooled, ordinary men, they were astonished and they took note that these men had been with Jesus. ¹⁴But since they could see the man who had been healed standing there with them, there was nothing they could say. ¹⁵So they ordered them to withdraw from the Sanhedrin and then conferred together. ¹⁶"What are we going to do with these men?" they asked. "Everyone living in Jerusalem knows they have performed a notable sign, and we cannot deny it. ¹⁷But to stop this thing from spreading any further among the people, we must warn them to speak no longer to anyone in this name."

¹⁸Then they called them in again and commanded them not to speak or teach at all in the name of Jesus. ¹⁹But Peter and John replied, "Which is right in God's eyes: to listen to you, or to him? You be the judges! ²⁰As for us, we cannot help speaking about what we have seen and heard."

²¹After further threats they let them go. They could not decide how to punish them, because all the people were praising God for what had happened. ²²For the man who was miraculously healed was over forty years old.

The Believers Pray

²³On their release, Peter and John went back to their own people and reported all that the chief priests and the elders had said to them. ²⁴When they heard this, they raised their voices together in prayer to God. "Sovereign Lord," they said, "you made the heavens and the earth and the sea, and everything in them. ²⁵You spoke by the Holy Spirit through the mouth of your servant, our father David:

" 'Why do the nations rage
    and the peoples plot in vain?

²⁶The kings of the earth rise up
     and the rulers band together
  against the Lord
     and against his anointed one.ᵃᵇ

²⁷Indeed Herod and Pontius Pilate met together with the Gentiles and the people of Israel in this city to conspire against your holy servant Jesus, whom you anointed. ²⁸They did what your power and will had decided beforehand should happen. ²⁹Now, Lord, consider their threats and enable your servants to speak your word with great boldness. ³⁰Stretch out your hand to heal and perform signs and wonders through the name of your holy servant Jesus."

³¹After they prayed, the place where they were meeting was shaken. And they were all filled with the Holy Spirit and spoke the word of God boldly.

The Believers Share Their Possessions

³²All the believers were one in heart and mind. No one claimed that any of their possessions was their own, but they shared everything they had. ³³With great power the apostles continued to testify to the resurrection of the Lord Jesus. And God's grace was so powerfully at work in them all ³⁴that there were no needy persons among them. For from time to time those who owned land or houses sold them, brought the money from the sales ³⁵and put it at the apostles' feet, and it was distributed to anyone who had need.

³⁶Joseph, a Levite from Cyprus, whom the apostles called Barnabas (which means "son of encouragement"), ³⁷sold a field he owned and brought the money and put it at the apostles' feet.

Ananias and Sapphira

5 Now a man named Ananias, together with his wife Sapphira, also sold a piece of property. ²With his wife's full knowledge he kept back part of the money for himself, but brought the rest and put it at the apostles' feet. ³Then Peter said, "Ananias, how is it that Satan has so filled your heart that you have lied to the Holy Spirit and have kept for yourself some of the money you received for the land? ⁴Didn't it belong to you before it was sold? And after it was sold, wasn't the mon-

ey at your disposal? What made you think of doing such a thing? You have not lied just to human beings but to God."

⁵When Ananias heard this, he fell down and died. And great fear seized all who heard what had happened. ⁶Then some young men came forward, wrapped up his body, and carried him out and buried him.

⁷About three hours later his wife came in, not knowing what had happened. ⁸Peter asked her, "Tell me, is this the price you and Ananias got for the land?"

"Yes," she said, "that is the price."

⁹Peter said to her, "How could you conspire to test the Spirit of the Lord? Listen! The feet of the men who buried your husband are at the door, and they will carry you out also."

¹⁰At that moment she fell down at his feet and died. Then the young men came in and, finding her dead, carried her out and buried her beside her husband. ¹¹Great fear seized the whole church and all who heard about these events.

The Apostles Heal Many

¹²The apostles performed many signs and wonders among the people. And all the believers used to meet together in Solomon's Colonnade. ¹³No one else dared join them, even though they were highly regarded by the people. ¹⁴Nevertheless, more and more men and women believed in the Lord and were added to their number. ¹⁵As a result, people brought the sick into the streets and laid them on beds and mats so that at least Peter's shadow might fall on some of them as he passed by. ¹⁶Crowds gathered also from the towns around Jerusalem, bringing their sick and those tormented by impure spirits, and all of them were healed.

The Apostles Persecuted

¹⁷Then the high priest and all his associates, who were members of the party of the Sadducees, were filled with jealousy. ¹⁸They arrested the apostles and put them in the public jail. ¹⁹But during the night an angel of the Lord opened the doors of the jail and brought them out. ²⁰"Go, stand in the temple courts," he said, "and tell the people all about this new life."

²¹At daybreak they entered the temple

ᵃ 26 That is, Messiah or Christ   ᵇ 26 Psalm 2:1,2

courts, as they had been told, and began to teach the people.

When the high priest and his associates arrived, they called together the Sanhedrin — the full assembly of the elders of Israel — and sent to the jail for the apostles. ²²But on arriving at the jail, the officers did not find them there. So they went back and reported, ²³"We found the jail securely locked, with the guards standing at the doors; but when we opened them, we found no one inside." ²⁴On hearing this report, the captain of the temple guard and the chief priests were at a loss, wondering what this might lead to.

²⁵Then someone came and said, "Look! The men you put in jail are standing in the temple courts teaching the people." ²⁶At that, the captain went with his officers and brought the apostles. They did not use force, because they feared that the people would stone them.

²⁷The apostles were brought in and made to appear before the Sanhedrin to be questioned by the high priest. ²⁸"We gave you strict orders not to teach in this name," he said. "Yet you have filled Jerusalem with your teaching and are determined to make us guilty of this man's blood."

²⁹Peter and the other apostles replied: "We must obey God rather than human beings! ³⁰The God of our ancestors raised Jesus from the dead — whom you killed by hanging him on a cross. ³¹God exalted him to his own right hand as Prince and Savior that he might bring Israel to repentance and forgive their sins. ³²We are witnesses of these things, and so is the Holy Spirit, whom God has given to those who obey him."

³³When they heard this, they were furious and wanted to put them to death. ³⁴But a Pharisee named Gamaliel, a teacher of the law, who was honored by all the people, stood up in the Sanhedrin and ordered that the men be put outside for a little while. ³⁵Then he addressed the Sanhedrin: "Men of Israel, consider carefully what you intend to do to these men. ³⁶Some time ago Theudas appeared, claiming to be somebody, and about four hundred men rallied to him. He was killed, all his followers were dispersed, and it all came to nothing. ³⁷After him, Judas the Galilean appeared in the days of the census and led a band of people in revolt. He too was killed, and all his followers were scattered. ³⁸Therefore, in the present case I advise you: Leave these men alone! Let them go! For if their purpose or activity is of human origin, it will fail. ³⁹But if it is from God, you will not be able to stop these men; you will only find yourselves fighting against God."

⁴⁰His speech persuaded them. They called the apostles in and had them flogged. Then they ordered them not to speak in the name of Jesus, and let them go.

⁴¹The apostles left the Sanhedrin, rejoicing because they had been counted worthy of suffering disgrace for the Name. ⁴²Day after day, in the temple courts and from house to house, they never stopped teaching and proclaiming the good news that Jesus is the Messiah.

The Choosing of the Seven

6 In those days when the number of disciples was increasing, the Hellenistic Jews^a among them complained against the Hebraic Jews because their widows were being overlooked in the daily distribution of food. ²So the Twelve gathered all the disciples together and said, "It would not be right for us to neglect the ministry of the word of God in order to wait on tables. ³Brothers and sisters, choose seven men from among you who are known to be full of the Spirit and wisdom. We will turn this responsibility over to them ⁴and will give our attention to prayer and the ministry of the word."

⁵This proposal pleased the whole group. They chose Stephen, a man full of faith and of the Holy Spirit; also Philip, Procorus, Nicanor, Timon, Parmenas, and Nicolas from Antioch, a convert to Judaism. ⁶They presented these men to the apostles, who prayed and laid their hands on them.

⁷So the word of God spread. The number of disciples in Jerusalem increased rapidly, and a large number of priests became obedient to the faith.

Stephen Seized

⁸Now Stephen, a man full of God's grace and power, performed great wonders and signs among the people. ⁹Opposition arose,

^a 1 That is, Jews who had adopted the Greek language and culture

however, from members of the Synagogue of the Freedmen (as it was called) — Jews of Cyrene and Alexandria as well as the provinces of Cilicia and Asia — who began to argue with Stephen. [10]But they could not stand up against the wisdom the Spirit gave him as he spoke.

[11]Then they secretly persuaded some men to say, "We have heard Stephen speak blasphemous words against Moses and against God."

[12]So they stirred up the people and the elders and the teachers of the law. They seized Stephen and brought him before the Sanhedrin. [13]They produced false witnesses, who testified, "This fellow never stops speaking against this holy place and against the law. [14]For we have heard him say that this Jesus of Nazareth will destroy this place and change the customs Moses handed down to us."

[15]All who were sitting in the Sanhedrin looked intently at Stephen, and they saw that his face was like the face of an angel.

Stephen's Speech to the Sanhedrin

7 Then the high priest asked Stephen, "Are these charges true?"

[2]To this he replied: "Brothers and fathers, listen to me! The God of glory appeared to our father Abraham while he was still in Mesopotamia, before he lived in Harran. [3]'Leave your country and your people,' God said, 'and go to the land I will show you.'[a]

[4]"So he left the land of the Chaldeans and settled in Harran. After the death of his father, God sent him to this land where you are now living. [5]He gave him no inheritance here, not even enough ground to set his foot on. But God promised him that he and his descendants after him would possess the land, even though at that time Abraham had no child. [6]God spoke to him in this way: 'For four hundred years your descendants will be strangers in a country not their own, and they will be enslaved and mistreated. [7]But I will punish the nation they serve as slaves,' God said, 'and afterward they will come out of that country and worship me in this place.'[b] [8]Then he gave Abraham the covenant of circumcision. And Abraham became the father of Isaac and circumcised

him eight days after his birth. Later Isaac became the father of Jacob, and Jacob became the father of the twelve patriarchs.

[9]"Because the patriarchs were jealous of Joseph, they sold him as a slave into Egypt. But God was with him [10]and rescued him from all his troubles. He gave Joseph wisdom and enabled him to gain the goodwill of Pharaoh king of Egypt. So Pharaoh made him ruler over Egypt and all his palace.

[11]"Then a famine struck all Egypt and Canaan, bringing great suffering, and our ancestors could not find food. [12]When Jacob heard that there was grain in Egypt, he sent our forefathers on their first visit. [13]On their second visit, Joseph told his brothers who he was, and Pharaoh learned about Joseph's family. [14]After this, Joseph sent for his father Jacob and his whole family, seventy-five in all. [15]Then Jacob went down to Egypt, where he and our ancestors died. [16]Their bodies were brought back to Shechem and placed in the tomb that Abraham had bought from the sons of Hamor at Shechem for a certain sum of money.

[17]"As the time drew near for God to fulfill his promise to Abraham, the number of our people in Egypt had greatly increased. [18]Then 'a new king, to whom Joseph meant nothing, came to power in Egypt.'[c] [19]He dealt treacherously with our people and oppressed our ancestors by forcing them to throw out their newborn babies so that they would die.

[20]"At that time Moses was born, and he was no ordinary child.[d] For three months he was cared for by his family. [21]When he was placed outside, Pharaoh's daughter took him and brought him up as her own son. [22]Moses was educated in all the wisdom of the Egyptians and was powerful in speech and action.

[23]"When Moses was forty years old, he decided to visit his own people, the Israelites. [24]He saw one of them being mistreated by an Egyptian, so he went to his defense and avenged him by killing the Egyptian. [25]Moses thought that his own people would realize that God was using him to rescue them, but they did not. [26]The next day Moses came upon two Israelites who were fighting. He tried to reconcile them by saying, 'Men, you

---

[a] 3 Gen. 12:1   [b] 7 Gen. 15:13,14   [c] 18 Exodus 1:8   [d] 20 Or *was fair in the sight of God*

are brothers; why do you want to hurt each other?'

²⁷ "But the man who was mistreating the other pushed Moses aside and said, 'Who made you ruler and judge over us? ²⁸ Are you thinking of killing me as you killed the Egyptian yesterday?'ᵃ ²⁹ When Moses heard this, he fled to Midian, where he settled as a foreigner and had two sons.

³⁰ "After forty years had passed, an angel appeared to Moses in the flames of a burning bush in the desert near Mount Sinai. ³¹ When he saw this, he was amazed at the sight. As he went over to get a closer look, he heard the Lord say: ³² 'I am the God of your fathers, the God of Abraham, Isaac and Jacob.'ᵇ Moses trembled with fear and did not dare to look.

³³ "Then the Lord said to him, 'Take off your sandals, for the place where you are standing is holy ground. ³⁴ I have indeed seen the oppression of my people in Egypt. I have heard their groaning and have come down to set them free. Now come, I will send you back to Egypt.'ᶜ

³⁵ "This is the same Moses they had rejected with the words, 'Who made you ruler and judge?' He was sent to be their ruler and deliverer by God himself, through the angel who appeared to him in the bush. ³⁶ He led them out of Egypt and performed wonders and signs in Egypt, at the Red Sea and for forty years in the wilderness.

³⁷ "This is the Moses who told the Israelites, 'God will raise up for you a prophet like me from your own people.'ᵈ ³⁸ He was in the assembly in the wilderness, with the angel who spoke to him on Mount Sinai, and with our ancestors; and he received living words to pass on to us.

³⁹ "But our ancestors refused to obey him. Instead, they rejected him and in their hearts turned back to Egypt. ⁴⁰ They told Aaron, 'Make us gods who will go before us. As for this fellow Moses who led us out of Egypt— we don't know what has happened to him!'ᵉ ⁴¹ That was the time they made an idol in the form of a calf. They brought sacrifices to it and reveled in what their own hands had made. ⁴² But God turned away from them and gave them over to the worship of the sun, moon and stars. This agrees with what is written in the book of the prophets:

> " 'Did you bring me sacrifices and
>   offerings
>   forty years in the wilderness, people of
>   Israel?
> ⁴³ You have taken up the tabernacle of
>   Molek
>   and the star of your god Rephan,
>   the idols you made to worship.
> Therefore I will send you into exile'ᶠ
>   beyond Babylon.

⁴⁴ "Our ancestors had the tabernacle of the covenant law with them in the wilderness. It had been made as God directed Moses, according to the pattern he had seen. ⁴⁵ After receiving the tabernacle, our ancestors under Joshua brought it with them when they took the land from the nations God drove out before them. It remained in the land until the time of David, ⁴⁶ who enjoyed God's favor and asked that he might provide a dwelling place for the God of Jacob.ᵍ ⁴⁷ But it was Solomon who built a house for him.

⁴⁸ "However, the Most High does not live in houses made by human hands. As the prophet says:

> ⁴⁹ " 'Heaven is my throne,
>   and the earth is my footstool.
>   What kind of house will you build for me?
>   says the Lord.
>   Or where will my resting place be?
> ⁵⁰ Has not my hand made all these things?'ʰ

⁵¹ "You stiff-necked people! Your hearts and ears are still uncircumcised. You are just like your ancestors: You always resist the Holy Spirit! ⁵² Was there ever a prophet your ancestors did not persecute? They even killed those who predicted the coming of the Righteous One. And now you have betrayed and murdered him— ⁵³ you who have received the law that was given through angels but have not obeyed it."

The Stoning of Stephen

⁵⁴ When the members of the Sanhedrin heard this, they were furious and gnashed their teeth at him. ⁵⁵ But Stephen, full of the Holy Spirit, looked up to heaven and saw the

---

ᵃ 28 Exodus 2:14   ᵇ 32 Exodus 3:6   ᶜ 34 Exodus 3:5,7,8,10   ᵈ 37 Deut. 18:15   ᵉ 40 Exodus 32:1
ᶠ 43 Amos 5:25-27 (see Septuagint)   ᵍ 46 Some early manuscripts the house of Jacob
ʰ 50 Isaiah 66:1,2

glory of God, and Jesus standing at the right hand of God. [56]"Look," he said, "I see heaven open and the Son of Man standing at the right hand of God."

[57]At this they covered their ears and, yelling at the top of their voices, they all rushed at him, [58]dragged him out of the city and began to stone him. Meanwhile, the witnesses laid their coats at the feet of a young man named Saul.

[59]While they were stoning him, Stephen prayed, "Lord Jesus, receive my spirit." [60]Then he fell on his knees and cried out, "Lord, do not hold this sin against them." When he had said this, he fell asleep.

8

And Saul approved of their killing him.

The Church Persecuted and Scattered

On that day a great persecution broke out against the church in Jerusalem, and all except the apostles were scattered throughout Judea and Samaria. [2]Godly men buried Stephen and mourned deeply for him. [3]But Saul began to destroy the church. Going from house to house, he dragged off both men and women and put them in prison.

Philip in Samaria

[4]Those who had been scattered preached the word wherever they went. [5]Philip went down to a city in Samaria and proclaimed the Messiah there. [6]When the crowds heard Philip and saw the signs he performed, they all paid close attention to what he said. [7]For with shrieks, impure spirits came out of many, and many who were paralyzed or lame were healed. [8]So there was great joy in that city.

Simon the Sorcerer

[9]Now for some time a man named Simon had practiced sorcery in the city and amazed all the people of Samaria. He boasted that he was someone great, [10]and all the people, both high and low, gave him their attention and exclaimed, "This man is rightly called the Great Power of God." [11]They followed him because he had amazed them for a long time with his sorcery. [12]But when they believed Philip as he proclaimed the good news of the kingdom of God and the name of Jesus Christ, they were baptized, both men

and women. [13]Simon himself believed and was baptized. And he followed Philip everywhere, astonished by the great signs and miracles he saw.

[14]When the apostles in Jerusalem heard that Samaria had accepted the word of God, they sent Peter and John to Samaria. [15]When they arrived, they prayed for the new believers there that they might receive the Holy Spirit, [16]because the Holy Spirit had not yet come on any of them; they had simply been baptized in the name of the Lord Jesus. [17]Then Peter and John placed their hands on them, and they received the Holy Spirit.

[18]When Simon saw that the Spirit was given at the laying on of the apostles' hands, he offered them money [19]and said, "Give me also this ability so that everyone on whom I lay my hands may receive the Holy Spirit."

[20]Peter answered: "May your money perish with you, because you thought you could buy the gift of God with money! [21]You have no part or share in this ministry, because your heart is not right before God. [22]Repent of this wickedness and pray to the Lord in the hope that he may forgive you for having such a thought in your heart. [23]For I see that you are full of bitterness and captive to sin."

[24]Then Simon answered, "Pray to the Lord for me so that nothing you have said may happen to me."

[25]After they had further proclaimed the word of the Lord and testified about Jesus, Peter and John returned to Jerusalem, preaching the gospel in many Samaritan villages.

Philip and the Ethiopian

[26]Now an angel of the Lord said to Philip, "Go south to the road — the desert road — that goes down from Jerusalem to Gaza." [27]So he started out, and on his way he met an Ethiopian[a] eunuch, an important official in charge of all the treasury of the Kandake (which means "queen of the Ethiopians"). This man had gone to Jerusalem to worship, [28]and on his way home was sitting in his chariot reading the Book of Isaiah the prophet. [29]The Spirit told Philip, "Go to that chariot and stay near it."

[30]Then Philip ran up to the chariot and heard the man reading Isaiah the prophet.

[a] 27 That is, from the southern Nile region

"Do you understand what you are reading?" Philip asked.

[31] "How can I," he said, "unless someone explains it to me?" So he invited Philip to come up and sit with him.

[32] This is the passage of Scripture the eunuch was reading:

"He was led like a sheep to the slaughter,
    and as a lamb before its shearer is
    silent,
so he did not open his mouth.
[33] In his humiliation he was deprived of
    justice.
Who can speak of his descendants?
For his life was taken from the earth."[a]

[34] The eunuch asked Philip, "Tell me, please, who is the prophet talking about, himself or someone else?" [35] Then Philip began with that very passage of Scripture and told him the good news about Jesus.

[36] As they traveled along the road, they came to some water and the eunuch said, "Look, here is water. What can stand in the way of my being baptized?" [37][b] [38] And he gave orders to stop the chariot. Then both Philip and the eunuch went down into the water and Philip baptized him. [39] When they came up out of the water, the Spirit of the Lord suddenly took Philip away, and the eunuch did not see him again, but went on his way rejoicing. [40] Philip, however, appeared at Azotus and traveled about, preaching the gospel in all the towns until he reached Caesarea.

Saul's Conversion

9 Meanwhile, Saul was still breathing out murderous threats against the Lord's disciples. He went to the high priest [2] and asked him for letters to the synagogues in Damascus, so that if he found any there who belonged to the Way, whether men or women, he might take them as prisoners to Jerusalem. [3] As he neared Damascus on his journey, suddenly a light from heaven flashed around him. [4] He fell to the ground and heard a voice say to him, "Saul, Saul, why do you persecute me?"

[5] "Who are you, Lord?" Saul asked.

"I am Jesus, whom you are persecuting," he replied. [6] "Now get up and go into the city, and you will be told what you must do."

[7] The men traveling with Saul stood there speechless; they heard the sound but did not see anyone. [8] Saul got up from the ground, but when he opened his eyes he could see nothing. So they led him by the hand into Damascus. [9] For three days he was blind, and did not eat or drink anything.

[10] In Damascus there was a disciple named Ananias. The Lord called to him in a vision, "Ananias!"

"Yes, Lord," he answered.

[11] The Lord told him, "Go to the house of Judas on Straight Street and ask for a man from Tarsus named Saul, for he is praying. [12] In a vision he has seen a man named Ananias come and place his hands on him to restore his sight."

[13] "Lord," Ananias answered, "I have heard many reports about this man and all the harm he has done to your holy people in Jerusalem. [14] And he has come here with authority from the chief priests to arrest all who call on your name."

[15] But the Lord said to Ananias, "Go! This man is my chosen instrument to proclaim my name to the Gentiles and their kings and to the people of Israel. [16] I will show him how much he must suffer for my name."

[17] Then Ananias went to the house and entered it. Placing his hands on Saul, he said, "Brother Saul, the Lord — Jesus, who appeared to you on the road as you were coming here — has sent me so that you may see again and be filled with the Holy Spirit." [18] Immediately, something like scales fell from Saul's eyes, and he could see again. He got up and was baptized, [19] and after taking some food, he regained his strength.

Saul in Damascus and Jerusalem

Saul spent several days with the disciples in Damascus. [20] At once he began to preach in the synagogues that Jesus is the Son of God. [21] All those who heard him were astonished and asked, "Isn't he the man who raised havoc in Jerusalem among those who call on this name? And hasn't he come here to take them as prisoners to the chief priests?" [22] Yet Saul grew more and more

---

[a] 33 Isaiah 53:7,8 (see Septuagint)   [b] 37 Some manuscripts include here *Philip said, "If you believe with all your heart, you may." The eunuch answered, "I believe that Jesus Christ is the Son of God."*

Hope for the Unsaved

By Jocelyn Green

READ: Acts 9:1–31

Saul was notorious for persecuting those who "belonged to the Way" (see Acts 9:1–2). If there was anyone the early Christians would have given up as a lost cause for conversion, it surely would have been Saul.

But God had other plans. Saul became the apostle Paul, the Lord Jesus' "chosen instrument to proclaim [the Lord's] name to the Gentiles and their kings and to the people of Israel" (verse 15).

If your husband is not a believer, Acts 9:1–31 can give you hope that even the staunchest opposers of the gospel can be saved. If your husband once believed but has since walked away from his faith, be encouraged by the fact that Peter denied knowing Jesus three times (see Mark 14:66–72), yet Jesus symbolically redeemed and restored him three times (see John 21:15–19). He can restore your husband too.

It took an act of God to get Saul's attention, and it may take something dramatic to soften your husband's heart as well. But maybe, the act of God leading to your husband's salvation will come through the act of prayer. *Your* prayers.

Author Dineen Miller is a Christian whose husband is an atheist. In *Praying God's Word for Your Husband*, she shares how she uses the Scriptures to intercede for the man she loves. Here's an example:

2 Corinthians 2:14–16

But thanks be to God, who always leads us as captives in Christ's triumphal procession and uses us to spread the aroma of the knowledge of him everywhere. For we are to God the pleasing aroma of Christ among those who are being saved and those who are perishing. To the one we are an aroma that brings death; to the other, an aroma that brings life. And who is equal to such a task?

Prayer: Lord, help me to be the aroma of Christ in my husband's life. Where I am "stinky," help me to change. Fragrance my words and actions, Lord Jesus, so that my husband catches glimpses of you through me.

No matter how closed to God's Word your husband seems now, the Holy Spirit can work the miracle of saving grace in his heart. One day, your husband may have his own amazing testimony of the moment when the scales came off his eyes and he was no longer blind to the Truth.

Immediately, something like scales fell from Saul's eyes, and he could see again. He got up and was baptized.
ACTS 9:18

DEBRIEF
- Do the unsaved see glimpses of Jesus in me?
- Am I diligently praying for the lost, including my husband if he fits into this category?

REPORT
Lord, make me bold for you in word and deed. Paul preached fearlessly in the name of Jesus. I pray that I am able to do the same and that in the process I may help those who are lost to see the Truth. May I be the pleasing aroma of Christ to you and those around me. Amen.

---

for your next devotional reading, go to page 159

powerful and baffled the Jews living in Damascus by proving that Jesus is the Messiah.

²³After many days had gone by, there was a conspiracy among the Jews to kill him, ²⁴but Saul learned of their plan. Day and night they kept close watch on the city gates in order to kill him. ²⁵But his followers took him by night and lowered him in a basket through an opening in the wall.

²⁶When he came to Jerusalem, he tried to join the disciples, but they were all afraid of him, not believing that he really was a disciple. ²⁷But Barnabas took him and brought him to the apostles. He told them how Saul on his journey had seen the Lord and that the Lord had spoken to him, and how in Damascus he had preached fearlessly in the name of Jesus. ²⁸So Saul stayed with them and moved about freely in Jerusalem, speaking boldly in the name of the Lord. ²⁹He talked and debated with the Hellenistic Jews,*ᵃ* but they tried to kill him. ³⁰When the believers learned of this, they took him down to Caesarea and sent him off to Tarsus.

³¹Then the church throughout Judea, Galilee and Samaria enjoyed a time of peace and was strengthened. Living in the fear of the Lord and encouraged by the Holy Spirit, it increased in numbers.

Aeneas and Dorcas

³²As Peter traveled about the country, he went to visit the Lord's people who lived in Lydda. ³³There he found a man named Aeneas, who was paralyzed and had been bedridden for eight years. ³⁴"Aeneas," Peter said to him, "Jesus Christ heals you. Get up and roll up your mat." Immediately Aeneas got up. ³⁵All those who lived in Lydda and Sharon saw him and turned to the Lord.

³⁶In Joppa there was a disciple named Tabitha (in Greek her name is Dorcas); she was always doing good and helping the poor. ³⁷About that time she became sick and died, and her body was washed and placed in an upstairs room. ³⁸Lydda was near Joppa; so when the disciples heard that Peter was in Lydda, they sent two men to him and urged him, "Please come at once!"

³⁹Peter went with them, and when he arrived he was taken upstairs to the room. All the widows stood around him, crying and showing him the robes and other clothing that Dorcas had made while she was still with them.

⁴⁰Peter sent them all out of the room; then he got down on his knees and prayed. Turning toward the dead woman, he said, "Tabitha, get up." She opened her eyes, and seeing Peter she sat up. ⁴¹He took her by the hand and helped her to her feet. Then he called for the believers, especially the widows, and presented her to them alive. ⁴²This became known all over Joppa, and many people believed in the Lord. ⁴³Peter stayed in Joppa for some time with a tanner named Simon.

Cornelius Calls for Peter

10 At Caesarea there was a man named Cornelius, a centurion in what was known as the Italian Regiment. ²He and all his family were devout and God-fearing; he gave generously to those in need and prayed to God regularly. ³One day at about three in the afternoon he had a vision. He distinctly saw an angel of God, who came to him and said, "Cornelius!"

⁴Cornelius stared at him in fear. "What is it, Lord?" he asked.

The angel answered, "Your prayers and gifts to the poor have come up as a memorial offering before God. ⁵Now send men to Joppa to bring back a man named Simon who is called Peter. ⁶He is staying with Simon the tanner, whose house is by the sea."

⁷When the angel who spoke to him had gone, Cornelius called two of his servants and a devout soldier who was one of his attendants. ⁸He told them everything that had happened and sent them to Joppa.

Peter's Vision

⁹About noon the following day as they were on their journey and approaching the city, Peter went up on the roof to pray. ¹⁰He became hungry and wanted something to eat, and while the meal was being prepared, he fell into a trance. ¹¹He saw heaven opened and something like a large sheet being let down to earth by its four corners. ¹²It contained all kinds of four-footed animals, as well as reptiles and birds. ¹³Then a voice told him, "Get up, Peter. Kill and eat."

ᵃ 29 That is, Jews who had adopted the Greek language and culture

[14] "Surely not, Lord!" Peter replied. "I have never eaten anything impure or unclean."

[15] The voice spoke to him a second time, "Do not call anything impure that God has made clean."

[16] This happened three times, and immediately the sheet was taken back to heaven.

[17] While Peter was wondering about the meaning of the vision, the men sent by Cornelius found out where Simon's house was and stopped at the gate. [18] They called out, asking if Simon who was known as Peter was staying there.

[19] While Peter was still thinking about the vision, the Spirit said to him, "Simon, three[a] men are looking for you. [20] So get up and go downstairs. Do not hesitate to go with them, for I have sent them."

[21] Peter went down and said to the men, "I'm the one you're looking for. Why have you come?"

[22] The men replied, "We have come from Cornelius the centurion. He is a righteous and God-fearing man, who is respected by all the Jewish people. A holy angel told him to ask you to come to his house so that he could hear what you have to say." [23] Then Peter invited the men into the house to be his guests.

Peter at Cornelius's House

The next day Peter started out with them, and some of the believers from Joppa went along. [24] The following day he arrived in Caesarea. Cornelius was expecting them and had called together his relatives and close friends. [25] As Peter entered the house, Cornelius met him and fell at his feet in reverence. [26] But Peter made him get up. "Stand up," he said, "I am only a man myself."

[27] While talking with him, Peter went inside and found a large gathering of people. [28] He said to them: "You are well aware that it is against our law for a Jew to associate with or visit a Gentile. But God has shown me that I should not call anyone impure or unclean. [29] So when I was sent for, I came without raising any objection. May I ask why you sent for me?"

[30] Cornelius answered: "Three days ago I was in my house praying at this hour, at three in the afternoon. Suddenly a man in shining clothes stood before me [31] and said, 'Cornelius, God has heard your prayer and remembered your gifts to the poor. [32] Send to Joppa for Simon who is called Peter. He is a guest in the home of Simon the tanner, who lives by the sea.' [33] So I sent for you immediately, and it was good of you to come. Now we are all here in the presence of God to listen to everything the Lord has commanded you to tell us."

[34] Then Peter began to speak: "I now realize how true it is that God does not show favoritism [35] but accepts from every nation the one who fears him and does what is right. [36] You know the message God sent to the people of Israel, announcing the good news of peace through Jesus Christ, who is Lord of all. [37] You know what has happened throughout the province of Judea, beginning in Galilee after the baptism that John preached— [38] how God anointed Jesus of Nazareth with the Holy Spirit and power, and how he went around doing good and healing all who were under the power of the devil, because God was with him.

[39] "We are witnesses of everything he did in the country of the Jews and in Jerusalem. They killed him by hanging him on a cross, [40] but God raised him from the dead on the third day and caused him to be seen. [41] He was not seen by all the people, but by witnesses whom God had already chosen—by us who ate and drank with him after he rose from the dead. [42] He commanded us to preach to the people and to testify that he is the one whom God appointed as judge of the living and the dead. [43] All the prophets testify about him that everyone who believes in him receives forgiveness of sins through his name."

[44] While Peter was still speaking these words, the Holy Spirit came on all who heard the message. [45] The circumcised believers who had come with Peter were astonished that the gift of the Holy Spirit had been poured out even on Gentiles. [46] For they heard them speaking in tongues[b] and praising God.

Then Peter said, [47] "Surely no one can stand in the way of their being baptized with water. They have received the Holy Spirit just as we have." [48] So he ordered that they be baptized in the name of Jesus Christ. Then

---

[a] 19 One early manuscript *two*; other manuscripts do not have the number.   [b] 46 Or *other languages*

ACTS 11:1

they asked Peter to stay with them for a few days.

Peter Explains His Actions

11 The apostles and the believers throughout Judea heard that the Gentiles also had received the word of God. [2]So when Peter went up to Jerusalem, the circumcised believers criticized him [3]and said, "You went into the house of uncircumcised men and ate with them."

[4]Starting from the beginning, Peter told them the whole story: [5]"I was in the city of Joppa praying, and in a trance I saw a vision. I saw something like a large sheet being let down from heaven by its four corners, and it came down to where I was. [6]I looked into it and saw four-footed animals of the earth, wild beasts, reptiles and birds. [7]Then I heard a voice telling me, 'Get up, Peter. Kill and eat.'

[8]"I replied, 'Surely not, Lord! Nothing impure or unclean has ever entered my mouth.'

[9]"The voice spoke from heaven a second time, 'Do not call anything impure that God has made clean.' [10]This happened three times, and then it was all pulled up to heaven again.

[11]"Right then three men who had been sent to me from Caesarea stopped at the house where I was staying. [12]The Spirit told me to have no hesitation about going with them. These six brothers also went with me, and we entered the man's house. [13]He told us how he had seen an angel appear in his house and say, 'Send to Joppa for Simon who is called Peter. [14]He will bring you a message through which you and all your household will be saved.'

[15]"As I began to speak, the Holy Spirit came on them as he had come on us at the beginning. [16]Then I remembered what the Lord had said: 'John baptized with[a] water, but you will be baptized with[a] the Holy Spirit.' [17]So if God gave them the same gift he gave us who believed in the Lord Jesus Christ, who was I to think that I could stand in God's way?"

[18]When they heard this, they had no further objections and praised God, saying, "So then, even to Gentiles God has granted repentance that leads to life."

The Church in Antioch

[19]Now those who had been scattered by the persecution that broke out when Stephen was killed traveled as far as Phoenicia, Cyprus and Antioch, spreading the word only among Jews. [20]Some of them, however, men from Cyprus and Cyrene, went to Antioch and began to speak to Greeks also, telling them the good news about the Lord Jesus. [21]The Lord's hand was with them, and a great number of people believed and turned to the Lord.

[22]News of this reached the church in Jerusalem, and they sent Barnabas to Antioch. [23]When he arrived and saw what the grace of God had done, he was glad and encouraged them all to remain true to the Lord with all their hearts. [24]He was a good man, full of the Holy Spirit and faith, and a great number of people were brought to the Lord.

[25]Then Barnabas went to Tarsus to look for Saul, [26]and when he found him, he brought him to Antioch. So for a whole year Barnabas and Saul met with the church and taught great numbers of people. The disciples were called Christians first at Antioch.

[27]During this time some prophets came down from Jerusalem to Antioch. [28]One of them, named Agabus, stood up and through the Spirit predicted that a severe famine would spread over the entire Roman world. (This happened during the reign of Claudius.) [29]The disciples, as each one was able, decided to provide help for the brothers and sisters living in Judea. [30]This they did, sending their gift to the elders by Barnabas and Saul.

Peter's Miraculous Escape From Prison

12 It was about this time that King Herod arrested some who belonged to the church, intending to persecute them. [2]He had James, the brother of John, put to death with the sword. [3]When he saw that this met with approval among the Jews, he proceeded to seize Peter also. This happened during the Festival of Unleavened Bread. [4]After arresting him, he put him in prison, handing him over to be guarded by four squads of four soldiers each. Herod intended to bring him out for public trial after the Passover.

[a] *16 Or in*

[5]So Peter was kept in prison, but the church was earnestly praying to God for him.

[6]The night before Herod was to bring him to trial, Peter was sleeping between two soldiers, bound with two chains, and sentries stood guard at the entrance. [7]Suddenly an angel of the Lord appeared and a light shone in the cell. He struck Peter on the side and woke him up. "Quick, get up!" he said, and the chains fell off Peter's wrists.

[8]Then the angel said to him, "Put on your clothes and sandals." And Peter did so. "Wrap your cloak around you and follow me," the angel told him. [9]Peter followed him out of the prison, but he had no idea that what the angel was doing was really happening; he thought he was seeing a vision. [10]They passed the first and second guards and came to the iron gate leading to the city. It opened for them by itself, and they went through it. When they had walked the length of one street, suddenly the angel left him.

[11]Then Peter came to himself and said, "Now I know without a doubt that the Lord has sent his angel and rescued me from Herod's clutches and from everything the Jewish people were hoping would happen."

[12]When this had dawned on him, he went to the house of Mary the mother of John, also called Mark, where many people had gathered and were praying. [13]Peter knocked at the outer entrance, and a servant named Rhoda came to answer the door. [14]When she recognized Peter's voice, she was so overjoyed she ran back without opening it and exclaimed, "Peter is at the door!"

[15]"You're out of your mind," they told her. When she kept insisting that it was so, they said, "It must be his angel."

[16]But Peter kept on knocking, and when they opened the door and saw him, they were astonished. [17]Peter motioned with his hand for them to be quiet and described how the Lord had brought him out of prison. "Tell James and the other brothers and sisters about this," he said, and then he left for another place.

[18]In the morning, there was no small commotion among the soldiers as to what had become of Peter. [19]After Herod had a thorough search made for him and did not find him, he cross-examined the guards and ordered that they be executed.

Herod's Death

Then Herod went from Judea to Caesarea and stayed there. [20]He had been quarreling with the people of Tyre and Sidon; they now joined together and sought an audience with him. After securing the support of Blastus, a trusted personal servant of the king, they asked for peace, because they depended on the king's country for their food supply.

[21]On the appointed day Herod, wearing his royal robes, sat on his throne and delivered a public address to the people. [22]They shouted, "This is the voice of a god, not of a man." [23]Immediately, because Herod did not give praise to God, an angel of the Lord struck him down, and he was eaten by worms and died.

[24]But the word of God continued to spread and flourish.

Barnabas and Saul Sent Off

[25]When Barnabas and Saul had finished their mission, they returned from[a] Jerusalem, taking with them John, also called Mark. 13 [1]Now in the church at Antioch there were prophets and teachers: Barnabas, Simeon called Niger, Lucius of Cyrene, Manaen (who had been brought up with Herod the tetrarch) and Saul. [2]While they were worshiping the Lord and fasting, the Holy Spirit said, "Set apart for me Barnabas and Saul for the work to which I have called them." [3]So after they had fasted and prayed, they placed their hands on them and sent them off.

On Cyprus

[4]The two of them, sent on their way by the Holy Spirit, went down to Seleucia and sailed from there to Cyprus. [5]When they arrived at Salamis, they proclaimed the word of God in the Jewish synagogues. John was with them as their helper.

[6]They traveled through the whole island until they came to Paphos. There they met a Jewish sorcerer and false prophet named Bar-Jesus, [7]who was an attendant of the proconsul, Sergius Paulus. The proconsul, an intelligent man, sent for Barnabas and

[a] 25 Some manuscripts to

Saul because he wanted to hear the word of God. [8]But Elymas the sorcerer (for that is what his name means) opposed them and tried to turn the proconsul from the faith. [9]Then Saul, who was also called Paul, filled with the Holy Spirit, looked straight at Elymas and said, [10]"You are a child of the devil and an enemy of everything that is right! You are full of all kinds of deceit and trickery. Will you never stop perverting the right ways of the Lord? [11]Now the hand of the Lord is against you. You are going to be blind for a time, not even able to see the light of the sun."

Immediately mist and darkness came over him, and he groped about, seeking someone to lead him by the hand. [12]When the proconsul saw what had happened, he believed, for he was amazed at the teaching about the Lord.

In Pisidian Antioch

[13]From Paphos, Paul and his companions sailed to Perga in Pamphylia, where John left them to return to Jerusalem. [14]From Perga they went on to Pisidian Antioch. On the Sabbath they entered the synagogue and sat down. [15]After the reading from the Law and the Prophets, the leaders of the synagogue sent word to them, saying, "Brothers, if you have a word of exhortation for the people, please speak."

[16]Standing up, Paul motioned with his hand and said: "Fellow Israelites and you Gentiles who worship God, listen to me! [17]The God of the people of Israel chose our ancestors; he made the people prosper during their stay in Egypt; with mighty power he led them out of that country; [18]for about forty years he endured their conduct[a] in the wilderness; [19]and he overthrew seven nations in Canaan, giving their land to his people as their inheritance. [20]All this took about 450 years.

"After this, God gave them judges until the time of Samuel the prophet. [21]Then the people asked for a king, and he gave them Saul son of Kish, of the tribe of Benjamin, who ruled forty years. [22]After removing Saul, he made David their king. God testified concerning him: 'I have found David son of Jesse, a man after my own heart; he will do everything I want him to do.'

[23]"From this man's descendants God has brought to Israel the Savior Jesus, as he promised. [24]Before the coming of Jesus, John preached repentance and baptism to all the people of Israel. [25]As John was completing his work, he said: 'Who do you suppose I am? I am not the one you are looking for. But there is one coming after me whose sandals I am not worthy to untie.'

[26]"Fellow children of Abraham and you God-fearing Gentiles, it is to us that this message of salvation has been sent. [27]The people of Jerusalem and their rulers did not recognize Jesus, yet in condemning him they fulfilled the words of the prophets that are read every Sabbath. [28]Though they found no proper ground for a death sentence, they asked Pilate to have him executed. [29]When they had carried out all that was written about him, they took him down from the cross and laid him in a tomb. [30]But God raised him from the dead, [31]and for many days he was seen by those who had traveled with him from Galilee to Jerusalem. They are now his witnesses to our people.

[32]"We tell you the good news: What God promised our ancestors [33]he has fulfilled for us, their children, by raising up Jesus. As it is written in the second Psalm:

> "'You are my son;
>   today I have become your father.'[b]

[34]God raised him from the dead so that he will never be subject to decay. As God has said,

> "'I will give you the holy and sure
>   blessings promised to David.'[c]

[35]So it is also stated elsewhere:

> "'You will not let your holy one see
>   decay.'[d]

[36]"Now when David had served God's purpose in his own generation, he fell asleep; he was buried with his ancestors and his body decayed. [37]But the one whom God raised from the dead did not see decay.

[38]"Therefore, my friends, I want you to know that through Jesus the forgiveness of sins is proclaimed to you. [39]Through him everyone who believes is set free from every sin, a justification you were not able to

---

[a] 18 Some manuscripts *he cared for them*   [b] 33 Psalm 2:7   [c] 34 Isaiah 55:3   [d] 35 Psalm 16:10 (see Septuagint)

obtain under the law of Moses. [40]Take care that what the prophets have said does not happen to you:

[41]" 'Look, you scoffers,
    wonder and perish,
for I am going to do something in
        your days
    that you would never believe,
    even if someone told you.'[a]"

[42]As Paul and Barnabas were leaving the synagogue, the people invited them to speak further about these things on the next Sabbath. [43]When the congregation was dismissed, many of the Jews and devout converts to Judaism followed Paul and Barnabas, who talked with them and urged them to continue in the grace of God.

[44]On the next Sabbath almost the whole city gathered to hear the word of the Lord. [45]When the Jews saw the crowds, they were filled with jealousy. They began to contradict what Paul was saying and heaped abuse on him.

[46]Then Paul and Barnabas answered them boldly: "We had to speak the word of God to you first. Since you reject it and do not consider yourselves worthy of eternal life, we now turn to the Gentiles. [47]For this is what the Lord has commanded us:

" 'I have made you[b] a light for the
        Gentiles,
    that you[b] may bring salvation to the
        ends of the earth.'[c]"

[48]When the Gentiles heard this, they were glad and honored the word of the Lord; and all who were appointed for eternal life believed.

[49]The word of the Lord spread through the whole region. [50]But the Jewish leaders incited the God-fearing women of high standing and the leading men of the city. They stirred up persecution against Paul and Barnabas, and expelled them from their region. [51]So they shook the dust off their feet as a warning to them and went to Iconium. [52]And the disciples were filled with joy and with the Holy Spirit.

In Iconium

14 At Iconium Paul and Barnabas went as usual into the Jewish synagogue.

There they spoke so effectively that a great number of Jews and Greeks believed. [2]But the Jews who refused to believe stirred up the other Gentiles and poisoned their minds against the brothers. [3]So Paul and Barnabas spent considerable time there, speaking boldly for the Lord, who confirmed the message of his grace by enabling them to perform signs and wonders. [4]The people of the city were divided; some sided with the Jews, others with the apostles. [5]There was a plot afoot among both Gentiles and Jews, together with their leaders, to mistreat them and stone them. [6]But they found out about it and fled to the Lycaonian cities of Lystra and Derbe and to the surrounding country, [7]where they continued to preach the gospel.

In Lystra and Derbe

[8]In Lystra there sat a man who was lame. He had been that way from birth and had never walked. [9]He listened to Paul as he was speaking. Paul looked directly at him, saw that he had faith to be healed [10]and called out, "Stand up on your feet!" At that, the man jumped up and began to walk.

[11]When the crowd saw what Paul had done, they shouted in the Lycaonian language, "The gods have come down to us in human form!" [12]Barnabas they called Zeus, and Paul they called Hermes because he was the chief speaker. [13]The priest of Zeus, whose temple was just outside the city, brought bulls and wreaths to the city gates because he and the crowd wanted to offer sacrifices to them.

[14]But when the apostles Barnabas and Paul heard of this, they tore their clothes and rushed out into the crowd, shouting: [15]"Friends, why are you doing this? We too are only human, like you. We are bringing you good news, telling you to turn from these worthless things to the living God, who made the heavens and the earth and the sea and everything in them. [16]In the past, he let all nations go their own way. [17]Yet he has not left himself without testimony: He has shown kindness by giving you rain from heaven and crops in their seasons; he provides you with plenty of food and fills your hearts with joy." [18]Even with these words, they had difficulty keeping the crowd from sacrificing to them.

[a] 41 Hab. 1:5   [b] 47 The Greek is singular.   [c] 47 Isaiah 49:6

[19]Then some Jews came from Antioch and Iconium and won the crowd over. They stoned Paul and dragged him outside the city, thinking he was dead. [20]But after the disciples had gathered around him, he got up and went back into the city. The next day he and Barnabas left for Derbe.

The Return to Antioch in Syria

[21]They preached the gospel in that city and won a large number of disciples. Then they returned to Lystra, Iconium and Antioch, [22]strengthening the disciples and encouraging them to remain true to the faith. "We must go through many hardships to enter the kingdom of God," they said. [23]Paul and Barnabas appointed elders[a] for them in each church and, with prayer and fasting, committed them to the Lord, in whom they had put their trust. [24]After going through Pisidia, they came into Pamphylia, [25]and when they had preached the word in Perga, they went down to Attalia.

[26]From Attalia they sailed back to Antioch, where they had been committed to the grace of God for the work they had now completed. [27]On arriving there, they gathered the church together and reported all that God had done through them and how he had opened a door of faith to the Gentiles. [28]And they stayed there a long time with the disciples.

The Council at Jerusalem

15 Certain people came down from Judea to Antioch and were teaching the believers: "Unless you are circumcised, according to the custom taught by Moses, you cannot be saved." [2]This brought Paul and Barnabas into sharp dispute and debate with them. So Paul and Barnabas were appointed, along with some other believers, to go up to Jerusalem to see the apostles and elders about this question. [3]The church sent them on their way, and as they traveled through Phoenicia and Samaria, they told how the Gentiles had been converted. This news made all the believers very glad. [4]When they came to Jerusalem, they were welcomed by the church and the apostles and elders, to whom they reported everything God had done through them.

[5]Then some of the believers who belonged to the party of the Pharisees stood up and said, "The Gentiles must be circumcised and required to keep the law of Moses."

[6]The apostles and elders met to consider this question. [7]After much discussion, Peter got up and addressed them: "Brothers, you know that some time ago God made a choice among you that the Gentiles might hear from my lips the message of the gospel and believe. [8]God, who knows the heart, showed that he accepted them by giving the Holy Spirit to them, just as he did to us. [9]He did not discriminate between us and them, for he purified their hearts by faith. [10]Now then, why do you try to test God by putting on the necks of Gentiles a yoke that neither we nor our ancestors have been able to bear? [11]No! We believe it is through the grace of our Lord Jesus that we are saved, just as they are."

[12]The whole assembly became silent as they listened to Barnabas and Paul telling about the signs and wonders God had done among the Gentiles through them. [13]When they finished, James spoke up. "Brothers," he said, "listen to me. [14]Simon[b] has described to us how God first intervened to choose a people for his name from the Gentiles. [15]The words of the prophets are in agreement with this, as it is written:

[16] " 'After this I will return
    and rebuild David's fallen tent.
  Its ruins I will rebuild,
    and I will restore it,
[17] that the rest of mankind may seek
      the Lord,
    even all the Gentiles who bear
      my name,
    says the Lord, who does these things'[c] —
[18]   things known from long ago.[d]

[19]"It is my judgment, therefore, that we should not make it difficult for the Gentiles who are turning to God. [20]Instead we should write to them, telling them to abstain from food polluted by idols, from sexual immorality, from the meat of strangled animals and from blood. [21]For the law of Moses has been preached in every city from the earliest

---

[a] 23 Or Barnabas ordained elders; or Barnabas had elders elected   [b] 14 Greek Simeon, a variant of Simon; that is, Peter   [c] 17 Amos 9:11,12 (see Septuagint)   [d] 17,18 Some manuscripts things' — / [18]the Lord's work is known to him from long ago

times and is read in the synagogues on every Sabbath."

The Council's Letter to Gentile Believers

22 Then the apostles and elders, with the whole church, decided to choose some of their own men and send them to Antioch with Paul and Barnabas. They chose Judas (called Barsabbas) and Silas, men who were leaders among the believers. 23 With them they sent the following letter:

The apostles and elders, your brothers,

To the Gentile believers in Antioch, Syria and Cilicia:

Greetings.

24 We have heard that some went out from us without our authorization and disturbed you, troubling your minds by what they said. 25 So we all agreed to choose some men and send them to you with our dear friends Barnabas and Paul— 26 men who have risked their lives for the name of our Lord Jesus Christ. 27 Therefore we are sending Judas and Silas to confirm by word of mouth what we are writing. 28 It seemed good to the Holy Spirit and to us not to burden you with anything beyond the following requirements: 29 You are to abstain from food sacrificed to idols, from blood, from the meat of strangled animals and from sexual immorality. You will do well to avoid these things.

Farewell.

30 So the men were sent off and went down to Antioch, where they gathered the church together and delivered the letter. 31 The people read it and were glad for its encouraging message. 32 Judas and Silas, who themselves were prophets, said much to encourage and strengthen the believers. 33 After spending some time there, they were sent off by the believers with the blessing of peace to return to those who had sent them. [34] a 35 But Paul and Barnabas remained in Antioch, where they and many others taught and preached the word of the Lord.

Disagreement Between Paul and Barnabas

36 Some time later Paul said to Barnabas, "Let us go back and visit the believers in all the towns where we preached the word of the Lord and see how they are doing." 37 Barnabas wanted to take John, also called Mark, with them, 38 but Paul did not think it wise to take him, because he had deserted them in Pamphylia and had not continued with them in the work. 39 They had such a sharp disagreement that they parted company. Barnabas took Mark and sailed for Cyprus, 40 but Paul chose Silas and left, commended by the believers to the grace of the Lord. 41 He went through Syria and Cilicia, strengthening the churches.

Timothy Joins Paul and Silas

16 Paul came to Derbe and then to Lystra, where a disciple named Timothy lived, whose mother was Jewish and a believer but whose father was a Greek. 2 The believers at Lystra and Iconium spoke well of him. 3 Paul wanted to take him along on the journey, so he circumcised him because of the Jews who lived in that area, for they all knew that his father was a Greek. 4 As they traveled from town to town, they delivered the decisions reached by the apostles and elders in Jerusalem for the people to obey. 5 So the churches were strengthened in the faith and grew daily in numbers.

Paul's Vision of the Man of Macedonia

6 Paul and his companions traveled throughout the region of Phrygia and Galatia, having been kept by the Holy Spirit from preaching the word in the province of Asia. 7 When they came to the border of Mysia, they tried to enter Bithynia, but the Spirit of Jesus would not allow them to. 8 So they passed by Mysia and went down to Troas. 9 During the night Paul had a vision of a man of Macedonia standing and begging him, "Come over to Macedonia and help us." 10 After Paul had seen the vision, we got ready at once to leave for Macedonia, concluding that God had called us to preach the gospel to them.

Lydia's Conversion in Philippi

11 From Troas we put out to sea and sailed straight for Samothrace, and the next day we

---

a 34 Some manuscripts include here But Silas decided to remain there.

went on to Neapolis. [12] From there we traveled to Philippi, a Roman colony and the leading city of that district[a] of Macedonia. And we stayed there several days.

[13] On the Sabbath we went outside the city gate to the river, where we expected to find a place of prayer. We sat down and began to speak to the women who had gathered there. [14] One of those listening was a woman from the city of Thyatira named Lydia, a dealer in purple cloth. She was a worshiper of God. The Lord opened her heart to respond to Paul's message. [15] When she and the members of her household were baptized, she invited us to her home. "If you consider me a believer in the Lord," she said, "come and stay at my house." And she persuaded us.

Paul and Silas in Prison

[16] Once when we were going to the place of prayer, we were met by a female slave who had a spirit by which she predicted the future. She earned a great deal of money for her owners by fortune-telling. [17] She followed Paul and the rest of us, shouting, "These men are servants of the Most High God, who are telling you the way to be saved." [18] She kept this up for many days. Finally Paul became so annoyed that he turned around and said to the spirit, "In the name of Jesus Christ I command you to come out of her!" At that moment the spirit left her.

[19] When her owners realized that their hope of making money was gone, they seized Paul and Silas and dragged them into the marketplace to face the authorities. [20] They brought them before the magistrates and said, "These men are Jews, and are throwing our city into an uproar [21] by advocating customs unlawful for us Romans to accept or practice."

[22] The crowd joined in the attack against Paul and Silas, and the magistrates ordered them to be stripped and beaten with rods. [23] After they had been severely flogged, they were thrown into prison, and the jailer was commanded to guard them carefully. [24] When he received these orders, he put them in the inner cell and fastened their feet in the stocks.

[25] About midnight Paul and Silas were praying and singing hymns to God, and the other prisoners were listening to them. [26] Suddenly there was such a violent earthquake that the foundations of the prison were shaken. At once all the prison doors flew open, and everyone's chains came loose. [27] The jailer woke up, and when he saw the prison doors open, he drew his sword and was about to kill himself because he thought the prisoners had escaped. [28] But Paul shouted, "Don't harm yourself! We are all here!"

[29] The jailer called for lights, rushed in and fell trembling before Paul and Silas. [30] He then brought them out and asked, "Sirs, what must I do to be saved?"

[31] They replied, "Believe in the Lord Jesus, and you will be saved — you and your household." [32] Then they spoke the word of the Lord to him and to all the others in his house. [33] At that hour of the night the jailer took them and washed their wounds; then immediately he and all his household were baptized. [34] The jailer brought them into his house and set a meal before them; he was filled with joy because he had come to believe in God — he and his whole household.

[35] When it was daylight, the magistrates sent their officers to the jailer with the order: "Release those men." [36] The jailer told Paul, "The magistrates have ordered that you and Silas be released. Now you can leave. Go in peace."

[37] But Paul said to the officers: "They beat us publicly without a trial, even though we are Roman citizens, and threw us into prison. And now do they want to get rid of us quietly? No! Let them come themselves and escort us out."

[38] The officers reported this to the magistrates, and when they heard that Paul and Silas were Roman citizens, they were alarmed. [39] They came to appease them and escorted them from the prison, requesting them to leave the city. [40] After Paul and Silas came out of the prison, they went to Lydia's house, where they met with the brothers and sisters and encouraged them. Then they left.

In Thessalonica

17 When Paul and his companions had passed through Amphipolis and Apollonia, they came to Thessalonica, where

---

[a] 12 The text and meaning of the Greek for *the leading city of that district* are uncertain.

Praise From Prison

By Catherine Fitzgerald

READ: Acts 16:16–34

I n an instant, every military wife's greatest fear became a reality for my friend: She received the news that her husband had been killed. But a few months later, when she made the coast-to-coast journey to get some respite at my home, I could see that she was not held captive by her grief. Instead, she praised God for his goodness even during a personal nightmare. Her response to a tragedy and my recollection of it in the days that followed began to release me from the bondage of my own anxieties.

In Acts 16:16–26, we see another example of imprisonment and praise. Paul and Silas were confined to the four walls of a prison cell. Their fate remained unknown as they were unfairly imprisoned for doing something that was good. They had liberated a young girl from demon possession, yet they found themselves shackled and alone.

These apostles knew something about confinement. They also knew that praise had power. Imagine the disbelief of those overhearing the singing and thanksgiving echoing through the halls of the jail in the night (see verse 25). It seemed unnatural to be praising God in such a dire situation.

Two missionaries provided a special lesson about praise that day. Long after the doors of that jail swung open, the inmates who were imprisoned with Paul and Silas had a lifelong example to reflect on. Praise could *release* them (see verse 26).

Military life is an inherently good thing. It is the laying down of ourselves for the benefit of others. It is learning the art of sacrifice. Nevertheless, because of it we can find ourselves unjustly incarcerated in the prison of fear, loneliness or despair. How can we fling open the doors of these cells while all the other prisoners watch?

We can start by following the example of Paul and Silas: We can pray, meditate on God's Word, sing hymns and praise God. Praise has the incredible ability to change a circumstance. When our mouths overflow with worship, our eyes no longer fixate on the bars that surround us but instead focus on the freedom that belongs to us. This freedom, according to Jesus in John 8:31–36, means we are no longer slaves to sin, which shackles our spirit.

As you battle whatever incarcerates your soul, start praising the Lord, and watch what happens. Those in the cell next to you are watching you too. Are you ready and willing to show them how to break free?

About midnight Paul and Silas were praying and singing hymns to God, and the other prisoners were listening to them. Suddenly there was such a violent earthquake that the foundations of the prison were shaken. At once all the prison doors flew open, and everyone's chains came loose.

ACTS 16:25–26

DEBRIEF
- What can I praise God for today?
- Whom might my example influence?

REPORT
Lord, strengthen me so that I may sing your praises inside the prison I am in. Use my songs of thanksgiving to show others how they can live in freedom in Christ, which brings freedom from the fears, loneliness or despair that seeks to restrain them. In Jesus' name I pray. Amen.

for your next devotional reading, go to page 178

there was a Jewish synagogue. [2]As was his custom, Paul went into the synagogue, and on three Sabbath days he reasoned with them from the Scriptures, [3]explaining and proving that the Messiah had to suffer and rise from the dead. "This Jesus I am proclaiming to you is the Messiah," he said. [4]Some of the Jews were persuaded and joined Paul and Silas, as did a large number of God-fearing Greeks and quite a few prominent women.

[5]But other Jews were jealous; so they rounded up some bad characters from the marketplace, formed a mob and started a riot in the city. They rushed to Jason's house in search of Paul and Silas in order to bring them out to the crowd.[a] [6]But when they did not find them, they dragged Jason and some other believers before the city officials, shouting: "These men who have caused trouble all over the world have now come here, [7]and Jason has welcomed them into his house. They are all defying Caesar's decrees, saying that there is another king, one called Jesus." [8]When they heard this, the crowd and the city officials were thrown into turmoil. [9]Then they made Jason and the others post bond and let them go.

In Berea

[10]As soon as it was night, the believers sent Paul and Silas away to Berea. On arriving there, they went to the Jewish synagogue. [11]Now the Berean Jews were of more noble character than those in Thessalonica, for they received the message with great eagerness and examined the Scriptures every day to see if what Paul said was true. [12]As a result, many of them believed, as did also a number of prominent Greek women and many Greek men.

[13]But when the Jews in Thessalonica learned that Paul was preaching the word of God at Berea, some of them went there too, agitating the crowds and stirring them up. [14]The believers immediately sent Paul to the coast, but Silas and Timothy stayed at Berea. [15]Those who escorted Paul brought him to Athens and then left with instructions for Silas and Timothy to join him as soon as possible.

In Athens

[16]While Paul was waiting for them in Athens, he was greatly distressed to see that the city was full of idols. [17]So he reasoned in the synagogue with both Jews and God-fearing Greeks, as well as in the marketplace day by day with those who happened to be there. [18]A group of Epicurean and Stoic philosophers began to debate with him. Some of them asked, "What is this babbler trying to say?" Others remarked, "He seems to be advocating foreign gods." They said this because Paul was preaching the good news about Jesus and the resurrection. [19]Then they took him and brought him to a meeting of the Areopagus, where they said to him, "May we know what this new teaching is that you are presenting? [20]You are bringing some strange ideas to our ears, and we would like to know what they mean." [21](All the Athenians and the foreigners who lived there spent their time doing nothing but talking about and listening to the latest ideas.)

[22]Paul then stood up in the meeting of the Areopagus and said: "People of Athens! I see that in every way you are very religious. [23]For as I walked around and looked carefully at your objects of worship, I even found an altar with this inscription: TO AN UNKNOWN GOD. So you are ignorant of the very thing you worship—and this is what I am going to proclaim to you.

[24]"The God who made the world and everything in it is the Lord of heaven and earth and does not live in temples built by human hands. [25]And he is not served by human hands, as if he needed anything. Rather, he himself gives everyone life and breath and everything else. [26]From one man he made all the nations, that they should inhabit the whole earth; and he marked out their appointed times in history and the boundaries of their lands. [27]God did this so that they would seek him and perhaps reach out for him and find him, though he is not far from any one of us. [28]'For in him we live and move and have our being.'[b] As some of your own poets have said, 'We are his offspring.'[c]

[29]"Therefore since we are God's offspring, we should not think that the divine being is like gold or silver or stone—an image made by human design and skill. [30]In the past God overlooked such ignorance, but now he commands all people everywhere to repent. [31]For he has set a day when he will judge the

---

[a] 5 Or *the assembly of the people*   [b] 28 From the Cretan philosopher Epimenides   [c] 28 From the Cilician Stoic philosopher Aratus

world with justice by the man he has appointed. He has given proof of this to everyone by raising him from the dead."

³²When they heard about the resurrection of the dead, some of them sneered, but others said, "We want to hear you again on this subject." ³³At that, Paul left the Council. ³⁴Some of the people became followers of Paul and believed. Among them was Dionysius, a member of the Areopagus, also a woman named Damaris, and a number of others.

In Corinth

18 After this, Paul left Athens and went to Corinth. ²There he met a Jew named Aquila, a native of Pontus, who had recently come from Italy with his wife Priscilla, because Claudius had ordered all Jews to leave Rome. Paul went to see them, ³and because he was a tentmaker as they were, he stayed and worked with them. ⁴Every Sabbath he reasoned in the synagogue, trying to persuade Jews and Greeks.

⁵When Silas and Timothy came from Macedonia, Paul devoted himself exclusively to preaching, testifying to the Jews that Jesus was the Messiah. ⁶But when they opposed Paul and became abusive, he shook out his clothes in protest and said to them, "Your blood be on your own heads! I am innocent of it. From now on I will go to the Gentiles."

⁷Then Paul left the synagogue and went next door to the house of Titius Justus, a worshiper of God. ⁸Crispus, the synagogue leader, and his entire household believed in the Lord; and many of the Corinthians who heard Paul believed and were baptized.

⁹One night the Lord spoke to Paul in a vision: "Do not be afraid; keep on speaking, do not be silent. ¹⁰For I am with you, and no one is going to attack and harm you, because I have many people in this city." ¹¹So Paul stayed in Corinth for a year and a half, teaching them the word of God.

¹²While Gallio was proconsul of Achaia, the Jews of Corinth made a united attack on Paul and brought him to the place of judgment. ¹³"This man," they charged, "is persuading the people to worship God in ways contrary to the law."

¹⁴Just as Paul was about to speak, Gallio said to them, "If you Jews were making a complaint about some misdemeanor or serious crime, it would be reasonable for me to listen to you. ¹⁵But since it involves questions about words and names and your own law—settle the matter yourselves. I will not be a judge of such things." ¹⁶So he drove them off. ¹⁷Then the crowd there turned on Sosthenes the synagogue leader and beat him in front of the proconsul; and Gallio showed no concern whatever.

Priscilla, Aquila and Apollos

¹⁸Paul stayed on in Corinth for some time. Then he left the brothers and sisters and sailed for Syria, accompanied by Priscilla and Aquila. Before he sailed, he had his hair cut off at Cenchreae because of a vow he had taken. ¹⁹They arrived at Ephesus, where Paul left Priscilla and Aquila. He himself went into the synagogue and reasoned with the Jews. ²⁰When they asked him to spend more time with them, he declined. ²¹But as he left, he promised, "I will come back if it is God's will." Then he set sail from Ephesus. ²²When he landed at Caesarea, he went up to Jerusalem and greeted the church and then went down to Antioch.

²³After spending some time in Antioch, Paul set out from there and traveled from place to place throughout the region of Galatia and Phrygia, strengthening all the disciples.

²⁴Meanwhile a Jew named Apollos, a native of Alexandria, came to Ephesus. He was a learned man, with a thorough knowledge of the Scriptures. ²⁵He had been instructed in the way of the Lord, and he spoke with great fervor[a] and taught about Jesus accurately, though he knew only the baptism of John. ²⁶He began to speak boldly in the synagogue. When Priscilla and Aquila heard him, they invited him to their home and explained to him the way of God more adequately.

²⁷When Apollos wanted to go to Achaia, the brothers and sisters encouraged him and wrote to the disciples there to welcome him. When he arrived, he was a great help to those who by grace had believed. ²⁸For he vigorously refuted his Jewish opponents in

[a] 25 Or *with fervor in the Spirit*

public debate, proving from the Scriptures that Jesus was the Messiah.

Paul in Ephesus

19 While Apollos was at Corinth, Paul took the road through the interior and arrived at Ephesus. There he found some disciples ²and asked them, "Did you receive the Holy Spirit when*a* you believed?"

They answered, "No, we have not even heard that there is a Holy Spirit."

³So Paul asked, "Then what baptism did you receive?"

"John's baptism," they replied.

⁴Paul said, "John's baptism was a baptism of repentance. He told the people to believe in the one coming after him, that is, in Jesus." ⁵On hearing this, they were baptized in the name of the Lord Jesus. ⁶When Paul placed his hands on them, the Holy Spirit came on them, and they spoke in tongues*b* and prophesied. ⁷There were about twelve men in all.

⁸Paul entered the synagogue and spoke boldly there for three months, arguing persuasively about the kingdom of God. ⁹But some of them became obstinate; they refused to believe and publicly maligned the Way. So Paul left them. He took the disciples with him and had discussions daily in the lecture hall of Tyrannus. ¹⁰This went on for two years, so that all the Jews and Greeks who lived in the province of Asia heard the word of the Lord.

¹¹God did extraordinary miracles through Paul, ¹²so that even handkerchiefs and aprons that had touched him were taken to the sick, and their illnesses were cured and the evil spirits left them.

¹³Some Jews who went around driving out evil spirits tried to invoke the name of the Lord Jesus over those who were demon-possessed. They would say, "In the name of the Jesus whom Paul preaches, I command you to come out." ¹⁴Seven sons of Sceva, a Jewish chief priest, were doing this. ¹⁵One day the evil spirit answered them, "Jesus I know, and Paul I know about, but who are you?" ¹⁶Then the man who had the evil spirit jumped on them and overpowered them all. He gave them such a beating that they ran out of the house naked and bleeding.

¹⁷When this became known to the Jews and Greeks living in Ephesus, they were all seized with fear, and the name of the Lord Jesus was held in high honor. ¹⁸Many of those who believed now came and openly confessed what they had done. ¹⁹A number who had practiced sorcery brought their scrolls together and burned them publicly. When they calculated the value of the scrolls, the total came to fifty thousand drachmas.*c* ²⁰In this way the word of the Lord spread widely and grew in power.

²¹After all this had happened, Paul decided*d* to go to Jerusalem, passing through Macedonia and Achaia. "After I have been there," he said, "I must visit Rome also." ²²He sent two of his helpers, Timothy and Erastus, to Macedonia, while he stayed in the province of Asia a little longer.

The Riot in Ephesus

²³About that time there arose a great disturbance about the Way. ²⁴A silversmith named Demetrius, who made silver shrines of Artemis, brought in a lot of business for the craftsmen there. ²⁵He called them together, along with the workers in related trades, and said: "You know, my friends, that we receive a good income from this business. ²⁶And you see and hear how this fellow Paul has convinced and led astray large numbers of people here in Ephesus and in practically the whole province of Asia. He says that gods made by human hands are no gods at all. ²⁷There is danger not only that our trade will lose its good name, but also that the temple of the great goddess Artemis will be discredited; and the goddess herself, who is worshiped throughout the province of Asia and the world, will be robbed of her divine majesty."

²⁸When they heard this, they were furious and began shouting: "Great is Artemis of the Ephesians!" ²⁹Soon the whole city was in an uproar. The people seized Gaius and Aristarchus, Paul's traveling companions from Macedonia, and all of them rushed into the theater together. ³⁰Paul wanted to appear before the crowd, but the disciples would not let him. ³¹Even some of the officials of the province, friends of Paul, sent him a

---

a 2 Or *after*   *b* 6 Or *other languages*   *c* 19 A drachma was a silver coin worth about a day's wages.
d 21 Or *decided in the Spirit*

message begging him not to venture into the theater.

[32] The assembly was in confusion: Some were shouting one thing, some another. Most of the people did not even know why they were there. [33] The Jews in the crowd pushed Alexander to the front, and they shouted instructions to him. He motioned for silence in order to make a defense before the people. [34] But when they realized he was a Jew, they all shouted in unison for about two hours: "Great is Artemis of the Ephesians!"

[35] The city clerk quieted the crowd and said: "Fellow Ephesians, doesn't all the world know that the city of Ephesus is the guardian of the temple of the great Artemis and of her image, which fell from heaven? [36] Therefore, since these facts are undeniable, you ought to calm down and not do anything rash. [37] You have brought these men here, though they have neither robbed temples nor blasphemed our goddess. [38] If, then, Demetrius and his fellow craftsmen have a grievance against anybody, the courts are open and there are proconsuls. They can press charges. [39] If there is anything further you want to bring up, it must be settled in a legal assembly. [40] As it is, we are in danger of being charged with rioting because of what happened today. In that case we would not be able to account for this commotion, since there is no reason for it." [41] After he had said this, he dismissed the assembly.

Through Macedonia and Greece

20 When the uproar had ended, Paul sent for the disciples and, after encouraging them, said goodbye and set out for Macedonia. [2] He traveled through that area, speaking many words of encouragement to the people, and finally arrived in Greece, [3] where he stayed three months. Because some Jews had plotted against him just as he was about to sail for Syria, he decided to go back through Macedonia. [4] He was accompanied by Sopater son of Pyrrhus from Berea, Aristarchus and Secundus from Thessalonica, Gaius from Derbe, Timothy also, and Tychicus and Trophimus from the province of Asia. [5] These men went on ahead and waited for us at Troas. [6] But we sailed from Philippi after the Festival of Unleavened Bread, and five days later joined the others at Troas, where we stayed seven days.

Eutychus Raised From the Dead at Troas

[7] On the first day of the week we came together to break bread. Paul spoke to the people and, because he intended to leave the next day, kept on talking until midnight. [8] There were many lamps in the upstairs room where we were meeting. [9] Seated in a window was a young man named Eutychus, who was sinking into a deep sleep as Paul talked on and on. When he was sound asleep, he fell to the ground from the third story and was picked up dead. [10] Paul went down, threw himself on the young man and put his arms around him. "Don't be alarmed," he said. "He's alive!" [11] Then he went upstairs again and broke bread and ate. After talking until daylight, he left. [12] The people took the young man home alive and were greatly comforted.

Paul's Farewell to the Ephesian Elders

[13] We went on ahead to the ship and sailed for Assos, where we were going to take Paul aboard. He had made this arrangement because he was going there on foot. [14] When he met us at Assos, we took him aboard and went on to Mitylene. [15] The next day we set sail from there and arrived off Chios. The day after that we crossed over to Samos, and on the following day arrived at Miletus. [16] Paul had decided to sail past Ephesus to avoid spending time in the province of Asia, for he was in a hurry to reach Jerusalem, if possible, by the day of Pentecost.

[17] From Miletus, Paul sent to Ephesus for the elders of the church. [18] When they arrived, he said to them: "You know how I lived the whole time I was with you, from the first day I came into the province of Asia. [19] I served the Lord with great humility and with tears and in the midst of severe testing by the plots of my Jewish opponents. [20] You know that I have not hesitated to preach anything that would be helpful to you but have taught you publicly and from house to house. [21] I have declared to both Jews and Greeks that they must turn to God in repentance and have faith in our Lord Jesus.

[22] "And now, compelled by the Spirit, I am going to Jerusalem, not knowing what will happen to me there. [23] I only know that in every city the Holy Spirit warns me that prison and hardships are facing me. [24] However,

I consider my life worth nothing to me; my only aim is to finish the race and complete the task the Lord Jesus has given me — the task of testifying to the good news of God's grace.

25 "Now I know that none of you among whom I have gone about preaching the kingdom will ever see me again. 26 Therefore, I declare to you today that I am innocent of the blood of any of you. 27 For I have not hesitated to proclaim to you the whole will of God. 28 Keep watch over yourselves and all the flock of which the Holy Spirit has made you overseers. Be shepherds of the church of God,ᵃ which he bought with his own blood.ᵇ 29 I know that after I leave, savage wolves will come in among you and will not spare the flock. 30 Even from your own number men will arise and distort the truth in order to draw away disciples after them. 31 So be on your guard! Remember that for three years I never stopped warning each of you night and day with tears.

32 "Now I commit you to God and to the word of his grace, which can build you up and give you an inheritance among all those who are sanctified. 33 I have not coveted anyone's silver or gold or clothing. 34 You yourselves know that these hands of mine have supplied my own needs and the needs of my companions. 35 In everything I did, I showed you that by this kind of hard work we must help the weak, remembering the words the Lord Jesus himself said: 'It is more blessed to give than to receive.'"

36 When Paul had finished speaking, he knelt down with all of them and prayed. 37 They all wept as they embraced him and kissed him. 38 What grieved them most was his statement that they would never see his face again. Then they accompanied him to the ship.

On to Jerusalem

21 After we had torn ourselves away from them, we put out to sea and sailed straight to Kos. The next day we went to Rhodes and from there to Patara. 2 We found a ship crossing over to Phoenicia, went on board and set sail. 3 After sighting Cyprus and passing to the south of it, we sailed on to Syria. We landed at Tyre, where our ship

was to unload its cargo. 4 We sought out the disciples there and stayed with them seven days. Through the Spirit they urged Paul not to go on to Jerusalem. 5 When it was time to leave, we left and continued on our way. All of them, including wives and children, accompanied us out of the city, and there on the beach we knelt to pray. 6 After saying goodbye to each other, we went aboard the ship, and they returned home.

7 We continued our voyage from Tyre and landed at Ptolemais, where we greeted the brothers and sisters and stayed with them for a day. 8 Leaving the next day, we reached Caesarea and stayed at the house of Philip the evangelist, one of the Seven. 9 He had four unmarried daughters who prophesied.

10 After we had been there a number of days, a prophet named Agabus came down from Judea. 11 Coming over to us, he took Paul's belt, tied his own hands and feet with it and said, "The Holy Spirit says, 'In this way the Jewish leaders in Jerusalem will bind the owner of this belt and will hand him over to the Gentiles.'"

12 When we heard this, we and the people there pleaded with Paul not to go up to Jerusalem. 13 Then Paul answered, "Why are you weeping and breaking my heart? I am ready not only to be bound, but also to die in Jerusalem for the name of the Lord Jesus." 14 When he would not be dissuaded, we gave up and said, "The Lord's will be done."

15 After this, we started on our way up to Jerusalem. 16 Some of the disciples from Caesarea accompanied us and brought us to the home of Mnason, where we were to stay. He was a man from Cyprus and one of the early disciples.

Paul's Arrival at Jerusalem

17 When we arrived at Jerusalem, the brothers and sisters received us warmly. 18 The next day Paul and the rest of us went to see James, and all the elders were present. 19 Paul greeted them and reported in detail what God had done among the Gentiles through his ministry.

20 When they heard this, they praised God. Then they said to Paul: "You see, brother, how many thousands of Jews have believed, and all of them are zealous for the

---

ᵃ 28 Many manuscripts *of the Lord*   ᵇ 28 Or *with the blood of his own Son.*

law. ²¹They have been informed that you teach all the Jews who live among the Gentiles to turn away from Moses, telling them not to circumcise their children or live according to our customs. ²²What shall we do? They will certainly hear that you have come, ²³so do what we tell you. There are four men with us who have made a vow. ²⁴Take these men, join in their purification rites and pay their expenses, so that they can have their heads shaved. Then everyone will know there is no truth in these reports about you, but that you yourself are living in obedience to the law. ²⁵As for the Gentile believers, we have written to them our decision that they should abstain from food sacrificed to idols, from blood, from the meat of strangled animals and from sexual immorality."

²⁶The next day Paul took the men and purified himself along with them. Then he went to the temple to give notice of the date when the days of purification would end and the offering would be made for each of them.

Paul Arrested

²⁷When the seven days were nearly over, some Jews from the province of Asia saw Paul at the temple. They stirred up the whole crowd and seized him, ²⁸shouting, "Fellow Israelites, help us! This is the man who teaches everyone everywhere against our people and our law and this place. And besides, he has brought Greeks into the temple and defiled this holy place." ²⁹(They had previously seen Trophimus the Ephesian in the city with Paul and assumed that Paul had brought him into the temple.)

³⁰The whole city was aroused, and the people came running from all directions. Seizing Paul, they dragged him from the temple, and immediately the gates were shut. ³¹While they were trying to kill him, news reached the commander of the Roman troops that the whole city of Jerusalem was in an uproar. ³²He at once took some officers and soldiers and ran down to the crowd. When the rioters saw the commander and his soldiers, they stopped beating Paul.

³³The commander came up and arrested him and ordered him to be bound with two chains. Then he asked who he was and what he had done. ³⁴Some in the crowd shouted one thing and some another, and since the commander could not get at the truth because of the uproar, he ordered that Paul be taken into the barracks. ³⁵When Paul reached the steps, the violence of the mob was so great he had to be carried by the soldiers. ³⁶The crowd that followed kept shouting, "Get rid of him!"

Paul Speaks to the Crowd

³⁷As the soldiers were about to take Paul into the barracks, he asked the commander, "May I say something to you?"

"Do you speak Greek?" he replied. ³⁸"Aren't you the Egyptian who started a revolt and led four thousand terrorists out into the wilderness some time ago?"

³⁹Paul answered, "I am a Jew, from Tarsus in Cilicia, a citizen of no ordinary city. Please let me speak to the people."

⁴⁰After receiving the commander's permission, Paul stood on the steps and motioned to the crowd. When they were all silent, he said

22 to them in Aramaic^a: ¹"Brothers and fathers, listen now to my defense."

²When they heard him speak to them in Aramaic, they became very quiet.

Then Paul said: ³"I am a Jew, born in Tarsus of Cilicia, but brought up in this city. I studied under Gamaliel and was thoroughly trained in the law of our ancestors. I was just as zealous for God as any of you are today. ⁴I persecuted the followers of this Way to their death, arresting both men and women and throwing them into prison, ⁵as the high priest and all the Council can themselves testify. I even obtained letters from them to their associates in Damascus, and went there to bring these people as prisoners to Jerusalem to be punished.

⁶"About noon as I came near Damascus, suddenly a bright light from heaven flashed around me. ⁷I fell to the ground and heard a voice say to me, 'Saul! Saul! Why do you persecute me?'

⁸"'Who are you, Lord?' I asked.

"'I am Jesus of Nazareth, whom you are persecuting,' he replied. ⁹My companions saw the light, but they did not understand the voice of him who was speaking to me.

¹⁰"'What shall I do, Lord?' I asked.

^a 40 Or possibly *Hebrew*; also in 22:2

" 'Get up,' the Lord said, 'and go into Damascus. There you will be told all that you have been assigned to do.' [11]My companions led me by the hand into Damascus, because the brilliance of the light had blinded me.

[12]"A man named Ananias came to see me. He was a devout observer of the law and highly respected by all the Jews living there. [13]He stood beside me and said, 'Brother Saul, receive your sight!' And at that very moment I was able to see him.

[14]"Then he said: 'The God of our ancestors has chosen you to know his will and to see the Righteous One and to hear words from his mouth. [15]You will be his witness to all people of what you have seen and heard. [16]And now what are you waiting for? Get up, be baptized and wash your sins away, calling on his name.'

[17]"When I returned to Jerusalem and was praying at the temple, I fell into a trance [18]and saw the Lord speaking to me. 'Quick!' he said. 'Leave Jerusalem immediately, because the people here will not accept your testimony about me.'

[19]" 'Lord,' I replied, 'these people know that I went from one synagogue to another to imprison and beat those who believe in you. [20]And when the blood of your martyr[a] Stephen was shed, I stood there giving my approval and guarding the clothes of those who were killing him.'

[21]"Then the Lord said to me, 'Go; I will send you far away to the Gentiles.' "

Paul the Roman Citizen

[22]The crowd listened to Paul until he said this. Then they raised their voices and shouted, "Rid the earth of him! He's not fit to live!"

[23]As they were shouting and throwing off their cloaks and flinging dust into the air, [24]the commander ordered that Paul be taken into the barracks. He directed that he be flogged and interrogated in order to find out why the people were shouting at him like this. [25]As they stretched him out to flog him, Paul said to the centurion standing there, "Is it legal for you to flog a Roman citizen who hasn't even been found guilty?"

[26]When the centurion heard this, he went to the commander and reported it. "What are you going to do?" he asked. "This man is a Roman citizen."

[27]The commander went to Paul and asked, "Tell me, are you a Roman citizen?"

"Yes, I am," he answered.

[28]Then the commander said, "I had to pay a lot of money for my citizenship."

"But I was born a citizen," Paul replied.

[29]Those who were about to interrogate him withdrew immediately. The commander himself was alarmed when he realized that he had put Paul, a Roman citizen, in chains.

Paul Before the Sanhedrin

[30]The commander wanted to find out exactly why Paul was being accused by the Jews. So the next day he released him and ordered the chief priests and all the members of the Sanhedrin to assemble. Then he brought Paul and had him stand before them.

23 Paul looked straight at the Sanhedrin and said, "My brothers, I have fulfilled my duty to God in all good conscience to this day." [2]At this the high priest Ananias ordered those standing near Paul to strike him on the mouth. [3]Then Paul said to him, "God will strike you, you whitewashed wall! You sit there to judge me according to the law, yet you yourself violate the law by commanding that I be struck!"

[4]Those who were standing near Paul said, "How dare you insult God's high priest!"

[5]Paul replied, "Brothers, I did not realize that he was the high priest; for it is written: 'Do not speak evil about the ruler of your people.'[b]"

[6]Then Paul, knowing that some of them were Sadducees and the others Pharisees, called out in the Sanhedrin, "My brothers, I am a Pharisee, descended from Pharisees. I stand on trial because of the hope of the resurrection of the dead." [7]When he said this, a dispute broke out between the Pharisees and the Sadducees, and the assembly was divided. [8](The Sadducees say that there is no resurrection, and that there are neither angels nor spirits, but the Pharisees believe all these things.)

[9]There was a great uproar, and some of the teachers of the law who were Pharisees stood

_____
[a] 20 Or witness   [b] 5 Exodus 22:28

up and argued vigorously. "We find nothing wrong with this man," they said. "What if a spirit or an angel has spoken to him?" ¹⁰The dispute became so violent that the commander was afraid Paul would be torn to pieces by them. He ordered the troops to go down and take him away from them by force and bring him into the barracks.

¹¹The following night the Lord stood near Paul and said, "Take courage! As you have testified about me in Jerusalem, so you must also testify in Rome."

The Plot to Kill Paul

¹²The next morning some Jews formed a conspiracy and bound themselves with an oath not to eat or drink until they had killed Paul. ¹³More than forty men were involved in this plot. ¹⁴They went to the chief priests and the elders and said, "We have taken a solemn oath not to eat anything until we have killed Paul. ¹⁵Now then, you and the Sanhedrin petition the commander to bring him before you on the pretext of wanting more accurate information about his case. We are ready to kill him before he gets here."

¹⁶But when the son of Paul's sister heard of this plot, he went into the barracks and told Paul.

¹⁷Then Paul called one of the centurions and said, "Take this young man to the commander; he has something to tell him." ¹⁸So he took him to the commander.

The centurion said, "Paul, the prisoner, sent for me and asked me to bring this young man to you because he has something to tell you."

¹⁹The commander took the young man by the hand, drew him aside and asked, "What is it you want to tell me?"

²⁰He said: "Some Jews have agreed to ask you to bring Paul before the Sanhedrin tomorrow on the pretext of wanting more accurate information about him. ²¹Don't give in to them, because more than forty of them are waiting in ambush for him. They have taken an oath not to eat or drink until they have killed him. They are ready now, waiting for your consent to their request."

²²The commander dismissed the young man with this warning: "Don't tell anyone that you have reported this to me."

Paul Transferred to Caesarea

²³Then he called two of his centurions and ordered them, "Get ready a detachment of two hundred soldiers, seventy horsemen and two hundred spearmen*a* to go to Caesarea at nine tonight. ²⁴Provide horses for Paul so that he may be taken safely to Governor Felix."

²⁵He wrote a letter as follows:

²⁶Claudius Lysias,

To His Excellency, Governor Felix:

Greetings.

²⁷This man was seized by the Jews and they were about to kill him, but I came with my troops and rescued him, for I had learned that he is a Roman citizen. ²⁸I wanted to know why they were accusing him, so I brought him to their Sanhedrin. ²⁹I found that the accusation had to do with questions about their law, but there was no charge against him that deserved death or imprisonment. ³⁰When I was informed of a plot to be carried out against the man, I sent him to you at once. I also ordered his accusers to present to you their case against him.

³¹So the soldiers, carrying out their orders, took Paul with them during the night and brought him as far as Antipatris. ³²The next day they let the cavalry go on with him, while they returned to the barracks. ³³When the cavalry arrived in Caesarea, they delivered the letter to the governor and handed Paul over to him. ³⁴The governor read the letter and asked what province he was from. Learning that he was from Cilicia, ³⁵he said, "I will hear your case when your accusers get here." Then he ordered that Paul be kept under guard in Herod's palace.

Paul's Trial Before Felix

24 Five days later the high priest Ananias went down to Caesarea with some of the elders and a lawyer named Tertullus, and they brought their charges against Paul before the governor. ²When Paul was called in, Tertullus presented his case before Felix:

"We have enjoyed a long period of peace under you, and your foresight has brought about reforms in this nation. [3] Everywhere and in every way, most excellent Felix, we acknowledge this with profound gratitude. [4] But in order not to weary you further, I would request that you be kind enough to hear us briefly.

[5] "We have found this man to be a troublemaker, stirring up riots among the Jews all over the world. He is a ringleader of the Nazarene sect [6] and even tried to desecrate the temple; so we seized him. [7] [a] [8] By examining him yourself you will be able to learn the truth about all these charges we are bringing against him."

[9] The other Jews joined in the accusation, asserting that these things were true.

[10] When the governor motioned for him to speak, Paul replied: "I know that for a number of years you have been a judge over this nation; so I gladly make my defense. [11] You can easily verify that no more than twelve days ago I went up to Jerusalem to worship. [12] My accusers did not find me arguing with anyone at the temple, or stirring up a crowd in the synagogues or anywhere else in the city. [13] And they cannot prove to you the charges they are now making against me. [14] However, I admit that I worship the God of our ancestors as a follower of the Way, which they call a sect. I believe everything that is in accordance with the Law and that is written in the Prophets, [15] and I have the same hope in God as these men themselves have, that there will be a resurrection of both the righteous and the wicked. [16] So I strive always to keep my conscience clear before God and man.

[17] "After an absence of several years, I came to Jerusalem to bring my people gifts for the poor and to present offerings. [18] I was ceremonially clean when they found me in the temple courts doing this. There was no crowd with me, nor was I involved in any disturbance. [19] But there are some Jews from the province of Asia, who ought to be here before you and bring charges if they have anything against me. [20] Or these who are here should state what crime they found in me when I stood before the Sanhedrin—

[21] unless it was this one thing I shouted as I stood in their presence: 'It is concerning the resurrection of the dead that I am on trial before you today.' "

[22] Then Felix, who was well acquainted with the Way, adjourned the proceedings. "When Lysias the commander comes," he said, "I will decide your case." [23] He ordered the centurion to keep Paul under guard but to give him some freedom and permit his friends to take care of his needs.

[24] Several days later Felix came with his wife Drusilla, who was Jewish. He sent for Paul and listened to him as he spoke about faith in Christ Jesus. [25] As Paul talked about righteousness, self-control and the judgment to come, Felix was afraid and said, "That's enough for now! You may leave. When I find it convenient, I will send for you." [26] At the same time he was hoping that Paul would offer him a bribe, so he sent for him frequently and talked with him.

[27] When two years had passed, Felix was succeeded by Porcius Festus, but because Felix wanted to grant a favor to the Jews, he left Paul in prison.

Paul's Trial Before Festus

25 Three days after arriving in the province, Festus went up from Caesarea to Jerusalem, [2] where the chief priests and the Jewish leaders appeared before him and presented the charges against Paul. [3] They requested Festus, as a favor to them, to have Paul transferred to Jerusalem, for they were preparing an ambush to kill him along the way. [4] Festus answered, "Paul is being held at Caesarea, and I myself am going there soon. [5] Let some of your leaders come with me, and if the man has done anything wrong, they can press charges against him there."

[6] After spending eight or ten days with them, Festus went down to Caesarea. The next day he convened the court and ordered that Paul be brought before him. [7] When Paul came in, the Jews who had come down from Jerusalem stood around him. They brought many serious charges against him, but they could not prove them.

---

[a] 6-8 Some manuscripts include here *him, and we would have judged him in accordance with our law.* [7] *But the commander Lysias came and took him from us with much violence,* [8] *ordering his accusers to come before you.*

⁸Then Paul made his defense: "I have done nothing wrong against the Jewish law or against the temple or against Caesar."

⁹Festus, wishing to do the Jews a favor, said to Paul, "Are you willing to go up to Jerusalem and stand trial before me there on these charges?"

¹⁰Paul answered: "I am now standing before Caesar's court, where I ought to be tried. I have not done any wrong to the Jews, as you yourself know very well. ¹¹If, however, I am guilty of doing anything deserving death, I do not refuse to die. But if the charges brought against me by these Jews are not true, no one has the right to hand me over to them. I appeal to Caesar!"

¹²After Festus had conferred with his council, he declared: "You have appealed to Caesar. To Caesar you will go!"

Festus Consults King Agrippa

¹³A few days later King Agrippa and Bernice arrived at Caesarea to pay their respects to Festus. ¹⁴Since they were spending many days there, Festus discussed Paul's case with the king. He said: "There is a man here whom Felix left as a prisoner. ¹⁵When I went to Jerusalem, the chief priests and the elders of the Jews brought charges against him and asked that he be condemned.

¹⁶"I told them that it is not the Roman custom to hand over anyone before they have faced their accusers and have had an opportunity to defend themselves against the charges. ¹⁷When they came here with me, I did not delay the case, but convened the court the next day and ordered the man to be brought in. ¹⁸When his accusers got up to speak, they did not charge him with any of the crimes I had expected. ¹⁹Instead, they had some points of dispute with him about their own religion and about a dead man named Jesus who Paul claimed was alive. ²⁰I was at a loss how to investigate such matters; so I asked if he would be willing to go to Jerusalem and stand trial there on these charges. ²¹But when Paul made his appeal to be held over for the Emperor's decision, I ordered him held until I could send him to Caesar."

²²Then Agrippa said to Festus, "I would like to hear this man myself."

He replied, "Tomorrow you will hear him."

Paul Before Agrippa

²³The next day Agrippa and Bernice came with great pomp and entered the audience room with the high-ranking military officers and the prominent men of the city. At the command of Festus, Paul was brought in. ²⁴Festus said: "King Agrippa, and all who are present with us, you see this man! The whole Jewish community has petitioned me about him in Jerusalem and here in Caesarea, shouting that he ought not to live any longer. ²⁵I found he had done nothing deserving of death, but because he made his appeal to the Emperor I decided to send him to Rome. ²⁶But I have nothing definite to write to His Majesty about him. Therefore I have brought him before all of you, and especially before you, King Agrippa, so that as a result of this investigation I may have something to write. ²⁷For I think it is unreasonable to send a prisoner on to Rome without specifying the charges against him."

26 Then Agrippa said to Paul, "You have permission to speak for yourself."

So Paul motioned with his hand and began his defense: ²"King Agrippa, I consider myself fortunate to stand before you today as I make my defense against all the accusations of the Jews, ³and especially so because you are well acquainted with all the Jewish customs and controversies. Therefore, I beg you to listen to me patiently.

⁴"The Jewish people all know the way I have lived ever since I was a child, from the beginning of my life in my own country, and also in Jerusalem. ⁵They have known me for a long time and can testify, if they are willing, that I conformed to the strictest sect of our religion, living as a Pharisee. ⁶And now it is because of my hope in what God has promised our ancestors that I am on trial today. ⁷This is the promise our twelve tribes are hoping to see fulfilled as they earnestly serve God day and night. King Agrippa, it is because of this hope that these Jews are accusing me. ⁸Why should any of you consider it incredible that God raises the dead?

⁹"I too was convinced that I ought to do all that was possible to oppose the name of Jesus of Nazareth. ¹⁰And that is just what I did in Jerusalem. On the authority of the chief priests I put many of the Lord's people in prison, and when they were put to death, I cast my vote against them. ¹¹Many a time I went

from one synagogue to another to have them punished, and I tried to force them to blaspheme. I was so obsessed with persecuting them that I even hunted them down in foreign cities.

[12] "On one of these journeys I was going to Damascus with the authority and commission of the chief priests. [13] About noon, King Agrippa, as I was on the road, I saw a light from heaven, brighter than the sun, blazing around me and my companions. [14] We all fell to the ground, and I heard a voice saying to me in Aramaic,[a] 'Saul, Saul, why do you persecute me? It is hard for you to kick against the goads.'

[15] "Then I asked, 'Who are you, Lord?'

" 'I am Jesus, whom you are persecuting,' the Lord replied. [16] 'Now get up and stand on your feet. I have appeared to you to appoint you as a servant and as a witness of what you have seen and will see of me. [17] I will rescue you from your own people and from the Gentiles. I am sending you to them [18] to open their eyes and turn them from darkness to light, and from the power of Satan to God, so that they may receive forgiveness of sins and a place among those who are sanctified by faith in me.'

[19] "So then, King Agrippa, I was not disobedient to the vision from heaven. [20] First to those in Damascus, then to those in Jerusalem and in all Judea, and then to the Gentiles, I preached that they should repent and turn to God and demonstrate their repentance by their deeds. [21] That is why some Jews seized me in the temple courts and tried to kill me. [22] But God has helped me to this very day; so I stand here and testify to small and great alike. I am saying nothing beyond what the prophets and Moses said would happen— [23] that the Messiah would suffer and, as the first to rise from the dead, would bring the message of light to his own people and to the Gentiles."

[24] At this point Festus interrupted Paul's defense. "You are out of your mind, Paul!" he shouted. "Your great learning is driving you insane."

[25] "I am not insane, most excellent Festus," Paul replied. "What I am saying is true and reasonable. [26] The king is familiar with these things, and I can speak freely to him.

I am convinced that none of this has escaped his notice, because it was not done in a corner. [27] King Agrippa, do you believe the prophets? I know you do."

[28] Then Agrippa said to Paul, "Do you think that in such a short time you can persuade me to be a Christian?"

[29] Paul replied, "Short time or long—I pray to God that not only you but all who are listening to me today may become what I am, except for these chains."

[30] The king rose, and with him the governor and Bernice and those sitting with them. [31] After they left the room, they began saying to one another, "This man is not doing anything that deserves death or imprisonment."

[32] Agrippa said to Festus, "This man could have been set free if he had not appealed to Caesar."

Paul Sails for Rome

27 When it was decided that we would sail for Italy, Paul and some other prisoners were handed over to a centurion named Julius, who belonged to the Imperial Regiment. [2] We boarded a ship from Adramyttium about to sail for ports along the coast of the province of Asia, and we put out to sea. Aristarchus, a Macedonian from Thessalonica, was with us.

[3] The next day we landed at Sidon; and Julius, in kindness to Paul, allowed him to go to his friends so they might provide for his needs. [4] From there we put out to sea again and passed to the lee of Cyprus because the winds were against us. [5] When we had sailed across the open sea off the coast of Cilicia and Pamphylia, we landed at Myra in Lycia. [6] There the centurion found an Alexandrian ship sailing for Italy and put us on board. [7] We made slow headway for many days and had difficulty arriving off Cnidus. When the wind did not allow us to hold our course, we sailed to the lee of Crete, opposite Salmone. [8] We moved along the coast with difficulty and came to a place called Fair Havens, near the town of Lasea.

[9] Much time had been lost, and sailing had already become dangerous because by now it was after the Day of Atonement.[b] So Paul warned them, [10] "Men, I can see that our

---

[a] 14 Or Hebrew   [b] 9 That is, Yom Kippur

voyage is going to be disastrous and bring great loss to ship and cargo, and to our own lives also." [11] But the centurion, instead of listening to what Paul said, followed the advice of the pilot and of the owner of the ship. [12] Since the harbor was unsuitable to winter in, the majority decided that we should sail on, hoping to reach Phoenix and winter there. This was a harbor in Crete, facing both southwest and northwest.

The Storm

[13] When a gentle south wind began to blow, they saw their opportunity; so they weighed anchor and sailed along the shore of Crete. [14] Before very long, a wind of hurricane force, called the Northeaster, swept down from the island. [15] The ship was caught by the storm and could not head into the wind; so we gave way to it and were driven along. [16] As we passed to the lee of a small island called Cauda, we were hardly able to make the lifeboat secure, [17] so the men hoisted it aboard. Then they passed ropes under the ship itself to hold it together. Because they were afraid they would run aground on the sandbars of Syrtis, they lowered the sea anchor[a] and let the ship be driven along. [18] We took such a violent battering from the storm that the next day they began to throw the cargo overboard. [19] On the third day, they threw the ship's tackle overboard with their own hands. [20] When neither sun nor stars appeared for many days and the storm continued raging, we finally gave up all hope of being saved.

[21] After they had gone a long time without food, Paul stood up before them and said: "Men, you should have taken my advice not to sail from Crete; then you would have spared yourselves this damage and loss. [22] But now I urge you to keep up your courage, because not one of you will be lost; only the ship will be destroyed. [23] Last night an angel of the God to whom I belong and whom I serve stood beside me [24] and said, 'Do not be afraid, Paul. You must stand trial before Caesar; and God has graciously given you the lives of all who sail with you.' [25] So keep up your courage, men, for I have faith in God that it will happen just as he told me.

[26] Nevertheless, we must run aground on some island."

The Shipwreck

[27] On the fourteenth night we were still being driven across the Adriatic[b] Sea, when about midnight the sailors sensed they were approaching land. [28] They took soundings and found that the water was a hundred and twenty feet[c] deep. A short time later they took soundings again and found it was ninety feet[d] deep. [29] Fearing that we would be dashed against the rocks, they dropped four anchors from the stern and prayed for daylight. [30] In an attempt to escape from the ship, the sailors let the lifeboat down into the sea, pretending they were going to lower some anchors from the bow. [31] Then Paul said to the centurion and the soldiers, "Unless these men stay with the ship, you cannot be saved." [32] So the soldiers cut the ropes that held the lifeboat and let it drift away.

[33] Just before dawn Paul urged them all to eat. "For the last fourteen days," he said, "you have been in constant suspense and have gone without food — you haven't eaten anything. [34] Now I urge you to take some food. You need it to survive. Not one of you will lose a single hair from his head." [35] After he said this, he took some bread and gave thanks to God in front of them all. Then he broke it and began to eat. [36] They were all encouraged and ate some food themselves. [37] Altogether there were 276 of us on board. [38] When they had eaten as much as they wanted, they lightened the ship by throwing the grain into the sea.

[39] When daylight came, they did not recognize the land, but they saw a bay with a sandy beach, where they decided to run the ship aground if they could. [40] Cutting loose the anchors, they left them in the sea and at the same time untied the ropes that held the rudders. Then they hoisted the foresail to the wind and made for the beach. [41] But the ship struck a sandbar and ran aground. The bow stuck fast and would not move, and the stern was broken to pieces by the pounding of the surf.

[42] The soldiers planned to kill the prisoners to prevent any of them from swimming away

---

[a] 17 Or *the sails*   [b] 27 In ancient times the name referred to an area extending well south of Italy.
[c] 28 Or about 37 meters   [d] 28 Or about 27 meters

and escaping. [43]But the centurion wanted to spare Paul's life and kept them from carrying out their plan. He ordered those who could swim to jump overboard first and get to land. [44]The rest were to get there on planks or on other pieces of the ship. In this way everyone reached land safely.

Paul Ashore on Malta

28 Once safely on shore, we found out that the island was called Malta. [2]The islanders showed us unusual kindness. They built a fire and welcomed us all because it was raining and cold. [3]Paul gathered a pile of brushwood and, as he put it on the fire, a viper, driven out by the heat, fastened itself on his hand. [4]When the islanders saw the snake hanging from his hand, they said to each other, "This man must be a murderer; for though he escaped from the sea, the goddess Justice has not allowed him to live." [5]But Paul shook the snake off into the fire and suffered no ill effects. [6]The people expected him to swell up or suddenly fall dead; but after waiting a long time and seeing nothing unusual happen to him, they changed their minds and said he was a god.

[7]There was an estate nearby that belonged to Publius, the chief official of the island. He welcomed us to his home and showed us generous hospitality for three days. [8]His father was sick in bed, suffering from fever and dysentery. Paul went in to see him and, after prayer, placed his hands on him and healed him. [9]When this had happened, the rest of the sick on the island came and were cured. [10]They honored us in many ways; and when we were ready to sail, they furnished us with the supplies we needed.

Paul's Arrival at Rome

[11]After three months we put out to sea in a ship that had wintered in the island — it was an Alexandrian ship with the figurehead of the twin gods Castor and Pollux. [12]We put in at Syracuse and stayed there three days. [13]From there we set sail and arrived at Rhegium. The next day the south wind came up, and on the following day we reached Puteoli. [14]There we found some brothers and sisters who invited us to spend a week with them. And so we came to Rome. [15]The brothers and sisters there had heard that we were coming, and they traveled as far as the Forum of Appius and the Three Taverns to meet us. At the sight of these people Paul thanked God and was encouraged. [16]When we got to Rome, Paul was allowed to live by himself, with a soldier to guard him.

Paul Preaches at Rome Under Guard

[17]Three days later he called together the local Jewish leaders. When they had assembled, Paul said to them: "My brothers, although I have done nothing against our people or against the customs of our ancestors, I was arrested in Jerusalem and handed over to the Romans. [18]They examined me and wanted to release me, because I was not guilty of any crime deserving death. [19]The Jews objected, so I was compelled to make an appeal to Caesar. I certainly did not intend to bring any charge against my own people. [20]For this reason I have asked to see you and talk with you. It is because of the hope of Israel that I am bound with this chain."

[21]They replied, "We have not received any letters from Judea concerning you, and none of our people who have come from there has reported or said anything bad about you. [22]But we want to hear what your views are, for we know that people everywhere are talking against this sect."

[23]They arranged to meet Paul on a certain day, and came in even larger numbers to the place where he was staying. He witnessed to them from morning till evening, explaining about the kingdom of God, and from the Law of Moses and from the Prophets he tried to persuade them about Jesus. [24]Some were convinced by what he said, but others would not believe. [25]They disagreed among themselves and began to leave after Paul had made this final statement: "The Holy Spirit spoke the truth to your ancestors when he said through Isaiah the prophet:

[26] " 'Go to this people and say,
    "You will be ever hearing but never
        understanding;
    you will be ever seeing but never
        perceiving."
[27] For this people's heart has become
        calloused;
    they hardly hear with their ears,
    and they have closed their eyes.
Otherwise they might see with their eyes,
    hear with their ears,

understand with their hearts
and turn, and I would heal them.'[a]

28 "Therefore I want you to know that God's salvation has been sent to the Gentiles, and they will listen!" [29][b]

30 For two whole years Paul stayed there in his own rented house and welcomed all who came to see him. 31 He proclaimed the kingdom of God and taught about the Lord Jesus Christ — with all boldness and without hindrance!

[a] 27 Isaiah 6:9,10 (see Septuagint)   [b] 29 Some manuscripts include here After he said this, the Jews left, arguing vigorously among themselves.

Romans

1 Paul, a servant of Christ Jesus, called to be an apostle and set apart for the gospel of God — [2]the gospel he promised beforehand through his prophets in the Holy Scriptures [3]regarding his Son, who as to his earthly life[a] was a descendant of David, [4]and who through the Spirit of holiness was appointed the Son of God in power[b] by his resurrection from the dead: Jesus Christ our Lord. [5]Through him we received grace and apostleship to call all the Gentiles to the obedience that comes from[c] faith for his name's sake. [6]And you also are among those Gentiles who are called to belong to Jesus Christ.

[7]To all in Rome who are loved by God and called to be his holy people:

Grace and peace to you from God our Father and from the Lord Jesus Christ.

Paul's Longing to Visit Rome

[8]First, I thank my God through Jesus Christ for all of you, because your faith is being reported all over the world. [9]God, whom I serve in my spirit in preaching the gospel of his Son, is my witness how constantly I remember you [10]in my prayers at all times; and I pray that now at last by God's will the way may be opened for me to come to you.

[11]I long to see you so that I may impart to you some spiritual gift to make you strong — [12]that is, that you and I may be mutually encouraged by each other's faith. [13]I do not want you to be unaware, brothers and sisters,[d] that I planned many times to come to you (but have been prevented from doing so until now) in order that I might have a harvest among you, just as I have had among the other Gentiles.

[14]I am obligated both to Greeks and non-Greeks, both to the wise and the foolish.

[15]That is why I am so eager to preach the gospel also to you who are in Rome.

[16]For I am not ashamed of the gospel, because it is the power of God that brings salvation to everyone who believes: first to the Jew, then to the Gentile. [17]For in the gospel the righteousness of God is revealed — a righteousness that is by faith from first to last,[e] just as it is written: "The righteous will live by faith."[f]

God's Wrath Against Sinful Humanity

[18]The wrath of God is being revealed from heaven against all the godlessness and wickedness of people, who suppress the truth by their wickedness, [19]since what may be known about God is plain to them, because God has made it plain to them. [20]For since the creation of the world God's invisible qualities — his eternal power and divine nature — have been clearly seen, being understood from what has been made, so that people are without excuse.

[21]For although they knew God, they neither glorified him as God nor gave thanks to him, but their thinking became futile and their foolish hearts were darkened. [22]Although they claimed to be wise, they became fools [23]and exchanged the glory of the immortal God for images made to look like a mortal human being and birds and animals and reptiles.

[24]Therefore God gave them over in the sinful desires of their hearts to sexual impurity for the degrading of their bodies with one another. [25]They exchanged the truth about God for a lie, and worshiped and served created things rather than the Creator — who is forever praised. Amen.

[26]Because of this, God gave them over to shameful lusts. Even their women exchanged natural sexual relations for unnatural ones.

---

[a] 3 Or *who according to the flesh*   [b] 4 Or *was declared with power to be the Son of God*   [c] 5 Or *that is*
[d] 13 The Greek word for *brothers and sisters* (*adelphoi*) refers here to believers, both men and women, as part of God's family; also in 7:1, 4; 8:12, 29; 10:1; 11:25; 12:1; 15:14, 30; 16:14, 17.   [e] 17 Or *is from faith to faith*   [f] 17 Hab. 2:4

[27] In the same way the men also abandoned natural relations with women and were inflamed with lust for one another. Men committed shameful acts with other men, and received in themselves the due penalty for their error.

[28] Furthermore, just as they did not think it worthwhile to retain the knowledge of God, so God gave them over to a depraved mind, so that they do what ought not to be done. [29] They have become filled with every kind of wickedness, evil, greed and depravity. They are full of envy, murder, strife, deceit and malice. They are gossips, [30] slanderers, God-haters, insolent, arrogant and boastful; they invent ways of doing evil; they disobey their parents; [31] they have no understanding, no fidelity, no love, no mercy. [32] Although they know God's righteous decree that those who do such things deserve death, they not only continue to do these very things but also approve of those who practice them.

God's Righteous Judgment

2 You, therefore, have no excuse, you who pass judgment on someone else, for at whatever point you judge another, you are condemning yourself, because you who pass judgment do the same things. [2] Now we know that God's judgment against those who do such things is based on truth. [3] So when you, a mere human being, pass judgment on them and yet do the same things, do you think you will escape God's judgment? [4] Or do you show contempt for the riches of his kindness, forbearance and patience, not realizing that God's kindness is intended to lead you to repentance?

[5] But because of your stubbornness and your unrepentant heart, you are storing up wrath against yourself for the day of God's wrath, when his righteous judgment will be revealed. [6] God "will repay each person according to what they have done."[a] [7] To those who by persistence in doing good seek glory, honor and immortality, he will give eternal life. [8] But for those who are self-seeking and who reject the truth and follow evil, there will be wrath and anger. [9] There will be trouble and distress for every human being who does evil: first for the Jew, then for the Gentile; [10] but glory, honor and peace for every-one who does good: first for the Jew, then for the Gentile. [11] For God does not show favoritism.

[12] All who sin apart from the law will also perish apart from the law, and all who sin under the law will be judged by the law. [13] For it is not those who hear the law who are righteous in God's sight, but it is those who obey the law who will be declared righteous. [14] (Indeed, when Gentiles, who do not have the law, do by nature things required by the law, they are a law for themselves, even though they do not have the law. [15] They show that the requirements of the law are written on their hearts, their consciences also bearing witness, and their thoughts sometimes accusing them and at other times even defending them.) [16] This will take place on the day when God judges people's secrets through Jesus Christ, as my gospel declares.

The Jews and the Law

[17] Now you, if you call yourself a Jew; if you rely on the law and boast in God; [18] if you know his will and approve of what is superior because you are instructed by the law; [19] if you are convinced that you are a guide for the blind, a light for those who are in the dark, [20] an instructor of the foolish, a teacher of little children, because you have in the law the embodiment of knowledge and truth— [21] you, then, who teach others, do you not teach yourself? You who preach against stealing, do you steal? [22] You who say that people should not commit adultery, do you commit adultery? You who abhor idols, do you rob temples? [23] You who boast in the law, do you dishonor God by breaking the law? [24] As it is written: "God's name is blasphemed among the Gentiles because of you."[b]

[25] Circumcision has value if you observe the law, but if you break the law, you have become as though you had not been circumcised. [26] So then, if those who are not circumcised keep the law's requirements, will they not be regarded as though they were circumcised? [27] The one who is not circumcised physically and yet obeys the law will condemn you who, even though you have the[c] written code and circumcision, are a lawbreaker.

---

[a] 6 Psalm 62:12; Prov. 24:12   [b] 24 Isaiah 52:5 (see Septuagint); Ezek. 36:20,22   [c] 27 Or who, by means of a

[28] A person is not a Jew who is one only outwardly, nor is circumcision merely outward and physical. [29] No, a person is a Jew who is one inwardly; and circumcision is circumcision of the heart, by the Spirit, not by the written code. Such a person's praise is not from other people, but from God.

God's Faithfulness

3 What advantage, then, is there in being a Jew, or what value is there in circumcision? [2] Much in every way! First of all, the Jews have been entrusted with the very words of God.

[3] What if some were unfaithful? Will their unfaithfulness nullify God's faithfulness? [4] Not at all! Let God be true, and every human being a liar. As it is written:

"So that you may be proved right when
        you speak
    and prevail when you judge."[a]

[5] But if our unrighteousness brings out God's righteousness more clearly, what shall we say? That God is unjust in bringing his wrath on us? (I am using a human argument.) [6] Certainly not! If that were so, how could God judge the world? [7] Someone might argue, "If my falsehood enhances God's truthfulness and so increases his glory, why am I still condemned as a sinner?" [8] Why not say — as some slanderously claim that we say — "Let us do evil that good may result"? Their condemnation is just!

No One Is Righteous

[9] What shall we conclude then? Do we have any advantage? Not at all! For we have already made the charge that Jews and Gentiles alike are all under the power of sin. [10] As it is written:

"There is no one righteous, not even one;
[11]   there is no one who understands;
        there is no one who seeks God.
[12] All have turned away,
        they have together become worthless;
    there is no one who does good,
        not even one."[b]

[13] "Their throats are open graves;
        their tongues practice deceit."[c]
    "The poison of vipers is on their lips."[d]
[14]   "Their mouths are full of cursing
            and bitterness."[e]
[15] "Their feet are swift to shed blood;
[16]   ruin and misery mark their ways,
[17] and the way of peace they do not
            know."[f]
[18]   "There is no fear of God before
            their eyes."[g]

[19] Now we know that whatever the law says, it says to those who are under the law, so that every mouth may be silenced and the whole world held accountable to God. [20] Therefore no one will be declared righteous in God's sight by the works of the law; rather, through the law we become conscious of our sin.

Righteousness Through Faith

[21] But now apart from the law the righteousness of God has been made known, to which the Law and the Prophets testify. [22] This righteousness is given through faith in[h] Jesus Christ to all who believe. There is no difference between Jew and Gentile, [23] for all have sinned and fall short of the glory of God, [24] and all are justified freely by his grace through the redemption that came by Christ Jesus. [25] God presented Christ as a sacrifice of atonement,[i] through the shedding of his blood — to be received by faith. He did this to demonstrate his righteousness, because in his forbearance he had left the sins committed beforehand unpunished — [26] he did it to demonstrate his righteousness at the present time, so as to be just and the one who justifies those who have faith in Jesus.

[27] Where, then, is boasting? It is excluded. Because of what law? The law that requires works? No, because of the law that requires faith. [28] For we maintain that a person is justified by faith apart from the works of the law. [29] Or is God the God of Jews only? Is he not the God of Gentiles too? Yes, of Gentiles too, [30] since there is only one God, who will justify the circumcised by faith and the uncircumcised through that same faith. [31] Do

---

[a] 4 Psalm 51:4   [b] 12 Psalms 14:1-3; 53:1-3; Eccles. 7:20   [c] 13 Psalm 5:9   [d] 13 Psalm 140:3
[e] 14 Psalm 10:7 (see Septuagint)   [f] 17 Isaiah 59:7,8   [g] 18 Psalm 36:1   [h] 22 Or through the
faithfulness of   [i] 25 The Greek for sacrifice of atonement refers to the atonement cover on the ark of the
covenant (see Lev. 16:15,16).

we, then, nullify the law by this faith? Not at all! Rather, we uphold the law.

Abraham Justified by Faith

4 What then shall we say that Abraham, our forefather according to the flesh, discovered in this matter? ²If, in fact, Abraham was justified by works, he had something to boast about—but not before God. ³What does Scripture say? "Abraham believed God, and it was credited to him as righteousness."ᵃ

⁴Now to the one who works, wages are not credited as a gift but as an obligation. ⁵However, to the one who does not work but trusts God who justifies the ungodly, their faith is credited as righteousness. ⁶David says the same thing when he speaks of the blessedness of the one to whom God credits righteousness apart from works:

⁷"Blessed are those
    whose transgressions are forgiven,
    whose sins are covered.
⁸Blessed is the one
    whose sin the Lord will never count
        against them."ᵇ

⁹Is this blessedness only for the circumcised, or also for the uncircumcised? We have been saying that Abraham's faith was credited to him as righteousness. ¹⁰Under what circumstances was it credited? Was it after he was circumcised, or before? It was not after, but before! ¹¹And he received circumcision as a sign, a seal of the righteousness that he had by faith while he was still uncircumcised. So then, he is the father of all who believe but have not been circumcised, in order that righteousness might be credited to them. ¹²And he is then also the father of the circumcised who not only are circumcised but who also follow in the footsteps of the faith that our father Abraham had before he was circumcised.

¹³It was not through the law that Abraham and his offspring received the promise that he would be heir of the world, but through the righteousness that comes by faith. ¹⁴For if those who depend on the law are heirs, faith means nothing and the promise is worthless, ¹⁵because the law brings wrath. And where there is no law there is no transgression.

¹⁶Therefore, the promise comes by faith, so that it may be by grace and may be guaranteed to all Abraham's offspring—not only to those who are of the law but also to those who have the faith of Abraham. He is the father of us all. ¹⁷As it is written: "I have made you a father of many nations."ᶜ He is our father in the sight of God, in whom he believed—the God who gives life to the dead and calls into being things that were not.

¹⁸Against all hope, Abraham in hope believed and so became the father of many nations, just as it had been said to him, "So shall your offspring be."ᵈ ¹⁹Without weakening in his faith, he faced the fact that his body was as good as dead—since he was about a hundred years old—and that Sarah's womb was also dead. ²⁰Yet he did not waver through unbelief regarding the promise of God, but was strengthened in his faith and gave glory to God, ²¹being fully persuaded that God had power to do what he had promised. ²²This is why "it was credited to him as righteousness." ²³The words "it was credited to him" were written not for him alone, ²⁴but also for us, to whom God will credit righteousness—for us who believe in him who raised Jesus our Lord from the dead. ²⁵He was delivered over to death for our sins and was raised to life for our justification.

Peace and Hope

5 Therefore, since we have been justified through faith, weᵉ have peace with God through our Lord Jesus Christ, ²through whom we have gained access by faith into this grace in which we now stand. And weᶠ boast in the hope of the glory of God. ³Not only so, but weᶠ also glory in our sufferings, because we know that suffering produces perseverance; ⁴perseverance, character; and character, hope. ⁵And hope does not put us to shame, because God's love has been poured out into our hearts through the Holy Spirit, who has been given to us.

⁶You see, at just the right time, when we were still powerless, Christ died for the ungodly. ⁷Very rarely will anyone die for a righteous person, though for a good person someone might possibly dare to die. ⁸But God demonstrates his own love for us in this: While we were still sinners, Christ died for us.

ᵃ 3 Gen. 15:6; also in verse 22   ᵇ 8 Psalm 32:1,2   ᶜ 17 Gen. 17:5   ᵈ 18 Gen. 15:5   ᵉ 1 Many manuscripts *let us*   ᶠ 2,3 Or *let us*

LOVE WITHOUT EXPECTING A RETURN

By Jane Hampton Cook

Lucy Rumney and her four children needed help. Inadequate soldier's pay made it difficult for them to survive financially. During the early 1800s, women did not have many options to bring in income. She wrote to First Lady Dolley Madison on July 17, 1813:

"He enlisted while under the influence of liquor, and [was] not aware of the evil that he was going to bring upon his family. We are poor and dependant on our daily labor, and principally on him, for subsistence."

Lucy's husband turned out to be a wayward soldier whose poor choices cost him dearly.

"He is now again in custody for desertion and I fear that the sentence of a court martial will affect his life. You, Madam, can feel — I cannot express — the grief and misery in which the danger of my husband plunges me, and those of my children who are capable of estimating their loss!"

Dolley knew what it was like to lose a husband. Her first husband and their infant had died years earlier in the yellow fever epidemic in Philadelphia. Dolley understood that the death of a husband could sink women and children into poverty.

Lucy knew this too and asked for mercy. "Justice and the law I do not ask — They I know would condemn my unhappy husband's desertions — But I beg for pardon for my husband — mercy, for him, for me and for my innocent and helpless children. If you, Madam, can be induced to ask this boon for me from the President, I hope it will be granted, and to whom could I go with greater propriety with my petition."

Dolley received numerous letters from women like Lucy. It is unclear from Dolley's collection of papers exactly what happened to Lucy. However, touched by the experiences of her countrywomen and never forgetting what it was like to be a widow, Dolley made an important decision. She became the first wife of a president to establish a charity while her husband was in office.

Dolley created an orphanage for girls whose fathers had died in the war. She called on the ladies of Washington to meet in the hall of representatives to contribute money for an Asylum for Orphans.

The Washington newspaper observed "that these orphans, by the death of their parents, are in a particular manner placed by Providence under the protection of society." The ladies of the town responded with open pocketbooks and open hearts. The return of their investment was not monetary but was the smiles on the faces of those orphans who now had hope for a brighter future. Dolley and the ladies loved without expecting anything in return. They gave the way Christ still asks us to give today: unconditionally.

Prayer: I will seek to give all I am capable of giving — whether through my service, my money or my words of encouragement — without asking anything in return. Amen.

**God demonstrates his own love for us in this: While we were still
sinners, Christ died for us.**
ROMANS 5:8

for your next devotional reading, go to page 182

[9]Since we have now been justified by his blood, how much more shall we be saved from God's wrath through him! [10]For if, while we were God's enemies, we were reconciled to him through the death of his Son, how much more, having been reconciled, shall we be saved through his life! [11]Not only is this so, but we also boast in God through our Lord Jesus Christ, through whom we have now received reconciliation.

Death Through Adam, Life Through Christ

[12]Therefore, just as sin entered the world through one man, and death through sin, and in this way death came to all people, because all sinned— [13]To be sure, sin was in the world before the law was given, but sin is not charged against anyone's account where there is no law. [14]Nevertheless, death reigned from the time of Adam to the time of Moses, even over those who did not sin by breaking a command, as did Adam, who is a pattern of the one to come.

[15]But the gift is not like the trespass. For if the many died by the trespass of the one man, how much more did God's grace and the gift that came by the grace of the one man, Jesus Christ, overflow to the many! [16]Nor can the gift of God be compared with the result of one man's sin: The judgment followed one sin and brought condemnation, but the gift followed many trespasses and brought justification. [17]For if, by the trespass of the one man, death reigned through that one man, how much more will those who receive God's abundant provision of grace and of the gift of righteousness reign in life through the one man, Jesus Christ!

[18]Consequently, just as one trespass resulted in condemnation for all people, so also one righteous act resulted in justification and life for all people. [19]For just as through the disobedience of the one man the many were made sinners, so also through the obedience of the one man the many will be made righteous.

[20]The law was brought in so that the trespass might increase. But where sin increased, grace increased all the more, [21]so that, just as sin reigned in death, so also grace might reign through righteousness to

bring eternal life through Jesus Christ our Lord.

Dead to Sin, Alive in Christ

6 What shall we say, then? Shall we go on sinning so that grace may increase? [2]By no means! We are those who have died to sin; how can we live in it any longer? [3]Or don't you know that all of us who were baptized into Christ Jesus were baptized into his death? [4]We were therefore buried with him through baptism into death in order that, just as Christ was raised from the dead through the glory of the Father, we too may live a new life.

[5]For if we have been united with him in a death like his, we will certainly also be united with him in a resurrection like his. [6]For we know that our old self was crucified with him so that the body ruled by sin might be done away with,[a] that we should no longer be slaves to sin— [7]because anyone who has died has been set free from sin.

[8]Now if we died with Christ, we believe that we will also live with him. [9]For we know that since Christ was raised from the dead, he cannot die again; death no longer has mastery over him. [10]The death he died, he died to sin once for all; but the life he lives, he lives to God.

[11]In the same way, count yourselves dead to sin but alive to God in Christ Jesus. [12]Therefore do not let sin reign in your mortal body so that you obey its evil desires. [13]Do not offer any part of yourself to sin as an instrument of wickedness, but rather offer yourselves to God as those who have been brought from death to life; and offer every part of yourself to him as an instrument of righteousness. [14]For sin shall no longer be your master, because you are not under the law, but under grace.

Slaves to Righteousness

[15]What then? Shall we sin because we are not under the law but under grace? By no means! [16]Don't you know that when you offer yourselves to someone as obedient slaves, you are slaves of the one you obey—whether you are slaves to sin, which leads to death, or to obedience, which leads to righteousness? [17]But thanks be to God that, though you used to be slaves to sin, you have come to

[a] 6 Or *be rendered powerless*

obey from your heart the pattern of teaching that has now claimed your allegiance. [18]You have been set free from sin and have become slaves to righteousness.

[19]I am using an example from everyday life because of your human limitations. Just as you used to offer yourselves as slaves to impurity and to ever-increasing wickedness, so now offer yourselves as slaves to righteousness leading to holiness. [20]When you were slaves to sin, you were free from the control of righteousness. [21]What benefit did you reap at that time from the things you are now ashamed of? Those things result in death! [22]But now that you have been set free from sin and have become slaves of God, the benefit you reap leads to holiness, and the result is eternal life. [23]For the wages of sin is death, but the gift of God is eternal life in[a] Christ Jesus our Lord.

Released From the Law, Bound to Christ

7 Do you not know, brothers and sisters — for I am speaking to those who know the law — that the law has authority over someone only as long as that person lives? [2]For example, by law a married woman is bound to her husband as long as he is alive, but if her husband dies, she is released from the law that binds her to him. [3]So then, if she has sexual relations with another man while her husband is still alive, she is called an adulteress. But if her husband dies, she is released from that law and is not an adulteress if she marries another man.

[4]So, my brothers and sisters, you also died to the law through the body of Christ, that you might belong to another, to him who was raised from the dead, in order that we might bear fruit for God. [5]For when we were in the realm of the flesh,[b] the sinful passions aroused by the law were at work in us, so that we bore fruit for death. [6]But now, by dying to what once bound us, we have been released from the law so that we serve in the new way of the Spirit, and not in the old way of the written code.

The Law and Sin

[7]What shall we say, then? Is the law sinful? Certainly not! Nevertheless, I would not

have known what sin was had it not been for the law. For I would not have known what coveting really was if the law had not said, "You shall not covet."[c] [8]But sin, seizing the opportunity afforded by the commandment, produced in me every kind of coveting. For apart from the law, sin was dead. [9]Once I was alive apart from the law; but when the commandment came, sin sprang to life and I died. [10]I found that the very commandment that was intended to bring life actually brought death. [11]For sin, seizing the opportunity afforded by the commandment, deceived me, and through the commandment put me to death. [12]So then, the law is holy, and the commandment is holy, righteous and good.

[13]Did that which is good, then, become death to me? By no means! Nevertheless, in order that sin might be recognized as sin, it used what is good to bring about my death, so that through the commandment sin might become utterly sinful.

[14]We know that the law is spiritual; but I am unspiritual, sold as a slave to sin. [15]I do not understand what I do. For what I want to do I do not do, but what I hate I do. [16]And if I do what I do not want to do, I agree that the law is good. [17]As it is, it is no longer I myself who do it, but it is sin living in me. [18]For I know that good itself does not dwell in me, that is, in my sinful nature.[d] For I have the desire to do what is good, but I cannot carry it out. [19]For I do not do the good I want to do, but the evil I do not want to do — this I keep on doing. [20]Now if I do what I do not want to do, it is no longer I who do it, but it is sin living in me that does it.

[21]So I find this law at work: Although I want to do good, evil is right there with me. [22]For in my inner being I delight in God's law; [23]but I see another law at work in me, waging war against the law of my mind and making me a prisoner of the law of sin at work within me. [24]What a wretched man I am! Who will rescue me from this body that is subject to death? [25]Thanks be to God, who delivers me through Jesus Christ our Lord!

So then, I myself in my mind am a slave to God's law, but in my sinful nature[e] a slave to the law of sin.

---

[a] 23 Or *through*   [b] 5 In contexts like this, the Greek word for *flesh* (*sarx*) refers to the sinful state of human beings, often presented as a power in opposition to the Spirit.   [c] 7 Exodus 20:17; Deut. 5:21
[d] 18 Or *my flesh*   [e] 25 Or *in the flesh*

Life Through the Spirit

8 Therefore, there is now no condemnation for those who are in Christ Jesus, [2] because through Christ Jesus the law of the Spirit who gives life has set you*a* free from the law of sin and death. [3] For what the law was powerless to do because it was weakened by the flesh,*b* God did by sending his own Son in the likeness of sinful flesh to be a sin offering.*c* And so he condemned sin in the flesh, [4] in order that the righteous requirement of the law might be fully met in us, who do not live according to the flesh but according to the Spirit.

[5] Those who live according to the flesh have their minds set on what the flesh desires; but those who live in accordance with the Spirit have their minds set on what the Spirit desires. [6] The mind governed by the flesh is death, but the mind governed by the Spirit is life and peace. [7] The mind governed by the flesh is hostile to God; it does not submit to God's law, nor can it do so. [8] Those who are in the realm of the flesh cannot please God.

[9] You, however, are not in the realm of the flesh but are in the realm of the Spirit, if indeed the Spirit of God lives in you. And if anyone does not have the Spirit of Christ, they do not belong to Christ. [10] But if Christ is in you, then even though your body is subject to death because of sin, the Spirit gives life*d* because of righteousness. [11] And if the Spirit of him who raised Jesus from the dead is living in you, he who raised Christ from the dead will also give life to your mortal bodies because of*e* his Spirit who lives in you.

[12] Therefore, brothers and sisters, we have an obligation — but it is not to the flesh, to live according to it. [13] For if you live according to the flesh, you will die; but if by the Spirit you put to death the misdeeds of the body, you will live.

[14] For those who are led by the Spirit of God are the children of God. [15] The Spirit you received does not make you slaves, so that you live in fear again; rather, the Spirit you received brought about your adoption to sonship.*f* And by him we cry, *"Abba,*g* Father."* [16] The Spirit himself testifies with our spirit that we are God's children. [17] Now if we are children, then we are heirs — heirs of God and co-heirs with Christ, if indeed we share in his sufferings in order that we may also share in his glory.

Present Suffering and Future Glory

[18] I consider that our present sufferings are not worth comparing with the glory that will be revealed in us. [19] For the creation waits in eager expectation for the children of God to be revealed. [20] For the creation was subjected to frustration, not by its own choice, but by the will of the one who subjected it, in hope [21] that*h* the creation itself will be liberated from its bondage to decay and brought into the freedom and glory of the children of God.

[22] We know that the whole creation has been groaning as in the pains of childbirth right up to the present time. [23] Not only so, but we ourselves, who have the firstfruits of the Spirit, groan inwardly as we wait eagerly for our adoption to sonship, the redemption of our bodies. [24] For in this hope we were saved. But hope that is seen is no hope at all. Who hopes for what they already have? [25] But if we hope for what we do not yet have, we wait for it patiently.

[26] In the same way, the Spirit helps us in our weakness. We do not know what we ought to pray for, but the Spirit himself intercedes for us through wordless groans. [27] And he who searches our hearts knows the mind of the Spirit, because the Spirit intercedes for God's people in accordance with the will of God.

[28] And we know that in all things God works for the good of those who love him, who*i* have been called according to his purpose. [29] For those God foreknew he also

---

a 2 The Greek is singular; some manuscripts *me*   *b 3* In contexts like this, the Greek word for *flesh* (*sarx*) refers to the sinful state of human beings, often presented as a power in opposition to the Spirit; also in verses 4-13.   *c 3* Or *flesh, for sin*   *d 10* Or *you, your body is dead because of sin, yet your spirit is alive*   *e 11* Some manuscripts *bodies through*   *f 15* The Greek word for *adoption to sonship* is a term referring to the full legal standing of an adopted male heir in Roman culture; also in verse 23.   *g 15* Aramaic for *father*   *h 20,21* Or *subjected it in hope.* *21For*   *i 28* Or *that all things work together for good to those who love God, who*; or *that in all things God works together with those who love him to bring about what is good — with those who*

THE COUPON QUEEN

By Jocelyn Green

Ellie Kay left a successful business as a broker to marry her pilot husband Bob and follow him around the country. She called it a 3-for-1 deal, because she also became stepmother to Bob's two daughters. "Now my new identity was mother and wife, not business profession-al," she said. "I'm a very driven, Type-A personality, so that was a bit of a challenge for me."

The other challenge built into the bargain was $40,000 of debt. Living under this financial burden was out of the question for Ellie, a born saver. "I took all my business background and skills and put that into saving money in our household," she recalled. "I remember those early years, coming back from the grocery store with a receipt for $220 before coupons, and $80 after coupons. I showed that to my husband and said, 'This is what I've done today.' "

Ellie's efforts paid off. Even though she stayed home with their growing family (five children in their first seven years of marriage) instead of working for a paycheck, they were completely debt free in two and a half years. Soon she was saving money not just at the grocery store but on everything from life insurance to automobiles.

"That allowed me to find the identity that Christ had for me," said Ellie. "That was based in something as simple as couponing that could be a blessing to my family and a provision for others as well. Through that, I've learned how to get things for free and give money away to causes and ministries I support."

To share what she had learned with other military families, Ellie gave "Shop, Save, and Share" seminars that were so successful the material eventually grew into her first book. Bethany House published *Shop, Save, and Share* in 1998, and it became a bestseller.

"When I found my identity and purpose in helping my family save money, God took that and expanded it so I could begin to help other people learn to save money too," she said.

Today, Ellie Kay is the bestselling author of 14 books, including *Heroes at Home: Help and Hope for America's Military Families*. She is a popular international speaker and has appeared on more than 600 radio and TV stations.

"My business skills were not wasted when I married a military man and gave up my career . . . God just used those skills in a new place," she said.

We may not know yet what God is doing through the various chapters of our lives, but we can trust that he is working with a specific purpose in mind.

Prayer: Lord, thank you for orchestrating all the details of my life. Help me trust you even before I know how the circumstances of my life will all work out.

And we know that in all things God works for the good of those who love him, who have been called according to his purpose.

ROMANS 8:28

predestined to be conformed to the image of his Son, that he might be the firstborn among many brothers and sisters. [30] And those he predestined, he also called; those he called, he also justified; those he justified, he also glorified.

More Than Conquerors

[31] What, then, shall we say in response to these things? If God is for us, who can be against us? [32] He who did not spare his own Son, but gave him up for us all — how will he not also, along with him, graciously give us all things? [33] Who will bring any charge against those whom God has chosen? It is God who justifies. [34] Who then is the one who condemns? No one. Christ Jesus who died — more than that, who was raised to life — is at the right hand of God and is also interceding for us. [35] Who shall separate us from the love of Christ? Shall trouble or hardship or persecution or famine or nakedness or danger or sword? [36] As it is written:

"For your sake we face death all day long;
    we are considered as sheep to be
        slaughtered."[a]

[37] No, in all these things we are more than conquerors through him who loved us. [38] For I am convinced that neither death nor life, neither angels nor demons,[b] neither the present nor the future, nor any powers, [39] neither height nor depth, nor anything else in all creation, will be able to separate us from the love of God that is in Christ Jesus our Lord.

Paul's Anguish Over Israel

9 I speak the truth in Christ — I am not lying, my conscience confirms it through the Holy Spirit — [2] I have great sorrow and unceasing anguish in my heart. [3] For I could wish that I myself were cursed and cut off from Christ for the sake of my people, those of my own race, [4] the people of Israel. Theirs is the adoption to sonship; theirs the divine glory, the covenants, the receiving of the law, the temple worship and the promises. [5] Theirs are the patriarchs, and from them is traced the human ancestry of the Messiah, who is God over all, forever praised![c] Amen.

God's Sovereign Choice

[6] It is not as though God's word had failed. For not all who are descended from Israel are Israel. [7] Nor because they are his descendants are they all Abraham's children. On the contrary, "It is through Isaac that your offspring will be reckoned."[d] [8] In other words, it is not the children by physical descent who are God's children, but it is the children of the promise who are regarded as Abraham's offspring. [9] For this was how the promise was stated: "At the appointed time I will return, and Sarah will have a son."[e]

[10] Not only that, but Rebekah's children were conceived at the same time by our father Isaac. [11] Yet, before the twins were born or had done anything good or bad — in order that God's purpose in election might stand: [12] not by works but by him who calls — she was told, "The older will serve the younger."[f] [13] Just as it is written: "Jacob I loved, but Esau I hated."[g]

[14] What then shall we say? Is God unjust? Not at all! [15] For he says to Moses,

"I will have mercy on whom I have mercy,
    and I will have compassion on whom I
        have compassion."[h]

[16] It does not, therefore, depend on human desire or effort, but on God's mercy. [17] For Scripture says to Pharaoh: "I raised you up for this very purpose, that I might display my power in you and that my name might be proclaimed in all the earth."[i] [18] Therefore God has mercy on whom he wants to have mercy, and he hardens whom he wants to harden.

[19] One of you will say to me: "Then why does God still blame us? For who is able to resist his will?" [20] But who are you, a human being, to talk back to God? "Shall what is formed say to the one who formed it, 'Why did you make me like this?'"[j] [21] Does not the potter have the right to make out of the same lump of clay some pottery for special purposes and some for common use?

[22] What if God, although choosing to show his wrath and make his power known, bore with great patience the objects of his wrath — prepared for destruction? [23] What

---

[a] 36 Psalm 44:22   [b] 38 Or *nor heavenly rulers*   [c] 5 Or *Messiah, who is over all. God be forever praised!*
Or *Messiah. God who is over all be forever praised!*   [d] 7 Gen. 21:12   [e] 9 Gen. 18:10,14   [f] 12 Gen. 25:23
[g] 13 Mal. 1:2,3   [h] 15 Exodus 33:19   [i] 17 Exodus 9:16   [j] 20 Isaiah 29:16; 45:9

Never Separated

By Sarah Ball

READ: Romans 8:31–39

What does 'friends forever' mean?" my four-year-old asked me. Since his conversations usually involve robots, superheroes or light sabers, I thought it an unusual question.

"It means you will be friends with someone for your whole life," I explained. He thought for a long moment before responding, "Or until you move."

Military life brings a lot of separation from people we love. My son has already lived in four states, and we'll be moving again in six months. We wave good-bye to Daddy for year-long deployments, month-long field exercises and week-long training sessions. Friend and family are scattered thousands of miles away.

If I had my way, I would never choose separation. I draw emotional strength from the presence of my husband and loved ones. Yet God does not want me to look at my husband, family or friends as my sustaining sources of love. Each new separation reminds me that my only eternal source of love and strength is my heavenly Father. The painful moments of good-bye help me refocus on the security of God's love, and I am comforted by verses like Romans 8:35: "Who shall separate us from the love of Christ? Shall trouble or hardship or persecution or famine or nakedness or danger or sword?"

Can you hear the ringing conviction of personal experience in those words? The apostle Paul had been through those kinds of circumstances. In each experience, though, Paul's understanding of the love of Christ grew deeper and richer.

The obvious answers to his questions in verse 35 are "No one!" and "No way!" Because Paul couldn't overstate the amazing love of God, he created a beautiful word picture for us in verses 38 and 39. Death, life, angels, demons, present, future, powers, height, depth — nothing in all of creation can separate us from the love of God. The military can send me away from my family, move my friends to new locations, and deploy my husband, but it can't separate me from the love of God. In fact my life as a military wife offers the great blessing of separation from everyone but God.

What challenges or separations are you facing right now? Read Romans 8:38 – 39 again; personalize it by listing all the things you fear. "For I am convinced that neither [deployment, a move to _____, relationship problems, illness, financial stress, depression, job loss], nor anything else in all creation, will be able to separate [me] from the love of God that is in Christ Jesus [my] Lord."

For I am convinced that neither death nor life, neither angels nor demons, neither the present nor the future, nor any powers, neither height nor depth, nor anything else in all creation, will be able to separate us from the love of God that is in Christ Jesus our Lord.
ROMANS 8:38 – 39

DEBRIEF
- Have I personally received the amazing love of God that is in Christ Jesus?
- What can I learn about God's love during times of difficulty or separation?

REPORT
Lord, thank you for your eternal, unchanging love for me. Hold me close to you through every difficulty and separation, so that I may say with Paul that I am convinced of your inseparable love. In Jesus' name I pray. Amen.

if he did this to make the riches of his glory known to the objects of his mercy, whom he prepared in advance for glory — [24]even us, whom he also called, not only from the Jews but also from the Gentiles? [25]As he says in Hosea:

> "I will call them 'my people' who are not
>   my people;
> and I will call her 'my loved one' who is
>   not my loved one,"[a]

[26]and,

> "In the very place where it was said to
>   them,
>   'You are not my people,'
> there they will be called 'children of
>   the living God.'"[b]

[27]Isaiah cries out concerning Israel:

> "Though the number of the Israelites be
>   like the sand by the sea,
> only the remnant will be saved.
> [28]For the Lord will carry out
>   his sentence on earth with speed and
>   finality."[c]

[29]It is just as Isaiah said previously:

> "Unless the Lord Almighty
>   had left us descendants,
> we would have become like Sodom,
>   we would have been like Gomorrah."[d]

Israel's Unbelief

[30]What then shall we say? That the Gentiles, who did not pursue righteousness, have obtained it, a righteousness that is by faith; [31]but the people of Israel, who pursued the law as the way of righteousness, have not attained their goal. [32]Why not? Because they pursued it not by faith but as if it were by works. They stumbled over the stumbling stone. [33]As it is written:

> "See, I lay in Zion a stone that causes
>   people to stumble
> and a rock that makes them fall,
>   and the one who believes in him will
>   never be put to shame."[e]

10 Brothers and sisters, my heart's desire and prayer to God for the Isra-

elites is that they may be saved. [2]For I can testify about them that they are zealous for God, but their zeal is not based on knowledge. [3]Since they did not know the righteousness of God and sought to establish their own, they did not submit to God's righteousness. [4]Christ is the culmination of the law so that there may be righteousness for everyone who believes.

[5]Moses writes this about the righteousness that is by the law: "The person who does these things will live by them."[f] [6]But the righteousness that is by faith says: "Do not say in your heart, 'Who will ascend into heaven?'"[g] (that is, to bring Christ down) [7]"or 'Who will descend into the deep?'"[h] (that is, to bring Christ up from the dead). [8]But what does it say? "The word is near you; it is in your mouth and in your heart,"[i] that is, the message concerning faith that we proclaim: [9]If you declare with your mouth, "Jesus is Lord," and believe in your heart that God raised him from the dead, you will be saved. [10]For it is with your heart that you believe and are justified, and it is with your mouth that you profess your faith and are saved. [11]As Scripture says, "Anyone who believes in him will never be put to shame."[j] [12]For there is no difference between Jew and Gentile — the same Lord is Lord of all and richly blesses all who call on him, [13]for, "Everyone who calls on the name of the Lord will be saved."[k]

[14]How, then, can they call on the one they have not believed in? And how can they believe in the one of whom they have not heard? And how can they hear without someone preaching to them? [15]And how can anyone preach unless they are sent? As it is written: "How beautiful are the feet of those who bring good news!"[l]

[16]But not all the Israelites accepted the good news. For Isaiah says, "Lord, who has believed our message?"[m] [17]Consequently, faith comes from hearing the message, and the message is heard through the word about Christ. [18]But I ask: Did they not hear? Of course they did:

> "Their voice has gone out into all the
>   earth,
>   their words to the ends of the world."[n]

---

[a]25 Hosea 2:23   [b]26 Hosea 1:10   [c]28 Isaiah 10:22,23 (see Septuagint)   [d]29 Isaiah 1:9   [e]33 Isaiah 8:14; 28:16   [f]5 Lev. 18:5   [g]6 Deut. 30:12   [h]7 Deut. 30:13   [i]8 Deut. 30:14   [j]11 Isaiah 28:16 (see Septuagint)   [k]13 Joel 2:32   [l]15 Isaiah 52:7   [m]16 Isaiah 53:1   [n]18 Psalm 19:4

[19]Again I ask: Did Israel not understand? First, Moses says,

> "I will make you envious by those who
>   are not a nation;
> I will make you angry by a nation that
>   has no understanding."[a]

[20]And Isaiah boldly says,

> "I was found by those who did not seek me;
> I revealed myself to those who did not
>   ask for me."[b]

[21]But concerning Israel he says,

> "All day long I have held out my hands
>   to a disobedient and obstinate people."[c]

The Remnant of Israel

11 I ask then: Did God reject his people? By no means! I am an Israelite myself, a descendant of Abraham, from the tribe of Benjamin. [2]God did not reject his people, whom he foreknew. Don't you know what Scripture says in the passage about Elijah—how he appealed to God against Israel: [3]"Lord, they have killed your prophets and torn down your altars; I am the only one left, and they are trying to kill me"[d]? [4]And what was God's answer to him? "I have reserved for myself seven thousand who have not bowed the knee to Baal."[e] [5]So too, at the present time there is a remnant chosen by grace. [6]And if by grace, then it cannot be based on works; if it were, grace would no longer be grace.

[7]What then? What the people of Israel sought so earnestly they did not obtain. The elect among them did, but the others were hardened, [8]as it is written:

> "God gave them a spirit of stupor,
>   eyes that could not see
>   and ears that could not hear,
> to this very day."[f]

[9]And David says:

> "May their table become a snare and
>   a trap,
>   a stumbling block and a retribution
>   for them.
> [10]May their eyes be darkened so they
>   cannot see,
>   and their backs be bent forever."[g]

Ingrafted Branches

[11]Again I ask: Did they stumble so as to fall beyond recovery? Not at all! Rather, because of their transgression, salvation has come to the Gentiles to make Israel envious. [12]But if their transgression means riches for the world, and their loss means riches for the Gentiles, how much greater riches will their full inclusion bring!

[13]I am talking to you Gentiles. Inasmuch as I am the apostle to the Gentiles, I take pride in my ministry [14]in the hope that I may somehow arouse my own people to envy and save some of them. [15]For if their rejection brought reconciliation to the world, what will their acceptance be but life from the dead? [16]If the part of the dough offered as firstfruits is holy, then the whole batch is holy; if the root is holy, so are the branches.

[17]If some of the branches have been broken off, and you, though a wild olive shoot, have been grafted in among the others and now share in the nourishing sap from the olive root, [18]do not consider yourself to be superior to those other branches. If you do, consider this: You do not support the root, but the root supports you. [19]You will say then, "Branches were broken off so that I could be grafted in." [20]Granted. But they were broken off because of unbelief, and you stand by faith. Do not be arrogant, but tremble. [21]For if God did not spare the natural branches, he will not spare you either.

[22]Consider therefore the kindness and sternness of God: sternness to those who fell, but kindness to you, provided that you continue in his kindness. Otherwise, you also will be cut off. [23]And if they do not persist in unbelief, they will be grafted in, for God is able to graft them in again. [24]After all, if you were cut out of an olive tree that is wild by nature, and contrary to nature were grafted into a cultivated olive tree, how much more readily will these, the natural branches, be grafted into their own olive tree!

All Israel Will Be Saved

[25]I do not want you to be ignorant of this mystery, brothers and sisters, so that you may not be conceited: Israel has experienced a hardening in part until the full number of

---

[a] 19 Deut. 32:21   [b] 20 Isaiah 65:1   [c] 21 Isaiah 65:2   [d] 3 1 Kings 19:10,14   [e] 4 1 Kings 19:18
[f] 8 Deut. 29:4; Isaiah 29:10   [g] 10 Psalm 69:22,23

the Gentiles has come in, [26] and in this way[a] all Israel will be saved. As it is written:

"The deliverer will come from Zion;
    he will turn godlessness away from
        Jacob.
[27] And this is[b] my covenant with them
    when I take away their sins."[c]

[28] As far as the gospel is concerned, they are enemies for your sake; but as far as election is concerned, they are loved on account of the patriarchs, [29] for God's gifts and his call are irrevocable. [30] Just as you who were at one time disobedient to God have now received mercy as a result of their disobedience, [31] so they too have now become disobedient in order that they too may now[d] receive mercy as a result of God's mercy to you. [32] For God has bound everyone over to disobedience so that he may have mercy on them all.

Doxology

[33] Oh, the depth of the riches of the wisdom
        and[e] knowledge of God!
    How unsearchable his judgments,
        and his paths beyond tracing out!
[34] "Who has known the mind of the Lord?
        Or who has been his counselor?"[f]
[35] "Who has ever given to God,
        that God should repay them?"[g]
[36] For from him and through him and for
        him are all things.
    To him be the glory forever! Amen.

A Living Sacrifice

12 Therefore, I urge you, brothers and sisters, in view of God's mercy, to offer your bodies as a living sacrifice, holy and pleasing to God — this is your true and proper worship. [2] Do not conform to the pattern of this world, but be transformed by the renewing of your mind. Then you will be able to test and approve what God's will is — his good, pleasing and perfect will.

Humble Service in the Body of Christ

[3] For by the grace given me I say to every one of you: Do not think of yourself more highly than you ought, but rather think of yourself with sober judgment, in accordance

with the faith God has distributed to each of you. [4] For just as each of us has one body with many members, and these members do not all have the same function, [5] so in Christ we, though many, form one body, and each member belongs to all the others. [6] We have different gifts, according to the grace given to each of us. If your gift is prophesying, then prophesy in accordance with your[h] faith; [7] if it is serving, then serve; if it is teaching, then teach; [8] if it is to encourage, then give encouragement; if it is giving, then give generously; if it is to lead,[i] do it diligently; if it is to show mercy, do it cheerfully.

Love in Action

[9] Love must be sincere. Hate what is evil; cling to what is good. [10] Be devoted to one another in love. Honor one another above yourselves. [11] Never be lacking in zeal, but keep your spiritual fervor, serving the Lord. [12] Be joyful in hope, patient in affliction, faithful in prayer. [13] Share with the Lord's people who are in need. Practice hospitality.

[14] Bless those who persecute you; bless and do not curse. [15] Rejoice with those who rejoice; mourn with those who mourn. [16] Live in harmony with one another. Do not be proud, but be willing to associate with people of low position.[j] Do not be conceited.

[17] Do not repay anyone evil for evil. Be careful to do what is right in the eyes of everyone. [18] If it is possible, as far as it depends on you, live at peace with everyone. [19] Do not take revenge, my dear friends, but leave room for God's wrath, for it is written: "It is mine to avenge; I will repay,"[k] says the Lord. [20] On the contrary:

"If your enemy is hungry, feed him;
    if he is thirsty, give him something to
        drink.
In doing this, you will heap burning coals
    on his head."[l]

[21] Do not be overcome by evil, but overcome evil with good.

Submission to Governing Authorities

13 Let everyone be subject to the governing authorities, for there is no

---

[a] 26 Or *and so*   [b] 27 Or *will be*   [c] 27 Isaiah 59:20,21; 27:9 (see Septuagint); Jer. 31:33,34   [d] 31 Some manuscripts do not have *now.*   [e] 33 Or *riches and the wisdom and the*   [f] 34 Isaiah 40:13
[g] 35 Job 41:11   [h] 6 Or *the*   [i] 8 Or *to provide for others*   [j] 16 Or *willing to do menial work*
[k] 19 Deut. 32:35   [l] 20 Prov. 25:21,22

Atmosphere of the Home

By Linda Montgomery

READ: Romans 12:12–13

As the story goes, a military family recently arrived at their new duty station. The wife and young daughter made a quick run to the commissary, where they encountered the squadron commander's wife. She asked, "Have you found a home yet?" The little girl quickly replied, "Oh, we have a home. We just haven't found a house to put it in!"

Truly it is the peaceful atmosphere of a loving Christian home that creates strength and security within the walls of the dwelling and the hearts of each family member. In Romans 12:12–13, we find five realities that are characteristic of a gracious, Christian home, each of which is echoed elsewhere in the Scriptures:

1. *Be joyful in hope.* Military service can be difficult — with moves, frequent absences, uncertainties. But it can also be a time of making great memories with close friends, experiencing exciting travel and offering noble service. A wise military wife maintains an attitude of joyful hope, not frustration, in her home. "The LORD delights in those who fear him, who put their hope in his unfailing love" (Psalm 147:11).

2. *Be patient in affliction.* Military wives face huge pressure at various times. Neighbors, friends, children and even strangers are watching us to see how we cope. A wise military wife demonstrates patience before a watching world when she approaches each day's challenges with confidence and trust in her Lord. "The righteous person may have many troubles, but the LORD delivers him from them all" (Psalm 34:19).

3. *Be faithful in prayer.* A wise military wife sets an example of a prayer-filled life, looking to her Lord for comfort, direction, provision, strength and peace. "Pray continually" (1 Thessalonians 5:17).

4. *Share with the Lord's people who are in need.* You don't have to look far in a military community to find others in need. Babysitting, bringing a meal, helping around the house — all of these and so many more can be opportunities to reveal the servant heart of a humble military wife. "Command them to do good, to be rich in good deeds, and to be generous and willing to share" (1 Timothy 6:18).

5. *Practice hospitality.* When a military wife opens her home to others, it is a powerful way to demonstrate Christ's love in a lonely and hurting world. "Offer hospitality to one another without grumbling" (1 Peter 4:9).

Individually, each of these commands reveals the character of God in a home. Taken together, they show how the character of God is demonstrated in community.

Be joyful in hope, patient in affliction, faithful in prayer. Share with the Lord's people who are in need. Practice hospitality.
ROMANS 12:12–13

DEBRIEF

- Which of the five Scripture commands mentioned above is easiest for me to obey?
- What steps can I take to grow in the commands that are more difficult for me?

REPORT

Lord, I want my home to have an atmosphere of peace and love. Guide me in the ways you call me to serve others. I pray this in Jesus' name. Amen.

authority except that which God has established. The authorities that exist have been established by God. [2]Consequently, whoever rebels against the authority is rebelling against what God has instituted, and those who do so will bring judgment on themselves. [3]For rulers hold no terror for those who do right, but for those who do wrong. Do you want to be free from fear of the one in authority? Then do what is right and you will be commended. [4]For the one in authority is God's servant for your good. But if you do wrong, be afraid, for rulers do not bear the sword for no reason. They are God's servants, agents of wrath to bring punishment on the wrongdoer. [5]Therefore, it is necessary to submit to the authorities, not only because of possible punishment but also as a matter of conscience.

[6]This is also why you pay taxes, for the authorities are God's servants, who give their full time to governing. [7]Give to everyone what you owe them: If you owe taxes, pay taxes; if revenue, then revenue; if respect, then respect; if honor, then honor.

Love Fulfills the Law

[8]Let no debt remain outstanding, except the continuing debt to love one another, for whoever loves others has fulfilled the law. [9]The commandments, "You shall not commit adultery," "You shall not murder," "You shall not steal," "You shall not covet,"[a] and whatever other command there may be, are summed up in this one command: "Love your neighbor as yourself."[b] [10]Love does no harm to a neighbor. Therefore love is the fulfillment of the law.

The Day Is Near

[11]And do this, understanding the present time: The hour has already come for you to wake up from your slumber, because our salvation is nearer now than when we first believed. [12]The night is nearly over; the day is almost here. So let us put aside the deeds of darkness and put on the armor of light. [13]Let us behave decently, as in the daytime, not in carousing and drunkenness, not in

sexual immorality and debauchery, not in dissension and jealousy. [14]Rather, clothe yourselves with the Lord Jesus Christ, and do not think about how to gratify the desires of the flesh.[c]

The Weak and the Strong

14 Accept the one whose faith is weak, without quarreling over disputable matters. [2]One person's faith allows them to eat anything, but another, whose faith is weak, eats only vegetables. [3]The one who eats everything must not treat with contempt the one who does not, and the one who does not eat everything must not judge the one who does, for God has accepted them. [4]Who are you to judge someone else's servant? To their own master, servants stand or fall. And they will stand, for the Lord is able to make them stand.

[5]One person considers one day more sacred than another; another considers every day alike. Each of them should be fully convinced in their own mind. [6]Whoever regards one day as special does so to the Lord. Whoever eats meat does so to the Lord, for they give thanks to God; and whoever abstains does so to the Lord and gives thanks to God. [7]For none of us lives for ourselves alone, and none of us dies for ourselves alone. [8]If we live, we live for the Lord; and if we die, we die for the Lord. So, whether we live or die, we belong to the Lord. [9]For this very reason, Christ died and returned to life so that he might be the Lord of both the dead and the living.

[10]You, then, why do you judge your brother or sister[d]? Or why do you treat them with contempt? For we will all stand before God's judgment seat. [11]It is written:

"'As surely as I live,' says the Lord,
'every knee will bow before me;
    every tongue will acknowledge God.'"[e]

[12]So then, each of us will give an account of ourselves to God.

[13]Therefore let us stop passing judgment on one another. Instead, make up your mind not to put any stumbling block or obstacle

---

[a] 9 Exodus 20:13-15,17; Deut. 5:17-19,21   [b] 9 Lev. 19:18   [c] 14 In contexts like this, the Greek word for *flesh* (*sarx*) refers to the sinful state of human beings, often presented as a power in opposition to the Spirit.   [d] 10 The Greek word for *brother or sister* (*adelphos*) refers here to a believer, whether man or woman, as part of God's family; also in verses 13, 15 and 21.   [e] 11 Isaiah 45:23

in the way of a brother or sister. [14]I am convinced, being fully persuaded in the Lord Jesus, that nothing is unclean in itself. But if anyone regards something as unclean, then for that person it is unclean. [15]If your brother or sister is distressed because of what you eat, you are no longer acting in love. Do not by your eating destroy someone for whom Christ died. [16]Therefore do not let what you know is good be spoken of as evil. [17]For the kingdom of God is not a matter of eating and drinking, but of righteousness, peace and joy in the Holy Spirit, [18]because anyone who serves Christ in this way is pleasing to God and receives human approval.

[19]Let us therefore make every effort to do what leads to peace and to mutual edification. [20]Do not destroy the work of God for the sake of food. All food is clean, but it is wrong for a person to eat anything that causes someone else to stumble. [21]It is better not to eat meat or drink wine or to do anything else that will cause your brother or sister to fall.

[22]So whatever you believe about these things keep between yourself and God. Blessed is the one who does not condemn himself by what he approves. [23]But whoever has doubts is condemned if they eat, because their eating is not from faith; and everything that does not come from faith is sin.[a]

15 We who are strong ought to bear with the failings of the weak and not to please ourselves. [2]Each of us should please our neighbors for their good, to build them up. [3]For even Christ did not please himself but, as it is written: "The insults of those who insult you have fallen on me."[b] [4]For everything that was written in the past was written to teach us, so that through the endurance taught in the Scriptures and the encouragement they provide we might have hope.

[5]May the God who gives endurance and encouragement give you the same attitude of mind toward each other that Christ Jesus had, [6]so that with one mind and one voice you may glorify the God and Father of our Lord Jesus Christ.

[7]Accept one another, then, just as Christ accepted you, in order to bring praise to God. [8]For I tell you that Christ has become a servant of the Jews[c] on behalf of God's truth, so that the promises made to the patriarchs might be confirmed [9]and, moreover, that the Gentiles might glorify God for his mercy. As it is written:

"Therefore I will praise you among the
   Gentiles;
   I will sing the praises of your name."[d]

[10]Again, it says,

"Rejoice, you Gentiles, with his people."[e]

[11]And again,

"Praise the Lord, all you Gentiles;
   let all the peoples extol him."[f]

[12]And again, Isaiah says,

"The Root of Jesse will spring up,
   one who will arise to rule over the
      nations;
   in him the Gentiles will hope."[g]

[13]May the God of hope fill you with all joy and peace as you trust in him, so that you may overflow with hope by the power of the Holy Spirit.

Paul the Minister to the Gentiles

[14]I myself am convinced, my brothers and sisters, that you yourselves are full of goodness, filled with knowledge and competent to instruct one another. [15]Yet I have written you quite boldly on some points to remind you of them again, because of the grace God gave me [16]to be a minister of Christ Jesus to the Gentiles. He gave me the priestly duty of proclaiming the gospel of God, so that the Gentiles might become an offering acceptable to God, sanctified by the Holy Spirit.

[17]Therefore I glory in Christ Jesus in my service to God. [18]I will not venture to speak of anything except what Christ has accomplished through me in leading the Gentiles to obey God by what I have said and done— [19]by the power of signs and wonders, through the power of the Spirit of God. So from Jerusalem all the way around to Illyricum, I have fully proclaimed the gospel of Christ. [20]It has always been my ambition

---

[a] 23 Some manuscripts place 16:25-27 here; others after 15:33.   [b] 3 Psalm 69:9   [c] 8 Greek *circumcision*   [d] 9 2 Samuel 22:50; Psalm 18:49   [e] 10 Deut. 32:43   [f] 11 Psalm 117:1
[g] 12 Isaiah 11:10 (see Septuagint)

Do Not Give Up!

By Ronda Sturgill

READ: Romans 15:1–13

E ndurance. Just hearing the word makes me feel weary and worn out! But I'm convinced it's the backbone of our military lifestyle, and I praise God for giving us both endurance *and* encouragement (see Romans 15:5).

A quick search of the definition of *endurance* brings up words such as fortitude, persistence, resolution, durability, staying power, stamina and even survival. All of these words seem to tell us the same thing: Do *not* give up!

Have you ever felt like giving up? We recently made our eighth military move. On moving day as the boxes came rolling into the house, one after another, I became completely overwhelmed. How was I ever going to get through this? Seven tons of stuff needed to be unpacked and put away in a house barely big enough to hold it all. What I really wanted to do was call an airline and get on the first plane out of here!

None of us have the personal resources or strength to live through what we face as military families. But God does! Reread Romans 15:5–6. When we ask him, God pours out his strength to us generously and in abundance. How? The answer is in verse 13: as we trust in him. When we trust God, the Holy Spirit fills us with his power and we are encouraged. Hope rises and our spirits become refreshed. We gain a new perspective — God's — on our situation. Trusting God allows us to take a step back and see the big picture. It means we give up control, ultimately believing God is good.

Trusting God is how we endure the daily challenges we face. What may not look good at the time might be the very thing God uses to strengthen our faith. The situation that makes us want to quit might be the very thing God uses to lead us to our sweet spot, the spot God created for us in this world. But we must choose to hang in there and trust God.

Thanks to a visit from our son, the boxes that were stacked to the ceiling are now empty, and most things have found their place in our home. Leaving on a jet plane would not have been a good idea. Instead, I'm trusting God sent us here to do a specific work. I can't wait to see what that work is!

May the God who gives endurance and encouragement give you the same attitude of mind toward each other that Christ Jesus had, so that with one mind and one voice you may glorify the God and Father of our Lord Jesus Christ … May the God of hope fill you with all joy and peace as you trust in him, so that you may overflow with hope by the power of the Holy Spirit.

ROMANS 15:5–6, 13

DEBRIEF

- When was the last time I felt like leaving on a jet plane?
- Using the word T-R-U-S-T, I will make an acronym to help me remember to trust God in challenging situations, both now and in the future.

REPORT

Dear heavenly Father, oh, how I want to trust you more! My life can be hard, and I sometimes feel like giving up. Please come and fill me anew with hope by the power of your Holy Spirit. Grant me the peace that comes with surrendering my life to your control, knowing you are good. In Jesus' name I pray. Amen.

for your next devotional reading, go to page 201

to preach the gospel where Christ was not known, so that I would not be building on someone else's foundation. [21]Rather, as it is written:

"Those who were not told about him
    will see,
and those who have not heard will
    understand."[a]

[22]This is why I have often been hindered from coming to you.

Paul's Plan to Visit Rome

[23]But now that there is no more place for me to work in these regions, and since I have been longing for many years to visit you, [24]I plan to do so when I go to Spain. I hope to see you while passing through and to have you assist me on my journey there, after I have enjoyed your company for a while. [25]Now, however, I am on my way to Jerusalem in the service of the Lord's people there. [26]For Macedonia and Achaia were pleased to make a contribution for the poor among the Lord's people in Jerusalem. [27]They were pleased to do it, and indeed they owe it to them. For if the Gentiles have shared in the Jews' spiritual blessings, they owe it to the Jews to share with them their material blessings. [28]So after I have completed this task and have made sure that they have received this contribution, I will go to Spain and visit you on the way. [29]I know that when I come to you, I will come in the full measure of the blessing of Christ.

[30]I urge you, brothers and sisters, by our Lord Jesus Christ and by the love of the Spirit, to join me in my struggle by praying to God for me. [31]Pray that I may be kept safe from the unbelievers in Judea and that the contribution I take to Jerusalem may be favorably received by the Lord's people there, [32]so that I may come to you with joy, by God's will, and in your company be refreshed. [33]The God of peace be with you all. Amen.

Personal Greetings

16 I commend to you our sister Phoebe, a deacon[b,c] of the church in Cenchreae. [2]I ask you to receive her in the Lord in a way worthy of his people and to give her any help she may need from you, for she has been the benefactor of many people, including me.

[3]Greet Priscilla[d] and Aquila, my co-workers in Christ Jesus. [4]They risked their lives for me. Not only I but all the churches of the Gentiles are grateful to them.
[5]Greet also the church that meets at their house.
Greet my dear friend Epenetus, who was the first convert to Christ in the province of Asia.
[6]Greet Mary, who worked very hard for you.
[7]Greet Andronicus and Junia, my fellow Jews who have been in prison with me. They are outstanding among[e] the apostles, and they were in Christ before I was.
[8]Greet Ampliatus, my dear friend in the Lord.
[9]Greet Urbanus, our co-worker in Christ, and my dear friend Stachys.
[10]Greet Apelles, whose fidelity to Christ has stood the test.
Greet those who belong to the household of Aristobulus.
[11]Greet Herodion, my fellow Jew.
Greet those in the household of Narcissus who are in the Lord.
[12]Greet Tryphena and Tryphosa, those women who work hard in the Lord.
Greet my dear friend Persis, another woman who has worked very hard in the Lord.
[13]Greet Rufus, chosen in the Lord, and his mother, who has been a mother to me, too.
[14]Greet Asyncritus, Phlegon, Hermes, Patrobas, Hermas and the other brothers and sisters with them.
[15]Greet Philologus, Julia, Nereus and his sister, and Olympas and all the Lord's people who are with them.
[16]Greet one another with a holy kiss.
All the churches of Christ send greetings.

[17]I urge you, brothers and sisters, to watch out for those who cause divisions and put obstacles in your way that are contrary to

---

[a]21 Isaiah 52:15 (see Septuagint)   [b]1 Or *servant*   [c]1 The word *deacon* refers here to a Christian designated to serve with the overseers/elders of the church in a variety of ways; similarly in Phil. 1:1 and 1 Tim. 3:8,12.   [d]3 Greek *Prisca*, a variant of *Priscilla*   [e]7 Or *are esteemed by*

the teaching you have learned. Keep away from them. [18]For such people are not serving our Lord Christ, but their own appetites. By smooth talk and flattery they deceive the minds of naive people. [19]Everyone has heard about your obedience, so I rejoice because of you; but I want you to be wise about what is good, and innocent about what is evil.

[20]The God of peace will soon crush Satan under your feet.

The grace of our Lord Jesus be with you.

[21]Timothy, my co-worker, sends his greetings to you, as do Lucius, Jason and Sosipater, my fellow Jews.

[22]I, Tertius, who wrote down this letter, greet you in the Lord.

[23]Gaius, whose hospitality I and the whole church here enjoy, sends you his greetings.

Erastus, who is the city's director of public works, and our brother Quartus send you their greetings. [24]*a*

[25]Now to him who is able to establish you in accordance with my gospel, the message I proclaim about Jesus Christ, in keeping with the revelation of the mystery hidden for long ages past, [26]but now revealed and made known through the prophetic writings by the command of the eternal God, so that all the Gentiles might come to the obedience that comes from*b* faith — [27]to the only wise God be glory forever through Jesus Christ! Amen.

---

a 24 Some manuscripts include here *May the grace of our Lord Jesus Christ be with all of you. Amen.*
b 26 Or *that is*

1 Corinthians

1 Paul, called to be an apostle of Christ Jesus by the will of God, and our brother Sosthenes,

[2] To the church of God in Corinth, to those sanctified in Christ Jesus and called to be his holy people, together with all those everywhere who call on the name of our Lord Jesus Christ — their Lord and ours:

[3] Grace and peace to you from God our Father and the Lord Jesus Christ.

Thanksgiving

[4] I always thank my God for you because of his grace given you in Christ Jesus. [5] For in him you have been enriched in every way — with all kinds of speech and with all knowledge — [6] God thus confirming our testimony about Christ among you. [7] Therefore you do not lack any spiritual gift as you eagerly wait for our Lord Jesus Christ to be revealed. [8] He will also keep you firm to the end, so that you will be blameless on the day of our Lord Jesus Christ. [9] God is faithful, who has called you into fellowship with his Son, Jesus Christ our Lord.

A Church Divided Over Leaders

[10] I appeal to you, brothers and sisters,[a] in the name of our Lord Jesus Christ, that all of you agree with one another in what you say and that there be no divisions among you, but that you be perfectly united in mind and thought. [11] My brothers and sisters, some from Chloe's household have informed me that there are quarrels among you. [12] What I mean is this: One of you says, "I follow Paul"; another, "I follow Apollos"; another, "I follow Cephas[b]"; still another, "I follow Christ."

[13] Is Christ divided? Was Paul crucified for you? Were you baptized in the name of Paul? [14] I thank God that I did not baptize any of you except Crispus and Gaius, [15] so no one can say that you were baptized in my name. [16] (Yes, I also baptized the household of Stephanas; beyond that, I don't remember if I baptized anyone else.) [17] For Christ did not send me to baptize, but to preach the gospel — not with wisdom and eloquence, lest the cross of Christ be emptied of its power.

Christ Crucified Is God's Power and Wisdom

[18] For the message of the cross is foolishness to those who are perishing, but to us who are being saved it is the power of God. [19] For it is written:

"I will destroy the wisdom of the wise;
   the intelligence of the intelligent I will
      frustrate."[c]

[20] Where is the wise person? Where is the teacher of the law? Where is the philosopher of this age? Has not God made foolish the wisdom of the world? [21] For since in the wisdom of God the world through its wisdom did not know him, God was pleased through the foolishness of what was preached to save those who believe. [22] Jews demand signs and Greeks look for wisdom, [23] but we preach Christ crucified: a stumbling block to Jews and foolishness to Gentiles, [24] but to those whom God has called, both Jews and Greeks, Christ the power of God and the wisdom of God. [25] For the foolishness of God is wiser than human wisdom, and the weakness of God is stronger than human strength.

[26] Brothers and sisters, think of what you were when you were called. Not many of you were wise by human standards; not many were influential; not many were of noble birth. [27] But God chose the foolish things of the world to shame the wise; God chose the weak things of the world to shame the strong. [28] God chose the lowly things of this world and the despised things — and the

---

[a] 10 The Greek word for *brothers and sisters* (*adelphoi*) refers here to believers, both men and women, as part of God's family; also in verses 11 and 26; and in 2:1; 3:1; 4:6; 6:8; 7:24, 29; 10:1; 11:33; 12:1; 14:6, 20, 26, 39; 15:1, 6, 50, 58; 16:15, 20.   [b] 12 That is, Peter   [c] 19 Isaiah 29:14

things that are not—to nullify the things that are, [29] so that no one may boast before him. [30] It is because of him that you are in Christ Jesus, who has become for us wisdom from God—that is, our righteousness, holiness and redemption. [31] Therefore, as it is written: "Let the one who boasts boast in the Lord."[a]

2 And so it was with me, brothers and sisters. When I came to you, I did not come with eloquence or human wisdom as I proclaimed to you the testimony about God.[b] [2] For I resolved to know nothing while I was with you except Jesus Christ and him crucified. [3] I came to you in weakness with great fear and trembling. [4] My message and my preaching were not with wise and persuasive words, but with a demonstration of the Spirit's power, [5] so that your faith might not rest on human wisdom, but on God's power.

God's Wisdom Revealed by the Spirit

[6] We do, however, speak a message of wisdom among the mature, but not the wisdom of this age or of the rulers of this age, who are coming to nothing. [7] No, we declare God's wisdom, a mystery that has been hidden and that God destined for our glory before time began. [8] None of the rulers of this age understood it, for if they had, they would not have crucified the Lord of glory. [9] However, as it is written:

"What no eye has seen,
    what no ear has heard,
and what no human mind has
        conceived"[c]—
    the things God has prepared for those
        who love him—

[10] these are the things God has revealed to us by his Spirit.

The Spirit searches all things, even the deep things of God. [11] For who knows a person's thoughts except their own spirit within them? In the same way no one knows the thoughts of God except the Spirit of God. [12] What we have received is not the spirit of the world, but the Spirit who is from God, so that we may understand what God has freely given us. [13] This is what we speak, not in words taught us by human wisdom but in words taught by the Spirit, explaining spir-

itual realities with Spirit-taught words.[d] [14] The person without the Spirit does not accept the things that come from the Spirit of God but considers them foolishness, and cannot understand them because they are discerned only through the Spirit. [15] The person with the Spirit makes judgments about all things, but such a person is not subject to merely human judgments, [16] for,

"Who has known the mind of
        the Lord
    so as to instruct him?"[e]

But we have the mind of Christ.

The Church and Its Leaders

3 Brothers and sisters, I could not address you as people who live by the Spirit but as people who are still worldly—mere infants in Christ. [2] I gave you milk, not solid food, for you were not yet ready for it. Indeed, you are still not ready. [3] You are still worldly. For since there is jealousy and quarreling among you, are you not worldly? Are you not acting like mere humans? [4] For when one says, "I follow Paul," and another, "I follow Apollos," are you not mere human beings?

[5] What, after all, is Apollos? And what is Paul? Only servants, through whom you came to believe—as the Lord has assigned to each his task. [6] I planted the seed, Apollos watered it, but God has been making it grow. [7] So neither the one who plants nor the one who waters is anything, but only God, who makes things grow. [8] The one who plants and the one who waters have one purpose, and they will each be rewarded according to their own labor. [9] For we are co-workers in God's service; you are God's field, God's building.

[10] By the grace God has given me, I laid a foundation as a wise builder, and someone else is building on it. But each one should build with care. [11] For no one can lay any foundation other than the one already laid, which is Jesus Christ. [12] If anyone builds on this foundation using gold, silver, costly stones, wood, hay or straw, [13] their work will be shown for what it is, because the Day will bring it to light. It will be revealed with fire, and the fire will test the quality of each person's work. [14] If what has been built survives,

---

[a] 31 Jer. 9:24   [b] 1 Some manuscripts *proclaimed to you God's mystery*   [c] 9 Isaiah 64:4   [d] 13 Or *Spirit, interpreting spiritual truths to those who are spiritual*   [e] 16 Isaiah 40:13

the builder will receive a reward. [15]If it is burned up, the builder will suffer loss but yet will be saved — even though only as one escaping through the flames.

[16]Don't you know that you yourselves are God's temple and that God's Spirit dwells in your midst? [17]If anyone destroys God's temple, God will destroy that person; for God's temple is sacred, and you together are that temple.

[18]Do not deceive yourselves. If any of you think you are wise by the standards of this age, you should become "fools" so that you may become wise. [19]For the wisdom of this world is foolishness in God's sight. As it is written: "He catches the wise in their craftiness"[a]; [20]and again, "The Lord knows that the thoughts of the wise are futile."[b] [21]So then, no more boasting about human leaders! All things are yours, [22]whether Paul or Apollos or Cephas[c] or the world or life or death or the present or the future — all are yours, [23]and you are of Christ, and Christ is of God.

The Nature of True Apostleship

4 This, then, is how you ought to regard us: as servants of Christ and as those entrusted with the mysteries God has revealed. [2]Now it is required that those who have been given a trust must prove faithful. [3]I care very little if I am judged by you or by any human court; indeed, I do not even judge myself. [4]My conscience is clear, but that does not make me innocent. It is the Lord who judges me. [5]Therefore judge nothing before the appointed time; wait until the Lord comes. He will bring to light what is hidden in darkness and will expose the motives of the heart. At that time each will receive their praise from God.

[6]Now, brothers and sisters, I have applied these things to myself and Apollos for your benefit, so that you may learn from us the meaning of the saying, "Do not go beyond what is written." Then you will not be puffed up in being a follower of one of us over against the other. [7]For who makes you different from anyone else? What do you have that you did not receive? And if you did receive it, why do you boast as though you did not?

[8]Already you have all you want! Already you have become rich! You have begun to reign — and that without us! How I wish that you really had begun to reign so that we also might reign with you! [9]For it seems to me that God has put us apostles on display at the end of the procession, like those condemned to die in the arena. We have been made a spectacle to the whole universe, to angels as well as to human beings. [10]We are fools for Christ, but you are so wise in Christ! We are weak, but you are strong! You are honored, we are dishonored! [11]To this very hour we go hungry and thirsty, we are in rags, we are brutally treated, we are homeless. [12]We work hard with our own hands. When we are cursed, we bless; when we are persecuted, we endure it; [13]when we are slandered, we answer kindly. We have become the scum of the earth, the garbage of the world — right up to this moment.

Paul's Appeal and Warning

[14]I am writing this not to shame you but to warn you as my dear children. [15]Even if you had ten thousand guardians in Christ, you do not have many fathers, for in Christ Jesus I became your father through the gospel. [16]Therefore I urge you to imitate me. [17]For this reason I have sent to you Timothy, my son whom I love, who is faithful in the Lord. He will remind you of my way of life in Christ Jesus, which agrees with what I teach everywhere in every church.

[18]Some of you have become arrogant, as if I were not coming to you. [19]But I will come to you very soon, if the Lord is willing, and then I will find out not only how these arrogant people are talking, but what power they have. [20]For the kingdom of God is not a matter of talk but of power. [21]What do you prefer? Shall I come to you with a rod of discipline, or shall I come in love and with a gentle spirit?

Dealing With a Case of Incest

5 It is actually reported that there is sexual immorality among you, and of a kind that even pagans do not tolerate: A man is sleeping with his father's wife. [2]And you are proud! Shouldn't you rather have gone into mourning and have put out of your fellowship the man who has been doing this? [3]For my part, even though I am not physically

---

[a] *19* Job 5:13   [b] *20* Psalm 94:11   [c] *22* That is, Peter

present, I am with you in spirit. As one who is present with you in this way, I have already passed judgment in the name of our Lord Jesus on the one who has been doing this. ⁴So when you are assembled and I am with you in spirit, and the power of our Lord Jesus is present, ⁵hand this man over to Satan for the destruction of the flesh,ᵃ,ᵇ so that his spirit may be saved on the day of the Lord.

⁶Your boasting is not good. Don't you know that a little yeast leavens the whole batch of dough? ⁷Get rid of the old yeast, so that you may be a new unleavened batch — as you really are. For Christ, our Passover lamb, has been sacrificed. ⁸Therefore let us keep the Festival, not with the old bread leavened with malice and wickedness, but with the unleavened bread of sincerity and truth.

⁹I wrote to you in my letter not to associate with sexually immoral people — ¹⁰not at all meaning the people of this world who are immoral, or the greedy and swindlers, or idolaters. In that case you would have to leave this world. ¹¹But now I am writing to you that you must not associate with anyone who claims to be a brother or sisterᶜ but is sexually immoral or greedy, an idolater or slanderer, a drunkard or swindler. Do not even eat with such people.

¹²What business is it of mine to judge those outside the church? Are you not to judge those inside? ¹³God will judge those outside. "Expel the wicked person from among you."ᵈ

Lawsuits Among Believers

6 If any of you has a dispute with another, do you dare to take it before the ungodly for judgment instead of before the Lord's people? ²Or do you not know that the Lord's people will judge the world? And if you are to judge the world, are you not competent to judge trivial cases? ³Do you not know that we will judge angels? How much more the things of this life! ⁴Therefore, if you have disputes about such matters, do you ask for a ruling from those whose way of life is scorned in the church? ⁵I say this to shame you. Is it possible that there is nobody among you wise enough to judge a dispute between believers? ⁶But instead, one brother takes another to court — and this in front of unbelievers!

⁷The very fact that you have lawsuits among you means you have been completely defeated already. Why not rather be wronged? Why not rather be cheated? ⁸Instead, you yourselves cheat and do wrong, and you do this to your brothers and sisters. ⁹Or do you not know that wrongdoers will not inherit the kingdom of God? Do not be deceived: Neither the sexually immoral nor idolaters nor adulterers nor men who have sex with menᵉ ¹⁰nor thieves nor the greedy nor drunkards nor slanderers nor swindlers will inherit the kingdom of God. ¹¹And that is what some of you were. But you were washed, you were sanctified, you were justified in the name of the Lord Jesus Christ and by the Spirit of our God.

Sexual Immorality

¹²"I have the right to do anything," you say — but not everything is beneficial. "I have the right to do anything" — but I will not be mastered by anything. ¹³You say, "Food for the stomach and the stomach for food, and God will destroy them both." The body, however, is not meant for sexual immorality but for the Lord, and the Lord for the body. ¹⁴By his power God raised the Lord from the dead, and he will raise us also. ¹⁵Do you not know that your bodies are members of Christ himself? Shall I then take the members of Christ and unite them with a prostitute? Never! ¹⁶Do you not know that he who unites himself with a prostitute is one with her in body? For it is said, "The two will become one flesh."ᶠ ¹⁷But whoever is united with the Lord is one with him in spirit.ᵍ

¹⁸Flee from sexual immorality. All other sins a person commits are outside the body, but whoever sins sexually, sins against their own body. ¹⁹Do you not know that your bodies are temples of the Holy Spirit, who is in

---

ᵃ 5 In contexts like this, the Greek word for *flesh* (*sarx*) refers to the sinful state of human beings, often presented as a power in opposition to the Spirit.   ᵇ 5 Or *of his body*   ᶜ 11 The Greek word for *brother or sister* (*adelphos*) refers here to a believer, whether man or woman, as part of God's family; also in 8:11, 13.   ᵈ 13 Deut. 13:5; 17:7; 19:19; 21:21; 22:21,24; 24:7   ᵉ 9 The words *men who have sex with men* translate two Greek words that refer to the passive and active participants in homosexual acts.   ᶠ 16 Gen. 2:24   ᵍ 17 Or *in the Spirit*

you, whom you have received from God? You are not your own; [20]you were bought at a price. Therefore honor God with your bodies.

Concerning Married Life

7 Now for the matters you wrote about: "It is good for a man not to have sexual relations with a woman." [2]But since sexual immorality is occurring, each man should have sexual relations with his own wife, and each woman with her own husband. [3]The husband should fulfill his marital duty to his wife, and likewise the wife to her husband. [4]The wife does not have authority over her own body but yields it to her husband. In the same way, the husband does not have authority over his own body but yields it to his wife. [5]Do not deprive each other except perhaps by mutual consent and for a time, so that you may devote yourselves to prayer. Then come together again so that Satan will not tempt you because of your lack of self-control. [6]I say this as a concession, not as a command. [7]I wish that all of you were as I am. But each of you has your own gift from God; one has this gift, another has that.

[8]Now to the unmarried[a] and the widows I say: It is good for them to stay unmarried, as I do. [9]But if they cannot control themselves, they should marry, for it is better to marry than to burn with passion.

[10]To the married I give this command (not I, but the Lord): A wife must not separate from her husband. [11]But if she does, she must remain unmarried or else be reconciled to her husband. And a husband must not divorce his wife.

[12]To the rest I say this (I, not the Lord): If any brother has a wife who is not a believer and she is willing to live with him, he must not divorce her. [13]And if a woman has a husband who is not a believer and he is willing to live with her, she must not divorce him. [14]For the unbelieving husband has been sanctified through his wife, and the unbelieving wife has been sanctified through her believing husband. Otherwise your children would be unclean, but as it is, they are holy.

[15]But if the unbeliever leaves, let it be so. The brother or the sister is not bound in such circumstances; God has called us to live in peace. [16]How do you know, wife, whether you will save your husband? Or, how do you know, husband, whether you will save your wife?

Concerning Change of Status

[17]Nevertheless, each person should live as a believer in whatever situation the Lord has assigned to them, just as God has called them. This is the rule I lay down in all the churches. [18]Was a man already circumcised when he was called? He should not become uncircumcised. Was a man uncircumcised when he was called? He should not be circumcised. [19]Circumcision is nothing and uncircumcision is nothing. Keeping God's commands is what counts. [20]Each person should remain in the situation they were in when God called them.

[21]Were you a slave when you were called? Don't let it trouble you—although if you can gain your freedom, do so. [22]For the one who was a slave when called to faith in the Lord is the Lord's freed person; similarly, the one who was free when called is Christ's slave. [23]You were bought at a price; do not become slaves of human beings. [24]Brothers and sisters, each person, as responsible to God, should remain in the situation they were in when God called them.

Concerning the Unmarried

[25]Now about virgins: I have no command from the Lord, but I give a judgment as one who by the Lord's mercy is trustworthy. [26]Because of the present crisis, I think that it is good for a man to remain as he is. [27]Are you pledged to a woman? Do not seek to be released. Are you free from such a commitment? Do not look for a wife. [28]But if you do marry, you have not sinned; and if a virgin marries, she has not sinned. But those who marry will face many troubles in this life, and I want to spare you this.

[29]What I mean, brothers and sisters, is that the time is short. From now on those who have wives should live as if they do not; [30]those who mourn, as if they did not; those who are happy, as if they were not; those who buy something, as if it were not theirs to keep; [31]those who use the things of the

world, as if not engrossed in them. For this world in its present form is passing away.

³²I would like you to be free from concern. An unmarried man is concerned about the Lord's affairs — how he can please the Lord. ³³But a married man is concerned about the affairs of this world — how he can please his wife — ³⁴and his interests are divided. An unmarried woman or virgin is concerned about the Lord's affairs: Her aim is to be devoted to the Lord in both body and spirit. But a married woman is concerned about the affairs of this world — how she can please her husband. ³⁵I am saying this for your own good, not to restrict you, but that you may live in a right way in undivided devotion to the Lord.

³⁶If anyone is worried that he might not be acting honorably toward the virgin he is engaged to, and if his passions are too strong[a] and he feels he ought to marry, he should do as he wants. He is not sinning. They should get married. ³⁷But the man who has settled the matter in his own mind, who is under no compulsion but has control over his own will, and who has made up his mind not to marry the virgin — this man also does the right thing. ³⁸So then, he who marries the virgin does right, but he who does not marry her does better.[b]

³⁹A woman is bound to her husband as long as he lives. But if her husband dies, she is free to marry anyone she wishes, but he must belong to the Lord. ⁴⁰In my judgment, she is happier if she stays as she is — and I think that I too have the Spirit of God.

Concerning Food Sacrificed to Idols

8 Now about food sacrificed to idols: We know that "We all possess knowledge." But knowledge puffs up while love builds up. ²Those who think they know something do not yet know as they ought to know. ³But whoever loves God is known by God.[c]

⁴So then, about eating food sacrificed to idols: We know that "An idol is nothing at all in the world" and that "There is no God but one." ⁵For even if there are so-called gods, whether in heaven or on earth (as indeed there are many "gods" and many "lords"), ⁶yet for us there is but one God, the Father, from whom all things came and for whom we live; and there is but one Lord, Jesus Christ, through whom all things came and through whom we live.

⁷But not everyone possesses this knowledge. Some people are still so accustomed to idols that when they eat sacrificial food they think of it as having been sacrificed to a god, and since their conscience is weak, it is defiled. ⁸But food does not bring us near to God; we are no worse if we do not eat, and no better if we do.

⁹Be careful, however, that the exercise of your rights does not become a stumbling block to the weak. ¹⁰For if someone with a weak conscience sees you, with all your knowledge, eating in an idol's temple, won't that person be emboldened to eat what is sacrificed to idols? ¹¹So this weak brother or sister, for whom Christ died, is destroyed by your knowledge. ¹²When you sin against them in this way and wound their weak conscience, you sin against Christ. ¹³Therefore, if what I eat causes my brother or sister to fall into sin, I will never eat meat again, so that I will not cause them to fall.

Paul's Rights as an Apostle

9 Am I not free? Am I not an apostle? Have I not seen Jesus our Lord? Are you not the result of my work in the Lord? ²Even though I may not be an apostle to others, surely I am to you! For you are the seal of my apostleship in the Lord.

³This is my defense to those who sit in judgment on me. ⁴Don't we have the right to food and drink? ⁵Don't we have the right to take a believing wife along with us, as do the other apostles and the Lord's brothers and Cephas[d]? ⁶Or is it only I and Barnabas who lack the right to not work for a living?

---

[a] 36 Or *if she is getting beyond the usual age for marriage*   [b] 36-38 Or ³⁶*If anyone thinks he is not treating his daughter properly, and if she is getting along in years (or if her passions are too strong), and he feels she ought to marry, he should do as he wants. He is not sinning. He should let her get married.* ³⁷*But the man who has settled the matter in his own mind, who is under no compulsion but has control over his own will, and who has made up his mind to keep the virgin unmarried — this man also does the right thing.* ³⁸*So then, he who gives his virgin in marriage does right, but he who does not give her in marriage does better.*
[c] 2,3 An early manuscript and another ancient witness *think they have knowledge do not yet know as they ought to know.* ³*But whoever loves truly knows.*   [d] 5 That is, Peter

[7]Who serves as a soldier at his own expense? Who plants a vineyard and does not eat its grapes? Who tends a flock and does not drink the milk? [8]Do I say this merely on human authority? Doesn't the Law say the same thing? [9]For it is written in the Law of Moses: "Do not muzzle an ox while it is treading out the grain."[a] Is it about oxen that God is concerned? [10]Surely he says this for us, doesn't he? Yes, this was written for us, because whoever plows and threshes should be able to do so in the hope of sharing in the harvest. [11]If we have sown spiritual seed among you, is it too much if we reap a material harvest from you? [12]If others have this right of support from you, shouldn't we have it all the more?

But we did not use this right. On the contrary, we put up with anything rather than hinder the gospel of Christ.

[13]Don't you know that those who serve in the temple get their food from the temple, and that those who serve at the altar share in what is offered on the altar? [14]In the same way, the Lord has commanded that those who preach the gospel should receive their living from the gospel.

[15]But I have not used any of these rights. And I am not writing this in the hope that you will do such things for me, for I would rather die than allow anyone to deprive me of this boast. [16]For when I preach the gospel, I cannot boast, since I am compelled to preach. Woe to me if I do not preach the gospel! [17]If I preach voluntarily, I have a reward; if not voluntarily, I am simply discharging the trust committed to me. [18]What then is my reward? Just this: that in preaching the gospel I may offer it free of charge, and so not make full use of my rights as a preacher of the gospel.

Paul's Use of His Freedom

[19]Though I am free and belong to no one, I have made myself a slave to everyone, to win as many as possible. [20]To the Jews I became like a Jew, to win the Jews. To those under the law I became like one under the law (though I myself am not under the law), so as to win those under the law. [21]To those not having the law I became like one not having the law (though I am not free from God's law but am under Christ's law), so as to win those not having the law. [22]To the weak I became weak, to win the weak. I have become all things to all people so that by all possible means I might save some. [23]I do all this for the sake of the gospel, that I may share in its blessings.

The Need for Self-Discipline

[24]Do you not know that in a race all the runners run, but only one gets the prize? Run in such a way as to get the prize. [25]Everyone who competes in the games goes into strict training. They do it to get a crown that will not last, but we do it to get a crown that will last forever. [26]Therefore I do not run like someone running aimlessly; I do not fight like a boxer beating the air. [27]No, I strike a blow to my body and make it my slave so that after I have preached to others, I myself will not be disqualified for the prize.

Warnings From Israel's History

10 For I do not want you to be ignorant of the fact, brothers and sisters, that our ancestors were all under the cloud and that they all passed through the sea. [2]They were all baptized into Moses in the cloud and in the sea. [3]They all ate the same spiritual food [4]and drank the same spiritual drink; for they drank from the spiritual rock that accompanied them, and that rock was Christ. [5]Nevertheless, God was not pleased with most of them; their bodies were scattered in the wilderness.

[6]Now these things occurred as examples to keep us from setting our hearts on evil things as they did. [7]Do not be idolaters, as some of them were; as it is written: "The people sat down to eat and drink and got up to indulge in revelry."[b] [8]We should not commit sexual immorality, as some of them did — and in one day twenty-three thousand of them died. [9]We should not test Christ,[c] as some of them did — and were killed by snakes. [10]And do not grumble, as some of them did — and were killed by the destroying angel.

[11]These things happened to them as examples and were written down as warnings for us, on whom the culmination of the ages has come. [12]So, if you think you are standing

---

[a] 9 Deut. 25:4   [b] 7 Exodus 32:6   [c] 9 Some manuscripts *test the Lord*

God Casts a Lifeline

By Penny Monetti

READ: 1 Corinthians 10:1–13

"Counseling means divorce!" My husband of 19 years had had enough. We needed professional help, but Tony would have none of it. He angrily launched his wedding ring across the room as my cutting words echoed, "Fine! Get a divorce! I'm done!"

Through the years, we had lost our ability to communicate. Unresolved issues stockpiled as I stuffed into my mental drawer all the hurtful words, unrealized ambitions, time-consuming business and military demands that robbed our family time. I turned to church, friends and community activities to fill the void. The repressed emotions prevented me from meeting Tony's needs. Tony felt out of control and got angry easily. I grew depressed. Temptation to divorce kept surfacing like a life preserver in a raging sea.

All of us deal with temptations. In 1 Corinthians 10:7 – 10, Paul lists a few, but the list for each of us could fill pages. But whatever your temptation, God throws a lifeline — you only have to grasp it and follow it back to safety (see verse 13).

The lifeline God threw me came in the form of a novel whose main character's marriage bore an uncanny resemblance to mine, causing me to do some deep soul-searching. By the time I read the last page, I had made a recommitment to honor my marriage vows — even though the feelings of love still remained buried.

I knew that proving my commitment to our marriage demanded a monumental gesture, so I booked a next-day flight to London, where Tony was chairing an aviation conference. After paying a ridiculously expensive airfare, I arrived at the conference. Feeling like a schoolgirl, I handed a message written on a napkin to the conference coordinator to pass to Tony. I then waited in the reception room. As I heard Tony's voice among the arriving executives, I lowered my newspaper. Tony's eyes met mine. He rushed toward me and lifted me in a tight embrace. He held up the message like a trophy, displaying three life-changing words: *I Choose Us.*

Healing through counseling demanded tremendous commitment and daily trust in God; however, resolving to work through our painful issues created a love richer than that of the day we married. You may feel that your marriage is a sinking ship and divorcing is the only way to stay afloat. But remember that God's faithfulness is even stronger. Choose to honor the "for worse" part of your marriage vows, and accept God's lifeline of hope and healing.

No temptation has overtaken you except what is common to mankind. And God is faithful; he will not let you be tempted beyond what you can bear. But when you are tempted, he will also provide a way out so that you can endure it.

1 CORINTHIANS 10:13

DEBRIEF
- What is my biggest temptation right now?
- Where do I see God throwing me a lifeline?

REPORT
Heavenly Father, you know my vulnerabilities and temptations. Thank you for providing a way out, for picking me up when I fall, and for encompassing me with your insurmountable love. Amen.

for your next devotional reading, go to page 205

firm, be careful that you don't fall! [13]No temptation[a] has overtaken you except what is common to mankind. And God is faithful; he will not let you be tempted[a] beyond what you can bear. But when you are tempted,[a] he will also provide a way out so that you can endure it.

Idol Feasts and the Lord's Supper

[14]Therefore, my dear friends, flee from idolatry. [15]I speak to sensible people; judge for yourselves what I say. [16]Is not the cup of thanksgiving for which we give thanks a participation in the blood of Christ? And is not the bread that we break a participation in the body of Christ? [17]Because there is one loaf, we, who are many, are one body, for we all share the one loaf.

[18]Consider the people of Israel: Do not those who eat the sacrifices participate in the altar? [19]Do I mean then that food sacrificed to an idol is anything, or that an idol is anything? [20]No, but the sacrifices of pagans are offered to demons, not to God, and I do not want you to be participants with demons. [21]You cannot drink the cup of the Lord and the cup of demons too; you cannot have a part in both the Lord's table and the table of demons. [22]Are we trying to arouse the Lord's jealousy? Are we stronger than he?

The Believer's Freedom

[23]"I have the right to do anything," you say — but not everything is beneficial. "I have the right to do anything" — but not everything is constructive. [24]No one should seek their own good, but the good of others.

[25]Eat anything sold in the meat market without raising questions of conscience, [26]for, "The earth is the Lord's, and everything in it."[b]

[27]If an unbeliever invites you to a meal and you want to go, eat whatever is put before you without raising questions of conscience. [28]But if someone says to you, "This has been offered in sacrifice," then do not eat it, both for the sake of the one who told you and for the sake of conscience. [29]I am referring to the other person's conscience, not yours. For why is my freedom being judged by another's conscience? [30]If I take part in the meal with thankfulness, why am I denounced because of something I thank God for?

[31]So whether you eat or drink or whatever you do, do it all for the glory of God. [32]Do not cause anyone to stumble, whether Jews, Greeks or the church of God— [33]even as I try to please everyone in every way. For I am not seeking my own good but the good of many,

11 so that they may be saved. [1]Follow my example, as I follow the example of Christ.

On Covering the Head in Worship

[2]I praise you for remembering me in everything and for holding to the traditions just as I passed them on to you. [3]But I want you to realize that the head of every man is Christ, and the head of the woman is man,[c] and the head of Christ is God. [4]Every man who prays or prophesies with his head covered dishonors his head. [5]But every woman who prays or prophesies with her head uncovered dishonors her head—it is the same as having her head shaved. [6]For if a woman does not cover her head, she might as well have her hair cut off; but if it is a disgrace for a woman to have her hair cut off or her head shaved, then she should cover her head.

[7]A man ought not to cover his head,[d] since he is the image and glory of God; but woman is the glory of man. [8]For man did not come from woman, but woman from man; [9]neither was man created for woman, but woman for man. [10]It is for this reason that a woman ought to have authority over her own[e] head, because of the angels. [11]Nevertheless, in the Lord woman is not independent of man, nor is man independent of woman. [12]For as woman came from man, so also man is born of woman. But everything comes from God.

[13]Judge for yourselves: Is it proper for a woman to pray to God with her head uncovered? [14]Does not the very nature of things

---

[a]13 The Greek for *temptation* and *tempted* can also mean *testing* and *tested*.   [b]26 Psalm 24:1
[c]3 Or *of the wife is her husband*   [d]4-7 Or [4]*Every man who prays or prophesies with long hair dishonors his head.* [5]*But every woman who prays or prophesies with no covering of hair dishonors her head—she is just like one of the "shorn women."* [6]*If a woman has no covering, let her be for now with short hair; but since it is a disgrace for a woman to have her hair shorn or shaved, she should grow it again.* [7]*A man ought not to have long hair*   [e]10 Or *have a sign of authority on her*

teach you that if a man has long hair, it is a disgrace to him, [15]but that if a woman has long hair, it is her glory? For long hair is given to her as a covering. [16]If anyone wants to be contentious about this, we have no other practice — nor do the churches of God.

Correcting an Abuse of the Lord's Supper

[17]In the following directives I have no praise for you, for your meetings do more harm than good. [18]In the first place, I hear that when you come together as a church, there are divisions among you, and to some extent I believe it. [19]No doubt there have to be differences among you to show which of you have God's approval. [20]So then, when you come together, it is not the Lord's Supper you eat, [21]for when you are eating, some of you go ahead with your own private suppers. As a result, one person remains hungry and another gets drunk. [22]Don't you have homes to eat and drink in? Or do you despise the church of God by humiliating those who have nothing? What shall I say to you? Shall I praise you? Certainly not in this matter!

[23]For I received from the Lord what I also passed on to you: The Lord Jesus, on the night he was betrayed, took bread, [24]and when he had given thanks, he broke it and said, "This is my body, which is for you; do this in remembrance of me." [25]In the same way, after supper he took the cup, saying, "This cup is the new covenant in my blood; do this, whenever you drink it, in remembrance of me." [26]For whenever you eat this bread and drink this cup, you proclaim the Lord's death until he comes.

[27]So then, whoever eats the bread or drinks the cup of the Lord in an unworthy manner will be guilty of sinning against the body and blood of the Lord. [28]Everyone ought to examine themselves before they eat of the bread and drink from the cup. [29]For those who eat and drink without discerning the body of Christ eat and drink judgment on themselves. [30]That is why many among you are weak and sick, and a number of you have fallen asleep. [31]But if we were more discerning with regard to ourselves, we would not come under such judgment. [32]Nevertheless, when we are judged in this way by the Lord,

we are being disciplined so that we will not be finally condemned with the world.

[33]So then, my brothers and sisters, when you gather to eat, you should all eat together. [34]Anyone who is hungry should eat something at home, so that when you meet together it may not result in judgment.

And when I come I will give further directions.

Concerning Spiritual Gifts

12 Now about the gifts of the Spirit, brothers and sisters, I do not want you to be uninformed. [2]You know that when you were pagans, somehow or other you were influenced and led astray to mute idols. [3]Therefore I want you to know that no one who is speaking by the Spirit of God says, "Jesus be cursed," and no one can say, "Jesus is Lord," except by the Holy Spirit.

[4]There are different kinds of gifts, but the same Spirit distributes them. [5]There are different kinds of service, but the same Lord. [6]There are different kinds of working, but in all of them and in everyone it is the same God at work.

[7]Now to each one the manifestation of the Spirit is given for the common good. [8]To one there is given through the Spirit a message of wisdom, to another a message of knowledge by means of the same Spirit, [9]to another faith by the same Spirit, to another gifts of healing by that one Spirit, [10]to another miraculous powers, to another prophecy, to another distinguishing between spirits, to another speaking in different kinds of tongues,[a] and to still another the interpretation of tongues.[a] [11]All these are the work of one and the same Spirit, and he distributes them to each one, just as he determines.

Unity and Diversity in the Body

[12]Just as a body, though one, has many parts, but all its many parts form one body, so it is with Christ. [13]For we were all baptized by[b] one Spirit so as to form one body — whether Jews or Gentiles, slave or free — and we were all given the one Spirit to drink. [14]Even so the body is not made up of one part but of many.

[15]Now if the foot should say, "Because I am not a hand, I do not belong to the body," it would not for that reason stop being part

---

[a] 10 Or languages; also in verse 28   [b] 13 Or with; or in

of the body. [16] And if the ear should say, "Because I am not an eye, I do not belong to the body," it would not for that reason stop being part of the body. [17] If the whole body were an eye, where would the sense of hearing be? If the whole body were an ear, where would the sense of smell be? [18] But in fact God has placed the parts in the body, every one of them, just as he wanted them to be. [19] If they were all one part, where would the body be? [20] As it is, there are many parts, but one body.

[21] The eye cannot say to the hand, "I don't need you!" And the head cannot say to the feet, "I don't need you!" [22] On the contrary, those parts of the body that seem to be weaker are indispensable, [23] and the parts that we think are less honorable we treat with special honor. And the parts that are unpresentable are treated with special modesty, [24] while our presentable parts need no special treatment. But God has put the body together, giving greater honor to the parts that lacked it, [25] so that there should be no division in the body, but that its parts should have equal concern for each other. [26] If one part suffers, every part suffers with it; if one part is honored, every part rejoices with it.

[27] Now you are the body of Christ, and each one of you is a part of it. [28] And God has placed in the church first of all apostles, second prophets, third teachers, then miracles, then gifts of healing, of helping, of guidance, and of different kinds of tongues. [29] Are all apostles? Are all prophets? Are all teachers? Do all work miracles? [30] Do all have gifts of healing? Do all speak in tongues[a]? Do all interpret? [31] Now eagerly desire the greater gifts.

Love Is Indispensable

And yet I will show you the most excellent way.

13 If I speak in the tongues[b] of men or of angels, but do not have love, I am only a resounding gong or a clanging cymbal. [2] If I have the gift of prophecy and can fathom all mysteries and all knowledge, and if I have a faith that can move mountains, but do not have love, I am nothing. [3] If I give all I possess to the poor and give over my body to hardship that I may boast,[c] but do not have love, I gain nothing.

[4] Love is patient, love is kind. It does not envy, it does not boast, it is not proud. [5] It does not dishonor others, it is not self-seeking, it is not easily angered, it keeps no record of wrongs. [6] Love does not delight in evil but rejoices with the truth. [7] It always protects, always trusts, always hopes, always perseveres.

[8] Love never fails. But where there are prophecies, they will cease; where there are tongues, they will be stilled; where there is knowledge, it will pass away. [9] For we know in part and we prophesy in part, [10] but when completeness comes, what is in part disappears. [11] When I was a child, I talked like a child, I thought like a child, I reasoned like a child. When I became a man, I put the ways of childhood behind me. [12] For now we see only a reflection as in a mirror; then we shall see face to face. Now I know in part; then I shall know fully, even as I am fully known.

[13] And now these three remain: faith, hope and love. But the greatest of these is love.

Intelligibility in Worship

14 Follow the way of love and eagerly desire gifts of the Spirit, especially prophecy. [2] For anyone who speaks in a tongue[d] does not speak to people but to God. Indeed, no one understands them; they utter mysteries by the Spirit. [3] But the one who prophesies speaks to people for their strengthening, encouraging and comfort. [4] Anyone who speaks in a tongue edifies themselves, but the one who prophesies edifies the church. [5] I would like every one of you to speak in tongues,[e] but I would rather have you prophesy. The one who prophesies is greater than the one who speaks in tongues,[e] unless someone interprets, so that the church may be edified.

[6] Now, brothers and sisters, if I come to you and speak in tongues, what good will I be to you, unless I bring you some revelation or knowledge or prophecy or word of instruction? [7] Even in the case of lifeless things that make sounds, such as the pipe or harp,

---

[a] 30 Or *other languages*   [b] 1 Or *languages*   [c] 3 Some manuscripts *body to the flames*   [d] 2 Or *in another language*; also in verses 4, 13, 14, 19, 26 and 27   [e] 5 Or *in other languages*; also in verses 6, 18, 22, 23 and 39

UNFAILING LOVE

By Jocelyn Green

Twenty-year-old Brenda Roever had her suitcase packed and by the door as she got ready to meet her husband, Dave, for his leave in 16 days. Her eagerness was understandable — they had been married just two years, and eight months before, Uncle Sam's draft had whisked Dave away to the Mekong Delta in Vietnam. Brenda could hardly wait to see him again.

But on July 26, 1969, she saw two Naval officers in dress whites at her door. Nausea and dizziness overtook her as she read the telegram they placed in her hands: An enemy had fired a shot into a grenade Dave had been holding, and the explosion had nearly killed him.

The officers' words sounded faraway, and she dismissed them so she could cry out to God alone. As she did, "a supernatural spirit of grace and peace filled me," she told a magazine reporter. "I knew everything would be all right."

After spending eight days clinging to life in a hospital in Japan, Dave's health stabilized, and he was transported to Brooke Army Medical Center in San Antonio, Texas. This was where Brenda was finally able to see him.

"Dave's body was horrifically swollen, his head to the width of his shoulders, with no hair and only one ear. From the waist up he was black from the burns and covered with a milky-white medication that could not hide the huge chunks of missing flesh. His charred body was almost unrecognizable," she said. And yet Brenda peered into his eyes, gently kissed what was left of his lips and said, "Welcome home, Davey. I love you."

What she didn't know then was that Dave had just watched another wife take off her wedding ring and drop it at the feet of her own badly burned husband. Dave was terrified of what Brenda's reaction would be — but Brenda never wavered from her faith in God or her devotion to her husband.

"Love is commitment—for richer, for poorer, for better, for worse, in sickness, and in health, till death do us part," Brenda wrote in an article. "I did not marry Dave Roever because he was the most handsome man I had ever seen or because he had the strongest body. I married him because he was gentle and kind. He was patient and longsuffering. He was loyal and a faithful friend. Our commitment of fidelity could not be broken, though the flames of hell tried," said Brenda.

Though the doctors had predicted that Dave would not be able to have children, they now have two adult children, both married, and two grandchildren. Since Dave suffered his injuries, he and Brenda have shared their story, which Brenda says is one of "an overcoming faith and an uncompromising love," all over the world.

Prayer: Lord, help me show love that protects, trusts, hopes, perseveres and never fails.

Love does not delight in evil but rejoices with the truth. It always protects, always trusts, always hopes, always perseveres. Love never fails.

1 CORINTHIANS 13:6 – 8

for your next devotional reading, go to page 209

how will anyone know what tune is being played unless there is a distinction in the notes? [8]Again, if the trumpet does not sound a clear call, who will get ready for battle? [9]So it is with you. Unless you speak intelligible words with your tongue, how will anyone know what you are saying? You will just be speaking into the air. [10]Undoubtedly there are all sorts of languages in the world, yet none of them is without meaning. [11]If then I do not grasp the meaning of what someone is saying, I am a foreigner to the speaker, and the speaker is a foreigner to me. [12]So it is with you. Since you are eager for gifts of the Spirit, try to excel in those that build up the church.

[13]For this reason the one who speaks in a tongue should pray that they may interpret what they say. [14]For if I pray in a tongue, my spirit prays, but my mind is unfruitful. [15]So what shall I do? I will pray with my spirit, but I will also pray with my understanding; I will sing with my spirit, but I will also sing with my understanding. [16]Otherwise when you are praising God in the Spirit, how can someone else, who is now put in the position of an inquirer,[a] say "Amen" to your thanksgiving, since they do not know what you are saying? [17]You are giving thanks well enough, but no one else is edified.

[18]I thank God that I speak in tongues more than all of you. [19]But in the church I would rather speak five intelligible words to instruct others than ten thousand words in a tongue.

[20]Brothers and sisters, stop thinking like children. In regard to evil be infants, but in your thinking be adults. [21]In the Law it is written:

"With other tongues
    and through the lips of foreigners
I will speak to this people,
    but even then they will not listen to me,
        says the Lord."[b]

[22]Tongues, then, are a sign, not for believers but for unbelievers; prophecy, however, is not for unbelievers but for believers. [23]So if the whole church comes together and everyone speaks in tongues, and inquirers or un-believers come in, will they not say that you are out of your mind? [24]But if an unbeliever or an inquirer comes in while everyone is prophesying, they are convicted of sin and are brought under judgment by all, [25]as the secrets of their hearts are laid bare. So they will fall down and worship God, exclaiming, "God is really among you!"

Good Order in Worship

[26]What then shall we say, brothers and sisters? When you come together, each of you has a hymn, or a word of instruction, a revelation, a tongue or an interpretation. Everything must be done so that the church may be built up. [27]If anyone speaks in a tongue, two — or at the most three — should speak, one at a time, and someone must interpret. [28]If there is no interpreter, the speaker should keep quiet in the church and speak to himself and to God.

[29]Two or three prophets should speak, and the others should weigh carefully what is said. [30]And if a revelation comes to someone who is sitting down, the first speaker should stop. [31]For you can all prophesy in turn so that everyone may be instructed and encouraged. [32]The spirits of prophets are subject to the control of prophets. [33]For God is not a God of disorder but of peace — as in all the congregations of the Lord's people.

[34]Women[c] should remain silent in the churches. They are not allowed to speak, but must be in submission, as the law says. [35]If they want to inquire about something, they should ask their own husbands at home; for it is disgraceful for a woman to speak in the church.[d]

[36]Or did the word of God originate with you? Or are you the only people it has reached? [37]If anyone thinks they are a prophet or otherwise gifted by the Spirit, let them acknowledge that what I am writing to you is the Lord's command. [38]But if anyone ignores this, they will themselves be ignored.[e]

[39]Therefore, my brothers and sisters, be eager to prophesy, and do not forbid speaking in tongues. [40]But everything should be done in a fitting and orderly way.

---

[a] 16 The Greek word for *inquirer* is a technical term for someone not fully initiated into a religion; also in verses 23 and 24.   [b] 21 Isaiah 28:11,12   [c] 33,34 Or *peace. As in all the congregations of the Lord's people,* [34]*women*   [d] 34,35 In a few manuscripts these verses come after verse 40.   [e] 38 Some manuscripts *But anyone who is ignorant of this will be ignorant*

The Resurrection of Christ

15 Now, brothers and sisters, I want to remind you of the gospel I preached to you, which you received and on which you have taken your stand. ²By this gospel you are saved, if you hold firmly to the word I preached to you. Otherwise, you have believed in vain.

³For what I received I passed on to you as of first importance*a*: that Christ died for our sins according to the Scriptures, ⁴that he was buried, that he was raised on the third day according to the Scriptures, ⁵and that he appeared to Cephas,*b* and then to the Twelve. ⁶After that, he appeared to more than five hundred of the brothers and sisters at the same time, most of whom are still living, though some have fallen asleep. ⁷Then he appeared to James, then to all the apostles, ⁸and last of all he appeared to me also, as to one abnormally born.

⁹For I am the least of the apostles and do not even deserve to be called an apostle, because I persecuted the church of God. ¹⁰But by the grace of God I am what I am, and his grace to me was not without effect. No, I worked harder than all of them—yet not I, but the grace of God that was with me. ¹¹Whether, then, it is I or they, this is what we preach, and this is what you believed.

The Resurrection of the Dead

¹²But if it is preached that Christ has been raised from the dead, how can some of you say that there is no resurrection of the dead? ¹³If there is no resurrection of the dead, then not even Christ has been raised. ¹⁴And if Christ has not been raised, our preaching is useless and so is your faith. ¹⁵More than that, we are then found to be false witnesses about God, for we have testified about God that he raised Christ from the dead. But he did not raise him if in fact the dead are not raised. ¹⁶For if the dead are not raised, then Christ has not been raised either. ¹⁷And if Christ has not been raised, your faith is futile; you are still in your sins. ¹⁸Then those also who have fallen asleep in Christ are lost. ¹⁹If only for this life we have hope in Christ, we are of all people most to be pitied.

²⁰But Christ has indeed been raised from the dead, the firstfruits of those who have fallen asleep. ²¹For since death came through a man, the resurrection of the dead comes also through a man. ²²For as in Adam all die, so in Christ all will be made alive. ²³But each in turn: Christ, the firstfruits; then, when he comes, those who belong to him. ²⁴Then the end will come, when he hands over the kingdom to God the Father after he has destroyed all dominion, authority and power. ²⁵For he must reign until he has put all his enemies under his feet. ²⁶The last enemy to be destroyed is death. ²⁷For he "has put everything under his feet."*c* Now when it says that "everything" has been put under him, it is clear that this does not include God himself, who put everything under Christ. ²⁸When he has done this, then the Son himself will be made subject to him who put everything under him, so that God may be all in all.

²⁹Now if there is no resurrection, what will those do who are baptized for the dead? If the dead are not raised at all, why are people baptized for them? ³⁰And as for us, why do we endanger ourselves every hour? ³¹I face death every day—yes, just as surely as I boast about you in Christ Jesus our Lord. ³²If I fought wild beasts in Ephesus with no more than human hopes, what have I gained? If the dead are not raised,

"Let us eat and drink,
for tomorrow we die."*d*

³³Do not be misled: "Bad company corrupts good character."*e* ³⁴Come back to your senses as you ought, and stop sinning; for there are some who are ignorant of God—I say this to your shame.

The Resurrection Body

³⁵But someone will ask, "How are the dead raised? With what kind of body will they come?" ³⁶How foolish! What you sow does not come to life unless it dies. ³⁷When you sow, you do not plant the body that will be, but just a seed, perhaps of wheat or of something else. ³⁸But God gives it a body as he has determined, and to each kind of seed he gives its own body. ³⁹Not all flesh is the same: People have one kind of flesh, animals

a 3 Or *you at the first*   *b 5* That is, Peter   *c 27* Psalm 8:6   *d 32* Isaiah 22:13   *e 33* From the Greek poet Menander

have another, birds another and fish another. [40]There are also heavenly bodies and there are earthly bodies; but the splendor of the heavenly bodies is one kind, and the splendor of the earthly bodies is another. [41]The sun has one kind of splendor, the moon another and the stars another; and star differs from star in splendor.

[42]So will it be with the resurrection of the dead. The body that is sown is perishable, it is raised imperishable; [43]it is sown in dishonor, it is raised in glory; it is sown in weakness, it is raised in power; [44]it is sown a natural body, it is raised a spiritual body.

If there is a natural body, there is also a spiritual body. [45]So it is written: "The first man Adam became a living being"[a]; the last Adam, a life-giving spirit. [46]The spiritual did not come first, but the natural, and after that the spiritual. [47]The first man was of the dust of the earth; the second man is of heaven. [48]As was the earthly man, so are those who are of the earth; and as is the heavenly man, so also are those who are of heaven. [49]And just as we have borne the image of the earthly man, so shall we[b] bear the image of the heavenly man.

[50]I declare to you, brothers and sisters, that flesh and blood cannot inherit the kingdom of God, nor does the perishable inherit the imperishable. [51]Listen, I tell you a mystery: We will not all sleep, but we will all be changed— [52]in a flash, in the twinkling of an eye, at the last trumpet. For the trumpet will sound, the dead will be raised imperishable, and we will be changed. [53]For the perishable must clothe itself with the imperishable, and the mortal with immortality. [54]When the perishable has been clothed with the imperishable, and the mortal with immortality, then the saying that is written will come true: "Death has been swallowed up in victory."[c]

[55]"Where, O death, is your victory?
    Where, O death, is your sting?"[d]

[56]The sting of death is sin, and the power of sin is the law. [57]But thanks be to God! He gives us the victory through our Lord Jesus Christ.

[58]Therefore, my dear brothers and sisters, stand firm. Let nothing move you. Always give yourselves fully to the work of the Lord, because you know that your labor in the Lord is not in vain.

The Collection for the Lord's People

16 Now about the collection for the Lord's people: Do what I told the Galatian churches to do. [2]On the first day of every week, each one of you should set aside a sum of money in keeping with your income, saving it up, so that when I come no collections will have to be made. [3]Then, when I arrive, I will give letters of introduction to the men you approve and send them with your gift to Jerusalem. [4]If it seems advisable for me to go also, they will accompany me.

Personal Requests

[5]After I go through Macedonia, I will come to you—for I will be going through Macedonia. [6]Perhaps I will stay with you for a while, or even spend the winter, so that you can help me on my journey, wherever I go. [7]For I do not want to see you now and make only a passing visit; I hope to spend some time with you, if the Lord permits. [8]But I will stay on at Ephesus until Pentecost, [9]because a great door for effective work has opened to me, and there are many who oppose me.

[10]When Timothy comes, see to it that he has nothing to fear while he is with you, for he is carrying on the work of the Lord, just as I am. [11]No one, then, should treat him with contempt. Send him on his way in peace so that he may return to me. I am expecting him along with the brothers.

[12]Now about our brother Apollos: I strongly urged him to go to you with the brothers. He was quite unwilling to go now, but he will go when he has the opportunity.

[13]Be on your guard; stand firm in the faith; be courageous; be strong. [14]Do everything in love.

[15]You know that the household of Stephanas were the first converts in Achaia, and they have devoted themselves to the service of the Lord's people. I urge you, brothers and sisters, [16]to submit to such people and to everyone who joins in the work and labors at it. [17]I was glad when Stephanas, Fortunatus and Achaicus arrived, because they have

---

[a] 45 Gen. 2:7   [b] 49 Some early manuscripts *so let us*   [c] 54 Isaiah 25:8   [d] 55 Hosea 13:14

ALL FOR GOD'S GLORY

By Jocelyn Green

The day Christy Goetz's husband deployed to Afghanistan, she and her family spent the morning in church together. It was Chaplain Captain Dale Goetz's second deployment, but that didn't make his leaving any easier.

"The last hymn we sang was 'Take My Life and Let It Be,'"* Christy later said in a radio broadcast. "I was bawling, the words were so rich. In my heart I was saying it, but I couldn't sing. I realized I was giving my husband to God."

Their final moments were excruciating. Dale wept over each of his three sons, and when he and Christy said good-bye, Christy said she "literally felt like part of [her] body was being ripped away from [her]."

Two days later, on August 4, 2010, Dale e-mailed Christy to tell her he had led a soldier to Christ the previous night. His goal was to see 300 soldiers come to Jesus and help 10 commit to full-time ministry. He never met that goal because on August 30, Dale was killed by a roadside bomb, making him the first chaplain to be killed in the line of duty since the Vietnam War.

Hours later Christy opened the door to find a chaplain in blue and a soldier in green. Her knees barely held her up. Her heart buckled. A surreal moment passed while Christy grappled with what was happening. "Can I touch you?" she asked. She touched them to make sure they were really there.

After hearing the news confirmed, Christy's mind reeled as she tried to imagine how she would break the news to her two sons, who would be arriving home from school shortly. (Her 18-month-old son, Joel, was taking a nap.)

Ten-year-old Landon and eight-year-old Caleb soon came in, sensed a change in the home, and asked, "Was Daddy killed?"

"Boys, I need to talk to you." Christy pulled them close. "Where's the best place to be?"

"Home."

"Where's home?"

"Heaven," they answered.

"That's where Daddy is."

Today Christy and her sons miss Dale intensely, but she still trusts in God's plan. Before Dale deployed, he told her, "When it's our time, it's our time. And we need to live to the glory of God."

And though she hated the idea of losing him, she agreed. She still does. "That is why we live," she later said. "To glorify God and enjoy him. And with all of the disappointments and losses that I have gone through, I can still say my God reigns, he lives, and he will see me through."

---

*Read the words to "Take My Life and Let It Be" on page 495.

Prayer: *Lord, thank you that death on earth is not the end for your children! Help me live for your glory until I see you face to face.*

"Where, O death, is your victory? Where, O death, is your sting?"

1 CORINTHIANS 15:55

supplied what was lacking from you. [18] For they refreshed my spirit and yours also. Such men deserve recognition.

Final Greetings

[19] The churches in the province of Asia send you greetings. Aquila and Priscilla[a] greet you warmly in the Lord, and so does the church that meets at their house. [20] All the brothers and sisters here send you greetings. Greet one another with a holy kiss.

[21] I, Paul, write this greeting in my own hand.

[22] If anyone does not love the Lord, let that person be cursed! Come, Lord[b]!

[23] The grace of the Lord Jesus be with you.

[24] My love to all of you in Christ Jesus. Amen.[c]

---

[a] 19 Greek *Prisca*, a variant of *Priscilla*   [b] 22 The Greek for *Come, Lord* reproduces an Aramaic expression (*Marana tha*) used by early Christians.   [c] 24 Some manuscripts do not have *Amen*.

2 Corinthians

1 Paul, an apostle of Christ Jesus by the will of God, and Timothy our brother,

To the church of God in Corinth, together with all his holy people throughout Achaia:

² Grace and peace to you from God our Father and the Lord Jesus Christ.

Praise to the God of All Comfort

³ Praise be to the God and Father of our Lord Jesus Christ, the Father of compassion and the God of all comfort, ⁴ who comforts us in all our troubles, so that we can comfort those in any trouble with the comfort we ourselves receive from God. ⁵ For just as we share abundantly in the sufferings of Christ, so also our comfort abounds through Christ. ⁶ If we are distressed, it is for your comfort and salvation; if we are comforted, it is for your comfort, which produces in you patient endurance of the same sufferings we suffer. ⁷ And our hope for you is firm, because we know that just as you share in our sufferings, so also you share in our comfort.

⁸ We do not want you to be uninformed, brothers and sisters,ᵃ about the troubles we experienced in the province of Asia. We were under great pressure, far beyond our ability to endure, so that we despaired of life itself. ⁹ Indeed, we felt we had received the sentence of death. But this happened that we might not rely on ourselves but on God, who raises the dead. ¹⁰ He has delivered us from such a deadly peril, and he will deliver us again. On him we have set our hope that he will continue to deliver us, ¹¹ as you help us by your prayers. Then many will give thanks on our behalf for the gracious favor granted us in answer to the prayers of many.

Paul's Change of Plans

¹² Now this is our boast: Our conscience testifies that we have conducted ourselves in the world, and especially in our relations with you, with integrityᵇ and godly sincerity. We have done so, relying not on worldly wisdom but on God's grace. ¹³ For we do not write you anything you cannot read or understand. And I hope that, ¹⁴ as you have understood us in part, you will come to understand fully that you can boast of us just as we will boast of you in the day of the Lord Jesus.

¹⁵ Because I was confident of this, I wanted to visit you first so that you might benefit twice. ¹⁶ I wanted to visit you on my way to Macedonia and to come back to you from Macedonia, and then to have you send me on my way to Judea. ¹⁷ Was I fickle when I intended to do this? Or do I make my plans in a worldly manner so that in the same breath I say both "Yes, yes" and "No, no"?

¹⁸ But as surely as God is faithful, our message to you is not "Yes" and "No." ¹⁹ For the Son of God, Jesus Christ, who was preached among you by us — by me and Silasᶜ and Timothy — was not "Yes" and "No," but in him it has always been "Yes." ²⁰ For no matter how many promises God has made, they are "Yes" in Christ. And so through him the "Amen" is spoken by us to the glory of God. ²¹ Now it is God who makes both us and you stand firm in Christ. He anointed us, ²² set his seal of ownership on us, and put his Spirit in our hearts as a deposit, guaranteeing what is to come.

²³ I call God as my witness — and I stake my life on it — that it was in order to spare you that I did not return to Corinth. ²⁴ Not that we lord it over your faith, but we work with you for your joy, because it is by faith **2** you stand firm. ¹ So I made up my mind that I would not make another painful visit to you. ² For if I grieve you, who is left to make me glad but you whom I have grieved? ³ I wrote as I did, so that when I came I would not be distressed by those who should have

---

ᵃ 8 The Greek word for *brothers and sisters* (*adelphoi*) refers here to believers, both men and women, as part of God's family; also in 8:1; 13:11.   ᵇ 12 Many manuscripts *holiness*   ᶜ 19 Greek *Silvanus*, a variant of *Silas*

COMFORTING THOSE IN TROUBLE

By Jocelyn Green

Sergeant Joel House was 22 years old on the day of his second deployment to Iraq in 2007. He'd experienced a dozen or more explosions and had survived a suicide bombing on his post. "When he came home in March for R&R, you could see it on his face," recalled his father, Paul. "He said it was a big shock coming back home after seeing the tragedies of war. But we figured since he had made it through that ordeal, he was going to be okay."

He wasn't. On June 22, 2007 — his mom Deanna's birthday — an IED took Joel's life.

Though he grieved deeply, Paul never felt so close to God as he did the first few months after his son's death. Paul had led Joel to Christ as a child, so he was able to focus on what Joel must be experiencing in heaven.

Paul and Deanna still trust that God is sovereign. "God doesn't make mistakes," Paul said. "We recognize his deity, his sovereignty, and his plan, even though we don't always know what his plan is. And we ask him for strength to help others."

In August 2007, Paul and Deanna went to a memorial service at Fort Hood, Texas, where they gathered with the family members of 18 other fallen heroes. The morning after the memorial service, with tears spilling down his face, Paul thought, There has to be a way to help these families!

Paul was inspired to create House in the Woods Military and Family Retreat, now a year-round program that brings veterans and their families to Maine virtually cost free. "I don't preach to the guys here, but when they ask me how I get through my grief, I share with them that Joel is in heaven, that we'll see him some day, and that God gives us the strength," said Paul.

Veterans from Iraq, Afghanistan, Vietnam, Korea and World War II have all visited House in the Woods. While licensed counselors are not part of the program, veterans inevitably share with each other their experiences, some of them crying for the first time in decades.

The gatherings also help heal Paul and Deanna. "Talking to the soldiers gives us more perspective about what our son went through," said Paul. "I feel a bond with them because God was there. It's rewarding to see the soldiers and veterans laugh, even if it's for a short time. It could change their lives forever."

Paul attributes the healing power of House in the Woods to the camaraderie among military families and to being immersed in nature, which points to the Creator. He's sure Joel would have loved it.

Prayer: Lord, show me how you'd like to use me. Amen.

> **Praise be to the God and Father of our Lord Jesus Christ, the Father of compassion and the God of all comfort, who comforts us in all our troubles, so that we can comfort those in any trouble with the comfort we ourselves receive from God.**
>
> 2 CORINTHIANS 1:3 – 4

for your next devotional reading, go to page 214

made me rejoice. I had confidence in all of you, that you would all share my joy. [4]For I wrote you out of great distress and anguish of heart and with many tears, not to grieve you but to let you know the depth of my love for you.

Forgiveness for the Offender

[5]If anyone has caused grief, he has not so much grieved me as he has grieved all of you to some extent — not to put it too severely. [6]The punishment inflicted on him by the majority is sufficient. [7]Now instead, you ought to forgive and comfort him, so that he will not be overwhelmed by excessive sorrow. [8]I urge you, therefore, to reaffirm your love for him. [9]Another reason I wrote you was to see if you would stand the test and be obedient in everything. [10]Anyone you forgive, I also forgive. And what I have forgiven — if there was anything to forgive — I have forgiven in the sight of Christ for your sake, [11]in order that Satan might not outwit us. For we are not unaware of his schemes.

Ministers of the New Covenant

[12]Now when I went to Troas to preach the gospel of Christ and found that the Lord had opened a door for me, [13]I still had no peace of mind, because I did not find my brother Titus there. So I said goodbye to them and went on to Macedonia.

[14]But thanks be to God, who always leads us as captives in Christ's triumphal procession and uses us to spread the aroma of the knowledge of him everywhere. [15]For we are to God the pleasing aroma of Christ among those who are being saved and those who are perishing. [16]To the one we are an aroma that brings death; to the other, an aroma that brings life. And who is equal to such a task? [17]Unlike so many, we do not peddle the word of God for profit. On the contrary, in Christ we speak before God with sincerity, as those sent from God.

3 Are we beginning to commend ourselves again? Or do we need, like some people, letters of recommendation to you or from you? [2]You yourselves are our letter, written on our hearts, known and read by everyone. [3]You show that you are a letter from Christ, the result of our ministry, written not with ink but with the Spirit of the living God, not on tablets of stone but on tablets of human hearts.

[4]Such confidence we have through Christ before God. [5]Not that we are competent in ourselves to claim anything for ourselves, but our competence comes from God. [6]He has made us competent as ministers of a new covenant — not of the letter but of the Spirit; for the letter kills, but the Spirit gives life.

The Greater Glory of the New Covenant

[7]Now if the ministry that brought death, which was engraved in letters on stone, came with glory, so that the Israelites could not look steadily at the face of Moses because of its glory, transitory though it was, [8]will not the ministry of the Spirit be even more glorious? [9]If the ministry that brought condemnation was glorious, how much more glorious is the ministry that brings righteousness! [10]For what was glorious has no glory now in comparison with the surpassing glory. [11]And if what was transitory came with glory, how much greater is the glory of that which lasts!

[12]Therefore, since we have such a hope, we are very bold. [13]We are not like Moses, who would put a veil over his face to prevent the Israelites from seeing the end of what was passing away. [14]But their minds were made dull, for to this day the same veil remains when the old covenant is read. It has not been removed, because only in Christ is it taken away. [15]Even to this day when Moses is read, a veil covers their hearts. [16]But whenever anyone turns to the Lord, the veil is taken away. [17]Now the Lord is the Spirit, and where the Spirit of the Lord is, there is freedom. [18]And we all, who with unveiled faces contemplate[a] the Lord's glory, are being transformed into his image with ever-increasing glory, which comes from the Lord, who is the Spirit.

Present Weakness and Resurrection Life

4 Therefore, since through God's mercy we have this ministry, we do not lose heart. [2]Rather, we have renounced secret and shameful ways; we do not use deception, nor do we distort the word of God. On the

The Ritual of Responsibility

By Leeana Tankersley

READ: 2 Corinthians 4

If there was ever a time when I felt "hard pressed" and "struck down" (2 Corinthians 4:8 – 9), it was the summer of 2011, when we PCSed to the Middle East with two-year-old twins and a baby on the way. In the middle of July. During Ramadan. With nausea and no belongings, I found myself in a personal tailspin.

One of my most toxic go-to rituals to make myself feel better in times of stress is blame. For example, if my kids would just give me a break and play quietly, then I wouldn't have to yell. If this tour wasn't so demanding, then I could be happy.

What I'm learning, though, is that when I feel stressed, I need to side-step self-pity and take personal responsibility for myself. Blaming others for my problems is not the solution. Waiting for circumstances to change in order to begin really living is a ruse. And exaggerating never helps — in fact, it only makes things worse.

The apostle Paul must have known this. He wasn't in denial about his hardships, and God doesn't ask us to pretend everything is fine in our own lives when it isn't. But notice how careful Paul was to be accurate about his circumstances. The picture might be dim, but let's not paint it pitch black.

The first couple of months in the Middle East, I was on the verge of panic at some moments. Yet when I could slow myself down enough to bring my true self to Christ — when that became my default ritual — tiny beams of hope showed up. I realized I wasn't crushed. I wasn't abandoned. Life hadn't been destroyed after all.

When I would fillet myself open before Christ and ask him to come into my feelings of self-contempt and exhaustion, life would begin again. I could breathe again. I didn't blame (God, my husband, the Navy) but instead chose to take personal responsibility for my feelings … laying it all at the feet of Christ, my comforter.

We don't have to live as though we are victims of the behavior and choices of those around us or of the circumstances we find ourselves in. We cannot control everyone and everything — in fact, there's very little we can control. But we can choose what we do with our feelings every day.

Christ invites us to find healing and hope in his presence. "Therefore we do not lose heart. Though outwardly we are wasting away, yet inwardly we are being renewed day by day" (2 Corinthians 4:16).

We are hard pressed on every side, but not crushed; perplexed, but not in despair; persecuted, but not abandoned; struck down, but not destroyed.

2 CORINTHIANS 4:8 – 9

DEBRIEF

- Am I blaming others for my unhappiness or exaggerating my hardships in my own mind?
- Do I need to take personal responsibility for my life?

REPORT

God, grant me the serenity to accept the things I cannot change; courage to change the things I can; and wisdom to know the difference. Amen.

---

for your next devotional reading, go to page 219

contrary, by setting forth the truth plainly we commend ourselves to everyone's conscience in the sight of God. [3] And even if our gospel is veiled, it is veiled to those who are perishing. [4] The god of this age has blinded the minds of unbelievers, so that they cannot see the light of the gospel that displays the glory of Christ, who is the image of God. [5] For what we preach is not ourselves, but Jesus Christ as Lord, and ourselves as your servants for Jesus' sake. [6] For God, who said, "Let light shine out of darkness,"[a] made his light shine in our hearts to give us the light of the knowledge of God's glory displayed in the face of Christ.

[7] But we have this treasure in jars of clay to show that this all-surpassing power is from God and not from us. [8] We are hard pressed on every side, but not crushed; perplexed, but not in despair; [9] persecuted, but not abandoned; struck down, but not destroyed. [10] We always carry around in our body the death of Jesus, so that the life of Jesus may also be revealed in our body. [11] For we who are alive are always being given over to death for Jesus' sake, so that his life may also be revealed in our mortal body. [12] So then, death is at work in us, but life is at work in you.

[13] It is written: "I believed; therefore I have spoken."[b] Since we have that same spirit of[c] faith, we also believe and therefore speak, [14] because we know that the one who raised the Lord Jesus from the dead will also raise us with Jesus and present us with you to himself. [15] All this is for your benefit, so that the grace that is reaching more and more people may cause thanksgiving to overflow to the glory of God.

[16] Therefore we do not lose heart. Though outwardly we are wasting away, yet inwardly we are being renewed day by day. [17] For our light and momentary troubles are achieving for us an eternal glory that far outweighs them all. [18] So we fix our eyes not on what is seen, but on what is unseen, since what is seen is temporary, but what is unseen is eternal.

Awaiting the New Body

5 For we know that if the earthly tent we live in is destroyed, we have a build-ing from God, an eternal house in heaven, not built by human hands. [2] Meanwhile we groan, longing to be clothed instead with our heavenly dwelling, [3] because when we are clothed, we will not be found naked. [4] For while we are in this tent, we groan and are burdened, because we do not wish to be unclothed but to be clothed instead with our heavenly dwelling, so that what is mortal may be swallowed up by life. [5] Now the one who has fashioned us for this very purpose is God, who has given us the Spirit as a deposit, guaranteeing what is to come.

[6] Therefore we are always confident and know that as long as we are at home in the body we are away from the Lord. [7] For we live by faith, not by sight. [8] We are confident, I say, and would prefer to be away from the body and at home with the Lord. [9] So we make it our goal to please him, whether we are at home in the body or away from it. [10] For we must all appear before the judgment seat of Christ, so that each of us may receive what is due us for the things done while in the body, whether good or bad.

The Ministry of Reconciliation

[11] Since, then, we know what it is to fear the Lord, we try to persuade others. What we are is plain to God, and I hope it is also plain to your conscience. [12] We are not trying to commend ourselves to you again, but are giving you an opportunity to take pride in us, so that you can answer those who take pride in what is seen rather than in what is in the heart. [13] If we are "out of our mind," as some say, it is for God; if we are in our right mind, it is for you. [14] For Christ's love compels us, because we are convinced that one died for all, and therefore all died. [15] And he died for all, that those who live should no longer live for themselves but for him who died for them and was raised again.

[16] So from now on we regard no one from a worldly point of view. Though we once regarded Christ in this way, we do so no longer. [17] Therefore, if anyone is in Christ, the new creation has come:[d] The old has gone, the new is here! [18] All this is from God, who reconciled us to himself through Christ and gave us the ministry of reconciliation: [19] that

---

[a] 6 Gen. 1:3   [b] 13 Psalm 116:10 (see Septuagint)   [c] 13 Or Spirit-given   [d] 17 Or Christ, that person is a new creation.

God was reconciling the world to himself in Christ, not counting people's sins against them. And he has committed to us the message of reconciliation. [20] We are therefore Christ's ambassadors, as though God were making his appeal through us. We implore you on Christ's behalf: Be reconciled to God. [21] God made him who had no sin to be sin[a] for us, so that in him we might become the righteousness of God.

6 As God's co-workers we urge you not to receive God's grace in vain. [2] For he says,

"In the time of my favor I
    heard you,
and in the day of salvation
    I helped you."[b]

I tell you, now is the time of God's favor, now is the day of salvation.

Paul's Hardships

[3] We put no stumbling block in anyone's path, so that our ministry will not be discredited. [4] Rather, as servants of God we commend ourselves in every way: in great endurance; in troubles, hardships and distresses; [5] in beatings, imprisonments and riots; in hard work, sleepless nights and hunger; [6] in purity, understanding, patience and kindness; in the Holy Spirit and in sincere love; [7] in truthful speech and in the power of God; with weapons of righteousness in the right hand and in the left; [8] through glory and dishonor, bad report and good report; genuine, yet regarded as impostors; [9] known, yet regarded as unknown; dying, and yet we live on; beaten, and yet not killed; [10] sorrowful, yet always rejoicing; poor, yet making many rich; having nothing, and yet possessing everything.

[11] We have spoken freely to you, Corinthians, and opened wide our hearts to you. [12] We are not withholding our affection from you, but you are withholding yours from us. [13] As a fair exchange — I speak as to my children — open wide your hearts also.

Warning Against Idolatry

[14] Do not be yoked together with unbelievers. For what do righteousness and wickedness have in common? Or what fellowship can light have with darkness? [15] What harmony is there between Christ and Belial[c]? Or what does a believer have in common with an unbeliever? [16] What agreement is there between the temple of God and idols? For we are the temple of the living God. As God has said:

"I will live with them
    and walk among them,
and I will be their God,
    and they will be my people."[d]

[17] Therefore,

"Come out from them
    and be separate,
                    says the Lord.
Touch no unclean thing,
    and I will receive you."[e]

[18] And,

"I will be a Father to you,
    and you will be my sons and
        daughters,
            says the Lord Almighty."[f]

7 Therefore, since we have these promises, dear friends, let us purify ourselves from everything that contaminates body and spirit, perfecting holiness out of reverence for God.

Paul's Joy Over the Church's Repentance

[2] Make room for us in your hearts. We have wronged no one, we have corrupted no one, we have exploited no one. [3] I do not say this to condemn you; I have said before that you have such a place in our hearts that we would live or die with you. [4] I have spoken to you with great frankness; I take great pride in you. I am greatly encouraged; in all our troubles my joy knows no bounds.

[5] For when we came into Macedonia, we had no rest, but we were harassed at every turn — conflicts on the outside, fears within. [6] But God, who comforts the downcast, comforted us by the coming of Titus, [7] and not only by his coming but also by the comfort you had given him. He told us about your longing for me, your deep sorrow, your ardent concern for me, so that my joy was greater than ever.

[8] Even if I caused you sorrow by my letter, I do not regret it. Though I did regret it — I

---

[a] 21 Or *be a sin offering*   [b] 2 Isaiah 49:8   [c] 15 Greek *Beliar*, a variant of *Belial*   [d] 16 Lev. 26:12;
Jer. 32:38; Ezek. 37:27   [e] 17 Isaiah 52:11; Ezek. 20:34,41   [f] 18 2 Samuel 7:14; 7:8

see that my letter hurt you, but only for a little while — [9]yet now I am happy, not because you were made sorry, but because your sorrow led you to repentance. For you became sorrowful as God intended and so were not harmed in any way by us. [10]Godly sorrow brings repentance that leads to salvation and leaves no regret, but worldly sorrow brings death. [11]See what this godly sorrow has produced in you: what earnestness, what eagerness to clear yourselves, what indignation, what alarm, what longing, what concern, what readiness to see justice done. At every point you have proved yourselves to be innocent in this matter. [12]So even though I wrote to you, it was neither on account of the one who did the wrong nor on account of the injured party, but rather that before God you could see for yourselves how devoted to us you are. [13]By all this we are encouraged.

In addition to our own encouragement, we were especially delighted to see how happy Titus was, because his spirit has been refreshed by all of you. [14]I had boasted to him about you, and you have not embarrassed me. But just as everything we said to you was true, so our boasting about you to Titus has proved to be true as well. [15]And his affection for you is all the greater when he remembers that you were all obedient, receiving him with fear and trembling. [16]I am glad I can have complete confidence in you.

The Collection for the Lord's People

8 And now, brothers and sisters, we want you to know about the grace that God has given the Macedonian churches. [2]In the midst of a very severe trial, their overflowing joy and their extreme poverty welled up in rich generosity. [3]For I testify that they gave as much as they were able, and even beyond their ability. Entirely on their own, [4]they urgently pleaded with us for the privilege of sharing in this service to the Lord's people. [5]And they exceeded our expectations: They gave themselves first of all to the Lord, and then by the will of God also to us. [6]So we urged Titus, just as he had earlier made a beginning, to bring also to completion this act of grace on your part. [7]But since you excel in everything — in faith, in speech, in knowledge, in complete earnestness and in

the love we have kindled in you[a] — see that you also excel in this grace of giving.

[8]I am not commanding you, but I want to test the sincerity of your love by comparing it with the earnestness of others. [9]For you know the grace of our Lord Jesus Christ, that though he was rich, yet for your sake he became poor, so that you through his poverty might become rich.

[10]And here is my judgment about what is best for you in this matter. Last year you were the first not only to give but also to have the desire to do so. [11]Now finish the work, so that your eager willingness to do it may be matched by your completion of it, according to your means. [12]For if the willingness is there, the gift is acceptable according to what one has, not according to what one does not have.

[13]Our desire is not that others might be relieved while you are hard pressed, but that there might be equality. [14]At the present time your plenty will supply what they need, so that in turn their plenty will supply what you need. The goal is equality, [15]as it is written: "The one who gathered much did not have too much, and the one who gathered little did not have too little."[b]

Titus Sent to Receive the Collection

[16]Thanks be to God, who put into the heart of Titus the same concern I have for you. [17]For Titus not only welcomed our appeal, but he is coming to you with much enthusiasm and on his own initiative. [18]And we are sending along with him the brother who is praised by all the churches for his service to the gospel. [19]What is more, he was chosen by the churches to accompany us as we carry the offering, which we administer in order to honor the Lord himself and to show our eagerness to help. [20]We want to avoid any criticism of the way we administer this liberal gift. [21]For we are taking pains to do what is right, not only in the eyes of the Lord but also in the eyes of man.

[22]In addition, we are sending with them our brother who has often proved to us in many ways that he is zealous, and now even more so because of his great confidence in you. [23]As for Titus, he is my partner and coworker among you; as for our brothers, they

---

[a] 7 Some manuscripts *and in your love for us*   [b] 15 Exodus 16:18

are representatives of the churches and an honor to Christ. [24] Therefore show these men the proof of your love and the reason for our pride in you, so that the churches can see it.

9 There is no need for me to write to you about this service to the Lord's people. [2] For I know your eagerness to help, and I have been boasting about it to the Macedonians, telling them that since last year you in Achaia were ready to give; and your enthusiasm has stirred most of them to action. [3] But I am sending the brothers in order that our boasting about you in this matter should not prove hollow, but that you may be ready, as I said you would be. [4] For if any Macedonians come with me and find you unprepared, we — not to say anything about you — would be ashamed of having been so confident. [5] So I thought it necessary to urge the brothers to visit you in advance and finish the arrangements for the generous gift you had promised. Then it will be ready as a generous gift, not as one grudgingly given.

Generosity Encouraged

[6] Remember this: Whoever sows sparingly will also reap sparingly, and whoever sows generously will also reap generously. [7] Each of you should give what you have decided in your heart to give, not reluctantly or under compulsion, for God loves a cheerful giver. [8] And God is able to bless you abundantly, so that in all things at all times, having all that you need, you will abound in every good work. [9] As it is written:

"They have freely scattered their gifts to
     the poor;
  their righteousness endures forever."[a]

[10] Now he who supplies seed to the sower and bread for food will also supply and increase your store of seed and will enlarge the harvest of your righteousness. [11] You will be enriched in every way so that you can be generous on every occasion, and through us your generosity will result in thanksgiving to God.

[12] This service that you perform is not only supplying the needs of the Lord's people but is also overflowing in many expressions of thanks to God. [13] Because of the service by

which you have proved yourselves, others will praise God for the obedience that accompanies your confession of the gospel of Christ, and for your generosity in sharing with them and with everyone else. [14] And in their prayers for you their hearts will go out to you, because of the surpassing grace God has given you. [15] Thanks be to God for his indescribable gift!

Paul's Defense of His Ministry

10 By the humility and gentleness of Christ, I appeal to you — I, Paul, who am "timid" when face to face with you, but "bold" toward you when away! [2] I beg you that when I come I may not have to be as bold as I expect to be toward some people who think that we live by the standards of this world. [3] For though we live in the world, we do not wage war as the world does. [4] The weapons we fight with are not the weapons of the world. On the contrary, they have divine power to demolish strongholds. [5] We demolish arguments and every pretension that sets itself up against the knowledge of God, and we take captive every thought to make it obedient to Christ. [6] And we will be ready to punish every act of disobedience, once your obedience is complete.

[7] You are judging by appearances.[b] If anyone is confident that they belong to Christ, they should consider again that we belong to Christ just as much as they do. [8] So even if I boast somewhat freely about the authority the Lord gave us for building you up rather than tearing you down, I will not be ashamed of it. [9] I do not want to seem to be trying to frighten you with my letters. [10] For some say, "His letters are weighty and forceful, but in person he is unimpressive and his speaking amounts to nothing." [11] Such people should realize that what we are in our letters when we are absent, we will be in our actions when we are present.

[12] We do not dare to classify or compare ourselves with some who commend themselves. When they measure themselves by themselves and compare themselves with themselves, they are not wise. [13] We, however, will not boast beyond proper limits, but will confine our boasting to the sphere of service God himself has assigned to us, a

[a] 9 Psalm 112:9   [b] 7 Or *Look at the obvious facts*

WAGING WAR ON BITTERNESS

By Jocelyn Green

"I would not exchange the hope I have now in my Savior for all that the world could give … My prayer is for a stronger faith, though I sometimes shrink at the tribulation I may be called to endure for this purpose. But Jesus is all sufficient."

Mary Custis, the wife of General Robert E. Lee, penned these words in 1830 shortly after she gave her life to Christ. Three decades later the Civil War brought great tribulation and tested her faith like never before.

Mary and her children were forced to flee their home early in the war. None of them could have dreamed, however, that they would never again live in the beloved family mansion in Arlington, Virginia. Instead, the federal government appropriated the stately property as a burial site for Union soldiers (Arlington National Cemetery).

Five months after the war ended, Mary wrote in a letter: "My heart yearns to the home of my youth … The knowledge of how it is occupied and desecrated is a bitter grief to me."

Mary had vehemently opposed the North, and yet she managed to acknowledge that God ordained all things, even those that are the most difficult to endure. Speaking of the defeat of the Confederate South in her memoir, she wrote: "We must do our duty as best we can and believe that the inscrutable Providence who permitted our present situation may be preparing us for a more useful and higher destiny."

When Mary heard of Jefferson Davis's imprisonment at Fort Monroe, she wrote to express her sympathy. Once again, she turned her thoughts heavenward and offered Davis the words to her favorite hymn, "Jesus, I My Cross Have Taken".*

Even when her husband, General Lee, passed away in October of 1870, Mary's faith remained solid. A well-meaning journalist labeled General Lee's death "untimely." How easy it would have been for the grieving widow, herself in ill health by this time, to agree. But Mary replied: "We must not deem that untimely which God ordains. He knows the best time to take us from this world and can we question either His love or wisdom?"

Throughout Mary's letters, journals and memoir, we see the battle she waged against bitterness by taking captive her thoughts and making them obedient to Christ (see 2 Corinthians 10:5). It is an example worth following, as we would be wise to examine our thoughts and emotions against the standard of God's truths, and make sure they align.

*Read the words to "Jesus, I My Cross Have Taken" on page 496.

Prayer: Lord, help me take captive any thought that sets itself up against your Word, and replace it with your truth instead.

> **We demolish arguments and every pretension that sets itself up against the knowledge of God, and we take captive every thought to make it obedient to Christ.**
>
> 2 CORINTHIANS 10:5

for your next devotional reading, go to page 222

sphere that also includes you. [14]We are not going too far in our boasting, as would be the case if we had not come to you, for we did get as far as you with the gospel of Christ. [15]Neither do we go beyond our limits by boasting of work done by others. Our hope is that, as your faith continues to grow, our sphere of activity among you will greatly expand, [16]so that we can preach the gospel in the regions beyond you. For we do not want to boast about work already done in someone else's territory. [17]But, "Let the one who boasts boast in the Lord."[a] [18]For it is not the one who commends himself who is approved, but the one whom the Lord commends.

Paul and the False Apostles

11 I hope you will put up with me in a little foolishness. Yes, please put up with me! [2]I am jealous for you with a godly jealousy. I promised you to one husband, to Christ, so that I might present you as a pure virgin to him. [3]But I am afraid that just as Eve was deceived by the serpent's cunning, your minds may somehow be led astray from your sincere and pure devotion to Christ. [4]For if someone comes to you and preaches a Jesus other than the Jesus we preached, or if you receive a different spirit from the Spirit you received, or a different gospel from the one you accepted, you put up with it easily enough.

[5]I do not think I am in the least inferior to those "super-apostles."[b] [6]I may indeed be untrained as a speaker, but I do have knowledge. We have made this perfectly clear to you in every way. [7]Was it a sin for me to lower myself in order to elevate you by preaching the gospel of God to you free of charge? [8]I robbed other churches by receiving support from them so as to serve you. [9]And when I was with you and needed something, I was not a burden to anyone, for the brothers who came from Macedonia supplied what I needed. I have kept myself from being a burden to you in any way, and will continue to do so. [10]As surely as the truth of Christ is in me, nobody in the regions of Achaia will stop this boasting of mine. [11]Why? Because I do not love you? God knows I do!

[12]And I will keep on doing what I am doing in order to cut the ground from under those who want an opportunity to be considered equal with us in the things they boast about. [13]For such people are false apostles, deceitful workers, masquerading as apostles of Christ. [14]And no wonder, for Satan himself masquerades as an angel of light. [15]It is not surprising, then, if his servants also masquerade as servants of righteousness. Their end will be what their actions deserve.

Paul Boasts About His Sufferings

[16]I repeat: Let no one take me for a fool. But if you do, then tolerate me just as you would a fool, so that I may do a little boasting. [17]In this self-confident boasting I am not talking as the Lord would, but as a fool. [18]Since many are boasting in the way the world does, I too will boast. [19]You gladly put up with fools since you are so wise! [20]In fact, you even put up with anyone who enslaves you or exploits you or takes advantage of you or puts on airs or slaps you in the face. [21]To my shame I admit that we were too weak for that!

Whatever anyone else dares to boast about — I am speaking as a fool — I also dare to boast about. [22]Are they Hebrews? So am I. Are they Israelites? So am I. Are they Abraham's descendants? So am I. [23]Are they servants of Christ? (I am out of my mind to talk like this.) I am more. I have worked much harder, been in prison more frequently, been flogged more severely, and been exposed to death again and again. [24]Five times I received from the Jews the forty lashes minus one. [25]Three times I was beaten with rods, once I was pelted with stones, three times I was shipwrecked, I spent a night and a day in the open sea, [26]I have been constantly on the move. I have been in danger from rivers, in danger from bandits, in danger from my fellow Jews, in danger from Gentiles; in danger in the city, in danger in the country, in danger at sea; and in danger from false believers. [27]I have labored and toiled and have often gone without sleep; I have known hunger and thirst and have often gone without food; I have been cold and naked. [28]Besides everything else, I face daily the pressure of my concern for all the churches. [29]Who is weak, and I do not feel weak? Who is led into sin, and I do not inwardly burn?

[30]If I must boast, I will boast of the things

---

[a] 17 Jer. 9:24   [b] 5 Or *to the most eminent apostles*

that show my weakness. [31] The God and Father of the Lord Jesus, who is to be praised forever, knows that I am not lying. [32] In Damascus the governor under King Aretas had the city of the Damascenes guarded in order to arrest me. [33] But I was lowered in a basket from a window in the wall and slipped through his hands.

Paul's Vision and His Thorn

12 I must go on boasting. Although there is nothing to be gained, I will go on to visions and revelations from the Lord. [2] I know a man in Christ who fourteen years ago was caught up to the third heaven. Whether it was in the body or out of the body I do not know — God knows. [3] And I know that this man — whether in the body or apart from the body I do not know, but God knows — [4] was caught up to paradise and heard inexpressible things, things that no one is permitted to tell. [5] I will boast about a man like that, but I will not boast about myself, except about my weaknesses. [6] Even if I should choose to boast, I would not be a fool, because I would be speaking the truth. But I refrain, so no one will think more of me than is warranted by what I do or say, [7] or because of these surpassingly great revelations. Therefore, in order to keep me from becoming conceited, I was given a thorn in my flesh, a messenger of Satan, to torment me. [8] Three times I pleaded with the Lord to take it away from me. [9] But he said to me, "My grace is sufficient for you, for my power is made perfect in weakness." Therefore I will boast all the more gladly about my weaknesses, so that Christ's power may rest on me. [10] That is why, for Christ's sake, I delight in weaknesses, in insults, in hardships, in persecutions, in difficulties. For when I am weak, then I am strong.

Paul's Concern for the Corinthians

[11] I have made a fool of myself, but you drove me to it. I ought to have been commended by you, for I am not in the least inferior to the "super-apostles,"[a] even though I am nothing. [12] I persevered in demonstrating among you the marks of a true apostle, including signs, wonders and miracles. [13] How were you inferior to the other churches, except that I was never a burden to you? Forgive me this wrong!

[14] Now I am ready to visit you for the third time, and I will not be a burden to you, because what I want is not your possessions but you. After all, children should not have to save up for their parents, but parents for their children. [15] So I will very gladly spend for you everything I have and expend myself as well. If I love you more, will you love me less? [16] Be that as it may, I have not been a burden to you. Yet, crafty fellow that I am, I caught you by trickery! [17] Did I exploit you through any of the men I sent to you? [18] I urged Titus to go to you and I sent our brother with him. Titus did not exploit you, did he? Did we not walk in the same footsteps by the same Spirit?

[19] Have you been thinking all along that we have been defending ourselves to you? We have been speaking in the sight of God as those in Christ; and everything we do, dear friends, is for your strengthening. [20] For I am afraid that when I come I may not find you as I want you to be, and you may not find me as you want me to be. I fear that there may be discord, jealousy, fits of rage, selfish ambition, slander, gossip, arrogance and disorder. [21] I am afraid that when I come again my God will humble me before you, and I will be grieved over many who have sinned earlier and have not repented of the impurity, sexual sin and debauchery in which they have indulged.

Final Warnings

13 This will be my third visit to you. "Every matter must be established by the testimony of two or three witnesses."[b] [2] I already gave you a warning when I was with you the second time. I now repeat it while absent: On my return I will not spare those who sinned earlier or any of the others, [3] since you are demanding proof that Christ is speaking through me. He is not weak in dealing with you, but is powerful among you. [4] For to be sure, he was crucified in weakness, yet he lives by God's power. Likewise, we are weak in him, yet by God's power we will live with him in our dealing with you.

[5] Examine yourselves to see whether you are in the faith; test yourselves. Do you not realize that Christ Jesus is in you — unless, of course, you fail the test? [6] And I trust that

[a] 11 Or the most eminent apostles   [b] 1 Deut. 19:15

Home Front
★ ★ ★
HEROES

SUSTAINED BY GRACE

By Jocelyn Green

When Captain Daniel Gade deployed to Iraq, his wife, Wendy, prepared herself for two possibilities: "Either he would come home and be perfectly fine in every way, or he wouldn't," she said. "I didn't think of the in-between — an injury."

But in January 2005, an IED made injury a life-altering reality.

Three days after she received the news, Wendy arranged childcare for their two-year-old daughter and met Daniel at Walter Reed Army Medical Center in Washington, D.C. He had a fractured skull, a broken bone in his neck and a massive wound from his sternum across his groin to his right knee. Sitting in the Humvee, the explosion came through the bottom of his right leg and out the top of the same leg. Tissue the size of an ice cream scoop had been carved out from behind his left knee. Two fists could fit in the gaping hole of his leg. The abdominal wall on the front was stripped away; the skin and flesh were pushed to the side.

Okay, this is where we start, she resolved when she saw him. "I had a job to do: To support my husband and be the leader of the family while he recovered," Wendy recalled. "I braced myself for what would be required of me, calling on prayer and God's strength to be my support."

Wendy poured herself into caring for her daughter and being Daniel's patient advocate. She got a crash course in medical terminology and human anatomy as she learned about Daniel's injuries and their complications, including kidney failure and pneumonia.

A week after his injury, Daniel's right leg was amputated at the hip to save his life. "The insurgents could take his leg, but not his faith and personality," Wendy said. "Watching him go through all that was inspiring. I couldn't wait for him to resume his position in our family because at that point I had taken on so much of the leadership role I wondered at times if I'd ever be able to go back to the way it was."

Wendy was right — life in the Gade family is not "the way it was." They forged a new normal and renegotiated their roles based on Daniel's physical limits.

Since then, Daniel has been promoted to the rank of major, earned a PhD from the University of Georgia, competed in triathlons, and is now on the faculty at West Point. In 2008, Daniel and Wendy welcomed twin sons into their family.

Looking back, Wendy says her strength was supernatural. "I was upheld by people's prayers. I felt God in the most personal way," she recalls. "Now when I learn that someone is facing a difficult time, I'm sad about what they're experiencing, but my immediate thought is that they are about to go on the most amazing ride of their lives. I get excited for them, because I've experienced how God draws so near and sustains you. It's unlike anything else."

Prayer: Lord, make your strength perfect in my weakness.

But he said to me, "My grace is sufficient for you, for my power is made perfect in weakness."

2 CORINTHIANS 12:9

you will discover that we have not failed the test. [7]Now we pray to God that you will not do anything wrong — not so that people will see that we have stood the test but so that you will do what is right even though we may seem to have failed. [8]For we cannot do anything against the truth, but only for the truth. [9]We are glad whenever we are weak but you are strong; and our prayer is that you may be fully restored. [10]This is why I write these things when I am absent, that when I come I may not have to be harsh in my use of authority — the authority the Lord gave me for building you up, not for tearing you down.

Final Greetings

[11]Finally, brothers and sisters, rejoice! Strive for full restoration, encourage one another, be of one mind, live in peace. And the God of love and peace will be with you.

[12]Greet one another with a holy kiss. [13]All God's people here send their greetings.

[14]May the grace of the Lord Jesus Christ, and the love of God, and the fellowship of the Holy Spirit be with you all.

Galatians

1 Paul, an apostle — sent not from men nor by a man, but by Jesus Christ and God the Father, who raised him from the dead — ²and all the brothers and sisters*a* with me,

To the churches in Galatia:

³Grace and peace to you from God our Father and the Lord Jesus Christ, ⁴who gave himself for our sins to rescue us from the present evil age, according to the will of our God and Father, ⁵to whom be glory for ever and ever. Amen.

No Other Gospel

⁶I am astonished that you are so quickly deserting the one who called you to live in the grace of Christ and are turning to a different gospel — ⁷which is really no gospel at all. Evidently some people are throwing you into confusion and are trying to pervert the gospel of Christ. ⁸But even if we or an angel from heaven should preach a gospel other than the one we preached to you, let them be under God's curse! ⁹As we have already said, so now I say again: If anybody is preaching to you a gospel other than what you accepted, let them be under God's curse!

¹⁰Am I now trying to win the approval of human beings, or of God? Or am I trying to please people? If I were still trying to please people, I would not be a servant of Christ.

Paul Called by God

¹¹I want you to know, brothers and sisters, that the gospel I preached is not of human origin. ¹²I did not receive it from any man, nor was I taught it; rather, I received it by revelation from Jesus Christ.

¹³For you have heard of my previous way of life in Judaism, how intensely I persecuted the church of God and tried to destroy it. ¹⁴I was advancing in Judaism beyond many of my own age among my people and was extremely zealous for the traditions of my fathers. ¹⁵But when God, who set me apart from my mother's womb and called me by his grace, was pleased ¹⁶to reveal his Son in me so that I might preach him among the Gentiles, my immediate response was not to consult any human being. ¹⁷I did not go up to Jerusalem to see those who were apostles before I was, but I went into Arabia. Later I returned to Damascus.

¹⁸Then after three years, I went up to Jerusalem to get acquainted with Cephas*b* and stayed with him fifteen days. ¹⁹I saw none of the other apostles — only James, the Lord's brother. ²⁰I assure you before God that what I am writing you is no lie.

²¹Then I went to Syria and Cilicia. ²²I was personally unknown to the churches of Judea that are in Christ. ²³They only heard the report: "The man who formerly persecuted us is now preaching the faith he once tried to destroy." ²⁴And they praised God because of me.

Paul Accepted by the Apostles

2 Then after fourteen years, I went up again to Jerusalem, this time with Barnabas. I took Titus along also. ²I went in response to a revelation and, meeting privately with those esteemed as leaders, I presented to them the gospel that I preach among the Gentiles. I wanted to be sure I was not running and had not been running my race in vain. ³Yet not even Titus, who was with me, was compelled to be circumcised, even though he was a Greek. ⁴This matter arose because some false believers had infiltrated our ranks to spy on the freedom we have in Christ Jesus and to make us slaves. ⁵We did not give in to them for a moment, so that the truth of the gospel might be preserved for you.

⁶As for those who were held in high esteem — whatever they were makes no difference to me; God does not show favoritism —

---

a 2 The Greek word for *brothers and sisters* (*adelphoi*) refers here to believers, both men and women, as part of God's family; also in verse 11; and in 3:15; 4:12, 28, 31; 5:11, 13; 6:1, 18.   *b 18* That is, Peter

they added nothing to my message. [7]On the contrary, they recognized that I had been entrusted with the task of preaching the gospel to the uncircumcised,[a] just as Peter had been to the circumcised.[b] [8]For God, who was at work in Peter as an apostle to the circumcised, was also at work in me as an apostle to the Gentiles. [9]James, Cephas[c] and John, those esteemed as pillars, gave me and Barnabas the right hand of fellowship when they recognized the grace given to me. They agreed that we should go to the Gentiles, and they to the circumcised. [10]All they asked was that we should continue to remember the poor, the very thing I had been eager to do all along.

Paul Opposes Cephas

[11]When Cephas came to Antioch, I opposed him to his face, because he stood condemned. [12]For before certain men came from James, he used to eat with the Gentiles. But when they arrived, he began to draw back and separate himself from the Gentiles because he was afraid of those who belonged to the circumcision group. [13]The other Jews joined him in his hypocrisy, so that by their hypocrisy even Barnabas was led astray.

[14]When I saw that they were not acting in line with the truth of the gospel, I said to Cephas in front of them all, "You are a Jew, yet you live like a Gentile and not like a Jew. How is it, then, that you force Gentiles to follow Jewish customs?

[15]"We who are Jews by birth and not sinful Gentiles [16]know that a person is not justified by the works of the law, but by faith in Jesus Christ. So we, too, have put our faith in Christ Jesus that we may be justified by faith in[d] Christ and not by the works of the law, because by the works of the law no one will be justified.

[17]"But if, in seeking to be justified in Christ, we Jews find ourselves also among the sinners, doesn't that mean that Christ promotes sin? Absolutely not! [18]If I rebuild what I destroyed, then I really would be a lawbreaker.

[19]"For through the law I died to the law so that I might live for God. [20]I have been crucified with Christ and I no longer live, but Christ lives in me. The life I now live in the body, I live by faith in the Son of God, who loved me and gave himself for me. [21]I do not set aside the grace of God, for if righteousness could be gained through the law, Christ died for nothing!"[e]

Faith or Works of the Law

3 You foolish Galatians! Who has bewitched you? Before your very eyes Jesus Christ was clearly portrayed as crucified. [2]I would like to learn just one thing from you: Did you receive the Spirit by the works of the law, or by believing what you heard? [3]Are you so foolish? After beginning by means of the Spirit, are you now trying to finish by means of the flesh?[f] [4]Have you experienced[g] so much in vain — if it really was in vain? [5]So again I ask, does God give you his Spirit and work miracles among you by the works of the law, or by your believing what you heard? [6]So also Abraham "believed God, and it was credited to him as righteousness."[h]

[7]Understand, then, that those who have faith are children of Abraham. [8]Scripture foresaw that God would justify the Gentiles by faith, and announced the gospel in advance to Abraham: "All nations will be blessed through you."[i] [9]So those who rely on faith are blessed along with Abraham, the man of faith.

[10]For all who rely on the works of the law are under a curse, as it is written: "Cursed is everyone who does not continue to do everything written in the Book of the Law."[j] [11]Clearly no one who relies on the law is justified before God, because "the righteous will live by faith."[k] [12]The law is not based on faith; on the contrary, it says, "The person who does these things will live by them."[l] [13]Christ redeemed us from the curse of the law by becoming a curse for us, for it is written: "Cursed is everyone who is hung on a pole."[m] [14]He redeemed us in order that the blessing given to Abraham might come to

---

[a] 7 That is, Gentiles   [b] 7 That is, Jews; also in verses 8 and 9   [c] 9 That is, Peter; also in verses 11 and 14   [d] 16 Or but through the faithfulness of . . . justified on the basis of the faithfulness of   [e] 21 Some interpreters end the quotation after verse 14.   [f] 3 In contexts like this, the Greek word for flesh (sarx) refers to the sinful state of human beings, often presented as a power in opposition to the Spirit.   [g] 4 Or suffered   [h] 6 Gen. 15:6   [i] 8 Gen. 12:3; 18:18; 22:18   [j] 10 Deut. 27:26   [k] 11 Hab. 2:4   [l] 12 Lev. 18:5   [m] 13 Deut. 21:23

the Gentiles through Christ Jesus, so that by faith we might receive the promise of the Spirit.

The Law and the Promise

[15] Brothers and sisters, let me take an example from everyday life. Just as no one can set aside or add to a human covenant that has been duly established, so it is in this case. [16] The promises were spoken to Abraham and to his seed. Scripture does not say "and to seeds," meaning many people, but "and to your seed,"[a] meaning one person, who is Christ. [17] What I mean is this: The law, introduced 430 years later, does not set aside the covenant previously established by God and thus do away with the promise. [18] For if the inheritance depends on the law, then it no longer depends on the promise; but God in his grace gave it to Abraham through a promise.

[19] Why, then, was the law given at all? It was added because of transgressions until the Seed to whom the promise referred had come. The law was given through angels and entrusted to a mediator. [20] A mediator, however, implies more than one party; but God is one. [21] Is the law, therefore, opposed to the promises of God? Absolutely not! For if a law had been given that could impart life, then righteousness would certainly have come by the law. [22] But Scripture has locked up everything under the control of sin, so that what was promised, being given through faith in Jesus Christ, might be given to those who believe.

Children of God

[23] Before the coming of this faith,[b] we were held in custody under the law, locked up until the faith that was to come would be revealed. [24] So the law was our guardian until Christ came that we might be justified by faith. [25] Now that this faith has come, we are no longer under a guardian.

[26] So in Christ Jesus you are all children of God through faith, [27] for all of you who were baptized into Christ have clothed yourselves with Christ. [28] There is neither Jew nor Gentile, neither slave nor free, nor is there male and female, for you are all one in Christ Jesus. [29] If you belong to Christ, then you are Abraham's seed, and heirs according to the promise.

4 What I am saying is that as long as an heir is underage, he is no different from a slave, although he owns the whole estate. [2] The heir is subject to guardians and trustees until the time set by his father. [3] So also, when we were underage, we were in slavery under the elemental spiritual forces[c] of the world. [4] But when the set time had fully come, God sent his Son, born of a woman, born under the law, [5] to redeem those under the law, that we might receive adoption to sonship.[d] [6] Because you are his sons, God sent the Spirit of his Son into our hearts, the Spirit who calls out, "Abba,[e] Father." [7] So you are no longer a slave, but God's child; and since you are his child, God has made you also an heir.

Paul's Concern for the Galatians

[8] Formerly, when you did not know God, you were slaves to those who by nature are not gods. [9] But now that you know God — or rather are known by God — how is it that you are turning back to those weak and miserable forces[f]? Do you wish to be enslaved by them all over again? [10] You are observing special days and months and seasons and years! [11] I fear for you, that somehow I have wasted my efforts on you.

[12] I plead with you, brothers and sisters, become like me, for I became like you. You did me no wrong. [13] As you know, it was because of an illness that I first preached the gospel to you, [14] and even though my illness was a trial to you, you did not treat me with contempt or scorn. Instead, you welcomed me as if I were an angel of God, as if I were Christ Jesus himself. [15] Where, then, is your blessing of me now? I can testify that, if you could have done so, you would have torn out your eyes and given them to me. [16] Have I now become your enemy by telling you the truth?

[17] Those people are zealous to win you over, but for no good. What they want is to

---

[a] 16 Gen. 12:7; 13:15; 24:7   [b] 22,23 Or through the faithfulness of Jesus . . . [23] Before faith came
[c] 3 Or under the basic principles   [d] 5 The Greek word for adoption to sonship is a legal term referring to the full legal standing of an adopted male heir in Roman culture.   [e] 6 Aramaic for Father
[f] 9 Or principles

alienate you from us, so that you may have zeal for them. ¹⁸It is fine to be zealous, provided the purpose is good, and to be so always, not just when I am with you. ¹⁹My dear children, for whom I am again in the pains of childbirth until Christ is formed in you, ²⁰how I wish I could be with you now and change my tone, because I am perplexed about you!

Hagar and Sarah

²¹Tell me, you who want to be under the law, are you not aware of what the law says? ²²For it is written that Abraham had two sons, one by the slave woman and the other by the free woman. ²³His son by the slave woman was born according to the flesh, but his son by the free woman was born as the result of a divine promise.

²⁴These things are being taken figuratively: The women represent two covenants. One covenant is from Mount Sinai and bears children who are to be slaves: This is Hagar. ²⁵Now Hagar stands for Mount Sinai in Arabia and corresponds to the present city of Jerusalem, because she is in slavery with her children. ²⁶But the Jerusalem that is above is free, and she is our mother. ²⁷For it is written:

"Be glad, barren woman,
    you who never bore a child;
shout for joy and cry aloud,
    you who were never in labor;
because more are the children of the
        desolate woman
    than of her who has a husband."ᵃ

²⁸Now you, brothers and sisters, like Isaac, are children of promise. ²⁹At that time the son born according to the flesh persecuted the son born by the power of the Spirit. It is the same now. ³⁰But what does Scripture say? "Get rid of the slave woman and her son, for the slave woman's son will never share in the inheritance with the free woman's son."ᵇ ³¹Therefore, brothers and sisters, we are not children of the slave woman, but of the free woman.

Freedom in Christ

5 It is for freedom that Christ has set us free. Stand firm, then, and do not let yourselves be burdened again by a yoke of slavery.

²Mark my words! I, Paul, tell you that if you let yourselves be circumcised, Christ will be of no value to you at all. ³Again I declare to every man who lets himself be circumcised that he is obligated to obey the whole law. ⁴You who are trying to be justified by the law have been alienated from Christ; you have fallen away from grace. ⁵For through the Spirit we eagerly await by faith the righteousness for which we hope. ⁶For in Christ Jesus neither circumcision nor uncircumcision has any value. The only thing that counts is faith expressing itself through love.

⁷You were running a good race. Who cut in on you to keep you from obeying the truth? ⁸That kind of persuasion does not come from the one who calls you. ⁹"A little yeast works through the whole batch of dough." ¹⁰I am confident in the Lord that you will take no other view. The one who is throwing you into confusion, whoever that may be, will have to pay the penalty. ¹¹Brothers and sisters, if I am still preaching circumcision, why am I still being persecuted? In that case the offense of the cross has been abolished. ¹²As for those agitators, I wish they would go the whole way and emasculate themselves!

Life by the Spirit

¹³You, my brothers and sisters, were called to be free. But do not use your freedom to indulge the fleshᶜ; rather, serve one another humbly in love. ¹⁴For the entire law is fulfilled in keeping this one command: "Love your neighbor as yourself."ᵈ ¹⁵If you bite and devour each other, watch out or you will be destroyed by each other.

¹⁶So I say, walk by the Spirit, and you will not gratify the desires of the flesh. ¹⁷For the flesh desires what is contrary to the Spirit, and the Spirit what is contrary to the flesh. They are in conflict with each other, so that you are not to do whateverᵉ you want. ¹⁸But if you are led by the Spirit, you are not under the law.

¹⁹The acts of the flesh are obvious: sexual immorality, impurity and debauchery; ²⁰idolatry and witchcraft; hatred, discord,

---

ᵃ 27 Isaiah 54:1   ᵇ 30 Gen. 21:10   ᶜ 13 In contexts like this, the Greek word for *flesh* (*sarx*) refers to the sinful state of human beings, often presented as a power in opposition to the Spirit; also in verses 16, 17, 19 and 24; and in 6:8.   ᵈ 14 Lev. 19:18   ᵉ 17 Or *you do not do what*

BEAR ONE ANOTHER'S BURDENS

By Jane Hampton Cook

Henry and Lucy Knox married in 1775, when the British occupied their hometown of Boston. They faced a difficult choice when Henry wanted to join the Continental Army, because Lucy was the daughter of a high-ranking loyalist. What would she do if Henry left to join the army fighting her father's king?

Lucy decided to escape with him. She sewed Henry's sword into the lining of her cloak and, disguised in modest coats, they escaped from Boston into Cambridge under cover of darkness. Lucy took refuge in a nearby town while Henry built fortifications with the patriots at Bunker Hill.

Two years later it was clear their decision had cost Lucy greatly. Her parents had disowned her and refused to answer her letters. Henry responded by thinking about the problem from her viewpoint. He stepped into her "slippers" and wrote her a beautiful letter of support. Knox encouragingly wrote on May 20, 1777:

> Though your parents are on the opposite side from your Henry, yet it's very strange it should divest them of humanity. Not a line! My God! What stuff is the human heart made of? Although father, mother, sister, and brother have forgotten you, yet, my love, your Henry will ever esteem you the best boon of Heaven.

At the time, Lucy was very lonely as she cared for their child in Brookline, Massachusetts. Her anguish intensified when a Frenchman arrived on America's shores and claimed he was the new commander of artillery, the very job Henry held. The news was a double-edged sword. If the Frenchman's claim was correct, then Henry would be out of a job and on his way back home to her. How she longed for their reunion! However, she also knew that promotions and positions were important to military men. Henry was no exception. As much as she wanted him home, she also wanted him to succeed and be promoted.

She assured Henry that the Frenchman's claims of knowing princes and holding high military titles were more boastful than believable and that she supported Henry's decision to bring the matter before General Washington. Washington kept Henry as the head of artillery and later promoted him to command West Point. When Washington stepped down as commander-in-chief at the end of the war, he named Knox as his replacement to finish the job of dissolving the army.

Throughout their separation, Lucy and Henry often considered each other's point of view. In this self-sacrificing way, they carried each other's burdens. In the end, their reunion was sweeter because of it.

Prayer: *Help me put my spouse's needs before my own, and enable me to see life from their point of view.*

Carry each other's burdens, and in this way you will fulfill the law of Christ.
GALATIANS 6:2

jealousy, fits of rage, selfish ambition, dissensions, factions [21] and envy; drunkenness, orgies, and the like. I warn you, as I did before, that those who live like this will not inherit the kingdom of God.

[22] But the fruit of the Spirit is love, joy, peace, forbearance, kindness, goodness, faithfulness, [23] gentleness and self-control. Against such things there is no law. [24] Those who belong to Christ Jesus have crucified the flesh with its passions and desires. [25] Since we live by the Spirit, let us keep in step with the Spirit. [26] Let us not become conceited, provoking and envying each other.

Doing Good to All

6 Brothers and sisters, if someone is caught in a sin, you who live by the Spirit should restore that person gently. But watch yourselves, or you also may be tempted. [2] Carry each other's burdens, and in this way you will fulfill the law of Christ. [3] If anyone thinks they are something when they are not, they deceive themselves. [4] Each one should test their own actions. Then they can take pride in themselves alone, without comparing themselves to someone else, [5] for each one should carry their own load. [6] Nevertheless, the one who receives instruction in the word should share all good things with their instructor.

[7] Do not be deceived: God cannot be mocked. A man reaps what he sows. [8] Whoever sows to please their flesh, from the flesh will reap destruction; whoever sows to please the Spirit, from the Spirit will reap eternal life. [9] Let us not become weary in doing good, for at the proper time we will reap a harvest if we do not give up. [10] Therefore, as we have opportunity, let us do good to all people, especially to those who belong to the family of believers.

Not Circumcision but the New Creation

[11] See what large letters I use as I write to you with my own hand!

[12] Those who want to impress people by means of the flesh are trying to compel you to be circumcised. The only reason they do this is to avoid being persecuted for the cross of Christ. [13] Not even those who are circumcised keep the law, yet they want you to be circumcised that they may boast about your circumcision in the flesh. [14] May I never boast except in the cross of our Lord Jesus Christ, through which[a] the world has been crucified to me, and I to the world. [15] Neither circumcision nor uncircumcision means anything; what counts is the new creation. [16] Peace and mercy to all who follow this rule — to[b] the Israel of God.

[17] From now on, let no one cause me trouble, for I bear on my body the marks of Jesus.

[18] The grace of our Lord Jesus Christ be with your spirit, brothers and sisters. Amen.

a 14 Or *whom*   *b* 16 Or *rule and to*

Ephesians

1 Paul, an apostle of Christ Jesus by the will of God,

To God's holy people in Ephesus,[a] the faithful in Christ Jesus:

[2]Grace and peace to you from God our Father and the Lord Jesus Christ.

Praise for Spiritual Blessings in Christ

[3]Praise be to the God and Father of our Lord Jesus Christ, who has blessed us in the heavenly realms with every spiritual blessing in Christ. [4]For he chose us in him before the creation of the world to be holy and blameless in his sight. In love [5]he[b] predestined us for adoption to sonship[c] through Jesus Christ, in accordance with his pleasure and will — [6]to the praise of his glorious grace, which he has freely given us in the One he loves. [7]In him we have redemption through his blood, the forgiveness of sins, in accordance with the riches of God's grace [8]that he lavished on us. With all wisdom and understanding, [9]he[d] made known to us the mystery of his will according to his good pleasure, which he purposed in Christ, [10]to be put into effect when the times reach their fulfillment — to bring unity to all things in heaven and on earth under Christ.

[11]In him we were also chosen,[e] having been predestined according to the plan of him who works out everything in conformity with the purpose of his will, [12]in order that we, who were the first to put our hope in Christ, might be for the praise of his glory. [13]And you also were included in Christ when you heard the message of truth, the gospel of your salvation. When you believed, you were marked in him with a seal, the promised Holy Spirit, [14]who is a deposit guaranteeing our inheritance until the redemption of those who are God's possession — to the praise of his glory.

Thanksgiving and Prayer

[15]For this reason, ever since I heard about your faith in the Lord Jesus and your love for all God's people, [16]I have not stopped giving thanks for you, remembering you in my prayers. [17]I keep asking that the God of our Lord Jesus Christ, the glorious Father, may give you the Spirit[f] of wisdom and revelation, so that you may know him better. [18]I pray that the eyes of your heart may be enlightened in order that you may know the hope to which he has called you, the riches of his glorious inheritance in his holy people, [19]and his incomparably great power for us who believe. That power is the same as the mighty strength [20]he exerted when he raised Christ from the dead and seated him at his right hand in the heavenly realms, [21]far above all rule and authority, power and dominion, and every name that is invoked, not only in the present age but also in the one to come. [22]And God placed all things under his feet and appointed him to be head over everything for the church, [23]which is his body, the fullness of him who fills everything in every way.

Made Alive in Christ

2 As for you, you were dead in your transgressions and sins, [2]in which you used to live when you followed the ways of this world and of the ruler of the kingdom of the air, the spirit who is now at work in those who are disobedient. [3]All of us also lived among them at one time, gratifying the cravings of our flesh[g] and following its desires and thoughts. Like the rest, we were by nature deserving of wrath. [4]But because of

---

[a] 1 Some early manuscripts do not have *in Ephesus.*   [b] 4,5 Or *sight in love.* [5]*He*   [c] 5 The Greek word for *adoption to sonship* is a legal term referring to the full legal standing of an adopted male heir in Roman culture.   [d] 8,9 Or *us with all wisdom and understanding.* [9]*And he*   [e] 11 Or *were made heirs* [f] 17 Or *a spirit*   [g] 3 In contexts like this, the Greek word for *flesh* (*sarx*) refers to the sinful state of human beings, often presented as a power in opposition to the Spirit.

his great love for us, God, who is rich in mercy, [5]made us alive with Christ even when we were dead in transgressions — it is by grace you have been saved. [6]And God raised us up with Christ and seated us with him in the heavenly realms in Christ Jesus, [7]in order that in the coming ages he might show the incomparable riches of his grace, expressed in his kindness to us in Christ Jesus. [8]For it is by grace you have been saved, through faith — and this is not from yourselves, it is the gift of God — [9]not by works, so that no one can boast. [10]For we are God's handiwork, created in Christ Jesus to do good works, which God prepared in advance for us to do.

Jew and Gentile Reconciled Through Christ

[11]Therefore, remember that formerly you who are Gentiles by birth and called "uncircumcised" by those who call themselves "the circumcision" (which is done in the body by human hands) — [12]remember that at that time you were separate from Christ, excluded from citizenship in Israel and foreigners to the covenants of the promise, without hope and without God in the world. [13]But now in Christ Jesus you who once were far away have been brought near by the blood of Christ.

[14]For he himself is our peace, who has made the two groups one and has destroyed the barrier, the dividing wall of hostility, [15]by setting aside in his flesh the law with its commands and regulations. His purpose was to create in himself one new humanity out of the two, thus making peace, [16]and in one body to reconcile both of them to God through the cross, by which he put to death their hostility. [17]He came and preached peace to you who were far away and peace to those who were near. [18]For through him we both have access to the Father by one Spirit.

[19]Consequently, you are no longer foreigners and strangers, but fellow citizens with God's people and also members of his household, [20]built on the foundation of the apostles and prophets, with Christ Jesus himself as the chief cornerstone. [21]In him the whole building is joined together and rises to become a holy temple in the Lord.

[22]And in him you too are being built together to become a dwelling in which God lives by his Spirit.

God's Marvelous Plan for the Gentiles

3 For this reason I, Paul, the prisoner of Christ Jesus for the sake of you Gentiles —

[2]Surely you have heard about the administration of God's grace that was given to me for you, [3]that is, the mystery made known to me by revelation, as I have already written briefly. [4]In reading this, then, you will be able to understand my insight into the mystery of Christ, [5]which was not made known to people in other generations as it has now been revealed by the Spirit to God's holy apostles and prophets. [6]This mystery is that through the gospel the Gentiles are heirs together with Israel, members together of one body, and sharers together in the promise in Christ Jesus.

[7]I became a servant of this gospel by the gift of God's grace given me through the working of his power. [8]Although I am less than the least of all the Lord's people, this grace was given me: to preach to the Gentiles the boundless riches of Christ, [9]and to make plain to everyone the administration of this mystery, which for ages past was kept hidden in God, who created all things. [10]His intent was that now, through the church, the manifold wisdom of God should be made known to the rulers and authorities in the heavenly realms, [11]according to his eternal purpose that he accomplished in Christ Jesus our Lord. [12]In him and through faith in him we may approach God with freedom and confidence. [13]I ask you, therefore, not to be discouraged because of my sufferings for you, which are your glory.

A Prayer for the Ephesians

[14]For this reason I kneel before the Father, [15]from whom every family[a] in heaven and on earth derives its name. [16]I pray that out of his glorious riches he may strengthen you with power through his Spirit in your inner being, [17]so that Christ may dwell in your hearts through faith. And I pray that you, being rooted and established in love, [18]may have power, together with all the Lord's holy

---

[a] 15 The Greek for *family* (*patria*) is derived from the Greek for *father* (*pater*).

A HARVEST

By Jocelyn Green

Mary Livermore looked out across waves of grain carpeting the land of Wisconsin and eastern Iowa. On this late summer day in 1863, an errand for the Sanitary Commission took her through fields dotted with women reaping the wheat harvest.

Mary approached a sunburned woman with calloused hands who was sitting atop her reaper to give her horses a breathing spell. Mary learned that in addition to the woman's husband, all three of her boys had enlisted, and one had already been killed. A short distance away, her daughters stood binding the fallen grain. In her book, *My Story of the War*, Mary recalls her conversation with the woman's daughters:

> "Well, you are like your mother, not afraid to lend a hand at the harvesting, it seems!" was my opening remark.
>
> "No, we're willing to help outdoors in these times. Harvesting isn't any harder if it's as hard as cooking, washing, and ironing over a red hot stove in July and August — only we have to do both now. My three brothers went into the army, all my cousins, most of the young men about here, and the men we used to hire. So there's no help to be got but women and the crops must be got in all the same, you know."
>
> "I tell Annie we can do anything to help along while the country's in such trouble," [said another sister.]
>
> "I tell mother," said the Annie referred to standing very erect, with flashing eyes, "that as long as the country can't get along without grain nor the army fight without food we're serving the country just as much here in the harvest field as our boys are on the battle field — and that sort o' takes the edge off from this business of doing men's work, you know." And a hearty laugh followed this statement.

In addition to working in house and field, these women also made shirts, drawers, currant wine, and blackberry jam, as well as pickles to be sent to the Union's sick and wounded in Southern hospitals. Mary Livermore praised these women as heroines.

Our salvation comes by grace, through faith, and we were created to do good works (see Ephesians 2:8 – 10). Though few people, if any, praised these women as Livermore did, their work in the fields allowed their husbands to fight for their country. It was work worth doing, and God equipped them for the task.

Prayer: Lord, show me the work you want me to do, working always to serve you.

For it is by grace you have been saved, through faith — and this is not from yourselves, it is the gift of God — not by works, so that no one can boast. For we are God's handiwork, created in Christ Jesus to do good works, which God prepared in advance for us to do.
EPHESIANS 2:8 – 10

people, to grasp how wide and long and high and deep is the love of Christ, [19] and to know this love that surpasses knowledge — that you may be filled to the measure of all the fullness of God.

[20] Now to him who is able to do immeasurably more than all we ask or imagine, according to his power that is at work within us, [21] to him be glory in the church and in Christ Jesus throughout all generations, for ever and ever! Amen.

Unity and Maturity in the Body of Christ

4 As a prisoner for the Lord, then, I urge you to live a life worthy of the calling you have received. [2] Be completely humble and gentle; be patient, bearing with one another in love. [3] Make every effort to keep the unity of the Spirit through the bond of peace. [4] There is one body and one Spirit, just as you were called to one hope when you were called; [5] one Lord, one faith, one baptism; [6] one God and Father of all, who is over all and through all and in all.

[7] But to each one of us grace has been given as Christ apportioned it. [8] This is why it[a] says:

"When he ascended on high,
    he took many captives
    and gave gifts to his people."[b]

[9] (What does "he ascended" mean except that he also descended to the lower, earthly regions[c]? [10] He who descended is the very one who ascended higher than all the heavens, in order to fill the whole universe.) [11] So Christ himself gave the apostles, the prophets, the evangelists, the pastors and teachers, [12] to equip his people for works of service, so that the body of Christ may be built up [13] until we all reach unity in the faith and in the knowledge of the Son of God and become mature, attaining to the whole measure of the fullness of Christ.

[14] Then we will no longer be infants, tossed back and forth by the waves, and blown here and there by every wind of teaching and by the cunning and craftiness of people in their deceitful scheming. [15] Instead, speaking the truth in love, we will grow to become in every respect the mature body of him who is the head, that is, Christ. [16] From him the

whole body, joined and held together by every supporting ligament, grows and builds itself up in love, as each part does its work.

Instructions for Christian Living

[17] So I tell you this, and insist on it in the Lord, that you must no longer live as the Gentiles do, in the futility of their thinking. [18] They are darkened in their understanding and separated from the life of God because of the ignorance that is in them due to the hardening of their hearts. [19] Having lost all sensitivity, they have given themselves over to sensuality so as to indulge in every kind of impurity, and they are full of greed.

[20] That, however, is not the way of life you learned [21] when you heard about Christ and were taught in him in accordance with the truth that is in Jesus. [22] You were taught, with regard to your former way of life, to put off your old self, which is being corrupted by its deceitful desires; [23] to be made new in the attitude of your minds; [24] and to put on the new self, created to be like God in true righteousness and holiness.

[25] Therefore each of you must put off falsehood and speak truthfully to your neighbor, for we are all members of one body. [26] "In your anger do not sin"[d]: Do not let the sun go down while you are still angry, [27] and do not give the devil a foothold. [28] Anyone who has been stealing must steal no longer, but must work, doing something useful with their own hands, that they may have something to share with those in need.

[29] Do not let any unwholesome talk come out of your mouths, but only what is helpful for building others up according to their needs, that it may benefit those who listen. [30] And do not grieve the Holy Spirit of God, with whom you were sealed for the day of redemption. [31] Get rid of all bitterness, rage and anger, brawling and slander, along with every form of malice. [32] Be kind and compassionate to one another, forgiving each other,

5 just as in Christ God forgave you. [1] Follow God's example, therefore, as dearly loved children [2] and walk in the way of love, just as Christ loved us and gave himself up for us as a fragrant offering and sacrifice to God.

[3] But among you there must not be even a

---

[a] 8 Or God   [b] 8 Psalm 68:18   [c] 9 Or *the depths of the earth*   [d] 26 Psalm 4:4 (see Septuagint)

HONORING HER HERO

By Jocelyn Green

Every shot from the 21-gun salute pierced Deanna House's heart, and the face of her son Joel surged before her. He had been killed on June 22, 2007 — Deanna's birthday — while serving his country in Iraq. (See also "Comforting Those in Trouble" on page 212.)

Now here she was, watching her son's body go into the ground at the edge of the woods he loved so much in their little town of Lee, Maine. The mournful notes of "Taps" rose in the air while an officer in dress uniform handed her the folded flag.

It was over.

"All I could think was how badly I wanted to touch Joel again, to see his face, to put him back in his place in the family photos," Deanna recalled. "I walked to the coffin and touched it, knowing it was all I would have. 'Good-bye, Baby, I love you so much,' I whispered, and with every force I could find within, I turned my back and walked into the empty days ahead through which the fallen soldier's mother must learn to live."

During the next several months, Deanna coped by imagining her son was still deployed. In her last conversation with Joel, Deanna had promised to meet him at Fort Hood when he returned. When his unit came back without him, she was there to prove to her grieving heart that her son really had been called up to heaven and was not still in Iraq.

She wrote in a blog post on February 5, 2008:

Instead of meeting you at the airplane as I have so many times before, I met some of your buddies, and we went to IHOP for Sunday brunch ... You didn't come back from war, Joel! I kept my promise to be there for you when you came back, but all that returned were stories over strawberry-stuffed French toast and coffee.

Joel, you were so strong. You didn't want to die. You battled that giant so valiantly. You tried to get home. You tried to let me fulfill my promise to you. "Yea, though I walk through the valley of the shadow of death, I will fear no evil: for thou art with me; thy rod and thy staff they comfort me." Surrender it all to Jesus and walk the last shadow with him.

Day by day, Deanna has learned to live without Joel. In extending comfort and sympathy to another family in town who also lost their son in Iraq, she explained her resolve to move on this way: "My son is a hero, and I am now a hero's mother. I choose to honor his life by continuing to live mine to the fullest potential I am given."

Prayer: Jesus, may I honor your life, death and resurrection by living a life worthy of the calling you have given me.

**As a prisoner for the Lord, then, I urge you to live a life worthy
of the calling you have received.**
EPHESIANS 4:1

for your next devotional reading, go to page 236

hint of sexual immorality, or of any kind of impurity, or of greed, because these are improper for God's holy people. [4]Nor should there be obscenity, foolish talk or coarse joking, which are out of place, but rather thanksgiving. [5]For of this you can be sure: No immoral, impure or greedy person — such a person is an idolater — has any inheritance in the kingdom of Christ and of God.[a] [6]Let no one deceive you with empty words, for because of such things God's wrath comes on those who are disobedient. [7]Therefore do not be partners with them.

[8]For you were once darkness, but now you are light in the Lord. Live as children of light [9](for the fruit of the light consists in all goodness, righteousness and truth) [10]and find out what pleases the Lord. [11]Have nothing to do with the fruitless deeds of darkness, but rather expose them. [12]It is shameful even to mention what the disobedient do in secret. [13]But everything exposed by the light becomes visible — and everything that is illuminated becomes a light. [14]This is why it is said:

> "Wake up, sleeper,
>   rise from the dead,
>   and Christ will shine on you."

[15]Be very careful, then, how you live — not as unwise but as wise, [16]making the most of every opportunity, because the days are evil. [17]Therefore do not be foolish, but understand what the Lord's will is. [18]Do not get drunk on wine, which leads to debauchery. Instead, be filled with the Spirit, [19]speaking to one another with psalms, hymns, and songs from the Spirit. Sing and make music from your heart to the Lord, [20]always giving thanks to God the Father for everything, in the name of our Lord Jesus Christ.

Instructions for Christian Households

[21]Submit to one another out of reverence for Christ.
[22]Wives, submit yourselves to your own husbands as you do to the Lord. [23]For the husband is the head of the wife as Christ is the head of the church, his body, of which he is the Savior. [24]Now as the church submits to Christ, so also wives should submit to their husbands in everything.

[25]Husbands, love your wives, just as Christ loved the church and gave himself up for her [26]to make her holy, cleansing[b] her by the washing with water through the word, [27]and to present her to himself as a radiant church, without stain or wrinkle or any other blemish, but holy and blameless. [28]In this same way, husbands ought to love their wives as their own bodies. He who loves his wife loves himself. [29]After all, no one ever hated their own body, but they feed and care for their body, just as Christ does the church — [30]for we are members of his body. [31]"For this reason a man will leave his father and mother and be united to his wife, and the two will become one flesh."[c] [32]This is a profound mystery — but I am talking about Christ and the church. [33]However, each one of you also must love his wife as he loves himself, and the wife must respect her husband.

6 Children, obey your parents in the Lord, for this is right. [2]"Honor your father and mother" — which is the first commandment with a promise — [3]"so that it may go well with you and that you may enjoy long life on the earth."[d]

[4]Fathers,[e] do not exasperate your children; instead, bring them up in the training and instruction of the Lord.

[5]Slaves, obey your earthly masters with respect and fear, and with sincerity of heart, just as you would obey Christ. [6]Obey them not only to win their favor when their eye is on you, but as slaves of Christ, doing the will of God from your heart. [7]Serve wholeheartedly, as if you were serving the Lord, not people, [8]because you know that the Lord will reward each one for whatever good they do, whether they are slave or free.

[9]And masters, treat your slaves in the same way. Do not threaten them, since you know that he who is both their Master and yours is in heaven, and there is no favoritism with him.

The Armor of God

[10]Finally, be strong in the Lord and in his mighty power. [11]Put on the full armor of God, so that you can take your stand against the devil's schemes. [12]For our struggle is not

---

[a] 5 Or *kingdom of the Messiah and God*   [b] 26 Or *having cleansed*   [c] 31 Gen. 2:24   [d] 3 Deut. 5:16
[e] 4 Or *Parents*

Getting Dressed

By Marshéle Carter Waddell

READ: Ephesians 6:10–20

Besides studying God's Word and spending time with family, my grandmother's favorite thing was getting dressed for the day. She found joy in the challenge of finding a new way to coordinate a skirt, blouse, shoes and accessories. Her carefully selected combination gave her a humble confidence as she served others.

That's why I laughed until my sides ached when she told me she had driven downtown half-dressed. Her mind must have been elsewhere as she'd pulled on her pantyhose, squeezed into her girdle and slithered into her slip. She put on her blouse, situated her scarf around her neck, grabbed her purse and headed to town. She proceeded to scurry about as she did her errands only to look down and see that she had left her skirt on the bed at home. I can hear her now, exclaiming, "Lawd, have mercy!" She did an about-face and headed home to finish getting dressed.

Let me ask you a question: Did you finish getting dressed today? The truth is that most of us leave home stark naked every day, spiritually speaking.

God has told us in Ephesians 6 to put on the *full* armor of God — not half of it and not just those accessories we are in the mood to wear that day. The *full* armor of God includes the belt of truth, breastplate of righteousness, shoes of readiness, shield of faith, helmet of salvation and sword of the Spirit.

A seasoned warrior headed into battle would never leave one piece of armor at home. Neither should we if we want to "take [our] stand against the devil's schemes" (verse 11). Spiritual attacks on military wives are just as deadly as physical assaults on our military members. Satan can kill your peace, your joy and your marriage. He can wreak havoc on your faith and tempt you into personal destruction.

A careful reading of Ephesians 6 tells us some vital things about the battles we face: (1) *We cannot hope to stand on our own* (verse 10). We need to draw on the Lord's strength through the Bible, prayer and fellow believers. (2) *Human opponents are never our true enemy* (verse 12). Though we can't see the devil and his cohorts, they are real and we must be alert to their tactics. (3) *We cannot choose the time of battle* (verse 13). It's only a matter of when, not if. (4) *We can only hope to stand if we are wearing the full armor of God* (verses 14 – 17). With all pieces worn together, we can stand firm. Before you begin your day, be sure to get dressed, complete with the armor of God!

Put on the full armor of God, so that you can take your stand against the devil's schemes.

EPHESIANS 6:11

DEBRIEF
- Did I get fully dressed today?
- Which piece of the armor of God do I sometimes forget to wear? How can I remind myself to put it on?

REPORT
Lord, thank you for providing this protective armor for me. Help me remember to put on every piece of it by prayer and faith before my feet hit the floor each morning. I trust that your armor will protect my life, my heart and my mind as I serve you today. In Jesus' name I pray. Amen.

against flesh and blood, but against the rulers, against the authorities, against the powers of this dark world and against the spiritual forces of evil in the heavenly realms. [13]Therefore put on the full armor of God, so that when the day of evil comes, you may be able to stand your ground, and after you have done everything, to stand. [14]Stand firm then, with the belt of truth buckled around your waist, with the breastplate of righteousness in place, [15]and with your feet fitted with the readiness that comes from the gospel of peace. [16]In addition to all this, take up the shield of faith, with which you can extinguish all the flaming arrows of the evil one. [17]Take the helmet of salvation and the sword of the Spirit, which is the word of God. [18]And pray in the Spirit on all occasions with all kinds of prayers and requests. With this in mind, be alert and always keep on praying for all the Lord's people. [19]Pray also for me, that whenever I speak, words may be given me so that I will fearlessly make known the mystery of the gospel, [20]for which I am an ambassador in chains. Pray that I may declare it fearlessly, as I should.

Final Greetings

[21]Tychicus, the dear brother and faithful servant in the Lord, will tell you everything, so that you also may know how I am and what I am doing. [22]I am sending him to you for this very purpose, that you may know how we are, and that he may encourage you.

[23]Peace to the brothers and sisters,[a] and love with faith from God the Father and the Lord Jesus Christ. [24]Grace to all who love our Lord Jesus Christ with an undying love.[b]

---

[a] 23 The Greek word for *brothers and sisters* (*adelphoi*) refers here to believers, both men and women, as part of God's family.   [b] 24 Or *Grace and immortality to all who love our Lord Jesus Christ.*

Philippians

1 Paul and Timothy, servants of Christ Jesus,

To all God's holy people in Christ Jesus at Philippi, together with the overseers and deacons[a]:

[2] Grace and peace to you from God our Father and the Lord Jesus Christ.

Thanksgiving and Prayer

[3] I thank my God every time I remember you. [4] In all my prayers for all of you, I always pray with joy [5] because of your partnership in the gospel from the first day until now, [6] being confident of this, that he who began a good work in you will carry it on to completion until the day of Christ Jesus.

[7] It is right for me to feel this way about all of you, since I have you in my heart and, whether I am in chains or defending and confirming the gospel, all of you share in God's grace with me. [8] God can testify how I long for all of you with the affection of Christ Jesus.

[9] And this is my prayer: that your love may abound more and more in knowledge and depth of insight, [10] so that you may be able to discern what is best and may be pure and blameless for the day of Christ, [11] filled with the fruit of righteousness that comes through Jesus Christ — to the glory and praise of God.

Paul's Chains Advance the Gospel

[12] Now I want you to know, brothers and sisters,[b] that what has happened to me has actually served to advance the gospel. [13] As a result, it has become clear throughout the whole palace guard[c] and to everyone else that I am in chains for Christ. [14] And because of my chains, most of the brothers and sisters have become confident in the Lord and dare all the more to proclaim the gospel without fear.

[15] It is true that some preach Christ out of envy and rivalry, but others out of goodwill. [16] The latter do so out of love, knowing that I am put here for the defense of the gospel. [17] The former preach Christ out of selfish ambition, not sincerely, supposing that they can stir up trouble for me while I am in chains. [18] But what does it matter? The important thing is that in every way, whether from false motives or true, Christ is preached. And because of this I rejoice.

Yes, and I will continue to rejoice, [19] for I know that through your prayers and God's provision of the Spirit of Jesus Christ what has happened to me will turn out for my deliverance.[d] [20] I eagerly expect and hope that I will in no way be ashamed, but will have sufficient courage so that now as always Christ will be exalted in my body, whether by life or by death. [21] For to me, to live is Christ and to die is gain. [22] If I am to go on living in the body, this will mean fruitful labor for me. Yet what shall I choose? I do not know! [23] I am torn between the two: I desire to depart and be with Christ, which is better by far; [24] but it is more necessary for you that I remain in the body. [25] Convinced of this, I know that I will remain, and I will continue with all of you for your progress and joy in the faith, [26] so that through my being with you again your boasting in Christ Jesus will abound on account of me.

Life Worthy of the Gospel

[27] Whatever happens, conduct yourselves in a manner worthy of the gospel of Christ. Then, whether I come and see you or only hear about you in my absence, I will know that you stand firm in the one Spirit,[e] striving together as one for the faith of the gospel

---

[a] 1 The word *deacons* refers here to Christians designated to serve with the overseers/elders of the church in a variety of ways; similarly in Romans 16:1 and 1 Tim. 3:8,12. [b] 12 The Greek word for *brothers and sisters* (*adelphoi*) refers here to believers, both men and women, as part of God's family; also in verse 14; and in 3:1, 13, 17; 4:1, 8, 21. [c] 13 Or *whole palace* [d] 19 Or *vindication*; or *salvation* [e] 27 Or *in one spirit*

Our Heavenly Citizenship

By Alane Pearce

READ: Philippians 3:12–21

W here are you from?" It sounds like a simple question, but it's hard for a military spouse to give a simple answer. We aren't from where we live now and probably aren't from the last place we lived either.

In Philippians 3:20, Paul reminds us all, military or not, that once we put our faith in Jesus, heaven is our new hometown. In John 14:1 – 2, Jesus promised to prepare a place for us in heaven — a perfect, permanent home.

When immigrants take the Oath of Allegiance to become United States citizens, they accept certain responsibilities that parallel our own as we also accept the privilege of our heavenly citizenship. The Oath published on the website for U.S. Naturalization & Immigration Services in 2012 reads like this:

> I hereby declare, on oath, that I absolutely and entirely renounce and abjure all allegiance and fidelity to any foreign prince, potentate, state or sovereignty, of whom or which I have heretofore been a subject or citizen; that I will support and defend the Constitution and laws of the United States of America against all enemies, foreign and domestic; that I will bear true faith and allegiance to the same; that I will bear arms on behalf of the United States when required by the law; that I will perform noncombatant service in the armed forces of the United States when required by the law; that I will perform work of national importance under civilian direction when required by the law; and that I take this obligation freely without any mental reservation or purpose of evasion; so help me God.

In addition to giving us a new permanent residence, citizenship in heaven requires something of us. We must:

1. *Renounce previous allegiances.* We must turn away from whatever things of the world we once held dear to be fully loyal to God's kingdom. Our new allegiance must be to righteousness (see Romans 6:17 – 18).

2. *Support and defend the laws.* Citizenship in heaven requires us to follow God's rules for godly living and to live a life worthy of the calling we have received (see Ephesians 4:1).

3. *Perform military service.* We are soldiers of Christ and should try to please our commanding officer (see 2 Timothy 2:3 – 4). We must "put on the full armor of God, so that [we] can take [our] stand against the devil's schemes" (Ephesians 6:11).

As we move from town to town here on earth, remember that one day we'll reach our permanent heavenly residence.

But our citizenship is in heaven. And we eagerly await a Savior from there, the Lord Jesus Christ.

PHILIPPIANS 3:20

DEBRIEF

• Am I honoring the responsibilities that come with my heavenly citizenship?

• What is one aspect I can work on this week?

REPORT

God, as I dwell in various temporary homes, help me focus on the things that matter in heaven, and help me look forward to being with you in my forever home. Help me let go of any allegiance to the things of this world, so I can be fully loyal to the kingdom of God. Amen.

---

for your next devotional reading, go to page 241

[28] without being frightened in any way by those who oppose you. This is a sign to them that they will be destroyed, but that you will be saved — and that by God. [29] For it has been granted to you on behalf of Christ not only to believe in him, but also to suffer for him, [30] since you are going through the same struggle you saw I had, and now hear that I still have.

Imitating Christ's Humility

2 Therefore if you have any encouragement from being united with Christ, if any comfort from his love, if any common sharing in the Spirit, if any tenderness and compassion, [2] then make my joy complete by being like-minded, having the same love, being one in spirit and of one mind. [3] Do nothing out of selfish ambition or vain conceit. Rather, in humility value others above yourselves, [4] not looking to your own interests but each of you to the interests of the others.

[5] In your relationships with one another, have the same mindset as Christ Jesus:

[6] Who, being in very nature[a] God,
   did not consider equality with God
      something to be used to his own
      advantage;
[7] rather, he made himself nothing
   by taking the very nature[b] of a servant,
   being made in human likeness.
[8] And being found in appearance as a man,
   he humbled himself
   by becoming obedient to death —
      even death on a cross!

[9] Therefore God exalted him to the highest
      place
   and gave him the name that is above
      every name,
[10] that at the name of Jesus every knee
      should bow,
   in heaven and on earth and under
      the earth,
[11] and every tongue acknowledge that Jesus
      Christ is Lord,
   to the glory of God the Father.

Do Everything Without Grumbling

[12] Therefore, my dear friends, as you have always obeyed — not only in my presence, but now much more in my absence — continue to work out your salvation with fear and trembling, [13] for it is God who works in you to will and to act in order to fulfill his good purpose.

[14] Do everything without grumbling or arguing, [15] so that you may become blameless and pure, "children of God without fault in a warped and crooked generation."[c] Then you will shine among them like stars in the sky [16] as you hold firmly to the word of life. And then I will be able to boast on the day of Christ that I did not run or labor in vain. [17] But even if I am being poured out like a drink offering on the sacrifice and service coming from your faith, I am glad and rejoice with all of you. [18] So you too should be glad and rejoice with me.

Timothy and Epaphroditus

[19] I hope in the Lord Jesus to send Timothy to you soon, that I also may be cheered when I receive news about you. [20] I have no one else like him, who will show genuine concern for your welfare. [21] For everyone looks out for their own interests, not those of Jesus Christ. [22] But you know that Timothy has proved himself, because as a son with his father he has served with me in the work of the gospel. [23] I hope, therefore, to send him as soon as I see how things go with me. [24] And I am confident in the Lord that I myself will come soon.

[25] But I think it is necessary to send back to you Epaphroditus, my brother, co-worker and fellow soldier, who is also your messenger, whom you sent to take care of my needs. [26] For he longs for all of you and is distressed because you heard he was ill. [27] Indeed he was ill, and almost died. But God had mercy on him, and not on him only but also on me, to spare me sorrow upon sorrow. [28] Therefore I am all the more eager to send him, so that when you see him again you may be glad and I may have less anxiety. [29] So then, welcome him in the Lord with great joy, and honor people like him, [30] because he almost died for the work of Christ. He risked his life to make up for the help you yourselves could not give me.

No Confidence in the Flesh

3 Further, my brothers and sisters, rejoice in the Lord! It is no trouble for me

---

[a] 6 Or *in the form of*   [b] 7 Or *the form*   [c] 15 Deut. 32:5

A Single Word

By Catherine Fitzgerald

READ: Philippians 4:4–8

As the New Year approached, I decided that instead of making a resolution that would most certainly be broken, I'd choose a word to work toward that God would reveal to me. My word, *joy*, came quickly. It was almost comical considering the circumstances the year was bringing. My husband deployed, I brought a new baby home shortly afterward, and my five-year-old struggled with the adjustment of a new brother and daddy leaving again. God seemed to be playing a cosmic joke on me with such a word as *joy*.

I had to dig deep to understand what this word meant for me. In my quiet time, I was studying Philippians and noticed that Paul was able to find joy in the midst of much more difficulty than I was enduring. Here he was, writing while under house arrest, chained to a prison guard and facing execution if convicted of the charges against him. Surely if he could find joy, so could I. His keys to having joy during trials are still applicable to us as we face challenges today as military wives:

1. *Rejoice in the Lord* (see verse 4). Joy is a steadiness of the soul, not the fluctuating instability of happiness. True joy is found in the Lord when we understand the gift of Christ's death and resurrection and gain knowledge of his character through his Word.

2. *Pray about everything.* Constant communication with our heavenly Father is the antidote for an anxious heart. Prayer is to be supplemented with thanksgiving in order for God's overwhelming peace to guard our hearts and minds from the plague of worry (see verses 6–7).

3. *Think about a few things.* The human mind is a wonderfully powerful creation. Paul knew this because he knew the One who created it. He knew our minds are prone to wander from the goodness of God and into the darkness of despair. He called for us to orient our thoughts to the things of the Lord — things that are true, noble, right, pure, lovely, admirable, excellent and praiseworthy (see verse 8). This requires that we be aware of those things that threaten to derail our thinking and be willing to rid our lives of the distractions that pull our minds away from our Father.

A single word can change our lives. When we rejoice in the Lord, pray about everything and think about the few things he tells us to, our situations no longer control our emotional state. He can fill our souls with an indescribable gladness if we allow him to!

Rejoice in the Lord always. I will say it again: Rejoice!

PHILIPPIANS 4:4

DEBRIEF
- Do I have joy in the hard times?
- What keeps me from finding true joy?

REPORT
Lord, while circumstances may be difficult, help me find the joy that comes from knowing you and the gift of Christ. Teach me to pray with an attitude of thanksgiving, and help my mind remain focused on your goodness. Amen.

for your next devotional reading, go to page 243

to write the same things to you again, and it is a safeguard for you. ²Watch out for those dogs, those evildoers, those mutilators of the flesh. ³For it is we who are the circumcision, we who serve God by his Spirit, who boast in Christ Jesus, and who put no confidence in the flesh— ⁴though I myself have reasons for such confidence.

If someone else thinks they have reasons to put confidence in the flesh, I have more: ⁵circumcised on the eighth day, of the people of Israel, of the tribe of Benjamin, a Hebrew of Hebrews; in regard to the law, a Pharisee; ⁶as for zeal, persecuting the church; as for righteousness based on the law, faultless.

⁷But whatever were gains to me I now consider loss for the sake of Christ. ⁸What is more, I consider everything a loss because of the surpassing worth of knowing Christ Jesus my Lord, for whose sake I have lost all things. I consider them garbage, that I may gain Christ ⁹and be found in him, not having a righteousness of my own that comes from the law, but that which is through faith in*ᵃ* Christ—the righteousness that comes from God on the basis of faith. ¹⁰I want to know Christ—yes, to know the power of his resurrection and participation in his sufferings, becoming like him in his death, ¹¹and so, somehow, attaining to the resurrection from the dead.

¹²Not that I have already obtained all this, or have already arrived at my goal, but I press on to take hold of that for which Christ Jesus took hold of me. ¹³Brothers and sisters, I do not consider myself yet to have taken hold of it. But one thing I do: Forgetting what is behind and straining toward what is ahead, ¹⁴I press on toward the goal to win the prize for which God has called me heavenward in Christ Jesus.

Following Paul's Example

¹⁵All of us, then, who are mature should take such a view of things. And if on some point you think differently, that too God will make clear to you. ¹⁶Only let us live up to what we have already attained.

¹⁷Join together in following my example, brothers and sisters, and just as you have us as a model, keep your eyes on those who live as we do. ¹⁸For, as I have often told you before and now tell you again even with tears, many live as enemies of the cross of Christ. ¹⁹Their destiny is destruction, their god is their stomach, and their glory is in their shame. Their mind is set on earthly things. ²⁰But our citizenship is in heaven. And we eagerly await a Savior from there, the Lord Jesus Christ, ²¹who, by the power that enables him to bring everything under his control, will transform our lowly bodies so that they will be like his glorious body.

Closing Appeal for Steadfastness and Unity

4 Therefore, my brothers and sisters, you whom I love and long for, my joy and crown, stand firm in the Lord in this way, dear friends!

²I plead with Euodia and I plead with Syntyche to be of the same mind in the Lord. ³Yes, and I ask you, my true companion, help these women since they have contended at my side in the cause of the gospel, along with Clement and the rest of my co-workers, whose names are in the book of life.

Final Exhortations

⁴Rejoice in the Lord always. I will say it again: Rejoice! ⁵Let your gentleness be evident to all. The Lord is near. ⁶Do not be anxious about anything, but in every situation, by prayer and petition, with thanksgiving, present your requests to God. ⁷And the peace of God, which transcends all understanding, will guard your hearts and your minds in Christ Jesus.

⁸Finally, brothers and sisters, whatever is true, whatever is noble, whatever is right, whatever is pure, whatever is lovely, whatever is admirable—if anything is excellent or praiseworthy—think about such things. ⁹Whatever you have learned or received or heard from me, or seen in me—put it into practice. And the God of peace will be with you.

Thanks for Their Gifts

¹⁰I rejoiced greatly in the Lord that at last you renewed your concern for me. Indeed, you were concerned, but you had no opportunity to show it. ¹¹I am not saying this

ᵃ 9 Or *through the faithfulness of*

Is it "Tenor Play Eep"?

By Sarah Ball

READ: Philippians 4:8–9

Mom, is *Star Wars* 'tenor play eep'?" my daughter asked one evening. "What?" I asked, confused. "I mean, is *Star Wars* okay by Philippians 4:8? Is it true, noble, pure and all that?"

I finally understood what she was asking. During our family devotions, we had been memorizing Philippians 4:8. The length of the verse was challenging for my younger children, so we were using an acronym recommended in *Sword Fighting*, by Karyn Henley: TeNoR PLAy EeP. True, Noble, Right, Pure, Lovely, Admirable, Excellent, Praiseworthy. It sounds strange, but it worked for my children. Now it sounded as if they were a step ahead of me on the application of it.

My son and daughter had been discussing the "Tenor Play Eep" qualities of *Star Wars* and had decided that some parts weren't pure and noble but that fighting to protect the innocent and stop evil should be considered right and praiseworthy.

I was challenged by their application of the verse to start filtering my own entertainment more carefully. If *Star Wars* was deserving of scrutiny, what about my TV choices?

As Paul was concluding his letter to the Philippians, he instructed them on the right kinds of thoughts to seek. Why? Because the things we see and hear become the contents of our minds, which influence what we say and do.

Jesus taught about this when he said, "The mouth speaks what the heart is full of. A good man brings good things out of the good stored up in him, and an evil man brings evil things out of the evil stored up in him" (Matthew 12:34–35). Paul's list helps us evaluate our hearts and mouths. Rumors about people in my husband's unit: true? Late night TV shows: noble? Ending a friendship over a questionable quarrel: right? The music playing in my car: pure? Conflicts within my family support group: lovely? My attitude toward my employer: admirable? My interactions with difficult neighbors: excellent? Complaints about our current housing: praiseworthy?

Many things in our environment fall short of God's standards. How can we possibly avoid them all when we live in a world corrupted by sin? Notice Paul's instruction to the Philippian believers: Think about things that are true, noble, right, pure, lovely, admirable, excellent, praiseworthy. Our challenge is to consciously choose thoughts that are "Tenor Play Eep." In doing so, we become more able to do as Jesus taught: Bring good things out of the good stored up in our minds and hearts.

Finally, brothers and sisters, whatever is true, whatever is noble, whatever is right, whatever is pure, whatever is lovely, whatever is admirable — if anything is excellent or praiseworthy — think about such things.
PHILIPPIANS 4:8

DEBRIEF
- Do I focus my mind on thoughts that are "Tenor Play Eep"?
- What choices can I make today to fill my heart and mind with good things?

REPORT
Lord, I ask you to turn my mind away from sinful words and thoughts. Help me to be mindful of the choices I make each day. And please fill my heart and mind with thoughts that are true, noble, right, pure, lovely, admirable, excellent and praiseworthy. In Jesus' name I pray. Amen.

for your next devotional reading, go to page 247

because I am in need, for I have learned to be content whatever the circumstances. [12] I know what it is to be in need, and I know what it is to have plenty. I have learned the secret of being content in any and every situation, whether well fed or hungry, whether living in plenty or in want. [13] I can do all this through him who gives me strength.

[14] Yet it was good of you to share in my troubles. [15] Moreover, as you Philippians know, in the early days of your acquaintance with the gospel, when I set out from Macedonia, not one church shared with me in the matter of giving and receiving, except you only; [16] for even when I was in Thessalonica, you sent me aid more than once when I was in need. [17] Not that I desire your gifts; what I desire is that more be credited to your account. [18] I have received full payment and have more than enough. I am amply supplied, now that I have received from Epaphroditus the gifts you sent. They are a fragrant offering, an acceptable sacrifice, pleasing to God. [19] And my God will meet all your needs according to the riches of his glory in Christ Jesus.

[20] To our God and Father be glory for ever and ever. Amen.

Final Greetings

[21] Greet all God's people in Christ Jesus. The brothers and sisters who are with me send greetings. [22] All God's people here send you greetings, especially those who belong to Caesar's household.

[23] The grace of the Lord Jesus Christ be with your spirit. Amen.[a]

---

[a] 23 Some manuscripts do not have *Amen*.

Colossians

1 Paul, an apostle of Christ Jesus by the will of God, and Timothy our brother,

² To God's holy people in Colossae, the faithful brothers and sisters*a* in Christ:

Grace and peace to you from God our Father.*b*

Thanksgiving and Prayer

³ We always thank God, the Father of our Lord Jesus Christ, when we pray for you, ⁴ because we have heard of your faith in Christ Jesus and of the love you have for all God's people — ⁵ the faith and love that spring from the hope stored up for you in heaven and about which you have already heard in the true message of the gospel ⁶ that has come to you. In the same way, the gospel is bearing fruit and growing throughout the whole world — just as it has been doing among you since the day you heard it and truly understood God's grace. ⁷ You learned it from Epaphras, our dear fellow servant,*c* who is a faithful minister of Christ on our*d* behalf, ⁸ and who also told us of your love in the Spirit.

⁹ For this reason, since the day we heard about you, we have not stopped praying for you. We continually ask God to fill you with the knowledge of his will through all the wisdom and understanding that the Spirit gives,*e* ¹⁰ so that you may live a life worthy of the Lord and please him in every way: bearing fruit in every good work, growing in the knowledge of God, ¹¹ being strengthened with all power according to his glorious might so that you may have great endurance and patience, ¹² and giving joyful thanks to the Father, who has qualified you*f* to share in the inheritance of his holy people in the kingdom of light. ¹³ For he has rescued us from the dominion of darkness and brought us into the kingdom of the Son he loves, ¹⁴ in whom we have redemption, the forgiveness of sins.

The Supremacy of the Son of God

¹⁵ The Son is the image of the invisible God, the firstborn over all creation. ¹⁶ For in him all things were created: things in heaven and on earth, visible and invisible, whether thrones or powers or rulers or authorities; all things have been created through him and for him. ¹⁷ He is before all things, and in him all things hold together. ¹⁸ And he is the head of the body, the church; he is the beginning and the firstborn from among the dead, so that in everything he might have the supremacy. ¹⁹ For God was pleased to have all his fullness dwell in him, ²⁰ and through him to reconcile to himself all things, whether things on earth or things in heaven, by making peace through his blood, shed on the cross.

²¹ Once you were alienated from God and were enemies in your minds because of*g* your evil behavior. ²² But now he has reconciled you by Christ's physical body through death to present you holy in his sight, without blemish and free from accusation — ²³ if you continue in your faith, established and firm, and do not move from the hope held out in the gospel. This is the gospel that you heard and that has been proclaimed to every creature under heaven, and of which I, Paul, have become a servant.

Paul's Labor for the Church

²⁴ Now I rejoice in what I am suffering for you, and I fill up in my flesh what is still lacking in regard to Christ's afflictions, for the sake of his body, which is the church. ²⁵ I have become its servant by the commission God gave me to present to you the word of

---

a 2 The Greek word for *brothers and sisters* (*adelphoi*) refers here to believers, both men and women, as part of God's family; also in 4:15.   *b* 2 Some manuscripts *Father and the Lord Jesus Christ*   *c* 7 Or *slave*
d 7 Some manuscripts *your*   *e* 9 Or *all spiritual wisdom and understanding*   *f* 12 Some manuscripts *us*
g 21 Or *minds, as shown by*

God in its fullness— [26]the mystery that has been kept hidden for ages and generations, but is now disclosed to the Lord's people. [27]To them God has chosen to make known among the Gentiles the glorious riches of this mystery, which is Christ in you, the hope of glory.

[28]He is the one we proclaim, admonishing and teaching everyone with all wisdom, so that we may present everyone fully mature in Christ. [29]To this end I strenuously contend with all the energy Christ so powerfully works in me.

2 I want you to know how hard I am contending for you and for those at Laodicea, and for all who have not met me personally. [2]My goal is that they may be encouraged in heart and united in love, so that they may have the full riches of complete understanding, in order that they may know the mystery of God, namely, Christ, [3]in whom are hidden all the treasures of wisdom and knowledge. [4]I tell you this so that no one may deceive you by fine-sounding arguments. [5]For though I am absent from you in body, I am present with you in spirit and delight to see how disciplined you are and how firm your faith in Christ is.

Spiritual Fullness in Christ

[6]So then, just as you received Christ Jesus as Lord, continue to live your lives in him, [7]rooted and built up in him, strengthened in the faith as you were taught, and overflowing with thankfulness.

[8]See to it that no one takes you captive through hollow and deceptive philosophy, which depends on human tradition and the elemental spiritual forces[a] of this world rather than on Christ.

[9]For in Christ all the fullness of the Deity lives in bodily form, [10]and in Christ you have been brought to fullness. He is the head over every power and authority. [11]In him you were also circumcised with a circumcision not performed by human hands. Your whole self ruled by the flesh[b] was put off when you were circumcised by[c] Christ, [12]having been buried with him in baptism, in which you were also raised with him through your faith

in the working of God, who raised him from the dead.

[13]When you were dead in your sins and in the uncircumcision of your flesh, God made you[d] alive with Christ. He forgave us all our sins, [14]having canceled the charge of our legal indebtedness, which stood against us and condemned us; he has taken it away, nailing it to the cross. [15]And having disarmed the powers and authorities, he made a public spectacle of them, triumphing over them by the cross.[e]

Freedom From Human Rules

[16]Therefore do not let anyone judge you by what you eat or drink, or with regard to a religious festival, a New Moon celebration or a Sabbath day. [17]These are a shadow of the things that were to come; the reality, however, is found in Christ. [18]Do not let anyone who delights in false humility and the worship of angels disqualify you. Such a person also goes into great detail about what they have seen; they are puffed up with idle notions by their unspiritual mind. [19]They have lost connection with the head, from whom the whole body, supported and held together by its ligaments and sinews, grows as God causes it to grow.

[20]Since you died with Christ to the elemental spiritual forces of this world, why, as though you still belonged to the world, do you submit to its rules: [21]"Do not handle! Do not taste! Do not touch!"? [22]These rules, which have to do with things that are all destined to perish with use, are based on merely human commands and teachings. [23]Such regulations indeed have an appearance of wisdom, with their self-imposed worship, their false humility and their harsh treatment of the body, but they lack any value in restraining sensual indulgence.

Living as Those Made Alive in Christ

3 Since, then, you have been raised with Christ, set your hearts on things above, where Christ is, seated at the right hand of God. [2]Set your minds on things above, not on earthly things. [3]For you died, and your life is now hidden with Christ in God. [4]When

---

[a] 8 Or *the basic principles*; also in verse 20   [b] 11 In contexts like this, the Greek word for *flesh (sarx)* refers to the sinful state of human beings, often presented as a power in opposition to the Spirit; also in verse 13.   [c] 11 Or *put off in the circumcision of*   [d] 13 Some manuscripts *us*   [e] 15 Or *them in him*

Rooted in Christ

By Ronda Sturgill

READ: Colossians 2:6–15

How many major life changes have you experienced in the past two years? As a military wife, my guess is that you've experienced at least one. If I had to describe one aspect of my husband's 26-year military career that has affected me the most, it would be all the changes we've had to make — changes in housing, friends, jobs, schools, churches, ministry opportunities. I'm sure you could add a few more items of your own to this list.

No matter whether or not the change is good for us and our families, we initially process all change as loss. We must leave behind what is familiar to us and start all over again in most areas of our day-to-day lives. Even simple tasks such as turning on the utilities or arranging Internet service at our new living quarters can become overwhelming. Changes are emotionally charged and physically draining, even for those who have years of experience.

So how do we cope with all the changes that are thrust upon us? What keeps us steady when everything else around us is a-rocking and a-rolling? We remain rooted in Christ.

To be rooted in something means that we are firmly established. We are embedded, entwined and entangled to the point that it's hard to separate us from what we're rooted in. Paul says in Colossians 2:6–7 that being rooted in Christ is what will keep us steady and constant when the world we live in is turning upside down.

Being rooted in Christ means that we spend time with him. We read God's Word and regularly attend church. We look for mentors and friends who will keep us accountable and help us live out our faith in everyday life. We can grow stronger internally by making every effort to add to our faith goodness, knowledge, self-control, perseverance, godliness, mutual affection and love. For if we have these things, they will keep us from being ineffective and unproductive in our knowledge of our Lord Jesus Christ (see 2 Peter 1:5–8). These internal things remain constant when our external situation keeps changing.

Paul wraps up Colossians 2:7 by challenging us to overflow with thankfulness. A grateful heart acknowledges that God is the giver of all things and that all things given from his hand are ultimately good. When we're deeply rooted and established in Christ, we *can* be thankful for each one of the changes that comes. The deeper our roots, the more established we are in Christ. This is the *only* thing we have that won't change!

So then, just as you received Christ Jesus as Lord, continue to live your lives in him, rooted and built up in him, strengthened in the faith as you were taught, and overflowing with thankfulness.

COLOSSIANS 2:6 – 7

DEBRIEF
- What value do I see in being rooted and established in Christ?
- What can I commit to doing every day for the next 30 days that will help my roots grow deeper? How can I motivate myself to stick with it?

REPORT
Dear heavenly Father, I want my roots to be deeply established in Jesus. When changes come, help me remain strong and steady. Help my heart to always overflow with thankfulness, even in the midst of the most difficult changes. Thank you for being constant in my life. Amen.

for your next devotional reading, go to page 248

A SOLDIER'S WIFE

By Karen Whiting

A tall, slender woman in her 50s moved from bed to bed gently speaking to wounded soldiers. She knew each man by name, his hometown, family situation and the nature of his wounds. When asked her name, she simply responded, "I'm a soldier's wife," and let them know her husband had been wounded in France during World War II.

Her name was Ava Harrison, wife of Lieutenant General William K. Harrison, and she spent her days ministering in a hospital in Japan while her husband served as chief negotiator for peace with Korea. They had married on December 13, 1917, only months after William graduated from West Point Military Academy. They raised three children and faithfully read the Bible with them.

When Ava and her husband moved to Japan during the Korean conflict, her children had all married, so she spent her time comforting soldiers. No wound frightened the smile off her face or the encouraging words from her lips. One young man, considered a "basket case," had had both arms and legs amputated, and was blind. Reporters left the ward because the sight made them feel so miserable and hopeless. But Ava shared about that man's strength and faith. He had told her that although he could no longer see with his eyes, he could see God now as he never had before.

When visiting the soldiers, she always brought the conversation around to Jesus and shared her faith. When a soldier wanted to know more about salvation, she found a chaplain or missionary to lead the soldier to Christ.

In addition, Ava ran errands for the men and inspired many of them to start knitting as a way to strengthen their hands and arms. Knitting also gave them something to do to distract their minds from their pain and sorrow. She wrote to many of their mothers to share updates and give encouragement to worried parents far away.

Ava always celebrated victories. Once recovered enough to go home, soldiers received invitations to dine at her home, where they usually became aware of her identity. She also had several servants in her home in Japan and led them in reading the Bible daily. She focused on the Lord and not the misery of war.

Upon her death, her husband wrote: "She was a faithful servant of Christ, a faithful and loving wife and mother, a gracious woman. She was God's gift to me."

Prayer: *Lord, help us keep our minds on things above.*

Since, then, you have been raised with Christ, set your hearts on things above, where Christ is, seated at the right hand of God. Set your minds on things above, not on earthly things. For you died, and your life is now hidden with Christ in God. When Christ, who is your life, appears, then you also will appear with him in glory.

COLOSSIANS 3:1 – 4

 for your next devotional reading, go to page 253

Christ, who is your *a* life, appears, then you also will appear with him in glory.

⁵Put to death, therefore, whatever belongs to your earthly nature: sexual immorality, impurity, lust, evil desires and greed, which is idolatry. ⁶Because of these, the wrath of God is coming.*b* ⁷You used to walk in these ways, in the life you once lived. ⁸But now you must also rid yourselves of all such things as these: anger, rage, malice, slander, and filthy language from your lips. ⁹Do not lie to each other, since you have taken off your old self with its practices ¹⁰and have put on the new self, which is being renewed in knowledge in the image of its Creator. ¹¹Here there is no Gentile or Jew, circumcised or uncircumcised, barbarian, Scythian, slave or free, but Christ is all, and is in all.

¹²Therefore, as God's chosen people, holy and dearly loved, clothe yourselves with compassion, kindness, humility, gentleness and patience. ¹³Bear with each other and forgive one another if any of you has a grievance against someone. Forgive as the Lord forgave you. ¹⁴And over all these virtues put on love, which binds them all together in perfect unity.

¹⁵Let the peace of Christ rule in your hearts, since as members of one body you were called to peace. And be thankful. ¹⁶Let the message of Christ dwell among you richly as you teach and admonish one another with all wisdom through psalms, hymns, and songs from the Spirit, singing to God with gratitude in your hearts. ¹⁷And whatever you do, whether in word or deed, do it all in the name of the Lord Jesus, giving thanks to God the Father through him.

Instructions for Christian Households

¹⁸Wives, submit yourselves to your husbands, as is fitting in the Lord.

¹⁹Husbands, love your wives and do not be harsh with them.

²⁰Children, obey your parents in everything, for this pleases the Lord.

²¹Fathers,*c* do not embitter your children, or they will become discouraged.

²²Slaves, obey your earthly masters in everything; and do it, not only when their eye is on you and to curry their favor, but with sincerity of heart and reverence for the Lord. ²³Whatever you do, work at it with all your heart, as working for the Lord, not for human masters, ²⁴since you know that you will receive an inheritance from the Lord as a reward. It is the Lord Christ you are serving. ²⁵Anyone who does wrong will be repaid for their wrongs, and there is no favoritism.

4 Masters, provide your slaves with what is right and fair, because you know that you also have a Master in heaven.

Further Instructions

²Devote yourselves to prayer, being watchful and thankful. ³And pray for us, too, that God may open a door for our message, so that we may proclaim the mystery of Christ, for which I am in chains. ⁴Pray that I may proclaim it clearly, as I should. ⁵Be wise in the way you act toward outsiders; make the most of every opportunity. ⁶Let your conversation be always full of grace, seasoned with salt, so that you may know how to answer everyone.

Final Greetings

⁷Tychicus will tell you all the news about me. He is a dear brother, a faithful minister and fellow servant*d* in the Lord. ⁸I am sending him to you for the express purpose that you may know about our*e* circumstances and that he may encourage your hearts. ⁹He is coming with Onesimus, our faithful and dear brother, who is one of you. They will tell you everything that is happening here.

¹⁰My fellow prisoner Aristarchus sends you his greetings, as does Mark, the cousin of Barnabas. (You have received instructions about him; if he comes to you, welcome him.) ¹¹Jesus, who is called Justus, also sends greetings. These are the only Jews*f* among my co-workers for the kingdom of God, and they have proved a comfort to me. ¹²Epaphras, who is one of you and a servant of Christ Jesus, sends greetings. He is always wrestling in prayer for you, that you may stand firm in all the will of God, mature and fully assured. ¹³I vouch for him that he

---

a 4 Some manuscripts *our*   *b* 6 Some early manuscripts *coming on those who are disobedient*
c 21 Or *Parents*   *d* 7 Or *slave*; also in verse 12   *e* 8 Some manuscripts *that he may know about your*
f 11 Greek *only ones of the circumcision group*

is working hard for you and for those at Laodicea and Hierapolis. [14]Our dear friend
Luke, the doctor, and Demas send greetings.
[15]Give my greetings to the brothers and sisters at Laodicea, and to Nympha and the
church in her house.

[16]After this letter has been read to you, see
that it is also read in the church of the Laod-
iceans and that you in turn read the letter
from Laodicea.

[17]Tell Archippus: "See to it that you complete the ministry you have received in the
Lord."

[18]I, Paul, write this greeting in my own
hand. Remember my chains. Grace be with
you.

1 Thessalonians

1 Paul, Silas[a] and Timothy,

To the church of the Thessalonians in God the Father and the Lord Jesus Christ:

Grace and peace to you.

Thanksgiving for the Thessalonians' Faith

[2] We always thank God for all of you and continually mention you in our prayers. [3] We remember before our God and Father your work produced by faith, your labor prompted by love, and your endurance inspired by hope in our Lord Jesus Christ.

[4] For we know, brothers and sisters[b] loved by God, that he has chosen you, [5] because our gospel came to you not simply with words but also with power, with the Holy Spirit and deep conviction. You know how we lived among you for your sake. [6] You became imitators of us and of the Lord, for you welcomed the message in the midst of severe suffering with the joy given by the Holy Spirit. [7] And so you became a model to all the believers in Macedonia and Achaia. [8] The Lord's message rang out from you not only in Macedonia and Achaia — your faith in God has become known everywhere. Therefore we do not need to say anything about it, [9] for they themselves report what kind of reception you gave us. They tell how you turned to God from idols to serve the living and true God, [10] and to wait for his Son from heaven, whom he raised from the dead — Jesus, who rescues us from the coming wrath.

Paul's Ministry in Thessalonica

2 You know, brothers and sisters, that our visit to you was not without results. [2] We had previously suffered and been treated outrageously in Philippi, as you know, but with the help of our God we dared to tell you his gospel in the face of strong opposition. [3] For the appeal we make does not spring from error or impure motives, nor are we trying to trick you. [4] On the contrary, we speak as those approved by God to be entrusted with the gospel. We are not trying to please people but God, who tests our hearts. [5] You know we never used flattery, nor did we put on a mask to cover up greed — God is our witness. [6] We were not looking for praise from people, not from you or anyone else, even though as apostles of Christ we could have asserted our authority. [7] Instead, we were like young children[c] among you.

Just as a nursing mother cares for her children, [8] so we cared for you. Because we loved you so much, we were delighted to share with you not only the gospel of God but our lives as well. [9] Surely you remember, brothers and sisters, our toil and hardship; we worked night and day in order not to be a burden to anyone while we preached the gospel of God to you. [10] You are witnesses, and so is God, of how holy, righteous and blameless we were among you who believed. [11] For you know that we dealt with each of you as a father deals with his own children, [12] encouraging, comforting and urging you to live lives worthy of God, who calls you into his kingdom and glory.

[13] And we also thank God continually because, when you received the word of God, which you heard from us, you accepted it not as a human word, but as it actually is, the word of God, which is indeed at work in you who believe. [14] For you, brothers and sisters, became imitators of God's churches in Judea, which are in Christ Jesus: You suffered from your own people the same things those churches suffered from the Jews [15] who killed the Lord Jesus and the prophets and also drove us out. They displease God and are hostile to everyone [16] in their

---

[a] 1 Greek *Silvanus*, a variant of *Silas*   [b] 4 The Greek word for *brothers and sisters* (*adelphoi*) refers here to believers, both men and women, as part of God's family; also in 2:1, 9, 14, 17; 3:7; 4:1, 10, 13; 5:1, 4, 12, 14, 25, 27.   [c] 7 Some manuscripts *were gentle*

effort to keep us from speaking to the Gentiles so that they may be saved. In this way they always heap up their sins to the limit. The wrath of God has come upon them at last.[a]

Paul's Longing to See the Thessalonians

[17]But, brothers and sisters, when we were orphaned by being separated from you for a short time (in person, not in thought), out of our intense longing we made every effort to see you. [18]For we wanted to come to you — certainly I, Paul, did, again and again — but Satan blocked our way. [19]For what is our hope, our joy, or the crown in which we will glory in the presence of our Lord Jesus when he comes? Is it not you? [20]Indeed, you are our glory and joy.

3 So when we could stand it no longer, we thought it best to be left by ourselves in Athens. [2]We sent Timothy, who is our brother and co-worker in God's service in spreading the gospel of Christ, to strengthen and encourage you in your faith, [3]so that no one would be unsettled by these trials. For you know quite well that we are destined for them. [4]In fact, when we were with you, we kept telling you that we would be persecuted. And it turned out that way, as you well know. [5]For this reason, when I could stand it no longer, I sent to find out about your faith. I was afraid that in some way the tempter had tempted you and that our labors might have been in vain.

Timothy's Encouraging Report

[6]But Timothy has just now come to us from you and has brought good news about your faith and love. He has told us that you always have pleasant memories of us and that you long to see us, just as we also long to see you. [7]Therefore, brothers and sisters, in all our distress and persecution we were encouraged about you because of your faith. [8]For now we really live, since you are standing firm in the Lord. [9]How can we thank God enough for you in return for all the joy we have in the presence of our God because of you? [10]Night and day we pray most earnestly that we may see you again and supply what is lacking in your faith.

[11]Now may our God and Father himself and our Lord Jesus clear the way for us to come to you. [12]May the Lord make your love increase and overflow for each other and for everyone else, just as ours does for you. [13]May he strengthen your hearts so that you will be blameless and holy in the presence of our God and Father when our Lord Jesus comes with all his holy ones.

Living to Please God

4 As for other matters, brothers and sisters, we instructed you how to live in order to please God, as in fact you are living. Now we ask you and urge you in the Lord Jesus to do this more and more. [2]For you know what instructions we gave you by the authority of the Lord Jesus.

[3]It is God's will that you should be sanctified: that you should avoid sexual immorality; [4]that each of you should learn to control your own body[b] in a way that is holy and honorable, [5]not in passionate lust like the pagans, who do not know God; [6]and that in this matter no one should wrong or take advantage of a brother or sister.[c] The Lord will punish all those who commit such sins, as we told you and warned you before. [7]For God did not call us to be impure, but to live a holy life. [8]Therefore, anyone who rejects this instruction does not reject a human being but God, the very God who gives you his Holy Spirit.

[9]Now about your love for one another we do not need to write to you, for you yourselves have been taught by God to love each other. [10]And in fact, you do love all of God's family throughout Macedonia. Yet we urge you, brothers and sisters, to do so more and more, [11]and to make it your ambition to lead a quiet life: You should mind your own business and work with your hands, just as we told you, [12]so that your daily life may win the respect of outsiders and so that you will not be dependent on anybody.

Believers Who Have Died

[13]Brothers and sisters, we do not want you to be uninformed about those who sleep in death, so that you do not grieve like the rest of mankind, who have no hope. [14]For we

---

[a] 16 Or *them fully*   [b] 4 Or *learn to live with your own wife*; or *learn to acquire a wife*   [c] 6 The Greek word for *brother or sister* (*adelphos*) refers here to a believer, whether man or woman, as part of God's family.

Give Thanks

By Catherine Fitzgerald

READ: 1 Thessalonians 5:12–24

As I wrestled with my emotions and thoughts one day, God brought 1 Thessalonians 5:18 to my mind: "Give thanks," he whispered. *Of course!* It was a simple solution to such a complicated problem.

It had come on quickly, starting with shortness in my words and an overall bad attitude. Deployment was imminent and instead of enjoying our last few moments together, I was wasting them with an increasingly bitter heart.

The fear of having my husband gone during the birth of our second child was taking its toll on me. The thought of parenting my four-year-old and a newborn alone overwhelmed me. Anger welled up inside as I was reminded that this was our fifth deployment in three years. I had "done my time," and it just wasn't fair to go through yet another deployment.

Give thanks, God's Word reminded me.

So I started a gratitude journal, listing things I was thankful for. Slowly but surely, my focus was taken off the challenges ahead and put back on all the blessings God had given me.

It seems like such a simplistic answer: *Give thanks.* But it truly is what makes the difference between those who trudge through this life with a complaining mouth and hostile heart and those who flourish in the challenges that come their way. Our lives are riddled with tests, trials, hardships and reasons to be resentful. Even when our military member is *home*, there is still the constant stress of an unpredictable schedule and long work hours.

Yet when we start to give thanks in light of those things, we can see an incredible work being done within our heart. Our eyes can be opened to God's provision and blessing in our life. Our mouth can start to speak of the joy that manifests from the depths of our soul. Our ears can hear the sweetness that he has already done.

The question then becomes *how*? "Rejoice always, pray continually, give thanks in all circumstances" (1 Thessalonians 5:16–18). When we blend rejoicing, prayer and thanksgiving into our lives, the result can be extraordinary. We cannot, however, expect that we will naturally fall into these habits. It requires work to look at our life through the lens of the gospel: We deserved nothing; God gave us everything. With an outlook like that, anything else can be seen as a gift!

The will of our Father is for us to live a life that is filled with gratitude, not griping. This is not always easy to do, yet he is faithful when we try!

Give thanks in all circumstances; for this is God's will for you in Christ Jesus.

1 THESSALONIANS 5:18

DEBRIEF

- In what areas of my life am I not expressing my thanks to God?
- What are some practical ways to start being thankful?

REPORT

Lord, help me see the blessings you have given me. Show me how to give thanks in the midst of difficulty. Teach me to live a life of joy, prayer and gratitude in every circumstance. Amen.

for your next devotional reading, go to page 259

believe that Jesus died and rose again, and so we believe that God will bring with Jesus those who have fallen asleep in him. [15]According to the Lord's word, we tell you that we who are still alive, who are left until the coming of the Lord, will certainly not precede those who have fallen asleep. [16]For the Lord himself will come down from heaven, with a loud command, with the voice of the archangel and with the trumpet call of God, and the dead in Christ will rise first. [17]After that, we who are still alive and are left will be caught up together with them in the clouds to meet the Lord in the air. And so we will be with the Lord forever. [18]Therefore encourage one another with these words.

The Day of the Lord

5 Now, brothers and sisters, about times and dates we do not need to write to you, [2]for you know very well that the day of the Lord will come like a thief in the night. [3]While people are saying, "Peace and safety," destruction will come on them suddenly, as labor pains on a pregnant woman, and they will not escape.

[4]But you, brothers and sisters, are not in darkness so that this day should surprise you like a thief. [5]You are all children of the light and children of the day. We do not belong to the night or to the darkness. [6]So then, let us not be like others, who are asleep, but let us be awake and sober. [7]For those who sleep, sleep at night, and those who get drunk, get drunk at night. [8]But since we belong to the day, let us be sober, putting on faith and love as a breastplate, and the hope of salvation as a helmet. [9]For God did not appoint us to suffer wrath but to receive salvation through our Lord Jesus Christ. [10]He died for us so that, whether we are awake or asleep, we may live together with him. [11]Therefore encourage one another and build each other up, just as in fact you are doing.

Final Instructions

[12]Now we ask you, brothers and sisters, to acknowledge those who work hard among you, who care for you in the Lord and who admonish you. [13]Hold them in the highest regard in love because of their work. Live in peace with each other. [14]And we urge you, brothers and sisters, warn those who are idle and disruptive, encourage the disheartened, help the weak, be patient with everyone. [15]Make sure that nobody pays back wrong for wrong, but always strive to do what is good for each other and for everyone else.

[16]Rejoice always, [17]pray continually, [18]give thanks in all circumstances; for this is God's will for you in Christ Jesus.

[19]Do not quench the Spirit. [20]Do not treat prophecies with contempt [21]but test them all; hold on to what is good, [22]reject every kind of evil.

[23]May God himself, the God of peace, sanctify you through and through. May your whole spirit, soul and body be kept blameless at the coming of our Lord Jesus Christ. [24]The one who calls you is faithful, and he will do it.

[25]Brothers and sisters, pray for us. [26]Greet all God's people with a holy kiss. [27]I charge you before the Lord to have this letter read to all the brothers and sisters.

[28]The grace of our Lord Jesus Christ be with you.

2 Thessalonians

1

Paul, Silas[a] and Timothy,

To the church of the Thessalonians in God our Father and the Lord Jesus Christ:

[2]Grace and peace to you from God the Father and the Lord Jesus Christ.

Thanksgiving and Prayer

[3]We ought always to thank God for you, brothers and sisters,[b] and rightly so, because your faith is growing more and more, and the love all of you have for one another is increasing. [4]Therefore, among God's churches we boast about your perseverance and faith in all the persecutions and trials you are enduring.

[5]All this is evidence that God's judgment is right, and as a result you will be counted worthy of the kingdom of God, for which you are suffering. [6]God is just: He will pay back trouble to those who trouble you [7]and give relief to you who are troubled, and to us as well. This will happen when the Lord Jesus is revealed from heaven in blazing fire with his powerful angels. [8]He will punish those who do not know God and do not obey the gospel of our Lord Jesus. [9]They will be punished with everlasting destruction and shut out from the presence of the Lord and from the glory of his might [10]on the day he comes to be glorified in his holy people and to be marveled at among all those who have believed. This includes you, because you believed our testimony to you.

[11]With this in mind, we constantly pray for you, that our God may make you worthy of his calling, and that by his power he may bring to fruition your every desire for goodness and your every deed prompted by faith. [12]We pray this so that the name of our Lord Jesus may be glorified in you, and you in him, according to the grace of our God and the Lord Jesus Christ.[c]

The Man of Lawlessness

2

Concerning the coming of our Lord Jesus Christ and our being gathered to him, we ask you, brothers and sisters, [2]not to become easily unsettled or alarmed by the teaching allegedly from us — whether by a prophecy or by word of mouth or by letter — asserting that the day of the Lord has already come. [3]Don't let anyone deceive you in any way, for that day will not come until the rebellion occurs and the man of lawlessness[d] is revealed, the man doomed to destruction. [4]He will oppose and will exalt himself over everything that is called God or is worshiped, so that he sets himself up in God's temple, proclaiming himself to be God.

[5]Don't you remember that when I was with you I used to tell you these things? [6]And now you know what is holding him back, so that he may be revealed at the proper time. [7]For the secret power of lawlessness is already at work; but the one who now holds it back will continue to do so till he is taken out of the way. [8]And then the lawless one will be revealed, whom the Lord Jesus will overthrow with the breath of his mouth and destroy by the splendor of his coming. [9]The coming of the lawless one will be in accordance with how Satan works. He will use all sorts of displays of power through signs and wonders that serve the lie, [10]and all the ways that wickedness deceives those who are perishing. They perish because they refused to love the truth and so be saved. [11]For this reason God sends them a powerful delusion so that they will believe the lie [12]and so that all will be condemned who have not believed the truth but have delighted in wickedness.

Stand Firm

[13]But we ought always to thank God for you, brothers and sisters loved by the Lord,

---

[a] 1 Greek *Silvanus*, a variant of *Silas*   [b] 3 The Greek word for *brothers and sisters* (*adelphoi*) refers here to believers, both men and women, as part of God's family; also in 2:1, 13, 15; 3:1, 6, 13.   [c] 12 Or *God and Lord, Jesus Christ*   [d] 3 Some manuscripts *sin*

because God chose you as firstfruits*a* to be saved through the sanctifying work of the Spirit and through belief in the truth. [14]He called you to this through our gospel, that you might share in the glory of our Lord Jesus Christ.

[15]So then, brothers and sisters, stand firm and hold fast to the teachings*b* we passed on to you, whether by word of mouth or by letter. [16]May our Lord Jesus Christ himself and God our Father, who loved us and by his grace gave us eternal encouragement and good hope, [17]encourage your hearts and strengthen you in every good deed and word.

Request for Prayer

3 As for other matters, brothers and sisters, pray for us that the message of the Lord may spread rapidly and be honored, just as it was with you. [2]And pray that we may be delivered from wicked and evil people, for not everyone has faith. [3]But the Lord is faithful, and he will strengthen you and protect you from the evil one. [4]We have confidence in the Lord that you are doing and will continue to do the things we command. [5]May the Lord direct your hearts into God's love and Christ's perseverance.

Warning Against Idleness

[6]In the name of the Lord Jesus Christ, we command you, brothers and sisters, to keep away from every believer who is idle and disruptive and does not live according to the teaching*c* you received from us. [7]For you yourselves know how you ought to follow our example. We were not idle when we were with you, [8]nor did we eat anyone's food without paying for it. On the contrary, we worked night and day, laboring and toiling so that we would not be a burden to any of you. [9]We did this, not because we do not have the right to such help, but in order to offer ourselves as a model for you to imitate. [10]For even when we were with you, we gave you this rule: "The one who is unwilling to work shall not eat."

[11]We hear that some among you are idle and disruptive. They are not busy; they are busybodies. [12]Such people we command and urge in the Lord Jesus Christ to settle down and earn the food they eat. [13]And as for you, brothers and sisters, never tire of doing what is good.

[14]Take special note of anyone who does not obey our instruction in this letter. Do not associate with them, in order that they may feel ashamed. [15]Yet do not regard them as an enemy, but warn them as you would a fellow believer.

Final Greetings

[16]Now may the Lord of peace himself give you peace at all times and in every way. The Lord be with all of you.

[17]I, Paul, write this greeting in my own hand, which is the distinguishing mark in all my letters. This is how I write.

[18]The grace of our Lord Jesus Christ be with you all.

---

a 13 Some manuscripts *because from the beginning God chose you*   *b*15 Or *traditions*   *c*6 Or *tradition*

1 Timothy

1 Paul, an apostle of Christ Jesus by the command of God our Savior and of Christ Jesus our hope,

²To Timothy my true son in the faith:

Grace, mercy and peace from God the Father and Christ Jesus our Lord.

Timothy Charged to Oppose False Teachers

³As I urged you when I went into Macedonia, stay there in Ephesus so that you may command certain people not to teach false doctrines any longer ⁴or to devote themselves to myths and endless genealogies. Such things promote controversial speculations rather than advancing God's work—which is by faith. ⁵The goal of this command is love, which comes from a pure heart and a good conscience and a sincere faith. ⁶Some have departed from these and have turned to meaningless talk. ⁷They want to be teachers of the law, but they do not know what they are talking about or what they so confidently affirm.

⁸We know that the law is good if one uses it properly. ⁹We also know that the law is made not for the righteous but for lawbreakers and rebels, the ungodly and sinful, the unholy and irreligious, for those who kill their fathers or mothers, for murderers, ¹⁰for the sexually immoral, for those practicing homosexuality, for slave traders and liars and perjurers—and for whatever else is contrary to the sound doctrine ¹¹that conforms to the gospel concerning the glory of the blessed God, which he entrusted to me.

The Lord's Grace to Paul

¹²I thank Christ Jesus our Lord, who has given me strength, that he considered me trustworthy, appointing me to his service. ¹³Even though I was once a blasphemer and a persecutor and a violent man, I was shown mercy because I acted in ignorance and unbelief. ¹⁴The grace of our Lord was poured out on me abundantly, along with the faith and love that are in Christ Jesus.

¹⁵Here is a trustworthy saying that deserves full acceptance: Christ Jesus came into the world to save sinners—of whom I am the worst. ¹⁶But for that very reason I was shown mercy so that in me, the worst of sinners, Christ Jesus might display his immense patience as an example for those who would believe in him and receive eternal life. ¹⁷Now to the King eternal, immortal, invisible, the only God, be honor and glory for ever and ever. Amen.

The Charge to Timothy Renewed

¹⁸Timothy, my son, I am giving you this command in keeping with the prophecies once made about you, so that by recalling them you may fight the battle well, ¹⁹holding on to faith and a good conscience, which some have rejected and so have suffered shipwreck with regard to the faith. ²⁰Among them are Hymenaeus and Alexander, whom I have handed over to Satan to be taught not to blaspheme.

Instructions on Worship

2 I urge, then, first of all, that petitions, prayers, intercession and thanksgiving be made for all people— ²for kings and all those in authority, that we may live peaceful and quiet lives in all godliness and holiness. ³This is good, and pleases God our Savior, ⁴who wants all people to be saved and to come to a knowledge of the truth. ⁵For there is one God and one mediator between God and mankind, the man Christ Jesus, ⁶who gave himself as a ransom for all people. This has now been witnessed to at the proper time. ⁷And for this purpose I was appointed a herald and an apostle—I am telling the truth, I am not lying—and a true and faithful teacher of the Gentiles.

⁸Therefore I want the men everywhere to pray, lifting up holy hands without anger or disputing. ⁹I also want the women to

dress modestly, with decency and propriety, adorning themselves, not with elaborate hairstyles or gold or pearls or expensive clothes, [10] but with good deeds, appropriate for women who profess to worship God.

[11] A woman[a] should learn in quietness and full submission. [12] I do not permit a woman to teach or to assume authority over a man;[b] she must be quiet. [13] For Adam was formed first, then Eve. [14] And Adam was not the one deceived; it was the woman who was deceived and became a sinner. [15] But women[c] will be saved through childbearing — if they continue in faith, love and holiness with propriety.

Qualifications for Overseers and Deacons

3 Here is a trustworthy saying: Whoever aspires to be an overseer desires a noble task. [2] Now the overseer is to be above reproach, faithful to his wife, temperate, self-controlled, respectable, hospitable, able to teach, [3] not given to drunkenness, not violent but gentle, not quarrelsome, not a lover of money. [4] He must manage his own family well and see that his children obey him, and he must do so in a manner worthy of full[d] respect. [5] (If anyone does not know how to manage his own family, how can he take care of God's church?) [6] He must not be a recent convert, or he may become conceited and fall under the same judgment as the devil. [7] He must also have a good reputation with outsiders, so that he will not fall into disgrace and into the devil's trap.

[8] In the same way, deacons[e] are to be worthy of respect, sincere, not indulging in much wine, and not pursuing dishonest gain. [9] They must keep hold of the deep truths of the faith with a clear conscience. [10] They must first be tested; and then if there is nothing against them, let them serve as deacons.

[11] In the same way, the women[f] are to be worthy of respect, not malicious talkers but temperate and trustworthy in everything.

[12] A deacon must be faithful to his wife and must manage his children and his household well. [13] Those who have served well gain an excellent standing and great assurance in their faith in Christ Jesus.

Reasons for Paul's Instructions

[14] Although I hope to come to you soon, I am writing you these instructions so that, [15] if I am delayed, you will know how people ought to conduct themselves in God's household, which is the church of the living God, the pillar and foundation of the truth. [16] Beyond all question, the mystery from which true godliness springs is great:

He appeared in the flesh,
    was vindicated by the Spirit,[g]
was seen by angels,
    was preached among the nations,
was believed on in the world,
    was taken up in glory.

4 The Spirit clearly says that in later times some will abandon the faith and follow deceiving spirits and things taught by demons. [2] Such teachings come through hypocritical liars, whose consciences have been seared as with a hot iron. [3] They forbid people to marry and order them to abstain from certain foods, which God created to be received with thanksgiving by those who believe and who know the truth. [4] For everything God created is good, and nothing is to be rejected if it is received with thanksgiving, [5] because it is consecrated by the word of God and prayer.

[6] If you point these things out to the brothers and sisters,[h] you will be a good minister of Christ Jesus, nourished on the truths of the faith and of the good teaching that you have followed. [7] Have nothing to do with godless myths and old wives' tales; rather, train yourself to be godly. [8] For physical training is of some value, but godliness has value for all things, holding promise for both the present life and the life to come. [9] This is a trustworthy saying that deserves full acceptance. [10] That is why we labor and strive, because we have put our hope in the living God, who is the Savior of all people, and especially of those who believe.

---

[a] 11 Or wife; also in verse 12   [b] 12 Or over her husband   [c] 15 Greek she   [d] 4 Or him with proper
[e] 8 The word deacons refers here to Christians designated to serve with the overseers/elders of the church in a variety of ways; similarly in verse 12; and in Romans 16:1 and Phil. 1:1.   [f] 11 Possibly deacons' wives or women who are deacons   [g] 16 Or vindicated in spirit   [h] 6 The Greek word for brothers and sisters (adelphoi) refers here to believers, both men and women, as part of God's family.

Training Days

By Bettina Dowell

READ: 1 Timothy 4:6 – 16

Our first sea duty in the Navy as newlyweds provided many opportunities for new training. Stationed aboard a frigate, my husband learned about everything from ordering military parts to landing helicopters on the deck of a ship at sea. But while my husband learned the many different facets of ship life, I was receiving training of my own. In later years, I realized I had received exactly the kind of training talked about in 1 Timothy 4:7 – 8: training in godliness. But at the time, most of this training just seemed unpleasant.

What did my training look like? Extended deployments. Stressful working conditions for my husband. One in three 24-hour duty rotations. Lack of communication from my husband due to the ship's extended travels at sea. PCS moves. Orders that were delayed, changed, canceled or enacted at the last minute. Being hundreds of miles away from family for the first time in my life. All these things provided training for me, even though I did not recognize it at the time.

First Timothy 4:7 – 8 talks about training that holds promise for us in the present and in the future. As a young bride, I thought the military just wanted to make our lives miserable. And quite frankly, I was mad at God for allowing all these stresses into our young marriage. But the young among us are not exempt from training. In fact, Paul's letter to Timothy tells us that even as young people, we are to set an example for others (see verse 12). What I failed to see at the time was that God was using each and every stress to help me mature. The maturity of learning to trust God, even when my life circumstances were far from what I wanted them to be, was beneficial not only in our early days together but also throughout our marriage.

In some ways, spiritual training is no different than physical training. If you go to the gym kicking and screaming, you will have little time to benefit from the muscles that can be built under stress and hard work. If, however, you choose to work with the gym equipment, you can see significant progress. No pain, no gain.

So in what areas of life is God training you? Are you kicking against him or allowing the friction of difficult days to build character in you? May I encourage you? Embrace your training days, difficult as they may be. You will find benefit not just for today but also for the life to come. As 1 Timothy 4:7 – 8 says, godliness benefits you in *all* things.

> Train yourself to be godly. For physical training is of some value, but godliness has value for all things, holding promise for both the present life and the life to come.
>
> 1 TIMOTHY 4:7 – 8

DEBRIEF

- What challenging circumstances in my life right now could God be using to train me?
- Am I cooperating with my training or protesting against it?

REPORT

Dear God, please help me to cooperate as you train me right now. Thank you for loving me just as I am but not leaving me there. In Jesus' name I pray. Amen.

for your next devotional reading, go to page 263

[11] Command and teach these things. [12] Don't let anyone look down on you because you are young, but set an example for the believers in speech, in conduct, in love, in faith and in purity. [13] Until I come, devote yourself to the public reading of Scripture, to preaching and to teaching. [14] Do not neglect your gift, which was given you through prophecy when the body of elders laid their hands on you.

[15] Be diligent in these matters; give yourself wholly to them, so that everyone may see your progress. [16] Watch your life and doctrine closely. Persevere in them, because if you do, you will save both yourself and your hearers.

Widows, Elders and Slaves

5 Do not rebuke an older man harshly, but exhort him as if he were your father. Treat younger men as brothers, [2] older women as mothers, and younger women as sisters, with absolute purity.

[3] Give proper recognition to those widows who are really in need. [4] But if a widow has children or grandchildren, these should learn first of all to put their religion into practice by caring for their own family and so repaying their parents and grandparents, for this is pleasing to God. [5] The widow who is really in need and left all alone puts her hope in God and continues night and day to pray and to ask God for help. [6] But the widow who lives for pleasure is dead even while she lives. [7] Give the people these instructions, so that no one may be open to blame. [8] Anyone who does not provide for their relatives, and especially for their own household, has denied the faith and is worse than an unbeliever.

[9] No widow may be put on the list of widows unless she is over sixty, has been faithful to her husband, [10] and is well known for her good deeds, such as bringing up children, showing hospitality, washing the feet of the Lord's people, helping those in trouble and devoting herself to all kinds of good deeds.

[11] As for younger widows, do not put them on such a list. For when their sensual desires overcome their dedication to Christ, they want to marry. [12] Thus they bring judgment on themselves, because they have broken their first pledge. [13] Besides, they get into the habit of being idle and going about from house to house. And not only do they become idlers, but also busybodies who talk nonsense, saying things they ought not to. [14] So I counsel younger widows to marry, to have children, to manage their homes and to give the enemy no opportunity for slander. [15] Some have in fact already turned away to follow Satan.

[16] If any woman who is a believer has widows in her care, she should continue to help them and not let the church be burdened with them, so that the church can help those widows who are really in need.

[17] The elders who direct the affairs of the church well are worthy of double honor, especially those whose work is preaching and teaching. [18] For Scripture says, "Do not muzzle an ox while it is treading out the grain,"[a] and "The worker deserves his wages."[b] [19] Do not entertain an accusation against an elder unless it is brought by two or three witnesses. [20] But those elders who are sinning you are to reprove before everyone, so that the others may take warning. [21] I charge you, in the sight of God and Christ Jesus and the elect angels, to keep these instructions without partiality, and to do nothing out of favoritism.

[22] Do not be hasty in the laying on of hands, and do not share in the sins of others. Keep yourself pure.

[23] Stop drinking only water, and use a little wine because of your stomach and your frequent illnesses.

[24] The sins of some are obvious, reaching the place of judgment ahead of them; the sins of others trail behind them. [25] In the same way, good deeds are obvious, and even those that are not obvious cannot remain hidden forever.

6 All who are under the yoke of slavery should consider their masters worthy of full respect, so that God's name and our teaching may not be slandered. [2] Those who have believing masters should not show them disrespect just because they are fellow believers. Instead, they should serve them even better because their masters are dear to them as fellow believers and are devoted to the welfare[c] of their slaves.

---

[a] 18 Deut. 25:4   [b] 18 Luke 10:7   [c] 2 Or and benefit from the service

False Teachers and the Love of Money

These are the things you are to teach and insist on. [3]If anyone teaches otherwise and does not agree to the sound instruction of our Lord Jesus Christ and to godly teaching, [4]they are conceited and understand nothing. They have an unhealthy interest in controversies and quarrels about words that result in envy, strife, malicious talk, evil suspicions [5]and constant friction between people of corrupt mind, who have been robbed of the truth and who think that godliness is a means to financial gain.

[6]But godliness with contentment is great gain. [7]For we brought nothing into the world, and we can take nothing out of it. [8]But if we have food and clothing, we will be content with that. [9]Those who want to get rich fall into temptation and a trap and into many foolish and harmful desires that plunge people into ruin and destruction. [10]For the love of money is a root of all kinds of evil. Some people, eager for money, have wandered from the faith and pierced themselves with many griefs.

Final Charge to Timothy

[11]But you, man of God, flee from all this, and pursue righteousness, godliness, faith, love, endurance and gentleness. [12]Fight the good fight of the faith. Take hold of the eternal life to which you were called when you made your good confession in the presence of many witnesses. [13]In the sight of God, who gives life to everything, and of Christ Jesus, who while testifying before Pontius Pilate made the good confession, I charge you [14]to keep this command without spot or blame until the appearing of our Lord Jesus Christ, [15]which God will bring about in his own time — God, the blessed and only Ruler, the King of kings and Lord of lords, [16]who alone is immortal and who lives in unapproachable light, whom no one has seen or can see. To him be honor and might forever. Amen.

[17]Command those who are rich in this present world not to be arrogant nor to put their hope in wealth, which is so uncertain, but to put their hope in God, who richly provides us with everything for our enjoyment. [18]Command them to do good, to be rich in good deeds, and to be generous and willing to share. [19]In this way they will lay up treasure for themselves as a firm foundation for the coming age, so that they may take hold of the life that is truly life.

[20]Timothy, guard what has been entrusted to your care. Turn away from godless chatter and the opposing ideas of what is falsely called knowledge, [21]which some have professed and in so doing have departed from the faith.

Grace be with you all.

2 Timothy

1 Paul, an apostle of Christ Jesus by the will of God, in keeping with the promise of life that is in Christ Jesus,

²To Timothy, my dear son:

Grace, mercy and peace from God the Father and Christ Jesus our Lord.

Thanksgiving

³I thank God, whom I serve, as my ancestors did, with a clear conscience, as night and day I constantly remember you in my prayers. ⁴Recalling your tears, I long to see you, so that I may be filled with joy. ⁵I am reminded of your sincere faith, which first lived in your grandmother Lois and in your mother Eunice and, I am persuaded, now lives in you also.

Appeal for Loyalty to Paul and the Gospel

⁶For this reason I remind you to fan into flame the gift of God, which is in you through the laying on of my hands. ⁷For the Spirit God gave us does not make us timid, but gives us power, love and self-discipline. ⁸So do not be ashamed of the testimony about our Lord or of me his prisoner. Rather, join with me in suffering for the gospel, by the power of God. ⁹He has saved us and called us to a holy life — not because of anything we have done but because of his own purpose and grace. This grace was given us in Christ Jesus before the beginning of time, ¹⁰but it has now been revealed through the appearing of our Savior, Christ Jesus, who has destroyed death and has brought life and immortality to light through the gospel. ¹¹And of this gospel I was appointed a herald and an apostle and a teacher. ¹²That is why I am suffering as I am. Yet this is no cause for shame, because I know whom I have believed, and am convinced that he is able to guard what I have entrusted to him until that day.

¹³What you heard from me, keep as the pattern of sound teaching, with faith and love in Christ Jesus. ¹⁴Guard the good deposit that was entrusted to you — guard it with the help of the Holy Spirit who lives in us.

Examples of Disloyalty and Loyalty

¹⁵You know that everyone in the province of Asia has deserted me, including Phygelus and Hermogenes.

¹⁶May the Lord show mercy to the household of Onesiphorus, because he often refreshed me and was not ashamed of my chains. ¹⁷On the contrary, when he was in Rome, he searched hard for me until he found me. ¹⁸May the Lord grant that he will find mercy from the Lord on that day! You know very well in how many ways he helped me in Ephesus.

The Appeal Renewed

2 You then, my son, be strong in the grace that is in Christ Jesus. ²And the things you have heard me say in the presence of many witnesses entrust to reliable people who will also be qualified to teach others. ³Join with me in suffering, like a good soldier of Christ Jesus. ⁴No one serving as a soldier gets entangled in civilian affairs, but rather tries to please his commanding officer. ⁵Similarly, anyone who competes as an athlete does not receive the victor's crown except by competing according to the rules. ⁶The hardworking farmer should be the first to receive a share of the crops. ⁷Reflect on what I am saying, for the Lord will give you insight into all this.

⁸Remember Jesus Christ, raised from the dead, descended from David. This is my gospel, ⁹for which I am suffering even to the point of being chained like a criminal. But God's word is not chained. ¹⁰Therefore I endure everything for the sake of the elect, that they too may obtain the salvation that is in Christ Jesus, with eternal glory.

¹¹Here is a trustworthy saying:

Home Front
★★★
HEROES

NO FEAR

By Jane Hampton Cook

Dolley Madison grew up in the Quaker faith, whose members were typically pacifists and opponents of war. The irony haunted her years later when her husband, President James Madison, declared war against Great Britain (known as the War of 1812). James Madison, a scholar and author of the U.S. Constitution, became an unlikely commander-in-chief, and Dolley became an unlikely military wife who rose to the occasion with bravery.

In May of 1813 one of Madison's generals uncovered a secret British plan to overtake the White House. How did Dolley respond to the enemy's threats? "I have always been an advocate for fighting when assailed, though Quaker," she wrote to her cousin Edward Coles. "I therefore keep the old Tunisian saber within my reach."

The British did not come in May 1813, but they came a year later. On August 24, 1814, the British marched nearly 4,000 men to Bladensburg, Maryland, which was seven miles from the president's house in Washington, D.C. When President Madison left for Bladensburg, he asked Dolley if she was willing to stay behind to protect valuables in the house and wait for his return. She agreed, making a self-sacrificing pledge to him. She waited all day, but James did not return. When the Americans failed to defeat the British at Bladensburg, their retreat allowed the redcoats to easily march into Washington, D.C.

Dolley had no choice but to leave her post at the White House. Before she escaped she ordered her servants to remove a portrait of George Washington by Gilbert Stuart. A gift from Congress, the painting was a national treasure. Dolley knew that if the British captured it, they would parade it around the streets of London in triumph.

"I insist on waiting until the large picture of General Washington is secured, and it requires to be unscrewed from the wall. This process was found too tedious for these perilous moments; I have ordered the frame to be broken, and the canvass taken out. It is done, and the precious portrait placed in the hands of two gentlemen of New York, for safe keeping."

Because there were so few wagons available, Dolley left most of her clothing behind, saving the painting, her husband's papers, silver from the U.S. treasury and a few trinkets.

Dolley never forgot one key component of her Quaker faith: the light inside. Quakers believe that because everyone carries the potential for God's grace in their hearts, no one is greater than anyone else. This tenet allowed Dolley to think of others above and before herself. Thinking of her husband's reputation and honor enabled her to respond with courage, not fear, when the greatest threat against her became a reality.

Prayer: Thank you for your Spirit, who gives me power in times of trouble.

The Spirit God gave us does not make us timid, but gives us power, love and self-discipline.

2 TIMOTHY 1:7

for your next devotional reading, go to page 265

If we died with him,
   we will also live with him;
[12] if we endure,
   we will also reign with him.
If we disown him,
   he will also disown us;
[13] if we are faithless,
   he remains faithful,
   for he cannot disown himself.

Dealing With False Teachers

[14] Keep reminding God's people of these things. Warn them before God against quarreling about words; it is of no value, and only ruins those who listen. [15] Do your best to present yourself to God as one approved, a worker who does not need to be ashamed and who correctly handles the word of truth. [16] Avoid godless chatter, because those who indulge in it will become more and more ungodly. [17] Their teaching will spread like gangrene. Among them are Hymenaeus and Philetus, [18] who have departed from the truth. They say that the resurrection has already taken place, and they destroy the faith of some. [19] Nevertheless, God's solid foundation stands firm, sealed with this inscription: "The Lord knows those who are his," and, "Everyone who confesses the name of the Lord must turn away from wickedness."

[20] In a large house there are articles not only of gold and silver, but also of wood and clay; some are for special purposes and some for common use. [21] Those who cleanse themselves from the latter will be instruments for special purposes, made holy, useful to the Master and prepared to do any good work.

[22] Flee the evil desires of youth and pursue righteousness, faith, love and peace, along with those who call on the Lord out of a pure heart. [23] Don't have anything to do with foolish and stupid arguments, because you know they produce quarrels. [24] And the Lord's servant must not be quarrelsome but must be kind to everyone, able to teach, not resentful. [25] Opponents must be gently instructed, in the hope that God will grant them repentance leading them to a knowledge of the truth, [26] and that they will come to their senses and escape from the trap of the devil, who has taken them captive to do his will.

3 But mark this: There will be terrible times in the last days. [2] People will be lovers of themselves, lovers of money, boastful, proud, abusive, disobedient to their parents, ungrateful, unholy, [3] without love, unforgiving, slanderous, without self-control, brutal, not lovers of the good, [4] treacherous, rash, conceited, lovers of pleasure rather than lovers of God— [5] having a form of godliness but denying its power. Have nothing to do with such people.

[6] They are the kind who worm their way into homes and gain control over gullible women, who are loaded down with sins and are swayed by all kinds of evil desires, [7] always learning but never able to come to a knowledge of the truth. [8] Just as Jannes and Jambres opposed Moses, so also these teachers oppose the truth. They are men of depraved minds, who, as far as the faith is concerned, are rejected. [9] But they will not get very far because, as in the case of those men, their folly will be clear to everyone.

A Final Charge to Timothy

[10] You, however, know all about my teaching, my way of life, my purpose, faith, patience, love, endurance, [11] persecutions, sufferings—what kinds of things happened to me in Antioch, Iconium and Lystra, the persecutions I endured. Yet the Lord rescued me from all of them. [12] In fact, everyone who wants to live a godly life in Christ Jesus will be persecuted, [13] while evildoers and impostors will go from bad to worse, deceiving and being deceived. [14] But as for you, continue in what you have learned and have become convinced of, because you know those from whom you learned it, [15] and how from infancy you have known the Holy Scriptures, which are able to make you wise for salvation through faith in Christ Jesus. [16] All Scripture is God-breathed and is useful for teaching, rebuking, correcting and training in righteousness, [17] so that the servant of God[a] may be thoroughly equipped for every good work.

4 In the presence of God and of Christ Jesus, who will judge the living and the dead, and in view of his appearing and his kingdom, I give you this charge: [2] Preach the word; be prepared in season and out of

---

[a] 17 Or *that you, a man of God,*

THE WAR AT HOME

By Jocelyn Green

Her husband's battles were on the news, but Patti Katter fought her own battles much more privately. A page from her diary tells the story:

> I tell my children, "Everything is going to be okay," even when I had a phone call that morning from my husband saying, "If I don't make it back, know that I love you." I try to console them after having nightmares about Daddy not coming back, but I am having them too.
>
> I attend and help at another funeral without my children knowing because so many friends have been killed.
>
> When my husband calls, I try to sound cheerful when, in fact, tears are rolling down my face.
>
> I meet injured soldiers back at the base to help them with whatever they need without hesitation, whether at 2 a.m., 4 a.m., or high noon.
>
> My heart stops when the doorbell rings. I'm always wondering if I will have soldiers in dress uniform showing up at my door.

When her husband Ken was deployed to Iraq, Patti kept quiet about her struggles, mostly to protect her children. But since he returned with multiple injuries, she now spends much of her time caregiving and speaking out as a patient advocate for Ken, who suffers from combat trauma, traumatic brain injury, and nerve damage that causes chronic back pain. She hasn't limited the scope of her advocacy to her own family of five either. She is also the founder and president of two nonprofit organizations: Christian Military Wives and Voice of Warriors.

"Our experiences allow me to witness to other families in similar circumstances in a way I never would have been able to otherwise," said Patti. "If God uses our story to draw others closer to him, it's all worth it."

Patti has truly joined in the suffering of her husband and other veterans, just as the apostle Paul tells each of us to join in suffering "like a good soldier of Christ Jesus" (2 Timothy 2:3). She hopes to spread hope and healing to military families, but her ultimate goal is to please Jesus, her "commanding officer" (2 Timothy 2:4), and follow his leading.*

---

*Read "Lead On, O King Eternal" on page 497.

Prayer: *Lord, help me always to focus on pleasing and following you alone.*

> **Join with me in suffering, like a good soldier of Christ Jesus. No one serving as a soldier gets entangled in civilian affairs, but rather tries to please his commanding officer.**
>
> 2 TIMOTHY 2:3 – 4

for your next devotional reading, go to page 268

season; correct, rebuke and encourage —
with great patience and careful instruction.
[3]For the time will come when people will not
put up with sound doctrine. Instead, to suit
their own desires, they will gather around
them a great number of teachers to say what
their itching ears want to hear. [4]They will
turn their ears away from the truth and turn
aside to myths. [5]But you, keep your head in
all situations, endure hardship, do the work
of an evangelist, discharge all the duties of
your ministry.

[6]For I am already being poured out like a
drink offering, and the time for my departure is near. [7]I have fought the good fight, I
have finished the race, I have kept the faith.
[8]Now there is in store for me the crown of
righteousness, which the Lord, the righteous Judge, will award to me on that day —
and not only to me, but also to all who have
longed for his appearing.

Personal Remarks

[9]Do your best to come to me quickly, [10]for
Demas, because he loved this world, has
deserted me and has gone to Thessalonica. Crescens has gone to Galatia, and Titus
to Dalmatia. [11]Only Luke is with me. Get
Mark and bring him with you, because he is
helpful to me in my ministry. [12]I sent Tychicus to Ephesus. [13]When you come, bring the
cloak that I left with Carpus at Troas, and my
scrolls, especially the parchments.

[14]Alexander the metalworker did me a
great deal of harm. The Lord will repay him
for what he has done. [15]You too should be on
your guard against him, because he strongly
opposed our message.

[16]At my first defense, no one came to my
support, but everyone deserted me. May
it not be held against them. [17]But the Lord
stood at my side and gave me strength, so
that through me the message might be fully
proclaimed and all the Gentiles might hear
it. And I was delivered from the lion's mouth.
[18]The Lord will rescue me from every evil attack and will bring me safely to his heavenly
kingdom. To him be glory for ever and ever.
Amen.

Final Greetings

[19]Greet Priscilla[a] and Aquila and the
household of Onesiphorus. [20]Erastus stayed
in Corinth, and I left Trophimus sick in Miletus. [21]Do your best to get here before winter. Eubulus greets you, and so do Pudens,
Linus, Claudia and all the brothers and sisters.[b]

[22]The Lord be with your spirit. Grace be
with you all.

[a] 19 Greek *Prisca*, a variant of *Priscilla*   [b] 21 The Greek word for *brothers and sisters* (*adelphoi*) refers
here to believers, both men and women, as part of God's family.

Titus

Paul, a servant of God and an apostle of Jesus Christ to further the faith of God's elect and their knowledge of the truth that leads to godliness— ²in the hope of eternal life, which God, who does not lie, promised before the beginning of time, ³and which now at his appointed season he has brought to light through the preaching entrusted to me by the command of God our Savior,

⁴To Titus, my true son in our common faith:

Grace and peace from God the Father and Christ Jesus our Savior.

Appointing Elders Who Love What Is Good

⁵The reason I left you in Crete was that you might put in order what was left unfinished and appoint*a* elders in every town, as I directed you. ⁶An elder must be blameless, faithful to his wife, a man whose children believe*b* and are not open to the charge of being wild and disobedient. ⁷Since an overseer manages God's household, he must be blameless — not overbearing, not quick-tempered, not given to drunkenness, not violent, not pursuing dishonest gain. ⁸Rather, he must be hospitable, one who loves what is good, who is self-controlled, upright, holy and disciplined. ⁹He must hold firmly to the trustworthy message as it has been taught, so that he can encourage others by sound doctrine and refute those who oppose it.

Rebuking Those Who Fail to Do Good

¹⁰For there are many rebellious people, full of meaningless talk and deception, especially those of the circumcision group. ¹¹They must be silenced, because they are disrupting whole households by teaching things they ought not to teach — and that for the sake of dishonest gain. ¹²One of Crete's own prophets has said it: "Cretans are al-

ways liars, evil brutes, lazy gluttons."*c* ¹³This saying is true. Therefore rebuke them sharply, so that they will be sound in the faith ¹⁴and will pay no attention to Jewish myths or to the merely human commands of those who reject the truth. ¹⁵To the pure, all things are pure, but to those who are corrupted and do not believe, nothing is pure. In fact, both their minds and consciences are corrupted. ¹⁶They claim to know God, but by their actions they deny him. They are detestable, disobedient and unfit for doing anything good.

Doing Good for the Sake of the Gospel

You, however, must teach what is appropriate to sound doctrine. ²Teach the older men to be temperate, worthy of respect, self-controlled, and sound in faith, in love and in endurance.

³Likewise, teach the older women to be reverent in the way they live, not to be slanderers or addicted to much wine, but to teach what is good. ⁴Then they can urge the younger women to love their husbands and children, ⁵to be self-controlled and pure, to be busy at home, to be kind, and to be subject to their husbands, so that no one will malign the word of God.

⁶Similarly, encourage the young men to be self-controlled. ⁷In everything set them an example by doing what is good. In your teaching show integrity, seriousness ⁸and soundness of speech that cannot be condemned, so that those who oppose you may be ashamed because they have nothing bad to say about us.

⁹Teach slaves to be subject to their masters in everything, to try to please them, not to talk back to them, ¹⁰and not to steal from them, but to show that they can be fully trusted, so that in every way they will make the teaching about God our Savior attractive.

¹¹For the grace of God has appeared that offers salvation to all people. ¹²It teaches us

a 5 Or *ordain*   *b* 6 Or *children are trustworthy*   *c* 12 From the Cretan philosopher Epimenides

Down the Path

By Bettina Dowell

READ: Titus 2

In Titus 2 we are told that older women should teach younger women (see verses 3–5). Probably none of us is willing to sign up for the title of "older woman," even when we are octogenarians. So what happens if we redefine the term?

The original Greek word used in Titus is the feminine term for someone who is aged. An alternative definition is "advanced in life," or in more simple terms, someone who is down the path a little farther.

How encouraging! In order to share with someone the lessons God has taught us in our life as a military wife, we only have to be farther down the path than that person. Has your husband graduated from basic training? Then you are down the path from a wife whose husband has just begun!

When we moved to Washington, D.C., the ultimate military town, I imagined feeling very at home in an environment prevalent with military families. The problem was not a lack of military spouses in D.C. but actually being able to find and connect with them. In D.C. many military families do not live on a military base and many of the military wives have little or no connection with their husband's work assignment.

As my friend Tricia and I discussed these struggles to connect, we thought God might be leading us to start a Bible study for military wives. Instead, with the support of Immanuel Bible Church, we launched a monthly meeting for military wives led by military wives called Hearts Apart. Women gather each month for fun icebreakers and dinner and to hear an encouraging military wife speak or seasoned military wives lead table discussions around military life topics.

Do you have relationships with other military wives? Are you sharing your experiences with them? You don't have to attend a monthly meeting or be stationed on a military base to engage in these relationships. Thanks to modern technology, you can connect with military wives from almost any place on the globe.

Recently, we shared a panel night at Hearts Apart. Experienced military wives spent the evening answering questions from other military wives. The echoing theme throughout the evening was that God reigns and provides, even during the most challenging days of military life. How encouraging it was to see military wives from down the path "teach what is good," just as we are encouraged to do in Titus 2.

Likewise, teach the older women to be reverent in the way they live, not to be slanderers or addicted to much wine, but to teach what is good. Then they can urge the younger women to love their husbands and children, to be self-controlled and pure, to be busy at home, to be kind, and to be subject to their husbands, so that no one will malign the word of God.

TITUS 2:3–5

DEBRIEF

- Who has encouraged me from down the path? What has she taught me?
- Whom can I reach back and encourage from down the path?

REPORT

Dear Father, thank you for the fellow military wives who have encouraged and supported me in my calling as a military wife. Show me whom I can likewise encourage from the experiences you've given me. Amen.

to say "No" to ungodliness and worldly passions, and to live self-controlled, upright and godly lives in this present age, [13]while we wait for the blessed hope — the appearing of the glory of our great God and Savior, Jesus Christ, [14]who gave himself for us to redeem us from all wickedness and to purify for himself a people that are his very own, eager to do what is good.

[15]These, then, are the things you should teach. Encourage and rebuke with all authority. Do not let anyone despise you.

Saved in Order to Do Good

3 Remind the people to be subject to rulers and authorities, to be obedient, to be ready to do whatever is good, [2]to slander no one, to be peaceable and considerate, and always to be gentle toward everyone.

[3]At one time we too were foolish, disobedient, deceived and enslaved by all kinds of passions and pleasures. We lived in malice and envy, being hated and hating one another. [4]But when the kindness and love of God our Savior appeared, [5]he saved us, not because of righteous things we had done, but because of his mercy. He saved us through the washing of rebirth and renewal by the Holy Spirit, [6]whom he poured out on us generously through Jesus Christ our Savior, [7]so

that, having been justified by his grace, we might become heirs having the hope of eternal life. [8]This is a trustworthy saying. And I want you to stress these things, so that those who have trusted in God may be careful to devote themselves to doing what is good. These things are excellent and profitable for everyone.

[9]But avoid foolish controversies and genealogies and arguments and quarrels about the law, because these are unprofitable and useless. [10]Warn a divisive person once, and then warn them a second time. After that, have nothing to do with them. [11]You may be sure that such people are warped and sinful; they are self-condemned.

Final Remarks

[12]As soon as I send Artemas or Tychicus to you, do your best to come to me at Nicopolis, because I have decided to winter there. [13]Do everything you can to help Zenas the lawyer and Apollos on their way and see that they have everything they need. [14]Our people must learn to devote themselves to doing what is good, in order to provide for urgent needs and not live unproductive lives.

[15]Everyone with me sends you greetings. Greet those who love us in the faith.

Grace be with you all.

Philemon

[1] Paul, a prisoner of Christ Jesus, and Timothy our brother,

To Philemon our dear friend and fellow worker— [2] also to Apphia our sister and Archippus our fellow soldier—and to the church that meets in your home:

[3] Grace and peace to you[a] from God our Father and the Lord Jesus Christ.

Thanksgiving and Prayer

[4] I always thank my God as I remember you in my prayers, [5] because I hear about your love for all his holy people and your faith in the Lord Jesus. [6] I pray that your partnership with us in the faith may be effective in deepening your understanding of every good thing we share for the sake of Christ. [7] Your love has given me great joy and encouragement, because you, brother, have refreshed the hearts of the Lord's people.

Paul's Plea for Onesimus

[8] Therefore, although in Christ I could be bold and order you to do what you ought to do, [9] yet I prefer to appeal to you on the basis of love. It is as none other than Paul—an old man and now also a prisoner of Christ Jesus— [10] that I appeal to you for my son Onesimus,[b] who became my son while I was in chains. [11] Formerly he was useless to you, but now he has become useful both to you and to me.

[12] I am sending him—who is my very heart—back to you. [13] I would have liked to keep him with me so that he could take your place in helping me while I am in chains for the gospel. [14] But I did not want to do anything without your consent, so that any favor you do would not seem forced but would be voluntary. [15] Perhaps the reason he was separated from you for a little while was that you might have him back forever— [16] no longer as a slave, but better than a slave, as a dear brother. He is very dear to me but even dearer to you, both as a fellow man and as a brother in the Lord.

[17] So if you consider me a partner, welcome him as you would welcome me. [18] If he has done you any wrong or owes you anything, charge it to me. [19] I, Paul, am writing this with my own hand. I will pay it back—not to mention that you owe me your very self. [20] I do wish, brother, that I may have some benefit from you in the Lord; refresh my heart in Christ. [21] Confident of your obedience, I write to you, knowing that you will do even more than I ask.

[22] And one thing more: Prepare a guest room for me, because I hope to be restored to you in answer to your prayers.

[23] Epaphras, my fellow prisoner in Christ Jesus, sends you greetings. [24] And so do Mark, Aristarchus, Demas and Luke, my fellow workers.

[25] The grace of the Lord Jesus Christ be with your spirit.

---

[a] 3 The Greek is plural; also in verses 22 and 25; elsewhere in this letter "you" is singular.
[b] 10 Onesimus means useful.

Hebrews

God's Final Word: His Son

1 In the past God spoke to our ancestors through the prophets at many times and in various ways, ²but in these last days he has spoken to us by his Son, whom he appointed heir of all things, and through whom also he made the universe. ³The Son is the radiance of God's glory and the exact representation of his being, sustaining all things by his powerful word. After he had provided purification for sins, he sat down at the right hand of the Majesty in heaven. ⁴So he became as much superior to the angels as the name he has inherited is superior to theirs.

The Son Superior to Angels

⁵For to which of the angels did God ever say,

"You are my Son;
    today I have become your Father"[a]?

Or again,

"I will be his Father,
    and he will be my Son"[b]?

⁶And again, when God brings his firstborn into the world, he says,

"Let all God's angels worship him."[c]

⁷In speaking of the angels he says,

"He makes his angels spirits,
    and his servants flames of fire."[d]

⁸But about the Son he says,

"Your throne, O God, will last for ever
        and ever;
    a scepter of justice will be the scepter
        of your kingdom.
⁹You have loved righteousness and hated
        wickedness;
    therefore God, your God, has set you
        above your companions
    by anointing you with the oil of joy."[e]

¹⁰He also says,

"In the beginning, Lord, you laid the
        foundations of the earth,
    and the heavens are the work of your
        hands.
¹¹They will perish, but you remain;
    they will all wear out like a garment.
¹²You will roll them up like a robe;
    like a garment they will be changed.
But you remain the same,
    and your years will never end."[f]

¹³To which of the angels did God ever say,

"Sit at my right hand
    until I make your enemies
    a footstool for your feet"[g]?

¹⁴Are not all angels ministering spirits sent to serve those who will inherit salvation?

Warning to Pay Attention

2 We must pay the most careful attention, therefore, to what we have heard, so that we do not drift away. ²For since the message spoken through angels was binding, and every violation and disobedience received its just punishment, ³how shall we escape if we ignore so great a salvation? This salvation, which was first announced by the Lord, was confirmed to us by those who heard him. ⁴God also testified to it by signs, wonders and various miracles, and by gifts of the Holy Spirit distributed according to his will.

Jesus Made Fully Human

⁵It is not to angels that he has subjected the world to come, about which we are speaking. ⁶But there is a place where someone has testified:

"What is mankind that you are mindful
        of them,
    a son of man that you care for him?

---

[a] 5 Psalm 2:7   [b] 5 2 Samuel 7:14; 1 Chron. 17:13   [c] 6 Deut. 32:43 (see Dead Sea Scrolls and Septuagint)
[d] 7 Psalm 104:4   [e] 9 Psalm 45:6,7   [f] 12 Psalm 102:25-27   [g] 13 Psalm 110:1

[7] You made them a little[a] lower than
the angels;
you crowned them with glory and
honor
[8]   and put everything under their feet."[b,c]

In putting everything under them,[d] God left
nothing that is not subject to them.[d] Yet at
present we do not see everything subject to
them.[d] [9] But we do see Jesus, who was made
lower than the angels for a little while, now
crowned with glory and honor because he
suffered death, so that by the grace of God
he might taste death for everyone.
[10] In bringing many sons and daughters to
glory, it was fitting that God, for whom and
through whom everything exists, should
make the pioneer of their salvation perfect
through what he suffered. [11] Both the one
who makes people holy and those who are
made holy are of the same family. So Jesus is
not ashamed to call them brothers and sisters.[e] [12] He says,

"I will declare your name to my brothers
and sisters;
in the assembly I will sing your
praises."[f]

[13] And again,

"I will put my trust in him."[g]

And again he says,

"Here am I, and the children God has
given me."[h]

[14] Since the children have flesh and blood,
he too shared in their humanity so that by
his death he might break the power of him
who holds the power of death — that is, the
devil — [15] and free those who all their lives
were held in slavery by their fear of death.
[16] For surely it is not angels he helps, but
Abraham's descendants. [17] For this reason
he had to be made like them,[i] fully human in
every way, in order that he might become a
merciful and faithful high priest in service to
God, and that he might make atonement for
the sins of the people. [18] Because he himself
suffered when he was tempted, he is able to
help those who are being tempted.

Jesus Greater Than Moses

3 Therefore, holy brothers and sisters,
who share in the heavenly calling, fix
your thoughts on Jesus, whom we acknowledge as our apostle and high priest. [2] He was
faithful to the one who appointed him, just
as Moses was faithful in all God's house.
[3] Jesus has been found worthy of greater hon-
or than Moses, just as the builder of a house
has greater honor than the house itself. [4] For
every house is built by someone, but God is
the builder of everything. [5] "Moses was faithful as a servant in all God's house,"[j] bearing
witness to what would be spoken by God in
the future. [6] But Christ is faithful as the Son
over God's house. And we are his house, if indeed we hold firmly to our confidence and
the hope in which we glory.

Warning Against Unbelief

[7] So, as the Holy Spirit says:

"Today, if you hear his voice,
[8]   do not harden your hearts
as you did in the rebellion,
during the time of testing in the
wilderness,
[9] where your ancestors tested and
tried me,
though for forty years they saw what
I did.
[10] That is why I was angry with that
generation;
I said, 'Their hearts are always going
astray,
and they have not known
my ways.'
[11] So I declared on oath in my anger,
'They shall never enter my rest.' "[k]

[12] See to it, brothers and sisters, that none
of you has a sinful, unbelieving heart that
turns away from the living God. [13] But encourage one another daily, as long as it is
called "Today," so that none of you may be
hardened by sin's deceitfulness. [14] We have
come to share in Christ, if indeed we hold
our original conviction firmly to the very
end. [15] As has just been said:

---

[a] 7 Or *them for a little while*   [b] 6-8 Psalm 8:4-6   [c] 7,8 Or *7 You made him a little lower than the angels;/
you crowned him with glory and honor/ 8 and put everything under his feet."*   [d] 8 Or *him*   [e] 11 The
Greek word for *brothers and sisters* (*adelphoi*) refers here to believers, both men and women, as part of
God's family; also in verse 12; and in 3:1, 12; 10:19; 13:22.   [f] 12 Psalm 22:22   [g] 13 Isaiah 8:17
[h] 13 Isaiah 8:18   [i] 17 Or *like his brothers*   [j] 5 Num. 12:7   [k] 11 Psalm 95:7-11

"Today, if you hear his voice,
    do not harden your hearts
        as you did in the rebellion."[a]

[16]Who were they who heard and re-belled? Were they not all those Moses led out of Egypt? [17]And with whom was he an-gry for forty years? Was it not with those who sinned, whose bodies perished in the wilderness? [18]And to whom did God swear that they would never enter his rest if not to those who disobeyed? [19]So we see that they were not able to enter, because of their un-belief.

A Sabbath-Rest for the People of God

4 Therefore, since the promise of entering his rest still stands, let us be careful that none of you be found to have fallen short of it. [2]For we also have had the good news pro-claimed to us, just as they did; but the mes-sage they heard was of no value to them, because they did not share the faith of those who obeyed.[b] [3]Now we who have believed enter that rest, just as God has said,

"So I declared on oath in my anger,
    'They shall never enter my rest.' "[c]

And yet his works have been finished since the creation of the world. [4]For somewhere he has spoken about the seventh day in these words: "On the seventh day God rested from all his works."[d] [5]And again in the passage above he says, "They shall never enter my rest."

[6]Therefore since it still remains for some to enter that rest, and since those who for-merly had the good news proclaimed to them did not go in because of their disobe-dience, [7]God again set a certain day, calling it "Today." This he did when a long time later he spoke through David, as in the passage already quoted:

"Today, if you hear his voice,
    do not harden your hearts."[a]

[8]For if Joshua had given them rest, God would not have spoken later about another day. [9]There remains, then, a Sabbath-rest for the people of God; [10]for anyone who enters God's rest also rests from their works,[e] just as

God did from his. [11]Let us, therefore, make every effort to enter that rest, so that no one will perish by following their example of dis-obedience.

[12]For the word of God is alive and active. Sharper than any double-edged sword, it penetrates even to dividing soul and spirit, joints and marrow; it judges the thoughts and attitudes of the heart. [13]Nothing in all creation is hidden from God's sight. Every-thing is uncovered and laid bare before the eyes of him to whom we must give account.

Jesus the Great High Priest

[14]Therefore, since we have a great high priest who has ascended into heaven,[f] Jesus the Son of God, let us hold firmly to the faith we profess. [15]For we do not have a high priest who is unable to empathize with our weaknesses, but we have one who has been tempted in every way, just as we are — yet he did not sin. [16]Let us then approach God's throne of grace with confidence, so that we may receive mercy and find grace to help us in our time of need.

5 Every high priest is selected from among the people and is appointed to represent the people in matters related to God, to of-fer gifts and sacrifices for sins. [2]He is able to deal gently with those who are ignorant and are going astray, since he himself is subject to weakness. [3]This is why he has to offer sac-rifices for his own sins, as well as for the sins of the people. [4]And no one takes this honor on himself, but he receives it when called by God, just as Aaron was.

[5]In the same way, Christ did not take on himself the glory of becoming a high priest. But God said to him,

"You are my Son;
    today I have become your Father."[g]

[6]And he says in another place,

"You are a priest forever,
    in the order of Melchizedek."[h]

[7]During the days of Jesus' life on earth, he offered up prayers and petitions with fervent cries and tears to the one who could save him from death, and he was heard because of his reverent submission. [8]Son

[a] 15,7 Psalm 95:7,8   [b] 2 Some manuscripts *because those who heard did not combine it with faith*
[c] 3 Psalm 95:11; also in verse 5   [d] 4 Gen. 2:2   [e] 10 Or *labor*   [f] 14 Greek *has gone through the heavens*
[g] 5 Psalm 2:7   [h] 6 Psalm 110:4

WIELDING THE WORD

By Jocelyn Green

No one ever told Sonja Mannarino that deployment would be easy. But they didn't tell her it would be this hard either.

Her daughter was 15 and her sons were 11 and 4 years old when her husband of 16 years deployed. While Jason encountered enemy fire in Iraq, Sonja felt like the home front was under attack as well. After saying good-bye to his daddy, her 4-year-old son cried for days, especially at night because Jason always tucked him into bed. Her 11-year-old son went through depression and gained a lot of weight, eating to fill the void caused by his dad's absence.

"It was hard for him; he was Dad's helper working on cars or in the yard together," said Sonja. "He had a lot of anger too, and he took it out on me verbally. I had to sit down with him and say, 'What you're doing is not right. You don't need to act this way because Dad's gone.' It tore my heart out because there was nothing I could do."

As Sonja held down the fort, she quickly saw the need to go on the offensive against fear, worry, resentment, anger and bitterness. Her tactic was simple: She printed Scripture verses from her computer and stuck them with Scotch tape all around her house so God's Word would constantly be before her eyes and the eyes of her children.

Taped next to her bathroom mirror: "Be exalted in your strength, LORD; we will sing and praise your might" (Psalm 21:13). Taped inside her kitchen cupboard: "Even though I walk through the darkest valley, I will fear no evil, for you are with me" (Psalm 23:4). Above her dresser: Psalm 112:7. In her living room: Psalm 73:28.

The result was powerful. Instead of dwelling on the unknown, Sonja chose to dwell on what she did know: God is good, and God is in control. Even after Jason returned from deployment the following year, Sonja left those verses taped up throughout her home.

"Without God, I couldn't have made it," she said. "I needed comfort and peace, and he gave it to me. That is just amazing. Jason and I prayed with each other through email; we would speak to each other about God and Scriptures to lift our spirits. God's presence was really strong."

Sonja was able to ward off attacks from the enemy by claiming God's truths. Meditating on Scripture cleared her mind and heart of the swirling negative thoughts that threatened to consume her.

Prayer: Lord, give me the discipline I need to study and memorize your Word, so that I can use it as my source of strength.

The word of God is alive and active. Sharper than any double-edged sword, it penetrates even to dividing soul and spirit, joints and marrow; it judges the thoughts and attitudes of the heart.

HEBREWS 4:12

though he was, he learned obedience from what he suffered [9]and, once made perfect, he became the source of eternal salvation for all who obey him [10]and was designated by God to be high priest in the order of Melchizedek.

Warning Against Falling Away

[11]We have much to say about this, but it is hard to make it clear to you because you no longer try to understand. [12]In fact, though by this time you ought to be teachers, you need someone to teach you the elementary truths of God's word all over again. You need milk, not solid food! [13]Anyone who lives on milk, being still an infant, is not acquainted with the teaching about righteousness. [14]But solid food is for the mature, who by constant use have trained themselves to distinguish good from evil.

6 Therefore let us move beyond the elementary teachings about Christ and be taken forward to maturity, not laying again the foundation of repentance from acts that lead to death,[a] and of faith in God, [2]instruction about cleansing rites,[b] the laying on of hands, the resurrection of the dead, and eternal judgment. [3]And God permitting, we will do so.

[4]It is impossible for those who have once been enlightened, who have tasted the heavenly gift, who have shared in the Holy Spirit, [5]who have tasted the goodness of the word of God and the powers of the coming age [6]and who have fallen[c] away, to be brought back to repentance. To their loss they are crucifying the Son of God all over again and subjecting him to public disgrace. [7]Land that drinks in the rain often falling on it and that produces a crop useful to those for whom it is farmed receives the blessing of God. [8]But land that produces thorns and thistles is worthless and is in danger of being cursed. In the end it will be burned.

[9]Even though we speak like this, dear friends, we are convinced of better things in your case — the things that have to do with salvation. [10]God is not unjust; he will not forget your work and the love you have shown him as you have helped his people and continue to help them. [11]We want each of you to show this same diligence to the very end, so that what you hope for may be fully realized. [12]We do not want you to become lazy, but to imitate those who through faith and patience inherit what has been promised.

The Certainty of God's Promise

[13]When God made his promise to Abraham, since there was no one greater for him to swear by, he swore by himself, [14]saying, "I will surely bless you and give you many descendants."[d] [15]And so after waiting patiently, Abraham received what was promised.

[16]People swear by someone greater than themselves, and the oath confirms what is said and puts an end to all argument. [17]Because God wanted to make the unchanging nature of his purpose very clear to the heirs of what was promised, he confirmed it with an oath. [18]God did this so that, by two unchangeable things in which it is impossible for God to lie, we who have fled to take hold of the hope set before us may be greatly encouraged. [19]We have this hope as an anchor for the soul, firm and secure. It enters the inner sanctuary behind the curtain, [20]where our forerunner, Jesus, has entered on our behalf. He has become a high priest forever, in the order of Melchizedek.

Melchizedek the Priest

7 This Melchizedek was king of Salem and priest of God Most High. He met Abraham returning from the defeat of the kings and blessed him, [2]and Abraham gave him a tenth of everything. First, the name Melchizedek means "king of righteousness"; then also, "king of Salem" means "king of peace." [3]Without father or mother, without genealogy, without beginning of days or end of life, resembling the Son of God, he remains a priest forever.

[4]Just think how great he was: Even the patriarch Abraham gave him a tenth of the plunder! [5]Now the law requires the descendants of Levi who become priests to collect a tenth from the people — that is, from their fellow Israelites — even though they also are descended from Abraham. [6]This man, however, did not trace his descent from Levi, yet he collected a tenth from Abraham and blessed him who had the promises. [7]And

---

[a] 1 Or *from useless rituals*   [b] 2 Or *about baptisms*   [c] 6 Or *age,* [6]*if they fall*   [d] 14 Gen. 22:17

THE HEROINE OF GETTYSBURG

By Jocelyn Green

Elizabeth Masser Thorn, a German immigrant to Gettysburg, Pennsylvania, led a quiet life. She and her husband, Peter, were caretakers of Evergreen Cemetery, and they lived in the cemetery gatehouse with their three sons and Elizabeth's parents. Peter enlisted in the Union army in 1862, which left Elizabeth to tend the cemetery and dig graves in her husband's absence. Then in July 1863, when she was 31 years old and six-months pregnant with her fourth child, Elizabeth's peaceful existence was shattered by the Battle of Gettysburg.

Before the battle began on July 1, she fed the Rebels who came to her house begging for bread until there was no food for her own family, and the next day she and her sons carried water to Union soldiers passing by until the boys' hands were blistered. That night they brought their best things to the cellar and hid there during the cannonading until a Union soldier ordered them to flee for their lives. She wrote upon returning home:

> When we looked at the house I could only say "O my!" There were no window glass in the whole house. Some of the frames were knock[ed] out and the pump was broken. Fifteen soldiers were buried beside the pump shed. I went to the cellar to look for the good things I had put there on the first night. One chest was packed with good German linen, others packed with other good things — everything gone, but three featherbeds and they were full of blood and mud.

The cemetery president instructed her to bury the many deceased soldiers as fast as she could. The stench from the bloated corpses, both human and horse, was nauseating, but she and her father, aged 63, had little choice. The longer the bodies lay sweltering in the sun, the more of a health hazard they became.

Elizabeth telegraphed friends outside of town for help. "Two came, but one only stayed two days, then got deathly sick and left. The other stayed five days, then he went away very sick, and I had to pay their fare here and very good wages for their work . . . Then father and I had to dig on harder again."

Elizabeth and her father buried 102 soldiers in Evergreen Cemetery. Art Kennell, retired superintendent of Evergreen Cemetery, called her "the heroine of Gettysburg." She was never compensated for her work or for the damages to her home. Elizabeth had her baby three months later, but her health failed after that.

Peter survived the war and lived with Elizabeth until they both died in 1907. Though her work was unrewarded on earth, God was surely pleased with her diligence.

Prayer: Lord, thank you for seeing my work when no one else does.

**God is not unjust; he will not forget your work and the love you have
shown him as you have helped his people and continue to help them.**

HEBREWS 6:10

without doubt the lesser is blessed by the greater. ⁸In the one case, the tenth is collected by people who die; but in the other case, by him who is declared to be living. ⁹One might even say that Levi, who collects the tenth, paid the tenth through Abraham, ¹⁰because when Melchizedek met Abraham, Levi was still in the body of his ancestor.

Jesus Like Melchizedek

¹¹If perfection could have been attained through the Levitical priesthood—and indeed the law given to the people established that priesthood—why was there still need for another priest to come, one in the order of Melchizedek, not in the order of Aaron? ¹²For when the priesthood is changed, the law must be changed also. ¹³He of whom these things are said belonged to a different tribe, and no one from that tribe has ever served at the altar. ¹⁴For it is clear that our Lord descended from Judah, and in regard to that tribe Moses said nothing about priests. ¹⁵And what we have said is even more clear if another priest like Melchizedek appears, ¹⁶one who has become a priest not on the basis of a regulation as to his ancestry but on the basis of the power of an indestructible life. ¹⁷For it is declared:

"You are a priest forever,
    in the order of Melchizedek."[a]

¹⁸The former regulation is set aside because it was weak and useless ¹⁹(for the law made nothing perfect), and a better hope is introduced, by which we draw near to God.

²⁰And it was not without an oath! Others became priests without any oath, ²¹but he became a priest with an oath when God said to him:

"The Lord has sworn
    and will not change his mind:
    'You are a priest forever.'"[a]

²²Because of this oath, Jesus has become the guarantor of a better covenant.

²³Now there have been many of those priests, since death prevented them from continuing in office; ²⁴but because Jesus lives forever, he has a permanent priesthood. ²⁵Therefore he is able to save completely[b] those who come to God through him, because he always lives to intercede for them.

²⁶Such a high priest truly meets our need—one who is holy, blameless, pure, set apart from sinners, exalted above the heavens. ²⁷Unlike the other high priests, he does not need to offer sacrifices day after day, first for his own sins, and then for the sins of the people. He sacrificed for their sins once for all when he offered himself. ²⁸For the law appoints as high priests men in all their weakness; but the oath, which came after the law, appointed the Son, who has been made perfect forever.

The High Priest of a New Covenant

8 Now the main point of what we are saying is this: We do have such a high priest, who sat down at the right hand of the throne of the Majesty in heaven, ²and who serves in the sanctuary, the true tabernacle set up by the Lord, not by a mere human being.

³Every high priest is appointed to offer both gifts and sacrifices, and so it was necessary for this one also to have something to offer. ⁴If he were on earth, he would not be a priest, for there are already priests who offer the gifts prescribed by the law. ⁵They serve at a sanctuary that is a copy and shadow of what is in heaven. This is why Moses was warned when he was about to build the tabernacle: "See to it that you make everything according to the pattern shown you on the mountain."[c] ⁶But in fact the ministry Jesus has received is as superior to theirs as the covenant of which he is mediator is superior to the old one, since the new covenant is established on better promises.

⁷For if there had been nothing wrong with that first covenant, no place would have been sought for another. ⁸But God found fault with the people and said[d]:

"The days are coming, declares the Lord,
    when I will make a new covenant
with the people of Israel
    and with the people of Judah.
⁹It will not be like the covenant
    I made with their ancestors
when I took them by the hand
    to lead them out of Egypt,

because they did not remain faithful to
my covenant,
and I turned away from them,
declares the Lord.
[10] This is the covenant I will establish with
the people of Israel
after that time, declares the Lord.
I will put my laws in their minds
and write them on their hearts.
I will be their God,
and they will be my people.
[11] No longer will they teach their
neighbor,
or say to one another, 'Know
the Lord,'
because they will all know me,
from the least of them to the
greatest.
[12] For I will forgive their wickedness
and will remember their sins
no more."[a]

[13] By calling this covenant "new," he has
made the first one obsolete; and what is obsolete and outdated will soon disappear.

Worship in the Earthly Tabernacle

9 Now the first covenant had regulations
for worship and also an earthly sanctuary. [2] A tabernacle was set up. In its first
room were the lampstand and the table with
its consecrated bread; this was called the
Holy Place. [3] Behind the second curtain was
a room called the Most Holy Place, [4] which
had the golden altar of incense and the gold-
covered ark of the covenant. This ark contained the gold jar of manna, Aaron's staff
that had budded, and the stone tablets of the
covenant. [5] Above the ark were the cherubim
of the Glory, overshadowing the atonement
cover. But we cannot discuss these things in
detail now.

[6] When everything had been arranged like
this, the priests entered regularly into the
outer room to carry on their ministry. [7] But
only the high priest entered the inner room,
and that only once a year, and never without
blood, which he offered for himself and for
the sins the people had committed in ignorance. [8] The Holy Spirit was showing by this
that the way into the Most Holy Place had not
yet been disclosed as long as the first taber-

nacle was still functioning. [9] This is an illus-
tration for the present time, indicating that
the gifts and sacrifices being offered were
not able to clear the conscience of the worshiper. [10] They are only a matter of food and
drink and various ceremonial washings —
external regulations applying until the time
of the new order.

The Blood of Christ

[11] But when Christ came as high priest of
the good things that are now already here,[b]
he went through the greater and more perfect tabernacle that is not made with human
hands, that is to say, is not a part of this creation. [12] He did not enter by means of the
blood of goats and calves; but he entered
the Most Holy Place once for all by his own
blood, thus obtaining[c] eternal redemption.
[13] The blood of goats and bulls and the ashes
of a heifer sprinkled on those who are ceremonially unclean sanctify them so that they
are outwardly clean. [14] How much more,
then, will the blood of Christ, who through
the eternal Spirit offered himself unblem-
ished to God, cleanse our consciences from
acts that lead to death,[d] so that we may serve
the living God!

[15] For this reason Christ is the mediator of
a new covenant, that those who are called
may receive the promised eternal inheritance — now that he has died as a ransom to
set them free from the sins committed under
the first covenant.

[16] In the case of a will,[e] it is necessary to
prove the death of the one who made it, [17] because a will is in force only when somebody
has died; it never takes effect while the one
who made it is living. [18] This is why even the
first covenant was not put into effect without blood. [19] When Moses had proclaimed
every command of the law to all the people,
he took the blood of calves, together with
water, scarlet wool and branches of hyssop,
and sprinkled the scroll and all the people.
[20] He said, "This is the blood of the covenant,
which God has commanded you to keep."[f]
[21] In the same way, he sprinkled with the
blood both the tabernacle and everything
used in its ceremonies. [22] In fact, the law requires that nearly everything be cleansed

---

[a] 12 Jer. 31:31-34   [b] 11 Some early manuscripts *are to come*   [c] 12 Or *blood, having obtained*
[d] 14 Or *from useless rituals*   [e] 16 Same Greek word as *covenant*; also in verse 17   [f] 20 Exodus 24:8

with blood, and without the shedding of blood there is no forgiveness.

²³It was necessary, then, for the copies of the heavenly things to be purified with these sacrifices, but the heavenly things themselves with better sacrifices than these. ²⁴For Christ did not enter a sanctuary made with human hands that was only a copy of the true one; he entered heaven itself, now to appear for us in God's presence. ²⁵Nor did he enter heaven to offer himself again and again, the way the high priest enters the Most Holy Place every year with blood that is not his own. ²⁶Otherwise Christ would have had to suffer many times since the creation of the world. But he has appeared once for all at the culmination of the ages to do away with sin by the sacrifice of himself. ²⁷Just as people are destined to die once, and after that to face judgment, ²⁸so Christ was sacrificed once to take away the sins of many; and he will appear a second time, not to bear sin, but to bring salvation to those who are waiting for him.

Christ's Sacrifice Once for All

10 The law is only a shadow of the good things that are coming — not the realities themselves. For this reason it can never, by the same sacrifices repeated endlessly year after year, make perfect those who draw near to worship. ²Otherwise, would they not have stopped being offered? For the worshipers would have been cleansed once for all, and would no longer have felt guilty for their sins. ³But those sacrifices are an annual reminder of sins. ⁴It is impossible for the blood of bulls and goats to take away sins.

⁵Therefore, when Christ came into the world, he said:

"Sacrifice and offering you did not desire,
    but a body you prepared for me;
⁶with burnt offerings and sin offerings
    you were not pleased.
⁷Then I said, 'Here I am — it is written
    about me in the scroll —
I have come to do your will, my God.'"ᵃ

⁸First he said, "Sacrifices and offerings, burnt offerings and sin offerings you did not desire, nor were you pleased with them" — though they were offered in accordance with

the law. ⁹Then he said, "Here I am, I have come to do your will." He sets aside the first to establish the second. ¹⁰And by that will, we have been made holy through the sacrifice of the body of Jesus Christ once for all.

¹¹Day after day every priest stands and performs his religious duties; again and again he offers the same sacrifices, which can never take away sins. ¹²But when this priest had offered for all time one sacrifice for sins, he sat down at the right hand of God, ¹³and since that time he waits for his enemies to be made his footstool. ¹⁴For by one sacrifice he has made perfect forever those who are being made holy.

¹⁵The Holy Spirit also testifies to us about this. First he says:

¹⁶"This is the covenant I will make with
        them
    after that time, says the Lord.
I will put my laws in their hearts,
    and I will write them on their minds."ᵇ

¹⁷Then he adds:

"Their sins and lawless acts
    I will remember no more."ᶜ

¹⁸And where these have been forgiven, sacrifice for sin is no longer necessary.

A Call to Persevere in Faith

¹⁹Therefore, brothers and sisters, since we have confidence to enter the Most Holy Place by the blood of Jesus, ²⁰by a new and living way opened for us through the curtain, that is, his body, ²¹and since we have a great priest over the house of God, ²²let us draw near to God with a sincere heart and with the full assurance that faith brings, having our hearts sprinkled to cleanse us from a guilty conscience and having our bodies washed with pure water. ²³Let us hold unswervingly to the hope we profess, for he who promised is faithful. ²⁴And let us consider how we may spur one another on toward love and good deeds, ²⁵not giving up meeting together, as some are in the habit of doing, but encouraging one another — and all the more as you see the Day approaching.

²⁶If we deliberately keep on sinning after we have received the knowledge of the truth, no sacrifice for sins is left, ²⁷but only a fearful

---

ᵃ 7 Psalm 40:6-8 (see Septuagint)   ᵇ 16 Jer. 31:33   ᶜ 17 Jer. 31:34

Created for Community

By Ronda Sturgill

READ: Hebrews 10:19–25

From the very beginning we were created for community. Think about it. After observing that all he had created was "very good" (Genesis 1:31), God looked at Adam, who was alone in the beautiful garden, and declared, "It is not good for the man to be alone" (Genesis 2:18). And what did God do? He created Eve. He provided Adam with a companion and a friend. In their book, *Creating Community: Five Keys to Building a Small Group Culture*, Andy Stanley and Bill Willits make the following observation about the Genesis passage: God made people with a God-shaped void that no other person can fill, but he also made people with a human-shaped void that God himself cannot fill.

If we allow it to be, the life of a military wife can be very lonely. During the brief time we spend at the same geographic location, we can easily be tempted to think, "We'll be moving in a few years anyway, so why bother getting involved with others?" The problem is that when we aren't in meaningful relationships, we suffer natural consequences. We simply were not made to live in isolation. Living in isolation can cause selfishness, fear of intimacy, poor health and loss of perspective. Sheep are not usually attacked in flocks; they are attacked when isolated from the flock.

Therefore, believers are encouraged to make every effort to live in community with one another. This is expressed very well in Hebrews 10:23–25. Within the context of an authentic church community, life-giving relationships that foster hope, encouragement, love and good deeds are established. Since most military families live far away from their biological families, developing close relationships with other military families can help ease the separation from moms, dads, brothers, sisters and grandparents.

A vibrant church community helps us become the person God created us to be. When others see and affirm our natural skills, gifts and talents, we are encouraged to pursue areas of service where we can be the most fruitful. Members of an authentic church body support one another with mutual feelings of love and respect. In John 17:20–21, Jesus prayed for us, his disciples, to experience the same close relationship that he shares with the Father. Without such intimacy, it's almost impossible to become spiritually mature.

Are you living in relationship with other believers? Are you connected to a church body that loves and supports you? One of God's greatest desires for us is authentic community.

Let us consider how we may spur one another on toward love and good deeds, not giving up meeting together, as some are in the habit of doing, but encouraging one another—and all the more as you see the Day approaching.

HEBREWS 10:24–25

DEBRIEF
- How am I being fulfilled by other believers right now?
- If I'm not part of an authentic church community right now, what would it take for me to become part of one? I will ask God to meet this need for me.

REPORT
Dear heavenly Father, just as I desire to give hope and encouragement to others, I also need to be encouraged through loving and respectful relationships. I desire to live in relationship with members of an authentic Christian community. Help me build relationships within the church that will be a good fit for me and my family. Amen.

expectation of judgment and of raging fire that will consume the enemies of God. [28]Anyone who rejected the law of Moses died without mercy on the testimony of two or three witnesses. [29]How much more severely do you think someone deserves to be punished who has trampled the Son of God underfoot, who has treated as an unholy thing the blood of the covenant that sanctified them, and who has insulted the Spirit of grace? [30]For we know him who said, "It is mine to avenge; I will repay,"[a] and again, "The Lord will judge his people."[b] [31]It is a dreadful thing to fall into the hands of the living God.

[32]Remember those earlier days after you had received the light, when you endured in a great conflict full of suffering. [33]Sometimes you were publicly exposed to insult and persecution; at other times you stood side by side with those who were so treated. [34]You suffered along with those in prison and joyfully accepted the confiscation of your property, because you knew that you yourselves had better and lasting possessions. [35]So do not throw away your confidence; it will be richly rewarded.

[36]You need to persevere so that when you have done the will of God, you will receive what he has promised. [37]For,

"In just a little while,
    he who is coming will come
    and will not delay."[c]

[38]And,

"But my righteous[d] one will live by faith.
    And I take no pleasure
    in the one who shrinks back."[e]

[39]But we do not belong to those who shrink back and are destroyed, but to those who have faith and are saved.

Faith in Action

11 Now faith is confidence in what we hope for and assurance about what we do not see. [2]This is what the ancients were commended for.

[3]By faith we understand that the universe was formed at God's command, so that what is seen was not made out of what was visible.

[4]By faith Abel brought God a better offering than Cain did. By faith he was commended as righteous, when God spoke well of his offerings. And by faith Abel still speaks, even though he is dead.

[5]By faith Enoch was taken from this life, so that he did not experience death: "He could not be found, because God had taken him away."[f] For before he was taken, he was commended as one who pleased God. [6]And without faith it is impossible to please God, because anyone who comes to him must believe that he exists and that he rewards those who earnestly seek him.

[7]By faith Noah, when warned about things not yet seen, in holy fear built an ark to save his family. By his faith he condemned the world and became heir of the righteousness that is in keeping with faith.

[8]By faith Abraham, when called to go to a place he would later receive as his inheritance, obeyed and went, even though he did not know where he was going. [9]By faith he made his home in the promised land like a stranger in a foreign country; he lived in tents, as did Isaac and Jacob, who were heirs with him of the same promise. [10]For he was looking forward to the city with foundations, whose architect and builder is God. [11]And by faith even Sarah, who was past childbearing age, was enabled to bear children because she[g] considered him faithful who had made the promise. [12]And so from this one man, and he as good as dead, came descendants as numerous as the stars in the sky and as countless as the sand on the seashore.

[13]All these people were still living by faith when they died. They did not receive the things promised; they only saw them and welcomed them from a distance, admitting that they were foreigners and strangers on earth. [14]People who say such things show that they are looking for a country of their own. [15]If they had been thinking of the country they had left, they would have had opportunity to return. [16]Instead, they were longing for a better country — a heavenly one. Therefore God is not ashamed to be called their God, for he has prepared a city for them.

---

[a] 30 Deut. 32:35   [b] 30 Deut. 32:36; Psalm 135:14   [c] 37 Isaiah 26:20; Hab. 2:3   [d] 38 Some early manuscripts But the righteous   [e] 38 Hab. 2:4 (see Septuagint)   [f] 5 Gen. 5:24   [g] 11 Or By faith Abraham, even though he was too old to have children — and Sarah herself was not able to conceive — was enabled to become a father because he

[17] By faith Abraham, when God tested him, offered Isaac as a sacrifice. He who had embraced the promises was about to sacrifice his one and only son, [18] even though God had said to him, "It is through Isaac that your offspring will be reckoned."[a] [19] Abraham reasoned that God could even raise the dead, and so in a manner of speaking he did receive Isaac back from death.

[20] By faith Isaac blessed Jacob and Esau in regard to their future.

[21] By faith Jacob, when he was dying, blessed each of Joseph's sons, and worshiped as he leaned on the top of his staff.

[22] By faith Joseph, when his end was near, spoke about the exodus of the Israelites from Egypt and gave instructions concerning the burial of his bones.

[23] By faith Moses' parents hid him for three months after he was born, because they saw he was no ordinary child, and they were not afraid of the king's edict.

[24] By faith Moses, when he had grown up, refused to be known as the son of Pharaoh's daughter. [25] He chose to be mistreated along with the people of God rather than to enjoy the fleeting pleasures of sin. [26] He regarded disgrace for the sake of Christ as of greater value than the treasures of Egypt, because he was looking ahead to his reward. [27] By faith he left Egypt, not fearing the king's anger; he persevered because he saw him who is invisible. [28] By faith he kept the Passover and the application of blood, so that the destroyer of the firstborn would not touch the firstborn of Israel.

[29] By faith the people passed through the Red Sea as on dry land; but when the Egyptians tried to do so, they were drowned.

[30] By faith the walls of Jericho fell, after the army had marched around them for seven days.

[31] By faith the prostitute Rahab, because she welcomed the spies, was not killed with those who were disobedient.[b]

[32] And what more shall I say? I do not have time to tell about Gideon, Barak, Samson and Jephthah, about David and Samuel and the prophets, [33] who through faith conquered kingdoms, administered justice, and gained what was promised; who shut the mouths of lions, [34] quenched the fury of the

flames, and escaped the edge of the sword; whose weakness was turned to strength; and who became powerful in battle and routed foreign armies. [35] Women received back their dead, raised to life again. There were others who were tortured, refusing to be released so that they might gain an even better resurrection. [36] Some faced jeers and flogging, and even chains and imprisonment. [37] They were put to death by stoning;[c] they were sawed in two; they were killed by the sword. They went about in sheepskins and goatskins, destitute, persecuted and mistreated — [38] the world was not worthy of them. They wandered in deserts and mountains, living in caves and in holes in the ground.

[39] These were all commended for their faith, yet none of them received what had been promised, [40] since God had planned something better for us so that only together with us would they be made perfect.

12 Therefore, since we are surrounded by such a great cloud of witnesses, let us throw off everything that hinders and the sin that so easily entangles. And let us run with perseverance the race marked out for us, [2] fixing our eyes on Jesus, the pioneer and perfecter of faith. For the joy set before him he endured the cross, scorning its shame, and sat down at the right hand of the throne of God. [3] Consider him who endured such opposition from sinners, so that you will not grow weary and lose heart.

God Disciplines His Children

[4] In your struggle against sin, you have not yet resisted to the point of shedding your blood. [5] And have you completely forgotten this word of encouragement that addresses you as a father addresses his son? It says,

"My son, do not make light of the Lord's
    discipline,
and do not lose heart when he
        rebukes you,
[6] because the Lord disciplines the one
        he loves,
and he chastens everyone he accepts
        as his son."[d]

[7] Endure hardship as discipline; God is treating you as his children. For what children

---

[a] 18 Gen. 21:12   [b] 31 Or unbelieving   [c] 37 Some early manuscripts stoning; they were put to the test;
[d] 5,6 Prov. 3:11,12 (see Septuagint)

JOURNEY OF FAITH

By Jocelyn Green

In June 1846, during the Mexican-American War, Susan Shelby Magoffin accompanied her husband, Samuel, a trader, and his brother, James, on a journey down the Santa Fe Trail. Due to personal hardship and the rugged terrain, both Susan's courage and her faith were greatly challenged.

In August, Susan gave birth to a stillborn child and credited it to "the ruling hand of a Mighty Providence." In addition, Susan knew the war with Mexico added to their danger. What she didn't know was that her brother-in-law secretly carried critical information and instructions concerning the war directly from President James Polk.

The letters in James's pocket were discovered, and he was imprisoned for espionage. This, of course, put Susan and Samuel in danger as well. Still, Susan carried on by Samuel's side through the 2,000-mile journey, persevering in spite of wild beasts, hostile Native American tribes, bandits, miles of waterless desert and the threat of Mexican troops. She prayed for their safety and for James's protection. She also prayed that her fierce love for her husband, would never surpass her love for her Savior. She wrote in her diary:

> What a satisfaction would it be ... that loving my dear husband as I do, I am not excluding an Image more precious to the soul of mortals, than all things earthly ... Oh, that there may be no cause for severe judgment against either of us in this thing! but that the deep devotion felt for each other here may be but a small type of that felt for our Redeemer above!

In January 1847, trapped between a band of hostile Native Americans and Mexican troops, death or capture seeemed imminent. She wrote: "I wonder if I shall ever get home again. But it is all the same if I do or do not, I must look farther ahead than to earthly things."

Susan, Samuel and even James survived the Mexican-American War without harm. But Susan clearly understood that her life's journey would ultimately end in heaven, regardless of whether or not it ended on the Santa Fe Trail. At every turn in the road, Susan persevered physically, emotionally and spiritually. She fixed her eyes on Jesus so that she would not grow weary and lose heart.

Prayer: *Lord, give me strength to persevere and keep my eyes on you!*

Let us run with perseverance the race marked out for us, fixing our eyes on Jesus, the pioneer and perfecter of faith. For the joy set before him he endured the cross, scorning its shame, and sat down at the right hand of the throne of God. Consider him who endured such opposition from sinners, so that you will not grow weary and lose heart.

HEBREWS 12:1 – 3

for your next devotional reading, go to page 287

are not disciplined by their father? [8]If you are not disciplined—and everyone undergoes discipline—then you are not legitimate, not true sons and daughters at all. [9]Moreover, we have all had human fathers who disciplined us and we respected them for it. How much more should we submit to the Father of spirits and live! [10]They disciplined us for a little while as they thought best; but God disciplines us for our good, in order that we may share in his holiness. [11]No discipline seems pleasant at the time, but painful. Later on, however, it produces a harvest of righteousness and peace for those who have been trained by it.

[12]Therefore, strengthen your feeble arms and weak knees. [13]"Make level paths for your feet,"[a] so that the lame may not be disabled, but rather healed.

Warning and Encouragement

[14]Make every effort to live in peace with everyone and to be holy; without holiness no one will see the Lord. [15]See to it that no one falls short of the grace of God and that no bitter root grows up to cause trouble and defile many. [16]See that no one is sexually immoral, or is godless like Esau, who for a single meal sold his inheritance rights as the oldest son. [17]Afterward, as you know, when he wanted to inherit this blessing, he was rejected. Even though he sought the blessing with tears, he could not change what he had done.

The Mountain of Fear and the Mountain of Joy

[18]You have not come to a mountain that can be touched and that is burning with fire; to darkness, gloom and storm; [19]to a trumpet blast or to such a voice speaking words that those who heard it begged that no further word be spoken to them, [20]because they could not bear what was commanded: "If even an animal touches the mountain, it must be stoned to death."[b] [21]The sight was so terrifying that Moses said, "I am trembling with fear."[c]

[22]But you have come to Mount Zion, to the city of the living God, the heavenly Jerusalem. You have come to thousands upon thousands of angels in joyful assembly, [23]to the church of the firstborn, whose names are written in heaven. You have come to God, the Judge of all, to the spirits of the righteous made perfect, [24]to Jesus the mediator of a new covenant, and to the sprinkled blood that speaks a better word than the blood of Abel.

[25]See to it that you do not refuse him who speaks. If they did not escape when they refused him who warned them on earth, how much less will we, if we turn away from him who warns us from heaven? [26]At that time his voice shook the earth, but now he has promised, "Once more I will shake not only the earth but also the heavens."[d] [27]The words "once more" indicate the removing of what can be shaken—that is, created things—so that what cannot be shaken may remain.

[28]Therefore, since we are receiving a kingdom that cannot be shaken, let us be thankful, and so worship God acceptably with reverence and awe, [29]for our "God is a consuming fire."[e]

Concluding Exhortations

13 Keep on loving one another as brothers and sisters. [2]Do not forget to show hospitality to strangers, for by so doing some people have shown hospitality to angels without knowing it. [3]Continue to remember those in prison as if you were together with them in prison, and those who are mistreated as if you yourselves were suffering.

[4]Marriage should be honored by all, and the marriage bed kept pure, for God will judge the adulterer and all the sexually immoral. [5]Keep your lives free from the love of money and be content with what you have, because God has said,

"Never will I leave you;
    never will I forsake you."[f]

[6]So we say with confidence,

"The Lord is my helper; I will not be
    afraid.
What can mere mortals do to me?"[g]

[7]Remember your leaders, who spoke the word of God to you. Consider the outcome of their way of life and imitate their faith. [8]Jesus Christ is the same yesterday and today and forever.

[a] 13 Prov. 4:26   [b] 20 Exodus 19:12,13   [c] 21 See Deut. 9:19.   [d] 26 Haggai 2:6   [e] 29 Deut. 4:24   [f] 5 Deut. 31:6   [g] 6 Psalm 118:6,7

⁹Do not be carried away by all kinds of strange teachings. It is good for our hearts to be strengthened by grace, not by eating ceremonial foods, which is of no benefit to those who do so. ¹⁰We have an altar from which those who minister at the tabernacle have no right to eat.

¹¹The high priest carries the blood of animals into the Most Holy Place as a sin offering, but the bodies are burned outside the camp. ¹²And so Jesus also suffered outside the city gate to make the people holy through his own blood. ¹³Let us, then, go to him outside the camp, bearing the disgrace he bore. ¹⁴For here we do not have an enduring city, but we are looking for the city that is to come.

¹⁵Through Jesus, therefore, let us continually offer to God a sacrifice of praise — the fruit of lips that openly profess his name. ¹⁶And do not forget to do good and to share with others, for with such sacrifices God is pleased.

¹⁷Have confidence in your leaders and submit to their authority, because they keep watch over you as those who must give an account. Do this so that their work will be a joy, not a burden, for that would be of no benefit to you.

¹⁸Pray for us. We are sure that we have a clear conscience and desire to live honorably in every way. ¹⁹I particularly urge you to pray so that I may be restored to you soon.

Benediction and Final Greetings

²⁰Now may the God of peace, who through the blood of the eternal covenant brought back from the dead our Lord Jesus, that great Shepherd of the sheep, ²¹equip you with everything good for doing his will, and may he work in us what is pleasing to him, through Jesus Christ, to whom be glory for ever and ever. Amen.

²²Brothers and sisters, I urge you to bear with my word of exhortation, for in fact I have written to you quite briefly.

²³I want you to know that our brother Timothy has been released. If he arrives soon, I will come with him to see you.

²⁴Greet all your leaders and all the Lord's people. Those from Italy send you their greetings.

²⁵Grace be with you all.

James

1 James, a servant of God and of the Lord Jesus Christ,

To the twelve tribes scattered among the nations:

Greetings.

Trials and Temptations

[2] Consider it pure joy, my brothers and sisters,[a] whenever you face trials of many kinds, [3] because you know that the testing of your faith produces perseverance. [4] Let perseverance finish its work so that you may be mature and complete, not lacking anything. [5] If any of you lacks wisdom, you should ask God, who gives generously to all without finding fault, and it will be given to you. [6] But when you ask, you must believe and not doubt, because the one who doubts is like a wave of the sea, blown and tossed by the wind. [7] That person should not expect to receive anything from the Lord. [8] Such a person is double-minded and unstable in all they do.

[9] Believers in humble circumstances ought to take pride in their high position. [10] But the rich should take pride in their humiliation — since they will pass away like a wild flower. [11] For the sun rises with scorching heat and withers the plant; its blossom falls and its beauty is destroyed. In the same way, the rich will fade away even while they go about their business.

[12] Blessed is the one who perseveres under trial because, having stood the test, that person will receive the crown of life that the Lord has promised to those who love him. [13] When tempted, no one should say, "God is tempting me." For God cannot be tempted by evil, nor does he tempt anyone; [14] but each person is tempted when they are dragged away by their own evil desire and enticed. [15] Then, after desire has conceived, it gives birth to sin; and sin, when it is full-grown, gives birth to death.

[16] Don't be deceived, my dear brothers and sisters. [17] Every good and perfect gift is from above, coming down from the Father of the heavenly lights, who does not change like shifting shadows. [18] He chose to give us birth through the word of truth, that we might be a kind of firstfruits of all he created.

Listening and Doing

[19] My dear brothers and sisters, take note of this: Everyone should be quick to listen, slow to speak and slow to become angry, [20] because human anger does not produce the righteousness that God desires. [21] Therefore, get rid of all moral filth and the evil that is so prevalent and humbly accept the word planted in you, which can save you.

[22] Do not merely listen to the word, and so deceive yourselves. Do what it says. [23] Anyone who listens to the word but does not do what it says is like someone who looks at his face in a mirror [24] and, after looking at himself, goes away and immediately forgets what he looks like. [25] But whoever looks intently into the perfect law that gives freedom, and continues in it — not forgetting what they have heard, but doing it — they will be blessed in what they do.

[26] Those who consider themselves religious and yet do not keep a tight rein on their tongues deceive themselves, and their religion is worthless. [27] Religion that God our Father accepts as pure and faultless is this: to look after orphans and widows in their distress and to keep oneself from being polluted by the world.

Favoritism Forbidden

2 My brothers and sisters, believers in our glorious Lord Jesus Christ must not show favoritism. [2] Suppose a man comes into your meeting wearing a gold ring and fine clothes, and a poor man in filthy old clothes also comes in. [3] If you show special

---

[a] 2 The Greek word for *brothers and sisters* (*adelphoi*) refers here to believers, both men and women, as part of God's family; also in verses 16 and 19; and in 2:1, 5, 14; 3:10, 12; 4:11; 5:7, 9, 10, 12, 19.

Joy in the Crucible

By Sarah Ball

READ: James 1:2–18

What brings you joy? I hope you could make a long list of people and things that bring joy to your life. If you are like me, though, I doubt "trials of many kinds" (James 1:2) would make the list.

Our God takes a much bigger view of joy and life than we do. He created a world full of things that grow in beauty under stress. Consider silver, for example. Silver begins as ore that is mined from deep underground. At first, it looks like rock. Under the skillful hands of a silversmith, however, it is crumbled and heated in a container called a crucible. The steady high temperature liquefies the silver, and impurities rise to the surface. The silversmith watches carefully, skimming away the impurities as they appear.

The process takes time; constant heat continues to separate out the dross (impurities) from the silver. When the silversmith can finally see his own reflection clearly in the liquid silver, he knows the silver is pure. Finally, the silver is ready to be shaped into something beautiful.

When we begin our walk with God, we are much like the silver ore freshly taken from the ground. God, our great Refiner, values us as children created in his image. However, his image in us is marred by the many impurities we carry. Our sinful nature makes the image of God difficult to see in our natural selves. The trials we face challenge us, pushing our flaws and sins to the surface. When we yield them to God, he removes them from us. His image in us becomes clearer.

In *As Silver Refined*, Kay Arthur describes God's attentive care: "Our Refiner never leaves the crucible, never steps away from the fire … He knows the precise temperature to maintain so we don't face more than we can bear." Through the process of persevering, we become "mature and complete, not lacking anything" (James 1:4).

We military spouses share many of the same trials — deployments, cross-country moves, separations and loneliness. Other trials can feel like our own personal fires. These trials may refine and grow us, but we struggle to persevere through the pain of the fire.

The crucible is not an easy place to be. The only possible way to "consider it pure joy … whenever you face trials" (James 1:2) is to focus on the end result James describes. All of our impurities will finally be removed, and the image of our God will be mirror-clear in our lives. Knowing our future, we can have joy today while we are still in the crucible.

Consider it pure joy, my brothers and sisters, whenever you face trials of many kinds, because you know that the testing of your faith produces perseverance. Let perseverance finish its work so that you may be mature and complete, not lacking anything.
JAMES 1:2–4

DEBRIEF
- How has God used trials in my life to refine me?
- In what area of my life is God purifying me right now?

REPORT
Lord, thank you for loving me too much to leave me as I am. Help me yield my impurities to you. Grant me joy as I embrace the pure, refined silver that I am becoming. In Jesus' name I pray. Amen.

for your next devotional reading, go to page 290

attention to the man wearing fine clothes and say, "Here's a good seat for you," but say to the poor man, "You stand there" or "Sit on the floor by my feet," ⁴have you not discriminated among yourselves and become judges with evil thoughts?

⁵Listen, my dear brothers and sisters: Has not God chosen those who are poor in the eyes of the world to be rich in faith and to inherit the kingdom he promised those who love him? ⁶But you have dishonored the poor. Is it not the rich who are exploiting you? Are they not the ones who are dragging you into court? ⁷Are they not the ones who are blaspheming the noble name of him to whom you belong?

⁸If you really keep the royal law found in Scripture, "Love your neighbor as yourself,"ᵃ you are doing right. ⁹But if you show favoritism, you sin and are convicted by the law as lawbreakers. ¹⁰For whoever keeps the whole law and yet stumbles at just one point is guilty of breaking all of it. ¹¹For he who said, "You shall not commit adultery,"ᵇ also said, "You shall not murder."ᶜ If you do not commit adultery but do commit murder, you have become a lawbreaker.

¹²Speak and act as those who are going to be judged by the law that gives freedom, ¹³because judgment without mercy will be shown to anyone who has not been merciful. Mercy triumphs over judgment.

Faith and Deeds

¹⁴What good is it, my brothers and sisters, if someone claims to have faith but has no deeds? Can such faith save them? ¹⁵Suppose a brother or a sister is without clothes and daily food. ¹⁶If one of you says to them, "Go in peace; keep warm and well fed," but does nothing about their physical needs, what good is it? ¹⁷In the same way, faith by itself, if it is not accompanied by action, is dead.

¹⁸But someone will say, "You have faith; I have deeds."

Show me your faith without deeds, and I will show you my faith by my deeds. ¹⁹You believe that there is one God. Good! Even the demons believe that—and shudder.

²⁰You foolish person, do you want evidence that faith without deeds is useless ᵈ?

²¹Was not our father Abraham considered righteous for what he did when he offered his son Isaac on the altar? ²²You see that his faith and his actions were working together, and his faith was made complete by what he did. ²³And the scripture was fulfilled that says, "Abraham believed God, and it was credited to him as righteousness,"ᵉ and he was called God's friend. ²⁴You see that a person is considered righteous by what they do and not by faith alone.

²⁵In the same way, was not even Rahab the prostitute considered righteous for what she did when she gave lodging to the spies and sent them off in a different direction? ²⁶As the body without the spirit is dead, so faith without deeds is dead.

Taming the Tongue

3 Not many of you should become teachers, my fellow believers, because you know that we who teach will be judged more strictly. ²We all stumble in many ways. Anyone who is never at fault in what they say is perfect, able to keep their whole body in check.

³When we put bits into the mouths of horses to make them obey us, we can turn the whole animal. ⁴Or take ships as an example. Although they are so large and are driven by strong winds, they are steered by a very small rudder wherever the pilot wants to go. ⁵Likewise, the tongue is a small part of the body, but it makes great boasts. Consider what a great forest is set on fire by a small spark. ⁶The tongue also is a fire, a world of evil among the parts of the body. It corrupts the whole body, sets the whole course of one's life on fire, and is itself set on fire by hell.

⁷All kinds of animals, birds, reptiles and sea creatures are being tamed and have been tamed by mankind, ⁸but no human being can tame the tongue. It is a restless evil, full of deadly poison.

⁹With the tongue we praise our Lord and Father, and with it we curse human beings, who have been made in God's likeness. ¹⁰Out of the same mouth come praise and cursing. My brothers and sisters, this should not be. ¹¹Can both fresh water and salt water flow

---

ᵃ 8 Lev. 19:18   ᵇ 11 Exodus 20:14; Deut. 5:18   ᶜ 11 Exodus 20:13; Deut. 5:17   ᵈ 20 Some early manuscripts *dead*   ᵉ 23 Gen. 15:6

from the same spring? [12]My brothers and sisters, can a fig tree bear olives, or a grapevine bear figs? Neither can a salt spring produce fresh water.

Two Kinds of Wisdom

[13]Who is wise and understanding among you? Let them show it by their good life, by deeds done in the humility that comes from wisdom. [14]But if you harbor bitter envy and selfish ambition in your hearts, do not boast about it or deny the truth. [15]Such "wisdom" does not come down from heaven but is earthly, unspiritual, demonic. [16]For where you have envy and selfish ambition, there you find disorder and every evil practice.

[17]But the wisdom that comes from heaven is first of all pure; then peace-loving, considerate, submissive, full of mercy and good fruit, impartial and sincere. [18]Peacemakers who sow in peace reap a harvest of righteousness.

Submit Yourselves to God

4 What causes fights and quarrels among you? Don't they come from your desires that battle within you? [2]You desire but do not have, so you kill. You covet but you cannot get what you want, so you quarrel and fight. You do not have because you do not ask God. [3]When you ask, you do not receive, because you ask with wrong motives, that you may spend what you get on your pleasures.

[4]You adulterous people,[a] don't you know that friendship with the world means enmity against God? Therefore, anyone who chooses to be a friend of the world becomes an enemy of God. [5]Or do you think Scripture says without reason that he jealously longs for the spirit he has caused to dwell in us[b]? [6]But he gives us more grace. That is why Scripture says:

"God opposes the proud
　but shows favor to the humble."[c]

[7]Submit yourselves, then, to God. Resist the devil, and he will flee from you. [8]Come near to God and he will come near to you. Wash your hands, you sinners, and purify your hearts, you double-minded. [9]Grieve, mourn and wail. Change your laughter to mourning and your joy to gloom. [10]Humble yourselves before the Lord, and he will lift you up.

[11]Brothers and sisters, do not slander one another. Anyone who speaks against a brother or sister[d] or judges them speaks against the law and judges it. When you judge the law, you are not keeping it, but sitting in judgment on it. [12]There is only one Lawgiver and Judge, the one who is able to save and destroy. But you—who are you to judge your neighbor?

Boasting About Tomorrow

[13]Now listen, you who say, "Today or tomorrow we will go to this or that city, spend a year there, carry on business and make money." [14]Why, you do not even know what will happen tomorrow. What is your life? You are a mist that appears for a little while and then vanishes. [15]Instead, you ought to say, "If it is the Lord's will, we will live and do this or that." [16]As it is, you boast in your arrogant schemes. All such boasting is evil. [17]If anyone, then, knows the good they ought to do and doesn't do it, it is sin for them.

Warning to Rich Oppressors

5 Now listen, you rich people, weep and wail because of the misery that is coming on you. [2]Your wealth has rotted, and moths have eaten your clothes. [3]Your gold and silver are corroded. Their corrosion will testify against you and eat your flesh like fire. You have hoarded wealth in the last days. [4]Look! The wages you failed to pay the workers who mowed your fields are crying out against you. The cries of the harvesters have reached the ears of the Lord Almighty. [5]You have lived on earth in luxury and self-indulgence. You have fattened yourselves in the day of slaughter.[e] [6]You have condemned and murdered the innocent one, who was not opposing you.

Patience in Suffering

[7]Be patient, then, brothers and sisters, until the Lord's coming. See how the farmer waits for the land to yield its valuable crop, patiently waiting for the autumn and spring

---

[a] 4 An allusion to covenant unfaithfulness; see Hosea 3:1.　[b] 5 Or *that the spirit he caused to dwell in us envies intensely;* or *that the Spirit he caused to dwell in us longs jealously*　[c] 6 Prov. 3:34　[d] 11 The Greek word for *brother or sister* (*adelphos*) refers here to a believer, whether man or woman, as part of God's family.　[e] 5 Or *yourselves as in a day of feasting*

I Know Who Holds Tomorrow

By Pattie Reitz

READ: James 4:13–17

I am the kind of person for whom the unknown is more than a little frustrating. I want to know everything. I thrive on information, making lists, hashing things out and taking careful notes. I like to know *right now* what is going to happen *later*.

Are you laughing yet? Shaking your head? Nodding in agreement? Those of us living the life of the military wife know that it is often frustrating to make careful plans, only to have them quickly change, sometimes more than once in a single day, throwing our lives and futures into the proverbial tailspin. To say there are many unknowns is an understatement. How long will we live here? When is his next training/TDY/deployment? Will he make his next promotion? It's enough to drive a woman crazy.

That is why passages like this one in James 4 give me pause, and rightly so. When I feel the stress of not knowing my future, I am reminded of the One who *is* in control. Verse 14 says, "Why, you do not even know what will happen tomorrow. What is your life? You are a mist that appears for a little while and then vanishes." Ouch.

We are not promised tomorrow. Or the next day or the next rank or the next duty station. So what are we to do? Certainly not worry. Proverbs 16:3 instructs us to "commit to the LORD whatever you do, and he will establish your plans." I think that's about as clear as any road map, don't you? And James does not leave us hanging either. In verse 15, he continues: "Instead, you ought to say, 'If it is the Lord's will, we will live and do this or that.' " It's evident that we must let go of our worrying and planning, and commit the future to the Lord's capable, eternal hands.

Years ago, when my husband was pastoring a small church, I learned a hymn penned by Ira Forest Stanphill. The chorus goes like this:

> *Many things about tomorrow I don't seem to understand*
> *But I know who holds tomorrow, and I know who holds my hand.*

I had no idea this song would come back to my mind again and again as a reminder that I don't have to know the future because the Lord's purpose will prevail (see Proverbs 19:21).

Many things about military life are unknown. But we can rest with certainty in God's promise in Isaiah 48:17: "I am the LORD your God ... who directs you in the way you should go."

Why, you do not even know what will happen tomorrow. What is your life? You are a mist that appears for a little while and then vanishes.

JAMES 4:14

DEBRIEF
- How can I trust God more fully with my future?
- How can I focus on God's will for my life, instead of on my own plans and worries?

REPORT
Lord, thank you for the promises in your Word that you will take care of the future. Please direct me in the way you would have me go—in my daily life, in my husband's career and in our home. I pray all of this in your name. Amen.

ALL THE WAY HOME

By Jocelyn Green

When Dr. LuAnn Callaway's only child, Jacob, told her he had joined the Georgia National Guard, she told him she was going to shoot him in the foot. His response was, "Mom, I will limp all the way to Afghanistan. I'm going to serve my country."

After Jacob deployed, LuAnn's opportunities to communicate with him dwindled to once a month at the most. LuAnn and her husband, Sid, woke up in the mornings with what they called "the dreads." She explained: "It is that pit in your stomach that won't go away with a cup of coffee, some Bible verses and a quick prayer. The dreads called for deep prayer, crying out to God and reading large passages of Scripture. Worship music was helpful too."

When three different people suggested that she pray Psalm 91 over her son, God had her attention. "Everything began to change. I got my scaredy-pants off and my cargo pants on."

LuAnn studied God's Word, claiming his promises, and prayed boldly. Six months into Jacob's deployment, LuAnn discovered Military Ministry's many resources and eventually joined the Military Ministry team and called on churches to hold out their arms to our troops and families. As a counselor herself for 30 years, she had counseled patients with Post Traumatic Stress Disorder hundreds of times. "But I was surprised to learn that the symptoms for combat trauma are different and the treatment could not be the same," she said. "I had to learn more, for me and for my counseling center."

LuAnn invited 93 churches in her county and chaplains at all the bases from central to north Georgia to participate in a 30-hour training program. She told them, "We have 4,000 soldiers, the 48th Infantry, who are coming home in six months, and we have to be ready for them." Twenty-two people came.

"We learned that soldiers are often hesitant to seek help from the Army because it could be a 'career killer' for them," she said. "So our Saturday group, ages 23 to 83, decided to provide, without charge, our counseling time to the 20 percent who would return from battle with PTSD. No record of their visits. No insurance filed. No notification to the military."

LuAnn prayed for strength and wisdom to help soldiers heal from combat trauma, and God answered. Today she is the national counseling director of Military Ministry and speaks on behalf of numerous groups. By the middle of April 2010, nearly all of the 48th Infantry had returned to Georgia (eight soldiers were killed in Afghanistan). "We have been privileged to help many of them come all the way home."

Prayer: Lord, show me how you want me to pray and how you want me to be involved in helping others.

Is anyone among you in trouble? Let them pray ... The prayer of a righteous person is powerful and effective.
JAMES 5:13,16

for your next devotional reading, go to page 294

rains. [8]You too, be patient and stand firm, because the Lord's coming is near. [9]Don't grumble against one another, brothers and sisters, or you will be judged. The Judge is standing at the door!

[10]Brothers and sisters, as an example of patience in the face of suffering, take the prophets who spoke in the name of the Lord. [11]As you know, we count as blessed those who have persevered. You have heard of Job's perseverance and have seen what the Lord finally brought about. The Lord is full of compassion and mercy.

[12]Above all, my brothers and sisters, do not swear—not by heaven or by earth or by anything else. All you need to say is a simple "Yes" or "No." Otherwise you will be condemned.

The Prayer of Faith

[13]Is anyone among you in trouble? Let them pray. Is anyone happy? Let them sing songs of praise. [14]Is anyone among you sick? Let them call the elders of the church to pray over them and anoint them with oil in the name of the Lord. [15]And the prayer offered in faith will make the sick person well; the Lord will raise them up. If they have sinned, they will be forgiven. [16]Therefore confess your sins to each other and pray for each other so that you may be healed. The prayer of a righteous person is powerful and effective.

[17]Elijah was a human being, even as we are. He prayed earnestly that it would not rain, and it did not rain on the land for three and a half years. [18]Again he prayed, and the heavens gave rain, and the earth produced its crops.

[19]My brothers and sisters, if one of you should wander from the truth and someone should bring that person back, [20]remember this: Whoever turns a sinner from the error of their way will save them from death and cover over a multitude of sins.

1 Peter

1 Peter, an apostle of Jesus Christ,

To God's elect, exiles scattered throughout the provinces of Pontus, Galatia, Cappadocia, Asia and Bithynia, [2] who have been chosen according to the foreknowledge of God the Father, through the sanctifying work of the Spirit, to be obedient to Jesus Christ and sprinkled with his blood:

Grace and peace be yours in abundance.

Praise to God for a Living Hope

[3] Praise be to the God and Father of our Lord Jesus Christ! In his great mercy he has given us new birth into a living hope through the resurrection of Jesus Christ from the dead, [4] and into an inheritance that can never perish, spoil or fade. This inheritance is kept in heaven for you, [5] who through faith are shielded by God's power until the coming of the salvation that is ready to be revealed in the last time. [6] In all this you greatly rejoice, though now for a little while you may have had to suffer grief in all kinds of trials. [7] These have come so that the proven genuineness of your faith — of greater worth than gold, which perishes even though refined by fire — may result in praise, glory and honor when Jesus Christ is revealed. [8] Though you have not seen him, you love him; and even though you do not see him now, you believe in him and are filled with an inexpressible and glorious joy, [9] for you are receiving the end result of your faith, the salvation of your souls.

[10] Concerning this salvation, the prophets, who spoke of the grace that was to come to you, searched intently and with the greatest care, [11] trying to find out the time and circumstances to which the Spirit of Christ in them was pointing when he predicted the sufferings of the Messiah and the glories that would follow. [12] It was revealed to them that they were not serving themselves but you, when they spoke of the things that have now been told you by those who have preached the gospel to you by the Holy Spirit sent from heaven. Even angels long to look into these things.

Be Holy

[13] Therefore, with minds that are alert and fully sober, set your hope on the grace to be brought to you when Jesus Christ is revealed at his coming. [14] As obedient children, do not conform to the evil desires you had when you lived in ignorance. [15] But just as he who called you is holy, so be holy in all you do; [16] for it is written: "Be holy, because I am holy."[a]

[17] Since you call on a Father who judges each person's work impartially, live out your time as foreigners here in reverent fear. [18] For you know that it was not with perishable things such as silver or gold that you were redeemed from the empty way of life handed down to you from your ancestors, [19] but with the precious blood of Christ, a lamb without blemish or defect. [20] He was chosen before the creation of the world, but was revealed in these last times for your sake. [21] Through him you believe in God, who raised him from the dead and glorified him, and so your faith and hope are in God.

[22] Now that you have purified yourselves by obeying the truth so that you have sincere love for each other, love one another deeply, from the heart.[b] [23] For you have been born again, not of perishable seed, but of imperishable, through the living and enduring word of God. [24] For,

> "All people are like grass,
>   and all their glory is like the flowers of
>   the field;
> the grass withers and the flowers fall,
> [25]   but the word of the Lord endures
>   forever."[c]

---

[a] 16 Lev. 11:44,45; 19:2   [b] 22 Some early manuscripts *from a pure heart*   [c] 25 Isaiah 40:6-8 (see Septuagint)

When No One Is Watching

By Alane Pearce

READ: 1 Peter 1:13—2:3

The choices we make when no one is watching are the ones that define who we *really* are.

As military wives, we spend a lot of time alone; our husbands are deployed, in the field or simply working long shifts and long days. Being alone can tempt us to act or think in ways that are not honoring to God or to our husbands; and since no one is watching, we may think there will not be consequences for our actions. But every action has a consequence — good or bad.

In 1 Peter 1:14, Peter tells us not to "conform" to evil desires. The word "conform" here implies that evil desires are the standard. Being holy means we need to make the conscious decision to do the opposite of our evil desires — a decision that always has good consequences.

When my husband and I were first married, I read a popular romance novel by an author whose books are often turned into movies. The book described long-lost lovers and the illicit passion that was rekindled between them at a chance meeting on the beach. As I read this book alone at home while my husband was at work, I daydreamed about having that kind of romance in my marriage.

I had to stop reading that book because it made me wish my husband was different from the man he is. My husband does romance me, but in a very personal way that suits me perfectly. However, if I had let myself get entangled in a book that gave me different expectations for romance, my marriage would not have honored God. I made the conscious decision not to conform to my desire for something else; instead, I chose to honor God by avoiding romance novels altogether. This helped me love my husband for who he is rather than despise him for who he isn't.

We can (and should) choose holiness in all we do; God gives us the ability and discernment to do so through his Spirit. When we choose to do the right thing simply because it is the right thing — no matter who is watching — we are choosing to live with an alert mind that focuses on grace and acts in holiness. When we ignore holiness, we default to our evil desires, which hurts us and our relationships — especially our relationship with God.

The next time you find yourself at a crossroads, be mindful of what you are choosing. We can choose either to obey God or to conform to those tempting evil desires. Choose holiness.

> Therefore, with minds that are alert and fully sober, set your hope on the grace to be brought to you when Jesus Christ is revealed at his coming. As obedient children, do not conform to the evil desires you had when you lived in ignorance. But just as he who called you is holy, so be holy in all you do.
>
> 1 PETER 1:13 – 15

DEBRIEF
- What kind of life do I lead when I'm alone and no one is watching me?
- What kind of consequences do my choices usually have on my relationships?

REPORT
Father, help me let go of my old ways and evil desires. Help me concentrate on your holiness so I can become holy in all I do. In Jesus' name I pray. Amen.

And this is the word that was preached to you.

2 Therefore, rid yourselves of all malice and all deceit, hypocrisy, envy, and slander of every kind. [2] Like newborn babies, crave pure spiritual milk, so that by it you may grow up in your salvation, [3] now that you have tasted that the Lord is good.

The Living Stone and a Chosen People

[4] As you come to him, the living Stone — rejected by humans but chosen by God and precious to him — [5] you also, like living stones, are being built into a spiritual house[a] to be a holy priesthood, offering spiritual sacrifices acceptable to God through Jesus Christ. [6] For in Scripture it says:

"See, I lay a stone in Zion,
    a chosen and precious cornerstone,
and the one who trusts in him
    will never be put to shame."[b]

[7] Now to you who believe, this stone is precious. But to those who do not believe,

"The stone the builders rejected
    has become the cornerstone,"[c]

[8] and,

"A stone that causes people to stumble
    and a rock that makes them fall."[d]

They stumble because they disobey the message — which is also what they were destined for.

[9] But you are a chosen people, a royal priesthood, a holy nation, God's special possession, that you may declare the praises of him who called you out of darkness into his wonderful light. [10] Once you were not a people, but now you are the people of God; once you had not received mercy, but now you have received mercy.

Living Godly Lives in a Pagan Society

[11] Dear friends, I urge you, as foreigners and exiles, to abstain from sinful desires, which wage war against your soul. [12] Live such good lives among the pagans that, though they accuse you of doing wrong, they may see your good deeds and glorify God on the day he visits us.

[13] Submit yourselves for the Lord's sake to every human authority: whether to the emperor, as the supreme authority, [14] or to governors, who are sent by him to punish those who do wrong and to commend those who do right. [15] For it is God's will that by doing good you should silence the ignorant talk of foolish people. [16] Live as free people, but do not use your freedom as a cover-up for evil; live as God's slaves. [17] Show proper respect to everyone, love the family of believers, fear God, honor the emperor.

[18] Slaves, in reverent fear of God submit yourselves to your masters, not only to those who are good and considerate, but also to those who are harsh. [19] For it is commendable if someone bears up under the pain of unjust suffering because they are conscious of God. [20] But how is it to your credit if you receive a beating for doing wrong and endure it? But if you suffer for doing good and you endure it, this is commendable before God. [21] To this you were called, because Christ suffered for you, leaving you an example, that you should follow in his steps.

[22] "He committed no sin,
    and no deceit was found in his
        mouth."[e]

[23] When they hurled their insults at him, he did not retaliate; when he suffered, he made no threats. Instead, he entrusted himself to him who judges justly. [24] "He himself bore our sins" in his body on the cross, so that we might die to sins and live for righteousness; "by his wounds you have been healed." [25] For "you were like sheep going astray,"[f] but now you have returned to the Shepherd and Overseer of your souls.

3 Wives, in the same way submit yourselves to your own husbands so that, if any of them do not believe the word, they may be won over without words by the behavior of their wives, [2] when they see the purity and reverence of your lives. [3] Your beauty should not come from outward adornment, such as elaborate hairstyles and the wearing of gold jewelry or fine clothes. [4] Rather, it should be that of your inner self, the unfading beauty of a gentle and quiet spirit, which is of great worth in God's sight. [5] For this is the way the holy women of the past who put their hope in God used to adorn themselves.

[a] 5 Or *into a temple of the Spirit*   [b] 6 Isaiah 28:16   [c] 7 Psalm 118:22   [d] 8 Isaiah 8:14
[e] 22 Isaiah 53:9   [f] 24,25 Isaiah 53:4,5,6 (see Septuagint)

They submitted themselves to their own husbands, [6]like Sarah, who obeyed Abraham and called him her lord. You are her daughters if you do what is right and do not give way to fear.

[7]Husbands, in the same way be considerate as you live with your wives, and treat them with respect as the weaker partner and as heirs with you of the gracious gift of life, so that nothing will hinder your prayers.

Suffering for Doing Good

[8]Finally, all of you, be like-minded, be sympathetic, love one another, be compassionate and humble. [9]Do not repay evil with evil or insult with insult. On the contrary, repay evil with blessing, because to this you were called so that you may inherit a blessing. [10]For,

> "Whoever would love life
>   and see good days
> must keep their tongue from evil
>   and their lips from deceitful speech.
> [11]They must turn from evil and do good;
>   they must seek peace and pursue it.
> [12]For the eyes of the Lord are on the
>   righteous
>   and his ears are attentive to their
>   prayer,
> but the face of the Lord is against those
>   who do evil."[a]

[13]Who is going to harm you if you are eager to do good? [14]But even if you should suffer for what is right, you are blessed. "Do not fear their threats[b]; do not be frightened."[c] [15]But in your hearts revere Christ as Lord. Always be prepared to give an answer to everyone who asks you to give the reason for the hope that you have. But do this with gentleness and respect, [16]keeping a clear conscience, so that those who speak maliciously against your good behavior in Christ may be ashamed of their slander. [17]For it is better, if it is God's will, to suffer for doing good than for doing evil. [18]For Christ also suffered once for sins, the righteous for the unrighteous, to bring you to God. He was put to death in the body but made alive in the Spirit. [19]After being made alive,[d] he went and made proclamation to the imprisoned spirits— [20]to those who were disobedient long ago when God waited patiently in the days of Noah while the ark was being built. In it only a few people, eight in all, were saved through water, [21]and this water symbolizes baptism that now saves you also—not the removal of dirt from the body but the pledge of a clear conscience toward God.[e] It saves you by the resurrection of Jesus Christ, [22]who has gone into heaven and is at God's right hand— with angels, authorities and powers in submission to him.

Living for God

4 Therefore, since Christ suffered in his body, arm yourselves also with the same attitude, because whoever suffers in the body is done with sin. [2]As a result, they do not live the rest of their earthly lives for evil human desires, but rather for the will of God. [3]For you have spent enough time in the past doing what pagans choose to do—living in debauchery, lust, drunkenness, orgies, carousing and detestable idolatry. [4]They are surprised that you do not join them in their reckless, wild living, and they heap abuse on you. [5]But they will have to give account to him who is ready to judge the living and the dead. [6]For this is the reason the gospel was preached even to those who are now dead, so that they might be judged according to human standards in regard to the body, but live according to God in regard to the spirit.

[7]The end of all things is near. Therefore be alert and of sober mind so that you may pray. [8]Above all, love each other deeply, because love covers over a multitude of sins. [9]Offer hospitality to one another without grumbling. [10]Each of you should use whatever gift you have received to serve others, as faithful stewards of God's grace in its various forms. [11]If anyone speaks, they should do so as one who speaks the very words of God. If anyone serves, they should do so with the strength God provides, so that in all things God may be praised through Jesus Christ. To him be the glory and the power for ever and ever. Amen.

Suffering for Being a Christian

[12]Dear friends, do not be surprised at the fiery ordeal that has come on you to test you,

---

[a] 12 Psalm 34:12-16   [b] 14 Or *fear what they fear*   [c] 14 Isaiah 8:12   [d] 18,19 Or *but made alive in the spirit,* [19]*in which also*   [e] 21 Or *but an appeal to God for a clear conscience*

Love Covers

By Bettina Dowell

READ: 1 Peter 4:1–11

The deployment had been long and stressful for everyone, including my children (ranging in age from elementary school to college). The details of the stress are not important. What's important is that it strained our ability to demonstrate our love for each other (see 1 Peter 4:8).

Just when I thought the end was in sight, the phone call came. It went something like this: "Hey, you know how I was scheduled to come home next month? Well, I'm not." *Ugh!*

Being a military wife is hard. As I struggled to wrap my brain around the disappointment that came with seeing a coveted goal extended into the horizon, I quickly found myself looking for somewhere to place the blame. Why was the command not more organized? Why had his replacement not arrived sooner? And then the questions turned toward my husband. Why had he volunteered for this assignment in the first place? Other, less polite thoughts also began to compete for my attention, causing me to shift blame to my husband.

Even during straining times such as this, 1 Peter 4:8 tells us to "love each other deeply, because love covers over a multitude of sins." What exactly does that mean for military wives? It means letting go of the whys and focusing on deeply loving our husbands. My questioning of God's sovereignty by looking for someone to blame for my unhappy predicament, instead of realizing our times were in his hands, needed to be covered with love. In fact, love was the one garment that would cover both me and my family.

So I began to focus my love on my husband. How was he feeling about all of this? How disappointed must he be about being delayed from coming home to his family? How hard it must have been for him to call and deliver the bad news? The more I focused my love and concern on my husband, the more my anger lost its fuel and fire.

Frustration and anger can be very flammable. Like a pile of dry kindling, they only need a spark to ignite quite a fire. Love, however, can act as a blanket to smother those burning flames. Thrown as a cover over the anger, frustration and stresses of military life, love can give us peace and strength for ourselves, our marriages and our families.

Christ's love for us, demonstrated by his death for us on the cross, covers our sin. Likewise, our love can cover over the flaws of those we love, allowing us to let go and appreciate all of our husband's qualities, calming many of the frustrations of military life before they become raging fires.

Above all, love each other deeply, because love covers over a multitude of sins.

1 PETER 4:8

DEBRIEF
- Where am I focusing on negatives in my husband that need instead to be covered with love?
- How can I love my husband more deeply and cover him in love?

REPORT
Dear Jesus, help me to cover my spouse in love as your love has covered my many sins. Amen.

for your next devotional reading, go to page 298

A SOLDIER'S HEROINE

By Karen Whiting

A loving wife is a soldier's heroine. U.S. Army General John "Jack" Pershing found such love in his wife.

The night he met Helen Frances Warren, known as Frances to her friends, he woke a friend and exclaimed, "I've met the girl God made for me!" And though Pershing was 20 years her senior, Frances wrote in her diary that she had "lost [her] heart to Captain Pershing irretrievably."

After they shared their first kiss, Pershing wrote, "I never kissed you until we both said we love each other. That kiss, as all others have been, is divinely sacred." After they married, Pershing wrote endearments that included "I am the happiest man in the world and have the dearest wife" and "Millions of kisses from the craziest lover that ever wrote a line to his sweetheart."

As with many military couples, the Pershings faced separations and rumors. While stationed in the Philippines, a rumor circulated that John had a mistress. He denied the allegations while newspapers reported Frances considered divorce. Frances immediately wrote a letter declaring her steadfast love and even admonished her father in a note, "If any stories about Jack come to you to his discredit, don't believe them. No matter how circumstantial they may be, nor how well they seem to be substantiated, they are not true, and you may be sure of it."

Unfortunately, the lives of this loving couple were destroyed by tragedy. On August 27, 1915, while the family was living in San Francisco, John was away from home when a fire broke out in their family home, killing Frances and their three daughters. Their six-year-old son, Warren, crawled into a hallway, where an orderly rescued him.

John never got over his loss.

During World War I, while he led the American Expeditionary Forces in Europe, Pershing showed great compassion for orphans in France and even sponsored a few. Even though Frances had died, her last letter sustained him through the Great War.

She wrote, "The world is so clean this morning. There is the sound of meadowlarks everywhere. And God be thanked for the sunshine and blue sky! Do you think there can be many people in the world as happy as we are? I would like to live to be a thousand years old if I could spend all of that time with you."

In YMCA huts throughout France, General Pershing's photo hung with his own words: "Hardship will be your lot, but trust in God will give you comfort. Temptation will befall you, but the teaching of our Savior will give you strength."

Prayer: Lord, help me cast my anxiety on you, turn from rumors and find strength in you.

Cast all your anxiety on him because he cares for you.

1 PETER 5:7

for your next devotional reading, go to page 305

as though something strange were happening to you. [13]But rejoice inasmuch as you participate in the sufferings of Christ, so that you may be overjoyed when his glory is revealed. [14]If you are insulted because of the name of Christ, you are blessed, for the Spirit of glory and of God rests on you. [15]If you suffer, it should not be as a murderer or thief or any other kind of criminal, or even as a meddler. [16]However, if you suffer as a Christian, do not be ashamed, but praise God that you bear that name. [17]For it is time for judgment to begin with God's household; and if it begins with us, what will the outcome be for those who do not obey the gospel of God? [18]And,

> "If it is hard for the righteous to be saved,
>   what will become of the ungodly and
>   the sinner?"[a]

[19]So then, those who suffer according to God's will should commit themselves to their faithful Creator and continue to do good.

To the Elders and the Flock

5 To the elders among you, I appeal as a fellow elder and a witness of Christ's sufferings who also will share in the glory to be revealed: [2]Be shepherds of God's flock that is under your care, watching over them — not because you must, but because you are willing, as God wants you to be; not pursuing dishonest gain, but eager to serve; [3]not lording it over those entrusted to you, but being examples to the flock. [4]And when the Chief Shepherd appears, you will receive the crown of glory that will never fade away.

[5]In the same way, you who are younger, submit yourselves to your elders. All of you, clothe yourselves with humility toward one another, because,

> "God opposes the proud
>   but shows favor to the humble."[b]

[6]Humble yourselves, therefore, under God's mighty hand, that he may lift you up in due time. [7]Cast all your anxiety on him because he cares for you.

[8]Be alert and of sober mind. Your enemy the devil prowls around like a roaring lion looking for someone to devour. [9]Resist him, standing firm in the faith, because you know that the family of believers throughout the world is undergoing the same kind of sufferings.

[10]And the God of all grace, who called you to his eternal glory in Christ, after you have suffered a little while, will himself restore you and make you strong, firm and steadfast. [11]To him be the power for ever and ever. Amen.

Final Greetings

[12]With the help of Silas,[c] whom I regard as a faithful brother, I have written to you briefly, encouraging you and testifying that this is the true grace of God. Stand fast in it.

[13]She who is in Babylon, chosen together with you, sends you her greetings, and so does my son Mark. [14]Greet one another with a kiss of love.

Peace to all of you who are in Christ.

---

[a] 18 Prov. 11:31 (see Septuagint)   [b] 5 Prov. 3:34   [c] 12 Greek Silvanus, a variant of Silas

2 Peter

1 Simon Peter, a servant and apostle of Jesus Christ,

To those who through the righteousness of our God and Savior Jesus Christ have received a faith as precious as ours:

[2]Grace and peace be yours in abundance through the knowledge of God and of Jesus our Lord.

Confirming One's Calling and Election

[3]His divine power has given us everything we need for a godly life through our knowledge of him who called us by his own glory and goodness. [4]Through these he has given us his very great and precious promises, so that through them you may participate in the divine nature, having escaped the corruption in the world caused by evil desires.

[5]For this very reason, make every effort to add to your faith goodness; and to goodness, knowledge; [6]and to knowledge, self-control; and to self-control, perseverance; and to perseverance, godliness; [7]and to godliness, mutual affection; and to mutual affection, love. [8]For if you possess these qualities in increasing measure, they will keep you from being ineffective and unproductive in your knowledge of our Lord Jesus Christ. [9]But whoever does not have them is nearsighted and blind, forgetting that they have been cleansed from their past sins.

[10]Therefore, my brothers and sisters,[a] make every effort to confirm your calling and election. For if you do these things, you will never stumble, [11]and you will receive a rich welcome into the eternal kingdom of our Lord and Savior Jesus Christ.

Prophecy of Scripture

[12]So I will always remind you of these things, even though you know them and are firmly established in the truth you now have. [13]I think it is right to refresh your memory as long as I live in the tent of this body, [14]because I know that I will soon put it aside, as our Lord Jesus Christ has made clear to me. [15]And I will make every effort to see that after my departure you will always be able to remember these things.

[16]For we did not follow cleverly devised stories when we told you about the coming of our Lord Jesus Christ in power, but we were eyewitnesses of his majesty. [17]He received honor and glory from God the Father when the voice came to him from the Majestic Glory, saying, "This is my Son, whom I love; with him I am well pleased."[b] [18]We ourselves heard this voice that came from heaven when we were with him on the sacred mountain.

[19]We also have the prophetic message as something completely reliable, and you will do well to pay attention to it, as to a light shining in a dark place, until the day dawns and the morning star rises in your hearts. [20]Above all, you must understand that no prophecy of Scripture came about by the prophet's own interpretation of things. [21]For prophecy never had its origin in the human will, but prophets, though human, spoke from God as they were carried along by the Holy Spirit.

False Teachers and Their Destruction

2 But there were also false prophets among the people, just as there will be false teachers among you. They will secretly introduce destructive heresies, even denying the sovereign Lord who bought them — bringing swift destruction on themselves. [2]Many will follow their depraved conduct and will bring the way of truth into disrepute. [3]In their greed these teachers will exploit you with fabricated stories. Their condemnation has long been hanging over them, and their destruction has not been sleeping.

---

[a] 10 The Greek word for *brothers and sisters* (*adelphoi*) refers here to believers, both men and women, as part of God's family.   [b] 17 Matt. 17:5; Mark 9:7; Luke 9:35

[4]For if God did not spare angels when they sinned, but sent them to hell,[a] putting them in chains of darkness[b] to be held for judgment; [5]if he did not spare the ancient world when he brought the flood on its ungodly people, but protected Noah, a preacher of righteousness, and seven others; [6]if he condemned the cities of Sodom and Gomorrah by burning them to ashes, and made them an example of what is going to happen to the ungodly; [7]and if he rescued Lot, a righteous man, who was distressed by the depraved conduct of the lawless [8](for that righteous man, living among them day after day, was tormented in his righteous soul by the lawless deeds he saw and heard)— [9]if this is so, then the Lord knows how to rescue the godly from trials and to hold the unrighteous for punishment on the day of judgment. [10]This is especially true of those who follow the corrupt desire of the flesh[c] and despise authority.

Bold and arrogant, they are not afraid to heap abuse on celestial beings; [11]yet even angels, although they are stronger and more powerful, do not heap abuse on such beings when bringing judgment on them from[d] the Lord. [12]But these people blaspheme in matters they do not understand. They are like unreasoning animals, creatures of instinct, born only to be caught and destroyed, and like animals they too will perish.

[13]They will be paid back with harm for the harm they have done. Their idea of pleasure is to carouse in broad daylight. They are blots and blemishes, reveling in their pleasures while they feast with you.[e] [14]With eyes full of adultery, they never stop sinning; they seduce the unstable; they are experts in greed—an accursed brood! [15]They have left the straight way and wandered off to follow the way of Balaam son of Bezer,[f] who loved the wages of wickedness. [16]But he was rebuked for his wrongdoing by a donkey—an animal without speech—who spoke with a human voice and restrained the prophet's madness.

[17]These people are springs without water and mists driven by a storm. Blackest darkness is reserved for them. [18]For they mouth empty, boastful words and, by appealing to the lustful desires of the flesh, they entice people who are just escaping from those who live in error. [19]They promise them freedom, while they themselves are slaves of depravity—for "people are slaves to whatever has mastered them." [20]If they have escaped the corruption of the world by knowing our Lord and Savior Jesus Christ and are again entangled in it and are overcome, they are worse off at the end than they were at the beginning. [21]It would have been better for them not to have known the way of righteousness, than to have known it and then to turn their backs on the sacred command that was passed on to them. [22]Of them the proverbs are true: "A dog returns to its vomit,"[g] and, "A sow that is washed returns to her wallowing in the mud."

The Day of the Lord

3 Dear friends, this is now my second letter to you. I have written both of them as reminders to stimulate you to wholesome thinking. [2]I want you to recall the words spoken in the past by the holy prophets and the command given by our Lord and Savior through your apostles.

[3]Above all, you must understand that in the last days scoffers will come, scoffing and following their own evil desires. [4]They will say, "Where is this 'coming' he promised? Ever since our ancestors died, everything goes on as it has since the beginning of creation." [5]But they deliberately forget that long ago by God's word the heavens came into being and the earth was formed out of water and by water. [6]By these waters also the world of that time was deluged and destroyed. [7]By the same word the present heavens and earth are reserved for fire, being kept for the day of judgment and destruction of the ungodly.

[8]But do not forget this one thing, dear friends: With the Lord a day is like a thousand years, and a thousand years are like a day. [9]The Lord is not slow in keeping his promise, as some understand slowness. Instead he is patient with you, not wanting anyone to perish, but everyone to come to repentance.

---

[a] 4 Greek *Tartarus*   [b] 4 Some manuscripts *in gloomy dungeons*   [c] 10 In contexts like this, the Greek word for *flesh (sarx)* refers to the sinful state of human beings, often presented as a power in opposition to the Spirit; also in verse 18.   [d] 11 Many manuscripts *beings in the presence of*   [e] 13 Some manuscripts *in their love feasts*   [f] 15 Greek *Bosor*   [g] 22 Prov. 26:11

[10] But the day of the Lord will come like a thief. The heavens will disappear with a roar; the elements will be destroyed by fire, and the earth and everything done in it will be laid bare.[a]

[11] Since everything will be destroyed in this way, what kind of people ought you to be? You ought to live holy and godly lives [12] as you look forward to the day of God and speed its coming.[b] That day will bring about the destruction of the heavens by fire, and the elements will melt in the heat. [13] But in keeping with his promise we are looking forward to a new heaven and a new earth, where righteousness dwells.

[14] So then, dear friends, since you are looking forward to this, make every effort to be found spotless, blameless and at peace with him. [15] Bear in mind that our Lord's patience means salvation, just as our dear brother Paul also wrote you with the wisdom that God gave him. [16] He writes the same way in all his letters, speaking in them of these matters. His letters contain some things that are hard to understand, which ignorant and unstable people distort, as they do the other Scriptures, to their own destruction.

[17] Therefore, dear friends, since you have been forewarned, be on your guard so that you may not be carried away by the error of the lawless and fall from your secure position. [18] But grow in the grace and knowledge of our Lord and Savior Jesus Christ. To him be glory both now and forever! Amen.

---

[a] 10 Some manuscripts *be burned up*   [b] 12 Or *as you wait eagerly for the day of God to come*

1 John

The Incarnation of the Word of Life

1 That which was from the beginning, which we have heard, which we have seen with our eyes, which we have looked at and our hands have touched — this we proclaim concerning the Word of life. ²The life appeared; we have seen it and testify to it, and we proclaim to you the eternal life, which was with the Father and has appeared to us. ³We proclaim to you what we have seen and heard, so that you also may have fellowship with us. And our fellowship is with the Father and with his Son, Jesus Christ. ⁴We write this to make our*ᵃ* joy complete.

Light and Darkness, Sin and Forgiveness

⁵This is the message we have heard from him and declare to you: God is light; in him there is no darkness at all. ⁶If we claim to have fellowship with him and yet walk in the darkness, we lie and do not live out the truth. ⁷But if we walk in the light, as he is in the light, we have fellowship with one another, and the blood of Jesus, his Son, purifies us from all*ᵇ* sin.

⁸If we claim to be without sin, we deceive ourselves and the truth is not in us. ⁹If we confess our sins, he is faithful and just and will forgive us our sins and purify us from all unrighteousness. ¹⁰If we claim we have not sinned, we make him out to be a liar and his word is not in us.

2 My dear children, I write this to you so that you will not sin. But if anybody does sin, we have an advocate with the Father — Jesus Christ, the Righteous One. ²He is the atoning sacrifice for our sins, and not only for ours but also for the sins of the whole world.

Love and Hatred for Fellow Believers

³We know that we have come to know him if we keep his commands. ⁴Whoever says, "I know him," but does not do what he commands is a liar, and the truth is not in that person. ⁵But if anyone obeys his word, love for God*ᶜ* is truly made complete in them. This is how we know we are in him: ⁶Whoever claims to live in him must live as Jesus did.

⁷Dear friends, I am not writing you a new command but an old one, which you have had since the beginning. This old command is the message you have heard. ⁸Yet I am writing you a new command; its truth is seen in him and in you, because the darkness is passing and the true light is already shining.

⁹Anyone who claims to be in the light but hates a brother or sister*ᵈ* is still in the darkness. ¹⁰Anyone who loves their brother and sister*ᵉ* lives in the light, and there is nothing in them to make them stumble. ¹¹But anyone who hates a brother or sister is in the darkness and walks around in the darkness. They do not know where they are going, because the darkness has blinded them.

Reasons for Writing

¹²I am writing to you, dear children,
  because your sins have been forgiven
    on account of his name.
¹³I am writing to you, fathers,
  because you know him who is from the
    beginning.
I am writing to you, young men,
  because you have overcome the
    evil one.

¹⁴I write to you, dear children,
  because you know the Father.
I write to you, fathers,
  because you know him who is from
    the beginning.
I write to you, young men,
  because you are strong,
  and the word of God lives in you,
  and you have overcome the evil one.

ᵃ 4 Some manuscripts *your*   *ᵇ 7* Or *every*   *ᶜ 5* Or *word, God's love*   *ᵈ 9* The Greek word for *brother or sister* (*adelphos*) refers here to a believer, whether man or woman, as part of God's family; also in verse 11; and in 3:15, 17; 4:20; 5:16.   *ᵉ 10* The Greek word for *brother and sister* (*adelphos*) refers here to a believer, whether man or woman, as part of God's family; also in 3:10; 4:20, 21.

On Not Loving the World

[15] Do not love the world or anything in the world. If anyone loves the world, love for the Father[a] is not in them. [16] For everything in the world — the lust of the flesh, the lust of the eyes, and the pride of life — comes not from the Father but from the world. [17] The world and its desires pass away, but whoever does the will of God lives forever.

Warnings Against Denying the Son

[18] Dear children, this is the last hour; and as you have heard that the antichrist is coming, even now many antichrists have come. This is how we know it is the last hour. [19] They went out from us, but they did not really belong to us. For if they had belonged to us, they would have remained with us; but their going showed that none of them belonged to us. [20] But you have an anointing from the Holy One, and all of you know the truth.[b] [21] I do not write to you because you do not know the truth, but because you do know it and because no lie comes from the truth. [22] Who is the liar? It is whoever denies that Jesus is the Christ. Such a person is the antichrist — denying the Father and the Son. [23] No one who denies the Son has the Father; whoever acknowledges the Son has the Father also.

[24] As for you, see that what you have heard from the beginning remains in you. If it does, you also will remain in the Son and in the Father. [25] And this is what he promised us — eternal life.

[26] I am writing these things to you about those who are trying to lead you astray. [27] As for you, the anointing you received from him remains in you, and you do not need anyone to teach you. But as his anointing teaches you about all things and as that anointing is real, not counterfeit — just as it has taught you, remain in him.

God's Children and Sin

[28] And now, dear children, continue in him, so that when he appears we may be confident and unashamed before him at his coming.

[29] If you know that he is righteous, you know that everyone who does what is right has been born of him.

3 See what great love the Father has lavished on us, that we should be called children of God! And that is what we are! The reason the world does not know us is that it did not know him. [2] Dear friends, now we are children of God, and what we will be has not yet been made known. But we know that when Christ appears,[c] we shall be like him, for we shall see him as he is. [3] All who have this hope in him purify themselves, just as he is pure.

[4] Everyone who sins breaks the law; in fact, sin is lawlessness. [5] But you know that he appeared so that he might take away our sins. And in him is no sin. [6] No one who lives in him keeps on sinning. No one who continues to sin has either seen him or known him.

[7] Dear children, do not let anyone lead you astray. The one who does what is right is righteous, just as he is righteous. [8] The one who does what is sinful is of the devil, because the devil has been sinning from the beginning. The reason the Son of God appeared was to destroy the devil's work. [9] No one who is born of God will continue to sin, because God's seed remains in them; they cannot go on sinning, because they have been born of God. [10] This is how we know who the children of God are and who the children of the devil are: Anyone who does not do what is right is not God's child, nor is anyone who does not love their brother and sister.

More on Love and Hatred

[11] For this is the message you heard from the beginning: We should love one another. [12] Do not be like Cain, who belonged to the evil one and murdered his brother. And why did he murder him? Because his own actions were evil and his brother's were righteous. [13] Do not be surprised, my brothers and sisters,[d] if the world hates you. [14] We know that we have passed from death to life, because we love each other. Anyone who does not love remains in death. [15] Anyone who hates a brother or sister is a murderer,

---

[a] 15 Or *world, the Father's love*   [b] 20 Some manuscripts *and you know all things*   [c] 2 Or *when it is made known*   [d] 13 The Greek word for *brothers and sisters* (*adelphoi*) refers here to believers, both men and women, as part of God's family; also in verse 16.

Loved

By Bettina Dowell

READ: 1 John 3:1–3; 4:7–12

Letters that cross in the mail, emails that struggle to show tone and true intent, voice mails from missed phone calls or Skype calls that fall apart — technically or emotionally. During my husband's years of military service we worked at keeping our relationship together, despite the miles, through each of these communication methods. Without exception, every single one of them has failed us from time to time. Sometimes the failures were mechanical ones. And sometimes, the failures were emotional ones.

"Why haven't you written to me?" "What did you mean by that email?" "Everyone else in the unit was able to call their spouse, why didn't I hear from you?" "How could you not have just a few minutes to sit at your computer and talk to me?" Yes, the questions were painful ones that came from my hurting heart. Fair or not, they sprang from loneliness and sometimes caused me to feel unloved. So where have your questions left you?

As women, we sometimes place the burden of our emotional security on our husbands. Looking to our husbands for love, support and emotional encouragement seems normal by the world's standards. The problem with this is that, just like our military communication methods, it invariably sets us up for failure. Our hearts can be like vast wells needing to be filled with the water of love. Unfortunately, even the best of husbands can add only little drops to our wells. These drops often just make the echo sound louder against the empty walls. What we need is an overflow.

First John 3:1 says God has lavished us with his great love. He offers us the very living water that can fill our wells to overflowing (see John 7:37–38). His love is unconditional, unchangeable and never fails due to communication struggles. God has reached into our deep, dark wells and made us his very own children. The love he fills us with will never run out.

The blessing for every wife who chooses to accept this lavish love is that it can fill the cavernous well of her heart. And a wife whose heart is full of God's love can offer grace to the husband whose communication may fail. When a wife's well is full, the love her husband offers becomes overflow. This overflow is generous and reaches out to bless children and others their marriage encounters. And for a soldier struggling to communicate from a distant land, it offers the peace of a secure woman at home who gives him the strength to do his job on difficult days. What a lavish love!

See what great love the Father has lavished on us, that we should be called children of God! And that is what we are!

1 JOHN 3:1

DEBRIEF

- Does my emotional security depend on my husband communicating his love to me?
- What steps can I take to embrace God's love for me to satisfy my longings?

REPORT

Dear Father, thank you for the love you have so richly lavished on me. Please teach me how to allow your love to fill the cavernous well of my heart. May the overflow bless many others. Amen.

---

for your next devotional reading, go to page 315

and you know that no murderer has eternal life residing in him.

[16] This is how we know what love is: Jesus Christ laid down his life for us. And we ought to lay down our lives for our brothers and sisters. [17] If anyone has material possessions and sees a brother or sister in need but has no pity on them, how can the love of God be in that person? [18] Dear children, let us not love with words or speech but with actions and in truth.

[19] This is how we know that we belong to the truth and how we set our hearts at rest in his presence: [20] If our hearts condemn us, we know that God is greater than our hearts, and he knows everything. [21] Dear friends, if our hearts do not condemn us, we have confidence before God [22] and receive from him anything we ask, because we keep his commands and do what pleases him. [23] And this is his command: to believe in the name of his Son, Jesus Christ, and to love one another as he commanded us. [24] The one who keeps God's commands lives in him, and he in them. And this is how we know that he lives in us: We know it by the Spirit he gave us.

On Denying the Incarnation

4 Dear friends, do not believe every spirit, but test the spirits to see whether they are from God, because many false prophets have gone out into the world. [2] This is how you can recognize the Spirit of God: Every spirit that acknowledges that Jesus Christ has come in the flesh is from God, [3] but every spirit that does not acknowledge Jesus is not from God. This is the spirit of the antichrist, which you have heard is coming and even now is already in the world.

[4] You, dear children, are from God and have overcome them, because the one who is in you is greater than the one who is in the world. [5] They are from the world and therefore speak from the viewpoint of the world, and the world listens to them. [6] We are from God, and whoever knows God listens to us; but whoever is not from God does not listen to us. This is how we recognize the Spirit[a] of truth and the spirit of falsehood.

God's Love and Ours

[7] Dear friends, let us love one another, for love comes from God. Everyone who loves

has been born of God and knows God. [8] Whoever does not love does not know God, because God is love. [9] This is how God showed his love among us: He sent his one and only Son into the world that we might live through him. [10] This is love: not that we loved God, but that he loved us and sent his Son as an atoning sacrifice for our sins. [11] Dear friends, since God so loved us, we also ought to love one another. [12] No one has ever seen God; but if we love one another, God lives in us and his love is made complete in us.

[13] This is how we know that we live in him and he in us: He has given us of his Spirit. [14] And we have seen and testify that the Father has sent his Son to be the Savior of the world. [15] If anyone acknowledges that Jesus is the Son of God, God lives in them and they in God. [16] And so we know and rely on the love God has for us.

God is love. Whoever lives in love lives in God, and God in them. [17] This is how love is made complete among us so that we will have confidence on the day of judgment: In this world we are like Jesus. [18] There is no fear in love. But perfect love drives out fear, because fear has to do with punishment. The one who fears is not made perfect in love.

[19] We love because he first loved us. [20] Whoever claims to love God yet hates a brother or sister is a liar. For whoever does not love their brother and sister, whom they have seen, cannot love God, whom they have not seen. [21] And he has given us this command: Anyone who loves God must also love their brother and sister.

Faith in the Incarnate Son of God

5 Everyone who believes that Jesus is the Christ is born of God, and everyone who loves the father loves his child as well. [2] This is how we know that we love the children of God: by loving God and carrying out his commands. [3] In fact, this is love for God: to keep his commands. And his commands are not burdensome, [4] for everyone born of God overcomes the world. This is the victory that has overcome the world, even our faith. [5] Who is it that overcomes the world? Only the one who believes that Jesus is the Son of God.

[a] 6 Or *spirit*

⁶This is the one who came by water and blood—Jesus Christ. He did not come by water only, but by water and blood. And it is the Spirit who testifies, because the Spirit is the truth. ⁷For there are three that testify: ⁸the*a* Spirit, the water and the blood; and the three are in agreement. ⁹We accept human testimony, but God's testimony is greater because it is the testimony of God, which he has given about his Son. ¹⁰Whoever believes in the Son of God accepts this testimony. Whoever does not believe God has made him out to be a liar, because they have not believed the testimony God has given about his Son. ¹¹And this is the testimony: God has given us eternal life, and this life is in his Son. ¹²Whoever has the Son has life; whoever does not have the Son of God does not have life.

Concluding Affirmations

¹³I write these things to you who believe in the name of the Son of God so that you may know that you have eternal life. ¹⁴This is the confidence we have in approaching God: that if we ask anything according to his will, he hears us. ¹⁵And if we know that he hears us—whatever we ask—we know that we have what we asked of him.

¹⁶If you see any brother or sister commit a sin that does not lead to death, you should pray and God will give them life. I refer to those whose sin does not lead to death. There is a sin that leads to death. I am not saying that you should pray about that. ¹⁷All wrongdoing is sin, and there is sin that does not lead to death.

¹⁸We know that anyone born of God does not continue to sin; the One who was born of God keeps them safe, and the evil one cannot harm them. ¹⁹We know that we are children of God, and that the whole world is under the control of the evil one. ²⁰We know also that the Son of God has come and has given us understanding, so that we may know him who is true. And we are in him who is true by being in his Son Jesus Christ. He is the true God and eternal life.

²¹Dear children, keep yourselves from idols.

---

a 7,8 Late manuscripts of the Vulgate *testify in heaven: the Father, the Word and the Holy Spirit, and these three are one. ⁸And there are three that testify on earth: the* (not found in any Greek manuscript before the fourteenth century)

2 John

¹The elder,

To the lady chosen by God and to her children, whom I love in the truth — and not I only, but also all who know the truth — ²because of the truth, which lives in us and will be with us forever:

³Grace, mercy and peace from God the Father and from Jesus Christ, the Father's Son, will be with us in truth and love.

⁴It has given me great joy to find some of your children walking in the truth, just as the Father commanded us. ⁵And now, dear lady, I am not writing you a new command but one we have had from the beginning. I ask that we love one another. ⁶And this is love: that we walk in obedience to his commands. As you have heard from the beginning, his command is that you walk in love. ⁷I say this because many deceivers, who do not acknowledge Jesus Christ as coming in the flesh, have gone out into the world. Any such person is the deceiver and the antichrist. ⁸Watch out that you do not lose what we*a* have worked for, but that you may be rewarded fully. ⁹Anyone who runs ahead and does not continue in the teaching of Christ does not have God; whoever continues in the teaching has both the Father and the Son. ¹⁰If anyone comes to you and does not bring this teaching, do not take them into your house or welcome them. ¹¹Anyone who welcomes them shares in their wicked work.

¹²I have much to write to you, but I do not want to use paper and ink. Instead, I hope to visit you and talk with you face to face, so that our joy may be complete.

¹³The children of your sister, who is chosen by God, send their greetings.

a 8 Some manuscripts *you*

3 John

¹The elder,

To my dear friend Gaius, whom I love in the truth.

²Dear friend, I pray that you may enjoy good health and that all may go well with you, even as your soul is getting along well. ³It gave me great joy when some believers came and testified about your faithfulness to the truth, telling how you continue to walk in it. ⁴I have no greater joy than to hear that my children are walking in the truth.

⁵Dear friend, you are faithful in what you are doing for the brothers and sisters,ᵃ even though they are strangers to you. ⁶They have told the church about your love. Please send them on their way in a manner that honors God. ⁷It was for the sake of the Name that they went out, receiving no help from the pagans. ⁸We ought therefore to show hospitality to such people so that we may work together for the truth.

⁹I wrote to the church, but Diotrephes, who loves to be first, will not welcome us. ¹⁰So when I come, I will call attention to what he is doing, spreading malicious nonsense about us. Not satisfied with that, he even refuses to welcome other believers. He also stops those who want to do so and puts them out of the church.

¹¹Dear friend, do not imitate what is evil but what is good. Anyone who does what is good is from God. Anyone who does what is evil has not seen God. ¹²Demetrius is well spoken of by everyone — and even by the truth itself. We also speak well of him, and you know that our testimony is true.

¹³I have much to write you, but I do not want to do so with pen and ink. ¹⁴I hope to see you soon, and we will talk face to face.

Peace to you. The friends here send their greetings. Greet the friends there by name.

ᵃ 5 The Greek word for *brothers and sisters* (*adelphoi*) refers here to believers, both men and women, as part of God's family.

Jude

[1]Jude, a servant of Jesus Christ and a brother of James,

To those who have been called, who are loved in God the Father and kept for[a] Jesus Christ:

[2]Mercy, peace and love be yours in abundance.

The Sin and Doom of Ungodly People

[3]Dear friends, although I was very eager to write to you about the salvation we share, I felt compelled to write and urge you to contend for the faith that was once for all entrusted to God's holy people. [4]For certain individuals whose condemnation was written about[b] long ago have secretly slipped in among you. They are ungodly people, who pervert the grace of our God into a license for immorality and deny Jesus Christ our only Sovereign and Lord. [5]Though you already know all this, I want to remind you that the Lord[c] at one time delivered his people out of Egypt, but later destroyed those who did not believe. [6]And the angels who did not keep their positions of authority but abandoned their proper dwelling—these he has kept in darkness, bound with everlasting chains for judgment on the great Day. [7]In a similar way, Sodom and Gomorrah and the surrounding towns gave themselves up to sexual immorality and perversion. They serve as an example of those who suffer the punishment of eternal fire.

[8]In the very same way, on the strength of their dreams these ungodly people pollute their own bodies, reject authority and heap abuse on celestial beings. [9]But even the archangel Michael, when he was disputing with the devil about the body of Moses, did not himself dare to condemn him for slander but said, "The Lord rebuke you!"[d] [10]Yet these people slander whatever they do not understand, and the very things they do understand by instinct—as irrational animals do—will destroy them.

[11]Woe to them! They have taken the way of Cain; they have rushed for profit into Balaam's error; they have been destroyed in Korah's rebellion.

[12]These people are blemishes at your love feasts, eating with you without the slightest qualm—shepherds who feed only themselves. They are clouds without rain, blown along by the wind; autumn trees, without fruit and uprooted—twice dead. [13]They are wild waves of the sea, foaming up their shame; wandering stars, for whom blackest darkness has been reserved forever.

[14]Enoch, the seventh from Adam, prophesied about them: "See, the Lord is coming with thousands upon thousands of his holy ones [15]to judge everyone, and to convict all of them of all the ungodly acts they have committed in their ungodliness, and of all the defiant words ungodly sinners have spoken against him."[e] [16]These people are grumblers and faultfinders; they follow their own evil desires; they boast about themselves and flatter others for their own advantage.

A Call to Persevere

[17]But, dear friends, remember what the apostles of our Lord Jesus Christ foretold. [18]They said to you, "In the last times there will be scoffers who will follow their own ungodly desires." [19]These are the people who divide you, who follow mere natural instincts and do not have the Spirit.

[20]But you, dear friends, by building yourselves up in your most holy faith and praying

---

[a] 1 Or by; or in   [b] 4 Or individuals who were marked out for condemnation   [c] 5 Some early manuscripts Jesus   [d] 9 Jude is alluding to the Jewish Testament of Moses (approximately the first century A.D.).   [e] 14,15 From the Jewish First Book of Enoch (approximately the first century B.C.)

in the Holy Spirit, [21] keep yourselves in God's love as you wait for the mercy of our Lord Jesus Christ to bring you to eternal life.

[22] Be merciful to those who doubt; [23] save others by snatching them from the fire; to others show mercy, mixed with fear — hating even the clothing stained by corrupted flesh.[a]

Doxology

[24] To him who is able to keep you from stumbling and to present you before his glorious presence without fault and with great joy — [25] to the only God our Savior be glory, majesty, power and authority, through Jesus Christ our Lord, before all ages, now and forevermore! Amen.

---

[a] 22,23 The Greek manuscripts of these verses vary at several points.

Revelation

Prologue

1 The revelation from Jesus Christ, which God gave him to show his servants what must soon take place. He made it known by sending his angel to his servant John, ²who testifies to everything he saw—that is, the word of God and the testimony of Jesus Christ. ³Blessed is the one who reads aloud the words of this prophecy, and blessed are those who hear it and take to heart what is written in it, because the time is near.

Greetings and Doxology

⁴John,

To the seven churches in the province of Asia:

Grace and peace to you from him who is, and who was, and who is to come, and from the seven spirits*ᵃ* before his throne, ⁵and from Jesus Christ, who is the faithful witness, the firstborn from the dead, and the ruler of the kings of the earth.

To him who loves us and has freed us from our sins by his blood, ⁶and has made us to be a kingdom and priests to serve his God and Father—to him be glory and power for ever and ever! Amen.

⁷"Look, he is coming with the clouds,"*ᵇ*
    and "every eye will see him,
    even those who pierced him";
    and all peoples on earth "will mourn
        because of him."*ᶜ*
                    So shall it be! Amen.

⁸"I am the Alpha and the Omega," says the Lord God, "who is, and who was, and who is to come, the Almighty."

John's Vision of Christ

⁹I, John, your brother and companion in the suffering and kingdom and patient endurance that are ours in Jesus, was on the island of Patmos because of the word of God and the testimony of Jesus. ¹⁰On the Lord's Day I was in the Spirit, and I heard behind me a loud voice like a trumpet, ¹¹which said: "Write on a scroll what you see and send it to the seven churches: to Ephesus, Smyrna, Pergamum, Thyatira, Sardis, Philadelphia and Laodicea."

¹²I turned around to see the voice that was speaking to me. And when I turned I saw seven golden lampstands, ¹³and among the lampstands was someone like a son of man,*ᵈ* dressed in a robe reaching down to his feet and with a golden sash around his chest. ¹⁴The hair on his head was white like wool, as white as snow, and his eyes were like blazing fire. ¹⁵His feet were like bronze glowing in a furnace, and his voice was like the sound of rushing waters. ¹⁶In his right hand he held seven stars, and coming out of his mouth was a sharp, double-edged sword. His face was like the sun shining in all its brilliance.

¹⁷When I saw him, I fell at his feet as though dead. Then he placed his right hand on me and said: "Do not be afraid. I am the First and the Last. ¹⁸I am the Living One; I was dead, and now look, I am alive for ever and ever! And I hold the keys of death and Hades.

¹⁹"Write, therefore, what you have seen, what is now and what will take place later. ²⁰The mystery of the seven stars that you saw in my right hand and of the seven golden lampstands is this: The seven stars are the angels*ᵉ* of the seven churches, and the seven lampstands are the seven churches.

To the Church in Ephesus

2 "To the angel*ᶠ* of the church in Ephesus write:

These are the words of him who holds the seven stars in his right hand

---

ᵃ 4 That is, the sevenfold Spirit   *ᵇ 7* Daniel 7:13   *ᶜ 7* Zech. 12:10   *ᵈ 13* See Daniel 7:13.
ᵉ 20 Or *messengers*   *ᶠ 1* Or *messenger*; also in verses 8, 12 and 18

and walks among the seven golden lampstands. ²I know your deeds, your hard work and your perseverance. I know that you cannot tolerate wicked people, that you have tested those who claim to be apostles but are not, and have found them false. ³You have persevered and have endured hardships for my name, and have not grown weary.

⁴Yet I hold this against you: You have forsaken the love you had at first. ⁵Consider how far you have fallen! Repent and do the things you did at first. If you do not repent, I will come to you and remove your lampstand from its place. ⁶But you have this in your favor: You hate the practices of the Nicolaitans, which I also hate.

⁷Whoever has ears, let them hear what the Spirit says to the churches. To the one who is victorious, I will give the right to eat from the tree of life, which is in the paradise of God.

To the Church in Smyrna

⁸"To the angel of the church in Smyrna write:

These are the words of him who is the First and the Last, who died and came to life again. ⁹I know your afflictions and your poverty—yet you are rich! I know about the slander of those who say they are Jews and are not, but are a synagogue of Satan. ¹⁰Do not be afraid of what you are about to suffer. I tell you, the devil will put some of you in prison to test you, and you will suffer persecution for ten days. Be faithful, even to the point of death, and I will give you life as your victor's crown.

¹¹Whoever has ears, let them hear what the Spirit says to the churches. The one who is victorious will not be hurt at all by the second death.

To the Church in Pergamum

¹²"To the angel of the church in Pergamum write:

These are the words of him who has the sharp, double-edged sword. ¹³I know where you live—where Satan has his throne. Yet you remain true to my name. You did not renounce your faith in me, not even in the days of An-

tipas, my faithful witness, who was put to death in your city—where Satan lives.

¹⁴Nevertheless, I have a few things against you: There are some among you who hold to the teaching of Balaam, who taught Balak to entice the Israelites to sin so that they ate food sacrificed to idols and committed sexual immorality. ¹⁵Likewise, you also have those who hold to the teaching of the Nicolaitans. ¹⁶Repent therefore! Otherwise, I will soon come to you and will fight against them with the sword of my mouth.

¹⁷Whoever has ears, let them hear what the Spirit says to the churches. To the one who is victorious, I will give some of the hidden manna. I will also give that person a white stone with a new name written on it, known only to the one who receives it.

To the Church in Thyatira

¹⁸"To the angel of the church in Thyatira write:

These are the words of the Son of God, whose eyes are like blazing fire and whose feet are like burnished bronze. ¹⁹I know your deeds, your love and faith, your service and perseverance, and that you are now doing more than you did at first.

²⁰Nevertheless, I have this against you: You tolerate that woman Jezebel, who calls herself a prophet. By her teaching she misleads my servants into sexual immorality and the eating of food sacrificed to idols. ²¹I have given her time to repent of her immorality, but she is unwilling. ²²So I will cast her on a bed of suffering, and I will make those who commit adultery with her suffer intensely, unless they repent of her ways. ²³I will strike her children dead. Then all the churches will know that I am he who searches hearts and minds, and I will repay each of you according to your deeds.

²⁴Now I say to the rest of you in Thyatira, to you who do not hold to her teaching and have not learned Satan's so-called deep secrets, 'I will not impose any other burden on you,

[25] except to hold on to what you have until I come.'

[26] To the one who is victorious and does my will to the end, I will give authority over the nations — [27] that one 'will rule them with an iron scepter and will dash them to pieces like pottery'[a] — just as I have received authority from my Father. [28] I will also give that one the morning star. [29] Whoever has ears, let them hear what the Spirit says to the churches.

To the Church in Sardis

3 "To the angel[b] of the church in Sardis write:

These are the words of him who holds the seven spirits[c] of God and the seven stars. I know your deeds; you have a reputation of being alive, but you are dead. [2] Wake up! Strengthen what remains and is about to die, for I have found your deeds unfinished in the sight of my God. [3] Remember, therefore, what you have received and heard; hold it fast, and repent. But if you do not wake up, I will come like a thief, and you will not know at what time I will come to you.

[4] Yet you have a few people in Sardis who have not soiled their clothes. They will walk with me, dressed in white, for they are worthy. [5] The one who is victorious will, like them, be dressed in white. I will never blot out the name of that person from the book of life, but will acknowledge that name before my Father and his angels. [6] Whoever has ears, let them hear what the Spirit says to the churches.

To the Church in Philadelphia

[7] "To the angel of the church in Philadelphia write:

These are the words of him who is holy and true, who holds the key of David. What he opens no one can shut, and what he shuts no one can open. [8] I know your deeds. See, I have placed before you an open door that no one can shut. I know that you have little

strength, yet you have kept my word and have not denied my name. [9] I will make those who are of the synagogue of Satan, who claim to be Jews though they are not, but are liars — I will make them come and fall down at your feet and acknowledge that I have loved you. [10] Since you have kept my command to endure patiently, I will also keep you from the hour of trial that is going to come on the whole world to test the inhabitants of the earth.

[11] I am coming soon. Hold on to what you have, so that no one will take your crown. [12] The one who is victorious I will make a pillar in the temple of my God. Never again will they leave it. I will write on them the name of my God and the name of the city of my God, the new Jerusalem, which is coming down out of heaven from my God; and I will also write on them my new name. [13] Whoever has ears, let them hear what the Spirit says to the churches.

To the Church in Laodicea

[14] "To the angel of the church in Laodicea write:

These are the words of the Amen, the faithful and true witness, the ruler of God's creation. [15] I know your deeds, that you are neither cold nor hot. I wish you were either one or the other! [16] So, because you are lukewarm — neither hot nor cold — I am about to spit you out of my mouth. [17] You say, 'I am rich; I have acquired wealth and do not need a thing.' But you do not realize that you are wretched, pitiful, poor, blind and naked. [18] I counsel you to buy from me gold refined in the fire, so you can become rich; and white clothes to wear, so you can cover your shameful nakedness; and salve to put on your eyes, so you can see.

[19] Those whom I love I rebuke and discipline. So be earnest and repent. [20] Here I am! I stand at the door and knock. If anyone hears my voice and opens the door, I will come in and eat with that person, and they with me. [21] To the one who is victorious, I

---

[a] 27 Psalm 2:9   [b] 1 Or *messenger*; also in verses 7 and 14   [c] 1 That is, the sevenfold Spirit

A LOVER'S PURSUIT

By Jocelyn Green

Eliza Allen loved William Billings with all her heart. The fact that she was from a wealthy family in Maine, and he was a day laborer from Canada didn't matter to her. Her parents, however, were intent on arranging a marriage for her with a man of social standing. They threatened to disinherit Eliza and throw her out of the family mansion if she married William.

When William quietly went off to fight in the Mexican-American War, Eliza devised a plan to be near her true love. Remembering the accounts of Deborah Sampson and Lucy Brewer, Eliza followed suit. She cut her hair, dressed in men's clothing, adopted the alias of "George Mead," and found an officer who would muster her without a physical examination. Soon she had joined General Zachary Taylor's forces in Texas.

Eliza was wounded at the battle of Cerro Gordo — and so was William. Even while the two were quartered in the same private house during the American occupation, she kept her identity hidden.

After the war, William and his friends sailed to California to pan for gold, but they became shipwrecked along the way. Eliza, in pursuit of William once again, was on the ship that rescued him and his friends in the Strait of Magellan. It wasn't until they both returned to the East Coast in September 1849 that Eliza shared her secret with William. The couple eventually married with the consent of Eliza's parents, and their love survived.

The ultimate love story, of course, is that of Jesus pursuing each one of us from the throne of heaven to the cross on earth. Jesus broke the boundaries of heaven and hell, of life and death, to provide a way for us to be with him forever. There is no greater sacrifice, and there never will be a greater love than that which he has for us.

Francis Thompson's poem "The Hound of Heaven" describes God's pursuit of our hearts. The first lines read: "I fled from Him, down the nights and down the days; / I fled Him, down the arches of the years; / I fled Him, down the labyrinthine ways / Of my own mind; and in the mist of tears / I hid from Him, and under running laughter."

Finally, after the writer describes his search for fulfillment in everything the world has to offer, the "Hound of Heaven" says: "Ah, fondest, blindest, weakest, / I am He Whom thou seekest!"

Jesus pursues us throughout our lives, but he won't break into our hearts uninvited. He does, however, stand at the door and knock. It's up to us to let him in.

Prayer: Lord, thank you for pursuing me with your steadfast love! I welcome you into my life and want to dwell with you forever.

"Here I am! I stand at the door and knock. If anyone hears my voice and opens the door, I will come in and eat with that person, and they with me."
REVELATION 3:20

for your next devotional reading, go to page 327

will give the right to sit with me on my throne, just as I was victorious and sat down with my Father on his throne. [22] Whoever has ears, let them hear what the Spirit says to the churches."

The Throne in Heaven

4 After this I looked, and there before me was a door standing open in heaven. And the voice I had first heard speaking to me like a trumpet said, "Come up here, and I will show you what must take place after this." [2] At once I was in the Spirit, and there before me was a throne in heaven with someone sitting on it. [3] And the one who sat there had the appearance of jasper and ruby. A rainbow that shone like an emerald encircled the throne. [4] Surrounding the throne were twenty-four other thrones, and seated on them were twenty-four elders. They were dressed in white and had crowns of gold on their heads. [5] From the throne came flashes of lightning, rumblings and peals of thunder. In front of the throne, seven lamps were blazing. These are the seven spirits[a] of God. [6] Also in front of the throne there was what looked like a sea of glass, clear as crystal.

In the center, around the throne, were four living creatures, and they were covered with eyes, in front and in back. [7] The first living creature was like a lion, the second was like an ox, the third had a face like a man, the fourth was like a flying eagle. [8] Each of the four living creatures had six wings and was covered with eyes all around, even under its wings. Day and night they never stop saying:

"'Holy, holy, holy
    is the Lord God Almighty,'[b]
who was, and is, and is to come."

[9] Whenever the living creatures give glory, honor and thanks to him who sits on the throne and who lives for ever and ever, [10] the twenty-four elders fall down before him who sits on the throne and worship him who lives for ever and ever. They lay their crowns before the throne and say:

[11] "You are worthy, our Lord and God,
    to receive glory and honor and power,
    for you created all things,

and by your will they were
    created
and have their being."

The Scroll and the Lamb

5 Then I saw in the right hand of him who sat on the throne a scroll with writing on both sides and sealed with seven seals. [2] And I saw a mighty angel proclaiming in a loud voice, "Who is worthy to break the seals and open the scroll?" [3] But no one in heaven or on earth or under the earth could open the scroll or even look inside it. [4] I wept and wept because no one was found who was worthy to open the scroll or look inside. [5] Then one of the elders said to me, "Do not weep! See, the Lion of the tribe of Judah, the Root of David, has triumphed. He is able to open the scroll and its seven seals."

[6] Then I saw a Lamb, looking as if it had been slain, standing at the center of the throne, encircled by the four living creatures and the elders. The Lamb had seven horns and seven eyes, which are the seven spirits[a] of God sent out into all the earth. [7] He went and took the scroll from the right hand of him who sat on the throne. [8] And when he had taken it, the four living creatures and the twenty-four elders fell down before the Lamb. Each one had a harp and they were holding golden bowls full of incense, which are the prayers of God's people. [9] And they sang a new song, saying:

"You are worthy to take the scroll
    and to open its seals,
because you were slain,
    and with your blood you purchased
        for God
    persons from every tribe and language
        and people and nation.
[10] You have made them to be a kingdom and
        priests to serve our God,
    and they will reign[c] on the earth."

[11] Then I looked and heard the voice of many angels, numbering thousands upon thousands, and ten thousand times ten thousand. They encircled the throne and the living creatures and the elders. [12] In a loud voice they were saying:

"Worthy is the Lamb, who was
    slain,

---

[a] 5,6 That is, the sevenfold Spirit   [b] 8 Isaiah 6:3   [c] 10 Some manuscripts *they reign*

to receive power and wealth and
wisdom and strength
and honor and glory and praise!"

¹³Then I heard every creature in heaven and on earth and under the earth and on the sea, and all that is in them, saying:

"To him who sits on the throne and to
the Lamb
be praise and honor and glory and
power,
for ever and ever!"

¹⁴The four living creatures said, "Amen," and the elders fell down and worshiped.

The Seals

6 I watched as the Lamb opened the first of the seven seals. Then I heard one of the four living creatures say in a voice like thunder, "Come!" ²I looked, and there before me was a white horse! Its rider held a bow, and he was given a crown, and he rode out as a conqueror bent on conquest.

³When the Lamb opened the second seal, I heard the second living creature say, "Come!" ⁴Then another horse came out, a fiery red one. Its rider was given power to take peace from the earth and to make people kill each other. To him was given a large sword.

⁵When the Lamb opened the third seal, I heard the third living creature say, "Come!" I looked, and there before me was a black horse! Its rider was holding a pair of scales in his hand. ⁶Then I heard what sounded like a voice among the four living creatures, saying, "Two pounds^a of wheat for a day's wages,^{b} and six pounds^c of barley for a day's wages,^{b} and do not damage the oil and the wine!"

⁷When the Lamb opened the fourth seal, I heard the voice of the fourth living creature say, "Come!" ⁸I looked, and there before me was a pale horse! Its rider was named Death, and Hades was following close behind him. They were given power over a fourth of the earth to kill by sword, famine and plague, and by the wild beasts of the earth.

⁹When he opened the fifth seal, I saw under the altar the souls of those who had been slain because of the word of God and the testimony they had maintained. ¹⁰They called out in a loud voice, "How long, Sovereign Lord, holy and true, until you judge the inhabitants of the earth and avenge our blood?" ¹¹Then each of them was given a white robe, and they were told to wait a little longer, until the full number of their fellow servants, their brothers and sisters,^{d} were killed just as they had been.

¹²I watched as he opened the sixth seal. There was a great earthquake. The sun turned black like sackcloth made of goat hair, the whole moon turned blood red, ¹³and the stars in the sky fell to earth, as figs drop from a fig tree when shaken by a strong wind. ¹⁴The heavens receded like a scroll being rolled up, and every mountain and island was removed from its place.

¹⁵Then the kings of the earth, the princes, the generals, the rich, the mighty, and everyone else, both slave and free, hid in caves and among the rocks of the mountains. ¹⁶They called to the mountains and the rocks, "Fall on us and hide us^e from the face of him who sits on the throne and from the wrath of the Lamb! ¹⁷For the great day of their^f wrath has come, and who can withstand it?"

144,000 Sealed

7 After this I saw four angels standing at the four corners of the earth, holding back the four winds of the earth to prevent any wind from blowing on the land or on the sea or on any tree. ²Then I saw another angel coming up from the east, having the seal of the living God. He called out in a loud voice to the four angels who had been given power to harm the land and the sea: ³"Do not harm the land or the sea or the trees until we put a seal on the foreheads of the servants of our God." ⁴Then I heard the number of those who were sealed: 144,000 from all the tribes of Israel.

⁵From the tribe of Judah 12,000 were
sealed,
from the tribe of Reuben 12,000,
from the tribe of Gad 12,000,
⁶from the tribe of Asher 12,000,
from the tribe of Naphtali 12,000,
from the tribe of Manasseh 12,000,

---

^{a} 6 Or about 1 kilogram ^{b} 6 Greek *a denarius* ^{c} 6 Or about 3 kilograms ^{d} 11 The Greek word for *brothers and sisters (adelphoi)* refers here to believers, both men and women, as part of God's family; also in 12:10; 19:10. ^{e} 16 See Hosea 10:8. ^{f} 17 Some manuscripts *his*

[7] from the tribe of Simeon 12,000,
from the tribe of Levi 12,000,
from the tribe of Issachar 12,000,
[8] from the tribe of Zebulun 12,000,
from the tribe of Joseph 12,000,
from the tribe of Benjamin 12,000.

The Great Multitude in White Robes

[9] After this I looked, and there before me was a great multitude that no one could count, from every nation, tribe, people and language, standing before the throne and before the Lamb. They were wearing white robes and were holding palm branches in their hands. [10] And they cried out in a loud voice:

"Salvation belongs to our God,
who sits on the throne,
and to the Lamb."

[11] All the angels were standing around the throne and around the elders and the four living creatures. They fell down on their faces before the throne and worshiped God, [12] saying:

"Amen!
Praise and glory
and wisdom and thanks and honor
and power and strength
be to our God for ever and ever.
Amen!"

[13] Then one of the elders asked me, "These in white robes — who are they, and where did they come from?"

[14] I answered, "Sir, you know."

And he said, "These are they who have come out of the great tribulation; they have washed their robes and made them white in the blood of the Lamb. [15] Therefore,

"they are before the throne of God
and serve him day and night in his
temple;
and he who sits on the throne
will shelter them with his
presence.
[16] 'Never again will they hunger;
never again will they thirst.
The sun will not beat down on them,'[a]
nor any scorching heat.
[17] For the Lamb at the center of the throne
will be their shepherd;

'he will lead them to springs of living
water.'[a]
'And God will wipe away every tear
from their eyes.'[b]"

The Seventh Seal and the Golden Censer

8 When he opened the seventh seal, there was silence in heaven for about half an hour.

[2] And I saw the seven angels who stand before God, and seven trumpets were given to them.

[3] Another angel, who had a golden censer, came and stood at the altar. He was given much incense to offer, with the prayers of all God's people, on the golden altar in front of the throne. [4] The smoke of the incense, together with the prayers of God's people, went up before God from the angel's hand. [5] Then the angel took the censer, filled it with fire from the altar, and hurled it on the earth; and there came peals of thunder, rumblings, flashes of lightning and an earthquake.

The Trumpets

[6] Then the seven angels who had the seven trumpets prepared to sound them.

[7] The first angel sounded his trumpet, and there came hail and fire mixed with blood, and it was hurled down on the earth. A third of the earth was burned up, a third of the trees were burned up, and all the green grass was burned up.

[8] The second angel sounded his trumpet, and something like a huge mountain, all ablaze, was thrown into the sea. A third of the sea turned into blood, [9] a third of the living creatures in the sea died, and a third of the ships were destroyed.

[10] The third angel sounded his trumpet, and a great star, blazing like a torch, fell from the sky on a third of the rivers and on the springs of water — [11] the name of the star is Wormwood.[c] A third of the waters turned bitter, and many people died from the waters that had become bitter.

[12] The fourth angel sounded his trumpet, and a third of the sun was struck, a third of the moon, and a third of the stars, so that a third of them turned dark. A third of the day was without light, and also a third of the night.

[a] 16,17 Isaiah 49:10   [b] 17 Isaiah 25:8   [c] 11 Wormwood is a bitter substance.

[13]As I watched, I heard an eagle that was flying in midair call out in a loud voice: "Woe! Woe! Woe to the inhabitants of the earth, because of the trumpet blasts about to be sounded by the other three angels!"

9 The fifth angel sounded his trumpet, and I saw a star that had fallen from the sky to the earth. The star was given the key to the shaft of the Abyss. [2]When he opened the Abyss, smoke rose from it like the smoke from a gigantic furnace. The sun and sky were darkened by the smoke from the Abyss. [3]And out of the smoke locusts came down on the earth and were given power like that of scorpions of the earth. [4]They were told not to harm the grass of the earth or any plant or tree, but only those people who did not have the seal of God on their foreheads. [5]They were not allowed to kill them but only to torture them for five months. And the agony they suffered was like that of the sting of a scorpion when it strikes. [6]During those days people will seek death but will not find it; they will long to die, but death will elude them.

[7]The locusts looked like horses prepared for battle. On their heads they wore something like crowns of gold, and their faces resembled human faces. [8]Their hair was like women's hair, and their teeth were like lions' teeth. [9]They had breastplates like breastplates of iron, and the sound of their wings was like the thundering of many horses and chariots rushing into battle. [10]They had tails with stingers, like scorpions, and in their tails they had power to torment people for five months. [11]They had as king over them the angel of the Abyss, whose name in Hebrew is Abaddon and in Greek is Apollyon (that is, Destroyer).

[12]The first woe is past; two other woes are yet to come.

[13]The sixth angel sounded his trumpet, and I heard a voice coming from the four horns of the golden altar that is before God. [14]It said to the sixth angel who had the trumpet, "Release the four angels who are bound at the great river Euphrates." [15]And the four angels who had been kept ready for this very hour and day and month and year were released to kill a third of mankind. [16]The number of the mounted troops was twice ten thousand times ten thousand. I heard their number.

[17]The horses and riders I saw in my vision looked like this: Their breastplates were fiery red, dark blue, and yellow as sulfur. The heads of the horses resembled the heads of lions, and out of their mouths came fire, smoke and sulfur. [18]A third of mankind was killed by the three plagues of fire, smoke and sulfur that came out of their mouths. [19]The power of the horses was in their mouths and in their tails; for their tails were like snakes, having heads with which they inflict injury.

[20]The rest of mankind who were not killed by these plagues still did not repent of the work of their hands; they did not stop worshiping demons, and idols of gold, silver, bronze, stone and wood — idols that cannot see or hear or walk. [21]Nor did they repent of their murders, their magic arts, their sexual immorality or their thefts.

The Angel and the Little Scroll

10 Then I saw another mighty angel coming down from heaven. He was robed in a cloud, with a rainbow above his head; his face was like the sun, and his legs were like fiery pillars. [2]He was holding a little scroll, which lay open in his hand. He planted his right foot on the sea and his left foot on the land, [3]and he gave a loud shout like the roar of a lion. When he shouted, the voices of the seven thunders spoke. [4]And when the seven thunders spoke, I was about to write; but I heard a voice from heaven say, "Seal up what the seven thunders have said and do not write it down."

[5]Then the angel I had seen standing on the sea and on the land raised his right hand to heaven. [6]And he swore by him who lives for ever and ever, who created the heavens and all that is in them, the earth and all that is in it, and the sea and all that is in it, and said, "There will be no more delay! [7]But in the days when the seventh angel is about to sound his trumpet, the mystery of God will be accomplished, just as he announced to his servants the prophets."

[8]Then the voice that I had heard from heaven spoke to me once more: "Go, take the scroll that lies open in the hand of the angel who is standing on the sea and on the land."

[9]So I went to the angel and asked him to give me the little scroll. He said to me, "Take it and eat it. It will turn your stomach sour, but 'in your mouth it will be as sweet as

honey.'[a]" [10]I took the little scroll from the angel's hand and ate it. It tasted as sweet as honey in my mouth, but when I had eaten it, my stomach turned sour. [11]Then I was told, "You must prophesy again about many peoples, nations, languages and kings."

The Two Witnesses

11 I was given a reed like a measuring rod and was told, "Go and measure the temple of God and the altar, with its worshipers. [2]But exclude the outer court; do not measure it, because it has been given to the Gentiles. They will trample on the holy city for 42 months. [3]And I will appoint my two witnesses, and they will prophesy for 1,260 days, clothed in sackcloth." [4]They are "the two olive trees" and the two lampstands, and "they stand before the Lord of the earth."[b] [5]If anyone tries to harm them, fire comes from their mouths and devours their enemies. This is how anyone who wants to harm them must die. [6]They have power to shut up the heavens so that it will not rain during the time they are prophesying; and they have power to turn the waters into blood and to strike the earth with every kind of plague as often as they want.

[7]Now when they have finished their testimony, the beast that comes up from the Abyss will attack them, and overpower and kill them. [8]Their bodies will lie in the public square of the great city—which is figuratively called Sodom and Egypt—where also their Lord was crucified. [9]For three and a half days some from every people, tribe, language and nation will gaze on their bodies and refuse them burial. [10]The inhabitants of the earth will gloat over them and will celebrate by sending each other gifts, because these two prophets had tormented those who live on the earth.

[11]But after the three and a half days the breath[c] of life from God entered them, and they stood on their feet, and terror struck those who saw them. [12]Then they heard a loud voice from heaven saying to them, "Come up here." And they went up to heaven in a cloud, while their enemies looked on.

[13]At that very hour there was a severe earthquake and a tenth of the city collapsed. Seven thousand people were killed in the earthquake, and the survivors were terrified and gave glory to the God of heaven.

[14]The second woe has passed; the third woe is coming soon.

The Seventh Trumpet

[15]The seventh angel sounded his trumpet, and there were loud voices in heaven, which said:

"The kingdom of the world has become
  the kingdom of our Lord and of his
    Messiah,
  and he will reign for ever and ever."

[16]And the twenty-four elders, who were seated on their thrones before God, fell on their faces and worshiped God, [17]saying:

"We give thanks to you, Lord God
    Almighty,
  the One who is and who was,
because you have taken your great
      power
  and have begun to reign.
[18]The nations were angry,
  and your wrath has come.
The time has come for judging the dead,
  and for rewarding your servants the
      prophets
and your people who revere your name,
  both great and small—
and for destroying those who destroy
    the earth."

[19]Then God's temple in heaven was opened, and within his temple was seen the ark of his covenant. And there came flashes of lightning, rumblings, peals of thunder, an earthquake and a severe hailstorm.

The Woman and the Dragon

12 A great sign appeared in heaven: a woman clothed with the sun, with the moon under her feet and a crown of twelve stars on her head. [2]She was pregnant and cried out in pain as she was about to give birth. [3]Then another sign appeared in heaven: an enormous red dragon with seven heads and ten horns and seven crowns on its heads. [4]Its tail swept a third of the stars out of the sky and flung them to the earth. The dragon stood in front of the woman who was about to give birth, so that it might devour

---

[a] 9 Ezek. 3:3   [b] 4 See Zech. 4:3,11,14.   [c] 11 Or *Spirit* (see Ezek. 37:5,14)

her child the moment he was born. [5] She gave birth to a son, a male child, who "will rule all the nations with an iron scepter." [a] And her child was snatched up to God and to his throne. [6] The woman fled into the wilderness to a place prepared for her by God, where she might be taken care of for 1,260 days.

[7] Then war broke out in heaven. Michael and his angels fought against the dragon, and the dragon and his angels fought back. [8] But he was not strong enough, and they lost their place in heaven. [9] The great dragon was hurled down—that ancient serpent called the devil, or Satan, who leads the whole world astray. He was hurled to the earth, and his angels with him.

[10] Then I heard a loud voice in heaven say:

"Now have come the salvation and the
        power
    and the kingdom of our God,
    and the authority of his Messiah.
For the accuser of our brothers and
        sisters,
    who accuses them before our God
        day and night,
    has been hurled down.
[11] They triumphed over him
    by the blood of the Lamb
    and by the word of their testimony;
    they did not love their lives so much
        as to shrink from death.
[12] Therefore rejoice, you heavens
    and you who dwell in them!
But woe to the earth and the sea,
    because the devil has gone down
        to you!
He is filled with fury,
    because he knows that his time
        is short."

[13] When the dragon saw that he had been hurled to the earth, he pursued the woman who had given birth to the male child. [14] The woman was given the two wings of a great eagle, so that she might fly to the place prepared for her in the wilderness, where she would be taken care of for a time, times and half a time, out of the serpent's reach. [15] Then from his mouth the serpent spewed water like a river, to overtake the woman and sweep her away with the torrent. [16] But the earth helped the woman by opening its mouth and swallowing the river that the dragon had spewed out of his mouth. [17] Then the dragon was enraged at the woman and went off to wage war against the rest of her offspring—those who keep God's commands and hold fast their testimony about Jesus.

The Beast out of the Sea

13 The dragon[b] stood on the shore of the sea. And I saw a beast coming out of the sea. It had ten horns and seven heads, with ten crowns on its horns, and on each head a blasphemous name. [2] The beast I saw resembled a leopard, but had feet like those of a bear and a mouth like that of a lion. The dragon gave the beast his power and his throne and great authority. [3] One of the heads of the beast seemed to have had a fatal wound, but the fatal wound had been healed. The whole world was filled with wonder and followed the beast. [4] People worshiped the dragon because he had given authority to the beast, and they also worshiped the beast and asked, "Who is like the beast? Who can wage war against it?"

[5] The beast was given a mouth to utter proud words and blasphemies and to exercise its authority for forty-two months. [6] It opened its mouth to blaspheme God, and to slander his name and his dwelling place and those who live in heaven. [7] It was given power to wage war against God's holy people and to conquer them. And it was given authority over every tribe, people, language and nation. [8] All inhabitants of the earth will worship the beast—all whose names have not been written in the Lamb's book of life, the Lamb who was slain from the creation of the world.[c]

[9] Whoever has ears, let them hear.

[10] "If anyone is to go into captivity,
    into captivity they will go.
If anyone is to be killed[d] with the sword,
    with the sword they will be killed."[e]

This calls for patient endurance and faithfulness on the part of God's people.

The Beast out of the Earth

[11] Then I saw a second beast, coming out of the earth. It had two horns like a lamb,

---

[a] 5 Psalm 2:9   [b] 1 Some manuscripts *And I*   [c] 8 Or *written from the creation of the world in the book of life belonging to the Lamb who was slain*   [d] 10 Some manuscripts *anyone kills*   [e] 10 Jer. 15:2

but it spoke like a dragon. [12] It exercised all the authority of the first beast on its behalf, and made the earth and its inhabitants worship the first beast, whose fatal wound had been healed. [13] And it performed great signs, even causing fire to come down from heaven to the earth in full view of the people. [14] Because of the signs it was given power to perform on behalf of the first beast, it deceived the inhabitants of the earth. It ordered them to set up an image in honor of the beast who was wounded by the sword and yet lived. [15] The second beast was given power to give breath to the image of the first beast, so that the image could speak and cause all who refused to worship the image to be killed. [16] It also forced all people, great and small, rich and poor, free and slave, to receive a mark on their right hands or on their foreheads, [17] so that they could not buy or sell unless they had the mark, which is the name of the beast or the number of its name.

[18] This calls for wisdom. Let the person who has insight calculate the number of the beast, for it is the number of a man.[a] That number is 666.

The Lamb and the 144,000

14 Then I looked, and there before me was the Lamb, standing on Mount Zion, and with him 144,000 who had his name and his Father's name written on their foreheads. [2] And I heard a sound from heaven like the roar of rushing waters and like a loud peal of thunder. The sound I heard was like that of harpists playing their harps. [3] And they sang a new song before the throne and before the four living creatures and the elders. No one could learn the song except the 144,000 who had been redeemed from the earth. [4] These are those who did not defile themselves with women, for they remained virgins. They follow the Lamb wherever he goes. They were purchased from among mankind and offered as firstfruits to God and the Lamb. [5] No lie was found in their mouths; they are blameless.

The Three Angels

[6] Then I saw another angel flying in midair, and he had the eternal gospel to proclaim to those who live on the earth — to every nation, tribe, language and people. [7] He said in a loud voice, "Fear God and give him glory, because the hour of his judgment has come. Worship him who made the heavens, the earth, the sea and the springs of water."

[8] A second angel followed and said, " 'Fallen! Fallen is Babylon the Great,'[b] which made all the nations drink the maddening wine of her adulteries."

[9] A third angel followed them and said in a loud voice: "If anyone worships the beast and its image and receives its mark on their forehead or on their hand, [10] they, too, will drink the wine of God's fury, which has been poured full strength into the cup of his wrath. They will be tormented with burning sulfur in the presence of the holy angels and of the Lamb. [11] And the smoke of their torment will rise for ever and ever. There will be no rest day or night for those who worship the beast and its image, or for anyone who receives the mark of its name." [12] This calls for patient endurance on the part of the people of God who keep his commands and remain faithful to Jesus.

[13] Then I heard a voice from heaven say, "Write this: Blessed are the dead who die in the Lord from now on."

"Yes," says the Spirit, "they will rest from their labor, for their deeds will follow them."

Harvesting the Earth and Trampling the Winepress

[14] I looked, and there before me was a white cloud, and seated on the cloud was one like a son of man[c] with a crown of gold on his head and a sharp sickle in his hand. [15] Then another angel came out of the temple and called in a loud voice to him who was sitting on the cloud, "Take your sickle and reap, because the time to reap has come, for the harvest of the earth is ripe." [16] So he who was seated on the cloud swung his sickle over the earth, and the earth was harvested.

[17] Another angel came out of the temple in heaven, and he too had a sharp sickle. [18] Still another angel, who had charge of the fire, came from the altar and called in a loud voice to him who had the sharp sickle, "Take your sharp sickle and gather the clusters of grapes from the earth's vine, because its grapes are ripe." [19] The angel swung his

---

[a] 18 Or is humanity's number   [b] 8 Isaiah 21:9   [c] 14 See Daniel 7:13.

sickle on the earth, gathered its grapes and threw them into the great winepress of God's wrath. [20]They were trampled in the winepress outside the city, and blood flowed out of the press, rising as high as the horses' bridles for a distance of 1,600 stadia.[a]

Seven Angels With Seven Plagues

15 I saw in heaven another great and marvelous sign: seven angels with the seven last plagues — last, because with them God's wrath is completed. [2]And I saw what looked like a sea of glass glowing with fire and, standing beside the sea, those who had been victorious over the beast and its image and over the number of its name. They held harps given them by God [3]and sang the song of God's servant Moses and of the Lamb:

"Great and marvelous are your deeds,
    Lord God Almighty.
Just and true are your ways,
    King of the nations.[b]
[4]Who will not fear you, Lord,
    and bring glory to your name?
For you alone are holy.
All nations will come
    and worship before you,
for your righteous acts have been
        revealed."[c]

[5]After this I looked, and I saw in heaven the temple — that is, the tabernacle of the covenant law — and it was opened. [6]Out of the temple came the seven angels with the seven plagues. They were dressed in clean, shining linen and wore golden sashes around their chests. [7]Then one of the four living creatures gave to the seven angels seven golden bowls filled with the wrath of God, who lives for ever and ever. [8]And the temple was filled with smoke from the glory of God and from his power, and no one could enter the temple until the seven plagues of the seven angels were completed.

The Seven Bowls of God's Wrath

16 Then I heard a loud voice from the temple saying to the seven angels, "Go, pour out the seven bowls of God's wrath on the earth."

[2]The first angel went and poured out his bowl on the land, and ugly, festering sores broke out on the people who had the mark of the beast and worshiped its image.

[3]The second angel poured out his bowl on the sea, and it turned into blood like that of a dead person, and every living thing in the sea died.

[4]The third angel poured out his bowl on the rivers and springs of water, and they became blood. [5]Then I heard the angel in charge of the waters say:

"You are just in these judgments,
        O Holy One,
    you who are and who were;
[6]for they have shed the blood of your holy
        people and your prophets,
    and you have given them blood to
        drink as they deserve."

[7]And I heard the altar respond:

"Yes, Lord God Almighty,
    true and just are your judgments."

[8]The fourth angel poured out his bowl on the sun, and the sun was allowed to scorch people with fire. [9]They were seared by the intense heat and they cursed the name of God, who had control over these plagues, but they refused to repent and glorify him.

[10]The fifth angel poured out his bowl on the throne of the beast, and its kingdom was plunged into darkness. People gnawed their tongues in agony [11]and cursed the God of heaven because of their pains and their sores, but they refused to repent of what they had done.

[12]The sixth angel poured out his bowl on the great river Euphrates, and its water was dried up to prepare the way for the kings from the East. [13]Then I saw three impure spirits that looked like frogs; they came out of the mouth of the dragon, out of the mouth of the beast and out of the mouth of the false prophet. [14]They are demonic spirits that perform signs, and they go out to the kings of the whole world, to gather them for the battle on the great day of God Almighty.

[15]"Look, I come like a thief! Blessed is the one who stays awake and remains clothed, so as not to go naked and be shamefully exposed."

---

[a] 20 That is, about 180 miles or about 300 kilometers   [b] 3 Some manuscripts ages   [c] 3,4 Phrases in this song are drawn from Psalm 111:2,3; Deut. 32:4; Jer. 10:7; Psalms 86:9; 98:2.

¹⁶Then they gathered the kings together to the place that in Hebrew is called Armageddon.

¹⁷The seventh angel poured out his bowl into the air, and out of the temple came a loud voice from the throne, saying, "It is done!" ¹⁸Then there came flashes of lightning, rumblings, peals of thunder and a severe earthquake. No earthquake like it has ever occurred since mankind has been on earth, so tremendous was the quake. ¹⁹The great city split into three parts, and the cities of the nations collapsed. God remembered Babylon the Great and gave her the cup filled with the wine of the fury of his wrath. ²⁰Every island fled away and the mountains could not be found. ²¹From the sky huge hailstones, each weighing about a hundred pounds,*a* fell on people. And they cursed God on account of the plague of hail, because the plague was so terrible.

Babylon, the Prostitute on the Beast

17 One of the seven angels who had the seven bowls came and said to me, "Come, I will show you the punishment of the great prostitute, who sits by many waters. ²With her the kings of the earth committed adultery, and the inhabitants of the earth were intoxicated with the wine of her adulteries."

³Then the angel carried me away in the Spirit into a wilderness. There I saw a woman sitting on a scarlet beast that was covered with blasphemous names and had seven heads and ten horns. ⁴The woman was dressed in purple and scarlet, and was glittering with gold, precious stones and pearls. She held a golden cup in her hand, filled with abominable things and the filth of her adulteries. ⁵The name written on her forehead was a mystery:

> BABYLON THE GREAT
> THE MOTHER OF PROSTITUTES
> AND OF THE ABOMINATIONS
> OF THE EARTH.

⁶I saw that the woman was drunk with the blood of God's holy people, the blood of those who bore testimony to Jesus.

When I saw her, I was greatly astonished. ⁷Then the angel said to me: "Why are you astonished? I will explain to you the mystery of the woman and of the beast she rides, which has the seven heads and ten horns. ⁸The beast, which you saw, once was, now is not, and yet will come up out of the Abyss and go to its destruction. The inhabitants of the earth whose names have not been written in the book of life from the creation of the world will be astonished when they see the beast, because it once was, now is not, and yet will come.

⁹"This calls for a mind with wisdom. The seven heads are seven hills on which the woman sits. ¹⁰They are also seven kings. Five have fallen, one is, the other has not yet come; but when he does come, he must remain for only a little while. ¹¹The beast who once was, and now is not, is an eighth king. He belongs to the seven and is going to his destruction.

¹²"The ten horns you saw are ten kings who have not yet received a kingdom, but who for one hour will receive authority as kings along with the beast. ¹³They have one purpose and will give their power and authority to the beast. ¹⁴They will wage war against the Lamb, but the Lamb will triumph over them because he is Lord of lords and King of kings — and with him will be his called, chosen and faithful followers."

¹⁵Then the angel said to me, "The waters you saw, where the prostitute sits, are peoples, multitudes, nations and languages. ¹⁶The beast and the ten horns you saw will hate the prostitute. They will bring her to ruin and leave her naked; they will eat her flesh and burn her with fire. ¹⁷For God has put it into their hearts to accomplish his purpose by agreeing to hand over to the beast their royal authority, until God's words are fulfilled. ¹⁸The woman you saw is the great city that rules over the kings of the earth."

Lament Over Fallen Babylon

18 After this I saw another angel coming down from heaven. He had great authority, and the earth was illuminated by his splendor. ²With a mighty voice he shouted:

> "'Fallen! Fallen is Babylon the Great!'*b*
> She has become a dwelling for demons
> and a haunt for every impure spirit,
> a haunt for every unclean bird,

---

a 21 Or about 45 kilograms   *b 2* Isaiah 21:9

a haunt for every unclean and
  detestable animal.
[3] For all the nations have drunk
  the maddening wine of her adulteries.
The kings of the earth committed
  adultery with her,
and the merchants of the earth grew
  rich from her excessive luxuries."

Warning to Escape Babylon's Judgment

[4] Then I heard another voice from heaven
say:

" 'Come out of her, my people,'[a]
  so that you will not share in her sins,
  so that you will not receive any of her
    plagues;
[5] for her sins are piled up to heaven,
  and God has remembered
    her crimes.
[6] Give back to her as she has given;
  pay her back double for what she has
    done.
Pour her a double portion from her
    own cup.
[7] Give her as much torment and grief
  as the glory and luxury she gave
    herself.
In her heart she boasts,
  'I sit enthroned as queen.
I am not a widow;[b]
I will never mourn.'
[8] Therefore in one day her plagues will
    overtake her:
  death, mourning and famine.
She will be consumed by fire,
  for mighty is the Lord God who
    judges her.

Threefold Woe Over Babylon's Fall

[9] "When the kings of the earth who committed adultery with her and shared her luxury see the smoke of her burning, they will
weep and mourn over her. [10] Terrified at her
torment, they will stand far off and cry:

" 'Woe! Woe to you, great city,
  you mighty city of Babylon!
In one hour your doom has come!'

[11] "The merchants of the earth will weep
and mourn over her because no one buys
their cargoes anymore — [12] cargoes of gold,
silver, precious stones and pearls; fine linen,

purple, silk and scarlet cloth; every sort of
citron wood, and articles of every kind made
of ivory, costly wood, bronze, iron and mar-
ble; [13] cargoes of cinnamon and spice, of incense, myrrh and frankincense, of wine and
olive oil, of fine flour and wheat; cattle and
sheep; horses and carriages; and human beings sold as slaves.

[14] "They will say, 'The fruit you longed for
is gone from you. All your luxury and splendor have vanished, never to be recovered.'
[15] The merchants who sold these things and
gained their wealth from her will stand far
off, terrified at her torment. They will weep
and mourn [16] and cry out:

" 'Woe! Woe to you, great city,
  dressed in fine linen, purple
    and scarlet,
  and glittering with gold, precious
    stones and pearls!
[17] In one hour such great wealth has been
    brought to ruin!'

"Every sea captain, and all who travel by
ship, the sailors, and all who earn their living from the sea, will stand far off. [18] When
they see the smoke of her burning, they will
exclaim, 'Was there ever a city like this great
city?' [19] They will throw dust on their heads,
and with weeping and mourning cry out:

" 'Woe! Woe to you, great city,
  where all who had ships on
    the sea
  became rich through her wealth!
In one hour she has been brought
    to ruin!'

[20] "Rejoice over her, you heavens!
  Rejoice, you people of God!
  Rejoice, apostles and prophets!
For God has judged her
  with the judgment she imposed
    on you."

The Finality of Babylon's Doom

[21] Then a mighty angel picked up a boul-
der the size of a large millstone and threw it
into the sea, and said:

"With such violence
  the great city of Babylon will be
    thrown down,
  never to be found again.

---

[a] 4 Jer. 51:45   [b] 7 See Isaiah 47:7,8.

²²The music of harpists and musicians,
    pipers and trumpeters,
  will never be heard in you again.
No worker of any trade
  will ever be found in you again.
The sound of a millstone
  will never be heard in you again.
²³The light of a lamp
  will never shine in you again.
The voice of bridegroom and bride
  will never be heard in you again.
Your merchants were the world's
    important people.
By your magic spell all the nations
    were led astray.
²⁴In her was found the blood of prophets
    and of God's holy people,
  of all who have been slaughtered on
    the earth."

Threefold Hallelujah Over Babylon's Fall

19 After this I heard what sounded like the roar of a great multitude in heaven shouting:

"Hallelujah!
Salvation and glory and power belong
    to our God,
² for true and just are his judgments.
He has condemned the great
    prostitute
  who corrupted the earth by her
    adulteries.
He has avenged on her the blood of his
    servants."

³And again they shouted:

"Hallelujah!
The smoke from her goes up for ever
    and ever."

⁴The twenty-four elders and the four living creatures fell down and worshiped God, who was seated on the throne. And they cried:

"Amen, Hallelujah!"

⁵Then a voice came from the throne, saying:

"Praise our God,
  all you his servants,
you who fear him,
  both great and small!"

⁶Then I heard what sounded like a great multitude, like the roar of rushing waters and like loud peals of thunder, shouting:

"Hallelujah!
  For our Lord God Almighty reigns.
⁷Let us rejoice and be glad
  and give him glory!
For the wedding of the Lamb has come,
  and his bride has made herself
    ready.
⁸Fine linen, bright and clean,
  was given her to wear."

(Fine linen stands for the righteous acts of God's holy people.)

⁹Then the angel said to me, "Write this: Blessed are those who are invited to the wedding supper of the Lamb!" And he added, "These are the true words of God."

¹⁰At this I fell at his feet to worship him. But he said to me, "Don't do that! I am a fellow servant with you and with your brothers and sisters who hold to the testimony of Jesus. Worship God! For it is the Spirit of prophecy who bears testimony to Jesus."

The Heavenly Warrior Defeats the Beast

¹¹I saw heaven standing open and there before me was a white horse, whose rider is called Faithful and True. With justice he judges and wages war. ¹²His eyes are like blazing fire, and on his head are many crowns. He has a name written on him that no one knows but he himself. ¹³He is dressed in a robe dipped in blood, and his name is the Word of God. ¹⁴The armies of heaven were following him, riding on white horses and dressed in fine linen, white and clean. ¹⁵Coming out of his mouth is a sharp sword with which to strike down the nations. "He will rule them with an iron scepter."[a] He treads the winepress of the fury of the wrath of God Almighty. ¹⁶On his robe and on his thigh he has this name written:

KING OF KINGS AND
LORD OF LORDS.

¹⁷And I saw an angel standing in the sun, who cried in a loud voice to all the birds flying in midair, "Come, gather together for the great supper of God, ¹⁸so that you may eat the flesh of kings, generals, and the mighty,

[a] 15 Psalm 2:9

Anticipating His Return

By Alane Pearce

READ: Revelation 19:6–9

I remember lying in bed one night, looking forward to my reunion with my husband. I thought about what I still needed to do to prepare for his return: clean the house, stock the fridge — not to mention hair and nail appointments and choosing an outfit for the homecoming! Then a memory from a previous tour in Hawaii nudged my mental to-do list aside.

My friend Becky, a Navy wife, always spent the last few weeks of each sea tour anticipating her husband's return (she didn't always know the exact day of the docking until the morning of it). Each night she went to bed hoping that tomorrow her love would come home. She shared with me that one day it struck her that the anticipation she had for her husband's return should be her daily attitude about the coming of Christ.

Remorse washed over me as I thought about Becky's words. I was making big plans for my husband's return, but how concerned was I about preparing for Christ's return?

The joy of reunion is complete in Revelation 19:6–8 because of two phrases: (1) "the wedding of the Lamb has come" and (2) "his bride has made herself ready."

I am convinced that just going to church is not enough to ready ourselves to meet Jesus, who is referred to in Scripture as both our bridegroom (Greek *numphios*; see Matthew 9:15) and our husband (Greek *aner*; see 2 Corinthians 11:2). So how do we prepare for it? Here are seven tips to help us:

1. Repent daily (see Matthew 3:2).
2. Serve others (see Galatians 5:13).
3. Forgive quickly (see Colossians 3:13).
4. Pray continually (see 1 Thessalonians 5:17).
5. Give thanks (see 1 Thessalonians 5:18).
6. Be generous (see 2 Corinthians 9:6–11).
7. Live in community with other believers (1 Corinthians 12:12–27).

Flip to Matthew 25:1–13, the parable of the ten virgins. The story ends with words that are still relevant for us today: "Therefore keep watch, because you do not know the day or the hour" (verse 13).

Let's keep watch for Jesus and ready ourselves for his return by pursuing a daily relationship with him through the Word and prayer. Also do what my friend Becky does: Go to bed tonight hoping that tomorrow he will come, and wake in the morning hoping today is the day you'll see him!

> Then I heard what sounded like a great multitude, like the roar of rushing waters and like loud peals of thunder, shouting: "Hallelujah! For our Lord God Almighty reigns. Let us rejoice and be glad and give him glory! For the wedding of the Lamb has come, and his bride has made herself ready."
>
> REVELATION 19:6–7

DEBRIEF
- What can I do today to prepare for the return of the Savior?
- How will I live in expectation of his return?

REPORT
Lord, help me ready myself spiritually for the moment when we meet face to face. Give me a sense of urgency to prepare for your coming and a joyful anticipation of being with you, my heavenly bridegroom. Amen.

for your next devotional reading, go to page 335

of horses and their riders, and the flesh of all people, free and slave, great and small."

¹⁹Then I saw the beast and the kings of the earth and their armies gathered together to wage war against the rider on the horse and his army. ²⁰But the beast was captured, and with it the false prophet who had performed the signs on its behalf. With these signs he had deluded those who had received the mark of the beast and worshiped its image. The two of them were thrown alive into the fiery lake of burning sulfur. ²¹The rest were killed with the sword coming out of the mouth of the rider on the horse, and all the birds gorged themselves on their flesh.

The Thousand Years

20 And I saw an angel coming down out of heaven, having the key to the Abyss and holding in his hand a great chain. ²He seized the dragon, that ancient serpent, who is the devil, or Satan, and bound him for a thousand years. ³He threw him into the Abyss, and locked and sealed it over him, to keep him from deceiving the nations anymore until the thousand years were ended. After that, he must be set free for a short time.

⁴I saw thrones on which were seated those who had been given authority to judge. And I saw the souls of those who had been beheaded because of their testimony about Jesus and because of the word of God. They[a] had not worshiped the beast or its image and had not received its mark on their foreheads or their hands. They came to life and reigned with Christ a thousand years. ⁵(The rest of the dead did not come to life until the thousand years were ended.) This is the first resurrection. ⁶Blessed and holy are those who share in the first resurrection. The second death has no power over them, but they will be priests of God and of Christ and will reign with him for a thousand years.

The Judgment of Satan

⁷When the thousand years are over, Satan will be released from his prison ⁸and will go out to deceive the nations in the four corners of the earth—Gog and Magog—and to gather them for battle. In number they are like the sand on the seashore. ⁹They

marched across the breadth of the earth and surrounded the camp of God's people, the city he loves. But fire came down from heaven and devoured them. ¹⁰And the devil, who deceived them, was thrown into the lake of burning sulfur, where the beast and the false prophet had been thrown. They will be tormented day and night for ever and ever.

The Judgment of the Dead

¹¹Then I saw a great white throne and him who was seated on it. The earth and the heavens fled from his presence, and there was no place for them. ¹²And I saw the dead, great and small, standing before the throne, and books were opened. Another book was opened, which is the book of life. The dead were judged according to what they had done as recorded in the books. ¹³The sea gave up the dead that were in it, and death and Hades gave up the dead that were in them, and each person was judged according to what they had done. ¹⁴Then death and Hades were thrown into the lake of fire. The lake of fire is the second death. ¹⁵Anyone whose name was not found written in the book of life was thrown into the lake of fire.

A New Heaven and a New Earth

21 Then I saw "a new heaven and a new earth,"[b] for the first heaven and the first earth had passed away, and there was no longer any sea. ²I saw the Holy City, the new Jerusalem, coming down out of heaven from God, prepared as a bride beautifully dressed for her husband. ³And I heard a loud voice from the throne saying, "Look! God's dwelling place is now among the people, and he will dwell with them. They will be his people, and God himself will be with them and be their God. ⁴'He will wipe every tear from their eyes. There will be no more death'[c] or mourning or crying or pain, for the old order of things has passed away."

⁵He who was seated on the throne said, "I am making everything new!" Then he said, "Write this down, for these words are trustworthy and true."

⁶He said to me: "It is done. I am the Alpha and the Omega, the Beginning and the End. To the thirsty I will give water without cost from the spring of the water of life. ⁷Those

---

a 4 Or *God; I also saw those who*   *b* 1 Isaiah 65:17   *c* 4 Isaiah 25:8

who are victorious will inherit all this, and I will be their God and they will be my children. [8]But the cowardly, the unbelieving, the vile, the murderers, the sexually immoral, those who practice magic arts, the idolaters and all liars — they will be consigned to the fiery lake of burning sulfur. This is the second death."

The New Jerusalem, the Bride of the Lamb

[9]One of the seven angels who had the seven bowls full of the seven last plagues came and said to me, "Come, I will show you the bride, the wife of the Lamb." [10]And he carried me away in the Spirit to a mountain great and high, and showed me the Holy City, Jerusalem, coming down out of heaven from God. [11]It shone with the glory of God, and its brilliance was like that of a very precious jewel, like a jasper, clear as crystal. [12]It had a great, high wall with twelve gates, and with twelve angels at the gates. On the gates were written the names of the twelve tribes of Israel. [13]There were three gates on the east, three on the north, three on the south and three on the west. [14]The wall of the city had twelve foundations, and on them were the names of the twelve apostles of the Lamb.

[15]The angel who talked with me had a measuring rod of gold to measure the city, its gates and its walls. [16]The city was laid out like a square, as long as it was wide. He measured the city with the rod and found it to be 12,000 stadia[a] in length, and as wide and high as it is long. [17]The angel measured the wall using human measurement, and it was 144 cubits[b] thick.[c] [18]The wall was made of jasper, and the city of pure gold, as pure as glass. [19]The foundations of the city walls were decorated with every kind of precious stone. The first foundation was jasper, the second sapphire, the third agate, the fourth emerald, [20]the fifth onyx, the sixth ruby, the seventh chrysolite, the eighth beryl, the ninth topaz, the tenth turquoise, the eleventh jacinth, and the twelfth amethyst.[d] [21]The twelve gates were twelve pearls, each gate made of a single pearl. The great street of the city was of gold, as pure as transparent glass.

[22]I did not see a temple in the city, because the Lord God Almighty and the Lamb are its temple. [23]The city does not need the sun or the moon to shine on it, for the glory of God gives it light, and the Lamb is its lamp. [24]The nations will walk by its light, and the kings of the earth will bring their splendor into it. [25]On no day will its gates ever be shut, for there will be no night there. [26]The glory and honor of the nations will be brought into it. [27]Nothing impure will ever enter it, nor will anyone who does what is shameful or deceitful, but only those whose names are written in the Lamb's book of life.

Eden Restored

22 Then the angel showed me the river of the water of life, as clear as crystal, flowing from the throne of God and of the Lamb [2]down the middle of the great street of the city. On each side of the river stood the tree of life, bearing twelve crops of fruit, yielding its fruit every month. And the leaves of the tree are for the healing of the nations. [3]No longer will there be any curse. The throne of God and of the Lamb will be in the city, and his servants will serve him. [4]They will see his face, and his name will be on their foreheads. [5]There will be no more night. They will not need the light of a lamp or the light of the sun, for the Lord God will give them light. And they will reign for ever and ever.

John and the Angel

[6]The angel said to me, "These words are trustworthy and true. The Lord, the God who inspires the prophets, sent his angel to show his servants the things that must soon take place."

[7]"Look, I am coming soon! Blessed is the one who keeps the words of the prophecy written in this scroll."

[8]I, John, am the one who heard and saw these things. And when I had heard and seen them, I fell down to worship at the feet of the angel who had been showing them to me. [9]But he said to me, "Don't do that! I am a fellow servant with you and with your fellow prophets and with all who keep the words of this scroll. Worship God!"

[a] 16 That is, about 1,400 miles or about 2,200 kilometers   [b] 17 That is, about 200 feet or about 65 meters   [c] 17 Or high   [d] 20 The precise identification of some of these precious stones is uncertain.

¹⁰Then he told me, "Do not seal up the words of the prophecy of this scroll, because the time is near. ¹¹Let the one who does wrong continue to do wrong; let the vile person continue to be vile; let the one who does right continue to do right; and let the holy person continue to be holy."

Epilogue: Invitation and Warning

¹²"Look, I am coming soon! My reward is with me, and I will give to each person according to what they have done. ¹³I am the Alpha and the Omega, the First and the Last, the Beginning and the End.

¹⁴"Blessed are those who wash their robes, that they may have the right to the tree of life and may go through the gates into the city. ¹⁵Outside are the dogs, those who practice magic arts, the sexually immoral, the murderers, the idolaters and everyone who loves and practices falsehood.

¹⁶"I, Jesus, have sent my angel to give you*a* this testimony for the churches. I am the Root and the Offspring of David, and the bright Morning Star."

¹⁷The Spirit and the bride say, "Come!" And let the one who hears say, "Come!" Let the one who is thirsty come; and let the one who wishes take the free gift of the water of life.

¹⁸I warn everyone who hears the words of the prophecy of this scroll: If anyone adds anything to them, God will add to that person the plagues described in this scroll. ¹⁹And if anyone takes words away from this scroll of prophecy, God will take away from that person any share in the tree of life and in the Holy City, which are described in this scroll.

²⁰He who testifies to these things says, "Yes, I am coming soon."

Amen. Come, Lord Jesus.

²¹The grace of the Lord Jesus be with God's people. Amen.

---

a 16 The Greek is plural.

Psalms & Proverbs

Psalms

BOOK I

Psalms 1–41

Psalm 1

¹ Blessed is the one
who does not walk in step with the
wicked
or stand in the way that sinners take
or sit in the company of mockers,
² but whose delight is in the law of the LORD,
and who meditates on his law day and
night.
³ That person is like a tree planted by
streams of water,
which yields its fruit in season
and whose leaf does not wither—
whatever they do prospers.

⁴ Not so the wicked!
They are like chaff
that the wind blows away.
⁵ Therefore the wicked will not stand in the
judgment,
nor sinners in the assembly of the
righteous.

⁶ For the LORD watches over the way of the
righteous,
but the way of the wicked leads to
destruction.

Psalm 2

¹ Why do the nations conspire*ᵃ*
and the peoples plot in vain?
² The kings of the earth rise up
and the rulers band together
against the LORD and against his
anointed, saying,
³ "Let us break their chains
and throw off their shackles."

⁴ The One enthroned in heaven laughs;
the Lord scoffs at them.

⁵ He rebukes them in his anger
and terrifies them in his wrath, saying,
⁶ "I have installed my king
on Zion, my holy mountain."

⁷ I will proclaim the LORD's decree:

He said to me, "You are my son;
today I have become your father.
⁸ Ask me,
and I will make the nations your
inheritance,
the ends of the earth your possession.
⁹ You will break them with a rod of iron*ᵇ*;
you will dash them to pieces like
pottery."

¹⁰ Therefore, you kings, be wise;
be warned, you rulers of the earth.
¹¹ Serve the LORD with fear
and celebrate his rule with trembling.
¹² Kiss his son, or he will be angry
and your way will lead to your
destruction,
for his wrath can flare up in a moment.
Blessed are all who take refuge in him.

Psalm 3*ᶜ*

A psalm of David.
When he fled from his son Absalom.

¹ LORD, how many are my foes!
How many rise up against me!
² Many are saying of me,
"God will not deliver him."*ᵈ*

³ But you, LORD, are a shield around me,
my glory, the One who lifts my head
high.
⁴ I call out to the LORD,
and he answers me from his holy
mountain.

⁵ I lie down and sleep;
I wake again, because the LORD
sustains me.

ᵃ 1 Hebrew; Septuagint *rage*   *ᵇ 9* Or *will rule them with an iron scepter* (see Septuagint and Syriac)
ᶜ In Hebrew texts 3:1-8 is numbered 3:2-9.   *ᵈ 2* The Hebrew has *Selah* (a word of uncertain meaning)
here and at the end of verses 4 and 8.

6 I will not fear though tens of thousands
  assail me on every side.

7 Arise, LORD!
  Deliver me, my God!
  Strike all my enemies on the jaw;
  break the teeth of the wicked.

8 From the LORD comes deliverance.
  May your blessing be on your people.

Psalm 4 [a]

For the director of music.
With stringed instruments. A psalm of David.

1 Answer me when I call to you,
  my righteous God.
  Give me relief from my distress;
  have mercy on me and hear my prayer.

2 How long will you people turn my glory
  into shame?
  How long will you love delusions and
  seek false gods [b]? [c]
3 Know that the LORD has set apart his
  faithful servant for himself;
  the LORD hears when I call to him.

4 Tremble and [d] do not sin;
  when you are on your beds,
  search your hearts and be silent.
5 Offer the sacrifices of the righteous
  and trust in the LORD.

6 Many, LORD, are asking, "Who will bring
  us prosperity?"
  Let the light of your face shine on us.
7 Fill my heart with joy
  when their grain and new wine abound.

8 In peace I will lie down and sleep,
  for you alone, LORD,
  make me dwell in safety.

Psalm 5 [e]

For the director of music. For pipes.
A psalm of David.

1 Listen to my words, LORD,
  consider my lament.
2 Hear my cry for help,
  my King and my God,
  for to you I pray.

3 In the morning, LORD, you hear my
  voice;
  in the morning I lay my requests
  before you
  and wait expectantly.
4 For you are not a God who is pleased with
  wickedness;
  with you, evil people are not welcome.
5 The arrogant cannot stand
  in your presence.
  You hate all who do wrong;
6   you destroy those who tell lies.
  The bloodthirsty and deceitful
  you, LORD, detest.
7 But I, by your great love,
  can come into your house;
  in reverence I bow down
  toward your holy temple.

8 Lead me, LORD, in your righteousness
  because of my enemies —
  make your way straight before me.
9 Not a word from their mouth can be
  trusted;
  their heart is filled with malice.
  Their throat is an open grave;
  with their tongues they tell lies.
10 Declare them guilty, O God!
  Let their intrigues be their downfall.
  Banish them for their many sins,
  for they have rebelled against you.
11 But let all who take refuge in you be glad;
  let them ever sing for joy.
  Spread your protection over them,
  that those who love your name may
  rejoice in you.

12 Surely, LORD, you bless the righteous;
  you surround them with your favor as
  with a shield.

Psalm 6 [f]

For the director of music. With stringed
instruments. According to sheminith. [g]
A psalm of David.

1 LORD, do not rebuke me in your anger
  or discipline me in your wrath.
2 Have mercy on me, LORD, for I am faint;
  heal me, LORD, for my bones are in
  agony.
3 My soul is in deep anguish.
  How long, LORD, how long?

---

[a] In Hebrew texts 4:1-8 is numbered 4:2-9.   [b] 2 Or *seek lies*   [c] 2 The Hebrew has *Selah* (a word of uncertain meaning) here and at the end of verse 4.   [d] 4 Or *In your anger* (see Septuagint)   [e] In Hebrew texts 5:1-12 is numbered 5:2-13.   [f] In Hebrew texts 6:1-10 is numbered 6:2-11.   [g] Title: Probably a musical term

Sleep in Peace

By Sarah Ball

READ: Psalm 4:8

True confession time: As much as I want to "in peace ... lie down and sleep" (Psalm 4:8), that doesn't always happen. I'm a sleepwalker. Many of my nighttime travels are harmless, like when I wake up in my kitchen with a wooden spoon in hand.

But there are also darker moments. My nightmares are sometimes so vivid that I act in response to them. Once I tried to beat through a window to escape the fires in my nightmare. My husband was deployed, and I had been worrying about fire safety. I wondered if my house caught on fire at night, could I get my children out safely? My daytime worry came to life in the dark.

We military spouses carry heavy loads of stress — frequent moves, financial decisions, family relationships, parenting issues. During separations, we carry our loads alone. Is it any wonder that we crawl into bed at night seeking rest, only to find that our cares of the day have come with us?

Self-help articles abound on getting a good night's sleep: Shut out noises. Turn on white noise. Take naps during the day. Don't ever take naps. Get lots of sunlight. Block out all light. While many of these suggestions are useful for encouraging sleep, none of them answer my deeper question: When my mind is struggling with stress and fear, how can I find real rest?

David, the writer of many psalms, knew a lot about struggling with fear. David spent years evading and fighting enemies, both before and after he became king. He came to God with the same issues we face: weariness, anger, loneliness and frustration. His words of desperation were raw and real.

God did not leave David in despair however. David's psalms chronicle his discoveries of God's love and protection: "I keep my eyes always on the LORD. With him at my right hand, I will not be shaken. Therefore my heart is glad and my tongue rejoices; my body also will rest secure" (Psalm 16:8 – 9).

David found true rest in God alone, and so can we. God loves us and the people we care about. He is in complete authority over every circumstance, and he holds the past, present and future in his sovereign hands.

When rest eludes you, spend some time reading the psalms of David. Let them remind you of God's loving care and protection (see Psalm 23) or of God's salvation and goodness (see Psalm 27). Lie down and sleep in peace, resting in the safety of the Lord.

In peace I will lie down and sleep, for you alone, LORD, make me dwell in safety.

PSALM 4:8

DEBRIEF

- What fears and anxieties keep me from truly resting?
- Do I believe that God is greater than anything I fear?

REPORT

Lord, I know you love me and watch over me. Take my fears and grant me true rest, knowing that you are my source of strength and protection. In Jesus' name I pray. Amen.

for your next devotional reading, go to page 340

⁴Turn, Lᴏʀᴅ, and deliver me;
  save me because of your unfailing love.
⁵Among the dead no one proclaims
  your name.
  Who praises you from the grave?

⁶I am worn out from my groaning.

All night long I flood my bed with weeping
  and drench my couch with tears.
⁷My eyes grow weak with sorrow;
  they fail because of all my foes.

⁸Away from me, all you who do evil,
  for the Lᴏʀᴅ has heard my weeping.
⁹The Lᴏʀᴅ has heard my cry for mercy;
  the Lᴏʀᴅ accepts my prayer.
¹⁰All my enemies will be overwhelmed
  with shame and anguish;
  they will turn back and suddenly be
  put to shame.

Psalm 7ᵃ

*A shiggaionᵇ of David,
which he sang to the Lᴏʀᴅ concerning
Cush, a Benjamite.*

¹Lᴏʀᴅ my God, I take refuge in you;
  save and deliver me from all who
  pursue me,
²or they will tear me apart like a lion
  and rip me to pieces with no one to
  rescue me.

³Lᴏʀᴅ my God, if I have done this
  and there is guilt on my hands—
⁴if I have repaid my ally with evil
  or without cause have robbed my foe—
⁵then let my enemy pursue and
  overtake me;
  let him trample my life to the ground
  and make me sleep in the dust.ᶜ

⁶Arise, Lᴏʀᴅ, in your anger;
  rise up against the rage of my enemies.
  Awake, my God; decree justice.
⁷Let the assembled peoples gather
  around you,
  while you sit enthroned over them
  on high.
⁸ Let the Lᴏʀᴅ judge the peoples.
  Vindicate me, Lᴏʀᴅ, according to my
  righteousness,

according to my integrity, O Most High.
⁹Bring to an end the violence of the wicked
  and make the righteous secure—
you, the righteous God
  who probes minds and hearts.

¹⁰My shieldᵈ is God Most High,
  who saves the upright in heart.
¹¹God is a righteous judge,
  a God who displays his wrath every day.
¹²If he does not relent,
  heᵉ will sharpen his sword;
  he will bend and string his bow.
¹³He has prepared his deadly weapons;
  he makes ready his flaming arrows.

¹⁴Whoever is pregnant with evil
  conceives trouble and gives birth to
  disillusionment.
¹⁵Whoever digs a hole and scoops it out
  falls into the pit they have made.
¹⁶The trouble they cause recoils on them;
  their violence comes down on their
  own heads.

¹⁷I will give thanks to the Lᴏʀᴅ because of
  his righteousness;
  I will sing the praises of the name of
  the Lᴏʀᴅ Most High.

Psalm 8ᶠ

For the director of music. According to gittith.ᵍ
A psalm of David.

¹Lᴏʀᴅ, our Lord,
  how majestic is your name in all the
  earth!

You have set your glory
  in the heavens.
²Through the praise of children and
  infants
  you have established a stronghold
  against your enemies,
  to silence the foe and the avenger.
³When I consider your heavens,
  the work of your fingers,
  the moon and the stars,
  which you have set in place,
⁴what is mankind that you are mindful of
  them,
  human beings that you care for them?ʰ

ᵃ In Hebrew texts 7:1-17 is numbered 7:2-18.   ᵇ Title: Probably a literary or musical term   ᶜ 5 The
Hebrew has *Selah* (a word of uncertain meaning) here.   ᵈ 10 Or *sovereign*   ᵉ 12 Or *If anyone does
not repent, / God*   ᶠ In Hebrew texts 8:1-9 is numbered 8:2-10.   ᵍ Title: Probably a musical term
ʰ 4 Or *what is a human being that you are mindful of him, / a son of man that you care for him?*

⁵ You have made them[a] a little lower than
        the angels[b]
    and crowned them[a] with glory and
        honor.
⁶ You made them rulers over the works of
        your hands;
    you put everything under their[c] feet:
⁷ all flocks and herds,
    and the animals of the wild,
⁸ the birds in the sky,
    and the fish in the sea,
    all that swim the paths of the seas.

⁹ LORD, our Lord,
    how majestic is your name in all
        the earth!

Psalm 9[d,e]

For the director of music.
To the tune of "The Death of the Son."
A psalm of David.

¹ I will give thanks to you, LORD, with all
        my heart;
    I will tell of all your wonderful deeds.
² I will be glad and rejoice in you;
    I will sing the praises of your name,
        O Most High.

³ My enemies turn back;
    they stumble and perish before you.
⁴ For you have upheld my right and my
        cause,
    sitting enthroned as the righteous
        judge.
⁵ You have rebuked the nations and
        destroyed the wicked;
    you have blotted out their name for
        ever and ever.
⁶ Endless ruin has overtaken my enemies,
    you have uprooted their cities;
    even the memory of them has
        perished.

⁷ The LORD reigns forever;
    he has established his throne for
        judgment.
⁸ He rules the world in righteousness
    and judges the peoples with equity.
⁹ The LORD is a refuge for the oppressed,
    a stronghold in times of trouble.

¹⁰ Those who know your name trust in you,
    for you, LORD, have never forsaken
        those who seek you.
¹¹ Sing the praises of the LORD, enthroned
        in Zion;
    proclaim among the nations what he
        has done.
¹² For he who avenges blood remembers;
    he does not ignore the cries of the
        afflicted.

¹³ LORD, see how my enemies persecute me!
    Have mercy and lift me up from the
        gates of death,
¹⁴ that I may declare your praises
    in the gates of Daughter Zion,
    and there rejoice in your salvation.

¹⁵ The nations have fallen into the pit they
        have dug;
    their feet are caught in the net they
        have hidden.
¹⁶ The LORD is known by his acts of justice;
    the wicked are ensnared by the work of
        their hands.[f]
¹⁷ The wicked go down to the realm of
        the dead,
    all the nations that forget God.
¹⁸ But God will never forget the needy;
    the hope of the afflicted will never
        perish.

¹⁹ Arise, LORD, do not let mortals triumph;
    let the nations be judged in your
        presence.
²⁰ Strike them with terror, LORD;
    let the nations know they are only
        mortal.

Psalm 10[d]

¹ Why, LORD, do you stand far off?
    Why do you hide yourself in times of
        trouble?

² In his arrogance the wicked man hunts
        down the weak,
    who are caught in the schemes he
        devises.
³ He boasts about the cravings of his
        heart;

---

[a] 5 Or *him*   [b] 5 Or *than God*   [c] 6 Or *made him ruler . . . ; / . . . his*   [d] Psalms 9 and 10 may originally
have been a single acrostic poem in which alternating lines began with the successive letters of the
Hebrew alphabet. In the Septuagint they constitute one psalm.   [e] In Hebrew texts 9:1-20 is numbered
9:2-21.   [f] 16 The Hebrew has *Higgaion* and *Selah* (words of uncertain meaning) here; *Selah* occurs also
at the end of verse 20.

he blesses the greedy and reviles the
LORD.
⁴ In his pride the wicked man does not
seek him;
in all his thoughts there is no room
for God.
⁵ His ways are always prosperous;
your laws are rejected by*a* him;
he sneers at all his enemies.
⁶ He says to himself, "Nothing will ever
shake me."
He swears, "No one will ever do me
harm."

⁷ His mouth is full of lies and threats;
trouble and evil are under his tongue.
⁸ He lies in wait near the villages;
from ambush he murders the
innocent.
His eyes watch in secret for his victims;
⁹   like a lion in cover he lies in wait.
He lies in wait to catch the helpless;
he catches the helpless and drags them
off in his net.
¹⁰ His victims are crushed, they collapse;
they fall under his strength.
¹¹ He says to himself, "God will never notice;
he covers his face and never sees."

¹² Arise, LORD! Lift up your hand, O God.
Do not forget the helpless.
¹³ Why does the wicked man revile God?
Why does he say to himself,
"He won't call me to account"?
¹⁴ But you, God, see the trouble of the
afflicted;
you consider their grief and take it
in hand.
The victims commit themselves to you;
you are the helper of the fatherless.
¹⁵ Break the arm of the wicked man;
call the evildoer to account for his
wickedness
that would not otherwise be found out.

¹⁶ The LORD is King for ever and ever;
the nations will perish from his land.
¹⁷ You, LORD, hear the desire of the
afflicted;
you encourage them, and you listen to
their cry,
¹⁸ defending the fatherless and the
oppressed,

so that mere earthly mortals
will never again strike terror.

Psalm 11

For the director of music. Of David.

¹ In the LORD I take refuge.
How then can you say to me:
"Flee like a bird to your mountain.
² For look, the wicked bend their bows;
they set their arrows against the
strings
to shoot from the shadows
at the upright in heart.
³ When the foundations are being
destroyed,
what can the righteous do?"

⁴ The LORD is in his holy temple;
the LORD is on his heavenly throne.
He observes everyone on earth;
his eyes examine them.
⁵ The LORD examines the righteous,
but the wicked, those who love
violence,
he hates with a passion.
⁶ On the wicked he will rain
fiery coals and burning sulfur;
a scorching wind will be their lot.

⁷ For the LORD is righteous,
he loves justice;
the upright will see his face.

Psalm 12*b*

For the director of music.
According to sheminith.*c A psalm of David.*

¹ Help, LORD, for no one is faithful anymore;
those who are loyal have vanished
from the human race.
² Everyone lies to their neighbor;
they flatter with their lips
but harbor deception in their hearts.

³ May the LORD silence all flattering lips
and every boastful tongue —
⁴ those who say,
"By our tongues we will prevail;
our own lips will defend us — who is
lord over us?"

⁵ "Because the poor are plundered and the
needy groan,

---

a 5 See Septuagint; Hebrew / *they are haughty, and your laws are far from*   *b* In Hebrew texts 12:1-8 is
numbered 12:2-9.   *c* Title: Probably a musical term

I will now arise," says the LORD.
"I will protect them from those who
malign them."
[6] And the words of the LORD are flawless,
like silver purified in a crucible,
like gold[a] refined seven times.

[7] You, LORD, will keep the needy safe
and will protect us forever from the
wicked,
[8] who freely strut about
when what is vile is honored by the
human race.

Psalm 13[b]

For the director of music. A psalm of David.

[1] How long, LORD? Will you forget me
forever?
How long will you hide your face
from me?
[2] How long must I wrestle with my
thoughts
and day after day have sorrow in
my heart?
How long will my enemy triumph
over me?

[3] Look on me and answer, LORD my God.
Give light to my eyes, or I will sleep in
death,
[4] and my enemy will say, "I have overcome
him,"
and my foes will rejoice when I fall.

[5] But I trust in your unfailing love;
my heart rejoices in your salvation.
[6] I will sing the LORD's praise,
for he has been good to me.

Psalm 14

For the director of music. Of David.

[1] The fool[c] says in his heart,
"There is no God."
They are corrupt, their deeds are vile;
there is no one who does good.

[2] The LORD looks down from heaven
on all mankind
to see if there are any who understand,
any who seek God.

[3] All have turned away, all have become
corrupt;
there is no one who does good,
not even one.

[4] Do all these evildoers know nothing?

They devour my people as though eating
bread;
they never call on the LORD.
[5] But there they are, overwhelmed with
dread,
for God is present in the company of
the righteous.
[6] You evildoers frustrate the plans of
the poor,
but the LORD is their refuge.

[7] Oh, that salvation for Israel would come
out of Zion!
When the LORD restores his people,
let Jacob rejoice and Israel be glad!

Psalm 15

A psalm of David.

[1] LORD, who may dwell in your sacred tent?
Who may live on your holy mountain?

[2] The one whose walk is blameless,
who does what is righteous,
who speaks the truth from their heart;
[3] whose tongue utters no slander,
who does no wrong to a neighbor,
and casts no slur on others;
[4] who despises a vile person
but honors those who fear the LORD;
who keeps an oath even when it hurts,
and does not change their mind;
[5] who lends money to the poor without
interest;
who does not accept a bribe against
the innocent.

Whoever does these things
will never be shaken.

Psalm 16

A miktam[d] of David.

[1] Keep me safe, my God,
for in you I take refuge.

[2] I say to the LORD, "You are my Lord;
apart from you I have no good thing."

---

[a] 6 Probable reading of the original Hebrew text; Masoretic Text *earth*   [b] In Hebrew texts 13:1-6 is
numbered 13:2-6.   [c] 1 The Hebrew words rendered *fool* in Psalms denote one who is morally deficient.
[d] Title: Probably a literary or musical term

TAKING REFUGE IN GOD

By Jocelyn Green

Just as 20-year-old Sarah Morgan was thinking she would not know what to save if she ever needed to flee her home in Baton Rouge, Louisiana, her sister Lilly burst through the front door. What happened next is recorded in Sarah's diary: "[Lilly screamed,] 'Mr. Castle has killed a Federal officer on a ship, and they are going to shell —' Bang! went a cannon at the word, and that was all our warning."

Sarah's mother grabbed the important papers of her deceased husband. Lilly gathered her children, and Lucy, a slave, grabbed Lilly's baby out of the bathwater and threw a quilt over her before rushing out the door. Sarah's father had died, and her brothers were away fighting for the Confederacy, so the women fled.

After running out of the city, their pace mercifully slowed to a walk. Three miles out of town, the Morgans began to overtake a thick, slow stream of fugitives who had left Baton Rouge ahead of them. On May 31, 1862, Sarah described the chaos in her diary:

> Women searching for their babies along the road ... others sitting in the dust crying and wringing their hands ... All the talk by the roadside was of burning homes, houses knocked to pieces by balls, famine, murder, desolation; so I comforted myself singing "Better days are coming" and "I hope to die shouting the Lord will provide."

This was the first place in Sarah's diary where she penned the hymn lyrics "I hope to die shouting, 'The Lord will provide,' " but it was not the last.* She also used these words four more times as she chronicled her life as a refugee during the Civil War.

In August, she and her family finally returned to their home only to find it had suffered worse damage than any other house in Baton Rouge. The only items salvaged were Sarah's guitar, the piano, a few mattresses and some forgotten law books and papers of her father's. "For which I say in all humility, Blessed be God who has spared us so much," Sarah wrote. "Have I cause to complain? True, the house, furniture, clothing, etc., are lost but — trust in God!"

Though the enemy had reduced her to poverty, Sarah's thinking was similar to that illustrated in Psalm 13: Acknowledgment of loss and defeat that ends with trusting and praising God.

---

*Read the words to "The Lord Will Provide" on page 489.

Prayer: Lord, give me the strength to always turn to your love and goodness.

> **How long must I wrestle with my thoughts and day after day have sorrow in my heart? How long will my enemy triumph over me? ... But I trust in your unfailing love; my heart rejoices in your salvation. I will sing the LORD's praise, for he has been good to me.**
>
> PSALM 13:2,5 – 6

 for your next devotional reading, go to page 342

[3] I say of the holy people who are in the
land,
"They are the noble ones in whom is all
my delight."
[4] Those who run after other gods will
suffer more and more.
I will not pour out libations of blood to
such gods
or take up their names on my lips.

[5] LORD, you alone are my portion and
my cup;
you make my lot secure.
[6] The boundary lines have fallen for me in
pleasant places;
surely I have a delightful inheritance.
[7] I will praise the LORD, who counsels me;
even at night my heart instructs me.
[8] I keep my eyes always on the LORD.
With him at my right hand, I will not
be shaken.

[9] Therefore my heart is glad and my tongue
rejoices;
my body also will rest secure,
[10] because you will not abandon me to the
realm of the dead,
nor will you let your faithful[a] one see
decay.
[11] You make known to me the path of life;
you will fill me with joy in your
presence,
with eternal pleasures at your right
hand.

Psalm 17

A prayer of David.

[1] Hear me, LORD, my plea is just;
listen to my cry.
Hear my prayer—
it does not rise from deceitful lips.
[2] Let my vindication come from you;
may your eyes see what is right.

[3] Though you probe my heart,
though you examine me at night and
test me,
you will find that I have planned no evil;
my mouth has not transgressed.
[4] Though people tried to bribe me,
I have kept myself from the ways of
the violent
through what your lips have
commanded.

[5] My steps have held to your paths;
my feet have not stumbled.

[6] I call on you, my God, for you will
answer me;
turn your ear to me and hear my
prayer.
[7] Show me the wonders of your great love,
you who save by your right hand
those who take refuge in you from
their foes.

[8] Keep me as the apple of your eye;
hide me in the shadow of your wings
[9] from the wicked who are out to destroy me,
from my mortal enemies who
surround me.

[10] They close up their callous hearts,
and their mouths speak with
arrogance.
[11] They have tracked me down, they now
surround me,
with eyes alert, to throw me to the
ground.
[12] They are like a lion hungry for prey,
like a fierce lion crouching in cover.

[13] Rise up, LORD, confront them, bring
them down;
with your sword rescue me from the
wicked.
[14] By your hand save me from such people,
LORD,
from those of this world whose reward
is in this life.
May what you have stored up for the
wicked fill their bellies;
may their children gorge themselves
on it,
and may there be leftovers for their
little ones.

[15] As for me, I will be vindicated and will
see your face;
when I awake, I will be satisfied with
seeing your likeness.

Psalm 18[b]

*For the director of music. Of David the servant of
the LORD. He sang to the LORD the words of this song
when the LORD delivered him from the hand of all
his enemies and from the hand of Saul. He said:*

[1] I love you, LORD, my strength.

[2] The LORD is my rock, my fortress and my
deliverer;

---

[a] 10 Or *holy*   [b] In Hebrew texts 18:1-50 is numbered 18:2-51.

WE ARE HERE!

By Jocelyn Green

Benita Koeman's experiences during her husband's two deployments to the Middle East were as different as combat boots and flip-flops.

During the deployment to Iraq in early 2003, support on the home front was clear.

"My mother-in-law kept me occupied on the day of Scott's departure," said Benita. "On the second day of deployment, one of our church friends brought us lunch and stayed to eat with us. Evidence of God's provision continued to be shown through his children: prayers, meals, companionship, childcare, and other gestures of support and encouragement."

In mid-March the invasion into Iraq began, and with parting words of love, encourage-ment and prayers, Benita wrote to her husband, "Know that we will be fine ... Don't worry about us. You know that so many people are caring for us here."

The deployment to Afghanistan in 2005 was a different story altogether. Benita had adopted a genuine "I can do this" attitude about the deployment — but she couldn't do it alone. "Most good intentions to help from the people we love fell by the wayside. As I struggled to take care of our young children (ages two, four and six years old), I felt alone and abandoned. At one point I bordered on depression. I tried my best to smile, to fake like all was okay and to convince myself it was. But it wasn't."

When Scott returned, it was time to PCS, and along with the luggage, Benita carried residual hurt and anger with her. Many nights she would lie awake and ask God, "What do I do with this? Where do I go from here?"

As time passed, she heard other military wives share similar stories of hurt and disap-pointment regarding the lack of support from their churches. "To create an awareness of our challenges on the military home front and to offer practical suggestions for support and encouragement, the concept of the website *Operation We Are Here* was born." The website is now a highly trafficked clearinghouse of resources for those who want to support military families but aren't sure how to do so.

"Over time, God removed my hurts and redeemed a very painful year for his glory," said Benita. "I was committed to honor him despite my circumstances. I learned, by experience, that people (even those who love us) will disappoint us, and that our circumstances hold no guarantees. But, most important, I was reminded that God will not abandon me."

All of us have been disappointed by others, and we're guaranteed to be disappointed again. But if we place our trust in God rather than people, our lives will be secure (see Psalm 16:5).

Prayer: Father, when life is tough and just doesn't make sense, help me take my eyes off myself and lift my gaze to you, for only you can satisfy.

LORD, you alone are my portion and my cup; you make my lot secure.

PSALM 16:5

for your next devotional reading, go to page 346

my God is my rock, in whom I take
refuge,
my shield*a* and the horn*b* of my
salvation, my stronghold.
³ I called to the LORD, who is worthy of
praise,
and I have been saved from my
enemies.
⁴ The cords of death entangled me;
the torrents of destruction
overwhelmed me.
⁵ The cords of the grave coiled around me;
the snares of death confronted me.

⁶ In my distress I called to the LORD;
I cried to my God for help.
From his temple he heard my voice;
my cry came before him, into his ears.
⁷ The earth trembled and quaked,
and the foundations of the mountains
shook;
they trembled because he was angry.
⁸ Smoke rose from his nostrils;
consuming fire came from his mouth,
burning coals blazed out of it.
⁹ He parted the heavens and came down;
dark clouds were under his feet.
¹⁰ He mounted the cherubim and flew;
he soared on the wings of the wind.
¹¹ He made darkness his covering, his
canopy around him —
the dark rain clouds of the sky.
¹² Out of the brightness of his presence
clouds advanced,
with hailstones and bolts of lightning.
¹³ The LORD thundered from heaven;
the voice of the Most High resounded.*c*
¹⁴ He shot his arrows and scattered the
enemy,
with great bolts of lightning he routed
them.
¹⁵ The valleys of the sea were exposed
and the foundations of the earth laid
bare
at your rebuke, LORD,
at the blast of breath from your
nostrils.
¹⁶ He reached down from on high and took
hold of me;
he drew me out of deep waters.

¹⁷ He rescued me from my powerful enemy,
from my foes, who were too strong
for me.
¹⁸ They confronted me in the day of my
disaster,
but the LORD was my support.
¹⁹ He brought me out into a spacious place;
he rescued me because he delighted
in me.

²⁰ The LORD has dealt with me according to
my righteousness;
according to the cleanness of my
hands he has rewarded me.
²¹ For I have kept the ways of the LORD;
I am not guilty of turning from my God.
²² All his laws are before me;
I have not turned away from his
decrees.
²³ I have been blameless before him
and have kept myself from sin.
²⁴ The LORD has rewarded me according to
my righteousness,
according to the cleanness of my
hands in his sight.

²⁵ To the faithful you show yourself faithful,
to the blameless you show yourself
blameless,
²⁶ to the pure you show yourself pure,
but to the devious you show yourself
shrewd.
²⁷ You save the humble
but bring low those whose eyes are
haughty.
²⁸ You, LORD, keep my lamp burning;
my God turns my darkness into light.
²⁹ With your help I can advance against
a troop*d*;
with my God I can scale a wall.

³⁰ As for God, his way is perfect:
The LORD's word is flawless;
he shields all who take refuge in him.
³¹ For who is God besides the LORD?
And who is the Rock except our God?
³² It is God who arms me with strength
and keeps my way secure.
³³ He makes my feet like the feet of a deer;
he causes me to stand on the heights.
³⁴ He trains my hands for battle;
my arms can bend a bow of bronze.

---

a 2 Or *sovereign*   *b* 2 *Horn* here symbolizes strength.   *c* 13 Some Hebrew manuscripts and
Septuagint (see also 2 Samuel 22:14); most Hebrew manuscripts *resounded, / amid hailstones and bolts of
lightning*   *d* 29 Or *can run through a barricade*

35 You make your saving help my shield,
and your right hand sustains me;
your help has made me great.
36 You provide a broad path for my feet,
so that my ankles do not give way.

37 I pursued my enemies and overtook
them;
I did not turn back till they were
destroyed.
38 I crushed them so that they could
not rise;
they fell beneath my feet.
39 You armed me with strength for battle;
you humbled my adversaries
before me.
40 You made my enemies turn their backs
in flight,
and I destroyed my foes.
41 They cried for help, but there was no one
to save them —
to the Lord, but he did not answer.
42 I beat them as fine as windblown dust;
I trampled them*a* like mud in the
streets.
43 You have delivered me from the attacks of
the people;
you have made me the head of nations.
People I did not know now serve me,
44   foreigners cower before me;
as soon as they hear of me, they
obey me.
45 They all lose heart;
they come trembling from their
strongholds.

46 The Lord lives! Praise be to my Rock!
Exalted be God my Savior!
47 He is the God who avenges me,
who subdues nations under me,
48   who saves me from my enemies.
You exalted me above my foes;
from a violent man you rescued me.
49 Therefore I will praise you, Lord, among
the nations;
I will sing the praises of your name.

50 He gives his king great victories;
he shows unfailing love to his
anointed,
to David and to his descendants
forever.

Psalm 19*b*

For the director of music. A psalm of David.

1 The heavens declare the glory of God;
the skies proclaim the work of his
hands.
2 Day after day they pour forth speech;
night after night they reveal
knowledge.
3 They have no speech, they use no words;
no sound is heard from them.
4 Yet their voice*c* goes out into all the earth,
their words to the ends of the world.
In the heavens God has pitched a tent for
the sun.
5   It is like a bridegroom coming out of
his chamber,
like a champion rejoicing to run his
course.
6 It rises at one end of the heavens
and makes its circuit to the other;
nothing is deprived of its warmth.

7 The law of the Lord is perfect,
refreshing the soul.
The statutes of the Lord are trustworthy,
making wise the simple.
8 The precepts of the Lord are right,
giving joy to the heart.
The commands of the Lord are radiant,
giving light to the eyes.
9 The fear of the Lord is pure,
enduring forever.
The decrees of the Lord are firm,
and all of them are righteous.

10 They are more precious than gold,
than much pure gold;
they are sweeter than honey,
than honey from the honeycomb.
11 By them your servant is warned;
in keeping them there is great reward.
12 But who can discern their own errors?
Forgive my hidden faults.
13 Keep your servant also from willful sins;
may they not rule over me.
Then I will be blameless,
innocent of great transgression.

14 May these words of my mouth and this
meditation of my heart
be pleasing in your sight,
Lord, my Rock and my Redeemer.

a 42 Many Hebrew manuscripts, Septuagint, Syriac and Targum (see also 2 Samuel 22:43); Masoretic Text
I poured them out   *b* In Hebrew texts 19:1-14 is numbered 19:2-15.   *c 4* Septuagint, Jerome and Syriac;
Hebrew *measuring line*

Psalm 20[a]

For the director of music. A psalm of David.

[1] May the LORD answer you when you are
      in distress;
    may the name of the God of Jacob
      protect you.
[2] May he send you help from the sanctuary
    and grant you support from Zion.
[3] May he remember all your sacrifices
    and accept your burnt offerings.[b]
[4] May he give you the desire of your heart
    and make all your plans succeed.
[5] May we shout for joy over your victory
    and lift up our banners in the name of
      our God.

May the LORD grant all your requests.

[6] Now this I know:
    The LORD gives victory to his anointed.
  He answers him from his heavenly
      sanctuary
    with the victorious power of his right
      hand.
[7] Some trust in chariots and some in
      horses,
    but we trust in the name of the LORD
      our God.
[8] They are brought to their knees and fall,
    but we rise up and stand firm.
[9] LORD, give victory to the king!
    Answer us when we call!

Psalm 21[c]

For the director of music. A psalm of David.

[1] The king rejoices in your strength, LORD.
    How great is his joy in the victories
      you give!

[2] You have granted him his heart's desire
    and have not withheld the request of
      his lips.[b]
[3] You came to greet him with rich blessings
    and placed a crown of pure gold on his
      head.
[4] He asked you for life, and you gave it
      to him—
    length of days, for ever and ever.
[5] Through the victories you gave, his glory
      is great;

you have bestowed on him splendor
      and majesty.
[6] Surely you have granted him unending
      blessings
    and made him glad with the joy of your
      presence.
[7] For the king trusts in the LORD;
    through the unfailing love of the Most
      High
  he will not be shaken.

[8] Your hand will lay hold on all your
      enemies;
    your right hand will seize your foes.
[9] When you appear for battle,
    you will burn them up as in a blazing
      furnace.
  The LORD will swallow them up in his
      wrath,
    and his fire will consume them.
[10] You will destroy their descendants from
      the earth,
    their posterity from mankind.
[11] Though they plot evil against you
    and devise wicked schemes, they
      cannot succeed.
[12] You will make them turn their backs
    when you aim at them with drawn
      bow.

[13] Be exalted in your strength, LORD;
    we will sing and praise your might.

Psalm 22[d]

*For the director of music. To the tune of
"The Doe of the Morning." A psalm of David.*

[1] My God, my God, why have you
      forsaken me?
    Why are you so far from saving me,
      so far from my cries of anguish?
[2] My God, I cry out by day, but you do not
      answer,
    by night, but I find no rest.[e]

[3] Yet you are enthroned as the Holy One;
    you are the one Israel praises.[f]
[4] In you our ancestors put their trust;
    they trusted and you delivered them.
[5] To you they cried out and were saved;
    in you they trusted and were not put
      to shame.

---

a In Hebrew texts 20:1-9 is numbered 20:2-10.   *b 3,2* The Hebrew has *Selah* (a word of uncertain
meaning) here.   *c* In Hebrew texts 21:1-13 is numbered 21:2-14.   *d* In Hebrew texts 22:1-31 is numbered
22:2-32.   *e 2* Or *night, and am not silent*   *f 3* Or *Yet you are holy, / enthroned on the praises of Israel*

In God or in Government Do I Trust?

By Sheryl Shearer

READ: Psalm 20:7

One of my family's favorite Christmas traditions includes watching the movie *The Nativity Story*, which narrates the Christmas story through the eyes of Mary and Joseph. The film shows the chilling reality of living under the ruthless rule of the Roman Empire. This ancient superpower demanded absolute obedience from its citizens and captives. But as long as the Jews paid their taxes and did not revolt, all was well. It was into this political environment that Jesus entered the world.

Understandably, the Jewish people yearned for a hero, a Messiah who would deliver them from their earthly prison. God's solution was different. An angel told Joseph that Jesus would "save his people from their sins" (Matthew 1:21). To the disappointment of many, Jesus came to redeem humanity, not overthrow the tyrannical Roman government. The government situation did not change after Jesus' resurrection. In fact, hostility toward Jesus' followers increased. Amid persecution and even martyrdom, however, the early church grew.

The late Chuck Colson once described government's role as "an enforcer of good, restrainer of evil, and promoter of justice" (see Romans 13:1 – 7). But what happens when a government loses sight of those precepts and instead becomes an enforcer of evil and restrainer of good? How should we — especially as families who work within the government — respond when government rules or laws force believers to act contrary to their faith and values?

Oppressive governments and leaders have always existed (see Ecclesiastes 1:9). Edmund Burke (1729 – 1797) said, "Those who don't know history are destined to repeat it." We can learn from those who have gone before us and have remained true to their faith and even flourished in overwhelming circumstances.

The common thread of Christians living amid any type of government persecution is resolute faith in Christ. From the first Christian martyr Stephen (see Acts 7:54 – 60) to Perpetua of the early church to the Russian soldier Ivan (Vanya) Moiseyev to present-day Iranian pastor Youcef Nadarkhani, who was sentenced to death by the Iranian government for apostasy — their attention was focused on Christ, not their oppressors.

When we "set [our] minds on things above, not on earthly things" (Colossians 3:2) and allow Christ to live through us, we protect ourselves from any unhealthy dependence we may have on government.

> Some trust in chariots and some in horses, but we trust in the name of the LORD our God.
>
> PSALM 20:7

DEBRIEF

- Does how I live my life bear witness of a person who is relying on God?
- When I feel governmental rules or laws have forced me to act contrary to my faith and values, how do I respond?

REPORT

Lord, strengthen my resolve to stay on the straight, narrow path and live for you, especially when government or others demand that I do otherwise. Help me to trust you for the provision and protection of my family. Amen.

⁶ But I am a worm and not a man,
  scorned by everyone, despised by the
  people.
⁷ All who see me mock me;
  they hurl insults, shaking their heads.
⁸ "He trusts in the LORD," they say,
  "let the LORD rescue him.
  Let him deliver him,
  since he delights in him."

⁹ Yet you brought me out of the womb;
  you made me trust in you, even at my
  mother's breast.
¹⁰ From birth I was cast on you;
  from my mother's womb you have
  been my God.

¹¹ Do not be far from me,
  for trouble is near
  and there is no one to help.

¹² Many bulls surround me;
  strong bulls of Bashan encircle me.
¹³ Roaring lions that tear their prey
  open their mouths wide against me.
¹⁴ I am poured out like water,
  and all my bones are out of joint.
  My heart has turned to wax;
  it has melted within me.
¹⁵ My mouth*a* is dried up like a potsherd,
  and my tongue sticks to the roof of my
  mouth;
  you lay me in the dust of death.

¹⁶ Dogs surround me,
  a pack of villains encircles me;
  they pierce*b* my hands and my feet.
¹⁷ All my bones are on display;
  people stare and gloat over me.
¹⁸ They divide my clothes among them
  and cast lots for my garment.

¹⁹ But you, LORD, do not be far from me.
  You are my strength; come quickly to
  help me.
²⁰ Deliver me from the sword,
  my precious life from the power of
  the dogs.
²¹ Rescue me from the mouth of the
  lions;
  save me from the horns of the wild
  oxen.

²² I will declare your name to my people;
  in the assembly I will praise you.
²³ You who fear the LORD, praise him!
  All you descendants of Jacob, honor
  him!
  Revere him, all you descendants of
  Israel!
²⁴ For he has not despised or scorned
  the suffering of the afflicted one;
  he has not hidden his face from him
  but has listened to his cry for help.

²⁵ From you comes the theme of my praise
  in the great assembly;
  before those who fear you*c* I will fulfill
  my vows.
²⁶ The poor will eat and be satisfied;
  those who seek the LORD will praise
  him—
  may your hearts live forever!

²⁷ All the ends of the earth
  will remember and turn to the LORD,
  and all the families of the nations
  will bow down before him,
²⁸ for dominion belongs to the LORD
  and he rules over the nations.

²⁹ All the rich of the earth will feast and
  worship;
  all who go down to the dust will kneel
  before him—
  those who cannot keep themselves
  alive.
³⁰ Posterity will serve him;
  future generations will be told about
  the Lord.
³¹ They will proclaim his righteousness,
  declaring to a people yet unborn:
  He has done it!

Psalm 23

A psalm of David.

¹ The LORD is my shepherd, I lack nothing.
²   He makes me lie down in green
    pastures,
  he leads me beside quiet waters,
³   he refreshes my soul.
  He guides me along the right paths
  for his name's sake.

a 15 Probable reading of the original Hebrew text; Masoretic Text *strength*   *b 16* Dead Sea Scrolls and some manuscripts of the Masoretic Text, Septuagint and Syriac; most manuscripts of the Masoretic Text *me, / like a lion*   *c 25* Hebrew *him*

4 Even though I walk
    through the darkest valley,[a]
I will fear no evil,
    for you are with me;
your rod and your staff,
    they comfort me.

5 You prepare a table before me
    in the presence of my enemies.
You anoint my head with oil;
    my cup overflows.
6 Surely your goodness and love will
        follow me
    all the days of my life,
and I will dwell in the house of the LORD
    forever.

Psalm 24

Of David. A psalm.

1 The earth is the LORD's, and everything
        in it,
    the world, and all who live in it;
2 for he founded it on the seas
    and established it on the waters.

3 Who may ascend the mountain of the
        LORD?
    Who may stand in his holy place?
4 The one who has clean hands and a
        pure heart,
    who does not trust in an idol
    or swear by a false god.[b]

5 They will receive blessing from the LORD
    and vindication from God their Savior.
6 Such is the generation of those who
        seek him,
    who seek your face, God of Jacob.[c,d]

7 Lift up your heads, you gates;
    be lifted up, you ancient doors,
    that the King of glory may come in.
8 Who is this King of glory?
    The LORD strong and mighty,
    the LORD mighty in battle.
9 Lift up your heads, you gates;
    lift them up, you ancient doors,
    that the King of glory may come in.
10 Who is he, this King of glory?
    The LORD Almighty —
    he is the King of glory.

Psalm 25[e]

Of David.

1 In you, LORD my God,
    I put my trust.

2 I trust in you;
    do not let me be put to shame,
    nor let my enemies triumph over me.
3 No one who hopes in you
    will ever be put to shame,
but shame will come on those
    who are treacherous without cause.

4 Show me your ways, LORD,
    teach me your paths.
5 Guide me in your truth and teach me,
    for you are God my Savior,
    and my hope is in you all day long.
6 Remember, LORD, your great mercy
        and love,
    for they are from of old.
7 Do not remember the sins of my youth
    and my rebellious ways;
according to your love remember me,
    for you, LORD, are good.

8 Good and upright is the LORD;
    therefore he instructs sinners in
        his ways.
9 He guides the humble in what is right
    and teaches them his way.
10 All the ways of the LORD are loving and
        faithful
    toward those who keep the demands of
        his covenant.
11 For the sake of your name, LORD,
    forgive my iniquity, though it is great.

12 Who, then, are those who fear the LORD?
    He will instruct them in the ways they
        should choose.[f]
13 They will spend their days in prosperity,
    and their descendants will inherit
        the land.
14 The LORD confides in those who fear him;
    he makes his covenant known
        to them.
15 My eyes are ever on the LORD,
    for only he will release my feet from
        the snare.

---

a 4 Or *the valley of the shadow of death*   b 4 Or *swear falsely*   c 6 Two Hebrew manuscripts and Syriac
(see also Septuagint); most Hebrew manuscripts *face, Jacob*   d 6 The Hebrew has *Selah* (a word of
uncertain meaning) here and at the end of verse 10.   e This psalm is an acrostic poem, the verses of
which begin with the successive letters of the Hebrew alphabet.   f 12 Or *ways he chooses*

NEVER-FAILING SOLACE

By Jocelyn Green

As much as Elizabeth longed for spring after a bitter winter on the western prairie, the first tiny blade of grass she spied filled her heart with dread. Warmer weather signaled fighting season, and her husband, General George Armstrong Custer, was always in the thick of it.

During the summer of 1876, General Custer led his men off to Montana Territory for a campaign against the American Indians. They departed into the distance "like a broad dark ribbon stretched smoothly over the plains," Elizabeth recalled in her memoir, *Boots and Saddles*. Elizabeth recalled one summer day during the men's absence:

> On Sunday afternoon, the 25th of June, our little group of saddened women, borne down with one common weight of anxiety, sought solace in gathering together in our house. We tried to find some slight surcease from trouble in the old hymns ... The words of the hymn, "E'en though a cross it be, Nearer, my God, to Thee," came forth with almost a sob from every throat.* At that very hour the fears that our tortured minds had portrayed in imagination were realities, and the souls of those we thought upon were ascending to meet their Maker.
>
> On the 5th of July — for it took that time for the news to come — the sun rose on a beautiful world, but with its earliest beams came the first knell of disaster. A steamer came down the river bearing the wounded from the battle of the Little Big Horn, of Sunday, June 25th. This battle wrecked the lives of twenty-six women at Fort Lincoln, and orphaned children of officers and soldiers joined their cry to that of their bereaved mothers.

The Battle of the Little Bighorn, also called Custer's Last Stand, was an overwhelming victory for the Lakota, Northern Cheyenne and Arapaho Indian tribes. The U.S. Seventh Cavalry, including the Custer Battalion, a force of 700 men, suffered a severe defeat. Five of the Seventh's twelve companies were destroyed. Custer was killed, along with two of his brothers, a nephew and a brother-in-law.

Closing her memoir, Elizabeth Custer wrote, "From that time the life went out of the hearts of the 'women who weep,' and God asked them to walk on alone and in the shadow."

Even in the darkest valley, however, God is still with us, though we may not see him (see Psalm 23:4). His quiet presence and gentle leading are our comfort. The Lord is our shepherd, and our never-failing solace.

---

*Read the words to "Nearer, My God, to Thee" on page 490.

Prayer: Lord, even when I feel completely in the dark, be my guide and comfort.

Even though I walk through the darkest valley, I will fear no evil, for you are with me; your rod and your staff, they comfort me.

PSALM 23:4

for your next devotional reading, go to page 352

16 Turn to me and be gracious to me,
for I am lonely and afflicted.
17 Relieve the troubles of my heart
and free me from my anguish.
18 Look on my affliction and my distress
and take away all my sins.
19 See how numerous are my enemies
and how fiercely they hate me!

20 Guard my life and rescue me;
do not let me be put to shame,
for I take refuge in you.
21 May integrity and uprightness
protect me,
because my hope, Lord,^a is in you.

22 Deliver Israel, O God,
from all their troubles!

Psalm 26

Of David.

1 Vindicate me, Lord,
for I have led a blameless life;
I have trusted in the Lord
and have not faltered.
2 Test me, Lord, and try me,
examine my heart and my mind;
3 for I have always been mindful of your
unfailing love
and have lived in reliance on your
faithfulness.

4 I do not sit with the deceitful,
nor do I associate with hypocrites.
5 I abhor the assembly of evildoers
and refuse to sit with the wicked.
6 I wash my hands in innocence,
and go about your altar, Lord,
7 proclaiming aloud your praise
and telling of all your wonderful deeds.

8 Lord, I love the house where you live,
the place where your glory dwells.
9 Do not take away my soul along with
sinners,
my life with those who are
bloodthirsty,
10 in whose hands are wicked schemes,
whose right hands are full of bribes.
11 I lead a blameless life;
deliver me and be merciful to me.

12 My feet stand on level ground;

in the great congregation I will praise
the Lord.

Psalm 27

Of David.

1 The Lord is my light and my salvation —
whom shall I fear?
The Lord is the stronghold of my life —
of whom shall I be afraid?

2 When the wicked advance against me
to devour^b me,
it is my enemies and my foes
who will stumble and fall.
3 Though an army besiege me,
my heart will not fear;
though war break out against me,
even then I will be confident.

4 One thing I ask from the Lord,
this only do I seek:
that I may dwell in the house of the Lord
all the days of my life,
to gaze on the beauty of the Lord
and to seek him in his temple.
5 For in the day of trouble
he will keep me safe in his dwelling;
he will hide me in the shelter of his
sacred tent
and set me high upon a rock.

6 Then my head will be exalted
above the enemies who surround me;
at his sacred tent I will sacrifice with
shouts of joy;
I will sing and make music to the
Lord.

7 Hear my voice when I call, Lord;
be merciful to me and answer me.
8 My heart says of you, "Seek his face!"
Your face, Lord, I will seek.
9 Do not hide your face from me,
do not turn your servant away in anger;
you have been my helper.
Do not reject me or forsake me,
God my Savior.
10 Though my father and mother
forsake me,
the Lord will receive me.
11 Teach me your way, Lord;
lead me in a straight path
because of my oppressors.

¹² Do not turn me over to the desire of
    my foes,
  for false witnesses rise up against me,
    spouting malicious accusations.

¹³ I remain confident of this:
  I will see the goodness of the LORD
    in the land of the living.
¹⁴ Wait for the LORD;
  be strong and take heart
    and wait for the LORD.

Psalm 28

Of David.

¹ To you, LORD, I call;
  you are my Rock,
  do not turn a deaf ear to me.
For if you remain silent,
  I will be like those who go down to
    the pit.
² Hear my cry for mercy
  as I call to you for help,
as I lift up my hands
  toward your Most Holy Place.

³ Do not drag me away with the wicked,
  with those who do evil,
who speak cordially with their neighbors
  but harbor malice in their hearts.
⁴ Repay them for their deeds
  and for their evil work;
repay them for what their hands have
    done
  and bring back on them what they
    deserve.

⁵ Because they have no regard for the
    deeds of the LORD
  and what his hands have done,
he will tear them down
  and never build them up again.

⁶ Praise be to the LORD,
  for he has heard my cry for mercy.
⁷ The LORD is my strength and my shield;
  my heart trusts in him, and he
    helps me.
My heart leaps for joy,
  and with my song I praise him.

⁸ The LORD is the strength of his people,
  a fortress of salvation for his anointed
    one.

⁹ Save your people and bless your
    inheritance;
  be their shepherd and carry them
    forever.

Psalm 29

A psalm of David.

¹ Ascribe to the LORD, you heavenly
    beings,
  ascribe to the LORD glory and strength.
² Ascribe to the LORD the glory due his
    name;
  worship the LORD in the splendor of
    his*ᵃ* holiness.

³ The voice of the LORD is over the waters;
  the God of glory thunders,
  the LORD thunders over the mighty
    waters.
⁴ The voice of the LORD is powerful;
  the voice of the LORD is majestic.
⁵ The voice of the LORD breaks the cedars;
  the LORD breaks in pieces the cedars
    of Lebanon.
⁶ He makes Lebanon leap like a calf,
  Sirionᵇ like a young wild ox.
⁷ The voice of the LORD strikes
  with flashes of lightning.
⁸ The voice of the LORD shakes the desert;
  the LORD shakes the Desert of Kadesh.
⁹ The voice of the LORD twists the oaksᶜ
  and strips the forests bare.
And in his temple all cry, "Glory!"

¹⁰ The LORD sits enthroned over the flood;
  the LORD is enthroned as King forever.
¹¹ The LORD gives strength to his people;
  the LORD blesses his people with
    peace.

Psalm 30ᵈ

A psalm. A song.
*For the dedication of the temple.*ᵉ *Of David.*

¹ I will exalt you, LORD,
  for you lifted me out of the depths
  and did not let my enemies gloat
    over me.
² LORD my God, I called to you for help,
  and you healed me.
³ You, LORD, brought me up from the realm
    of the dead;

ᵃ 2 Or LORD *with the splendor of*   ᵇ 6 That is, Mount Hermon   ᶜ 9 Or LORD *makes the deer give birth*
ᵈ In Hebrew texts 30:1-12 is numbered 30:2-13.   ᵉ Title: Or *palace*

WAITING

By Ouida DeDahlin Carter

"Mama, what's wrong?" ten-year-old Ouida asked her crying mother as she and her sisters hung clothes to dry. Her mother shook her head. "I don't know. Something's wrong with Recie. The word *forward* keeps coming to me, and I know Recie is in danger." Nothing they said consoled their mother, and a shadow of foreboding darkened Ouida's heart.

Ouida's brother, TEC4 Sergeant Tomlinson Recie Russ, landed in France in the second wave of the Normandy invasion. Through sketchy information heard on static-ridden battery radio, his family pieced together information about his unit. They moved pins on a large map to track locations and battles. One glance showed that Recie remained in the thick of the war. His battalion came ashore on Omaha Beach on June 18, 1944, and participated in Operation Cobra.

The family soon left to visit a sister 90 miles south, in Bonita Springs, Florida. Three days later, as they exited a store, their sister Emily stepped out of a truck, crying. Recie had died.

Recie's commanding officer sent a letter that began with the words, "He went forward in the face of danger." But Ouida longed for more information about her beloved brother.

Years later, a comrade who returned home explained the circumstances. On July 30, 1944, only days after Recie turned 23, their commanding officer summoned Recie and some of his buddies for a dangerous maneuver.

Recie's buddies all had wives and children. Recie, the only single man, volunteered. The army had chosen Recie to attend Officer's Candidate School, but he had turned down the offer. He never wanted to give orders that might result in a soldier's death.

Recie and a few others advanced forward into enemy territory, near Tessy-sur-Vire, and set up communications detailing the enemy's location. Recie climbed a tree to get a good view. Once spotted, enemy fire instantly killed him. Recie was buried in Saint-Lo, but his remains were later repatriated to Florida in the late 1940s.

In 2011, Ouida visited France and the region where Recie had fought, and she finally found healing. "It meant so much to walk where my brother walked to find closure and experience what he experienced," said Ouida.

Though it took decades for Ouida to find peace after her brother's death, she still believes God's timing is perfect. "I'm learning in my golden years that time is almost more important than anything else where God is concerned, and I'm seeing that all things happen in God's timing," Ouida said. "I see that my responsibility and my joy is to trust him in the meantime."

Prayer: Lord, show me how to wait on you, trusting your perfect timing in all things.

I remain confident of this: I will see the goodness of the LORD in the land of the living. Wait for the LORD; be strong and take heart and wait for the LORD.
PSALM 27:13 – 14

for your next devotional reading, go to page 354

you spared me from going down to
the pit.
[4] Sing the praises of the LORD, you his
faithful people;
praise his holy name.
[5] For his anger lasts only a moment,
but his favor lasts a lifetime;
weeping may stay for the night,
but rejoicing comes in the morning.

[6] When I felt secure, I said,
"I will never be shaken."
[7] LORD, when you favored me,
you made my royal mountain[a] stand
firm;
but when you hid your face,
I was dismayed.

[8] To you, LORD, I called;
to the Lord I cried for mercy:
[9] "What is gained if I am silenced,
if I go down to the pit?
Will the dust praise you?
Will it proclaim your faithfulness?
[10] Hear, LORD, and be merciful to me;
LORD, be my help."

[11] You turned my wailing into dancing;
you removed my sackcloth and clothed
me with joy,
[12] that my heart may sing your praises and
not be silent.
LORD my God, I will praise you forever.

Psalm 31[b]

For the director of music.
A psalm of David.

[1] In you, LORD, I have taken refuge;
let me never be put to shame;
deliver me in your righteousness.
[2] Turn your ear to me,
come quickly to my rescue;
be my rock of refuge,
a strong fortress to save me.
[3] Since you are my rock and my fortress,
for the sake of your name lead and
guide me.
[4] Keep me free from the trap that is set
for me,
for you are my refuge.
[5] Into your hands I commit my spirit;
deliver me, LORD, my faithful God.

[6] I hate those who cling to worthless idols;
as for me, I trust in the LORD.
[7] I will be glad and rejoice in your love,
for you saw my affliction
and knew the anguish of my soul.
[8] You have not given me into the hands of
the enemy
but have set my feet in a spacious
place.

[9] Be merciful to me, LORD, for I am in
distress;
my eyes grow weak with sorrow,
my soul and body with grief.
[10] My life is consumed by anguish
and my years by groaning;
my strength fails because of my
affliction,[c]
and my bones grow weak.
[11] Because of all my enemies,
I am the utter contempt of my
neighbors
and an object of dread to my closest
friends—
those who see me on the street flee
from me.
[12] I am forgotten as though I were dead;
I have become like broken pottery.
[13] For I hear many whispering,
"Terror on every side!"
They conspire against me
and plot to take my life.

[14] But I trust in you, LORD;
I say, "You are my God."
[15] My times are in your hands;
deliver me from the hands of my
enemies,
from those who pursue me.
[16] Let your face shine on your servant;
save me in your unfailing love.
[17] Let me not be put to shame, LORD,
for I have cried out to you;
but let the wicked be put to shame
and be silent in the realm of the dead.
[18] Let their lying lips be silenced,
for with pride and contempt
they speak arrogantly against the
righteous.

[19] How abundant are the good things
that you have stored up for those who
fear you,
that you bestow in the sight of all,
on those who take refuge in you.

---

[a] 7 That is, Mount Zion   [b] In Hebrew texts 31:1-24 is numbered 31:2-25.   [c] 10 Or *guilt*

Farewells and Homecomings

By Kathy Guzzo

READ: Psalm 30:5–6

One of the toughest realities military families face is the draining cycle of weeping and rejoicing. I've had the opportunity to serve at homecoming and farewell ceremonies of local military units. As I observed these heartfelt ceremonies, I reflected on my own son's two deployments and homecomings, realizing the seemingly opposing things that occur in our lives and how it's impossible to fully experience one without the other.

January days in northern Illinois are usually dreary and cold. Yet without the gloomy days, would we get as excited about the sunny ones? Don't we appreciate work more if we've been without a job? Joy isn't as strong if we've never experienced sorrow. Love's more precious when we've seen hatred. Can we know true peace if we haven't felt fear?

During my son's deployments life was a roller coaster of emotions complete with ups and downs, twists and turns. There were times I felt sad just eating something I knew he enjoyed but couldn't have; then, after hearing he had received a package of his favorite treats, I'd smile. Other times I would be extremely anxious; then a trusted friend would send me a word of encouragement. Each time I experienced a low, God was faithful in creating a high.

The author of Ecclesiastes explored the enigmas of God's creation. There is a time for everything (see Ecclesiastes 3:1 – 8), but without God everything is meaningless (see Ecclesiastes 1:2; 12:1,8,13). All the ups in our lives are more valuable because we lived through the downs. We can get through the valleys because we know there are mountains nearby to climb.

Whatever happens in our lives, our foundation is the same: Jesus. There is a reason our heavenly Father created the rain and sun, flowers and weeds, life and death, joy and sorrow, even hellos and good-byes. Does he allow us to experience what we consider "bad" so we are more appreciative of the "good"? Perhaps, but I do know that he can turn the bad into good if we will only choose to trust him.

With God the cloudy days aren't as dreary, fear isn't all-consuming, and the good-byes are never forever because as the psalmist stated, "Weeping may stay for the night, but rejoicing comes in the morning." If you're approaching or currently enduring a deployment, remember that God is always with you and that without the heart-wrenching good-byes, we'd never experience the heart-stopping hellos.

Weeping may stay for the night, but rejoicing comes in the morning.
PSALM 30:5

DEBRIEF
- When difficulties occur in life, do they cause me to anticipate the good or do I instead expect more difficulties?
- What can I do to better endure my husband's deployment?

REPORT
Heavenly Father, help me remember that although I will experience tough times, the difficulties won't last forever, and remind me that I need to anticipate the time of rejoicing that you will bring into my life. I thank you that I can appreciate new life because I once lived in darkness. Amen.

---

for your next devotional reading, go to page 359

20 In the shelter of your presence you
    hide them
  from all human intrigues;
  you keep them safe in your dwelling
    from accusing tongues.

21 Praise be to the Lord,
  for he showed me the wonders of
    his love
  when I was in a city under siege.
22 In my alarm I said,
  "I am cut off from your sight!"
  Yet you heard my cry for mercy
  when I called to you for help.

23 Love the Lord, all his faithful people!
  The Lord preserves those who are true
    to him,
  but the proud he pays back in full.
24 Be strong and take heart,
  all you who hope in the Lord.

Psalm 32

Of David. A maskil.[a]

1 Blessed is the one
  whose transgressions are forgiven,
  whose sins are covered.
2 Blessed is the one
  whose sin the Lord does not count
    against them
  and in whose spirit is no deceit.

3 When I kept silent,
  my bones wasted away
  through my groaning all day long.
4 For day and night
  your hand was heavy on me;
  my strength was sapped
  as in the heat of summer.[b]

5 Then I acknowledged my sin to you
  and did not cover up my iniquity.
  I said, "I will confess
  my transgressions to the Lord."
  And you forgave
  the guilt of my sin.

6 Therefore let all the faithful pray to you
  while you may be found;
  surely the rising of the mighty waters
  will not reach them.
7 You are my hiding place;
  you will protect me from trouble

and surround me with songs of
  deliverance.
8 I will instruct you and teach you in the
    way you should go;
  I will counsel you with my loving eye
    on you.
9 Do not be like the horse or the mule,
  which have no understanding
  but must be controlled by bit and bridle
  or they will not come to you.
10 Many are the woes of the wicked,
  but the Lord's unfailing love
  surrounds the one who trusts in him.

11 Rejoice in the Lord and be glad, you
    righteous;
  sing, all you who are upright in heart!

Psalm 33

1 Sing joyfully to the Lord, you righteous;
  it is fitting for the upright to praise
    him.
2 Praise the Lord with the harp;
  make music to him on the ten-stringed
    lyre.
3 Sing to him a new song;
  play skillfully, and shout for joy.

4 For the word of the Lord is right and true;
  he is faithful in all he does.
5 The Lord loves righteousness and
    justice;
  the earth is full of his unfailing love.

6 By the word of the Lord the heavens were
    made,
  their starry host by the breath of his
    mouth.
7 He gathers the waters of the sea into jars[c];
  he puts the deep into storehouses.
8 Let all the earth fear the Lord;
  let all the people of the world revere
    him.
9 For he spoke, and it came to be;
  he commanded, and it stood firm.

10 The Lord foils the plans of the nations;
  he thwarts the purposes of the
    peoples.
11 But the plans of the Lord stand firm
    forever,
  the purposes of his heart through all
    generations.

---

[a] Title: Probably a literary or musical term   [b] 4 The Hebrew has *Selah* (a word of uncertain meaning)
here and at the end of verses 5 and 7.   [c] 7 Or *sea as into a heap*

¹² Blessed is the nation whose God is the
      LORD,
   the people he chose for his
      inheritance.
¹³ From heaven the LORD looks down
   and sees all mankind;
¹⁴ from his dwelling place he watches
   all who live on earth —
¹⁵ he who forms the hearts of all,
   who considers everything they do.

¹⁶ No king is saved by the size of his army;
   no warrior escapes by his great
      strength.
¹⁷ A horse is a vain hope for deliverance;
   despite all its great strength it cannot
      save.
¹⁸ But the eyes of the LORD are on those who
      fear him,
   on those whose hope is in his unfailing
      love,
¹⁹ to deliver them from death
   and keep them alive in famine.

²⁰ We wait in hope for the LORD;
   he is our help and our shield.
²¹ In him our hearts rejoice,
   for we trust in his holy name.
²² May your unfailing love be with us, LORD,
   even as we put our hope in you.

Psalm 34 *a,b*

*Of David. When he pretended to be insane
before Abimelek, who drove him away, and he left.*

¹ I will extol the LORD at all times;
   his praise will always be on my lips.
² I will glory in the LORD;
   let the afflicted hear and rejoice.
³ Glorify the LORD with me;
   let us exalt his name together.

⁴ I sought the LORD, and he answered me;
   he delivered me from all my fears.
⁵ Those who look to him are radiant;
   their faces are never covered with
      shame.
⁶ This poor man called, and the LORD
      heard him;
   he saved him out of all his troubles.
⁷ The angel of the LORD encamps around
      those who fear him,
   and he delivers them.

⁸ Taste and see that the LORD is good;
   blessed is the one who takes refuge
      in him.
⁹ Fear the LORD, you his holy people,
   for those who fear him lack nothing.
¹⁰ The lions may grow weak and hungry,
   but those who seek the LORD lack no
      good thing.
¹¹ Come, my children, listen to me;
   I will teach you the fear of the LORD.
¹² Whoever of you loves life
   and desires to see many good days,
¹³ keep your tongue from evil
   and your lips from telling lies.
¹⁴ Turn from evil and do good;
   seek peace and pursue it.

¹⁵ The eyes of the LORD are on the
      righteous,
   and his ears are attentive to their cry;
¹⁶ but the face of the LORD is against those
      who do evil,
   to blot out their name from the earth.

¹⁷ The righteous cry out, and the LORD
      hears them;
   he delivers them from all their
      troubles.
¹⁸ The LORD is close to the brokenhearted
   and saves those who are crushed in
      spirit.

¹⁹ The righteous person may have many
      troubles,
   but the LORD delivers him from
      them all;
²⁰ he protects all his bones,
   not one of them will be broken.

²¹ Evil will slay the wicked;
   the foes of the righteous will be
      condemned.
²² The LORD will rescue his servants;
   no one who takes refuge in him will be
      condemned.

Psalm 35

Of David.

¹ Contend, LORD, with those who contend
      with me;
   fight against those who fight against me.
² Take up shield and armor;
   arise and come to my aid.

---

a This psalm is an acrostic poem, the verses of which begin with the successive letters of the Hebrew
alphabet.   *b* In Hebrew texts 34:1-22 is numbered 34:2-23.

³Brandish spear and javelin^a
  against those who pursue me.
Say to me,
  "I am your salvation."

⁴May those who seek my life
  be disgraced and put to shame;
may those who plot my ruin
  be turned back in dismay.
⁵May they be like chaff before the wind,
  with the angel of the Lᴏʀᴅ driving
    them away;
⁶may their path be dark and slippery,
  with the angel of the Lᴏʀᴅ pursuing
    them.

⁷Since they hid their net for me without
    cause
  and without cause dug a pit for me,
⁸may ruin overtake them by surprise—
  may the net they hid entangle them,
  may they fall into the pit, to their ruin.
⁹Then my soul will rejoice in the Lᴏʀᴅ
  and delight in his salvation.
¹⁰My whole being will exclaim,
  "Who is like you, Lᴏʀᴅ?
You rescue the poor from those too
    strong for them,
  the poor and needy from those who
    rob them."

¹¹Ruthless witnesses come forward;
  they question me on things I know
    nothing about.
¹²They repay me evil for good
  and leave me like one bereaved.
¹³Yet when they were ill, I put on sackcloth
  and humbled myself with fasting.
When my prayers returned to me
    unanswered,
¹⁴ I went about mourning
  as though for my friend or brother.
I bowed my head in grief
  as though weeping for my mother.
¹⁵But when I stumbled, they gathered
    in glee;
  assailants gathered against me
    without my knowledge.
They slandered me without ceasing.
¹⁶Like the ungodly they maliciously
    mocked;^b
  they gnashed their teeth at me.

¹⁷How long, Lord, will you look on?
  Rescue me from their ravages,
  my precious life from these lions.
¹⁸I will give you thanks in the great
    assembly;
  among the throngs I will praise you.
¹⁹Do not let those gloat over me
  who are my enemies without cause;
do not let those who hate me without
    reason
  maliciously wink the eye.
²⁰They do not speak peaceably,
  but devise false accusations
  against those who live quietly in
    the land.
²¹They sneer at me and say, "Aha! Aha!
  With our own eyes we have seen it."

²²Lᴏʀᴅ, you have seen this; do not be silent.
  Do not be far from me, Lord.
²³Awake, and rise to my defense!
  Contend for me, my God and Lord.
²⁴Vindicate me in your righteousness,
    Lᴏʀᴅ my God;
  do not let them gloat over me.
²⁵Do not let them think, "Aha, just what
    we wanted!"
  or say, "We have swallowed him up."

²⁶May all who gloat over my distress
  be put to shame and confusion;
may all who exalt themselves over me
  be clothed with shame and disgrace.
²⁷May those who delight in my vindication
  shout for joy and gladness;
may they always say, "The Lᴏʀᴅ be
    exalted,
  who delights in the well-being of his
    servant."

²⁸My tongue will proclaim your
    righteousness,
  your praises all day long.

Psalm 36^c

For the director of music.
Of David the servant of the Lᴏʀᴅ.

¹I have a message from God in my heart
  concerning the sinfulness of the
    wicked:^d
There is no fear of God
  before their eyes.

---

^a 3 Or *and block the way*   ^b 16 Septuagint; Hebrew may mean *Like an ungodly circle of mockers,*   ^c In Hebrew texts 36:1-12 is numbered 36:2-13.   ^d 1 Or *A message from God: The transgression of the wicked / resides in their hearts.*

2 In their own eyes they flatter themselves
  too much to detect or hate their sin.
3 The words of their mouths are wicked
      and deceitful;
  they fail to act wisely or do good.
4 Even on their beds they plot evil;
  they commit themselves to a sinful
      course
  and do not reject what is wrong.

5 Your love, LORD, reaches to the heavens,
  your faithfulness to the skies.
6 Your righteousness is like the highest
      mountains,
  your justice like the great deep.
  You, LORD, preserve both people and
      animals.
7 How priceless is your unfailing love,
      O God!
  People take refuge in the shadow of
      your wings.
8 They feast on the abundance of your
      house;
  you give them drink from your river
      of delights.
9 For with you is the fountain of life;
  in your light we see light.

10 Continue your love to those who
      know you,
  your righteousness to the upright in
      heart.
11 May the foot of the proud not come
      against me,
  nor the hand of the wicked drive
      me away.
12 See how the evildoers lie fallen —
  thrown down, not able to rise!

Psalm 37[a]

Of David.

1 Do not fret because of those who are evil
  or be envious of those who do wrong;
2 for like the grass they will soon wither,
  like green plants they will soon die
      away.

3 Trust in the LORD and do good;
  dwell in the land and enjoy safe
      pasture.
4 Take delight in the LORD,
  and he will give you the desires of your
      heart.

5 Commit your way to the LORD;
  trust in him and he will do this:
6 He will make your righteous reward
      shine like the dawn,
  your vindication like the noonday sun.

7 Be still before the LORD
  and wait patiently for him;
  do not fret when people succeed in
      their ways,
  when they carry out their wicked
      schemes.

8 Refrain from anger and turn from wrath;
  do not fret — it leads only to evil.
9 For those who are evil will be destroyed,
  but those who hope in the LORD will
      inherit the land.

10 A little while, and the wicked will be no
      more;
  though you look for them, they will not
      be found.
11 But the meek will inherit the land
  and enjoy peace and prosperity.

12 The wicked plot against the righteous
  and gnash their teeth at them;
13 but the Lord laughs at the wicked,
  for he knows their day is coming.

14 The wicked draw the sword
  and bend the bow
  to bring down the poor and needy,
  to slay those whose ways are upright.
15 But their swords will pierce their own
      hearts,
  and their bows will be broken.

16 Better the little that the righteous have
  than the wealth of many wicked;
17 for the power of the wicked will be
      broken,
  but the LORD upholds the righteous.

18 The blameless spend their days under the
      LORD's care,
  and their inheritance will endure
      forever.
19 In times of disaster they will not wither;
  in days of famine they will enjoy
      plenty.

20 But the wicked will perish:
  Though the LORD's enemies are like
      the flowers of the field,

[a] This psalm is an acrostic poem, the stanzas of which begin with the successive letters of the Hebrew
alphabet.

Finding Delight

By Catherine Fitzgerald

READ: Psalm 37:4

There comes a point in all of our lives when everyday words — words we've used and heard a thousand times before — become incomprehensible. Psalm 37:4 is full of these types of words. And there was a time when I could not comprehend this verse.

I had two miscarriages within months of each other and then, just weeks later, I said good-bye to my husband as he boarded a bus for another deployment. The promise of Psalm 37:4 was etched in my mind: "Take delight in the Lord, and he will give you the desires of your heart." My heart longed for a second child. Yet my arms remained empty and would be for an extended period of time. How could I understand what it meant to delight in anything when my heart was broken? Where could I find reconciliation between the truth of God's Word and my circumstances? It came down to one word my spirit needed to grasp for it all to make sense: *delight*.

Circumstances have the ability to distract our hearts from what they were created to do: find unadulterated joy in God alone. But ever since Eve deviated from finding pure enjoyment in her Creator alone, we have found ourselves struggling too. And then we come to a verse like Psalm 37:4 and find ourselves angry or confused as to why our longing remains unfulfilled.

It's not because God's Word is wrong. It's because we have missed a key component of it. After many tears and painful prayers, God revealed that I was expecting my desires to be fulfilled while not taking delight in him. My delight was contingent upon a plus or minus sign on a pregnancy test. My joy was dependent on an expanding waistline and the subsequent sleepless nights that come along with having a newborn. I had not truly learned to take *delight* in the Lord.

When we start to fully devote ourselves to finding sheer joy in him alone, we see something incredible start to happen. Our desires begin to change. Rather than simply wanting a certain thing, we instead begin to want more of him. We crave his presence. With a heart like that, circumstances can come into our lives that may not be our first choice, but they don't determine our joy. It is then that we fully realize the promise of this verse.

Sometimes longings remain unfulfilled for a long time — even a lifetime. Yet when we persevere and seek to delight in our Creator instead of our circumstances, we can experience his goodness in what he gives us.

Take delight in the Lord, and he will give you the desires of your heart.

PSALM 37:4

DEBRIEF

- What situations are keeping me from delighting in the Lord?
- How can I begin to find joy in him first and foremost?

REPORT

Lord, teach me the meaning of delighting in you. Please help me to not allow my circumstances to dictate my joy. Change my heart's desire to be your desire for me. Amen.

for your next devotional reading, go to page 364

they will be consumed, they will go up
in smoke.

²¹ The wicked borrow and do not repay,
but the righteous give generously;
²² those the LORD blesses will inherit the
land,
but those he curses will be destroyed.

²³ The LORD makes firm the steps
of the one who delights in him;
²⁴ though he may stumble, he will not fall,
for the LORD upholds him with his
hand.

²⁵ I was young and now I am old,
yet I have never seen the righteous
forsaken
or their children begging bread.
²⁶ They are always generous and lend
freely;
their children will be a blessing.ᵃ

²⁷ Turn from evil and do good;
then you will dwell in the land forever.
²⁸ For the LORD loves the just
and will not forsake his faithful ones.

Wrongdoers will be completely
destroyedᵇ;
the offspring of the wicked will perish.
²⁹ The righteous will inherit the land
and dwell in it forever.

³⁰ The mouths of the righteous utter
wisdom,
and their tongues speak what is just.
³¹ The law of their God is in their hearts;
their feet do not slip.

³² The wicked lie in wait for the righteous,
intent on putting them to death;
³³ but the LORD will not leave them in the
power of the wicked
or let them be condemned when
brought to trial.

³⁴ Hope in the LORD
and keep his way.
He will exalt you to inherit the land;
when the wicked are destroyed, you
will see it.

³⁵ I have seen a wicked and ruthless man
flourishing like a luxuriant native tree,

³⁶ but he soon passed away and was no more;
though I looked for him, he could not
be found.

³⁷ Consider the blameless, observe the
upright;
a future awaits those who seek peace.ᶜ
³⁸ But all sinners will be destroyed;
there will be no futureᵈ for the wicked.

³⁹ The salvation of the righteous comes
from the LORD;
he is their stronghold in time of
trouble.
⁴⁰ The LORD helps them and delivers them;
he delivers them from the wicked and
saves them,
because they take refuge in him.

Psalm 38ᵉ

A psalm of David. A petition.

¹ LORD, do not rebuke me in your anger
or discipline me in your wrath.
² Your arrows have pierced me,
and your hand has come down on me.
³ Because of your wrath there is no health
in my body;
there is no soundness in my bones
because of my sin.
⁴ My guilt has overwhelmed me
like a burden too heavy to bear.

⁵ My wounds fester and are loathsome
because of my sinful folly.
⁶ I am bowed down and brought very low;
all day long I go about mourning.
⁷ My back is filled with searing pain;
there is no health in my body.
⁸ I am feeble and utterly crushed;
I groan in anguish of heart.

⁹ All my longings lie open before you,
Lord;
my sighing is not hidden from you.
¹⁰ My heart pounds, my strength fails me;
even the light has gone from my eyes.
¹¹ My friends and companions avoid me
because of my wounds;
my neighbors stay far away.
¹² Those who want to kill me set their
traps,

ᵃ 26 Or *freely; / the names of their children will be used in blessings* (see Gen. 48:20); or *freely; / others will
see that their children are blessed*   ᵇ 28 See Septuagint; Hebrew *They will be protected forever*
ᶜ 37 Or *upright; / those who seek peace will have posterity*   ᵈ 38 Or *posterity*   ᵉ In Hebrew texts 38:1-22
is numbered 38:2-23.

those who would harm me talk of
    my ruin;
    all day long they scheme and lie.
¹³ I am like the deaf, who cannot hear,
    like the mute, who cannot speak;
¹⁴ I have become like one who does
        not hear,
    whose mouth can offer no reply.
¹⁵ LORD, I wait for you;
    you will answer, Lord my God.
¹⁶ For I said, "Do not let them gloat
    or exalt themselves over me when my
        feet slip."

¹⁷ For I am about to fall,
    and my pain is ever with me.
¹⁸ I confess my iniquity;
    I am troubled by my sin.
¹⁹ Many have become my enemies without
        cause*a*;
    those who hate me without reason are
        numerous.
²⁰ Those who repay my good with evil
    lodge accusations against me,
    though I seek only to do what is good.

²¹ LORD, do not forsake me;
    do not be far from me, my God.
²² Come quickly to help me,
    my Lord and my Savior.

Psalm 39*b*

For the director of music.
For Jeduthun. A psalm of David.

¹ I said, "I will watch my ways
    and keep my tongue from sin;
    I will put a muzzle on my mouth
    while in the presence of the wicked."
² So I remained utterly silent,
    not even saying anything good.
    But my anguish increased;
³   my heart grew hot within me.
    While I meditated, the fire burned;
    then I spoke with my tongue:

⁴ "Show me, LORD, my life's end
    and the number of my days;
    let me know how fleeting my life is.
⁵ You have made my days a mere
        handbreadth;
    the span of my years is as nothing
        before you.

Everyone is but a breath,
    even those who seem secure.*c*

⁶ "Surely everyone goes around like a mere
        phantom;
    in vain they rush about, heaping up
        wealth
    without knowing whose it will
        finally be.

⁷ "But now, Lord, what do I look for?
    My hope is in you.
⁸ Save me from all my transgressions;
    do not make me the scorn of fools.
⁹ I was silent; I would not open my mouth,
    for you are the one who has done this.
¹⁰ Remove your scourge from me;
    I am overcome by the blow of your
        hand.
¹¹ When you rebuke and discipline anyone
        for their sin,
    you consume their wealth like a
        moth—
    surely everyone is but a breath.

¹² "Hear my prayer, LORD,
    listen to my cry for help;
    do not be deaf to my weeping.
    I dwell with you as a foreigner,
    a stranger, as all my ancestors were.
¹³ Look away from me, that I may enjoy life
        again
    before I depart and am no more."

Psalm 40*d*

For the director of music.
Of David. A psalm.

¹ I waited patiently for the LORD;
    he turned to me and heard my cry.
² He lifted me out of the slimy pit,
    out of the mud and mire;
    he set my feet on a rock
    and gave me a firm place to stand.
³ He put a new song in my mouth,
    a hymn of praise to our God.
    Many will see and fear the LORD
    and put their trust in him.

⁴ Blessed is the one
    who trusts in the LORD,
    who does not look to the proud,
    to those who turn aside to false gods.*e*

a 19 One Dead Sea Scrolls manuscript; Masoretic Text *my vigorous enemies*   *b* In Hebrew texts 39:1-13 is
numbered 39:2-14.   *c 5* The Hebrew has *Selah* (a word of uncertain meaning) here and at the end of
verse 11.   *d* In Hebrew texts 40:1-17 is numbered 40:2-18.   *e 4* Or *to lies*

⁵ Many, LORD my God,
  are the wonders you have done,
  the things you planned for us.
  None can compare with you;
  were I to speak and tell of your deeds,
  they would be too many to declare.

⁶ Sacrifice and offering you did not
    desire —
  but my ears you have opened^a —
  burnt offerings and sin offerings^b you
    did not require.
⁷ Then I said, "Here I am, I have come —
  it is written about me in the scroll.^c
⁸ I desire to do your will, my God;
  your law is within my heart."

⁹ I proclaim your saving acts in the great
    assembly;
  I do not seal my lips, LORD,
    as you know.
¹⁰ I do not hide your righteousness in my
    heart;
  I speak of your faithfulness and your
    saving help.
  I do not conceal your love and your
    faithfulness
  from the great assembly.

¹¹ Do not withhold your mercy from me,
    LORD;
  may your love and faithfulness always
    protect me.
¹² For troubles without number surround
    me;
  my sins have overtaken me, and I
    cannot see.
  They are more than the hairs of my head,
    and my heart fails within me.
¹³ Be pleased to save me, LORD;
  come quickly, LORD, to help me.

¹⁴ May all who want to take my life
  be put to shame and confusion;
  may all who desire my ruin
  be turned back in disgrace.
¹⁵ May those who say to me, "Aha! Aha!"
  be appalled at their own shame.
¹⁶ But may all who seek you
  rejoice and be glad in you;
  may those who long for your saving help
    always say,
  "The LORD is great!"

¹⁷ But as for me, I am poor and needy;
  may the Lord think of me.
  You are my help and my deliverer;
  you are my God, do not delay.

Psalm 41^d

For the director of music. A psalm of David.

¹ Blessed are those who have regard for
    the weak;
  the LORD delivers them in times of
    trouble.
² The LORD protects and preserves them —
  they are counted among the blessed in
    the land —
  he does not give them over to the
    desire of their foes.
³ The LORD sustains them on their sickbed
  and restores them from their bed of
    illness.

⁴ I said, "Have mercy on me, LORD;
  heal me, for I have sinned against you."
⁵ My enemies say of me in malice,
  "When will he die and his name
    perish?"
⁶ When one of them comes to see me,
  he speaks falsely, while his heart
    gathers slander;
  then he goes out and spreads it around.

⁷ All my enemies whisper together
    against me;
  they imagine the worst for me, saying,
⁸ "A vile disease has afflicted him;
  he will never get up from the place
    where he lies."
⁹ Even my close friend,
    someone I trusted,
  one who shared my bread,
  has turned^e against me.

¹⁰ But may you have mercy on me, LORD;
  raise me up, that I may repay them.
¹¹ I know that you are pleased with me,
  for my enemy does not triumph
    over me.
¹² Because of my integrity you uphold me
  and set me in your presence forever.

¹³ Praise be to the LORD, the God of Israel,
  from everlasting to everlasting.
    Amen and Amen.

---

^a 6 Hebrew; some Septuagint manuscripts *but a body you have prepared for me*   ^b 6 Or *purification offerings*   ^c 7 Or *come / with the scroll written for me*   ^d In Hebrew texts 41:1-13 is numbered 41:2-14.   ^e 9 Hebrew *has lifted up his heel*

BOOK II

Psalms 42–72

Psalm 42[a,b]

For the director of music.
A maskil[c] of the Sons of Korah.

[1] As the deer pants for streams of water,
    so my soul pants for you, my God.
[2] My soul thirsts for God, for the living God.
    When can I go and meet with God?
[3] My tears have been my food
    day and night,
while people say to me all day long,
    "Where is your God?"
[4] These things I remember
    as I pour out my soul:
how I used to go to the house of God
    under the protection of the
        Mighty One[d]
with shouts of joy and praise
    among the festive throng.

[5] Why, my soul, are you downcast?
    Why so disturbed within me?
Put your hope in God,
    for I will yet praise him,
    my Savior and my God.

[6] My soul is downcast within me;
    therefore I will remember you
from the land of the Jordan,
    the heights of Hermon—from Mount
        Mizar.
[7] Deep calls to deep
    in the roar of your waterfalls;
all your waves and breakers
    have swept over me.

[8] By day the LORD directs his love,
    at night his song is with me—
    a prayer to the God of my life.

[9] I say to God my Rock,
    "Why have you forgotten me?
Why must I go about mourning,
    oppressed by the enemy?"
[10] My bones suffer mortal agony
    as my foes taunt me,
saying to me all day long,
    "Where is your God?"

[11] Why, my soul, are you downcast?
    Why so disturbed within me?
Put your hope in God,
    for I will yet praise him,
    my Savior and my God.

Psalm 43[a]

[1] Vindicate me, my God,
    and plead my cause
    against an unfaithful nation.
Rescue me from those who are
    deceitful and wicked.
[2] You are God my stronghold.
    Why have you rejected me?
Why must I go about mourning,
    oppressed by the enemy?
[3] Send me your light and your faithful care,
    let them lead me;
let them bring me to your holy
        mountain,
    to the place where you dwell.
[4] Then I will go to the altar of God,
    to God, my joy and my delight.
I will praise you with the lyre,
    O God, my God.

[5] Why, my soul, are you downcast?
    Why so disturbed within me?
Put your hope in God,
    for I will yet praise him,
    my Savior and my God.

Psalm 44[e]

For the director of music.
Of the Sons of Korah. A maskil.[c]

[1] We have heard it with our ears, O God;
    our ancestors have told us
what you did in their days,
    in days long ago.
[2] With your hand you drove out the nations
    and planted our ancestors;
you crushed the peoples
    and made our ancestors flourish.
[3] It was not by their sword that they won
        the land,
    nor did their arm bring them victory;
it was your right hand, your arm,
    and the light of your face, for you
        loved them.

---

[a] In many Hebrew manuscripts Psalms 42 and 43 constitute one psalm.   [b] In Hebrew texts 42:1-11 is numbered 42:2-12.   [c] Title: Probably a literary or musical term   [d] 4 See Septuagint and Syriac; the meaning of the Hebrew for this line is uncertain.   [e] In Hebrew texts 44:1-26 is numbered 44:2-27.

Talking to Yourself

By Linda Montgomery

READ: Psalms 42 and 43

Military service can bring times of loneliness — when you're far from your parents and extended family ... and possibly far from your husband during deployment.

Have those lonely times caused you to "talk to yourself?" Perhaps you feel that no one understands your situation. Even when surrounded by loved ones and friends, it's possible to feel that no one understands. Well-meaning people can offer a listening ear, but sometimes it just doesn't help!

When I read Psalm 42 and its companion Psalm 43, I get the impression that the psalmist was at a similar point in his circumstances and was talking to himself. He asked, "Why, my soul, are you downcast? Why so disturbed within me?" (Psalm 42:5,11; 43:5)

Do you see that the author then answered himself? Notice the author's diagnosis and prescription for his depression: "Put your hope in God, for I will yet praise him, my Savior and my God" (Psalm 42:5,11; 43:5).

This conversation within the soul of this psalmist, speaking thousands of years ago, applies to our lives today. Praise to the living God, who knows your situation and offers the curative powers of hope.

We find this same message, or "soul conversation," in other psalms. For example, "Yes, my soul, find rest in God; my hope comes from him. Truly he is my rock and my salvation; he is my fortress, I will not be shaken" (Psalm 62:5 – 6). For another example, check out Psalm 116:7 – 9.

Maybe now is one of those times when you're having a talk with yourself. Perhaps you're frustrated and crying out to the Lord, who hears when no one else is around. Do you take the opportunity to surrender those thoughts to the Lord by moving from words of sadness and lament to words of thanksgiving and praise?

Yes, tears and faith are compatible. Even though we do not know the circumstances of this psalmist's depression, he shows us how to look inward to the soul to analyze trouble, look upward to the Lord for help, and then look onward to the future with hope.

God hears ... God knows you need hope, and he is the God who gives hope. Whether you are truly alone or all alone in a crowd of people, he knows the inner cry of your soul and longs to hear your voice in prayer and praise.

Why, my soul, are you downcast? Why so disturbed within me? Put your hope in God, for I will yet praise him, my Savior and my God.
PSALM 42:5

DEBRIEF

- What concerns do I need to take to the Lord today in prayer?
- How can I praise the Lord today for the ways in which he gives me hope?

REPORT

Lord, you care about the concerns of my soul. Please turn my eyes toward you in every circumstance so I can take steps forward in faith. In Jesus' name I pray. Amen.

for your next devotional reading, go to page 367

⁴You are my King and my God,
  who decrees*ᵃ* victories for Jacob.
⁵Through you we push back our enemies;
  through your name we trample
    our foes.
⁶I put no trust in my bow,
  my sword does not bring me victory;
⁷but you give us victory over our enemies,
  you put our adversaries to shame.
⁸In God we make our boast all day long,
  and we will praise your name forever.*ᵇ*

⁹But now you have rejected and
    humbled us;
  you no longer go out with our armies.
¹⁰You made us retreat before the enemy,
  and our adversaries have plundered us.
¹¹You gave us up to be devoured like sheep
  and have scattered us among the
    nations.
¹²You sold your people for a pittance,
  gaining nothing from their sale.

¹³You have made us a reproach to our
    neighbors,
  the scorn and derision of those
    around us.
¹⁴You have made us a byword among the
    nations;
  the peoples shake their heads at us.
¹⁵I live in disgrace all day long,
  and my face is covered with shame
¹⁶at the taunts of those who reproach and
    revile me,
  because of the enemy, who is bent on
    revenge.

¹⁷All this came upon us,
  though we had not forgotten you;
  we had not been false to your
    covenant.
¹⁸Our hearts had not turned back;
  our feet had not strayed from your
    path.
¹⁹But you crushed us and made us a haunt
    for jackals;
  you covered us over with deep
    darkness.

²⁰If we had forgotten the name of our God
  or spread out our hands to a foreign
    god,
²¹would not God have discovered it,
  since he knows the secrets of the
    heart?
²²Yet for your sake we face death all day long;
  we are considered as sheep to be
    slaughtered.

²³Awake, Lord! Why do you sleep?
  Rouse yourself! Do not reject us forever.
²⁴Why do you hide your face
  and forget our misery and oppression?

²⁵We are brought down to the dust;
  our bodies cling to the ground.
²⁶Rise up and help us;
  rescue us because of your unfailing
    love.

Psalm 45*ᶜ*

For the director of music. To the tune of "Lilies."
*Of the Sons of Korah. A maskil.*ᵈ *A wedding song.*

¹My heart is stirred by a noble theme
  as I recite my verses for the king;
  my tongue is the pen of a skillful writer.

²You are the most excellent of men
  and your lips have been anointed with
    grace,
  since God has blessed you forever.

³Gird your sword on your side, you
    mighty one;
  clothe yourself with splendor and
    majesty.
⁴In your majesty ride forth victoriously
  in the cause of truth, humility and
    justice;
  let your right hand achieve awesome
    deeds.
⁵Let your sharp arrows pierce the hearts of
    the king's enemies;
  let the nations fall beneath your feet.
⁶Your throne, O God,*ᵉ* will last for ever
    and ever;
  a scepter of justice will be the scepter
    of your kingdom.
⁷You love righteousness and hate
    wickedness;
  therefore God, your God, has set you
    above your companions
  by anointing you with the oil of joy.

ᵃ 4 Septuagint, Aquila and Syriac; Hebrew *King, O God; / command*   *ᵇ 8* The Hebrew has *Selah* (a word of uncertain meaning) here.   *ᶜ* In Hebrew texts 45:1-17 is numbered 45:2-18.   *ᵈ* Title: Probably a literary or musical term   *ᵉ 6* Here the king is addressed as God's representative.

⁸ All your robes are fragrant with myrrh
and aloes and cassia;
from palaces adorned with ivory
the music of the strings makes you
glad.
⁹ Daughters of kings are among your
honored women;
at your right hand is the royal bride in
gold of Ophir.
¹⁰ Listen, daughter, and pay careful
attention:
Forget your people and your father's
house.
¹¹ Let the king be enthralled by your
beauty;
honor him, for he is your lord.
¹² The city of Tyre will come with a gift,^a
people of wealth will seek your favor.
¹³ All glorious is the princess within her
chamber;
her gown is interwoven with gold.
¹⁴ In embroidered garments she is led to
the king;
her virgin companions follow her —
those brought to be with her.
¹⁵ Led in with joy and gladness,
they enter the palace of the king.

¹⁶ Your sons will take the place of your
fathers;
you will make them princes
throughout the land.

¹⁷ I will perpetuate your memory through
all generations;
therefore the nations will praise you
for ever and ever.

Psalm 46^b

*For the director of music. Of the Sons of Korah.
According to* alamoth.^c *A song.*

¹ God is our refuge and strength,
an ever-present help in trouble.
² Therefore we will not fear, though the
earth give way
and the mountains fall into the heart
of the sea,
³ though its waters roar and foam
and the mountains quake with their
surging.^d

⁴ There is a river whose streams make glad
the city of God,
the holy place where the Most High
dwells.
⁵ God is within her, she will not fall;
God will help her at break of day.
⁶ Nations are in uproar, kingdoms fall;
he lifts his voice, the earth melts.

⁷ The LORD Almighty is with us;
the God of Jacob is our fortress.

⁸ Come and see what the LORD has done,
the desolations he has brought on
the earth.
⁹ He makes wars cease
to the ends of the earth.
He breaks the bow and shatters the
spear;
he burns the shields^e with fire.
¹⁰ He says, "Be still, and know that I
am God;
I will be exalted among the nations,
I will be exalted in the earth."

¹¹ The LORD Almighty is with us;
the God of Jacob is our fortress.

Psalm 47^f

*For the director of music.
Of the Sons of Korah. A psalm.*

¹ Clap your hands, all you nations;
shout to God with cries of joy.

² For the LORD Most High is awesome,
the great King over all the earth.
³ He subdued nations under us,
peoples under our feet.
⁴ He chose our inheritance for us,
the pride of Jacob, whom he loved.^g

⁵ God has ascended amid shouts of joy,
the LORD amid the sounding of
trumpets.
⁶ Sing praises to God, sing praises;
sing praises to our King, sing praises.
⁷ For God is the King of all the earth;
sing to him a psalm of praise.

⁸ God reigns over the nations;
God is seated on his holy throne.
⁹ The nobles of the nations assemble
as the people of the God of Abraham,

^a 12 Or *A Tyrian robe is among the gifts*   ^b In Hebrew texts 46:1-11 is numbered 46:2-12.   ^c Title:
Probably a musical term   ^d 3 The Hebrew has *Selah* (a word of uncertain meaning) here and at the end
of verses 7 and 11.   ^e 9 Or *chariots*   ^f In Hebrew texts 47:1-9 is numbered 47:2-10.   ^g 4 The Hebrew
has *Selah* (a word of uncertain meaning) here.

A JOYFUL END

By Jocelyn Green

Although Patti Smith had always been healthy, her body became weakened from stress when both her sons, Josey and Jesse, were deployed at once. A doctor suggested medication to cope, but she refused. Sleeping through the night became a thing of the past as she traded the comfort of her bed for the floor on which she knelt, pleading with God to protect her sons. "My total dependence came to be my faith in God, but, oh, how I wavered at times," she said.

As president of her local military support group, she had meetings to conduct, support to give others and service projects to complete. After delivering Condolence Books to Gold Star mothers, she drove home begging God not to let her be next.

When Josey came home, she wanted to collapse from relief, and her health began to improve. And when the time came for Josey to deploy again, despair did not consume Patti as it had before. "Although living through the deployments of my sons has been excruciatingly painful, I sense a deep strengthening has taken place," Patti said during Josey's second deployment. "I still do not know what tomorrow holds ... but I do know HIM who holds tomorrow."

As Patti combated the anxiety that threatened to overwhelm her, the classic hymn "Be Still, My Soul" was a gentle reminder to quiet her heart by trusting the Lord:

> Be still, my soul: thy best, thy heavenly Friend
> Through thorny ways leads to a joyful end.*

In Patti's case, the thorny ways of deployment did lead to a joyful end — not just for her family but also for thousands of others. Instead of exchanging Christmas gifts one year, Patti and her husband decided to send Christmas care packages to the 40 Marines in Josey's platoon. She enlisted the help of everyone she could. "The task seemed insurmountable," said Patti. "But enough donations came in for 200 Marines — and we were just getting started."

Patti and her husband founded Operation Santa, which has grown to become the largest Christmas drive for the troops in the Midwest. By 2011, Operation Santa had shipped nearly 175,000 stockings to deployed soldiers.

"This has been the most terrifying and purposeful chapter of my life to date," said Patti. "However, I intend to live the rest of my life serving our veterans in gratitude for their sacrifice and service and to pass on the torch of public service to generations younger than I am. Freedom isn't free!"

---

*Read the words to "Be Still, My Soul" on page 491.

Prayer: *Lord, calm my anxious heart and show me how to make a difference for you.*

**He says, "Be still, and know that I am God; I will be exalted among
the nations, I will be exalted in the earth."**

PSALM 46:10

for your next devotional reading, go to page 373

for the kings[a] of the earth belong to God;
he is greatly exalted.

Psalm 48[b]

A song. A psalm of the Sons of Korah.

[1] Great is the LORD, and most worthy of
praise,
in the city of our God, his holy
mountain.

[2] Beautiful in its loftiness,
the joy of the whole earth,
like the heights of Zaphon[c] is Mount Zion,
the city of the Great King.
[3] God is in her citadels;
he has shown himself to be her fortress.

[4] When the kings joined forces,
when they advanced together,
[5] they saw her and were astounded;
they fled in terror.
[6] Trembling seized them there,
pain like that of a woman in labor.
[7] You destroyed them like ships of Tarshish
shattered by an east wind.

[8] As we have heard,
so we have seen
in the city of the LORD Almighty,
in the city of our God:
God makes her secure
forever.[d]

[9] Within your temple, O God,
we meditate on your unfailing love.
[10] Like your name, O God,
your praise reaches to the ends of the
earth;
your right hand is filled with
righteousness.
[11] Mount Zion rejoices,
the villages of Judah are glad
because of your judgments.

[12] Walk about Zion, go around her,
count her towers,
[13] consider well her ramparts,
view her citadels,
that you may tell of them
to the next generation.

[14] For this God is our God for ever and ever;
he will be our guide even to the end.

Psalm 49[e]

*For the director of music.
Of the Sons of Korah. A psalm.*

[1] Hear this, all you peoples;
listen, all who live in this world,
[2] both low and high,
rich and poor alike:
[3] My mouth will speak words of wisdom;
the meditation of my heart will give
you understanding.
[4] I will turn my ear to a proverb;
with the harp I will expound my
riddle:

[5] Why should I fear when evil days come,
when wicked deceivers surround me —
[6] those who trust in their wealth
and boast of their great riches?
[7] No one can redeem the life of another
or give to God a ransom for them —
[8] the ransom for a life is costly,
no payment is ever enough —
[9] so that they should live on forever
and not see decay.
[10] For all can see that the wise die,
that the foolish and the senseless also
perish,
leaving their wealth to others.
[11] Their tombs will remain their houses[f]
forever,
their dwellings for endless
generations,
though they had[g] named lands after
themselves.

[12] People, despite their wealth, do not
endure;
they are like the beasts that perish.

[13] This is the fate of those who trust in
themselves,
and of their followers, who approve
their sayings.[h]
[14] They are like sheep and are destined
to die;
death will be their shepherd

---

[a] 9 Or *shields*   [b] In Hebrew texts 48:1-14 is numbered 48:2-15.   [c] 2 *Zaphon* was the most sacred
mountain of the Canaanites.   [d] 8 The Hebrew has *Selah* (a word of uncertain meaning) here.   [e] In
Hebrew texts 49:1-20 is numbered 49:2-21.   [f] 11 Septuagint and Syriac; Hebrew *In their thoughts their
houses will remain*   [g] 11 Or *generations, / for they have*   [h] 13 The Hebrew has *Selah* (a word of
uncertain meaning) here and at the end of verse 15.

(but the upright will prevail over them
  in the morning).
Their forms will decay in the grave,
  far from their princely mansions.
¹⁵ But God will redeem me from the realm
  of the dead;
  he will surely take me to himself.
¹⁶ Do not be overawed when others grow
  rich,
  when the splendor of their houses
  increases;
¹⁷ for they will take nothing with them
  when they die,
  their splendor will not descend
  with them.
¹⁸ Though while they live they count
  themselves blessed —
  and people praise you when you
  prosper —
¹⁹ they will join those who have gone
  before them,
  who will never again see the light
  of life.

²⁰ People who have wealth but lack
  understanding
  are like the beasts that perish.

Psalm 50

A psalm of Asaph.

¹ The Mighty One, God, the Lᴏʀᴅ,
  speaks and summons the earth
  from the rising of the sun to where
  it sets.
² From Zion, perfect in beauty,
  God shines forth.
³ Our God comes
  and will not be silent;
  a fire devours before him,
  and around him a tempest rages.
⁴ He summons the heavens above,
  and the earth, that he may judge
  his people:
⁵ "Gather to me this consecrated
  people,
  who made a covenant with me by
  sacrifice."
⁶ And the heavens proclaim his
  righteousness,
  for he is a God of justice.[a,b]

⁷ "Listen, my people, and I will speak;
  I will testify against you, Israel:
  I am God, your God.
⁸ I bring no charges against you
  concerning your sacrifices
  or concerning your burnt offerings,
  which are ever before me.
⁹ I have no need of a bull from your stall
  or of goats from your pens,
¹⁰ for every animal of the forest is mine,
  and the cattle on a thousand hills.
¹¹ I know every bird in the mountains,
  and the insects in the fields are
  mine.
¹² If I were hungry I would not tell you,
  for the world is mine, and all that is
  in it.
¹³ Do I eat the flesh of bulls
  or drink the blood of goats?

¹⁴ "Sacrifice thank offerings to God,
  fulfill your vows to the Most High,
¹⁵ and call on me in the day of trouble;
  I will deliver you, and you will
  honor me."

¹⁶ But to the wicked person, God says:

"What right have you to recite my laws
  or take my covenant on your lips?
¹⁷ You hate my instruction
  and cast my words behind you.
¹⁸ When you see a thief, you join
  with him;
  you throw in your lot with
  adulterers.
¹⁹ You use your mouth for evil
  and harness your tongue to deceit.
²⁰ You sit and testify against your brother
  and slander your own mother's son.
²¹ When you did these things and I kept
  silent,
  you thought I was exactly[c] like you.
But I now arraign you
  and set my accusations before you.

²² "Consider this, you who forget God,
  or I will tear you to pieces, with no one
  to rescue you:
²³ Those who sacrifice thank offerings
  honor me,
  and to the blameless[d] I will show my
  salvation."

---

[a] 6 With a different word division of the Hebrew; Masoretic Text *for God himself is judge*   [b] 6 The Hebrew has *Selah* (a word of uncertain meaning) here.   [c] 21 Or *thought the 'I ᴀᴍ' was*   [d] 23 Probable reading of the original Hebrew text; the meaning of the Masoretic Text for this phrase is uncertain.

Psalm 51 [a]

For the director of music. A psalm of David.
When the prophet Nathan came to him after
David had committed adultery with Bathsheba.

[1] Have mercy on me, O God,
    according to your unfailing love;
    according to your great compassion
    blot out my transgressions.
[2] Wash away all my iniquity
    and cleanse me from my sin.

[3] For I know my transgressions,
    and my sin is always before me.
[4] Against you, you only, have I sinned
    and done what is evil in your sight;
so you are right in your verdict
    and justified when you judge.
[5] Surely I was sinful at birth,
    sinful from the time my mother
        conceived me.
[6] Yet you desired faithfulness even in
        the womb;
    you taught me wisdom in that secret
        place.

[7] Cleanse me with hyssop, and I will be
        clean;
    wash me, and I will be whiter than
        snow.
[8] Let me hear joy and gladness;
    let the bones you have crushed rejoice.
[9] Hide your face from my sins
    and blot out all my iniquity.

[10] Create in me a pure heart, O God,
    and renew a steadfast spirit within me.
[11] Do not cast me from your presence
    or take your Holy Spirit from me.
[12] Restore to me the joy of your salvation
    and grant me a willing spirit, to
        sustain me.

[13] Then I will teach transgressors your ways,
    so that sinners will turn back to you.
[14] Deliver me from the guilt of bloodshed,
        O God,
    you who are God my Savior,
    and my tongue will sing of your
        righteousness.
[15] Open my lips, Lord,
    and my mouth will declare your
        praise.

[16] You do not delight in sacrifice, or I would
        bring it;
    you do not take pleasure in burnt
        offerings.
[17] My sacrifice, O God, is [b] a broken spirit;
    a broken and contrite heart
    you, God, will not despise.

[18] May it please you to prosper Zion,
    to build up the walls of Jerusalem.
[19] Then you will delight in the sacrifices of
        the righteous,
    in burnt offerings offered whole;
    then bulls will be offered on your altar.

Psalm 52 [c]

For the director of music. A maskil [d] *of David.*
When Doeg the Edomite had gone to Saul and told
him: "David has gone to the house of Ahimelek."

[1] Why do you boast of evil, you mighty
        hero?
    Why do you boast all day long,
    you who are a disgrace in the eyes
        of God?
[2] You who practice deceit,
    your tongue plots destruction;
    it is like a sharpened razor.
[3] You love evil rather than good,
    falsehood rather than speaking the
        truth. [e]
[4] You love every harmful word,
    you deceitful tongue!

[5] Surely God will bring you down to
        everlasting ruin:
    He will snatch you up and pluck you
        from your tent;
    he will uproot you from the land of
        the living.
[6] The righteous will see and fear;
    they will laugh at you, saying,
[7] "Here now is the man
    who did not make God his stronghold
but trusted in his great wealth
    and grew strong by destroying others!"

[8] But I am like an olive tree
    flourishing in the house of God;
I trust in God's unfailing love
    for ever and ever.
[9] For what you have done I will always
        praise you

---

[a] In Hebrew texts 51:1-19 is numbered 51:3-21.   [b] 17 Or *The sacrifices of God are*   [c] In Hebrew texts
52:1-9 is numbered 52:3-11.   [d] Title: Probably a literary or musical term   [e] 3 The Hebrew has *Selah*
(a word of uncertain meaning) here and at the end of verse 5.

in the presence of your faithful
people.
And I will hope in your name,
for your name is good.

Psalm 53[a]

For the director of music.
According to mahalath.[b] *A* maskil[c] *of David.*

[1] The fool says in his heart,
"There is no God."
They are corrupt, and their ways are vile;
there is no one who does good.

[2] God looks down from heaven
on all mankind
to see if there are any who understand,
any who seek God.
[3] Everyone has turned away, all have
become corrupt;
there is no one who does good,
not even one.

[4] Do all these evildoers know nothing?

They devour my people as though eating
bread;
they never call on God.
[5] But there they are, overwhelmed with
dread,
where there was nothing to dread.
God scattered the bones of those who
attacked you;
you put them to shame, for God
despised them.

[6] Oh, that salvation for Israel would come
out of Zion!
When God restores his people,
let Jacob rejoice and Israel be glad!

Psalm 54[d]

For the director of music.
With stringed instruments. A maskil[c] *of David.*
When the Ziphites had gone to Saul and said,
"Is not David hiding among us?"

[1] Save me, O God, by your name;
vindicate me by your might.
[2] Hear my prayer, O God;
listen to the words of my mouth.

[3] Arrogant foes are attacking me;
ruthless people are trying to kill me —
people without regard for God.[e]

[4] Surely God is my help;
the Lord is the one who sustains me.

[5] Let evil recoil on those who slander me;
in your faithfulness destroy them.

[6] I will sacrifice a freewill offering to you;
I will praise your name, LORD, for it
is good.
[7] You have delivered me from all my
troubles,
and my eyes have looked in triumph
on my foes.

Psalm 55[f]

For the director of music. With stringed
instruments. A maskil[c] *of David.*

[1] Listen to my prayer, O God,
do not ignore my plea;
[2]   hear me and answer me.
My thoughts trouble me and I am
distraught
[3]   because of what my enemy is saying,
because of the threats of the wicked;
for they bring down suffering on me
and assail me in their anger.

[4] My heart is in anguish within me;
the terrors of death have fallen on me.
[5] Fear and trembling have beset me;
horror has overwhelmed me.
[6] I said, "Oh, that I had the wings of
a dove!
I would fly away and be at rest.
[7] I would flee far away
and stay in the desert;[g]
[8] I would hurry to my place of shelter,
far from the tempest and storm."

[9] Lord, confuse the wicked, confound
their words,
for I see violence and strife in the city.
[10] Day and night they prowl about on its
walls;
malice and abuse are within it.
[11] Destructive forces are at work in the city;
threats and lies never leave its streets.

---

[a] In Hebrew texts 53:1-6 is numbered 53:2-7.   [b] Title: Probably a musical term   [c] Title: Probably a
literary or musical term   [d] In Hebrew texts 54:1-7 is numbered 54:3-9.   [e] 3 The Hebrew has *Selah* (a
word of uncertain meaning) here.   [f] In Hebrew texts 55:1-23 is numbered 55:2-24.   [g] 7 The Hebrew
has *Selah* (a word of uncertain meaning) here and in the middle of verse 19.

¹² If an enemy were insulting me,
　　I could endure it;
　if a foe were rising against me,
　　I could hide.
¹³ But it is you, a man like myself,
　　my companion, my close friend,
¹⁴ with whom I once enjoyed sweet
　　　fellowship
　　at the house of God,
　as we walked about
　　among the worshipers.

¹⁵ Let death take my enemies by surprise;
　　let them go down alive to the realm of
　　　the dead,
　　for evil finds lodging among them.

¹⁶ As for me, I call to God,
　　and the LORD saves me.
¹⁷ Evening, morning and noon
　　I cry out in distress,
　　and he hears my voice.
¹⁸ He rescues me unharmed
　　from the battle waged against me,
　　even though many oppose me.
¹⁹ God, who is enthroned from of old,
　　who does not change —
　he will hear them and humble them,
　　because they have no fear of God.

²⁰ My companion attacks his friends;
　　he violates his covenant.
²¹ His talk is smooth as butter,
　　yet war is in his heart;
　his words are more soothing than oil,
　　yet they are drawn swords.

²² Cast your cares on the LORD
　　and he will sustain you;
　he will never let
　　the righteous be shaken.
²³ But you, God, will bring down the wicked
　　into the pit of decay;
　the bloodthirsty and deceitful
　　will not live out half their days.

But as for me, I trust in you.

Psalm 56ᵃ

*For the director of music. To the tune of
"A Dove on Distant Oaks." Of David. A* miktam.ᵇ
When the Philistines had seized him in Gath.

¹ Be merciful to me, my God,
　　for my enemies are in hot pursuit;

all day long they press their
　　attack.
² My adversaries pursue me all day long;
　　in their pride many are attacking me.

³ When I am afraid, I put my trust in you.
⁴ 　In God, whose word I praise —
　in God I trust and am not afraid.
　　What can mere mortals do to me?

⁵ All day long they twist my words;
　　all their schemes are for my ruin.
⁶ They conspire, they lurk,
　　they watch my steps,
　　hoping to take my life.
⁷ Because of their wickedness do notᶜ let
　　　them escape;
　　in your anger, God, bring the nations
　　　down.

⁸ Record my misery;
　　list my tears on your scrollᵈ —
　　are they not in your record?
⁹ Then my enemies will turn back
　　when I call for help.
　　By this I will know that God is for me.

¹⁰ In God, whose word I praise,
　　in the LORD, whose word I praise —
¹¹ in God I trust and am not afraid.
　　What can man do to me?

¹² I am under vows to you, my God;
　　I will present my thank offerings
　　　to you.
¹³ For you have delivered me from death
　　and my feet from stumbling,
　that I may walk before God
　　in the light of life.

Psalm 57ᵉ

*For the director of music. To the tune of
"Do Not Destroy." Of David. A* miktam.ᵇ
When he had fled from Saul into the cave.

¹ Have mercy on me, my God, have mercy
　　on me,
　for in you I take refuge.
　I will take refuge in the shadow of your
　　　wings
　　until the disaster has passed.

² I cry out to God Most High,
　　to God, who vindicates me.

ᵃ In Hebrew texts 56:1-13 is numbered 56:2-14.　　ᵇ Title: Probably a literary or musical term
ᶜ 7 Probable reading of the original Hebrew text; Masoretic Text does not have *do not.*　　ᵈ 8 Or *misery; /
put my tears in your wineskin*　　ᵉ In Hebrew texts 57:1-11 is numbered 57:2-12.

Moving Forward With Fear

By Kathy Guzzo

READ: Psalm 56:3–4

Fear is real, and it manifests itself in many forms. There's fear of heights, fear of spiders, fear of rejection, and the one military moms and spouses are most familiar with: fear of loss. The truth is, when we're in a battle, our fear may be the only weapon the enemy needs to defeat us. Panic can immobilize us, giving the enemy the advantage in an attack. The best way to ensure the upper hand in any battle is to not allow fear to hinder us from making forward progress. How? The answer is in Psalm 56:3–4: Trust in the Lord.

One word we would all use to describe our troops is courageous. Courage is moving forward even when afraid. The courage that our loved ones portray wasn't born into them; it was acquired through months of extreme training and dealing with fear. When they're fearful, they don't turn and run; they stand firm. They trust in their training, their equipment, their mission, and in the reinforcements of their "battle buddies." Many of them trust in God and find comfort in the fact they are not alone.

When you are afraid, where do you place your trust? Like the troops, it's our responsibility to prepare ourselves for life's battles, knowing we are never alone.

Remember David and Goliath (see 1 Samuel 17)? Although the Bible doesn't mention David's apprehension as he marched toward the giant, David must have been at least a little nervous. Yet he continued. I imagine that with each step his anxiety was replaced by courage. He knew, just as he later said in Psalm 56:3–4, which was written in light of a future harrowing circumstance, that he could trust God and need not fear. Courage, not fear, is the lesson of David.

In recent years, I've experienced real fear as a result of serious situations in my life, including my son's deployments. There were days when I allowed anxiety to overwhelm me. Through those trying days and months, I learned that the only way to move forward was to praise God while trusting in his faithfulness. How amazing that we need not fear what people can do to us or to our loved ones.

I encourage those of you experiencing overwhelming fear of any kind to place your trust in God and allow him to help you move forward. A strong woman of God is not one who doesn't experience fear but one who acknowledges it and moves forward anyway.

When I am afraid, I put my trust in you. In God, whose word I praise — in God I trust and am not afraid. What can mere mortals do to me?

PSALM 56:3–4

DEBRIEF

- What fears are overwhelming me right now?
- How can I take the first step to move forward, away from fear and toward courage?

REPORT

Lord, I don't want to be afraid. I want to be strong and courageous. Help me face my fears and find strength in you to move forward. I know you are with me each step of the way, because you are my personal "battle buddy." Amen.

---

for your next devotional reading, go to page 375

³ He sends from heaven and saves me,
  rebuking those who hotly pursue
    me — ᵃ
God sends forth his love and his
    faithfulness.

⁴ I am in the midst of lions;
  I am forced to dwell among ravenous
    beasts —
men whose teeth are spears and arrows,
  whose tongues are sharp swords.

⁵ Be exalted, O God, above the heavens;
  let your glory be over all the earth.

⁶ They spread a net for my feet —
  I was bowed down in distress.
They dug a pit in my path —
  but they have fallen into it themselves.

⁷ My heart, O God, is steadfast,
  my heart is steadfast;
  I will sing and make music.
⁸ Awake, my soul!
  Awake, harp and lyre!
  I will awaken the dawn.

⁹ I will praise you, Lord, among the
    nations;
  I will sing of you among the peoples.
¹⁰ For great is your love, reaching to the
    heavens;
  your faithfulness reaches to the skies.

¹¹ Be exalted, O God, above the heavens;
  let your glory be over all the earth.

Psalm 58ᵇ

For the director of music. To the tune of
"Do Not Destroy." Of David. A miktam.ᶜ

¹ Do you rulers indeed speak justly?
  Do you judge people with equity?
² No, in your heart you devise injustice,
  and your hands mete out violence on
    the earth.

³ Even from birth the wicked go astray;
  from the womb they are wayward,
    spreading lies.
⁴ Their venom is like the venom of a snake,
  like that of a cobra that has stopped
    its ears,

⁵ that will not heed the tune of the
    charmer,
  however skillful the enchanter
    may be.

⁶ Break the teeth in their mouths, O God;
  LORD, tear out the fangs of those
    lions!
⁷ Let them vanish like water that flows
    away;
  when they draw the bow, let their
    arrows fall short.
⁸ May they be like a slug that melts away as
    it moves along,
  like a stillborn child that never sees
    the sun.

⁹ Before your pots can feel the heat of the
    thorns —
  whether they be green or dry — the
    wicked will be swept away.ᵈ
¹⁰ The righteous will be glad when they are
    avenged,
  when they dip their feet in the blood of
    the wicked.
¹¹ Then people will say,
  "Surely the righteous still are
    rewarded;
  surely there is a God who judges the
    earth."

Psalm 59ᵉ

For the director of music. To the tune of
"Do Not Destroy." Of David. A miktam.ᶜ
When Saul had sent men to watch David's
house in order to kill him.

¹ Deliver me from my enemies, O God;
  be my fortress against those who are
    attacking me.
² Deliver me from evildoers
  and save me from those who are after
    my blood.

³ See how they lie in wait for me!
  Fierce men conspire against me
  for no offense or sin of mine, LORD.
⁴ I have done no wrong, yet they are ready
    to attack me.
  Arise to help me; look on my plight!
⁵ You, LORD God Almighty,
  you who are the God of Israel,

ᵃ 3 The Hebrew has *Selah* (a word of uncertain meaning) here and at the end of verse 6.   ᵇ In Hebrew
texts 58:1-11 is numbered 58:2-12.   ᶜ Title: Probably a literary or musical term   ᵈ 9 The meaning of the
Hebrew for this verse is uncertain.   ᵉ In Hebrew texts 59:1-17 is numbered 59:2-18.

No Surprise

By Bettina Dowell

READ: Psalm 57

As the director of a preschool and kindergarten, I quickly learned that every day is full of surprises. From potty accidents to parent complaints, unexpected occurrences are the norm, not the exception. Still, nothing could have prepared me for the words I heard on September 11, 2001: "A plane has just hit one of the Twin Towers." As the morning progressed, we learned of three more plane crashes and the fall of both towers. Terrorist attacks on American soil? What would the next target be?

Parents began to file in long before our noon dismissal. Something about tragedy sparks a need in many of us to be close to those we love. The adults all spontaneously gathered in the courtyard for prayer before the children were dismissed. God graciously gave us words of comfort in that hour. Prayers of thanks were offered to him that though *we* were in shock, nothing that had happened that morning had surprised *him*. God still reigned. His throne had not been shaken in the least, though our world had been turned upside down.

Military life is nothing if not a life of surprises. Orders come that are unexpected. Orders do not come that are expected. Deployments, PCS moves or scheduled transfers rarely occur according to plan. Husbands return from deployments with mental and/or physical challenges we never expected. So, as women of faith, how do we endure these surprises? Where is our source of comfort when the circumstances of life seem to indicate our world has been turned upside down?

From the Bible, David shows us an example of faith when we encounter unexpected struggles. After being secretly anointed by the prophet Samuel to be Israel's next king, David spent years on the run from Saul, the jealous reigning king. Psalm 57:1 affirms that David believed God was not surprised by the circumstances of David's life.

Continuing to root ourselves in God's truth and encouraging one another with his words can make a difference in how we approach the circumstances of life. Some mornings, just getting out of bed and facing the day may feel like stepping into a boxing ring. As believers, we have the ultimate referee in the ring with us. Not only is he able to monitor the fight, he also knows exactly what will occur during each round. We can give up fretting over what the future may hold, comforted by the knowledge that someone else is in charge. And nothing surprises him.

Have mercy on me, my God, have mercy on me, for in you I take refuge. I will take refuge in the shadow of your wings until the disaster has passed.
PSALM 57:1

DEBRIEF
- Where in my life is God asking me to trust him and accept the peace of knowing that my circumstances are no surprise to him?
- What difference could it make to my family and those I come in contact with each day if I were to have more peace?

REPORT
Father, I am thankful that nothing surprises you. Help me always to remember that you see and know all. Thank you for caring about my well-being each day, even in a world where evil things happen. In Jesus' name I pray. Amen.

for your next devotional reading, go to page 380

rouse yourself to punish all the
   nations;
   show no mercy to wicked traitors.[a]

[6] They return at evening,
   snarling like dogs,
   and prowl about the city.
[7] See what they spew from their
      mouths—
   the words from their lips are sharp
      as swords,
   and they think, "Who can hear us?"
[8] But you laugh at them, LORD;
   you scoff at all those nations.

[9] You are my strength, I watch for you;
   you, God, are my fortress,
[10]   my God on whom I can rely.

God will go before me
   and will let me gloat over those who
      slander me.
[11] But do not kill them, Lord our shield,[b]
   or my people will forget.
In your might uproot them
   and bring them down.
[12] For the sins of their mouths,
   for the words of their lips,
   let them be caught in their pride.
For the curses and lies they utter,
[13]   consume them in your wrath,
   consume them till they are no
      more.
Then it will be known to the ends of
      the earth
   that God rules over Jacob.

[14] They return at evening,
   snarling like dogs,
   and prowl about the city.
[15] They wander about for food
   and howl if not satisfied.
[16] But I will sing of your strength,
   in the morning I will sing of your
      love;
for you are my fortress,
   my refuge in times of trouble.

[17] You are my strength, I sing praise
      to you;
   you, God, are my fortress,
   my God on whom I can rely.

Psalm 60[c]

*For the director of music. To the tune of "The Lily of
the Covenant." A* miktam[d] *of David. For teaching.
When he fought Aram Naharaim[e] and Aram
Zobah,[f] and when Joab returned and struck down
twelve thousand Edomites in the Valley of Salt.*

[1] You have rejected us, God, and burst
      upon us;
   you have been angry—now restore us!
[2] You have shaken the land and torn it
      open;
   mend its fractures, for it is quaking.
[3] You have shown your people desperate
      times;
   you have given us wine that makes us
      stagger.
[4] But for those who fear you, you have
      raised a banner
   to be unfurled against the bow.[g]

[5] Save us and help us with your right hand,
   that those you love may be delivered.
[6] God has spoken from his sanctuary:
   "In triumph I will parcel out Shechem
   and measure off the Valley of Sukkoth.
[7] Gilead is mine, and Manasseh is mine;
   Ephraim is my helmet,
   Judah is my scepter.
[8] Moab is my washbasin,
   on Edom I toss my sandal;
   over Philistia I shout in triumph."

[9] Who will bring me to the fortified city?
   Who will lead me to Edom?
[10] Is it not you, God, you who have now
      rejected us
   and no longer go out with our armies?
[11] Give us aid against the enemy,
   for human help is worthless.
[12] With God we will gain the victory,
   and he will trample down our enemies.

Psalm 61[h]

*For the director of music.
With stringed instruments. Of David.*

[1] Hear my cry, O God;
   listen to my prayer.

[2] From the ends of the earth I call to you,
   I call as my heart grows faint;

---

[a] 5 The Hebrew has *Selah* (a word of uncertain meaning) here and at the end of verse 13.   [b] 11 Or *sovereign*
[c] In Hebrew texts 60:1-12 is numbered 60:3-14.   [d] Title: Probably a literary or musical term   [e] Title: That
is, Arameans of Northwest Mesopotamia   [f] Title: That is, Arameans of central Syria   [g] 4 The Hebrew
has *Selah* (a word of uncertain meaning) here.   [h] In Hebrew texts 61:1-8 is numbered 61:2-9.

lead me to the rock that is higher
than I.
[3] For you have been my refuge,
a strong tower against the foe.

[4] I long to dwell in your tent forever
and take refuge in the shelter of your
wings.[a]
[5] For you, God, have heard my vows;
you have given me the heritage of
those who fear your name.

[6] Increase the days of the king's life,
his years for many generations.
[7] May he be enthroned in God's presence
forever;
appoint your love and faithfulness to
protect him.

[8] Then I will ever sing in praise of your
name
and fulfill my vows day after day.

Psalm 62[b]

For the director of music.
For Jeduthun. A psalm of David.

[1] Truly my soul finds rest in God;
my salvation comes from him.
[2] Truly he is my rock and my salvation;
he is my fortress, I will never be
shaken.

[3] How long will you assault me?
Would all of you throw me down —
this leaning wall, this tottering fence?
[4] Surely they intend to topple me
from my lofty place;
they take delight in lies.
With their mouths they bless,
but in their hearts they curse.[c]

[5] Yes, my soul, find rest in God;
my hope comes from him.
[6] Truly he is my rock and my salvation;
he is my fortress, I will not be shaken.
[7] My salvation and my honor depend
on God[d];
he is my mighty rock, my refuge.
[8] Trust in him at all times, you people;
pour out your hearts to him,
for God is our refuge.

[9] Surely the lowborn are but a breath,
the highborn are but a lie.

If weighed on a balance, they are
nothing;
together they are only a breath.
[10] Do not trust in extortion
or put vain hope in stolen goods;
though your riches increase,
do not set your heart on them.

[11] One thing God has spoken,
two things I have heard:
"Power belongs to you, God,
[12]   and with you, Lord, is unfailing love";
and, "You reward everyone
according to what they have done."

Psalm 63[e]

A psalm of David.
When he was in the Desert of Judah.

[1] You, God, are my God,
earnestly I seek you;
I thirst for you,
my whole being longs for you,
in a dry and parched land
where there is no water.

[2] I have seen you in the sanctuary
and beheld your power and your
glory.
[3] Because your love is better than life,
my lips will glorify you.
[4] I will praise you as long as I live,
and in your name I will lift up my
hands.
[5] I will be fully satisfied as with the richest
of foods;
with singing lips my mouth will
praise you.

[6] On my bed I remember you;
I think of you through the watches of
the night.
[7] Because you are my help,
I sing in the shadow of your wings.
[8] I cling to you;
your right hand upholds me.

[9] Those who want to kill me will be
destroyed;
they will go down to the depths of
the earth.
[10] They will be given over to the sword
and become food for jackals.

---

[a] 4 The Hebrew has *Selah* (a word of uncertain meaning) here.   [b] In Hebrew texts 62:1-12 is numbered
62:2-13.   [c] 4 The Hebrew has *Selah* (a word of uncertain meaning) here and at the end of verse 8.
[d] 7 Or / *God Most High is my salvation and my honor*   [e] In Hebrew texts 63:1-11 is numbered 63:2-12.

¹¹ But the king will rejoice in God;
    all who swear by God will glory in him,
    while the mouths of liars will be
        silenced.

Psalm 64ᵃ

For the director of music.
A psalm of David.

¹ Hear me, my God, as I voice my
        complaint;
    protect my life from the threat of the
        enemy.

² Hide me from the conspiracy of the
        wicked,
    from the plots of evildoers.
³ They sharpen their tongues like swords
    and aim cruel words like deadly
        arrows.
⁴ They shoot from ambush at the innocent;
    they shoot suddenly, without fear.

⁵ They encourage each other in evil plans,
    they talk about hiding their snares;
    they say, "Who will see it*ᵇ*?"
⁶ They plot injustice and say,
    "We have devised a perfect plan!"
    Surely the human mind and heart are
        cunning.

⁷ But God will shoot them with his arrows;
    they will suddenly be struck down.
⁸ He will turn their own tongues against
        them
    and bring them to ruin;
    all who see them will shake their
        heads in scorn.
⁹ All people will fear;
    they will proclaim the works of God
    and ponder what he has done.

¹⁰ The righteous will rejoice in the Lord
    and take refuge in him;
    all the upright in heart will glory
        in him!

Psalm 65ᶜ

For the director of music.
A psalm of David. A song.

¹ Praise awaitsᵈ you, our God, in Zion;
    to you our vows will be fulfilled.

² You who answer prayer,
    to you all people will come.
³ When we were overwhelmed by sins,
    you forgaveᵉ our transgressions.
⁴ Blessed are those you choose
    and bring near to live in your courts!
    We are filled with the good things of your
        house,
    of your holy temple.

⁵ You answer us with awesome and
        righteous deeds,
    God our Savior,
    the hope of all the ends of the earth
    and of the farthest seas,
⁶ who formed the mountains by your
        power,
    having armed yourself with strength,
⁷ who stilled the roaring of the seas,
    the roaring of their waves,
    and the turmoil of the nations.
⁸ The whole earth is filled with awe at your
        wonders;
    where morning dawns, where evening
        fades,
    you call forth songs of joy.

⁹ You care for the land and water it;
    you enrich it abundantly.
    The streams of God are filled with water
    to provide the people with grain,
    for so you have ordained it.ᶠ
¹⁰ You drench its furrows and level its
        ridges;
    you soften it with showers and bless
        its crops.
¹¹ You crown the year with your bounty,
    and your carts overflow with
        abundance.
¹² The grasslands of the wilderness
        overflow;
    the hills are clothed with gladness.
¹³ The meadows are covered with flocks
    and the valleys are mantled with
        grain;
    they shout for joy and sing.

Psalm 66

For the director of music. A song. A psalm.

¹ Shout for joy to God, all the earth!
²   Sing the glory of his name;
    make his praise glorious.

ᵃ In Hebrew texts 64:1-10 is numbered 64:2-11.   ᵇ 5 Or *us*   ᶜ In Hebrew texts 65:1-13 is numbered 65:2-14.   ᵈ 1 Or *befits*; the meaning of the Hebrew for this word is uncertain.   ᵉ 3 Or *made atonement for*   ᶠ 9 Or *for that is how you prepare the land*

³ Say to God, "How awesome are your
deeds!
So great is your power
that your enemies cringe before you.
⁴ All the earth bows down to you;
they sing praise to you,
they sing the praises of your name."^a

⁵ Come and see what God has done,
his awesome deeds for mankind!
⁶ He turned the sea into dry land,
they passed through the waters on
foot—
come, let us rejoice in him.
⁷ He rules forever by his power,
his eyes watch the nations—
let not the rebellious rise up
against him.

⁸ Praise our God, all peoples,
let the sound of his praise be heard;
⁹ he has preserved our lives
and kept our feet from slipping.
¹⁰ For you, God, tested us;
you refined us like silver.
¹¹ You brought us into prison
and laid burdens on our backs.
¹² You let people ride over our heads;
we went through fire and water,
but you brought us to a place of
abundance.

¹³ I will come to your temple with burnt
offerings
and fulfill my vows to you—
¹⁴ vows my lips promised and my mouth
spoke
when I was in trouble.
¹⁵ I will sacrifice fat animals to you
and an offering of rams;
I will offer bulls and goats.

¹⁶ Come and hear, all you who fear God;
let me tell you what he has done for me.
¹⁷ I cried out to him with my mouth;
his praise was on my tongue.
¹⁸ If I had cherished sin in my heart,
the Lord would not have listened;
¹⁹ but God has surely listened
and has heard my prayer.
²⁰ Praise be to God,
who has not rejected my prayer
or withheld his love from me!

Psalm 67^b

*For the director of music. With stringed
instruments. A psalm. A song.*

¹ May God be gracious to us and bless us
and make his face shine on us — ^c
² so that your ways may be known on
earth,
your salvation among all nations.

³ May the peoples praise you, God;
may all the peoples praise you.
⁴ May the nations be glad and sing for joy,
for you rule the peoples with equity
and guide the nations of the earth.
⁵ May the peoples praise you, God;
may all the peoples praise you.

⁶ The land yields its harvest;
God, our God, blesses us.
⁷ May God bless us still,
so that all the ends of the earth will
fear him.

Psalm 68^d

*For the director of music. Of David.
A psalm. A song.*

¹ May God arise, may his enemies be
scattered;
may his foes flee before him.
² May you blow them away like smoke —
as wax melts before the fire,
may the wicked perish before God.
³ But may the righteous be glad
and rejoice before God;
may they be happy and joyful.

⁴ Sing to God, sing in praise of his name,
extol him who rides on the clouds^e;
rejoice before him — his name is
the Lord.
⁵ A father to the fatherless, a defender of
widows,
is God in his holy dwelling.
⁶ God sets the lonely in families,^f
he leads out the prisoners with
singing;
but the rebellious live in a sun-
scorched land.

⁷ When you, God, went out before your
people,

---

^a 4 The Hebrew has *Selah* (a word of uncertain meaning) here and at the end of verses 7 and 15.   ^b In
Hebrew texts 67:1-7 is numbered 67:2-8.   ^c 1 The Hebrew has *Selah* (a word of uncertain meaning) here
and at the end of verse 4.   ^d In Hebrew texts 68:1-35 is numbered 68:2-36.   ^e 4 Or *name, / prepare the
way for him who rides through the deserts*   ^f 6 Or *the desolate in a homeland*

DISCOVERING DAD

By Karen Whiting

Carolyn didn't realize until she started school that most girls had dads. When she asked her mother about her father, Theodore K. Mister, the response was simply, "That's something we don't talk about." No one in her family would answer her questions.

But Carolyn wouldn't give up. By the time she was a teenager, she knew her father had died at Normandy in 1944, when she was only three months old, and that he had received the Distinguished Service Cross. Then one night during her college years, Carolyn's mother showed her his wedding ring, the bloody prayer book he had worn when he had died and his wallet. Then her mother closed and locked the box. The message was clear: The memory of her father was to be locked away.

The ache in Carolyn's heart to know her father only grew, yet time marched on. Carolyn joined the Navy reserves, married and became Carolyn Green, and raised a family.

When the Navy deployed Carolyn and her husband to Amsterdam in 1990, they took a trip to Normandy, where she found her father's grave. After her trip, an uncle told her that her father had wanted to be buried in the country where he had died to free the people.

In 2007, Carolyn returned to the Normandy American Cemetery and met Geert Van Den Bogaert, who ran the museum built by the American Battle Monuments Commission. He researched and shared information about her father she otherwise would have never known.

Mister landed in Normandy on June 9, 1944, and served as a courier. On June 13, he led a charge up an embankment while firing his rifle and yelling, "Come on. Follow me." He died that day, but he led the charge that freed the town of Cerisy-la-Forêt, France.

Geert introduced Carolyn to the town's mayor, who planned a celebration to honor Carolyn and her dad. The town held dinners, had a portrait of her father painted, and gave Carolyn the key to the city. Theodore Mister was even declared an honorary citizen of the town, and Carolyn was embraced as long-lost family.

Carolyn said, "[The Lord] knew I wanted to learn about my dad and what happened to him for the few days he survived in Normandy. The Lord answered my plea by placing Geert in my life at the right time. That was the beginning of beautiful, unfolding friendships and reconnecting with dad's family — relationships which have enabled me to learn more and more about my dad and the kind of man he was."

Each time Carolyn returns to Cerisy-la-Forêt, the town's people treat her like a daughter. And each time, Carolyn feels a little closer to the father she never met.

Prayer: Lord, fill the lives of those who have lost a loved one with family to love them.

A father to the fatherless, a defender of widows, is God in his holy dwelling. God sets the lonely in families.

PSALM 68:5 – 6

for your next devotional reading, go to page 388

when you marched through the
    wilderness,[a]
[8] the earth shook, the heavens poured
    down rain,
    before God, the One of Sinai,
    before God, the God of Israel.
[9] You gave abundant showers, O God;
    you refreshed your weary inheritance.
[10] Your people settled in it,
    and from your bounty, God, you
    provided for the poor.

[11] The Lord announces the word,
    and the women who proclaim it are a
    mighty throng:
[12] "Kings and armies flee in haste;
    the women at home divide the
    plunder.
[13] Even while you sleep among the sheep
    pens,[b]
    the wings of my dove are sheathed
    with silver,
    its feathers with shining gold."
[14] When the Almighty[c] scattered the kings
    in the land,
    it was like snow fallen on Mount
    Zalmon.

[15] Mount Bashan, majestic mountain,
    Mount Bashan, rugged mountain,
[16] why gaze in envy, you rugged mountain,
    at the mountain where God chooses to
    reign,
    where the Lord himself will dwell
    forever?
[17] The chariots of God are tens of thousands
    and thousands of thousands;
    the Lord has come from Sinai into his
    sanctuary.[d]
[18] When you ascended on high,
    you took many captives;
    you received gifts from people,
    even from[e] the rebellious—
    that you,[f] Lord God, might dwell there.

[19] Praise be to the Lord, to God our Savior,
    who daily bears our burdens.
[20] Our God is a God who saves;
    from the Sovereign Lord comes
    escape from death.

[21] Surely God will crush the heads of his
    enemies,
    the hairy crowns of those who go on in
    their sins.
[22] The Lord says, "I will bring them from
    Bashan;
    I will bring them from the depths of
    the sea,
[23] that your feet may wade in the blood
    of your foes,
    while the tongues of your dogs have
    their share."

[24] Your procession, God, has come into
    view,
    the procession of my God and King
    into the sanctuary.
[25] In front are the singers, after them the
    musicians;
    with them are the young women
    playing the timbrels.
[26] Praise God in the great congregation;
    praise the Lord in the assembly of
    Israel.
[27] There is the little tribe of Benjamin,
    leading them,
    there the great throng of Judah's
    princes,
    and there the princes of Zebulun and
    of Naphtali.

[28] Summon your power, God[g];
    show us your strength, our God, as you
    have done before.
[29] Because of your temple at Jerusalem
    kings will bring you gifts.
[30] Rebuke the beast among the reeds,
    the herd of bulls among the calves of
    the nations.
    Humbled, may the beast bring bars of
    silver.
    Scatter the nations who delight in war.
[31] Envoys will come from Egypt;
    Cush[h] will submit herself to God.

[32] Sing to God, you kingdoms of the earth,
    sing praise to the Lord,
[33] to him who rides across the highest
    heavens, the ancient heavens,
    who thunders with mighty voice.

[a] 7 The Hebrew has *Selah* (a word of uncertain meaning) here and at the end of verses 19 and 32.
  [b] 13 Or *the campfires;* or *the saddlebags*   [c] 14 Hebrew *Shaddai*   [d] 17 Probable reading of the original
Hebrew text; Masoretic Text *Lord is among them at Sinai in holiness*   [e] 18 Or *gifts for people, / even*
[f] 18 Or *they*   [g] 28 Many Hebrew manuscripts, Septuagint and Syriac; most Hebrew manuscripts *Your
God has summoned power for you*   [h] 31 That is, the upper Nile region

³⁴ Proclaim the power of God,
    whose majesty is over Israel,
    whose power is in the heavens.
³⁵ You, God, are awesome in your
       sanctuary;
    the God of Israel gives power and
       strength to his people.

Praise be to God!

Psalm 69ᵃ

For the director of music.
To the tune of "Lilies." Of David.

¹ Save me, O God,
    for the waters have come up to
      my neck.
² I sink in the miry depths,
    where there is no foothold.
I have come into the deep waters;
    the floods engulf me.
³ I am worn out calling for help;
    my throat is parched.
My eyes fail,
    looking for my God.
⁴ Those who hate me without reason
    outnumber the hairs of my head;
many are my enemies without cause,
    those who seek to destroy me.
I am forced to restore
    what I did not steal.

⁵ You, God, know my folly;
    my guilt is not hidden from you.

⁶ Lord, the LORD Almighty,
    may those who hope in you
    not be disgraced because of me;
God of Israel,
    may those who seek you
    not be put to shame because of me.
⁷ For I endure scorn for your sake,
    and shame covers my face.
⁸ I am a foreigner to my own family,
    a stranger to my own mother's
      children;
⁹ for zeal for your house consumes me,
    and the insults of those who insult you
    fall on me.
¹⁰ When I weep and fast,
    I must endure scorn;
¹¹ when I put on sackcloth,
    people make sport of me.

¹² Those who sit at the gate mock me,
    and I am the song of the drunkards.

¹³ But I pray to you, LORD,
    in the time of your favor;
in your great love, O God,
    answer me with your sure salvation.
¹⁴ Rescue me from the mire,
    do not let me sink;
deliver me from those who hate me,
    from the deep waters.
¹⁵ Do not let the floodwaters engulf me
    or the depths swallow me up
    or the pit close its mouth over me.

¹⁶ Answer me, LORD, out of the goodness of
      your love;
    in your great mercy turn to me.
¹⁷ Do not hide your face from your servant;
    answer me quickly, for I am in trouble.
¹⁸ Come near and rescue me;
    deliver me because of my foes.

¹⁹ You know how I am scorned, disgraced
      and shamed;
    all my enemies are before you.
²⁰ Scorn has broken my heart
    and has left me helpless;
I looked for sympathy, but there was
      none,
    for comforters, but I found none.
²¹ They put gall in my food
    and gave me vinegar for my thirst.

²² May the table set before them become
      a snare;
    may it become retribution andᵇ a trap.
²³ May their eyes be darkened so they
      cannot see,
    and their backs be bent forever.
²⁴ Pour out your wrath on them;
    let your fierce anger overtake them.
²⁵ May their place be deserted;
    let there be no one to dwell in their
      tents.
²⁶ For they persecute those you wound
    and talk about the pain of those
      you hurt.
²⁷ Charge them with crime upon crime;
    do not let them share in your salvation.
²⁸ May they be blotted out of the book of life
    and not be listed with the righteous.

²⁹ But as for me, afflicted and in pain —
    may your salvation, God, protect me.

ᵃ In Hebrew texts 69:1-36 is numbered 69:2-37.   ᵇ 22 Or *snare / and their fellowship become*

[30] I will praise God's name in song
  and glorify him with thanksgiving.
[31] This will please the LORD more than
    an ox,
  more than a bull with its horns and
    hooves.
[32] The poor will see and be glad —
  you who seek God, may your hearts
    live!
[33] The LORD hears the needy
  and does not despise his captive
    people.

[34] Let heaven and earth praise him,
  the seas and all that move in them,
[35] for God will save Zion
  and rebuild the cities of Judah.
  Then people will settle there and
    possess it;
[36] the children of his servants will
    inherit it,
  and those who love his name will
    dwell there.

Psalm 70[a]

For the director of music. Of David. A petition.

[1] Hasten, O God, to save me;
  come quickly, LORD, to help me.

[2] May those who want to take my life
  be put to shame and confusion;
  may all who desire my ruin
  be turned back in disgrace.
[3] May those who say to me, "Aha! Aha!"
  turn back because of their shame.
[4] But may all who seek you
  rejoice and be glad in you;
  may those who long for your saving help
    always say,
  "The LORD is great!"

[5] But as for me, I am poor and needy;
  come quickly to me, O God.
  You are my help and my deliverer;
  LORD, do not delay.

Psalm 71

[1] In you, LORD, I have taken refuge;
  let me never be put to shame.
[2] In your righteousness, rescue me and
    deliver me;
  turn your ear to me and save me.

[3] Be my rock of refuge,
  to which I can always go;
  give the command to save me,
  for you are my rock and my fortress.
[4] Deliver me, my God, from the hand of the
    wicked,
  from the grasp of those who are evil
    and cruel.

[5] For you have been my hope, Sovereign
    LORD,
  my confidence since my youth.
[6] From birth I have relied on you;
  you brought me forth from my
    mother's womb.
  I will ever praise you.
[7] I have become a sign to many;
  you are my strong refuge.
[8] My mouth is filled with your praise,
  declaring your splendor all day long.

[9] Do not cast me away when I am old;
  do not forsake me when my strength
    is gone.
[10] For my enemies speak against me;
  those who wait to kill me conspire
    together.
[11] They say, "God has forsaken him;
  pursue him and seize him,
  for no one will rescue him."
[12] Do not be far from me, my God;
  come quickly, God, to help me.
[13] May my accusers perish in shame;
  may those who want to harm me
  be covered with scorn and disgrace.

[14] As for me, I will always have hope;
  I will praise you more and more.
[15] My mouth will tell of your righteous
    deeds,
  of your saving acts all day long —
  though I know not how to relate
    them all.
[16] I will come and proclaim your mighty
    acts, Sovereign LORD;
  I will proclaim your righteous deeds,
    yours alone.
[17] Since my youth, God, you have taught me,
  and to this day I declare your
    marvelous deeds.
[18] Even when I am old and gray,
  do not forsake me, my God,
  till I declare your power to the next
    generation,

---

[a] In Hebrew texts 70:1-5 is numbered 70:2-6.

your mighty acts to all who are to
    come.

¹⁹ Your righteousness, God, reaches to the
    heavens,
    you who have done great things.
    Who is like you, God?
²⁰ Though you have made me see
    troubles,
    many and bitter,
    you will restore my life again;
    from the depths of the earth
    you will again bring me up.
²¹ You will increase my honor
    and comfort me once more.

²² I will praise you with the harp
    for your faithfulness, my God;
    I will sing praise to you with the lyre,
    Holy One of Israel.
²³ My lips will shout for joy
    when I sing praise to you —
    I whom you have delivered.
²⁴ My tongue will tell of your righteous acts
    all day long,
    for those who wanted to harm me
    have been put to shame and
    confusion.

Psalm 72

Of Solomon.

¹ Endow the king with your justice,
    O God,
    the royal son with your righteousness.
² May he judge your people in
    righteousness,
    your afflicted ones with justice.

³ May the mountains bring prosperity to
    the people,
    the hills the fruit of righteousness.
⁴ May he defend the afflicted among the
    people
    and save the children of the needy;
    may he crush the oppressor.
⁵ May he endure^a as long as the sun,
    as long as the moon, through all
    generations.
⁶ May he be like rain falling on a mown
    field,
    like showers watering the earth.

⁷ In his days may the righteous flourish
    and prosperity abound till the moon
    is no more.

⁸ May he rule from sea to sea
    and from the River^b to the ends of
    the earth.
⁹ May the desert tribes bow before him
    and his enemies lick the dust.
¹⁰ May the kings of Tarshish and of distant
    shores
    bring tribute to him.
    May the kings of Sheba and Seba
    present him gifts.
¹¹ May all kings bow down to him
    and all nations serve him.

¹² For he will deliver the needy who cry out,
    the afflicted who have no one to help.
¹³ He will take pity on the weak and the
    needy
    and save the needy from death.
¹⁴ He will rescue them from oppression and
    violence,
    for precious is their blood in his sight.

¹⁵ Long may he live!
    May gold from Sheba be given him.
    May people ever pray for him
    and bless him all day long.
¹⁶ May grain abound throughout the
    land;
    on the tops of the hills may it sway.
    May the crops flourish like Lebanon
    and thrive^c like the grass of the field.
¹⁷ May his name endure forever;
    may it continue as long as the sun.

Then all nations will be blessed through
    him,^d
    and they will call him blessed.

¹⁸ Praise be to the Lord God, the God
    of Israel,
    who alone does marvelous deeds.
¹⁹ Praise be to his glorious name forever;
    may the whole earth be filled with
    his glory.
        Amen and Amen.

²⁰ This concludes the prayers of David
    son of Jesse.

---

^a 5 Septuagint; Hebrew *You will be feared*   ^b 8 That is, the Euphrates   ^c 16 Probable reading of the
original Hebrew text; Masoretic Text *Lebanon, / from the city*   ^d 17 Or *will use his name in blessings* (see
Gen. 48:20)

BOOK III

Psalms 73–89

Psalm 73

A psalm of Asaph.

¹ Surely God is good to Israel,
   to those who are pure in heart.

² But as for me, my feet had almost slipped;
   I had nearly lost my foothold.
³ For I envied the arrogant
   when I saw the prosperity of the
      wicked.

⁴ They have no struggles;
   their bodies are healthy and strong.ᵃ
⁵ They are free from common human
      burdens;
   they are not plagued by human ills.
⁶ Therefore pride is their necklace;
   they clothe themselves with violence.
⁷ From their callous hearts comes
      iniquityᵇ;
   their evil imaginations have no limits.
⁸ They scoff, and speak with malice;
   with arrogance they threaten
      oppression.
⁹ Their mouths lay claim to heaven,
   and their tongues take possession of
      the earth.
¹⁰ Therefore their people turn to them
   and drink up waters in abundance.ᶜ
¹¹ They say, "How would God know?
   Does the Most High know anything?"

¹² This is what the wicked are like —
   always free of care, they go on
      amassing wealth.

¹³ Surely in vain I have kept my heart pure
   and have washed my hands in
      innocence.
¹⁴ All day long I have been afflicted,
   and every morning brings new
      punishments.

¹⁵ If I had spoken out like that,
   I would have betrayed your children.
¹⁶ When I tried to understand all this,
   it troubled me deeply
¹⁷ till I entered the sanctuary of God;
   then I understood their final destiny.

¹⁸ Surely you place them on slippery
      ground;
   you cast them down to ruin.
¹⁹ How suddenly are they destroyed,
   completely swept away by terrors!
²⁰ They are like a dream when one awakes;
   when you arise, Lord,
   you will despise them as fantasies.

²¹ When my heart was grieved
   and my spirit embittered,
²² I was senseless and ignorant;
   I was a brute beast before you.

²³ Yet I am always with you;
   you hold me by my right hand.
²⁴ You guide me with your counsel,
   and afterward you will take me into
      glory.
²⁵ Whom have I in heaven but you?
   And earth has nothing I desire
      besides you.
²⁶ My flesh and my heart may fail,
   but God is the strength of my heart
   and my portion forever.

²⁷ Those who are far from you will perish;
   you destroy all who are unfaithful
      to you.
²⁸ But as for me, it is good to be near God.
   I have made the Sovereign Lord my
      refuge;
   I will tell of all your deeds.

Psalm 74

A maskilᵈ of Asaph.

¹ O God, why have you rejected us forever?
   Why does your anger smolder against
      the sheep of your pasture?
² Remember the nation you purchased
      long ago,
   the people of your inheritance, whom
      you redeemed —
   Mount Zion, where you dwelt.
³ Turn your steps toward these everlasting
      ruins,
   all this destruction the enemy has
      brought on the sanctuary.

⁴ Your foes roared in the place where you
      met with us;
   they set up their standards as signs.

ᵃ 4 With a different word division of the Hebrew; Masoretic Text *struggles at their death; / their bodies are healthy*   ᵇ 7 Syriac (see also Septuagint); Hebrew *Their eyes bulge with fat*   ᶜ 10 The meaning of the Hebrew for this verse is uncertain.   ᵈ Title: Probably a literary or musical term

⁵ They behaved like men wielding axes
   to cut through a thicket of trees.
⁶ They smashed all the carved paneling
   with their axes and hatchets.
⁷ They burned your sanctuary to the
      ground;
   they defiled the dwelling place of your
      Name.
⁸ They said in their hearts, "We will crush
      them completely!"
   They burned every place where God
      was worshiped in the land.

⁹ We are given no signs from God;
   no prophets are left,
   and none of us knows how long this
      will be.
¹⁰ How long will the enemy mock you, God?
   Will the foe revile your name forever?
¹¹ Why do you hold back your hand, your
      right hand?
   Take it from the folds of your garment
      and destroy them!

¹² But God is my King from long ago;
   he brings salvation on the earth.

¹³ It was you who split open the sea by your
      power;
   you broke the heads of the monster in
      the waters.
¹⁴ It was you who crushed the heads of
      Leviathan
   and gave it as food to the creatures
      of the desert.
¹⁵ It was you who opened up springs and
      streams;
   you dried up the ever-flowing rivers.
¹⁶ The day is yours, and yours also the
      night;
   you established the sun and moon.
¹⁷ It was you who set all the boundaries of
      the earth;
   you made both summer and winter.

¹⁸ Remember how the enemy has mocked
      you, LORD,
   how foolish people have reviled your
      name.
¹⁹ Do not hand over the life of your dove to
      wild beasts;
   do not forget the lives of your afflicted
      people forever.

²⁰ Have regard for your covenant,
   because haunts of violence fill the dark
      places of the land.
²¹ Do not let the oppressed retreat in
      disgrace;
   may the poor and needy praise your
      name.
²² Rise up, O God, and defend your cause;
   remember how fools mock you all
      day long.
²³ Do not ignore the clamor of your
      adversaries,
   the uproar of your enemies, which
      rises continually.

Psalm 75 ᵃ

For the director of music.
To the tune of "Do Not Destroy."
A psalm of Asaph. A song.

¹ We praise you, God,
   we praise you, for your Name is near;
   people tell of your wonderful deeds.

² You say, "I choose the appointed time;
   it is I who judge with equity.
³ When the earth and all its people quake,
   it is I who hold its pillars firm.ᵇ
⁴ To the arrogant I say, 'Boast no more,'
   and to the wicked, 'Do not lift up your
      horns.ᶜ
⁵ Do not lift your horns against heaven;
   do not speak so defiantly.' "

⁶ No one from the east or the west
   or from the desert can exalt
      themselves.
⁷ It is God who judges:
   He brings one down, he exalts another.
⁸ In the hand of the LORD is a cup
   full of foaming wine mixed with
      spices;
   he pours it out, and all the wicked of
      the earth
   drink it down to its very dregs.

⁹ As for me, I will declare this forever;
   I will sing praise to the God of Jacob,
¹⁰ who says, "I will cut off the horns of all
      the wicked,
   but the horns of the righteous will be
      lifted up."

ᵃ In Hebrew texts 75:1-10 is numbered 75:2-11.   ᵇ 3 The Hebrew has *Selah* (a word of uncertain meaning)
here.   ᶜ 4 *Horns* here symbolize strength; also in verses 5 and 10.

Psalm 76[a]

For the director of music. With stringed
instruments. A psalm of Asaph. A song.

[1] God is renowned in Judah;
  in Israel his name is great.
[2] His tent is in Salem,
  his dwelling place in Zion.
[3] There he broke the flashing arrows,
  the shields and the swords, the
  weapons of war.[b]

[4] You are radiant with light,
  more majestic than mountains rich
  with game.
[5] The valiant lie plundered,
  they sleep their last sleep;
  not one of the warriors
  can lift his hands.
[6] At your rebuke, God of Jacob,
  both horse and chariot lie still.

[7] It is you alone who are to be feared.
  Who can stand before you when you
  are angry?
[8] From heaven you pronounced judgment,
  and the land feared and was quiet—
[9] when you, God, rose up to judge,
  to save all the afflicted of the land.
[10] Surely your wrath against mankind
  brings you praise,
  and the survivors of your wrath are
  restrained.[c]

[11] Make vows to the LORD your God and
  fulfill them;
  let all the neighboring lands
  bring gifts to the One to be feared.
[12] He breaks the spirit of rulers;
  he is feared by the kings of the earth.

Psalm 77[d]

For the director of music.
For Jeduthun. Of Asaph. A psalm.

[1] I cried out to God for help;
  I cried out to God to hear me.
[2] When I was in distress, I sought the
  Lord;
  at night I stretched out untiring hands,
  and I would not be comforted.

[3] I remembered you, God, and I groaned;
  I meditated, and my spirit grew faint.[e]
[4] You kept my eyes from closing;
  I was too troubled to speak.
[5] I thought about the former days,
  the years of long ago;
[6] I remembered my songs in the night.
  My heart meditated and my spirit
  asked:

[7] "Will the Lord reject forever?
  Will he never show his favor again?
[8] Has his unfailing love vanished forever?
  Has his promise failed for all time?
[9] Has God forgotten to be merciful?
  Has he in anger withheld his
  compassion?"

[10] Then I thought, "To this I will appeal:
  the years when the Most High
  stretched out his right hand.
[11] I will remember the deeds of the LORD;
  yes, I will remember your miracles of
  long ago.
[12] I will consider all your works
  and meditate on all your mighty deeds."

[13] Your ways, God, are holy.
  What god is as great as our God?
[14] You are the God who performs miracles;
  you display your power among the
  peoples.
[15] With your mighty arm you redeemed
  your people,
  the descendants of Jacob and Joseph.

[16] The waters saw you, God,
  the waters saw you and writhed;
  the very depths were convulsed.
[17] The clouds poured down water,
  the heavens resounded with thunder;
  your arrows flashed back and forth.
[18] Your thunder was heard in the
  whirlwind,
  your lightning lit up the world;
  the earth trembled and quaked.
[19] Your path led through the sea,
  your way through the mighty waters,
  though your footprints were not seen.
[20] You led your people like a flock
  by the hand of Moses and Aaron.

[a] In Hebrew texts 76:1-12 is numbered 76:2-13.   [b] 3 The Hebrew has *Selah* (a word of uncertain meaning)
here and at the end of verse 9.   [c] 10 Or *Surely the wrath of mankind brings you praise, / and with the*
remainder of wrath you arm yourself   [d] In Hebrew texts 77:1-20 is numbered 77:2-21.   [e] 3 The Hebrew
has *Selah* (a word of uncertain meaning) here and at the end of verses 9 and 15.

Hope Lies in Remembering

By Ronda Sturgill

READ: Psalm 77:1–12

As I read Psalm 77, all I can think of are the many nights I have lain awake in distress, calling out to God. My desperate pleas and prayers on behalf of my family seemed at times to fall on deaf ears. Like the psalmist who penned these words, my soul refused to be comforted (see verse 2). My spirit inquired, "Will you reject my prayers forever and never show your favor again? Has your promise failed for all time? Have I made you angry, causing you to withhold your compassion?" (see verses 7–9).

But the author of Psalm 77 made a conscious decision to remember the deeds of the Lord. He looked beyond his present troubles and decided to remember the miracles of long ago. He chose to meditate on all of God's works (see verses 10–12). As the psalmist did this, his troubled spirit was transformed from hopeless to hopeful. Perhaps if I remember what God has done for me, my troubled spirit will be transformed as well.

My restless soul quiets as I make the choice to reminisce. I remember the day I kissed my husband good-bye as he went off to war, and I remember how God kept me close while he was gone. I remember the many times we've moved and needed special, wheelchair-accessible housing for me, and I remember how God provided for us every time. I remember the time when I was very lonely and God sent me a friend.

Remembering God's mighty works has played an important part in the faith journey of believers for many generations. When God stopped the Jordan River from flowing so the Israelites could cross over on dry land, Joshua was instructed to take 12 stones from the middle of the river and carry them to their camp. These stones were to serve as a reminder to future generations of God's faithfulness at that place (see Joshua 4:1–9). The psalms are full of instances of the psalmists deliberately reminiscing about the Lord's work. Read Psalm 145 and notice that the psalmist remembered not only God's works but also God's character.

When we remember God's faithfulness in our lives, feelings of hope rise to the surface. Faltering faith is steadied and strengthened. Assurance and encouragement replace the bewilderment and despair that previously held our souls captive. We are awakened to God's goodness — right here, right now. Though his footprints remain unseen, God is not missing in action. His invisible hands are working silently to bring about his glorious plan for the rest of our lives and the lives of the ones we love.

> I will remember the deeds of the LORD; yes, I will remember your miracles of long ago. I will consider all your works and meditate on all your mighty deeds.
>
> PSALM 77:11–12

DEBRIEF

- What has God done for me in the past? I'll make a list of these things.
- How might remembering these things give me hope for today and for the days to come?

REPORT

Dear heavenly Father, thank you for what you have done in the past for me. Help me to never forget these things, especially during the times when my faith falters and I fall prey to doubts, questions and fears. Help me stand firm on the promises that you are always present and doing mighty work in my life and in the lives of those I love. Amen.

for your next devotional reading, go to page 399

Psalm 78

A maskil[a] of Asaph.

¹ My people, hear my teaching;
  listen to the words of my mouth.
² I will open my mouth with a parable;
  I will utter hidden things, things from
    of old —
³ things we have heard and known,
  things our ancestors have told us.
⁴ We will not hide them from their
    descendants;
  we will tell the next generation
  the praiseworthy deeds of the LORD,
    his power, and the wonders he has
    done.
⁵ He decreed statutes for Jacob
    and established the law in Israel,
  which he commanded our ancestors
    to teach their children,
⁶ so the next generation would know them,
    even the children yet to be born,
    and they in turn would tell their
    children.
⁷ Then they would put their trust in God
    and would not forget his deeds
    but would keep his commands.
⁸ They would not be like their ancestors —
    a stubborn and rebellious generation,
  whose hearts were not loyal to God,
    whose spirits were not faithful to him.

⁹ The men of Ephraim, though armed with
    bows,
    turned back on the day of battle;
¹⁰ they did not keep God's covenant
    and refused to live by his law.
¹¹ They forgot what he had done,
    the wonders he had shown them.
¹² He did miracles in the sight of their
    ancestors
  in the land of Egypt, in the region of
    Zoan.
¹³ He divided the sea and led them through;
    he made the water stand up like
    a wall.
¹⁴ He guided them with the cloud by day
    and with light from the fire all night.
¹⁵ He split the rocks in the wilderness
    and gave them water as abundant as
    the seas;
¹⁶ he brought streams out of a rocky crag
    and made water flow down like rivers.

¹⁷ But they continued to sin against him,
    rebelling in the wilderness against the
    Most High.
¹⁸ They willfully put God to the test
    by demanding the food they craved.
¹⁹ They spoke against God;
    they said, "Can God really
    spread a table in the wilderness?
²⁰ True, he struck the rock,
    and water gushed out,
    streams flowed abundantly,
  but can he also give us bread?
    Can he supply meat for his people?"
²¹ When the LORD heard them, he was
    furious;
    his fire broke out against Jacob,
    and his wrath rose against Israel,
²² for they did not believe in God
    or trust in his deliverance.
²³ Yet he gave a command to the skies above
    and opened the doors of the heavens;
²⁴ he rained down manna for the people
    to eat,
    he gave them the grain of heaven.
²⁵ Human beings ate the bread of angels;
    he sent them all the food they could eat.
²⁶ He let loose the east wind from the
    heavens
    and by his power made the south
    wind blow.
²⁷ He rained meat down on them like dust,
    birds like sand on the seashore.
²⁸ He made them come down inside their
    camp,
    all around their tents.
²⁹ They ate till they were gorged —
    he had given them what they craved.
³⁰ But before they turned from what they
    craved,
  even while the food was still in their
    mouths,
³¹ God's anger rose against them;
    he put to death the sturdiest among
    them,
    cutting down the young men of Israel.

³² In spite of all this, they kept on sinning;
    in spite of his wonders, they did not
    believe.
³³ So he ended their days in futility
    and their years in terror.
³⁴ Whenever God slew them, they would
    seek him;
    they eagerly turned to him again.

---

a Title: Probably a literary or musical term

³⁵ They remembered that God was their
Rock,
that God Most High was their
Redeemer.
³⁶ But then they would flatter him with
their mouths,
lying to him with their tongues;
³⁷ their hearts were not loyal to him,
they were not faithful to his covenant.
³⁸ Yet he was merciful;
he forgave their iniquities
and did not destroy them.
Time after time he restrained his anger
and did not stir up his full wrath.
³⁹ He remembered that they were but flesh,
a passing breeze that does not return.

⁴⁰ How often they rebelled against him in
the wilderness
and grieved him in the wasteland!
⁴¹ Again and again they put God to the test;
they vexed the Holy One of Israel.
⁴² They did not remember his power —
the day he redeemed them from the
oppressor,
⁴³ the day he displayed his signs in Egypt,
his wonders in the region of Zoan.
⁴⁴ He turned their river into blood;
they could not drink from their
streams.
⁴⁵ He sent swarms of flies that devoured
them,
and frogs that devastated them.
⁴⁶ He gave their crops to the grasshopper,
their produce to the locust.
⁴⁷ He destroyed their vines with hail
and their sycamore-figs with sleet.
⁴⁸ He gave over their cattle to the hail,
their livestock to bolts of lightning.
⁴⁹ He unleashed against them his hot anger,
his wrath, indignation and hostility —
a band of destroying angels.
⁵⁰ He prepared a path for his anger;
he did not spare them from death
but gave them over to the plague.
⁵¹ He struck down all the firstborn of Egypt,
the firstfruits of manhood in the tents
of Ham.
⁵² But he brought his people out like a flock;
he led them like sheep through the
wilderness.
⁵³ He guided them safely, so they were
unafraid;
but the sea engulfed their enemies.

⁵⁴ And so he brought them to the border of
his holy land,
to the hill country his right hand had
taken.
⁵⁵ He drove out nations before them
and allotted their lands to them as an
inheritance;
he settled the tribes of Israel in their
homes.

⁵⁶ But they put God to the test
and rebelled against the Most High;
they did not keep his statutes.
⁵⁷ Like their ancestors they were disloyal
and faithless,
as unreliable as a faulty bow.
⁵⁸ They angered him with their high places;
they aroused his jealousy with their
idols.
⁵⁹ When God heard them, he was furious;
he rejected Israel completely.
⁶⁰ He abandoned the tabernacle of Shiloh,
the tent he had set up among humans.
⁶¹ He sent the ark of his might into captivity,
his splendor into the hands of the
enemy.
⁶² He gave his people over to the sword;
he was furious with his inheritance.
⁶³ Fire consumed their young men,
and their young women had no
wedding songs;
⁶⁴ their priests were put to the sword,
and their widows could not weep.

⁶⁵ Then the Lord awoke as from sleep,
as a warrior wakes from the stupor
of wine.
⁶⁶ He beat back his enemies;
he put them to everlasting shame.
⁶⁷ Then he rejected the tents of Joseph,
he did not choose the tribe of
Ephraim;
⁶⁸ but he chose the tribe of Judah,
Mount Zion, which he loved.
⁶⁹ He built his sanctuary like the heights,
like the earth that he established
forever.
⁷⁰ He chose David his servant
and took him from the sheep pens;
⁷¹ from tending the sheep he brought him
to be the shepherd of his people Jacob,
of Israel his inheritance.
⁷² And David shepherded them with
integrity of heart;
with skillful hands he led them.

Psalm 79

A psalm of Asaph.

¹ O God, the nations have invaded your
inheritance;
they have defiled your holy temple,
they have reduced Jerusalem to
rubble.
² They have left the dead bodies of your
servants
as food for the birds of the sky,
the flesh of your own people for the
animals of the wild.
³ They have poured out blood like water
all around Jerusalem,
and there is no one to bury the dead.
⁴ We are objects of contempt to our
neighbors,
of scorn and derision to those
around us.

⁵ How long, LORD? Will you be angry
forever?
How long will your jealousy burn
like fire?
⁶ Pour out your wrath on the nations
that do not acknowledge you,
on the kingdoms
that do not call on your name;
⁷ for they have devoured Jacob
and devastated his homeland.

⁸ Do not hold against us the sins of past
generations;
may your mercy come quickly to
meet us,
for we are in desperate need.
⁹ Help us, God our Savior,
for the glory of your name;
deliver us and forgive our sins
for your name's sake.
¹⁰ Why should the nations say,
"Where is their God?"

Before our eyes, make known among the
nations
that you avenge the outpoured blood
of your servants.
¹¹ May the groans of the prisoners come
before you;
with your strong arm preserve those
condemned to die.
¹² Pay back into the laps of our neighbors
seven times

the contempt they have hurled at
you, Lord.
¹³ Then we your people, the sheep of your
pasture,
will praise you forever;
from generation to generation
we will proclaim your praise.

Psalm 80[a]

*For the director of music. To the tune of
"The Lilies of the Covenant." Of Asaph. A psalm.*

¹ Hear us, Shepherd of Israel,
you who lead Joseph like a flock.
You who sit enthroned between the
cherubim,
shine forth ²before Ephraim,
Benjamin and Manasseh.
Awaken your might;
come and save us.

³ Restore us, O God;
make your face shine on us,
that we may be saved.

⁴ How long, LORD God Almighty,
will your anger smolder
against the prayers of your people?
⁵ You have fed them with the bread of
tears;
you have made them drink tears by
the bowlful.
⁶ You have made us an object of derision[b]
to our neighbors,
and our enemies mock us.

⁷ Restore us, God Almighty;
make your face shine on us,
that we may be saved.

⁸ You transplanted a vine from Egypt;
you drove out the nations and
planted it.
⁹ You cleared the ground for it,
and it took root and filled the land.
¹⁰ The mountains were covered with its
shade,
the mighty cedars with its branches.
¹¹ Its branches reached as far as the Sea,[c]
its shoots as far as the River.[d]
¹² Why have you broken down its walls
so that all who pass by pick its grapes?
¹³ Boars from the forest ravage it,
and insects from the fields feed on it.

---

[a] In Hebrew texts 80:1-19 is numbered 80:2-20.   [b] 6 Probable reading of the original Hebrew text;
Masoretic Text *contention*   [c] 11 Probably the Mediterranean   [d] 11 That is, the Euphrates

¹⁴ Return to us, God Almighty!
  Look down from heaven and see!
  Watch over this vine,
¹⁵   the root your right hand has planted,
    the son*a* you have raised up for
      yourself.

¹⁶ Your vine is cut down, it is burned with
    fire;
  at your rebuke your people perish.
¹⁷ Let your hand rest on the man at your
    right hand,
  the son of man you have raised up for
    yourself.
¹⁸ Then we will not turn away from you;
  revive us, and we will call on your
    name.

¹⁹ Restore us, LORD God Almighty;
  make your face shine on us,
  that we may be saved.

Psalm 81*b*

For the director of music. According to gittith.*c*
  Of Asaph.

¹ Sing for joy to God our strength;
  shout aloud to the God of Jacob!
² Begin the music, strike the timbrel,
  play the melodious harp and lyre.

³ Sound the ram's horn at the New Moon,
  and when the moon is full, on the day
    of our festival;
⁴ this is a decree for Israel,
  an ordinance of the God of Jacob.
⁵ When God went out against Egypt,
  he established it as a statute for
    Joseph.

I heard an unknown voice say:

⁶ "I removed the burden from their
    shoulders;
  their hands were set free from the
    basket.
⁷ In your distress you called and I rescued
    you,
  I answered you out of a thundercloud;
  I tested you at the waters of Meribah.*d*
⁸ Hear me, my people, and I will warn
    you —
  if you would only listen to me, Israel!
⁹ You shall have no foreign god among you;

you shall not worship any god other
    than me.
¹⁰ I am the LORD your God,
  who brought you up out of Egypt.
  Open wide your mouth and I will fill it.

¹¹ "But my people would not listen to me;
  Israel would not submit to me.
¹² So I gave them over to their stubborn
    hearts
  to follow their own devices.

¹³ "If my people would only listen to me,
  if Israel would only follow my ways,
¹⁴ how quickly I would subdue their
    enemies
  and turn my hand against their foes!
¹⁵ Those who hate the LORD would cringe
    before him,
  and their punishment would last
    forever.
¹⁶ But you would be fed with the finest of
    wheat;
  with honey from the rock I would
    satisfy you."

Psalm 82

A psalm of Asaph.

¹ God presides in the great assembly;
  he renders judgment among the "gods":

² "How long will you*e* defend the unjust
  and show partiality to the wicked?*d*
³ Defend the weak and the fatherless;
  uphold the cause of the poor and the
    oppressed.
⁴ Rescue the weak and the needy;
  deliver them from the hand of the
    wicked.

⁵ "The 'gods' know nothing, they
    understand nothing.
  They walk about in darkness;
  all the foundations of the earth are
    shaken.

⁶ "I said, 'You are "gods";
  you are all sons of the Most High.'
⁷ But you will die like mere mortals;
  you will fall like every other ruler."

⁸ Rise up, O God, judge the earth,
  for all the nations are your
    inheritance.

---

a 15 Or *branch*   *b* In Hebrew texts 81:1-16 is numbered 81:2-17.   *c* Title: Probably a musical term
d 7,2 The Hebrew has *Selah* (a word of uncertain meaning) here.   *e 2* The Hebrew is plural.

Psalm 83[a]

A song. A psalm of Asaph.

[1] O God, do not remain silent;
do not turn a deaf ear,
do not stand aloof, O God.
[2] See how your enemies growl,
how your foes rear their heads.
[3] With cunning they conspire against your
people;
they plot against those you cherish.
[4] "Come," they say, "let us destroy them as
a nation,
so that Israel's name is remembered
no more."

[5] With one mind they plot together;
they form an alliance against you —
[6] the tents of Edom and the Ishmaelites,
of Moab and the Hagrites,
[7] Byblos, Ammon and Amalek,
Philistia, with the people of Tyre.
[8] Even Assyria has joined them
to reinforce Lot's descendants.[b]

[9] Do to them as you did to Midian,
as you did to Sisera and Jabin at the
river Kishon,
[10] who perished at Endor
and became like dung on the ground.
[11] Make their nobles like Oreb and Zeeb,
all their princes like Zebah and
Zalmunna,
[12] who said, "Let us take possession
of the pasturelands of God."

[13] Make them like tumbleweed, my God,
like chaff before the wind.
[14] As fire consumes the forest
or a flame sets the mountains
ablaze,
[15] so pursue them with your tempest
and terrify them with your storm.
[16] Cover their faces with shame, LORD,
so that they will seek your name.

[17] May they ever be ashamed and
dismayed;
may they perish in disgrace.
[18] Let them know that you, whose name is
the LORD —

that you alone are the Most High over
all the earth.

Psalm 84[c]

For the director of music.
According to gittith.[d] Of the Sons of Korah.
A psalm.

[1] How lovely is your dwelling place,
LORD Almighty!
[2] My soul yearns, even faints,
for the courts of the LORD;
my heart and my flesh cry out
for the living God.
[3] Even the sparrow has found a home,
and the swallow a nest for herself,
where she may have her young —
a place near your altar,
LORD Almighty, my King and my God.
[4] Blessed are those who dwell in your
house;
they are ever praising you.[e]

[5] Blessed are those whose strength is
in you,
whose hearts are set on pilgrimage.
[6] As they pass through the Valley of Baka,
they make it a place of springs;
the autumn rains also cover it with
pools.[f]
[7] They go from strength to strength,
till each appears before God in Zion.

[8] Hear my prayer, LORD God Almighty;
listen to me, God of Jacob.
[9] Look on our shield,[g] O God;
look with favor on your anointed
one.

[10] Better is one day in your courts
than a thousand elsewhere;
I would rather be a doorkeeper in the
house of my God
than dwell in the tents of the wicked.
[11] For the LORD God is a sun and shield;
the LORD bestows favor and honor;
no good thing does he withhold
from those whose walk is blameless.
[12] LORD Almighty,
blessed is the one who trusts in you.

---

[a] In Hebrew texts 83:1-18 is numbered 83:2-19.   [b] 8 The Hebrew has *Selah* (a word of uncertain
meaning) here.   [c] In Hebrew texts 84:1-12 is numbered 84:2-13.   [d] Title: Probably a musical term
[e] 4 The Hebrew has *Selah* (a word of uncertain meaning) here and at the end of verse 8.   [f] 6 Or *blessings*
[g] 9 Or *sovereign*

Psalm 85[a]

For the director of music.
Of the Sons of Korah. A psalm.

[1] You, Lord, showed favor to your land;
  you restored the fortunes of Jacob.
[2] You forgave the iniquity of your people
  and covered all their sins.[b]
[3] You set aside all your wrath
  and turned from your fierce anger.

[4] Restore us again, God our Savior,
  and put away your displeasure toward
  us.
[5] Will you be angry with us forever?
  Will you prolong your anger through
  all generations?
[6] Will you not revive us again,
  that your people may rejoice in you?
[7] Show us your unfailing love, Lord,
  and grant us your salvation.

[8] I will listen to what God the Lord says;
  he promises peace to his people, his
  faithful servants—
  but let them not turn to folly.
[9] Surely his salvation is near those who
  fear him,
  that his glory may dwell in our land.

[10] Love and faithfulness meet together;
  righteousness and peace kiss each
  other.
[11] Faithfulness springs forth from the earth,
  and righteousness looks down from
  heaven.
[12] The Lord will indeed give what is good,
  and our land will yield its harvest.
[13] Righteousness goes before him
  and prepares the way for his steps.

Psalm 86

A prayer of David.

[1] Hear me, Lord, and answer me,
  for I am poor and needy.
[2] Guard my life, for I am faithful to you;
  save your servant who trusts in you.
  You are my God; [3] have mercy on me,
  Lord,
  for I call to you all day long.
[4] Bring joy to your servant, Lord,
  for I put my trust in you.

[5] You, Lord, are forgiving and good,
  abounding in love to all who call
  to you.
[6] Hear my prayer, Lord;
  listen to my cry for mercy.
[7] When I am in distress, I call to you,
  because you answer me.

[8] Among the gods there is none like
  you, Lord;
  no deeds can compare with yours.
[9] All the nations you have made
  will come and worship before you, Lord;
  they will bring glory to your name.
[10] For you are great and do marvelous
  deeds;
  you alone are God.

[11] Teach me your way, Lord,
  that I may rely on your faithfulness;
  give me an undivided heart,
  that I may fear your name.
[12] I will praise you, Lord my God, with all
  my heart;
  I will glorify your name forever.
[13] For great is your love toward me;
  you have delivered me from the
  depths,
  from the realm of the dead.

[14] Arrogant foes are attacking me, O God;
  ruthless people are trying to kill me—
  they have no regard for you.
[15] But you, Lord, are a compassionate and
  gracious God,
  slow to anger, abounding in love and
  faithfulness.
[16] Turn to me and have mercy on me;
  show your strength in behalf of your
  servant;
  save me, because I serve you
  just as my mother did.
[17] Give me a sign of your goodness,
  that my enemies may see it and be put
  to shame,
  for you, Lord, have helped me and
  comforted me.

Psalm 87

Of the Sons of Korah. A psalm. A song.

[1] He has founded his city on the holy
  mountain.

[a] In Hebrew texts 85:1-13 is numbered 85:2-14.   [b] 2 The Hebrew has *Selah* (a word of uncertain
meaning) here.

²The LORD loves the gates of Zion
more than all the other dwellings of
Jacob.

³Glorious things are said of you,
city of God:ᵃ
⁴"I will record Rahabᵇ and Babylon
among those who acknowledge me —
Philistia too, and Tyre, along with
Cushᶜ —
and will say, 'This one was born in
Zion.'"ᵈ
⁵Indeed, of Zion it will be said,
"This one and that one were born in
her,
and the Most High himself will
establish her."
⁶The LORD will write in the register of the
peoples:
"This one was born in Zion."

⁷As they make music they will sing,
"All my fountains are in you."

Psalm 88ᵉ

*A song. A psalm of the Sons of Korah. For the
director of music. According to* mahalath
leannoth.ᶠ *A maskilᵍ of Heman the Ezrahite.*

¹LORD, you are the God who saves me;
day and night I cry out to you.
²May my prayer come before you;
turn your ear to my cry.

³I am overwhelmed with troubles
and my life draws near to death.
⁴I am counted among those who go down
to the pit;
I am like one without strength.
⁵I am set apart with the dead,
like the slain who lie in the grave,
whom you remember no more,
who are cut off from your care.

⁶You have put me in the lowest pit,
in the darkest depths.
⁷Your wrath lies heavily on me;
you have overwhelmed me with all
your waves.ʰ

⁸You have taken from me my closest
friends
and have made me repulsive to them.
I am confined and cannot escape;
⁹   my eyes are dim with grief.

I call to you, LORD, every day;
I spread out my hands to you.
¹⁰Do you show your wonders to the dead?
Do their spirits rise up and praise you?
¹¹Is your love declared in the grave,
your faithfulness in Destructionⁱ?
¹²Are your wonders known in the place of
darkness,
or your righteous deeds in the land of
oblivion?

¹³But I cry to you for help, LORD;
in the morning my prayer comes
before you.
¹⁴Why, LORD, do you reject me
and hide your face from me?

¹⁵From my youth I have suffered and been
close to death;
I have borne your terrors and am in
despair.
¹⁶Your wrath has swept over me;
your terrors have destroyed me.
¹⁷All day long they surround me like a
flood;
they have completely engulfed me.
¹⁸You have taken from me friend and
neighbor —
darkness is my closest friend.

Psalm 89ʲ

A maskilᵍ of Ethan the Ezrahite.

¹I will sing of the LORD's great love forever;
with my mouth I will make your
faithfulness known
through all generations.
²I will declare that your love stands firm
forever,
that you have established your
faithfulness in heaven itself.
³You said, "I have made a covenant with
my chosen one,

ᵃ 3 The Hebrew has *Selah* (a word of uncertain meaning) here and at the end of verse 6.   ᵇ 4 A poetic
name for Egypt   ᶜ 4 That is, the upper Nile region   ᵈ 4 Or *"I will record concerning those who
acknowledge me: / 'This one was born in Zion.' / Hear this, Rahab and Babylon, / and you too, Philistia, Tyre
and Cush."*   ᵉ In Hebrew texts 88:1-18 is numbered 88:2-19.   ᶠ Title: Possibly a tune, "The Suffering of
Affliction"   ᵍ Title: Probably a literary or musical term   ʰ 7 The Hebrew has *Selah* (a word of
uncertain meaning) here and at the end of verse 10.   ⁱ 11 Hebrew *Abaddon*   ʲ In Hebrew texts 89:1-52
is numbered 89:2-53.

I have sworn to David my servant,
⁴'I will establish your line forever
  and make your throne firm through all
    generations.' "*a*

⁵The heavens praise your wonders, LORD,
  your faithfulness too, in the assembly
    of the holy ones.
⁶For who in the skies above can compare
    with the LORD?
  Who is like the LORD among the
    heavenly beings?
⁷In the council of the holy ones God is
    greatly feared;
  he is more awesome than all who
    surround him.
⁸Who is like you, LORD God Almighty?
  You, LORD, are mighty, and your
    faithfulness surrounds you.

⁹You rule over the surging sea;
  when its waves mount up, you still
    them.
¹⁰You crushed Rahab like one of the slain;
  with your strong arm you scattered
    your enemies.
¹¹The heavens are yours, and yours also
    the earth;
  you founded the world and all that
    is in it.
¹²You created the north and the south;
  Tabor and Hermon sing for joy at your
    name.
¹³Your arm is endowed with power;
  your hand is strong, your right hand
    exalted.

¹⁴Righteousness and justice are the
    foundation of your throne;
  love and faithfulness go before you.
¹⁵Blessed are those who have learned to
    acclaim you,
  who walk in the light of your presence,
    LORD.
¹⁶They rejoice in your name all day long;
  they celebrate your righteousness.
¹⁷For you are their glory and strength,
  and by your favor you exalt our horn.*b*
¹⁸Indeed, our shield*c* belongs to the LORD,
  our king to the Holy One of Israel.

¹⁹Once you spoke in a vision,
  to your faithful people you said:

"I have bestowed strength on a warrior;
  I have raised up a young man from
    among the people.
²⁰I have found David my servant;
  with my sacred oil I have anointed him.
²¹My hand will sustain him;
  surely my arm will strengthen him.
²²The enemy will not get the better of him;
  the wicked will not oppress him.
²³I will crush his foes before him
  and strike down his adversaries.
²⁴My faithful love will be with him,
  and through my name his horn*d* will
    be exalted.
²⁵I will set his hand over the sea,
  his right hand over the rivers.
²⁶He will call out to me, 'You are my Father,
  my God, the Rock my Savior.'
²⁷And I will appoint him to be my firstborn,
  the most exalted of the kings of the
    earth.
²⁸I will maintain my love to him forever,
  and my covenant with him will
    never fail.
²⁹I will establish his line forever,
  his throne as long as the heavens
    endure.

³⁰"If his sons forsake my law
  and do not follow my statutes,
³¹if they violate my decrees
  and fail to keep my commands,
³²I will punish their sin with the rod,
  their iniquity with flogging;
³³but I will not take my love from him,
  nor will I ever betray my faithfulness.
³⁴I will not violate my covenant
  or alter what my lips have uttered.
³⁵Once for all, I have sworn by my
    holiness—
  and I will not lie to David—
³⁶that his line will continue forever
  and his throne endure before me like
    the sun;
³⁷it will be established forever like the
    moon,
  the faithful witness in the sky."

³⁸But you have rejected, you have
    spurned,
  you have been very angry with your
    anointed one.

---

³⁹ You have renounced the covenant with
      your servant
  and have defiled his crown in the
      dust.
⁴⁰ You have broken through all his walls
  and reduced his strongholds to ruins.
⁴¹ All who pass by have plundered him;
  he has become the scorn of his
      neighbors.
⁴² You have exalted the right hand of his foes;
  you have made all his enemies rejoice.
⁴³ Indeed, you have turned back the edge of
      his sword
  and have not supported him in battle.
⁴⁴ You have put an end to his splendor
  and cast his throne to the ground.
⁴⁵ You have cut short the days of his youth;
  you have covered him with a mantle
      of shame.

⁴⁶ How long, LORD? Will you hide yourself
      forever?
  How long will your wrath burn like fire?
⁴⁷ Remember how fleeting is my life.
  For what futility you have created all
      humanity!
⁴⁸ Who can live and not see death,
  or who can escape the power of the
      grave?
⁴⁹ Lord, where is your former great love,
  which in your faithfulness you swore
      to David?
⁵⁰ Remember, Lord, how your servant has^a
      been mocked,
  how I bear in my heart the taunts of all
      the nations,
⁵¹ the taunts with which your enemies,
      LORD, have mocked,
  with which they have mocked every
      step of your anointed one.

⁵² Praise be to the LORD forever!
  Amen and Amen.

BOOK IV

Psalms 90–106

Psalm 90

A prayer of Moses the man of God.

¹ Lord, you have been our dwelling place
  throughout all generations.

² Before the mountains were born
  or you brought forth the whole world,
  from everlasting to everlasting you
      are God.

³ You turn people back to dust,
  saying, "Return to dust, you mortals."
⁴ A thousand years in your sight
  are like a day that has just gone by,
  or like a watch in the night.
⁵ Yet you sweep people away in the sleep of
      death —
  they are like the new grass of the
      morning:
⁶ In the morning it springs up new,
  but by evening it is dry and withered.

⁷ We are consumed by your anger
  and terrified by your indignation.
⁸ You have set our iniquities before you,
  our secret sins in the light of your
      presence.
⁹ All our days pass away under your wrath;
  we finish our years with a moan.
¹⁰ Our days may come to seventy years,
  or eighty, if our strength endures;
  yet the best of them are but trouble and
      sorrow,
  for they quickly pass, and we fly away.
¹¹ If only we knew the power of your anger!
  Your wrath is as great as the fear that is
      your due.
¹² Teach us to number our days,
  that we may gain a heart of wisdom.

¹³ Relent, LORD! How long will it be?
  Have compassion on your servants.
¹⁴ Satisfy us in the morning with your
      unfailing love,
  that we may sing for joy and be glad all
      our days.
¹⁵ Make us glad for as many days as you
      have afflicted us,
  for as many years as we have seen
      trouble.
¹⁶ May your deeds be shown to your
      servants,
  your splendor to their children.

¹⁷ May the favor^b of the Lord our God rest
      on us;
  establish the work of our hands
      for us —
  yes, establish the work of our hands.

---

^a 50 Or *your servants have*   ^b 17 Or *beauty*

Psalm 91

[1] Whoever dwells in the shelter of the
     Most High
   will rest in the shadow of the
     Almighty.[a]
[2] I will say of the LORD, "He is my refuge
     and my fortress,
   my God, in whom I trust."

[3] Surely he will save you
   from the fowler's snare
   and from the deadly pestilence.
[4] He will cover you with his feathers,
   and under his wings you will find
     refuge;
   his faithfulness will be your shield and
     rampart.
[5] You will not fear the terror of night,
   nor the arrow that flies by day,
[6] nor the pestilence that stalks in the
     darkness,
   nor the plague that destroys at midday.
[7] A thousand may fall at your side,
   ten thousand at your right hand,
   but it will not come near you.
[8] You will only observe with your eyes
   and see the punishment of the wicked.

[9] If you say, "The LORD is my refuge,"
   and you make the Most High your
     dwelling,
[10] no harm will overtake you,
   no disaster will come near your tent.
[11] For he will command his angels
     concerning you
   to guard you in all your ways;
[12] they will lift you up in their hands,
   so that you will not strike your foot
     against a stone.
[13] You will tread on the lion and the cobra;
   you will trample the great lion and the
     serpent.

[14] "Because he[b] loves me," says the LORD, "I
     will rescue him;
   I will protect him, for he acknowledges
     my name.
[15] He will call on me, and I will answer him;
   I will be with him in trouble,
   I will deliver him and honor him.
[16] With long life I will satisfy him
   and show him my salvation."

Psalm 92[c]

A psalm. A song. For the Sabbath day.

[1] It is good to praise the LORD
   and make music to your name,
     O Most High,
[2] proclaiming your love in the morning
   and your faithfulness at night,
[3] to the music of the ten-stringed lyre
   and the melody of the harp.

[4] For you make me glad by your deeds,
     LORD;
   I sing for joy at what your hands have
     done.
[5] How great are your works, LORD,
   how profound your thoughts!
[6] Senseless people do not know,
   fools do not understand,
[7] that though the wicked spring up like
     grass
   and all evildoers flourish,
   they will be destroyed forever.

[8] But you, LORD, are forever exalted.

[9] For surely your enemies, LORD,
   surely your enemies will perish;
   all evildoers will be scattered.
[10] You have exalted my horn[d] like that of
     a wild ox;
   fine oils have been poured on me.
[11] My eyes have seen the defeat of my
     adversaries;
   my ears have heard the rout of my
     wicked foes.

[12] The righteous will flourish like a palm
     tree,
   they will grow like a cedar of Lebanon;
[13] planted in the house of the LORD,
   they will flourish in the courts of
     our God.
[14] They will still bear fruit in old age,
   they will stay fresh and green,
[15] proclaiming, "The LORD is upright;
   he is my Rock, and there is no
     wickedness in him."

Psalm 93

[1] The LORD reigns, he is robed in majesty;
   the LORD is robed in majesty and
     armed with strength;

---

[a] *1* Hebrew *Shaddai*   [b] *14* That is, probably the king   [c] In Hebrew texts 92:1-15 is numbered 92:2-16.
[d] *10 Horn* here symbolizes strength.

In Case of an Emergency

By Kathy Guzzo

READ: Psalm 91

Have you ever been caught in a terrible storm, the kind that drenched you in just seconds or one in which the wind was so fierce that you struggled to remain upright? Remember the physical chill, possibly the fear, and the desire to escape to someplace safe and dry? When storms break out, we need shelter.

How appropriate that Psalm 91, which lists the ways God will protect those who love him, begins by describing God as a place of refuge. Notice the numerals of this psalm: 9-1-1. What are we to do in case of an emergency? Dial 9-1-1.

Just as dialing 9-1-1 is how we get emergency responders to help us, so reading and meditating on Psalm 91:1 is how we get help when we're in spiritual distress and need to be reminded of and accept our Father's protection. His response to our request for shelter is instantaneous. Without him we remain exposed, but dwelling in his shelter brings calm and hope in the midst of any storm.

One storm we faced as a nation occurred on September 11, 2001, the day the enemy attacked and terror reigned. However, our country also cried out to God on that day. Strangers prayed with strangers, and Congress sang "God Bless America" from the Capitol steps that evening. In the immediate weeks that followed, the phrase "Pray for Our Nation" was on restaurant signs and billboards across the country. Churches filled, leaders encouraged prayer for our troops, and we became united as a nation. During that time, the United States of America was in extreme agony. Needing help, the people cried out to the God of Psalm 91 for shelter and protection.

Psalm 91 says specifically that God protects his people because of their love for him (see verse 14). God may not remove all the things that are creating the storms, but he will protect us in the midst of them and in the aftermath. For this reason, we don't have to run from the storms. Instead, we run to our Shelter, knowing that he will bring us through each one of them.

If deployments, finances, relationships, health issues, depression or other elements are creating storms in your life, I encourage you to focus on loving the Lord for who he is, for what he has done and what he will do in your life. Then you will sense his closeness and know you are resting in his shadow.

Whoever dwells in the shelter of the Most High will rest in the shadow of the Almighty.

PSALM 91:1

DEBRIEF

- Where do I turn for shelter in life's storms or when I feel attacked?
- What practical step can I take that will help me rely on God's protection in a crisis?

REPORT

Lord, when I'm in the eye of one of life's storms, please help me to run straight to you. Give me the strength to love and trust you enough to make you my only refuge and shelter. Amen.

---

indeed, the world is established, firm
and secure.
² Your throne was established long ago;
you are from all eternity.

³ The seas have lifted up, LORD,
the seas have lifted up their voice;
the seas have lifted up their pounding
waves.
⁴ Mightier than the thunder of the great
waters,
mightier than the breakers of the
sea —
the LORD on high is mighty.

⁵ Your statutes, LORD, stand firm;
holiness adorns your house
for endless days.

Psalm 94

¹ The LORD is a God who avenges.
O God who avenges, shine forth.
² Rise up, Judge of the earth;
pay back to the proud what they
deserve.
³ How long, LORD, will the wicked,
how long will the wicked be jubilant?

⁴ They pour out arrogant words;
all the evildoers are full of boasting.
⁵ They crush your people, LORD;
they oppress your inheritance.
⁶ They slay the widow and the foreigner;
they murder the fatherless.
⁷ They say, "The LORD does not see;
the God of Jacob takes no notice."

⁸ Take notice, you senseless ones among
the people;
you fools, when will you become wise?
⁹ Does he who fashioned the ear not hear?
Does he who formed the eye not see?
¹⁰ Does he who disciplines nations not
punish?
Does he who teaches mankind lack
knowledge?
¹¹ The LORD knows all human plans;
he knows that they are futile.

¹² Blessed is the one you discipline, LORD,
the one you teach from your law;
¹³ you grant them relief from days of
trouble,
till a pit is dug for the wicked.
¹⁴ For the LORD will not reject his people;
he will never forsake his inheritance.

¹⁵ Judgment will again be founded on
righteousness,
and all the upright in heart will
follow it.

¹⁶ Who will rise up for me against the
wicked?
Who will take a stand for me against
evildoers?
¹⁷ Unless the LORD had given me help,
I would soon have dwelt in the silence
of death.
¹⁸ When I said, "My foot is slipping,"
your unfailing love, LORD,
supported me.
¹⁹ When anxiety was great within me,
your consolation brought me joy.

²⁰ Can a corrupt throne be allied with
you —
a throne that brings on misery by its
decrees?
²¹ The wicked band together against the
righteous
and condemn the innocent to death.
²² But the LORD has become my fortress,
and my God the rock in whom I take
refuge.
²³ He will repay them for their sins
and destroy them for their
wickedness;
the LORD our God will destroy them.

Psalm 95

¹ Come, let us sing for joy to the LORD;
let us shout aloud to the Rock of our
salvation.
² Let us come before him with
thanksgiving
and extol him with music and song.

³ For the LORD is the great God,
the great King above all gods.
⁴ In his hand are the depths of the earth,
and the mountain peaks belong to
him.
⁵ The sea is his, for he made it,
and his hands formed the dry land.

⁶ Come, let us bow down in worship,
let us kneel before the LORD our
Maker;
⁷ for he is our God
and we are the people of his pasture,
the flock under his care.

Finally Out of Control

By Rosie Williams

READ: Psalm 94:17–19

Scripture often refers to having joy and trusting God even when life is hard (see Psalm 94:19). Although I had been a Christian for years, my faith and joy were put to the test like never before when my husband headed off to war at age 19. He had often talked about being in Christian ministry, but now I watched helplessly as he headed off — not for the mission field but for the battlefield! Anxiety came crashing over me, which led to fear, which then led to an overwhelming sense of helplessness. The plans we had made were put on hold, and I could do nothing to stop the chain of events that were about to turn our lives upside down.

My first coping method was to withdraw and suffer alone. As I watched the news and pondered the many what-ifs, my anxiety grew. My prayers became a desperate plea! It's natural to feel that we must hang on to control or our worst fears will be realized. The problem is that hanging on to control induces anxiety when we realize we really don't have much control at all.

A military wife often feels a loss of control when her husband leaves home, especially if he is going to be deployed to a war zone. Psalm 94:17–19 reminds us that the love of the Lord provides support and joy in the midst of anxious circumstances.

The phrase "When I *said,* 'My foot is slipping'" (verse 18, emphasis added) implies the need to verbalize our need for support. In her book, *God Strong,* Sara Horn shares a lesson about trusting God when her husband was deployed to Iraq: "That night, I learned what it means to leave my burdens at the feet of Jesus. And that if the worst were to happen — whether my husband were to die in combat far away or in a car accident close to home — God is still in control. And he would walk with me through the hurts and the pain. He would be strong for me in my weakness, and he would give me enough of his grace and love to keep going."

Coping with deployment anxiety may involve seeking counseling, sharing with a trusted friend or finding a Christian support group for military wives. It's important for you to find a safe environment to share your feelings and be reminded of God's tender care. Allow yourself to be supported by God's love, and let him replace your anxiety with his joy.

When I said, "My foot is slipping," your unfailing love, LORD, supported me. When anxiety was great within me, your consolation brought me joy.
PSALM 94:18–19

DEBRIEF

- Have I released control over the lives of my husband and myself to God?
- Where can I find further support during the many trying times I will face in this life?

REPORT

Dear Lord, help me to persevere in times of trial. Help me to overcome anxiety, cast my cares on you and learn to trust you fully. Help me believe in my heart what I know in my mind to be true from your Word. In Jesus' name I pray. Amen.

for your next devotional reading, go to page 413

Today, if only you would hear his voice,
⁸ "Do not harden your hearts as you did at
      Meribah,ᵃ
   as you did that day at Massahᵇ in the
      wilderness,
⁹ where your ancestors tested me;
   they tried me, though they had seen
      what I did.
¹⁰ For forty years I was angry with that
      generation;
   I said, 'They are a people whose hearts
      go astray,
   and they have not known my ways.'
¹¹ So I declared on oath in my anger,
   'They shall never enter my rest.' "

Psalm 96

¹ Sing to the Lᴏʀᴅ a new song;
   sing to the Lᴏʀᴅ, all the earth.
² Sing to the Lᴏʀᴅ, praise his name;
   proclaim his salvation day after day.
³ Declare his glory among the nations,
   his marvelous deeds among all peoples.

⁴ For great is the Lᴏʀᴅ and most worthy of
      praise;
   he is to be feared above all gods.
⁵ For all the gods of the nations are idols,
   but the Lᴏʀᴅ made the heavens.
⁶ Splendor and majesty are before him;
   strength and glory are in his
      sanctuary.

⁷ Ascribe to the Lᴏʀᴅ, all you families of
      nations,
   ascribe to the Lᴏʀᴅ glory and strength.
⁸ Ascribe to the Lᴏʀᴅ the glory due his
      name;
   bring an offering and come into his
      courts.
⁹ Worship the Lᴏʀᴅ in the splendor of hisᶜ
      holiness;
   tremble before him, all the earth.
¹⁰ Say among the nations, "The Lᴏʀᴅ
      reigns."
   The world is firmly established, it
      cannot be moved;
   he will judge the peoples with equity.

¹¹ Let the heavens rejoice, let the earth
      be glad;
   let the sea resound, and all that is in it.

¹² Let the fields be jubilant, and everything
      in them;
   let all the trees of the forest sing for joy.
¹³ Let all creation rejoice before the Lᴏʀᴅ,
      for he comes,
   he comes to judge the earth.
   He will judge the world in righteousness
      and the peoples in his faithfulness.

Psalm 97

¹ The Lᴏʀᴅ reigns, let the earth be glad;
   let the distant shores rejoice.
² Clouds and thick darkness surround
      him;
   righteousness and justice are the
      foundation of his throne.
³ Fire goes before him
   and consumes his foes on every side.
⁴ His lightning lights up the world;
   the earth sees and trembles.
⁵ The mountains melt like wax before the
      Lᴏʀᴅ,
   before the Lord of all the earth.
⁶ The heavens proclaim his righteousness,
   and all peoples see his glory.

⁷ All who worship images are put to shame,
   those who boast in idols—
   worship him, all you gods!

⁸ Zion hears and rejoices
   and the villages of Judah are glad
   because of your judgments, Lᴏʀᴅ.
⁹ For you, Lᴏʀᴅ, are the Most High over all
      the earth;
   you are exalted far above all gods.
¹⁰ Let those who love the Lᴏʀᴅ hate evil,
   for he guards the lives of his faithful
      ones
   and delivers them from the hand of the
      wicked.
¹¹ Light shinesᵈ on the righteous
   and joy on the upright in heart.
¹² Rejoice in the Lᴏʀᴅ, you who are
      righteous,
   and praise his holy name.

Psalm 98

A psalm.

¹ Sing to the Lᴏʀᴅ a new song,
   for he has done marvelous things;

ᵃ 8 *Meribah* means *quarreling.*   ᵇ 8 *Massah* means *testing.*   ᶜ 9 Or *Lᴏʀᴅ with the splendor of*   ᵈ 11 One
Hebrew manuscript and ancient versions (see also 112:4); most Hebrew manuscripts *Light is sown*

his right hand and his holy arm
   have worked salvation for him.
[2] The Lord has made his salvation known
   and revealed his righteousness to the
     nations.
[3] He has remembered his love
   and his faithfulness to Israel;
all the ends of the earth have seen
   the salvation of our God.

[4] Shout for joy to the Lord, all the earth,
   burst into jubilant song with music;
[5] make music to the Lord with the harp,
   with the harp and the sound of
     singing,
[6] with trumpets and the blast of the ram's
     horn—
   shout for joy before the Lord, the King.

[7] Let the sea resound, and everything in it,
   the world, and all who live in it.
[8] Let the rivers clap their hands,
   let the mountains sing together for joy;
[9] let them sing before the Lord,
   for he comes to judge the earth.
He will judge the world in righteousness
   and the peoples with equity.

Psalm 99

[1] The Lord reigns,
   let the nations tremble;
he sits enthroned between the cherubim,
   let the earth shake.
[2] Great is the Lord in Zion;
   he is exalted over all the nations.
[3] Let them praise your great and awesome
     name—
   he is holy.

[4] The King is mighty, he loves justice—
   you have established equity;
in Jacob you have done
   what is just and right.
[5] Exalt the Lord our God
   and worship at his footstool;
   he is holy.

[6] Moses and Aaron were among his
     priests,
   Samuel was among those who called
     on his name;
they called on the Lord
   and he answered them.
[7] He spoke to them from the pillar of cloud;

they kept his statutes and the decrees
   he gave them.
[8] Lord our God,
   you answered them;
you were to Israel a forgiving God,
   though you punished their misdeeds.[a]
[9] Exalt the Lord our God
   and worship at his holy mountain,
   for the Lord our God is holy.

Psalm 100

A psalm. For giving grateful praise.

[1] Shout for joy to the Lord, all the earth.
[2]   Worship the Lord with gladness;
   come before him with joyful songs.
[3] Know that the Lord is God.
   It is he who made us, and we are his[b];
   we are his people, the sheep of his
     pasture.

[4] Enter his gates with thanksgiving
   and his courts with praise;
   give thanks to him and praise his
     name.
[5] For the Lord is good and his love endures
     forever;
   his faithfulness continues through all
     generations.

Psalm 101

Of David. A psalm.

[1] I will sing of your love and justice;
   to you, Lord, I will sing praise.
[2] I will be careful to lead a blameless life—
   when will you come to me?

I will conduct the affairs of my house
   with a blameless heart.
[3] I will not look with approval
   on anything that is vile.

I hate what faithless people do;
   I will have no part in it.
[4] The perverse of heart shall be far from me;
   I will have nothing to do with what
     is evil.

[5] Whoever slanders their neighbor in
     secret,
   I will put to silence;
whoever has haughty eyes and a proud
     heart,
   I will not tolerate.

---

[a] 8 Or *God, / an avenger of the wrongs done to them*   [b] 3 Or *and not we ourselves*

6 My eyes will be on the faithful in the
land,
  that they may dwell with me;
the one whose walk is blameless
  will minister to me.

7 No one who practices deceit
  will dwell in my house;
no one who speaks falsely
  will stand in my presence.

8 Every morning I will put to silence
  all the wicked in the land;
I will cut off every evildoer
  from the city of the LORD.

Psalm 102*ᵃ*

*A prayer of an afflicted person who has grown
weak and pours out a lament before the LORD.*

1 Hear my prayer, LORD;
  let my cry for help come to you.
2 Do not hide your face from me
  when I am in distress.
Turn your ear to me;
  when I call, answer me quickly.

3 For my days vanish like smoke;
  my bones burn like glowing embers.
4 My heart is blighted and withered like
    grass;
  I forget to eat my food.
5 In my distress I groan aloud
  and am reduced to skin and bones.
6 I am like a desert owl,
  like an owl among the ruins.
7 I lie awake; I have become
  like a bird alone on a roof.
8 All day long my enemies taunt me;
  those who rail against me use my
    name as a curse.
9 For I eat ashes as my food
  and mingle my drink with tears
10 because of your great wrath,
  for you have taken me up and thrown
    me aside.
11 My days are like the evening shadow;
  I wither away like grass.

12 But you, LORD, sit enthroned forever;
  your renown endures through all
    generations.
13 You will arise and have compassion
  on Zion,

for it is time to show favor to her;
  the appointed time has come.
14 For her stones are dear to your
    servants;
  her very dust moves them to pity.
15 The nations will fear the name of the
    LORD,
  all the kings of the earth will revere
    your glory.
16 For the LORD will rebuild Zion
  and appear in his glory.
17 He will respond to the prayer of the
    destitute;
  he will not despise their plea.

18 Let this be written for a future
    generation,
  that a people not yet created may
    praise the LORD:
19 "The LORD looked down from his
    sanctuary on high,
  from heaven he viewed the earth,
20 to hear the groans of the prisoners
  and release those condemned to
    death."
21 So the name of the LORD will be declared
    in Zion
  and his praise in Jerusalem
22 when the peoples and the kingdoms
  assemble to worship the LORD.

23 In the course of my life*ᵇ* he broke my
    strength;
  he cut short my days.
24 So I said:
"Do not take me away, my God, in the
    midst of my days;
  your years go on through all
    generations.
25 In the beginning you laid the foundations
    of the earth,
  and the heavens are the work of your
    hands.
26 They will perish, but you remain;
  they will all wear out like a garment.
Like clothing you will change them
  and they will be discarded.
27 But you remain the same,
  and your years will never end.
28 The children of your servants will live in
    your presence;
  their descendants will be established
    before you."

ᵃ In Hebrew texts 102:1-28 is numbered 102:2-29.   *ᵇ* 23 Or *By his power*

Psalm 103

Of David.

¹ Praise the LORD, my soul;
   all my inmost being, praise his holy
      name.
² Praise the LORD, my soul,
   and forget not all his benefits —
³ who forgives all your sins
   and heals all your diseases,
⁴ who redeems your life from the pit
   and crowns you with love and
      compassion,
⁵ who satisfies your desires with good
      things
   so that your youth is renewed like the
      eagle's.

⁶ The LORD works righteousness
   and justice for all the oppressed.

⁷ He made known his ways to Moses,
   his deeds to the people of Israel:
⁸ The LORD is compassionate and gracious,
   slow to anger, abounding in love.
⁹ He will not always accuse,
   nor will he harbor his anger forever;
¹⁰ he does not treat us as our sins deserve
   or repay us according to our iniquities.
¹¹ For as high as the heavens are above
      the earth,
   so great is his love for those who fear
      him;
¹² as far as the east is from the west,
   so far has he removed our
      transgressions from us.

¹³ As a father has compassion on his
      children,
   so the LORD has compassion on those
      who fear him;
¹⁴ for he knows how we are formed,
   he remembers that we are dust.
¹⁵ The life of mortals is like grass,
   they flourish like a flower of the field;
¹⁶ the wind blows over it and it is gone,
   and its place remembers it no more.
¹⁷ But from everlasting to everlasting
   the LORD's love is with those who fear
      him,
   and his righteousness with their
      children's children —
¹⁸ with those who keep his covenant
   and remember to obey his precepts.

¹⁹ The LORD has established his throne
      in heaven,
   and his kingdom rules over all.

²⁰ Praise the LORD, you his angels,
   you mighty ones who do his bidding,
   who obey his word.
²¹ Praise the LORD, all his heavenly hosts,
   you his servants who do his will.
²² Praise the LORD, all his works
   everywhere in his dominion.

Praise the LORD, my soul.

Psalm 104

¹ Praise the LORD, my soul.

LORD my God, you are very great;
   you are clothed with splendor and
      majesty.

² The LORD wraps himself in light as with a
      garment;
   he stretches out the heavens like a tent
³   and lays the beams of his upper
         chambers on their waters.
   He makes the clouds his chariot
   and rides on the wings of the wind.
⁴ He makes winds his messengers,ᵃ
   flames of fire his servants.

⁵ He set the earth on its foundations;
   it can never be moved.
⁶ You covered it with the watery depths as
      with a garment;
   the waters stood above the mountains.
⁷ But at your rebuke the waters fled,
   at the sound of your thunder they took
      to flight;
⁸ they flowed over the mountains,
   they went down into the valleys,
   to the place you assigned for them.
⁹ You set a boundary they cannot cross;
   never again will they cover the earth.

¹⁰ He makes springs pour water into the
      ravines;
   it flows between the mountains.
¹¹ They give water to all the beasts of the
      field;
   the wild donkeys quench their thirst.
¹² The birds of the sky nest by the waters;
   they sing among the branches.
¹³ He waters the mountains from his upper
      chambers;

ᵃ 4 Or *angels*

the land is satisfied by the fruit of
his work.
[14] He makes grass grow for the cattle,
and plants for people to cultivate —
bringing forth food from the earth:
[15] wine that gladdens human hearts,
oil to make their faces shine,
and bread that sustains their hearts.
[16] The trees of the LORD are well watered,
the cedars of Lebanon that he planted.
[17] There the birds make their nests;
the stork has its home in the junipers.
[18] The high mountains belong to the wild
goats;
the crags are a refuge for the hyrax.

[19] He made the moon to mark the seasons,
and the sun knows when to go down.
[20] You bring darkness, it becomes night,
and all the beasts of the forest prowl.
[21] The lions roar for their prey
and seek their food from God.
[22] The sun rises, and they steal away;
they return and lie down in their dens.
[23] Then people go out to their work,
to their labor until evening.

[24] How many are your works, LORD!
In wisdom you made them all;
the earth is full of your creatures.
[25] There is the sea, vast and spacious,
teeming with creatures beyond
number —
living things both large and small.
[26] There the ships go to and fro,
and Leviathan, which you formed to
frolic there.

[27] All creatures look to you
to give them their food at the proper
time.
[28] When you give it to them,
they gather it up;
when you open your hand,
they are satisfied with good things.
[29] When you hide your face,
they are terrified;
when you take away their breath,
they die and return to the dust.
[30] When you send your Spirit,
they are created,
and you renew the face of the ground.

[31] May the glory of the LORD endure forever;
may the LORD rejoice in his works —

[32] he who looks at the earth, and it trembles,
who touches the mountains, and they
smoke.

[33] I will sing to the LORD all my life;
I will sing praise to my God as long as
I live.
[34] May my meditation be pleasing to him,
as I rejoice in the LORD.
[35] But may sinners vanish from the earth
and the wicked be no more.

Praise the LORD, my soul.

Praise the LORD.[a]

Psalm 105

[1] Give praise to the LORD, proclaim his
name;
make known among the nations what
he has done.
[2] Sing to him, sing praise to him;
tell of all his wonderful acts.
[3] Glory in his holy name;
let the hearts of those who seek the
LORD rejoice.
[4] Look to the LORD and his strength;
seek his face always.

[5] Remember the wonders he has done,
his miracles, and the judgments he
pronounced,
[6] you his servants, the descendants of
Abraham,
his chosen ones, the children of Jacob.
[7] He is the LORD our God;
his judgments are in all the earth.

[8] He remembers his covenant forever,
the promise he made, for a thousand
generations,
[9] the covenant he made with Abraham,
the oath he swore to Isaac.
[10] He confirmed it to Jacob as a decree,
to Israel as an everlasting covenant:
[11] "To you I will give the land of Canaan
as the portion you will inherit."

[12] When they were but few in number,
few indeed, and strangers in it,
[13] they wandered from nation to nation,
from one kingdom to another.
[14] He allowed no one to oppress them;
for their sake he rebuked kings:
[15] "Do not touch my anointed ones;
do my prophets no harm."

---

[a] 35 Hebrew *Hallelu Yah*; in the Septuagint this line stands at the beginning of Psalm 105.

＾〜22

22

16 He called down famine on the land
  and destroyed all their supplies
    of food;
17 and he sent a man before them—
  Joseph, sold as a slave.
18 They bruised his feet with shackles,
  his neck was put in irons,
19 till what he foretold came to pass,
  till the word of the LORD proved
    him true.
20 The king sent and released him,
  the ruler of peoples set him free.
21 He made him master of his household,
  ruler over all he possessed,
22 to instruct his princes as he pleased
  and teach his elders wisdom.

23 Then Israel entered Egypt;
  Jacob resided as a foreigner in the land
    of Ham.
24 The LORD made his people very fruitful;
  he made them too numerous for their
    foes,
25 whose hearts he turned to hate his
    people,
  to conspire against his servants.
26 He sent Moses his servant,
  and Aaron, whom he had chosen.
27 They performed his signs among them,
  his wonders in the land of Ham.
28 He sent darkness and made the land
    dark—
  for had they not rebelled against his
    words?
29 He turned their waters into blood,
  causing their fish to die.
30 Their land teemed with frogs,
  which went up into the bedrooms of
    their rulers.
31 He spoke, and there came swarms of flies,
  and gnats throughout their country.
32 He turned their rain into hail,
  with lightning throughout their land;
33 he struck down their vines and fig trees
  and shattered the trees of their
    country.
34 He spoke, and the locusts came,
  grasshoppers without number;
35 they ate up every green thing in their land,
  ate up the produce of their soil.
36 Then he struck down all the firstborn in
    their land,
  the firstfruits of all their manhood.

37 He brought out Israel, laden with silver
    and gold,
  and from among their tribes no one
    faltered.
38 Egypt was glad when they left,
  because dread of Israel had fallen
    on them.
39 He spread out a cloud as a covering,
  and a fire to give light at night.
40 They asked, and he brought them quail;
  he fed them well with the bread of
    heaven.
41 He opened the rock, and water gushed
    out;
  it flowed like a river in the desert.
42 For he remembered his holy promise
  given to his servant Abraham.
43 He brought out his people with rejoicing,
  his chosen ones with shouts of joy;
44 he gave them the lands of the nations,
  and they fell heir to what others had
    toiled for—
45 that they might keep his precepts
  and observe his laws.

  Praise the LORD.[a]

Psalm 106

1 Praise the LORD.[b]

  Give thanks to the LORD, for he is good;
  his love endures forever.

2 Who can proclaim the mighty acts of
    the LORD
  or fully declare his praise?
3 Blessed are those who act justly,
  who always do what is right.

4 Remember me, LORD, when you show
    favor to your people,
  come to my aid when you save them,
5 that I may enjoy the prosperity of your
    chosen ones,
  that I may share in the joy of your
    nation
  and join your inheritance in giving
    praise.

6 We have sinned, even as our ancestors
    did;
  we have done wrong and acted
    wickedly.
7 When our ancestors were in Egypt,

they gave no thought to your
    miracles;
they did not remember your many
    kindnesses,
and they rebelled by the sea, the
    Red Sea.*a*

[8] Yet he saved them for his name's sake,
    to make his mighty power known.
[9] He rebuked the Red Sea, and it dried up;
    he led them through the depths as
        through a desert.
[10] He saved them from the hand of the foe;
    from the hand of the enemy he
        redeemed them.
[11] The waters covered their adversaries;
    not one of them survived.
[12] Then they believed his promises
    and sang his praise.

[13] But they soon forgot what he had done
    and did not wait for his plan to unfold.
[14] In the desert they gave in to their craving;
    in the wilderness they put God to
        the test.
[15] So he gave them what they asked for,
    but sent a wasting disease among them.

[16] In the camp they grew envious of Moses
    and of Aaron, who was consecrated to
        the LORD.
[17] The earth opened up and swallowed
        Dathan;
    it buried the company of Abiram.
[18] Fire blazed among their followers;
    a flame consumed the wicked.
[19] At Horeb they made a calf
    and worshiped an idol cast from metal.
[20] They exchanged their glorious God
    for an image of a bull, which eats grass.
[21] They forgot the God who saved them,
    who had done great things in Egypt,
[22] miracles in the land of Ham
    and awesome deeds by the Red Sea.
[23] So he said he would destroy them —
    had not Moses, his chosen one,
    stood in the breach before him
    to keep his wrath from destroying
        them.

[24] Then they despised the pleasant land;
    they did not believe his promise.
[25] They grumbled in their tents
    and did not obey the LORD.
[26] So he swore to them with uplifted hand

that he would make them fall in the
    wilderness,
[27] make their descendants fall among the
    nations
    and scatter them throughout the lands.

[28] They yoked themselves to the Baal of Peor
    and ate sacrifices offered to lifeless
        gods;
[29] they aroused the LORD's anger by their
    wicked deeds,
    and a plague broke out among them.
[30] But Phinehas stood up and intervened,
    and the plague was checked.
[31] This was credited to him as
        righteousness
    for endless generations to come.
[32] By the waters of Meribah they angered
    the LORD,
    and trouble came to Moses because
        of them;
[33] for they rebelled against the Spirit of God,
    and rash words came from Moses' lips.*b*

[34] They did not destroy the peoples
    as the LORD had commanded them,
[35] but they mingled with the nations
    and adopted their customs.
[36] They worshiped their idols,
    which became a snare to them.
[37] They sacrificed their sons
    and their daughters to false gods.
[38] They shed innocent blood,
    the blood of their sons and daughters,
    whom they sacrificed to the idols of
        Canaan,
    and the land was desecrated by their
        blood.
[39] They defiled themselves by what
        they did;
    by their deeds they prostituted
        themselves.

[40] Therefore the LORD was angry with his
    people
    and abhorred his inheritance.
[41] He gave them into the hands of the
    nations,
    and their foes ruled over them.
[42] Their enemies oppressed them
    and subjected them to their power.
[43] Many times he delivered them,
    but they were bent on rebellion
    and they wasted away in their sin.

---

a 7 Or *the Sea of Reeds*; also in verses 9 and 22   *b* 33 Or *against his spirit, / and rash words came from his lips*

⁴⁴ Yet he took note of their distress
   when he heard their cry;
⁴⁵ for their sake he remembered his
   covenant
   and out of his great love he relented.
⁴⁶ He caused all who held them captive
   to show them mercy.

⁴⁷ Save us, LORD our God,
   and gather us from the nations,
   that we may give thanks to your holy name
   and glory in your praise.

⁴⁸ Praise be to the LORD, the God of Israel,
   from everlasting to everlasting.

Let all the people say, "Amen!"

Praise the LORD.

BOOK V

Psalms 107 – 150

Psalm 107

¹ Give thanks to the LORD, for he is good;
   his love endures forever.

² Let the redeemed of the LORD tell their
   story—
   those he redeemed from the hand of
   the foe,
³ those he gathered from the lands,
   from east and west, from north and
   south.ᵃ

⁴ Some wandered in desert wastelands,
   finding no way to a city where they
   could settle.
⁵ They were hungry and thirsty,
   and their lives ebbed away.
⁶ Then they cried out to the LORD in their
   trouble,
   and he delivered them from their
   distress.
⁷ He led them by a straight way
   to a city where they could settle.
⁸ Let them give thanks to the LORD for his
   unfailing love
   and his wonderful deeds for mankind,
⁹ for he satisfies the thirsty
   and fills the hungry with good things.

¹⁰ Some sat in darkness, in utter darkness,
   prisoners suffering in iron chains,

¹¹ because they rebelled against God's
   commands
   and despised the plans of the Most
   High.
¹² So he subjected them to bitter labor;
   they stumbled, and there was no one
   to help.
¹³ Then they cried to the LORD in their
   trouble,
   and he saved them from their distress.
¹⁴ He brought them out of darkness, the
   utter darkness,
   and broke away their chains.
¹⁵ Let them give thanks to the LORD for his
   unfailing love
   and his wonderful deeds for mankind,
¹⁶ for he breaks down gates of bronze
   and cuts through bars of iron.

¹⁷ Some became fools through their
   rebellious ways
   and suffered affliction because of their
   iniquities.
¹⁸ They loathed all food
   and drew near the gates of death.
¹⁹ Then they cried to the LORD in their
   trouble,
   and he saved them from their distress.
²⁰ He sent out his word and healed them;
   he rescued them from the grave.
²¹ Let them give thanks to the LORD for his
   unfailing love
   and his wonderful deeds for mankind.
²² Let them sacrifice thank offerings
   and tell of his works with songs of joy.

²³ Some went out on the sea in ships;
   they were merchants on the mighty
   waters.
²⁴ They saw the works of the LORD,
   his wonderful deeds in the deep.
²⁵ For he spoke and stirred up a tempest
   that lifted high the waves.
²⁶ They mounted up to the heavens and
   went down to the depths;
   in their peril their courage melted
   away.
²⁷ They reeled and staggered like
   drunkards;
   they were at their wits' end.
²⁸ Then they cried out to the LORD in their
   trouble,
   and he brought them out of their
   distress.

ᵃ 3 Hebrew *north and the sea*

²⁹ He stilled the storm to a whisper;
     the waves of the sea*a* were hushed.
³⁰ They were glad when it grew calm,
     and he guided them to their desired
         haven.
³¹ Let them give thanks to the LORD for his
         unfailing love
     and his wonderful deeds for mankind.
³² Let them exalt him in the assembly of the
         people
     and praise him in the council of the
         elders.

³³ He turned rivers into a desert,
     flowing springs into thirsty ground,
³⁴ and fruitful land into a salt waste,
     because of the wickedness of those
         who lived there.
³⁵ He turned the desert into pools of water
     and the parched ground into flowing
         springs;
³⁶ there he brought the hungry to live,
     and they founded a city where they
         could settle.
³⁷ They sowed fields and planted vineyards
     that yielded a fruitful harvest;
³⁸ he blessed them, and their numbers
         greatly increased,
     and he did not let their herds diminish.

³⁹ Then their numbers decreased, and they
         were humbled
     by oppression, calamity and sorrow;
⁴⁰ he who pours contempt on nobles
     made them wander in a trackless
         waste.
⁴¹ But he lifted the needy out of their
         affliction
     and increased their families like
         flocks.
⁴² The upright see and rejoice,
     but all the wicked shut their mouths.

⁴³ Let the one who is wise heed these things
     and ponder the loving deeds of the
         LORD.

Psalm 108*b*

A song. A psalm of David.

¹ My heart, O God, is steadfast;
     I will sing and make music with all my
         soul.
² Awake, harp and lyre!

I will awaken the dawn.
³ I will praise you, LORD, among the
         nations;
     I will sing of you among the peoples.
⁴ For great is your love, higher than the
         heavens;
     your faithfulness reaches to the skies.
⁵ Be exalted, O God, above the heavens;
     let your glory be over all the earth.

⁶ Save us and help us with your right hand,
     that those you love may be delivered.
⁷ God has spoken from his sanctuary:
     "In triumph I will parcel out Shechem
     and measure off the Valley of Sukkoth.
⁸ Gilead is mine, Manasseh is mine;
     Ephraim is my helmet,
     Judah is my scepter.
⁹ Moab is my washbasin,
     on Edom I toss my sandal;
     over Philistia I shout in triumph."

¹⁰ Who will bring me to the fortified city?
     Who will lead me to Edom?
¹¹ Is it not you, God, you who have
         rejected us
     and no longer go out with our armies?
¹² Give us aid against the enemy,
     for human help is worthless.
¹³ With God we will gain the victory,
     and he will trample down our
         enemies.

Psalm 109

*For the director of music.
Of David. A psalm.*

¹ My God, whom I praise,
     do not remain silent,
² for people who are wicked and deceitful
     have opened their mouths against me;
     they have spoken against me with
         lying tongues.
³ With words of hatred they surround me;
     they attack me without cause.
⁴ In return for my friendship they
         accuse me,
     but I am a man of prayer.
⁵ They repay me evil for good,
     and hatred for my friendship.

⁶ Appoint someone evil to oppose my
         enemy;
     let an accuser stand at his right hand.

---

a 29 Dead Sea Scrolls; Masoretic Text / *their waves*   *b* In Hebrew texts 108:1-13 is numbered 108:2-14.

[7] When he is tried, let him be found guilty,
    and may his prayers condemn him.
[8] May his days be few;
    may another take his place of
        leadership.
[9] May his children be fatherless
    and his wife a widow.
[10] May his children be wandering beggars;
    may they be driven[a] from their ruined
        homes.
[11] May a creditor seize all he has;
    may strangers plunder the fruits of
        his labor.
[12] May no one extend kindness to him
    or take pity on his fatherless children.
[13] May his descendants be cut off,
    their names blotted out from the next
        generation.
[14] May the iniquity of his fathers be
        remembered before the LORD;
    may the sin of his mother never be
        blotted out.
[15] May their sins always remain before the
        LORD,
    that he may blot out their name from
        the earth.

[16] For he never thought of doing a kindness,
    but hounded to death the poor
    and the needy and the brokenhearted.
[17] He loved to pronounce a curse —
    may it come back on him.
    He found no pleasure in blessing —
    may it be far from him.
[18] He wore cursing as his garment;
    it entered into his body like water,
    into his bones like oil.
[19] May it be like a cloak wrapped about him,
    like a belt tied forever around him.
[20] May this be the LORD's payment to my
        accusers,
    to those who speak evil of me.

[21] But you, Sovereign LORD,
    help me for your name's sake;
    out of the goodness of your love,
        deliver me.
[22] For I am poor and needy,
    and my heart is wounded within me.
[23] I fade away like an evening shadow;
    I am shaken off like a locust.
[24] My knees give way from fasting;
    my body is thin and gaunt.

[25] I am an object of scorn to my accusers;
    when they see me, they shake their
        heads.

[26] Help me, LORD my God;
    save me according to your unfailing
        love.
[27] Let them know that it is your hand,
    that you, LORD, have done it.
[28] While they curse, may you bless;
    may those who attack me be put to
        shame,
    but may your servant rejoice.
[29] May my accusers be clothed with
        disgrace
    and wrapped in shame as in a cloak.

[30] With my mouth I will greatly extol the
        LORD;
    in the great throng of worshipers I will
        praise him.
[31] For he stands at the right hand of the
        needy,
    to save their lives from those who
        would condemn them.

Psalm 110

Of David. A psalm.

[1] The LORD says to my lord:[b]

"Sit at my right hand
    until I make your enemies
    a footstool for your feet."

[2] The LORD will extend your mighty
        scepter from Zion, saying,
    "Rule in the midst of your enemies!"
[3] Your troops will be willing
    on your day of battle.
    Arrayed in holy splendor,
    your young men will come to you
    like dew from the morning's womb.[c]

[4] The LORD has sworn
    and will not change his mind:
"You are a priest forever,
    in the order of Melchizedek."

[5] The Lord is at your right hand[d];
    he will crush kings on the day of his
        wrath.
[6] He will judge the nations, heaping up
        the dead
    and crushing the rulers of the whole
        earth.

---

[a] 10 Septuagint; Hebrew *sought*   [b] 1 Or *Lord*   [c] 3 The meaning of the Hebrew for this sentence is uncertain.   [d] 5 Or *My lord is at your right hand,* LORD

[7] He will drink from a brook along the way,[a]
and so he will lift his head high.

Psalm 111[b]

[1] Praise the LORD.[c]

I will extol the LORD with all my heart
in the council of the upright and in the
assembly.

[2] Great are the works of the LORD;
they are pondered by all who delight
in them.
[3] Glorious and majestic are his deeds,
and his righteousness endures forever.
[4] He has caused his wonders to be
remembered;
the LORD is gracious and
compassionate.
[5] He provides food for those who fear him;
he remembers his covenant forever.

[6] He has shown his people the power of
his works,
giving them the lands of other nations.
[7] The works of his hands are faithful and
just;
all his precepts are trustworthy.
[8] They are established for ever and ever,
enacted in faithfulness and
uprightness.
[9] He provided redemption for his people;
he ordained his covenant forever —
holy and awesome is his name.

[10] The fear of the LORD is the beginning of
wisdom;
all who follow his precepts have good
understanding.
To him belongs eternal praise.

Psalm 112[b]

[1] Praise the LORD.[c]

Blessed are those who fear the LORD,
who find great delight in his
commands.

[2] Their children will be mighty in the
land;
the generation of the upright will be
blessed.
[3] Wealth and riches are in their houses,

and their righteousness endures
forever.
[4] Even in darkness light dawns for the
upright,
for those who are gracious and
compassionate and righteous.
[5] Good will come to those who are
generous and lend freely,
who conduct their affairs with justice.

[6] Surely the righteous will never be
shaken;
they will be remembered forever.
[7] They will have no fear of bad news;
their hearts are steadfast, trusting in
the LORD.
[8] Their hearts are secure, they will have
no fear;
in the end they will look in triumph on
their foes.
[9] They have freely scattered their gifts to
the poor,
their righteousness endures forever;
their horn[d] will be lifted high in honor.

[10] The wicked will see and be vexed,
they will gnash their teeth and waste
away;
the longings of the wicked will come
to nothing.

Psalm 113

[1] Praise the LORD.[e]

Praise the LORD, you his servants;
praise the name of the LORD.
[2] Let the name of the LORD be praised,
both now and forevermore.
[3] From the rising of the sun to the place
where it sets,
the name of the LORD is to be praised.

[4] The LORD is exalted over all the nations,
his glory above the heavens.
[5] Who is like the LORD our God,
the One who sits enthroned on high,
[6] who stoops down to look
on the heavens and the earth?

[7] He raises the poor from the dust
and lifts the needy from the ash heap;
[8] he seats them with princes,
with the princes of his people.

---

[a] 7 The meaning of the Hebrew for this clause is uncertain.   [b] This psalm is an acrostic poem, the lines of
which begin with the successive letters of the Hebrew alphabet.   [c] 1 Hebrew *Hallelu Yah*   [d] 9 *Horn* here
symbolizes dignity.   [e] 1 Hebrew *Hallelu Yah*; also in verse 9

Conquering Fear

By Rosie Williams

READ: Psalm 112

If we're honest with ourselves, what military wife doesn't fear bad news at one time or another?

In 1969, I found myself glued to the television. It wasn't the comedic antics of Lucille Ball that had me tuning in; it was the evening news — and it was usually bad. With my fiancé, Steve, a world away in the jungles of Vietnam, I was always hungry for any information to let me know he was safe. The images of war and the uncertainty about the future made my heart anything but steadfast.

Modern-day technology has brought war even closer to our lives. Code words mentioned in an email or tense body language picked up over an Internet call can produce a gut-wrenching fear for military wives today. In the face of fear, I find myself comforted by Scripture. "Blessed are those who fear the LORD, who find great delight in his commands ... They will have no fear of bad news; their hearts are steadfast, trusting in the LORD" (Psalm 112:1,7).

Here are some ways to deal with fear:

Pray and ask God what it means to "fear" him rather than fear your circumstances. To fear God means to respect that God's ways are higher than our ways (see Isaiah 55:9). Fearing God also involves relinquishing control of our lives to him. This includes trusting him with the lives of those we love.

Read, study and meditate on Scripture. Ask God to show you verses to guide you through your current situation so that you can delight in him. This will lead you to an inner peace, a steadfast heart and an assurance that God is in control.

Replace fear with trust. In the book *A Woman Who Trusts God*, Debbie Alsdorf says, "If you are fearful today, remember that God loves you, and sit with the truth of his love. Why love? First John 4:18. 'There is no fear in love. But perfect love drives out fear, because fear has to do with punishment. The one who fears is not made perfect in love.'"

There will always be something in our circumstances — or in our imaginations — to cause us to fear. But notice the second part of Psalm 112:7. Our hearts will be steadfast if we place our trust in the Lord. Not in the government, not in top-grade weaponry, not even in our own abilities. Trust and dwell in God's love and sovereignty, and you will have no fear.

They will have no fear of bad news; their hearts are steadfast, trusting in the LORD.
PSALM 112:7

DEBRIEF
- Am I willing to replace fear with trust?
- Is my heart steadfast and have I given my heart to Jesus Christ?

REPORT
Lord, I give my heart fully to you. I also give my fear to you and ask that you give me a steadfast and trusting heart. Show me how to delight in your Word, and help me learn to trust you more. Thank you for your perfect love! In Jesus' name I pray. Amen.

---

for your next devotional reading, go to page 415

⁹ He settles the childless woman in her
home
as a happy mother of children.

Praise the LORD.

Psalm 114

¹ When Israel came out of Egypt,
Jacob from a people of foreign tongue,
² Judah became God's sanctuary,
Israel his dominion.

³ The sea looked and fled,
the Jordan turned back;
⁴ the mountains leaped like rams,
the hills like lambs.

⁵ Why was it, sea, that you fled?
Why, Jordan, did you turn back?
⁶ Why, mountains, did you leap like rams,
you hills, like lambs?

⁷ Tremble, earth, at the presence of the
Lord,
at the presence of the God of Jacob,
⁸ who turned the rock into a pool,
the hard rock into springs of water.

Psalm 115

¹ Not to us, LORD, not to us
but to your name be the glory,
because of your love and faithfulness.

² Why do the nations say,
"Where is their God?"
³ Our God is in heaven;
he does whatever pleases him.
⁴ But their idols are silver and gold,
made by human hands.
⁵ They have mouths, but cannot speak,
eyes, but cannot see.
⁶ They have ears, but cannot hear,
noses, but cannot smell.
⁷ They have hands, but cannot feel,
feet, but cannot walk,
nor can they utter a sound with their
throats.
⁸ Those who make them will be like them,
and so will all who trust in them.

⁹ All you Israelites, trust in the LORD —
he is their help and shield.
¹⁰ House of Aaron, trust in the LORD —
he is their help and shield.

¹¹ You who fear him, trust in the LORD —
he is their help and shield.

¹² The LORD remembers us and will
bless us:
He will bless his people Israel,
he will bless the house of Aaron,
¹³ he will bless those who fear the LORD —
small and great alike.

¹⁴ May the LORD cause you to flourish,
both you and your children.
¹⁵ May you be blessed by the LORD,
the Maker of heaven and earth.

¹⁶ The highest heavens belong to the LORD,
but the earth he has given to mankind.
¹⁷ It is not the dead who praise the LORD,
those who go down to the place of
silence;
¹⁸ it is we who extol the LORD,
both now and forevermore.

Praise the LORD.*ᵃ*

Psalm 116

¹ I love the LORD, for he heard my voice;
he heard my cry for mercy.
² Because he turned his ear to me,
I will call on him as long as I live.

³ The cords of death entangled me,
the anguish of the grave came over me;
I was overcome by distress and sorrow.
⁴ Then I called on the name of the LORD:
"LORD, save me!"

⁵ The LORD is gracious and righteous;
our God is full of compassion.
⁶ The LORD protects the unwary;
when I was brought low, he saved me.

⁷ Return to your rest, my soul,
for the LORD has been good to you.

⁸ For you, LORD, have delivered me from
death,
my eyes from tears,
my feet from stumbling,
⁹ that I may walk before the LORD
in the land of the living.

¹⁰ I trusted in the LORD when I said,
"I am greatly afflicted";
¹¹ in my alarm I said,
"Everyone is a liar."

ᵃ 18 Hebrew *Hallelu Yah*

"Praying for the Troops" Gets Personal

By Rosie Williams

READ: Psalm 116:1–2

Though Christians in America are often reminded to "pray for the troops," there is no better incentive to intercede on our knees and call on the Lord (see Psalm 116:2) than when those troops are our own spouses at risk. Suddenly, it's personal.

One Midwest military wife confessed she was not prepared for her husband's first deployment. After a year of relying on her own strength and "resiliency," she entered two words in her journal prior to her husband's return: *I survived!*

And yet she learned in the following months and years that God wanted so much more for her than mere survival. She began meeting with other military wives who encouraged her to go to God in prayer as the first line of defense. As she learned to ask the Lord for wisdom and help, she began to grow in her faith. When the next deployment came, she was prepared as she relied more on God to fight the battle against fear for her husband's physical, emotional and spiritual well-being.

Prayer offers a vital connection to a very personal God who cares deeply for the needs of military wives. When waves of emotions threaten to sweep us from our foundation of faith, God's Word is our anchor, tethering us to the truth.

In *Praying God's Word Day by Day*, Beth Moore puts it this way: "In praying Scriptures, I not only find myself in intimate communication with God, but my mind is being retrained, or renewed (Romans 12:2), to think his thoughts about my situation rather than mine."

Just as praying the Scriptures over our loved ones in the military is powerful, so too is praying God's Word over ourselves as we keep the home fires burning. One of the passages I have often prayed is Psalm 116:1–2. No matter how alone we may feel, these verses remind us that God does hear us and that we can always pour out our hearts to him.

Beth Moore's advice to pray the Scriptures when suffering easily translates to the military wife. She writes: "You, the God of all grace, who called me to your eternal glory in Christ, will restore me and make me strong, firm, and steadfast after I have suffered a little while (1 Peter 5:10)."

Try praying the Scriptures yourself. You'll connect intimately with your Creator, remind yourself of the rock-solid truths of his Word, and intercede for your family in a powerful way.

I love the LORD, for he heard my voice; he heard my cry for mercy. Because he turned his ear to me, I will call on him as long as I live.

PSALM 116:1–2

DEBRIEF

- Which Scripture verses can I be praying for my spouse?
- Which passages in God's Word can I pray for myself?

REPORT

Lord, please hear the deepest cry of my heart. Help me bring my husband and my trials to you in prayer, leaning on the promises in your Word. In Jesus' name I pray. Amen.

---

for your next devotional reading, go to page 424

¹² What shall I return to the LORD
    for all his goodness to me?

¹³ I will lift up the cup of salvation
    and call on the name of the LORD.
¹⁴ I will fulfill my vows to the LORD
    in the presence of all his people.

¹⁵ Precious in the sight of the LORD
    is the death of his faithful servants.
¹⁶ Truly I am your servant, LORD;
    I serve you just as my mother did;
    you have freed me from my chains.

¹⁷ I will sacrifice a thank offering to you
    and call on the name of the LORD.
¹⁸ I will fulfill my vows to the LORD
    in the presence of all his people,
¹⁹ in the courts of the house of the LORD —
    in your midst, Jerusalem.

Praise the LORD.^a

Psalm 117

¹ Praise the LORD, all you nations;
    extol him, all you peoples.
² For great is his love toward us,
    and the faithfulness of the LORD
    endures forever.

Praise the LORD.^a

Psalm 118

¹ Give thanks to the LORD, for he is good;
    his love endures forever.

² Let Israel say:
    "His love endures forever."
³ Let the house of Aaron say:
    "His love endures forever."
⁴ Let those who fear the LORD say:
    "His love endures forever."

⁵ When hard pressed, I cried to the LORD;
    he brought me into a spacious place.
⁶ The LORD is with me; I will not be afraid.
    What can mere mortals do to me?
⁷ The LORD is with me; he is my helper.
    I look in triumph on my enemies.

⁸ It is better to take refuge in the LORD
    than to trust in humans.
⁹ It is better to take refuge in the LORD
    than to trust in princes.
¹⁰ All the nations surrounded me,

but in the name of the LORD I cut
    them down.
¹¹ They surrounded me on every side,
    but in the name of the LORD I cut them
    down.
¹² They swarmed around me like bees,
    but they were consumed as quickly as
        burning thorns;
    in the name of the LORD I cut them
        down.
¹³ I was pushed back and about to fall,
    but the LORD helped me.
¹⁴ The LORD is my strength and my
        defense^b;
    he has become my salvation.

¹⁵ Shouts of joy and victory
    resound in the tents of the righteous:
"The LORD's right hand has done mighty
        things!
¹⁶   The LORD's right hand is lifted high;
    the LORD's right hand has done mighty
        things!"
¹⁷ I will not die but live,
    and will proclaim what the LORD has
        done.
¹⁸ The LORD has chastened me severely,
    but he has not given me over to death.
¹⁹ Open for me the gates of the righteous;
    I will enter and give thanks to the
        LORD.
²⁰ This is the gate of the LORD
    through which the righteous may
        enter.
²¹ I will give you thanks, for you answered
        me;
    you have become my salvation.

²² The stone the builders rejected
    has become the cornerstone;
²³ the LORD has done this,
    and it is marvelous in our eyes.
²⁴ The LORD has done it this very day;
    let us rejoice today and be glad.

²⁵ LORD, save us!
    LORD, grant us success!

²⁶ Blessed is he who comes in the name of
        the LORD.
    From the house of the LORD we bless
        you.^c
²⁷ The LORD is God,
    and he has made his light shine on us.

^a 19,2 Hebrew *Hallelu Yah*   ^b 14 Or *song*   ^c 26 The Hebrew is plural.

With boughs in hand, join in the festal
procession
up[a] to the horns of the altar.

28 You are my God, and I will praise you;
you are my God, and I will exalt you.

29 Give thanks to the LORD, for he is good;
his love endures forever.

Psalm 119[b]

א Aleph

1 Blessed are those whose ways are
blameless,
who walk according to the law of the
LORD.
2 Blessed are those who keep his statutes
and seek him with all their heart—
3 they do no wrong
but follow his ways.
4 You have laid down precepts
that are to be fully obeyed.
5 Oh, that my ways were steadfast
in obeying your decrees!
6 Then I would not be put to shame
when I consider all your commands.
7 I will praise you with an upright heart
as I learn your righteous laws.
8 I will obey your decrees;
do not utterly forsake me.

ב Beth

9 How can a young person stay on the path
of purity?
By living according to your word.
10 I seek you with all my heart;
do not let me stray from your
commands.
11 I have hidden your word in my heart
that I might not sin against you.
12 Praise be to you, LORD;
teach me your decrees.
13 With my lips I recount
all the laws that come from your mouth.
14 I rejoice in following your statutes
as one rejoices in great riches.
15 I meditate on your precepts
and consider your ways.
16 I delight in your decrees;
I will not neglect your word.

ג Gimel

17 Be good to your servant while I live,
that I may obey your word.
18 Open my eyes that I may see
wonderful things in your law.
19 I am a stranger on earth;
do not hide your commands from me.
20 My soul is consumed with longing
for your laws at all times.
21 You rebuke the arrogant, who are
accursed,
those who stray from your commands.
22 Remove from me their scorn and
contempt,
for I keep your statutes.
23 Though rulers sit together and slander me,
your servant will meditate on your
decrees.
24 Your statutes are my delight;
they are my counselors.

ד Daleth

25 I am laid low in the dust;
preserve my life according to your word.
26 I gave an account of my ways and you
answered me;
teach me your decrees.
27 Cause me to understand the way of your
precepts,
that I may meditate on your wonderful
deeds.
28 My soul is weary with sorrow;
strengthen me according to your word.
29 Keep me from deceitful ways;
be gracious to me and teach me your
law.
30 I have chosen the way of faithfulness;
I have set my heart on your laws.
31 I hold fast to your statutes, LORD;
do not let me be put to shame.
32 I run in the path of your commands,
for you have broadened my
understanding.

ה He

33 Teach me, LORD, the way of your decrees,
that I may follow it to the end.[c]
34 Give me understanding, so that I may
keep your law
and obey it with all my heart.

---

[a] 27 Or *Bind the festal sacrifice with ropes / and take it*   [b] This psalm is an acrostic poem, the stanzas of
which begin with successive letters of the Hebrew alphabet; moreover, the verses of each stanza begin with
the same letter of the Hebrew alphabet.   [c] 33 Or *follow it for its reward*

³⁵ Direct me in the path of your commands,
    for there I find delight.
³⁶ Turn my heart toward your statutes
    and not toward selfish gain.
³⁷ Turn my eyes away from worthless
    things;
    preserve my life according to your
    word.^a
³⁸ Fulfill your promise to your servant,
    so that you may be feared.
³⁹ Take away the disgrace I dread,
    for your laws are good.
⁴⁰ How I long for your precepts!
    In your righteousness preserve my life.

ו Waw

⁴¹ May your unfailing love come to me,
    LORD,
    your salvation, according to your
    promise;
⁴² then I can answer anyone who taunts me,
    for I trust in your word.
⁴³ Never take your word of truth from my
    mouth,
    for I have put my hope in your laws.
⁴⁴ I will always obey your law,
    for ever and ever.
⁴⁵ I will walk about in freedom,
    for I have sought out your precepts.
⁴⁶ I will speak of your statutes before kings
    and will not be put to shame,
⁴⁷ for I delight in your commands
    because I love them.
⁴⁸ I reach out for your commands, which I
    love,
    that I may meditate on your decrees.

ז Zayin

⁴⁹ Remember your word to your servant,
    for you have given me hope.
⁵⁰ My comfort in my suffering is this:
    Your promise preserves my life.
⁵¹ The arrogant mock me unmercifully,
    but I do not turn from your law.
⁵² I remember, LORD, your ancient laws,
    and I find comfort in them.
⁵³ Indignation grips me because of the
    wicked,
    who have forsaken your law.
⁵⁴ Your decrees are the theme of my song
    wherever I lodge.

⁵⁵ In the night, LORD, I remember your
    name,
    that I may keep your law.
⁵⁶ This has been my practice:
    I obey your precepts.

ח Heth

⁵⁷ You are my portion, LORD;
    I have promised to obey your words.
⁵⁸ I have sought your face with all my heart;
    be gracious to me according to your
    promise.
⁵⁹ I have considered my ways
    and have turned my steps to your
    statutes.
⁶⁰ I will hasten and not delay
    to obey your commands.
⁶¹ Though the wicked bind me with ropes,
    I will not forget your law.
⁶² At midnight I rise to give you thanks
    for your righteous laws.
⁶³ I am a friend to all who fear you,
    to all who follow your precepts.
⁶⁴ The earth is filled with your love, LORD;
    teach me your decrees.

ט Teth

⁶⁵ Do good to your servant
    according to your word, LORD.
⁶⁶ Teach me knowledge and good judgment,
    for I trust your commands.
⁶⁷ Before I was afflicted I went astray,
    but now I obey your word.
⁶⁸ You are good, and what you do is good;
    teach me your decrees.
⁶⁹ Though the arrogant have smeared me
    with lies,
    I keep your precepts with all my heart.
⁷⁰ Their hearts are callous and unfeeling,
    but I delight in your law.
⁷¹ It was good for me to be afflicted
    so that I might learn your decrees.
⁷² The law from your mouth is more
    precious to me
    than thousands of pieces of silver and
    gold.

י Yodh

⁷³ Your hands made me and formed me;
    give me understanding to learn your
    commands.

^a 37 Two manuscripts of the Masoretic Text and Dead Sea Scrolls; most manuscripts of the Masoretic Text *life in your way*

[74] May those who fear you rejoice when
    they see me,
    for I have put my hope in your word.
[75] I know, LORD, that your laws are
    righteous,
    and that in faithfulness you have
    afflicted me.
[76] May your unfailing love be my comfort,
    according to your promise to your
    servant.
[77] Let your compassion come to me that I
    may live,
    for your law is my delight.
[78] May the arrogant be put to shame for
    wronging me without cause;
    but I will meditate on your precepts.
[79] May those who fear you turn to me,
    those who understand your statutes.
[80] May I wholeheartedly follow your decrees,
    that I may not be put to shame.

כ Kaph

[81] My soul faints with longing for your
    salvation,
    but I have put my hope in your word.
[82] My eyes fail, looking for your promise;
    I say, "When will you comfort me?"
[83] Though I am like a wineskin in the smoke,
    I do not forget your decrees.
[84] How long must your servant wait?
    When will you punish my persecutors?
[85] The arrogant dig pits to trap me,
    contrary to your law.
[86] All your commands are trustworthy;
    help me, for I am being persecuted
    without cause.
[87] They almost wiped me from the earth,
    but I have not forsaken your precepts.
[88] In your unfailing love preserve my life,
    that I may obey the statutes of your
    mouth.

ל Lamedh

[89] Your word, LORD, is eternal;
    it stands firm in the heavens.
[90] Your faithfulness continues through all
    generations;
    you established the earth, and it
    endures.
[91] Your laws endure to this day,
    for all things serve you.
[92] If your law had not been my delight,

I would have perished in my
    affliction.
[93] I will never forget your precepts,
    for by them you have preserved my life.
[94] Save me, for I am yours;
    I have sought out your precepts.
[95] The wicked are waiting to destroy me,
    but I will ponder your statutes.
[96] To all perfection I see a limit,
    but your commands are boundless.

מ Mem

[97] Oh, how I love your law!
    I meditate on it all day long.
[98] Your commands are always with me
    and make me wiser than my enemies.
[99] I have more insight than all my teachers,
    for I meditate on your statutes.
[100] I have more understanding than the
    elders,
    for I obey your precepts.
[101] I have kept my feet from every evil path
    so that I might obey your word.
[102] I have not departed from your laws,
    for you yourself have taught me.
[103] How sweet are your words to my taste,
    sweeter than honey to my mouth!
[104] I gain understanding from your
    precepts;
    therefore I hate every wrong path.

נ Nun

[105] Your word is a lamp for my feet,
    a light on my path.
[106] I have taken an oath and confirmed it,
    that I will follow your righteous laws.
[107] I have suffered much;
    preserve my life, LORD, according to
    your word.
[108] Accept, LORD, the willing praise of my
    mouth,
    and teach me your laws.
[109] Though I constantly take my life in my
    hands,
    I will not forget your law.
[110] The wicked have set a snare for me,
    but I have not strayed from your
    precepts.
[111] Your statutes are my heritage forever;
    they are the joy of my heart.
[112] My heart is set on keeping your decrees
    to the very end.[a]

[a] 112 Or decrees / for their enduring reward

ס Samekh

¹¹³ I hate double-minded people,
but I love your law.
¹¹⁴ You are my refuge and my shield;
I have put my hope in your word.
¹¹⁵ Away from me, you evildoers,
that I may keep the commands of
my God!
¹¹⁶ Sustain me, my God, according to your
promise, and I will live;
do not let my hopes be dashed.
¹¹⁷ Uphold me, and I will be delivered;
I will always have regard for your
decrees.
¹¹⁸ You reject all who stray from your
decrees,
for their delusions come to nothing.
¹¹⁹ All the wicked of the earth you discard
like dross;
therefore I love your statutes.
¹²⁰ My flesh trembles in fear of you;
I stand in awe of your laws.

ע Ayin

¹²¹ I have done what is righteous and just;
do not leave me to my oppressors.
¹²² Ensure your servant's well-being;
do not let the arrogant oppress me.
¹²³ My eyes fail, looking for your salvation,
looking for your righteous promise.
¹²⁴ Deal with your servant according to
your love
and teach me your decrees.
¹²⁵ I am your servant; give me discernment
that I may understand your statutes.
¹²⁶ It is time for you to act, LORD;
your law is being broken.
¹²⁷ Because I love your commands
more than gold, more than pure gold,
¹²⁸ and because I consider all your precepts
right,
I hate every wrong path.

פ Pe

¹²⁹ Your statutes are wonderful;
therefore I obey them.
¹³⁰ The unfolding of your words gives light;
it gives understanding to the simple.
¹³¹ I open my mouth and pant,
longing for your commands.
¹³² Turn to me and have mercy on me,
as you always do to those who love
your name.

¹³³ Direct my footsteps according to your
word;
let no sin rule over me.
¹³⁴ Redeem me from human oppression,
that I may obey your precepts.
¹³⁵ Make your face shine on your servant
and teach me your decrees.
¹³⁶ Streams of tears flow from my eyes,
for your law is not obeyed.

צ Tsadhe

¹³⁷ You are righteous, LORD,
and your laws are right.
¹³⁸ The statutes you have laid down are
righteous;
they are fully trustworthy.
¹³⁹ My zeal wears me out,
for my enemies ignore your words.
¹⁴⁰ Your promises have been thoroughly
tested,
and your servant loves them.
¹⁴¹ Though I am lowly and despised,
I do not forget your precepts.
¹⁴² Your righteousness is everlasting
and your law is true.
¹⁴³ Trouble and distress have come
upon me,
but your commands give me delight.
¹⁴⁴ Your statutes are always righteous;
give me understanding that I may live.

ק Qoph

¹⁴⁵ I call with all my heart; answer me,
LORD,
and I will obey your decrees.
¹⁴⁶ I call out to you; save me
and I will keep your statutes.
¹⁴⁷ I rise before dawn and cry for help;
I have put my hope in your word.
¹⁴⁸ My eyes stay open through the watches
of the night,
that I may meditate on your promises.
¹⁴⁹ Hear my voice in accordance with your
love;
preserve my life, LORD, according to
your laws.
¹⁵⁰ Those who devise wicked schemes are
near,
but they are far from your law.
¹⁵¹ Yet you are near, LORD,
and all your commands are true.
¹⁵² Long ago I learned from your statutes
that you established them to last
forever.

ר Resh

¹⁵³ Look on my suffering and deliver me,
for I have not forgotten your law.
¹⁵⁴ Defend my cause and redeem me;
preserve my life according to your
promise.
¹⁵⁵ Salvation is far from the wicked,
for they do not seek out your decrees.
¹⁵⁶ Your compassion, Lord, is great;
preserve my life according to your
laws.
¹⁵⁷ Many are the foes who persecute me,
but I have not turned from your
statutes.
¹⁵⁸ I look on the faithless with loathing,
for they do not obey your word.
¹⁵⁹ See how I love your precepts;
preserve my life, Lord, in accordance
with your love.
¹⁶⁰ All your words are true;
all your righteous laws are eternal.

ש Sin and Shin

¹⁶¹ Rulers persecute me without cause,
but my heart trembles at your word.
¹⁶² I rejoice in your promise
like one who finds great spoil.
¹⁶³ I hate and detest falsehood
but I love your law.
¹⁶⁴ Seven times a day I praise you
for your righteous laws.
¹⁶⁵ Great peace have those who love your
law,
and nothing can make them stumble.
¹⁶⁶ I wait for your salvation, Lord,
and I follow your commands.
¹⁶⁷ I obey your statutes,
for I love them greatly.
¹⁶⁸ I obey your precepts and your statutes,
for all my ways are known to you.

ת Taw

¹⁶⁹ May my cry come before you, Lord;
give me understanding according to
your word.
¹⁷⁰ May my supplication come before you;
deliver me according to your promise.
¹⁷¹ May my lips overflow with praise,
for you teach me your decrees.
¹⁷² May my tongue sing of your word,
for all your commands are righteous.
¹⁷³ May your hand be ready to help me,
for I have chosen your precepts.

¹⁷⁴ I long for your salvation, Lord,
and your law gives me delight.
¹⁷⁵ Let me live that I may praise you,
and may your laws sustain me.
¹⁷⁶ I have strayed like a lost sheep.
Seek your servant,
for I have not forgotten your commands.

Psalm 120

A song of ascents.

¹ I call on the Lord in my distress,
and he answers me.
² Save me, Lord,
from lying lips
and from deceitful tongues.

³ What will he do to you,
and what more besides,
you deceitful tongue?
⁴ He will punish you with a warrior's sharp
arrows,
with burning coals of the broom bush.

⁵ Woe to me that I dwell in Meshek,
that I live among the tents of Kedar!
⁶ Too long have I lived
among those who hate peace.
⁷ I am for peace;
but when I speak, they are for war.

Psalm 121

A song of ascents.

¹ I lift up my eyes to the mountains —
where does my help come from?
² My help comes from the Lord,
the Maker of heaven and earth.

³ He will not let your foot slip —
he who watches over you will not
slumber;
⁴ indeed, he who watches over Israel
will neither slumber nor sleep.

⁵ The Lord watches over you —
the Lord is your shade at your right
hand;
⁶ the sun will not harm you by day,
nor the moon by night.

⁷ The Lord will keep you from all harm —
he will watch over your life;
⁸ the Lord will watch over your coming
and going
both now and forevermore.

Psalm 122

A song of ascents. Of David.

[1] I rejoiced with those who said to me,
  "Let us go to the house of the LORD."
[2] Our feet are standing
  in your gates, Jerusalem.

[3] Jerusalem is built like a city
  that is closely compacted together.
[4] That is where the tribes go up—
  the tribes of the LORD—
to praise the name of the LORD
  according to the statute given to Israel.
[5] There stand the thrones for judgment,
  the thrones of the house of David.

[6] Pray for the peace of Jerusalem:
  "May those who love you be secure.
[7] May there be peace within your walls
  and security within your citadels."
[8] For the sake of my family and friends,
  I will say, "Peace be within you."
[9] For the sake of the house of the LORD
    our God,
  I will seek your prosperity.

Psalm 123

A song of ascents.

[1] I lift up my eyes to you,
  to you who sit enthroned in heaven.
[2] As the eyes of slaves look to the hand of
    their master,
  as the eyes of a female slave look to the
    hand of her mistress,
so our eyes look to the LORD our God,
  till he shows us his mercy.

[3] Have mercy on us, LORD, have mercy
    on us,
  for we have endured no end of
    contempt.
[4] We have endured no end
  of ridicule from the arrogant,
  of contempt from the proud.

Psalm 124

A song of ascents. Of David.

[1] If the LORD had not been on our side—
  let Israel say—
[2] if the LORD had not been on our side
  when people attacked us,

[3] they would have swallowed us alive
  when their anger flared against us;
[4] the flood would have engulfed us,
  the torrent would have swept over us,
[5] the raging waters
  would have swept us away.

[6] Praise be to the LORD,
  who has not let us be torn by their teeth.
[7] We have escaped like a bird
  from the fowler's snare;
the snare has been broken,
  and we have escaped.
[8] Our help is in the name of the LORD,
  the Maker of heaven and earth.

Psalm 125

A song of ascents.

[1] Those who trust in the LORD are like
    Mount Zion,
  which cannot be shaken but endures
    forever.
[2] As the mountains surround Jerusalem,
  so the LORD surrounds his people
  both now and forevermore.

[3] The scepter of the wicked will not remain
    over the land allotted to the righteous,
for then the righteous might use
    their hands to do evil.

[4] LORD, do good to those who are good,
  to those who are upright in heart.
[5] But those who turn to crooked ways
  the LORD will banish with the evildoers.

Peace be on Israel.

Psalm 126

A song of ascents.

[1] When the LORD restored the fortunes
    of[a] Zion,
  we were like those who dreamed.[b]
[2] Our mouths were filled with laughter,
  our tongues with songs of joy.
Then it was said among the nations,
  "The LORD has done great things for
    them."
[3] The LORD has done great things for us,
  and we are filled with joy.

[4] Restore our fortunes,[c] LORD,
  like streams in the Negev.

---

[a] 1 Or LORD *brought back the captives to*   [b] 1 Or *those restored to health*   [c] 4 Or *Bring back our captives*

⁵ Those who sow with tears
  will reap with songs of joy.
⁶ Those who go out weeping,
  carrying seed to sow,
will return with songs of joy,
  carrying sheaves with them.

Psalm 127

A song of ascents. Of Solomon.

¹ Unless the Lord builds the house,
  the builders labor in vain.
Unless the Lord watches over the city,
  the guards stand watch in vain.
² In vain you rise early
  and stay up late,
toiling for food to eat—
  for he grants sleep to*ᵃ* those he
    loves.

³ Children are a heritage from the
    Lord,
  offspring a reward from him.
⁴ Like arrows in the hands of a warrior
  are children born in one's youth.
⁵ Blessed is the man
  whose quiver is full of them.
They will not be put to shame
  when they contend with their
    opponents in court.

Psalm 128

A song of ascents.

¹ Blessed are all who fear the Lord,
  who walk in obedience to him.
² You will eat the fruit of your labor;
  blessings and prosperity will
    be yours.
³ Your wife will be like a fruitful vine
  within your house;
  your children will be like olive shoots
    around your table.
⁴ Yes, this will be the blessing
  for the man who fears the Lord.

⁵ May the Lord bless you from Zion;
  may you see the prosperity of
    Jerusalem
  all the days of your life.
⁶ May you live to see your children's
    children—
  peace be on Israel.

Psalm 129

A song of ascents.

¹ "They have greatly oppressed me from
    my youth,"
  let Israel say;
² "they have greatly oppressed me from
    my youth,
  but they have not gained the victory
    over me.
³ Plowmen have plowed my back
  and made their furrows long.
⁴ But the Lord is righteous;
  he has cut me free from the cords of
    the wicked."

⁵ May all who hate Zion
  be turned back in shame.
⁶ May they be like grass on the roof,
  which withers before it can grow;
⁷ a reaper cannot fill his hands with it,
  nor one who gathers fill his arms.
⁸ May those who pass by not say to them,
  "The blessing of the Lord be on you;
  we bless you in the name of the Lord."

Psalm 130

A song of ascents.

¹ Out of the depths I cry to you, Lord;
²   Lord, hear my voice.
Let your ears be attentive
  to my cry for mercy.

³ If you, Lord, kept a record of sins,
  Lord, who could stand?
⁴ But with you there is forgiveness,
  so that we can, with reverence,
    serve you.

⁵ I wait for the Lord, my whole being
    waits,
  and in his word I put my hope.
⁶ I wait for the Lord
  more than watchmen wait for the
    morning,
  more than watchmen wait for the
    morning.

⁷ Israel, put your hope in the Lord,
  for with the Lord is unfailing love
  and with him is full redemption.
⁸ He himself will redeem Israel
  from all their sins.

ᵃ 2 Or *eat — / for while they sleep he provides for*

Any Day Can Be Mother's Day

By Kathy Guzzo

READ: Psalm 127:3–4

Holidays are hard when your husband is deployed. Birthdays, anniversaries and Valentine's Day can easily feel empty without your "other half" by your side. But if your child has grown up and joined the military, Mother's Day can also be bittersweet. I know from personal experience that while being a mom is tough physically, emotionally and spiritually, being a military mom magnifies these challenges a hundred-fold. It's probably best that none of us knew while we were enduring the long days and even longer nights of pregnancy and infancy that someday our babies would grow up to be in the military, causing us to once again suffer through long days and even longer nights.

God entrusts us with a precious gift, a child, whom we nurture into the man or woman God created them to be. Psalm 127:4 compares our children to a warrior's arrows, and like arrows shot by a warrior, when the time is right, a mom must launch her children from her quiver toward God's plan for them. If the target her children are shooting toward is the harsh world of military life, it now becomes mom's turn to practice the very character qualities she has taught to her children.

The Bible tells us of several mothers whose arrows were targeted to serve God in amazing ways far from home. Hannah pleaded with God to have a child and then willingly sent Samuel away. Elizabeth and Jesus' mother, Mary, reared their children but then rarely saw them as adults as John and Jesus were serving others away from home. I'm sure these moms experienced the same loneliness and anxiety we do.

Mother's Day of 2005 was extremely emotional for me. It was the day we dropped our son off at the airport after his pre-deployment leave. My first thought when I heard that he was leaving on Mother's Day was, "How could the military do this to a mom?" Of course, I soon realized that dates make no difference to the military. I made a decision at that time to celebrate the blessing of being a mother *every* day, regardless of the amount of time spent apart or the day on the calendar.

Just as arrows are made to soar toward their marks, our children are created to grow and launch as well. If you are struggling with loneliness because your child is away, allow your memories of that child to lift your spirits, but look to God to fill your needs.

Like arrows in the hands of a warrior are children born in one's youth.

PSALM 127:4

DEBRIEF

- Have I thanked God for choosing me to rear a child that serves in the military?
- How can I change my thought process in order to allow God to fill the void created by loneliness?

REPORT

Dear Lord, thank you for allowing me to rear a child who chose to serve our country. You know I long to spend time with each of my children, and I feel lonely when they aren't near. Help me to remember that although I may be lonely, I'm never alone because you are always near. Amen.

Psalm 131

A song of ascents. Of David.

¹ My heart is not proud, LORD,
    my eyes are not haughty;
  I do not concern myself with great matters
    or things too wonderful for me.
² But I have calmed and quieted myself,
    I am like a weaned child with its
      mother;
    like a weaned child I am content.

³ Israel, put your hope in the LORD
    both now and forevermore.

Psalm 132

A song of ascents.

¹ LORD, remember David
    and all his self-denial.

² He swore an oath to the LORD,
    he made a vow to the Mighty One
      of Jacob:
³ "I will not enter my house
    or go to my bed,
⁴ I will allow no sleep to my eyes
    or slumber to my eyelids,
⁵ till I find a place for the LORD,
    a dwelling for the Mighty One of Jacob."

⁶ We heard it in Ephrathah,
    we came upon it in the fields of Jaar:ᵃ
⁷ "Let us go to his dwelling place,
    let us worship at his footstool, saying,
⁸ 'Arise, LORD, and come to your resting
      place,
    you and the ark of your might.
⁹ May your priests be clothed with your
      righteousness;
    may your faithful people sing for joy.'"

¹⁰ For the sake of your servant David,
    do not reject your anointed one.

¹¹ The LORD swore an oath to David,
    a sure oath he will not revoke:
  "One of your own descendants
    I will place on your throne.
¹² If your sons keep my covenant
    and the statutes I teach them,
  then their sons will sit
    on your throne for ever and ever."

¹³ For the LORD has chosen Zion,
    he has desired it for his dwelling,
      saying,
¹⁴ "This is my resting place for ever and ever;
    here I will sit enthroned, for I have
      desired it.
¹⁵ I will bless her with abundant provisions;
    her poor I will satisfy with food.
¹⁶ I will clothe her priests with salvation,
    and her faithful people will ever sing
      for joy.

¹⁷ "Here I will make a hornᵇ grow for David
    and set up a lamp for my anointed one.
¹⁸ I will clothe his enemies with shame,
    but his head will be adorned with a
      radiant crown."

Psalm 133

A song of ascents. Of David.

¹ How good and pleasant it is
    when God's people live together in
      unity!

² It is like precious oil poured on the head,
    running down on the beard,
  running down on Aaron's beard,
    down on the collar of his robe.
³ It is as if the dew of Hermon
    were falling on Mount Zion.
  For there the LORD bestows his blessing,
    even life forevermore.

Psalm 134

A song of ascents.

¹ Praise the LORD, all you servants of the
      LORD
    who minister by night in the house of
      the LORD.
² Lift up your hands in the sanctuary
    and praise the LORD.

³ May the LORD bless you from Zion,
    he who is the Maker of heaven and
      earth.

Psalm 135

¹ Praise the LORD.ᶜ

  Praise the name of the LORD;
    praise him, you servants of the LORD,

ᵃ 6 Or *heard of it in Ephrathah, / we found it in the fields of Jearim.* (See 1 Chron. 13:5,6) (And no quotation marks around verses 7-9)   ᵇ 17 *Horn* here symbolizes strong one, that is, king.   ᶜ 1 Hebrew *Hallelu Yah;* also in verses 3 and 21

[2] you who minister in the house of the
LORD,
in the courts of the house of our God.

[3] Praise the LORD, for the LORD is good;
sing praise to his name, for that is
pleasant.
[4] For the LORD has chosen Jacob to be
his own,
Israel to be his treasured possession.

[5] I know that the LORD is great,
that our Lord is greater than all gods.
[6] The LORD does whatever pleases him,
in the heavens and on the earth,
in the seas and all their depths.
[7] He makes clouds rise from the ends of
the earth;
he sends lightning with the rain
and brings out the wind from his
storehouses.

[8] He struck down the firstborn of Egypt,
the firstborn of people and animals.
[9] He sent his signs and wonders into your
midst, Egypt,
against Pharaoh and all his servants.
[10] He struck down many nations
and killed mighty kings —
[11] Sihon king of the Amorites,
Og king of Bashan,
and all the kings of Canaan —
[12] and he gave their land as an inheritance,
an inheritance to his people Israel.

[13] Your name, LORD, endures forever,
your renown, LORD, through all
generations.
[14] For the LORD will vindicate his people
and have compassion on his servants.

[15] The idols of the nations are silver and gold,
made by human hands.
[16] They have mouths, but cannot speak,
eyes, but cannot see.
[17] They have ears, but cannot hear,
nor is there breath in their mouths.
[18] Those who make them will be like them,
and so will all who trust in them.

[19] All you Israelites, praise the LORD;
house of Aaron, praise the LORD;
[20] house of Levi, praise the LORD;
you who fear him, praise the LORD.
[21] Praise be to the LORD from Zion,
to him who dwells in Jerusalem.

Praise the LORD.

Psalm 136

[1] Give thanks to the LORD, for he is good.
His love endures forever.
[2] Give thanks to the God of gods.
His love endures forever.
[3] Give thanks to the Lord of lords:
His love endures forever.

[4] to him who alone does great wonders,
His love endures forever.
[5] who by his understanding made the
heavens,
His love endures forever.
[6] who spread out the earth upon the waters,
His love endures forever.
[7] who made the great lights —
His love endures forever.
[8] the sun to govern the day,
His love endures forever.
[9] the moon and stars to govern the night;
His love endures forever.

[10] to him who struck down the firstborn
of Egypt
His love endures forever.
[11] and brought Israel out from among them
His love endures forever.
[12] with a mighty hand and outstretched
arm;
His love endures forever.

[13] to him who divided the Red Sea[a] asunder
His love endures forever.
[14] and brought Israel through the midst of it,
His love endures forever.
[15] but swept Pharaoh and his army into the
Red Sea;
His love endures forever.

[16] to him who led his people through the
wilderness;
His love endures forever.

[17] to him who struck down great kings,
His love endures forever.
[18] and killed mighty kings —
His love endures forever.
[19] Sihon king of the Amorites
His love endures forever.
[20] and Og king of Bashan —
His love endures forever.
[21] and gave their land as an inheritance,
His love endures forever.
[22] an inheritance to his servant Israel.
His love endures forever.

[a] 13 Or *the Sea of Reeds; also in verse 15*

²³ He remembered us in our low estate
　　　His love endures forever.
²⁴ and freed us from our enemies.
　　　His love endures forever.
²⁵ He gives food to every creature.
　　　His love endures forever.

²⁶ Give thanks to the God of heaven.
　　　His love endures forever.

Psalm 137

¹ By the rivers of Babylon we sat and wept
　　when we remembered Zion.
² There on the poplars
　　we hung our harps,
³ for there our captors asked us for songs,
　　our tormentors demanded songs
　　　of joy;
　　they said, "Sing us one of the songs
　　　of Zion!"

⁴ How can we sing the songs of the Lord
　　while in a foreign land?
⁵ If I forget you, Jerusalem,
　　may my right hand forget its skill.
⁶ May my tongue cling to the roof of my
　　mouth
　　if I do not remember you,
　if I do not consider Jerusalem
　　my highest joy.

⁷ Remember, Lord, what the Edomites did
　　on the day Jerusalem fell.
　"Tear it down," they cried,
　　"tear it down to its foundations!"
⁸ Daughter Babylon, doomed to
　　destruction,
　　happy is the one who repays you
　　according to what you have done to us.
⁹ Happy is the one who seizes your infants
　　and dashes them against the rocks.

Psalm 138

Of David.

¹ I will praise you, Lord, with all my heart;
　　before the "gods" I will sing your
　　　praise.
² I will bow down toward your holy temple
　　and will praise your name
　　for your unfailing love and your
　　　faithfulness,
　for you have so exalted your solemn
　　decree
　　that it surpasses your fame.

³ When I called, you answered me;
　　you greatly emboldened me.

⁴ May all the kings of the earth praise you,
　　Lord,
　　when they hear what you have
　　　decreed.
⁵ May they sing of the ways of the Lord,
　　for the glory of the Lord is great.

⁶ Though the Lord is exalted, he looks
　　kindly on the lowly;
　　though lofty, he sees them from afar.
⁷ Though I walk in the midst of trouble,
　　you preserve my life.
　You stretch out your hand against the
　　anger of my foes;
　　with your right hand you save me.
⁸ The Lord will vindicate me;
　　your love, Lord, endures forever —
　　do not abandon the works of your
　　　hands.

Psalm 139

*For the director of music.
Of David. A psalm.*

¹ You have searched me, Lord,
　　and you know me.
² You know when I sit and when I rise;
　　you perceive my thoughts from afar.
³ You discern my going out and my lying
　　down;
　　you are familiar with all my ways.
⁴ Before a word is on my tongue
　　you, Lord, know it completely.
⁵ You hem me in behind and before,
　　and you lay your hand upon me.
⁶ Such knowledge is too wonderful for me,
　　too lofty for me to attain.

⁷ Where can I go from your Spirit?
　　Where can I flee from your presence?
⁸ If I go up to the heavens, you are there;
　　if I make my bed in the depths, you are
　　　there.
⁹ If I rise on the wings of the dawn,
　　if I settle on the far side of the sea,
¹⁰ even there your hand will guide me,
　　your right hand will hold me fast.
¹¹ If I say, "Surely the darkness will hide me
　　and the light become night around me,"
¹² even the darkness will not be dark to you;
　　the night will shine like the day,
　　for darkness is as light to you.

Never Alone

By Linda Montgomery

READ: Psalm 139:7–10

Picture this scene: A military wife comes back in the front door after getting her energetic kids on the school bus and looks around her home to make sure everything is in order before heading out again. Her husband is overseas in a combat zone, but every room features pictures of him with the family. She takes a moment to email him with plans to Skype later in the day (if possible). Their time "together," thanks to modern technology, gives them a chance to "catch up" and pray together. On her way out the door, she grabs the letter to put in the mailbox (as mail call is still an anticipated event in his day).

Despite the children, the pictures, the emails, the letters and the chance to Skype, if she lets herself, she can be tricked by her feelings into believing she is all alone. But she knows better. She is never really alone.

The life of a military wife can be a picture (a metaphor) of the Christian faith. She is surrounded by visible reminders of her husband's abiding presence and provision in her home — just as her faith reminds her that she is surrounded by visible reminders of her Lord's abiding presence and provision in her life. Just as she and her husband can read each other's written messages of love, she can read God's Word, which proclaims God's love for her. Just as she and her husband try to be personally involved in each other's lives, her Lord personally and actively participates in her life, always for her good. Like the promise of her husband's return from deployment, Jesus has promised that he will return. And like she and her husband long to be together again, she longs to be together with the Lord in her heavenly home.

Psalm 139 takes us right into that scene and makes sure we don't forget that the Lord is omnipresent: "Where can I go from your Spirit? Where can I flee from your presence?" (verse 7). The psalmist immediately answers: "If I go up to the heavens, you are there; if I make my bed in the depths, you are there. If I rise on the wings of the dawn, if I settle on the far side of the sea, even there your hand will guide me, your right hand will hold me fast" (verses 8–10).

It's almost as if the Lord is saying, "No matter where the military sends you (air, sea, land) — I am there!" Psalm 139 is the perfect answer to any military orders. There is nowhere on earth you can go that you will be alone. The Lord is with you wherever you are assigned.

Where can I go from your Spirit? Where can I flee from your presence?
PSALM 139:7

DEBRIEF
- As I look around my world, how am I reminded of God's presence and provision?
- How can I encourage my husband when he feels lonely?

REPORT
Lord, I know you love me and I am not alone. But sometimes I feel lonely. Help me grow close to you so that I can see you and feel your presence in my life today. In Jesus' name I pray. Amen.

¹³ For you created my inmost being;
  you knit me together in my mother's
    womb.
¹⁴ I praise you because I am fearfully and
    wonderfully made;
  your works are wonderful,
  I know that full well.
¹⁵ My frame was not hidden from you
  when I was made in the secret place,
  when I was woven together in the
    depths of the earth.
¹⁶ Your eyes saw my unformed body;
  all the days ordained for me were
    written in your book
  before one of them came to be.
¹⁷ How precious to me are your thoughts,ᵃ
    God!
  How vast is the sum of them!
¹⁸ Were I to count them,
  they would outnumber the grains of
    sand —
  when I awake, I am still with you.

¹⁹ If only you, God, would slay the wicked!
  Away from me, you who are
    bloodthirsty!
²⁰ They speak of you with evil intent;
  your adversaries misuse your name.
²¹ Do I not hate those who hate you, Lord,
  and abhor those who are in rebellion
    against you?
²² I have nothing but hatred for them;
  I count them my enemies.
²³ Search me, God, and know my heart;
  test me and know my anxious
    thoughts.
²⁴ See if there is any offensive way in me,
  and lead me in the way everlasting.

Psalm 140ᵇ

For the director of music.
A psalm of David.

¹ Rescue me, Lord, from evildoers;
  protect me from the violent,
² who devise evil plans in their hearts
  and stir up war every day.
³ They make their tongues as sharp as a
    serpent's;
  the poison of vipers is on their lips.ᶜ

⁴ Keep me safe, Lord, from the hands of
    the wicked;
  protect me from the violent,
  who devise ways to trip my feet.
⁵ The arrogant have hidden a snare for me;
  they have spread out the cords of
    their net
  and have set traps for me along my
    path.

⁶ I say to the Lord, "You are my God."
  Hear, Lord, my cry for mercy.
⁷ Sovereign Lord, my strong deliverer,
  you shield my head in the day of battle.
⁸ Do not grant the wicked their desires,
    Lord;
  do not let their plans succeed.

⁹ Those who surround me proudly rear
    their heads;
  may the mischief of their lips engulf
    them.
¹⁰ May burning coals fall on them;
  may they be thrown into the fire,
  into miry pits, never to rise.
¹¹ May slanderers not be established in the
    land;
  may disaster hunt down the violent.

¹² I know that the Lord secures justice for
    the poor
  and upholds the cause of the needy.
¹³ Surely the righteous will praise your name,
  and the upright will live in your
    presence.

Psalm 141

A psalm of David.

¹ I call to you, Lord, come quickly to me;
  hear me when I call to you.
² May my prayer be set before you like
    incense;
  may the lifting up of my hands be like
    the evening sacrifice.

³ Set a guard over my mouth, Lord;
  keep watch over the door of my lips.
⁴ Do not let my heart be drawn to what is
    evil
  so that I take part in wicked deeds
  along with those who are evildoers;
  do not let me eat their delicacies.

⁵ Let a righteous man strike me — that is a
    kindness;

ᵃ *17* Or *How amazing are your thoughts concerning me*   ᵇ In Hebrew texts 140:1-13 is numbered 140:2-14.
ᶜ *3* The Hebrew has *Selah* (a word of uncertain meaning) here and at the end of verses 5 and 8.

let him rebuke me — that is oil on
my head.
My head will not refuse it,
for my prayer will still be against the
deeds of evildoers.

[6] Their rulers will be thrown down from
the cliffs,
and the wicked will learn that my
words were well spoken.
[7] They will say, "As one plows and breaks
up the earth,
so our bones have been scattered at
the mouth of the grave."

[8] But my eyes are fixed on you, Sovereign
LORD;
in you I take refuge — do not give me
over to death.
[9] Keep me safe from the traps set by
evildoers,
from the snares they have laid for me.
[10] Let the wicked fall into their own nets,
while I pass by in safety.

Psalm 142[a]

A maskil[b] of David. When he was in the cave.
A prayer.

[1] I cry aloud to the LORD;
I lift up my voice to the LORD for mercy.
[2] I pour out before him my complaint;
before him I tell my trouble.

[3] When my spirit grows faint within me,
it is you who watch over my way.
In the path where I walk
people have hidden a snare for me.
[4] Look and see, there is no one at my right
hand;
no one is concerned for me.
I have no refuge;
no one cares for my life.

[5] I cry to you, LORD;
I say, "You are my refuge,
my portion in the land of the living."

[6] Listen to my cry,
for I am in desperate need;
rescue me from those who pursue me,
for they are too strong for me.
[7] Set me free from my prison,
that I may praise your name.

Then the righteous will gather about me
because of your goodness to me.

Psalm 143

A psalm of David.

[1] LORD, hear my prayer,
listen to my cry for mercy;
in your faithfulness and righteousness
come to my relief.
[2] Do not bring your servant into
judgment,
for no one living is righteous before
you.
[3] The enemy pursues me,
he crushes me to the ground;
he makes me dwell in the darkness
like those long dead.
[4] So my spirit grows faint within me;
my heart within me is dismayed.
[5] I remember the days of long ago;
I meditate on all your works
and consider what your hands have
done.
[6] I spread out my hands to you;
I thirst for you like a parched land.[c]

[7] Answer me quickly, LORD;
my spirit fails.
Do not hide your face from me
or I will be like those who go down to
the pit.
[8] Let the morning bring me word of your
unfailing love,
for I have put my trust in you.
Show me the way I should go,
for to you I entrust my life.
[9] Rescue me from my enemies, LORD,
for I hide myself in you.
[10] Teach me to do your will,
for you are my God;
may your good Spirit
lead me on level ground.

[11] For your name's sake, LORD, preserve
my life;
in your righteousness, bring me out
of trouble.
[12] In your unfailing love, silence my
enemies;
destroy all my foes,
for I am your servant.

---

[a] In Hebrew texts 142:1-7 is numbered 142:2-8.   [b] Title: Probably a literary or musical term   [c] 6 The
Hebrew has *Selah* (a word of uncertain meaning) here.

Psalm 144

Of David.

[1] Praise be to the LORD my Rock,
    who trains my hands for war,
    my fingers for battle.
[2] He is my loving God and my fortress,
    my stronghold and my deliverer,
    my shield, in whom I take refuge,
    who subdues peoples[a] under me.

[3] LORD, what are human beings that you
        care for them,
    mere mortals that you think of them?
[4] They are like a breath;
    their days are like a fleeting shadow.

[5] Part your heavens, LORD, and come
        down;
    touch the mountains, so that they
        smoke.
[6] Send forth lightning and scatter the
        enemy;
    shoot your arrows and rout them.
[7] Reach down your hand from on high;
    deliver me and rescue me
from the mighty waters,
    from the hands of foreigners
[8] whose mouths are full of lies,
    whose right hands are deceitful.

[9] I will sing a new song to you, my God;
    on the ten-stringed lyre I will make
        music to you,
[10] to the One who gives victory to kings,
    who delivers his servant David.

From the deadly sword [11] deliver me;
    rescue me from the hands of foreigners
whose mouths are full of lies,
    whose right hands are deceitful.

[12] Then our sons in their youth
    will be like well-nurtured plants,
and our daughters will be like pillars
    carved to adorn a palace.
[13] Our barns will be filled
    with every kind of provision.
Our sheep will increase by thousands,
    by tens of thousands in our fields;
[14]   our oxen will draw heavy loads.[b]

There will be no breaching of walls,
    no going into captivity,
    no cry of distress in our streets.
[15] Blessed is the people of whom this is true;
    blessed is the people whose God is the
        LORD.

Psalm 145[c]

A psalm of praise. Of David.

[1] I will exalt you, my God the King;
    I will praise your name for ever and
        ever.
[2] Every day I will praise you
    and extol your name for ever and ever.

[3] Great is the LORD and most worthy of
        praise;
    his greatness no one can fathom.
[4] One generation commends your works to
        another;
    they tell of your mighty acts.
[5] They speak of the glorious splendor of
        your majesty —
    and I will meditate on your wonderful
        works.[d]
[6] They tell of the power of your awesome
        works —
    and I will proclaim your great deeds.
[7] They celebrate your abundant goodness
    and joyfully sing of your
        righteousness.

[8] The LORD is gracious and compassionate,
    slow to anger and rich in love.

[9] The LORD is good to all;
    he has compassion on all he has
        made.
[10] All your works praise you, LORD;
    your faithful people extol you.
[11] They tell of the glory of your kingdom
    and speak of your might,
[12] so that all people may know of your
        mighty acts
    and the glorious splendor of your
        kingdom.
[13] Your kingdom is an everlasting kingdom,
    and your dominion endures through
        all generations.

---

[a] 2 Many manuscripts of the Masoretic Text, Dead Sea Scrolls, Aquila, Jerome and Syriac; most manuscripts of the Masoretic Text *subdues my people*   [b] 14 Or *our chieftains will be firmly established*   [c] This psalm is an acrostic poem, the verses of which (including verse 13b) begin with the successive letters of the Hebrew alphabet.   [d] 5 Dead Sea Scrolls and Syriac (see also Septuagint); Masoretic Text *On the glorious splendor of your majesty / and on your wonderful works I will meditate*

SURROGATE MOTHER TO AN UNKNOWN SOLDIER

By Jocelyn Green

The special love a mother has for her son was vividly captured during the Spanish-American War in 1898, when Marion Couthouy Smith penned the poem "Our Gallant Sons," which includes the lines:

> *Oh, mother hearts, that dare not break! That feel the stress, the long, long ache,*
> *The tears that burn, the eyes that wake, For these our cherished ones —*

When women on the home front learned that their soldiers were sick or injured in camps in the United States, many of them traveled great distances to personally nurse them and bring them home. Other soldiers were not so fortunate. Here is the story of one soldier suffering from severe malarial fever at Camp Wikoff on Long Island, New York:

> The soldier alternated between unconsciousness and delirium, and all efforts to find out who he was were unavailing. His one glimmering of reason was when he called in plaintive iteration for his mother: "Mother! Mother! Isn't she coming at all?"
>
> Across from him was another soldier suffering from malarial fever in a lighter form. His mother had come on from the West, and had found him already on the road to recovery. She sat on the edge of his cot, holding his hand and talking in low, happy tones. When the surgeon came along on his rounds she rose and half turned. The unknown soldier turned on his side and saw her standing there. For a moment there could be seen in his eyes the struggle of returning consciousness; then a great peace shone on the wasted face. "Mother," he said meekly, "you've come at last." The woman turned and saw a stranger feebly holding out his arms to her. She stood amazed, but it was only a moment before the mother heart comprehended. "Yes, dear boy," she said softly. "I've come."
>
> "Lift me up," he said, "I want to go home. You've come to take me home; haven't you, mother?" She stooped over and kissed him, then sat on the edge of the cot and took the emaciated form in her arms. He leaned back, his eyes closed, and he smiled … His breathing grew slower and softer … "I've longed for you so, mother," he said, and died.
>
> The woman laid the body down and went back to her own son.

This soldier died unknown, but thanks to this woman's compassion for another mother's son, he did not die feeling unloved. Compassion is a characteristic of God that we should all strive to emulate. Everyone is some mother's son or daughter and, even more important, we are all made in the image of God.

Prayer: Lord, fill me with your compassion for the hurting people around me.

> **The Lord is gracious and compassionate, slow to anger and rich in love. The Lord is good to all; he has compassion on all he has made.**
> PSALM 145:8 – 9

for your next devotional reading, go to page 435

The Lord is trustworthy in all he
    promises
    and faithful in all he does.[a]
[14] The Lord upholds all who fall
    and lifts up all who are bowed down.
[15] The eyes of all look to you,
    and you give them their food at the
    proper time.
[16] You open your hand
    and satisfy the desires of every living
    thing.

[17] The Lord is righteous in all his ways
    and faithful in all he does.
[18] The Lord is near to all who call on him,
    to all who call on him in truth.
[19] He fulfills the desires of those who fear
    him;
    he hears their cry and saves them.
[20] The Lord watches over all who love him,
    but all the wicked he will destroy.

[21] My mouth will speak in praise of the Lord.
    Let every creature praise his holy name
    for ever and ever.

Psalm 146

[1] Praise the Lord.[b]

Praise the Lord, my soul.

[2] I will praise the Lord all my life;
    I will sing praise to my God as long as
    I live.
[3] Do not put your trust in princes,
    in human beings, who cannot save.
[4] When their spirit departs, they return to
    the ground;
    on that very day their plans come to
    nothing.
[5] Blessed are those whose help is the God
    of Jacob,
    whose hope is in the Lord their God.

[6] He is the Maker of heaven and earth,
    the sea, and everything in them —
    he remains faithful forever.
[7] He upholds the cause of the oppressed
    and gives food to the hungry.
    The Lord sets prisoners free,
[8]   the Lord gives sight to the blind,
    the Lord lifts up those who are bowed
    down,

the Lord loves the righteous.
[9] The Lord watches over the foreigner
    and sustains the fatherless and the
    widow,
    but he frustrates the ways of the
    wicked.

[10] The Lord reigns forever,
    your God, O Zion, for all generations.

Praise the Lord.

Psalm 147

[1] Praise the Lord.[c]

How good it is to sing praises to our God,
    how pleasant and fitting to praise him!

[2] The Lord builds up Jerusalem;
    he gathers the exiles of Israel.
[3] He heals the brokenhearted
    and binds up their wounds.
[4] He determines the number of the stars
    and calls them each by name.
[5] Great is our Lord and mighty in power;
    his understanding has no limit.
[6] The Lord sustains the humble
    but casts the wicked to the ground.

[7] Sing to the Lord with grateful praise;
    make music to our God on the harp.

[8] He covers the sky with clouds;
    he supplies the earth with rain
    and makes grass grow on the hills.
[9] He provides food for the cattle
    and for the young ravens when they
    call.

[10] His pleasure is not in the strength of the
    horse,
    nor his delight in the legs of the
    warrior;
[11] the Lord delights in those who fear him,
    who put their hope in his unfailing
    love.

[12] Extol the Lord, Jerusalem;
    praise your God, Zion.

[13] He strengthens the bars of your gates
    and blesses your people within you.
[14] He grants peace to your borders
    and satisfies you with the finest of
    wheat.

[a] 13 One manuscript of the Masoretic Text, Dead Sea Scrolls and Syriac (see also Septuagint); most
manuscripts of the Masoretic Text do not have the last two lines of verse 13.   [b] 1 Hebrew *Hallelu Yah*;
also in verse 10   [c] 1 Hebrew *Hallelu Yah*; also in verse 20

¹⁵ He sends his command to the earth;
  his word runs swiftly.
¹⁶ He spreads the snow like wool
  and scatters the frost like ashes.
¹⁷ He hurls down his hail like pebbles.
  Who can withstand his icy blast?
¹⁸ He sends his word and melts them;
  he stirs up his breezes, and the
    waters flow.

¹⁹ He has revealed his word to Jacob,
  his laws and decrees to Israel.
²⁰ He has done this for no other nation;
  they do not know his laws.[a]

Praise the LORD.

Psalm 148

¹ Praise the LORD.[b]

Praise the LORD from the heavens;
  praise him in the heights above.
² Praise him, all his angels;
  praise him, all his heavenly hosts.
³ Praise him, sun and moon;
  praise him, all you shining stars.
⁴ Praise him, you highest heavens
  and you waters above the skies.

⁵ Let them praise the name of the LORD,
  for at his command they were
    created,
⁶ and he established them for ever and
    ever —
  he issued a decree that will never pass
    away.

⁷ Praise the LORD from the earth,
  you great sea creatures and all ocean
    depths,
⁸ lightning and hail, snow and clouds,
  stormy winds that do his bidding,
⁹ you mountains and all hills,
  fruit trees and all cedars,
¹⁰ wild animals and all cattle,
  small creatures and flying birds,
¹¹ kings of the earth and all nations,
  you princes and all rulers on earth,
¹² young men and women,
  old men and children.

¹³ Let them praise the name of the LORD,
  for his name alone is exalted;

his splendor is above the earth and the
    heavens.
¹⁴ And he has raised up for his people a
    horn,[c]
  the praise of all his faithful servants,
  of Israel, the people close to his heart.

Praise the LORD.

Psalm 149

¹ Praise the LORD.[d]

Sing to the LORD a new song,
  his praise in the assembly of his
    faithful people.

² Let Israel rejoice in their Maker;
  let the people of Zion be glad in their
    King.
³ Let them praise his name with dancing
  and make music to him with timbrel
    and harp.
⁴ For the LORD takes delight in his
    people;
  he crowns the humble with victory.
⁵ Let his faithful people rejoice in this
    honor
  and sing for joy on their beds.

⁶ May the praise of God be in their
    mouths
  and a double-edged sword in their
    hands,
⁷ to inflict vengeance on the nations
  and punishment on the peoples,
⁸ to bind their kings with fetters,
  their nobles with shackles of iron,
⁹ to carry out the sentence written against
    them —
  this is the glory of all his faithful
    people.

Praise the LORD.

Psalm 150

¹ Praise the LORD.[e]

Praise God in his sanctuary;
  praise him in his mighty heavens.
² Praise him for his acts of power;
  praise him for his surpassing
    greatness.

---

[a] 20 Masoretic Text; Dead Sea Scrolls and Septuagint *nation; / he has not made his laws known to them*
[b] 1 Hebrew *Hallelu Yah*; also in verse 14   [c] 14 *Horn* here symbolizes strength.   [d] 1 Hebrew *Hallelu Yah*;
also in verse 9   [e] 1 Hebrew *Hallelu Yah*; also in verse 6

Praise the Lord!

By Rebekah Benimoff

READ: Psalm 150

I was born with a song in my heart, as music is a precious connection with God. From the moment I fell in love with Jesus, I reveled in praising him. Until that season when my life was broken open and my heart was dragged across shards of glass. Dreams shattered, ground into dust, and I clung to what (and *who*) I knew. I sought God, who understood my need to be held. I spent worship services crying out for healing. I wondered if I would ever sing again. Each time music would begin, my song was immersed in grief. I could not see beyond pain, yet I held on to hope. Or rather, God held on to me.

Now, years after diagnoses for my husband — including PTSD — that I thought would destroy my world, I am finding restoration within my marriage and my own heart. As healing comes, the challenge is to see life as it is now, not look through the lens of past realities. And praise, entwined with thanksgiving, has provided a life-giving cordial to refresh my soul, teaching me to see through the eyes of truth.

What is praise? It is worship, tribute, exaltation. Praise is born of gratitude but distinct from it. Thankfulness springs from remembering all God has done, praise is recognizing who he is. Praise allows us to see outside ourselves, to look beyond our moods, our challenges and our wounds. Praise opens our eyes to the glory of God.

Have you ever glimpsed the glory of God Most High? Reveled in his beauty? Reflected on his captivating splendor? Speaking of his vision of God, the prophet Isaiah said, "I saw the Lord, high and exalted, seated on a throne; and the train of his robe filled the temple" (Isaiah 6:1).

The *train* of his robe! Imagine! This glimpse was enough to fill an entire temple with God's glory. We cannot begin to grasp his majesty. Yet God, the One who created all there is, longs for a day-to-day relationship with each of us. "The whole earth is full of his glory" (Isaiah 6:3), yet he loves and chooses *me*! And if you are his child, rest assured that he also loves and chooses *you*.

Take time each day — when you lie down and when you rise up, when you walk, when you run, and, yes, even when you feel like you're crawling — to celebrate who God is. Delight in him when you weep and when you find joy. Know that he is stable no matter what is going on in your life. He is worthy to be praised — simply because of who he is.

Let everything that has breath praise the LORD. Praise the LORD.
PSALM 150:6

DEBRIEF

- How can I cultivate the habit of praising my great God on a daily basis?
- I will list five attributes of God for which he deserves praise.

REPORT

God, you are holy, without blemish, unselfish and pure. You are love! Almighty deliverer, faithful and true, you are King of kings! All sufficient lover of my soul, you are my strength, my refuge, my rock. Creative and giving, you are the Lord of my peace. Amen.

for your next devotional reading, go to page 438

[3] Praise him with the sounding of the
trumpet,
praise him with the harp and lyre,
[4] praise him with timbrel and dancing,
praise him with the strings and
pipe,

[5] praise him with the clash of cymbals,
praise him with resounding cymbals.

[6] Let everything that has breath praise
the LORD.

Praise the LORD.

Proverbs

Purpose and Theme

1 The proverbs of Solomon son of David, king of Israel:

[2] for gaining wisdom and instruction;
for understanding words of insight;
[3] for receiving instruction in prudent
behavior,
doing what is right and just and fair;
[4] for giving prudence to those who are
simple,[a]
knowledge and discretion to the
young—
[5] let the wise listen and add to their
learning,
and let the discerning get guidance—
[6] for understanding proverbs and parables,
the sayings and riddles of the wise.[b]

[7] The fear of the LORD is the beginning of
knowledge,
but fools[c] despise wisdom and
instruction.

Prologue:
Exhortations to Embrace Wisdom

Warning Against the Invitation
of Sinful Men

[8] Listen, my son, to your father's
instruction
and do not forsake your mother's
teaching.
[9] They are a garland to grace your head
and a chain to adorn your neck.

[10] My son, if sinful men entice you,
do not give in to them.
[11] If they say, "Come along with us;
let's lie in wait for innocent blood,
let's ambush some harmless soul;
[12] let's swallow them alive, like the grave,
and whole, like those who go down to
the pit;

[13] we will get all sorts of valuable things
and fill our houses with plunder;
[14] cast lots with us;
we will all share the loot"—
[15] my son, do not go along with them,
do not set foot on their paths;
[16] for their feet rush into evil,
they are swift to shed blood.
[17] How useless to spread a net
where every bird can see it!
[18] These men lie in wait for their own blood;
they ambush only themselves!
[19] Such are the paths of all who go after ill-
gotten gain;
it takes away the life of those who get it.

Wisdom's Rebuke

[20] Out in the open wisdom calls aloud,
she raises her voice in the public
square;
[21] on top of the wall[d] she cries out,
at the city gate she makes her speech:

[22] "How long will you who are simple love
your simple ways?
How long will mockers delight in
mockery
and fools hate knowledge?
[23] Repent at my rebuke!
Then I will pour out my thoughts to you,
I will make known to you my
teachings.
[24] But since you refuse to listen when I call
and no one pays attention when I
stretch out my hand,
[25] since you disregard all my advice
and do not accept my rebuke,
[26] I in turn will laugh when disaster
strikes you;
I will mock when calamity overtakes
you—
[27] when calamity overtakes you like a
storm,

---

[a] 4 The Hebrew word rendered *simple* in Proverbs denotes a person who is gullible, without moral direction and inclined to evil.   [b] 6 Or *understanding a proverb, namely, a parable, / and the sayings of the wise, their riddles*   [c] 7 The Hebrew words rendered *fool* in Proverbs, and often elsewhere in the Old Testament, denote a person who is morally deficient.   [d] 21 Septuagint; Hebrew / *at noisy street corners*

when disaster sweeps over you like a
   whirlwind,
when distress and trouble overwhelm
   you.

28 "Then they will call to me but I will not
   answer;
   they will look for me but will not
      find me,
29 since they hated knowledge
   and did not choose to fear the LORD.
30 Since they would not accept my advice
   and spurned my rebuke,
31 they will eat the fruit of their ways
   and be filled with the fruit of their
      schemes.
32 For the waywardness of the simple will
      kill them,
   and the complacency of fools will
      destroy them;
33 but whoever listens to me will live in
      safety
   and be at ease, without fear of harm."

Moral Benefits of Wisdom

2 My son, if you accept my words
   and store up my commands within you,
2 turning your ear to wisdom
   and applying your heart to
      understanding—
3 indeed, if you call out for insight
   and cry aloud for understanding,
4 and if you look for it as for silver
   and search for it as for hidden treasure,
5 then you will understand the fear of the
      LORD
   and find the knowledge of God.
6 For the LORD gives wisdom;
   from his mouth come knowledge and
      understanding.
7 He holds success in store for the upright,
   he is a shield to those whose walk is
      blameless,
8 for he guards the course of the just
   and protects the way of his faithful ones.
9 Then you will understand what is right
      and just
   and fair—every good path.
10 For wisdom will enter your heart,
   and knowledge will be pleasant to
      your soul.
11 Discretion will protect you,
   and understanding will guard you.

12 Wisdom will save you from the ways of
      wicked men,
   from men whose words are perverse,
13 who have left the straight paths
   to walk in dark ways,
14 who delight in doing wrong
   and rejoice in the perverseness of evil,
15 whose paths are crooked
   and who are devious in their ways.

16 Wisdom will save you also from the
      adulterous woman,
   from the wayward woman with her
      seductive words,
17 who has left the partner of her youth
   and ignored the covenant she made
      before God.^{a}
18 Surely her house leads down to death
   and her paths to the spirits of the dead.
19 None who go to her return
   or attain the paths of life.

20 Thus you will walk in the ways of the
      good
   and keep to the paths of the righteous.
21 For the upright will live in the land,
   and the blameless will remain in it;
22 but the wicked will be cut off from the
      land,
   and the unfaithful will be torn from it.

Wisdom Bestows Well-Being

3 My son, do not forget my teaching,
   but keep my commands in your heart,
2 for they will prolong your life many years
   and bring you peace and prosperity.

3 Let love and faithfulness never leave you;
   bind them around your neck,
   write them on the tablet of your heart.
4 Then you will win favor and a good name
   in the sight of God and man.

5 Trust in the LORD with all your heart
   and lean not on your own
      understanding;
6 in all your ways submit to him,
   and he will make your paths straight.^{b}

7 Do not be wise in your own eyes;
   fear the LORD and shun evil.
8 This will bring health to your body
   and nourishment to your bones.

9 Honor the LORD with your wealth,
   with the firstfruits of all your crops;

---

^{a} 17 Or *covenant of her God* ^{b} 6 Or *will direct your paths*

TRUST IN THE LORD

By Jane Hampton Cook

"The day — perhaps, the decisive day — is come, on which the fate of America depends. My bursting heart must find vent at my pen," Abigail Adams wrote to her husband, John, on June 18, 1775.

Massachusetts leaders had attempted to preempt a British strike by secretly ordering 1,200 men to build fortifications and trenches on Bunker Hill. Instead, the militia had fortified Breed's Hill because it was closer to Boston Harbor.

On the morning of June 17, the British awoke and saw the hill's fortifications. They responded by attacking and advanced three times before taking the hill. The battle became known as the Battle of Bunker Hill, although it occurred on Breed's Hill. After defeating the Continental Army, British soldiers burned the neighboring city of Charlestown.

From a hill near her farm south of Boston, Abigail could see smoke billowing into the air as the battle inched toward her doorstep. Since John was away serving the Continental Congress in Philadelphia, Abigail was left alone and wondered how she could possibly manage her small brood of children in the face of such danger.

Abigail immediately turned to her faith. "Almighty God, cover the heads of our countrymen, and be a shield to our dear friends," she wrote to John. "How many have fallen, we know not. The constant roar of the cannon is so distressing, that we cannot eat, drink, or sleep. May we be supported and sustained in the dreadful conflict."

Abigail took practical steps while maintaining a positive attitude rooted in her faith. She explained her plan to John to remain at their home and retreat if necessary to her brother-in-law's house. Her pen was her therapy; her faith was her compass.

"The race is not to the swift, nor the battle to the strong; but the God of Israel is he that giveth strength and power unto his people. Trust in him at all times, ye people, pour out your hearts before him; God is a refuge for us," she wrote, combining Ecclesiastes 9:11, Psalm 68:35 and Psalm 62:8 (KJV). Within a few days the militia retreated away from Abigail's home.

The British may have taken the hill, but their victory came at a cost. More than 200 redcoats perished and more than 800 were wounded. These casualties were approximately 40 percent of their force in Boston. The colonists, however, lost only 140 to death and only 300 were wounded. Bunker Hill bolstered the colonists' confidence. Though initially a defeat, the battle gave them hope of an ultimate victory.

Once the smoke cleared, Abigail and her fellow Bostonians could see God's hand during uncertain circumstances. The same is true today. We can trust God no matter our situation.

Prayer: Teach me to trust in you and pour out my heart to you always.

Trust in the LORD with all your heart and lean not on your own understanding; in all your ways submit to him, and he will make your paths straight.
PROVERBS 3:5 – 6

for your next devotional reading, go to page 442

¹⁰ then your barns will be filled to
overflowing,
and your vats will brim over with
new wine.

¹¹ My son, do not despise the LORD's
discipline,
and do not resent his rebuke,
¹² because the LORD disciplines those
he loves,
as a father the son he delights in.*

¹³ Blessed are those who find wisdom,
those who gain understanding,
¹⁴ for she is more profitable than silver
and yields better returns than gold.
¹⁵ She is more precious than rubies;
nothing you desire can compare
with her.
¹⁶ Long life is in her right hand;
in her left hand are riches and honor.
¹⁷ Her ways are pleasant ways,
and all her paths are peace.
¹⁸ She is a tree of life to those who take hold
of her;
those who hold her fast will be
blessed.

¹⁹ By wisdom the LORD laid the earth's
foundations,
by understanding he set the heavens
in place;
²⁰ by his knowledge the watery depths were
divided,
and the clouds let drop the dew.

²¹ My son, do not let wisdom and
understanding out of your sight,
preserve sound judgment and
discretion;
²² they will be life for you,
an ornament to grace your neck.
²³ Then you will go on your way in safety,
and your foot will not stumble.
²⁴ When you lie down, you will not be
afraid;
when you lie down, your sleep will be
sweet.
²⁵ Have no fear of sudden disaster
or of the ruin that overtakes the
wicked,
²⁶ for the LORD will be at your side
and will keep your foot from being
snared.

²⁷ Do not withhold good from those to
whom it is due,
when it is in your power to act.
²⁸ Do not say to your neighbor,
"Come back tomorrow and I'll give it
to you" —
when you already have it with you.
²⁹ Do not plot harm against your neighbor,
who lives trustfully near you.
³⁰ Do not accuse anyone for no reason —
when they have done you no harm.

³¹ Do not envy the violent
or choose any of their ways.

³² For the LORD detests the perverse
but takes the upright into his
confidence.
³³ The LORD's curse is on the house of the
wicked,
but he blesses the home of the
righteous.
³⁴ He mocks proud mockers
but shows favor to the humble and
oppressed.
³⁵ The wise inherit honor,
but fools get only shame.

Get Wisdom at Any Cost

4 Listen, my sons, to a father's
instruction;
pay attention and gain understanding.
² I give you sound learning,
so do not forsake my teaching.
³ For I too was a son to my father,
still tender, and cherished by my
mother.
⁴ Then he taught me, and he said to me,
"Take hold of my words with all your
heart;
keep my commands, and you will live.
⁵ Get wisdom, get understanding;
do not forget my words or turn away
from them.
⁶ Do not forsake wisdom, and she will
protect you;
love her, and she will watch over you.
⁷ The beginning of wisdom is this: Get*ᵇ*
wisdom.
Though it cost all you have,*ᶜ* get
understanding.
⁸ Cherish her, and she will exalt you;
embrace her, and she will honor you.

ᵃ 12 Hebrew; Septuagint *loves, / and he chastens everyone he accepts as his child*   *ᵇ 7* Or *Wisdom is
supreme; therefore get*   *ᶜ 7* Or *wisdom. / Whatever else you get*

⁹ She will give you a garland to grace
   your head
   and present you with a glorious crown."

¹⁰ Listen, my son, accept what I say,
   and the years of your life will be many.
¹¹ I instruct you in the way of wisdom
   and lead you along straight paths.
¹² When you walk, your steps will not be
   hampered;
   when you run, you will not stumble.
¹³ Hold on to instruction, do not let it go;
   guard it well, for it is your life.
¹⁴ Do not set foot on the path of the wicked
   or walk in the way of evildoers.
¹⁵ Avoid it, do not travel on it;
   turn from it and go on your way.
¹⁶ For they cannot rest until they do evil;
   they are robbed of sleep till they make
   someone stumble.
¹⁷ They eat the bread of wickedness
   and drink the wine of violence.

¹⁸ The path of the righteous is like the
   morning sun,
   shining ever brighter till the full light
   of day.
¹⁹ But the way of the wicked is like deep
   darkness;
   they do not know what makes them
   stumble.

²⁰ My son, pay attention to what I say;
   turn your ear to my words.
²¹ Do not let them out of your sight,
   keep them within your heart;
²² for they are life to those who find them
   and health to one's whole body.
²³ Above all else, guard your heart,
   for everything you do flows from it.
²⁴ Keep your mouth free of perversity;
   keep corrupt talk far from your lips.
²⁵ Let your eyes look straight ahead;
   fix your gaze directly before you.
²⁶ Give careful thought to the*ᵃ* paths for
   your feet
   and be steadfast in all your ways.
²⁷ Do not turn to the right or the left;
   keep your foot from evil.

Warning Against Adultery

5 My son, pay attention to my wisdom,
   turn your ear to my words of insight,
² that you may maintain discretion
   and your lips may preserve knowledge.

³ For the lips of the adulterous woman drip
   honey,
   and her speech is smoother than oil;
⁴ but in the end she is bitter as gall,
   sharp as a double-edged sword.
⁵ Her feet go down to death;
   her steps lead straight to the grave.
⁶ She gives no thought to the way of life;
   her paths wander aimlessly, but she
   does not know it.

⁷ Now then, my sons, listen to me;
   do not turn aside from what I say.
⁸ Keep to a path far from her,
   do not go near the door of her house,
⁹ lest you lose your honor to others
   and your dignity*ᵇ* to one who is cruel,
¹⁰ lest strangers feast on your wealth
   and your toil enrich the house of
   another.
¹¹ At the end of your life you will groan,
   when your flesh and body are spent.
¹² You will say, "How I hated discipline!
   How my heart spurned correction!
¹³ I would not obey my teachers
   or turn my ear to my instructors.
¹⁴ And I was soon in serious trouble
   in the assembly of God's people."

¹⁵ Drink water from your own cistern,
   running water from your own well.
¹⁶ Should your springs overflow in the
   streets,
   your streams of water in the public
   squares?
¹⁷ Let them be yours alone,
   never to be shared with strangers.
¹⁸ May your fountain be blessed,
   and may you rejoice in the wife of your
   youth.
¹⁹ A loving doe, a graceful deer—
   may her breasts satisfy you always,
   may you ever be intoxicated with
   her love.
²⁰ Why, my son, be intoxicated with another
   man's wife?
   Why embrace the bosom of a wayward
   woman?

²¹ For your ways are in full view of the LORD,
   and he examines all your paths.
²² The evil deeds of the wicked ensnare
   them;
   the cords of their sins hold them fast.

ᵃ 26 Or *Make level*   *ᵇ 9* Or *years*

Guard Your Gate

By Alane Pearce

READ: Proverbs 4:23

The idea of guarding our hearts (see Proverbs 4:23) takes on new meaning when we consider it from a military perspective. It's part of our everyday life. We drive onto a military installation and are stopped by a guard at the gate who ensures that we are authorized to have access. It's so common for military families that we don't even think about it; but I, for one, certainly appreciate the feeling of freedom and safety that comes with being on base.

This was especially true when my family was stationed at the Pentagon in the fall of 2002 when the Beltway Sniper was making national headlines. It was not safe to run errands, get groceries or buy gas anywhere in and around Washington, D.C., because no one knew when or where the sniper would attack next. I always breathed a sigh of relief as I gained access to Fort Belvoir for my grocery and gas run, because I knew the gate guards would not knowingly allow a sniper on post.

Proverbs 4:23 isn't talking about locking down our hearts and not allowing anyone in. Instead, we are to guard our hearts in the same way that the men and women of the armed forces guard the gates at our military installations.

Supervising entry and exit: Our gate guards stop every car and check IDs. Without an ID, you can't get in — you have to have authorization to gain access to the installation. When you guard your heart, you need to supervise the entry and exit of ideas, thoughts, actions, sins, etc. If something should not have access to your heart, you shouldn't let it in.

Protecting from harm: Our gate guards carry guns to protect us from harm. You also need to protect your heart from harm by watching over it. The Bible says our weapon of choice is God's Word (see Ephesians 6:17). You can protect your heart from harm by arming yourself with the Scriptures.

Maintaining control: Our gate guards maintain control of our installations by refusing access to those who would harm the mission. In the same way, we need to maintain control of our hearts and not allow things in that destroy God's mission for us. Keep sin outside of the gate of your heart, maintaining control of your life to ensure it reflects God's desires.

When you guard your heart, you create a safe place inside. When your heart is safe and filled with good, that good overflows into your life for your benefit and for the benefit of others.

Above all else, guard your heart, for everything you do flows from it.
PROVERBS 4:23

DEBRIEF
- What do I let into my heart that doesn't have authorized access?
- I will choose and memorize specific Scripture passages to guard against those things.

REPORT
God, help me remember every day to guard my heart as well as the gate guards who keep watch over our military installations. Help me determine which things have your authorization to enter, and help me be strong enough not to allow in that which causes harm. Amen.

for your next devotional reading, go to page 456

23 For lack of discipline they will die,
  led astray by their own great folly.

Warnings Against Folly

6 My son, if you have put up security for
  your neighbor,
  if you have shaken hands in pledge for
  a stranger,
2 you have been trapped by what you said,
  ensnared by the words of your mouth.
3 So do this, my son, to free yourself,
  since you have fallen into your
  neighbor's hands:
  Go — to the point of exhaustion — *a*
  and give your neighbor no rest!
4 Allow no sleep to your eyes,
  no slumber to your eyelids.
5 Free yourself, like a gazelle from the
  hand of the hunter,
  like a bird from the snare of the fowler.

6 Go to the ant, you sluggard;
  consider its ways and be wise!
7 It has no commander,
  no overseer or ruler,
8 yet it stores its provisions in summer
  and gathers its food at harvest.

9 How long will you lie there, you sluggard?
  When will you get up from your sleep?
10 A little sleep, a little slumber,
  a little folding of the hands to rest —
11 and poverty will come on you like a thief
  and scarcity like an armed man.

12 A troublemaker and a villain,
  who goes about with a corrupt mouth,
13 who winks maliciously with his eye,
  signals with his feet
  and motions with his fingers,
14 who plots evil with deceit in his
  heart —
  he always stirs up conflict.
15 Therefore disaster will overtake him in
  an instant;
  he will suddenly be destroyed —
  without remedy.

16 There are six things the LORD hates,
  seven that are detestable to him:
17 haughty eyes,
  a lying tongue,
  hands that shed innocent blood,
18 a heart that devises wicked schemes,
  feet that are quick to rush into evil,

19 a false witness who pours out lies
  and a person who stirs up conflict in
  the community.

Warning Against Adultery

20 My son, keep your father's command
  and do not forsake your mother's
  teaching.
21 Bind them always on your heart;
  fasten them around your neck.
22 When you walk, they will guide you;
  when you sleep, they will watch over
  you;
  when you awake, they will speak to you.
23 For this command is a lamp,
  this teaching is a light,
  and correction and instruction
  are the way to life,
24 keeping you from your neighbor's wife,
  from the smooth talk of a wayward
  woman.

25 Do not lust in your heart after her beauty
  or let her captivate you with her eyes.
26 For a prostitute can be had for a loaf of
  bread,
  but another man's wife preys on your
  very life.
27 Can a man scoop fire into his lap
  without his clothes being burned?
28 Can a man walk on hot coals
  without his feet being scorched?
29 So is he who sleeps with another man's
  wife;
  no one who touches her will go
  unpunished.

30 People do not despise a thief if he steals
  to satisfy his hunger when he is
  starving.
31 Yet if he is caught, he must pay sevenfold,
  though it costs him all the wealth of
  his house.
32 But a man who commits adultery has
  no sense;
  whoever does so destroys himself.
33 Blows and disgrace are his lot,
  and his shame will never be wiped
  away.

34 For jealousy arouses a husband's fury,
  and he will show no mercy when he
  takes revenge.

a 3 Or *Go and humble yourself,*

[35] He will not accept any compensation;
   he will refuse a bribe, however great
      it is.

Warning Against the Adulterous Woman

7 My son, keep my words
   and store up my commands within you.
[2] Keep my commands and you will live;
   guard my teachings as the apple of
      your eye.
[3] Bind them on your fingers;
   write them on the tablet of your heart.
[4] Say to wisdom, "You are my sister,"
   and to insight, "You are my relative."
[5] They will keep you from the adulterous
      woman,
   from the wayward woman with her
      seductive words.

[6] At the window of my house
   I looked down through the lattice.
[7] I saw among the simple,
   I noticed among the young men,
   a youth who had no sense.
[8] He was going down the street near her
      corner,
   walking along in the direction of her
      house
[9] at twilight, as the day was fading,
   as the dark of night set in.

[10] Then out came a woman to meet him,
   dressed like a prostitute and with
      crafty intent.
[11] (She is unruly and defiant,
   her feet never stay at home;
[12] now in the street, now in the squares,
   at every corner she lurks.)
[13] She took hold of him and kissed him
   and with a brazen face she said:

[14] "Today I fulfilled my vows,
   and I have food from my fellowship
      offering at home.
[15] So I came out to meet you;
   I looked for you and have found you!
[16] I have covered my bed
   with colored linens from Egypt.
[17] I have perfumed my bed
   with myrrh, aloes and cinnamon.
[18] Come, let's drink deeply of love till
      morning;
   let's enjoy ourselves with love!

[19] My husband is not at home;
   he has gone on a long journey.
[20] He took his purse filled with money
   and will not be home till full moon."

[21] With persuasive words she led him
      astray;
   she seduced him with her smooth talk.
[22] All at once he followed her
   like an ox going to the slaughter,
   like a deer[a] stepping into a noose[b]
[23]   till an arrow pierces his liver,
   like a bird darting into a snare,
      little knowing it will cost him his life.

[24] Now then, my sons, listen to me;
   pay attention to what I say.
[25] Do not let your heart turn to her ways
   or stray into her paths.
[26] Many are the victims she has brought
      down;
   her slain are a mighty throng.
[27] Her house is a highway to the grave,
   leading down to the chambers of
      death.

Wisdom's Call

8 Does not wisdom call out?
   Does not understanding raise her
      voice?
[2] At the highest point along the way,
   where the paths meet, she takes her
      stand;
[3] beside the gate leading into the city,
   at the entrance, she cries aloud:
[4] "To you, O people, I call out;
   I raise my voice to all mankind.
[5] You who are simple, gain prudence;
   you who are foolish, set your hearts
      on it.[c]
[6] Listen, for I have trustworthy things
      to say;
   I open my lips to speak what is right.
[7] My mouth speaks what is true,
   for my lips detest wickedness.
[8] All the words of my mouth are just;
   none of them is crooked or perverse.
[9] To the discerning all of them are right;
   they are upright to those who have
      found knowledge.
[10] Choose my instruction instead of silver,
   knowledge rather than choice gold,

---

[a] 22 Syriac (see also Septuagint); Hebrew *fool*   [b] 22 The meaning of the Hebrew for this line is
uncertain.   [c] 5 Septuagint; Hebrew *foolish, instruct your minds*

[11] for wisdom is more precious than rubies,
  and nothing you desire can compare
    with her.

[12] "I, wisdom, dwell together with
    prudence;
  I possess knowledge and discretion.
[13] To fear the LORD is to hate evil;
  I hate pride and arrogance,
    evil behavior and perverse speech.
[14] Counsel and sound judgment are mine;
  I have insight, I have power.
[15] By me kings reign
  and rulers issue decrees that are just;
[16] by me princes govern,
  and nobles — all who rule on earth.[a]
[17] I love those who love me,
  and those who seek me find me.
[18] With me are riches and honor,
  enduring wealth and prosperity.
[19] My fruit is better than fine gold;
  what I yield surpasses choice silver.
[20] I walk in the way of righteousness,
  along the paths of justice,
[21] bestowing a rich inheritance on those
    who love me
  and making their treasuries full.

[22] "The LORD brought me forth as the first of
    his works,[b,c]
  before his deeds of old;
[23] I was formed long ages ago,
  at the very beginning, when the world
    came to be.
[24] When there were no watery depths, I was
    given birth,
  when there were no springs
    overflowing with water;
[25] before the mountains were settled in
    place,
  before the hills, I was given birth,
[26] before he made the world or its fields
  or any of the dust of the earth.
[27] I was there when he set the heavens in
    place,
  when he marked out the horizon on
    the face of the deep,
[28] when he established the clouds above
  and fixed securely the fountains of
    the deep,

[29] when he gave the sea its boundary
  so the waters would not overstep his
    command,
  and when he marked out the foundations
    of the earth.
[30]   Then I was constantly[d] at his side.
  I was filled with delight day after day,
  rejoicing always in his presence,
[31] rejoicing in his whole world
  and delighting in mankind.

[32] "Now then, my children, listen to me;
  blessed are those who keep my ways.
[33] Listen to my instruction and be wise;
  do not disregard it.
[34] Blessed are those who listen to me,
  watching daily at my doors,
  waiting at my doorway.
[35] For those who find me find life
  and receive favor from the LORD.
[36] But those who fail to find me harm
    themselves;
  all who hate me love death."

Invitations of Wisdom and Folly

9 Wisdom has built her house;
  she has set up[e] its seven pillars.
[2] She has prepared her meat and mixed
    her wine;
  she has also set her table.
[3] She has sent out her servants, and she
    calls
  from the highest point of the city,
[4]   "Let all who are simple come to my
    house!"
  To those who have no sense she says,
[5]   "Come, eat my food
  and drink the wine I have mixed.
[6] Leave your simple ways and you will live;
  walk in the way of insight."

[7] Whoever corrects a mocker invites
    insults;
  whoever rebukes the wicked incurs
    abuse.
[8] Do not rebuke mockers or they will
    hate you;
  rebuke the wise and they will love you.
[9] Instruct the wise and they will be wiser
    still;

---

[a] 16 Some Hebrew manuscripts and Septuagint; other Hebrew manuscripts *all righteous rulers*
[b] 22 Or *way*; or *dominion*   [c] 22 Or *The LORD possessed me at the beginning of his work*; or *The LORD brought me forth at the beginning of his work*   [d] 30 Or *was the artisan*; or *was a little child*
[e] 1 Septuagint, Syriac and Targum; Hebrew *has hewn out*

teach the righteous and they will add
to their learning.

¹⁰ The fear of the LORD is the beginning of
wisdom,
and knowledge of the Holy One is
understanding.
¹¹ For through wisdom*ᵃ* your days will
be many,
and years will be added to your life.
¹² If you are wise, your wisdom will reward
you;
if you are a mocker, you alone will
suffer.

¹³ Folly is an unruly woman;
she is simple and knows nothing.
¹⁴ She sits at the door of her house,
on a seat at the highest point of the
city,
¹⁵ calling out to those who pass by,
who go straight on their way,
¹⁶   "Let all who are simple come to my
house!"
To those who have no sense she says,
¹⁷   "Stolen water is sweet;
food eaten in secret is delicious!"
¹⁸ But little do they know that the dead are
there,
that her guests are deep in the realm of
the dead.

Proverbs of Solomon

10 The proverbs of Solomon:

A wise son brings joy to his father,
but a foolish son brings grief to his
mother.

² Ill-gotten treasures have no lasting value,
but righteousness delivers from death.

³ The LORD does not let the righteous go
hungry,
but he thwarts the craving of the
wicked.

⁴ Lazy hands make for poverty,
but diligent hands bring wealth.

⁵ He who gathers crops in summer is a
prudent son,
but he who sleeps during harvest is a
disgraceful son.

⁶ Blessings crown the head of the
righteous,
but violence overwhelms the mouth of
the wicked.*ᵇ*

⁷ The name of the righteous is used in
blessings,*ᶜ*
but the name of the wicked will rot.

⁸ The wise in heart accept commands,
but a chattering fool comes to ruin.

⁹ Whoever walks in integrity walks
securely,
but whoever takes crooked paths will
be found out.

¹⁰ Whoever winks maliciously causes grief,
and a chattering fool comes to ruin.

¹¹ The mouth of the righteous is a fountain
of life,
but the mouth of the wicked conceals
violence.

¹² Hatred stirs up conflict,
but love covers over all wrongs.

¹³ Wisdom is found on the lips of the
discerning,
but a rod is for the back of one who has
no sense.

¹⁴ The wise store up knowledge,
but the mouth of a fool invites ruin.

¹⁵ The wealth of the rich is their fortified
city,
but poverty is the ruin of the poor.

¹⁶ The wages of the righteous is life,
but the earnings of the wicked are sin
and death.

¹⁷ Whoever heeds discipline shows the way
to life,
but whoever ignores correction leads
others astray.

¹⁸ Whoever conceals hatred with lying lips
and spreads slander is a fool.

¹⁹ Sin is not ended by multiplying words,
but the prudent hold their tongues.

²⁰ The tongue of the righteous is choice
silver,
but the heart of the wicked is of little
value.

ᵃ 11 Septuagint, Syriac and Targum; Hebrew *me
conceals violence*   *ᶜ 7* See Gen. 48:20.   *ᵇ 6* Or *righteous, / but the mouth of the wicked*

²¹ The lips of the righteous nourish many,
but fools die for lack of sense.

²² The blessing of the LORD brings wealth,
without painful toil for it.

²³ A fool finds pleasure in wicked schemes,
but a person of understanding delights
in wisdom.

²⁴ What the wicked dread will overtake
them;
what the righteous desire will be
granted.

²⁵ When the storm has swept by, the wicked
are gone,
but the righteous stand firm forever.

²⁶ As vinegar to the teeth and smoke to the
eyes,
so are sluggards to those who send
them.

²⁷ The fear of the LORD adds length to life,
but the years of the wicked are cut
short.

²⁸ The prospect of the righteous is joy,
but the hopes of the wicked come to
nothing.

²⁹ The way of the LORD is a refuge for the
blameless,
but it is the ruin of those who do evil.

³⁰ The righteous will never be uprooted,
but the wicked will not remain in
the land.

³¹ From the mouth of the righteous comes
the fruit of wisdom,
but a perverse tongue will be silenced.

³² The lips of the righteous know what finds
favor,
but the mouth of the wicked only what
is perverse.

11 The LORD detests dishonest scales,
but accurate weights find favor with
him.

² When pride comes, then comes disgrace,
but with humility comes wisdom.

³ The integrity of the upright guides them,
but the unfaithful are destroyed by
their duplicity.

⁴ Wealth is worthless in the day of wrath,
but righteousness delivers from death.

⁵ The righteousness of the blameless
makes their paths straight,
but the wicked are brought down by
their own wickedness.

⁶ The righteousness of the upright delivers
them,
but the unfaithful are trapped by evil
desires.

⁷ Hopes placed in mortals die with them;
all the promise ofª their power comes
to nothing.

⁸ The righteous person is rescued from
trouble,
and it falls on the wicked instead.

⁹ With their mouths the godless destroy
their neighbors,
but through knowledge the righteous
escape.

¹⁰ When the righteous prosper, the city
rejoices;
when the wicked perish, there are
shouts of joy.

¹¹ Through the blessing of the upright a city
is exalted,
but by the mouth of the wicked it is
destroyed.

¹² Whoever derides their neighbor has no
sense,
but the one who has understanding
holds their tongue.

¹³ A gossip betrays a confidence,
but a trustworthy person keeps a
secret.

¹⁴ For lack of guidance a nation falls,
but victory is won through many
advisers.

¹⁵ Whoever puts up security for a stranger
will surely suffer,
but whoever refuses to shake hands in
pledge is safe.

¹⁶ A kindhearted woman gains honor,
but ruthless men gain only wealth.

¹⁷ Those who are kind benefit themselves,
but the cruel bring ruin on themselves.

ª 7 Two Hebrew manuscripts; most Hebrew manuscripts, Vulgate, Syriac and Targum *When the wicked
die, their hope perishes; / all they expected from*

¹⁸ A wicked person earns deceptive wages,
but the one who sows righteousness
reaps a sure reward.

¹⁹ Truly the righteous attain life,
but whoever pursues evil finds death.

²⁰ The LORD detests those whose hearts are
perverse,
but he delights in those whose ways
are blameless.

²¹ Be sure of this: The wicked will not go
unpunished,
but those who are righteous will go free.

²² Like a gold ring in a pig's snout
is a beautiful woman who shows no
discretion.

²³ The desire of the righteous ends only in
good,
but the hope of the wicked only in
wrath.

²⁴ One person gives freely, yet gains even
more;
another withholds unduly, but comes
to poverty.

²⁵ A generous person will prosper;
whoever refreshes others will be
refreshed.

²⁶ People curse the one who hoards grain,
but they pray God's blessing on the one
who is willing to sell.

²⁷ Whoever seeks good finds favor,
but evil comes to one who searches
for it.

²⁸ Those who trust in their riches will fall,
but the righteous will thrive like a
green leaf.

²⁹ Whoever brings ruin on their family will
inherit only wind,
and the fool will be servant to the wise.

³⁰ The fruit of the righteous is a tree of life,
and the one who is wise saves lives.

³¹ If the righteous receive their due on
earth,
how much more the ungodly and the
sinner!

12 Whoever loves discipline loves
knowledge,
but whoever hates correction is stupid.

² Good people obtain favor from the LORD,
but he condemns those who devise
wicked schemes.

³ No one can be established through
wickedness,
but the righteous cannot be uprooted.

⁴ A wife of noble character is her husband's
crown,
but a disgraceful wife is like decay in
his bones.

⁵ The plans of the righteous are just,
but the advice of the wicked is
deceitful.

⁶ The words of the wicked lie in wait for
blood,
but the speech of the upright rescues
them.

⁷ The wicked are overthrown and are no
more,
but the house of the righteous stands
firm.

⁸ A person is praised according to their
prudence,
and one with a warped mind is
despised.

⁹ Better to be a nobody and yet have a
servant
than pretend to be somebody and have
no food.

¹⁰ The righteous care for the needs of their
animals,
but the kindest acts of the wicked are
cruel.

¹¹ Those who work their land will have
abundant food,
but those who chase fantasies have no
sense.

¹² The wicked desire the stronghold of
evildoers,
but the root of the righteous endures.

¹³ Evildoers are trapped by their sinful talk,
and so the innocent escape trouble.

¹⁴ From the fruit of their lips people are
filled with good things,
and the work of their hands brings
them reward.

¹⁵ The way of fools seems right to them,
but the wise listen to advice.

¹⁶ Fools show their annoyance at once,
  but the prudent overlook an insult.

¹⁷ An honest witness tells the truth,
  but a false witness tells lies.

¹⁸ The words of the reckless pierce like
    swords,
  but the tongue of the wise brings
    healing.

¹⁹ Truthful lips endure forever,
  but a lying tongue lasts only a moment.

²⁰ Deceit is in the hearts of those who plot
    evil,
  but those who promote peace have joy.

²¹ No harm overtakes the righteous,
  but the wicked have their fill of
    trouble.

²² The LORD detests lying lips,
  but he delights in people who are
    trustworthy.

²³ The prudent keep their knowledge to
    themselves,
  but a fool's heart blurts out folly.

²⁴ Diligent hands will rule,
  but laziness ends in forced labor.

²⁵ Anxiety weighs down the heart,
  but a kind word cheers it up.

²⁶ The righteous choose their friends
    carefully,
  but the way of the wicked leads them
    astray.

²⁷ The lazy do not roast[a] any game,
  but the diligent feed on the riches of
    the hunt.

²⁸ In the way of righteousness there is life;
  along that path is immortality.

13 A wise son heeds his father's
    instruction,
  but a mocker does not respond to
    rebukes.

² From the fruit of their lips people enjoy
    good things,
  but the unfaithful have an appetite for
    violence.

³ Those who guard their lips preserve their
    lives,

but those who speak rashly will come
    to ruin.

⁴ A sluggard's appetite is never filled,
  but the desires of the diligent are fully
    satisfied.

⁵ The righteous hate what is false,
  but the wicked make themselves
    a stench
  and bring shame on themselves.

⁶ Righteousness guards the person of
    integrity,
  but wickedness overthrows the
    sinner.

⁷ One person pretends to be rich, yet has
    nothing;
  another pretends to be poor, yet has
    great wealth.

⁸ A person's riches may ransom their life,
  but the poor cannot respond to
    threatening rebukes.

⁹ The light of the righteous shines
    brightly,
  but the lamp of the wicked is snuffed
    out.

¹⁰ Where there is strife, there is pride,
  but wisdom is found in those who take
    advice.

¹¹ Dishonest money dwindles away,
  but whoever gathers money little by
    little makes it grow.

¹² Hope deferred makes the heart sick,
  but a longing fulfilled is a tree of life.

¹³ Whoever scorns instruction will pay
    for it,
  but whoever respects a command is
    rewarded.

¹⁴ The teaching of the wise is a fountain
    of life,
  turning a person from the snares of
    death.

¹⁵ Good judgment wins favor,
  but the way of the unfaithful leads to
    their destruction.[b]

¹⁶ All who are prudent act with[c] knowledge,
  but fools expose their folly.

---

[a] 27 The meaning of the Hebrew for this word is uncertain.   [b] 15 Septuagint and Syriac; the meaning of
the Hebrew for this phrase is uncertain.   [c] 16 Or *prudent protect themselves through*

¹⁷ A wicked messenger falls into trouble,
  but a trustworthy envoy brings
    healing.

¹⁸ Whoever disregards discipline comes to
    poverty and shame,
  but whoever heeds correction is
    honored.

¹⁹ A longing fulfilled is sweet to the soul,
  but fools detest turning from evil.

²⁰ Walk with the wise and become wise,
  for a companion of fools suffers harm.

²¹ Trouble pursues the sinner,
  but the righteous are rewarded with
    good things.

²² A good person leaves an inheritance for
    their children's children,
  but a sinner's wealth is stored up for
    the righteous.

²³ An unplowed field produces food for the
    poor,
  but injustice sweeps it away.

²⁴ Whoever spares the rod hates their
    children,
  but the one who loves their children is
    careful to discipline them.

²⁵ The righteous eat to their hearts' content,
  but the stomach of the wicked goes
    hungry.

14 The wise woman builds her house,
  but with her own hands the foolish
    one tears hers down.

² Whoever fears the LORD walks uprightly,
  but those who despise him are devious
    in their ways.

³ A fool's mouth lashes out with pride,
  but the lips of the wise protect them.

⁴ Where there are no oxen, the manger is
    empty,
  but from the strength of an ox come
    abundant harvests.

⁵ An honest witness does not deceive,
  but a false witness pours out lies.

⁶ The mocker seeks wisdom and finds
    none,
  but knowledge comes easily to the
    discerning.

⁷ Stay away from a fool,
  for you will not find knowledge on
    their lips.

⁸ The wisdom of the prudent is to give
    thought to their ways,
  but the folly of fools is deception.

⁹ Fools mock at making amends for sin,
  but goodwill is found among the
    upright.

¹⁰ Each heart knows its own bitterness,
  and no one else can share its joy.

¹¹ The house of the wicked will be
    destroyed,
  but the tent of the upright will
    flourish.

¹² There is a way that appears to be right,
  but in the end it leads to death.

¹³ Even in laughter the heart may ache,
  and rejoicing may end in grief.

¹⁴ The faithless will be fully repaid for their
    ways,
  and the good rewarded for theirs.

¹⁵ The simple believe anything,
  but the prudent give thought to their
    steps.

¹⁶ The wise fear the LORD and shun evil,
  but a fool is hotheaded and yet feels
    secure.

¹⁷ A quick-tempered person does foolish
    things,
  and the one who devises evil schemes
    is hated.

¹⁸ The simple inherit folly,
  but the prudent are crowned with
    knowledge.

¹⁹ Evildoers will bow down in the presence
    of the good,
  and the wicked at the gates of the
    righteous.

²⁰ The poor are shunned even by their
    neighbors,
  but the rich have many friends.

²¹ It is a sin to despise one's neighbor,
  but blessed is the one who is kind to
    the needy.

²² Do not those who plot evil go astray?

But those who plan what is good find[a]
love and faithfulness.

²³ All hard work brings a profit,
but mere talk leads only to poverty.

²⁴ The wealth of the wise is their crown,
but the folly of fools yields folly.

²⁵ A truthful witness saves lives,
but a false witness is deceitful.

²⁶ Whoever fears the LORD has a secure
fortress,
and for their children it will be a refuge.

²⁷ The fear of the LORD is a fountain of life,
turning a person from the snares of
death.

²⁸ A large population is a king's glory,
but without subjects a prince is ruined.

²⁹ Whoever is patient has great
understanding,
but one who is quick-tempered
displays folly.

³⁰ A heart at peace gives life to the body,
but envy rots the bones.

³¹ Whoever oppresses the poor shows
contempt for their Maker,
but whoever is kind to the needy
honors God.

³² When calamity comes, the wicked are
brought down,
but even in death the righteous seek
refuge in God.

³³ Wisdom reposes in the heart of the
discerning
and even among fools she lets herself
be known.[b]

³⁴ Righteousness exalts a nation,
but sin condemns any people.

³⁵ A king delights in a wise servant,
but a shameful servant arouses
his fury.

15 A gentle answer turns away wrath,
but a harsh word stirs up anger.

² The tongue of the wise adorns
knowledge,
but the mouth of the fool gushes folly.

³ The eyes of the LORD are everywhere,
keeping watch on the wicked and the
good.

⁴ The soothing tongue is a tree of life,
but a perverse tongue crushes the spirit.

⁵ A fool spurns a parent's discipline,
but whoever heeds correction shows
prudence.

⁶ The house of the righteous contains great
treasure,
but the income of the wicked brings
ruin.

⁷ The lips of the wise spread knowledge,
but the hearts of fools are not upright.

⁸ The LORD detests the sacrifice of the
wicked,
but the prayer of the upright pleases
him.

⁹ The LORD detests the way of the wicked,
but he loves those who pursue
righteousness.

¹⁰ Stern discipline awaits anyone who
leaves the path;
the one who hates correction will die.

¹¹ Death and Destruction[c] lie open before
the LORD —
how much more do human hearts!

¹² Mockers resent correction,
so they avoid the wise.

¹³ A happy heart makes the face cheerful,
but heartache crushes the spirit.

¹⁴ The discerning heart seeks knowledge,
but the mouth of a fool feeds on folly.

¹⁵ All the days of the oppressed are
wretched,
but the cheerful heart has a continual
feast.

¹⁶ Better a little with the fear of the LORD
than great wealth with turmoil.

¹⁷ Better a small serving of vegetables with
love
than a fattened calf with hatred.

¹⁸ A hot-tempered person stirs up conflict,
but the one who is patient calms a
quarrel.

---

[a] 22 Or *show*   [b] 33 Hebrew; Septuagint and Syriac *discerning / but in the heart of fools she is not known*
[c] 11 Hebrew *Abaddon*

¹⁹ The way of the sluggard is blocked with
      thorns,
   but the path of the upright is a
      highway.

²⁰ A wise son brings joy to his father,
   but a foolish man despises his mother.

²¹ Folly brings joy to one who has no sense,
   but whoever has understanding keeps
      a straight course.

²² Plans fail for lack of counsel,
   but with many advisers they succeed.

²³ A person finds joy in giving an apt reply —
   and how good is a timely word!

²⁴ The path of life leads upward for the
      prudent
   to keep them from going down to the
      realm of the dead.

²⁵ The Lord tears down the house of the
      proud,
   but he sets the widow's boundary
      stones in place.

²⁶ The Lord detests the thoughts of the
      wicked,
   but gracious words are pure in his
      sight.

²⁷ The greedy bring ruin to their
      households,
   but the one who hates bribes will live.

²⁸ The heart of the righteous weighs its
      answers,
   but the mouth of the wicked gushes
      evil.

²⁹ The Lord is far from the wicked,
   but he hears the prayer of the
      righteous.

³⁰ Light in a messenger's eyes brings joy to
      the heart,
   and good news gives health to the
      bones.

³¹ Whoever heeds life-giving correction
   will be at home among the wise.

³² Those who disregard discipline despise
      themselves,
   but the one who heeds correction
      gains understanding.

³³ Wisdom's instruction is to fear the Lord,
   and humility comes before honor.

16 To humans belong the plans of the
      heart,
   but from the Lord comes the proper
      answer of the tongue.

² All a person's ways seem pure to them,
   but motives are weighed by the Lord.

³ Commit to the Lord whatever you do,
   and he will establish your plans.

⁴ The Lord works out everything to its
      proper end —
   even the wicked for a day of disaster.

⁵ The Lord detests all the proud of heart.
   Be sure of this: They will not go
      unpunished.

⁶ Through love and faithfulness sin is
      atoned for;
   through the fear of the Lord evil is
      avoided.

⁷ When the Lord takes pleasure in
      anyone's way,
   he causes their enemies to make peace
      with them.

⁸ Better a little with righteousness
   than much gain with injustice.

⁹ In their hearts humans plan their
      course,
   but the Lord establishes their steps.

¹⁰ The lips of a king speak as an oracle,
   and his mouth does not betray justice.

¹¹ Honest scales and balances belong to the
      Lord;
   all the weights in the bag are of his
      making.

¹² Kings detest wrongdoing,
   for a throne is established through
      righteousness.

¹³ Kings take pleasure in honest lips;
   they value the one who speaks what
      is right.

¹⁴ A king's wrath is a messenger of death,
   but the wise will appease it.

¹⁵ When a king's face brightens, it means
      life;
   his favor is like a rain cloud in spring.

¹⁶ How much better to get wisdom
      than gold,
   to get insight rather than silver!

¹⁷ The highway of the upright avoids evil;
  those who guard their ways preserve
    their lives.

¹⁸ Pride goes before destruction,
  a haughty spirit before a fall.

¹⁹ Better to be lowly in spirit along with the
    oppressed
  than to share plunder with the proud.

²⁰ Whoever gives heed to instruction
    prospers,ᵃ
  and blessed is the one who trusts in
    the Lᴏʀᴅ.

²¹ The wise in heart are called discerning,
  and gracious words promote
    instruction.ᵇ

²² Prudence is a fountain of life to the
    prudent,
  but folly brings punishment to fools.

²³ The hearts of the wise make their mouths
    prudent,
  and their lips promote instruction.ᶜ

²⁴ Gracious words are a honeycomb,
  sweet to the soul and healing to the
    bones.

²⁵ There is a way that appears to be right,
  but in the end it leads to death.

²⁶ The appetite of laborers works for them;
  their hunger drives them on.

²⁷ A scoundrel plots evil,
  and on their lips it is like a scorching
    fire.

²⁸ A perverse person stirs up conflict,
  and a gossip separates close friends.

²⁹ A violent person entices their neighbor
  and leads them down a path that is not
    good.

³⁰ Whoever winks with their eye is plotting
    perversity;
  whoever purses their lips is bent on
    evil.

³¹ Gray hair is a crown of splendor;
  it is attained in the way of
    righteousness.

³² Better a patient person than a warrior,
  one with self-control than one who
    takes a city.

³³ The lot is cast into the lap,
  but its every decision is from
    the Lᴏʀᴅ.

17 Better a dry crust with peace and
    quiet
  than a house full of feasting, with
    strife.

² A prudent servant will rule over a
    disgraceful son
  and will share the inheritance as one
    of the family.

³ The crucible for silver and the furnace
    for gold,
  but the Lᴏʀᴅ tests the heart.

⁴ A wicked person listens to deceitful lips;
  a liar pays attention to a destructive
    tongue.

⁵ Whoever mocks the poor shows
    contempt for their Maker;
  whoever gloats over disaster will not
    go unpunished.

⁶ Children's children are a crown to the
    aged,
  and parents are the pride of their
    children.

⁷ Eloquent lips are unsuited to a godless
    fool—
  how much worse lying lips to a ruler!

⁸ A bribe is seen as a charm by the one who
    gives it;
  they think success will come at every
    turn.

⁹ Whoever would foster love covers over an
    offense,
  but whoever repeats the matter
    separates close friends.

¹⁰ A rebuke impresses a discerning person
  more than a hundred lashes a fool.

¹¹ Evildoers foster rebellion against God;
  the messenger of death will be sent
    against them.

¹² Better to meet a bear robbed of her cubs
  than a fool bent on folly.

¹³ Evil will never leave the house
  of one who pays back evil for good.

ᵃ 20 Or *whoever speaks prudently finds what is good*
ᶜ 23 Or *prudent / and make their lips persuasive*

ᵇ 21 Or *words make a person persuasive*

¹⁴ Starting a quarrel is like breaching
     a dam;
  so drop the matter before a dispute
     breaks out.

¹⁵ Acquitting the guilty and condemning
     the innocent —
  the LORD detests them both.

¹⁶ Why should fools have money in hand to
     buy wisdom,
  when they are not able to understand it?

¹⁷ A friend loves at all times,
  and a brother is born for a time of
     adversity.

¹⁸ One who has no sense shakes hands in
     pledge
  and puts up security for a neighbor.

¹⁹ Whoever loves a quarrel loves sin;
  whoever builds a high gate invites
     destruction.

²⁰ One whose heart is corrupt does not
     prosper;
  one whose tongue is perverse falls into
     trouble.

²¹ To have a fool for a child brings grief;
  there is no joy for the parent of a
     godless fool.

²² A cheerful heart is good medicine,
  but a crushed spirit dries up the bones.

²³ The wicked accept bribes in secret
  to pervert the course of justice.

²⁴ A discerning person keeps wisdom in
     view,
  but a fool's eyes wander to the ends of
     the earth.

²⁵ A foolish son brings grief to his father
  and bitterness to the mother who bore
     him.

²⁶ If imposing a fine on the innocent is not
     good,
  surely to flog honest officials is not
     right.

²⁷ The one who has knowledge uses words
     with restraint,
  and whoever has understanding is
     even-tempered.

²⁸ Even fools are thought wise if they keep
     silent,
  and discerning if they hold their
     tongues.

18 An unfriendly person pursues
     selfish ends
  and against all sound judgment starts
     quarrels.

² Fools find no pleasure in understanding
  but delight in airing their own
     opinions.

³ When wickedness comes, so does
     contempt,
  and with shame comes reproach.

⁴ The words of the mouth are deep waters,
  but the fountain of wisdom is a rushing
     stream.

⁵ It is not good to be partial to the wicked
  and so deprive the innocent of justice.

⁶ The lips of fools bring them strife,
  and their mouths invite a beating.

⁷ The mouths of fools are their undoing,
  and their lips are a snare to their very
     lives.

⁸ The words of a gossip are like choice
     morsels;
  they go down to the inmost parts.

⁹ One who is slack in his work
  is brother to one who destroys.

¹⁰ The name of the LORD is a fortified tower;
  the righteous run to it and are safe.

¹¹ The wealth of the rich is their fortified
     city;
  they imagine it a wall too high to scale.

¹² Before a downfall the heart is haughty,
  but humility comes before honor.

¹³ To answer before listening —
  that is folly and shame.

¹⁴ The human spirit can endure in sickness,
  but a crushed spirit who can bear?

¹⁵ The heart of the discerning acquires
     knowledge,
  for the ears of the wise seek it out.

¹⁶ A gift opens the way
  and ushers the giver into the presence
     of the great.

¹⁷ In a lawsuit the first to speak seems right,
  until someone comes forward and
     cross-examines.

¹⁸ Casting the lot settles disputes
   and keeps strong opponents apart.

¹⁹ A brother wronged is more unyielding
      than a fortified city;
   disputes are like the barred gates of
      a citadel.

²⁰ From the fruit of their mouth a person's
      stomach is filled;
   with the harvest of their lips they are
      satisfied.

²¹ The tongue has the power of life and
      death,
   and those who love it will eat
      its fruit.

²² He who finds a wife finds what is good
   and receives favor from the LORD.

²³ The poor plead for mercy,
   but the rich answer harshly.

²⁴ One who has unreliable friends soon
      comes to ruin,
   but there is a friend who sticks closer
      than a brother.

19
Better the poor whose walk is
   blameless
than a fool whose lips are perverse.

² Desire without knowledge is not good —
   how much more will hasty feet miss
      the way!

³ A person's own folly leads to their ruin,
   yet their heart rages against the LORD.

⁴ Wealth attracts many friends,
   but even the closest friend of the poor
      person deserts them.

⁵ A false witness will not go unpunished,
   and whoever pours out lies will not
      go free.

⁶ Many curry favor with a ruler,
   and everyone is the friend of one who
      gives gifts.

⁷ The poor are shunned by all their
      relatives —
   how much more do their friends avoid
      them!
   Though the poor pursue them with
      pleading,
   they are nowhere to be found.^a

⁸ The one who gets wisdom loves life;
   the one who cherishes understanding
      will soon prosper.

⁹ A false witness will not go unpunished,
   and whoever pours out lies will perish.

¹⁰ It is not fitting for a fool to live in luxury —
   how much worse for a slave to rule over
      princes!

¹¹ A person's wisdom yields patience;
   it is to one's glory to overlook an offense.

¹² A king's rage is like the roar of a lion,
   but his favor is like dew on the grass.

¹³ A foolish child is a father's ruin,
   and a quarrelsome wife is like
      the constant dripping of a leaky roof.

¹⁴ Houses and wealth are inherited from
      parents,
   but a prudent wife is from the LORD.

¹⁵ Laziness brings on deep sleep,
   and the shiftless go hungry.

¹⁶ Whoever keeps commandments keeps
      their life,
   but whoever shows contempt for their
      ways will die.

¹⁷ Whoever is kind to the poor lends to the
      LORD,
   and he will reward them for what they
      have done.

¹⁸ Discipline your children, for in that there
      is hope;
   do not be a willing party to their death.

¹⁹ A hot-tempered person must pay the
      penalty;
   rescue them, and you will have to do
      it again.

²⁰ Listen to advice and accept discipline,
   and at the end you will be counted
      among the wise.

²¹ Many are the plans in a person's heart,
   but it is the LORD's purpose that
      prevails.

²² What a person desires is unfailing love^b;
   better to be poor than a liar.

²³ The fear of the LORD leads to life;
   then one rests content, untouched by
      trouble.

---

^a 7 The meaning of the Hebrew for this sentence is uncertain.   ^b 22 Or *Greed is a person's shame*

THE POWER OF OUR WORDS

By Jocelyn Green

Susan Anna Good wrestled with her emotions as her husband John's departure drew near. She was proud of John for answering Texas' call for troops to fight for the Confederacy but knew she and their children would miss him dearly. She wanted to send him off with words of hope and strength, but she imagined her tears and trembling voice would betray her at their final good-bye. So on July 9, 1861, she wrote him a letter:

> … You must not allow your mind to grow gloomy and sorrowful over our separation, but ever remember that we have a kind and indulgent Father who suffereth not even a sparrow to fall to the ground without notice … The world is but short at best, and whether prepared or unprepared, we will sooner or later be called to meet our God. I shall ever remember you at a throne of grace and pray our Heavenly Father to grant you a safe return. But, Oh, Father, if Thou in Thy divine wisdom dost not permit a reunion of our little family, grant that we may meet in a better world …

Susan Anna knew she had the power to send John off either with a sense of pride for following the path of duty or with a sense of neglect toward his family for leaving them. She chose to bolster John with words of truth and a prayer to God. Because of Susan Anna's words, John went to war filled with courage, not guilt.

Months later, a cloud began to settle on their plans for a Christmas reunion. Repeatedly in the fall of 1861, she wrote that while she and the children would be overjoyed to see him, she could not insist on his coming because she knew his stay would be short, and he would have to travel in the severe winter weather. She also predicted that, as an officer, his taking the luxury of an absence of leave might cause resentment among the men under him.

Finally, the matter was settled. John would not be coming home for Christmas after all. In response to the final decision, she wrote:

> I have never insisted upon your coming … but you must not imagine I have refrained from doing so without a severe struggle between affection and duty, and I think your boys ought to appreciate your wife very highly when she succeeds in conquering her affections enough to tell you to remain and do your duty by them.

Rather than allowing her words to be ruled by emotions, Susan Anna demonstrated the sacrificial love required of both spouses in a marriage, especially during wartime.

Prayer: Lord, help me choose the right words to edify my family.

**The tongue has the power of life and death, and those
who love it will eat its fruit.**
PROVERBS 18:21

for your next devotional reading, go to page 465

²⁴ A sluggard buries his hand in the dish;
　　he will not even bring it back to his
　　　mouth!

²⁵ Flog a mocker, and the simple will learn
　　prudence;
　　rebuke the discerning, and they will
　　　gain knowledge.

²⁶ Whoever robs their father and drives out
　　their mother
　　is a child who brings shame and
　　　disgrace.

²⁷ Stop listening to instruction, my son,
　　and you will stray from the words of
　　　knowledge.

²⁸ A corrupt witness mocks at justice,
　　and the mouth of the wicked gulps
　　　down evil.

²⁹ Penalties are prepared for mockers,
　　and beatings for the backs of fools.

20 Wine is a mocker and beer a brawler;
　　whoever is led astray by them is not
　　　wise.

² A king's wrath strikes terror like the roar
　　of a lion;
　　those who anger him forfeit their lives.

³ It is to one's honor to avoid strife,
　　but every fool is quick to quarrel.

⁴ Sluggards do not plow in season;
　　so at harvest time they look but find
　　　nothing.

⁵ The purposes of a person's heart are deep
　　waters,
　　but one who has insight draws
　　　them out.

⁶ Many claim to have unfailing love,
　　but a faithful person who can find?

⁷ The righteous lead blameless lives;
　　blessed are their children after them.

⁸ When a king sits on his throne to judge,
　　he winnows out all evil with his eyes.

⁹ Who can say, "I have kept my heart
　　pure;
　　I am clean and without sin"?

¹⁰ Differing weights and differing
　　measures —
　　the LORD detests them both.

¹¹ Even small children are known by their
　　actions,
　　so is their conduct really pure and
　　　upright?

¹² Ears that hear and eyes that see —
　　the LORD has made them both.

¹³ Do not love sleep or you will grow poor;
　　stay awake and you will have food
　　　to spare.

¹⁴ "It's no good, it's no good!" says the
　　buyer —
　　then goes off and boasts about the
　　　purchase.

¹⁵ Gold there is, and rubies in abundance,
　　but lips that speak knowledge are a
　　　rare jewel.

¹⁶ Take the garment of one who puts up
　　security for a stranger;
　　hold it in pledge if it is done for an
　　　outsider.

¹⁷ Food gained by fraud tastes sweet,
　　but one ends up with a mouth full
　　　of gravel.

¹⁸ Plans are established by seeking advice;
　　so if you wage war, obtain guidance.

¹⁹ A gossip betrays a confidence;
　　so avoid anyone who talks too much.

²⁰ If someone curses their father or mother,
　　their lamp will be snuffed out in pitch
　　　darkness.

²¹ An inheritance claimed too soon
　　will not be blessed at the end.

²² Do not say, "I'll pay you back for this
　　wrong!"
　　Wait for the LORD, and he will avenge
　　　you.

²³ The LORD detests differing weights,
　　and dishonest scales do not please him.

²⁴ A person's steps are directed by the LORD.
　　How then can anyone understand
　　　their own way?

²⁵ It is a trap to dedicate something
　　rashly
　　and only later to consider one's vows.

²⁶ A wise king winnows out the wicked;
　　he drives the threshing wheel over
　　　them.

²⁷ The human spirit is*ᵃ* the lamp of the Lᴏʀᴅ
that sheds light on one's inmost being.

²⁸ Love and faithfulness keep a king safe;
through love his throne is made
secure.

²⁹ The glory of young men is their strength,
gray hair the splendor of the old.

³⁰ Blows and wounds scrub away evil,
and beatings purge the inmost being.

21 In the Lᴏʀᴅ's hand the king's heart
is a stream of water
that he channels toward all who
please him.

² A person may think their own ways are
right,
but the Lᴏʀᴅ weighs the heart.

³ To do what is right and just
is more acceptable to the Lᴏʀᴅ than
sacrifice.

⁴ Haughty eyes and a proud heart —
the unplowed field of the wicked —
produce sin.

⁵ The plans of the diligent lead to profit
as surely as haste leads to poverty.

⁶ A fortune made by a lying tongue
is a fleeting vapor and a deadly snare.*ᵇ*

⁷ The violence of the wicked will drag them
away,
for they refuse to do what is right.

⁸ The way of the guilty is devious,
but the conduct of the innocent is
upright.

⁹ Better to live on a corner of the roof
than share a house with a quarrelsome
wife.

¹⁰ The wicked crave evil;
their neighbors get no mercy from them.

¹¹ When a mocker is punished, the simple
gain wisdom;
by paying attention to the wise they get
knowledge.

¹² The Righteous One*ᶜ* takes note of the
house of the wicked
and brings the wicked to ruin.

¹³ Whoever shuts their ears to the cry of the
poor
will also cry out and not be answered.

¹⁴ A gift given in secret soothes anger,
and a bribe concealed in the cloak
pacifies great wrath.

¹⁵ When justice is done, it brings joy to the
righteous
but terror to evildoers.

¹⁶ Whoever strays from the path of
prudence
comes to rest in the company of the
dead.

¹⁷ Whoever loves pleasure will become
poor;
whoever loves wine and olive oil will
never be rich.

¹⁸ The wicked become a ransom for the
righteous,
and the unfaithful for the upright.

¹⁹ Better to live in a desert
than with a quarrelsome and nagging
wife.

²⁰ The wise store up choice food and
olive oil,
but fools gulp theirs down.

²¹ Whoever pursues righteousness and love
finds life, prosperity*ᵈ* and honor.

²² One who is wise can go up against the
city of the mighty
and pull down the stronghold in which
they trust.

²³ Those who guard their mouths and their
tongues
keep themselves from calamity.

²⁴ The proud and arrogant person —
"Mocker" is his name —
behaves with insolent fury.

²⁵ The craving of a sluggard will be the
death of him,
because his hands refuse to work.

²⁶ All day long he craves for more,
but the righteous give without sparing.

²⁷ The sacrifice of the wicked is
detestable —

ᵃ 27 Or *A person's words are*   *ᵇ 6* Some Hebrew manuscripts, Septuagint and Vulgate; most Hebrew
manuscripts *vapor for those who seek death*   *ᶜ 12* Or *The righteous person*   *ᵈ 21* Or *righteousness*

how much more so when brought with evil intent!

²⁸ A false witness will perish,
but a careful listener will testify successfully.

²⁹ The wicked put up a bold front,
but the upright give thought to their ways.

³⁰ There is no wisdom, no insight, no plan
that can succeed against the LORD.

³¹ The horse is made ready for the day of battle,
but victory rests with the LORD.

22 A good name is more desirable than great riches;
to be esteemed is better than silver or gold.

² Rich and poor have this in common:
The LORD is the Maker of them all.

³ The prudent see danger and take refuge,
but the simple keep going and pay the penalty.

⁴ Humility is the fear of the LORD;
its wages are riches and honor and life.

⁵ In the paths of the wicked are snares and pitfalls,
but those who would preserve their life stay far from them.

⁶ Start children off on the way they should go,
and even when they are old they will not turn from it.

⁷ The rich rule over the poor,
and the borrower is slave to the lender.

⁸ Whoever sows injustice reaps calamity,
and the rod they wield in fury will be broken.

⁹ The generous will themselves be blessed,
for they share their food with the poor.

¹⁰ Drive out the mocker, and out goes strife;
quarrels and insults are ended.

¹¹ One who loves a pure heart and who speaks with grace
will have the king for a friend.

¹² The eyes of the LORD keep watch over knowledge,
but he frustrates the words of the unfaithful.

¹³ The sluggard says, "There's a lion outside!
I'll be killed in the public square!"

¹⁴ The mouth of an adulterous woman is a deep pit;
a man who is under the LORD's wrath falls into it.

¹⁵ Folly is bound up in the heart of a child,
but the rod of discipline will drive it far away.

¹⁶ One who oppresses the poor to increase his wealth
and one who gives gifts to the rich —
both come to poverty.

Thirty Sayings of the Wise

Saying 1

¹⁷ Pay attention and turn your ear to the sayings of the wise;
apply your heart to what I teach,
¹⁸ for it is pleasing when you keep them in your heart
and have all of them ready on your lips.
¹⁹ So that your trust may be in the LORD,
I teach you today, even you.
²⁰ Have I not written thirty sayings for you,
sayings of counsel and knowledge,
²¹ teaching you to be honest and to speak the truth,
so that you bring back truthful reports to those you serve?

Saying 2

²² Do not exploit the poor because they are poor
and do not crush the needy in court,
²³ for the LORD will take up their case
and will exact life for life.

Saying 3

²⁴ Do not make friends with a hot-tempered person,
do not associate with one easily angered,
²⁵ or you may learn their ways
and get yourself ensnared.

Saying 4

²⁶ Do not be one who shakes hands in pledge
or puts up security for debts;

²⁷ if you lack the means to pay,
    your very bed will be snatched from
      under you.

Saying 5

²⁸ Do not move an ancient boundary stone
    set up by your ancestors.

Saying 6

²⁹ Do you see someone skilled in their
      work?
    They will serve before kings;
    they will not serve before officials of
      low rank.

Saying 7

23 When you sit to dine with a ruler,
    note well what^{*a*} is before you,
² and put a knife to your throat
    if you are given to gluttony.
³ Do not crave his delicacies,
    for that food is deceptive.

Saying 8

⁴ Do not wear yourself out to get rich;
    do not trust your own cleverness.
⁵ Cast but a glance at riches, and they
      are gone,
    for they will surely sprout wings
    and fly off to the sky like an eagle.

Saying 9

⁶ Do not eat the food of a begrudging host,
    do not crave his delicacies;
⁷ for he is the kind of person
    who is always thinking about the cost.^{*b*}
    "Eat and drink," he says to you,
    but his heart is not with you.
⁸ You will vomit up the little you have
      eaten
    and will have wasted your
      compliments.

Saying 10

⁹ Do not speak to fools,
    for they will scorn your prudent words.

Saying 11

¹⁰ Do not move an ancient boundary stone
    or encroach on the fields of the
      fatherless,
¹¹ for their Defender is strong;
    he will take up their case against you.

Saying 12

¹² Apply your heart to instruction
    and your ears to words of knowledge.

Saying 13

¹³ Do not withhold discipline from a child;
    if you punish them with the rod, they
      will not die.
¹⁴ Punish them with the rod
    and save them from death.

Saying 14

¹⁵ My son, if your heart is wise,
    then my heart will be glad indeed;
¹⁶ my inmost being will rejoice
    when your lips speak what is right.

Saying 15

¹⁷ Do not let your heart envy sinners,
    but always be zealous for the fear of
      the Lord.
¹⁸ There is surely a future hope for you,
    and your hope will not be cut off.

Saying 16

¹⁹ Listen, my son, and be wise,
    and set your heart on the right path:
²⁰ Do not join those who drink too much
      wine
    or gorge themselves on meat,
²¹ for drunkards and gluttons become poor,
    and drowsiness clothes them in rags.

Saying 17

²² Listen to your father, who gave you life,
    and do not despise your mother when
      she is old.
²³ Buy the truth and do not sell it—
    wisdom, instruction and insight as
      well.
²⁴ The father of a righteous child has great
      joy;
    a man who fathers a wise son rejoices
      in him.
²⁵ May your father and mother rejoice;
    may she who gave you birth be joyful!

Saying 18

²⁶ My son, give me your heart
    and let your eyes delight in my ways,
²⁷ for an adulterous woman is a deep pit,
    and a wayward wife is a narrow well.

^{*a*} *1* Or *who*   ^{*b*} *7* Or *for as he thinks within himself, / so he is*; or *for as he puts on a feast, / so he is*

²⁸ Like a bandit she lies in wait
    and multiplies the unfaithful
        among men.

Saying 19

²⁹ Who has woe? Who has sorrow?
    Who has strife? Who has complaints?
    Who has needless bruises? Who has
        bloodshot eyes?
³⁰ Those who linger over wine,
    who go to sample bowls of mixed wine.
³¹ Do not gaze at wine when it is red,
    when it sparkles in the cup,
    when it goes down smoothly!
³² In the end it bites like a snake
    and poisons like a viper.
³³ Your eyes will see strange sights,
    and your mind will imagine confusing
        things.
³⁴ You will be like one sleeping on the high
        seas,
    lying on top of the rigging.
³⁵ "They hit me," you will say, "but I'm not
        hurt!
    They beat me, but I don't feel it!
    When will I wake up
        so I can find another drink?"

Saying 20

24 Do not envy the wicked,
    do not desire their company;
² for their hearts plot violence,
    and their lips talk about making
        trouble.

Saying 21

³ By wisdom a house is built,
    and through understanding it is
        established;
⁴ through knowledge its rooms are filled
    with rare and beautiful treasures.

Saying 22

⁵ The wise prevail through great power,
    and those who have knowledge muster
        their strength.
⁶ Surely you need guidance to wage war,
    and victory is won through many
        advisers.

Saying 23

⁷ Wisdom is too high for fools;
    in the assembly at the gate they must
        not open their mouths.

Saying 24

⁸ Whoever plots evil
    will be known as a schemer.
⁹ The schemes of folly are sin,
    and people detest a mocker.

Saying 25

¹⁰ If you falter in a time of trouble,
    how small is your strength!
¹¹ Rescue those being led away to death;
    hold back those staggering toward
        slaughter.
¹² If you say, "But we knew nothing about
        this,"
    does not he who weighs the heart
        perceive it?
    Does not he who guards your life
        know it?
    Will he not repay everyone according
        to what they have done?

Saying 26

¹³ Eat honey, my son, for it is good;
    honey from the comb is sweet to your
        taste.
¹⁴ Know also that wisdom is like honey for
        you:
    If you find it, there is a future hope
        for you,
    and your hope will not be cut off.

Saying 27

¹⁵ Do not lurk like a thief near the house of
        the righteous,
    do not plunder their dwelling place;
¹⁶ for though the righteous fall seven times,
        they rise again,
    but the wicked stumble when calamity
        strikes.

Saying 28

¹⁷ Do not gloat when your enemy falls;
    when they stumble, do not let your
        heart rejoice,
¹⁸ or the LORD will see and disapprove
    and turn his wrath away from
        them.

Saying 29

¹⁹ Do not fret because of evildoers
    or be envious of the wicked,
²⁰ for the evildoer has no future hope,
    and the lamp of the wicked will be
        snuffed out.

Saying 30

²¹ Fear the LORD and the king, my son,
     and do not join with rebellious
       officials,
²² for those two will send sudden
       destruction on them,
     and who knows what calamities they
       can bring?

Further Sayings of the Wise

²³ These also are sayings of the wise:

To show partiality in judging is not good:
²⁴ Whoever says to the guilty, "You are
       innocent,"
     will be cursed by peoples and
       denounced by nations.
²⁵ But it will go well with those who convict
       the guilty,
     and rich blessing will come on them.

²⁶ An honest answer
     is like a kiss on the lips.

²⁷ Put your outdoor work in order
     and get your fields ready;
     after that, build your house.

²⁸ Do not testify against your neighbor
       without cause —
     would you use your lips to mislead?
²⁹ Do not say, "I'll do to them as they have
       done to me;
     I'll pay them back for what they did."

³⁰ I went past the field of a sluggard,
     past the vineyard of someone who has
       no sense;
³¹ thorns had come up everywhere,
     the ground was covered with weeds,
     and the stone wall was in ruins.
³² I applied my heart to what I observed
     and learned a lesson from what I saw:
³³ A little sleep, a little slumber,
     a little folding of the hands to rest —
³⁴ and poverty will come on you like a thief
     and scarcity like an armed man.

More Proverbs of Solomon

25 These are more proverbs of Solomon,
     compiled by the men of Hezekiah
king of Judah:

² It is the glory of God to conceal a matter;

to search out a matter is the glory of
       kings.
³ As the heavens are high and the earth is
       deep,
     so the hearts of kings are
       unsearchable.

⁴ Remove the dross from the silver,
     and a silversmith can produce a vessel;
⁵ remove wicked officials from the king's
       presence,
     and his throne will be established
       through righteousness.

⁶ Do not exalt yourself in the king's
       presence,
     and do not claim a place among his
       great men;
⁷ it is better for him to say to you, "Come up
       here,"
     than for him to humiliate you before
       his nobles.

What you have seen with your eyes
⁸   do not bring*ᵃ* hastily to court,
     for what will you do in the end
       if your neighbor puts you to shame?

⁹ If you take your neighbor to court,
     do not betray another's confidence,
¹⁰ or the one who hears it may shame you
     and the charge against you will stand.

¹¹ Like apples*ᵇ* of gold in settings of silver
     is a ruling rightly given.
¹² Like an earring of gold or an ornament of
       fine gold
     is the rebuke of a wise judge to a
       listening ear.

¹³ Like a snow-cooled drink at harvest time
     is a trustworthy messenger to the one
       who sends him;
     he refreshes the spirit of his master.
¹⁴ Like clouds and wind without rain
     is one who boasts of gifts never given.

¹⁵ Through patience a ruler can be
       persuaded,
     and a gentle tongue can break a bone.

¹⁶ If you find honey, eat just enough —
     too much of it, and you will vomit.
¹⁷ Seldom set foot in your neighbor's
       house —
     too much of you, and they will hate you.

ᵃ 7,8 Or nobles / on whom you had set your eyes. / ᵇDo not go   *ᵇ 11 Or possibly apricots*

18 Like a club or a sword or a sharp arrow
    is one who gives false testimony
        against a neighbor.
19 Like a broken tooth or a lame foot
    is reliance on the unfaithful in a time
        of trouble.
20 Like one who takes away a garment on a
        cold day,
    or like vinegar poured on a wound,
    is one who sings songs to a heavy
        heart.

21 If your enemy is hungry, give him food
        to eat;
    if he is thirsty, give him water to drink.
22 In doing this, you will heap burning coals
        on his head,
    and the LORD will reward you.

23 Like a north wind that brings unexpected
        rain
    is a sly tongue — which provokes a
        horrified look.

24 Better to live on a corner of the roof
    than share a house with a quarrelsome
        wife.

25 Like cold water to a weary soul
    is good news from a distant land.
26 Like a muddied spring or a polluted well
    are the righteous who give way to the
        wicked.

27 It is not good to eat too much honey,
    nor is it honorable to search out
        matters that are too deep.

28 Like a city whose walls are broken
        through
    is a person who lacks self-control.

26 Like snow in summer or rain in
        harvest,
    honor is not fitting for a fool.
2 Like a fluttering sparrow or a darting
        swallow,
    an undeserved curse does not come
        to rest.
3 A whip for the horse, a bridle for the
        donkey,
    and a rod for the backs of fools!
4 Do not answer a fool according to his folly,
    or you yourself will be just like him.
5 Answer a fool according to his folly,
    or he will be wise in his own eyes.

6 Sending a message by the hands of a fool
    is like cutting off one's feet or drinking
        poison.
7 Like the useless legs of one who is lame
    is a proverb in the mouth of a fool.
8 Like tying a stone in a sling
    is the giving of honor to a fool.
9 Like a thornbush in a drunkard's hand
    is a proverb in the mouth of a fool.
10 Like an archer who wounds at random
    is one who hires a fool or any passer-by.
11 As a dog returns to its vomit,
    so fools repeat their folly.
12 Do you see a person wise in their own
        eyes?
    There is more hope for a fool than
        for them.

13 A sluggard says, "There's a lion in the
        road,
    a fierce lion roaming the streets!"
14 As a door turns on its hinges,
    so a sluggard turns on his bed.
15 A sluggard buries his hand in the dish;
    he is too lazy to bring it back to his
        mouth.
16 A sluggard is wiser in his own eyes
    than seven people who answer
        discreetly.

17 Like one who grabs a stray dog by
        the ears
    is someone who rushes into a quarrel
        not their own.

18 Like a maniac shooting
    flaming arrows of death
19 is one who deceives their neighbor
    and says, "I was only joking!"

20 Without wood a fire goes out;
    without a gossip a quarrel dies down.
21 As charcoal to embers and as wood
        to fire,
    so is a quarrelsome person for kindling
        strife.
22 The words of a gossip are like choice
        morsels;
    they go down to the inmost parts.

23 Like a coating of silver dross on
        earthenware
    are fervent*a* lips with an evil heart.
24 Enemies disguise themselves with their
        lips,
    but in their hearts they harbor deceit.

a 23 Hebrew; Septuagint *smooth*

²⁵ Though their speech is charming, do not
  believe them,
   for seven abominations fill their hearts.
²⁶ Their malice may be concealed by
  deception,
   but their wickedness will be exposed
   in the assembly.
²⁷ Whoever digs a pit will fall into it;
   if someone rolls a stone, it will roll back
   on them.
²⁸ A lying tongue hates those it hurts,
   and a flattering mouth works ruin.

27 Do not boast about tomorrow,
   for you do not know what a day may
   bring.

² Let someone else praise you, and not
   your own mouth;
   an outsider, and not your own lips.

³ Stone is heavy and sand a burden,
   but a fool's provocation is heavier
   than both.

⁴ Anger is cruel and fury overwhelming,
   but who can stand before jealousy?

⁵ Better is open rebuke
   than hidden love.

⁶ Wounds from a friend can be trusted,
   but an enemy multiplies kisses.

⁷ One who is full loathes honey from the
   comb,
   but to the hungry even what is bitter
   tastes sweet.

⁸ Like a bird that flees its nest
   is anyone who flees from home.

⁹ Perfume and incense bring joy to the
   heart,
   and the pleasantness of a friend
   springs from their heartfelt advice.

¹⁰ Do not forsake your friend or a friend of
   your family,
   and do not go to your relative's house
   when disaster strikes you —
   better a neighbor nearby than a
   relative far away.

¹¹ Be wise, my son, and bring joy to my
   heart;
   then I can answer anyone who treats
   me with contempt.

¹² The prudent see danger and take refuge,
   but the simple keep going and pay
   the penalty.

¹³ Take the garment of one who puts up
   security for a stranger;
   hold it in pledge if it is done for an
   outsider.

¹⁴ If anyone loudly blesses their neighbor
   early in the morning,
   it will be taken as a curse.

¹⁵ A quarrelsome wife is like the dripping
   of a leaky roof in a rainstorm;
¹⁶ restraining her is like restraining
   the wind
   or grasping oil with the hand.

¹⁷ As iron sharpens iron,
   so one person sharpens another.

¹⁸ The one who guards a fig tree will eat
   its fruit,
   and whoever protects their master will
   be honored.

¹⁹ As water reflects the face,
   so one's life reflects the heart.[a]

²⁰ Death and Destruction[b] are never
   satisfied,
   and neither are human eyes.

²¹ The crucible for silver and the furnace
   for gold,
   but people are tested by their praise.

²² Though you grind a fool in a mortar,
   grinding them like grain with a pestle,
   you will not remove their folly
   from them.

²³ Be sure you know the condition of your
   flocks,
   give careful attention to your herds;
²⁴ for riches do not endure forever,
   and a crown is not secure for all
   generations.
²⁵ When the hay is removed and new
   growth appears
   and the grass from the hills is
   gathered in,
²⁶ the lambs will provide you with clothing,
   and the goats with the price of a field.
²⁷ You will have plenty of goats' milk to feed
   your family
   and to nourish your female servants.

---

[a] 19 Or *so others reflect your heart back to you*   [b] 20 Hebrew *Abaddon*

IRON LADY

By Jane Hampton Cook

In 1777, meeting the wife of the highest-ranking military officer was an exciting opportunity for the women of Morristown, New Jersey. George Washington chose Morristown as the site of winter camp for the Continental Army. As she had done the previous year, Martha Washington joined her husband and the troops. Her presence influenced the townswomen.

"As she was said to be so grand a lady, we thought we must put on our best bibs and bands," one lady, Mrs. Troupe, recalled of her encounter with Martha.

These women knew Martha had been one of the wealthiest widows in Virginia when she had married George Washington years earlier. Perhaps they had read newspaper accounts of her beautiful gold and purple damask wedding dress with matching violet slippers that were imported from London dressmakers. But what the women found was Martha neatly dressed in a plain brown habit. Not only did Martha's choice of clothing surprise the ladies, but her behavior did as well.

"There we were without a stitch of work, and sitting in state, but General Washington's lady with her own hands was knitting stockings for herself and husband!" one woman wrote.

Martha received the ladies graciously and knitted while they talked. Then she conveyed a simple message, which was recorded by a woman there: " ... Her ladyship took the occasion to say ... that American ladies should be patterns of industry to their country women, because the separation from the mother country will dry up the sources whence many of our comforts have been derived."

Martha understood that in order to become truly free from England, Americans would have to make their own clothing and take other practical steps toward liberation. At first the ladies were ashamed and defensive. "We felt rebuked by the plainness of her apparel and her example of persistent industry, while we were extravagantly dressed idlers."

Upon further reflection, many of these women realized that Martha was merely setting a good example. Soon the ladies of Morristown created a sewing society to make clothing for soldiers.

"Mrs. Washington's remarks and example were not intended to point out a moral ... rather she was carrying out the habits of thrift industry that were, with her, cardinal virtues, not to be set aside even when she was entertaining."

Martha understood that as a military wife, she could best lead others by her actions. She was an iron lady, sharpening and directing the ladies of Morristown to fulfill a greater purpose in life. The same is true today. Leading by example never goes out of style.

Prayer: Father, may I become an iron lady, a woman of influence on those around me in positive, encouraging ways.

Better is open rebuke than hidden love. Wounds from a friend can be trusted, but an enemy multiplies kisses ... As iron sharpens iron, so one person sharpens another.

PROVERBS 27:5 – 6, 17

for your next devotional reading, go to page 469

28

The wicked flee though no one pursues,
but the righteous are as bold as a lion.

2 When a country is rebellious, it has many rulers,
but a ruler with discernment and knowledge maintains order.

3 A ruler[a] who oppresses the poor
is like a driving rain that leaves no crops.

4 Those who forsake instruction praise the wicked,
but those who heed it resist them.

5 Evildoers do not understand what is right,
but those who seek the LORD understand it fully.

6 Better the poor whose walk is blameless
than the rich whose ways are perverse.

7 A discerning son heeds instruction,
but a companion of gluttons disgraces his father.

8 Whoever increases wealth by taking interest or profit from the poor
amasses it for another, who will be kind to the poor.

9 If anyone turns a deaf ear to my instruction,
even their prayers are detestable.

10 Whoever leads the upright along an evil path
will fall into their own trap,
but the blameless will receive a good inheritance.

11 The rich are wise in their own eyes;
one who is poor and discerning sees how deluded they are.

12 When the righteous triumph, there is great elation;
but when the wicked rise to power, people go into hiding.

13 Whoever conceals their sins does not prosper,
but the one who confesses and renounces them finds mercy.

14 Blessed is the one who always trembles before God,
but whoever hardens their heart falls into trouble.

15 Like a roaring lion or a charging bear
is a wicked ruler over a helpless people.

16 A tyrannical ruler practices extortion,
but one who hates ill-gotten gain will enjoy a long reign.

17 Anyone tormented by the guilt of murder
will seek refuge in the grave;
let no one hold them back.

18 The one whose walk is blameless is kept safe,
but the one whose ways are perverse will fall into the pit.[b]

19 Those who work their land will have abundant food,
but those who chase fantasies will have their fill of poverty.

20 A faithful person will be richly blessed,
but one eager to get rich will not go unpunished.

21 To show partiality is not good —
yet a person will do wrong for a piece of bread.

22 The stingy are eager to get rich
and are unaware that poverty awaits them.

23 Whoever rebukes a person will in the end gain favor
rather than one who has a flattering tongue.

24 Whoever robs their father or mother
and says, "It's not wrong,"
is partner to one who destroys.

25 The greedy stir up conflict,
but those who trust in the LORD will prosper.

26 Those who trust in themselves are fools,
but those who walk in wisdom are kept safe.

27 Those who give to the poor will lack nothing,
but those who close their eyes to them receive many curses.

---

a 3 Or *A poor person*   *b 18* Syriac (see Septuagint); Hebrew *into one*

²⁸ When the wicked rise to power, people go
into hiding;
but when the wicked perish, the
righteous thrive.

29 Whoever remains stiff-necked after
many rebukes
will suddenly be destroyed — without
remedy.

² When the righteous thrive, the people
rejoice;
when the wicked rule, the people groan.

³ A man who loves wisdom brings joy to
his father,
but a companion of prostitutes
squanders his wealth.

⁴ By justice a king gives a country stability,
but those who are greedy for*a* bribes
tear it down.

⁵ Those who flatter their neighbors
are spreading nets for their feet.

⁶ Evildoers are snared by their own sin,
but the righteous shout for joy and
are glad.

⁷ The righteous care about justice for the
poor,
but the wicked have no such concern.

⁸ Mockers stir up a city,
but the wise turn away anger.

⁹ If a wise person goes to court with a fool,
the fool rages and scoffs, and there is
no peace.

¹⁰ The bloodthirsty hate a person of
integrity
and seek to kill the upright.

¹¹ Fools give full vent to their rage,
but the wise bring calm in the end.

¹² If a ruler listens to lies,
all his officials become wicked.

¹³ The poor and the oppressor have this in
common:
The LORD gives sight to the eyes of both.

¹⁴ If a king judges the poor with fairness,
his throne will be established forever.

¹⁵ A rod and a reprimand impart wisdom,
but a child left undisciplined disgraces
its mother.

¹⁶ When the wicked thrive, so does sin,
but the righteous will see their
downfall.

¹⁷ Discipline your children, and they will
give you peace;
they will bring you the delights you
desire.

¹⁸ Where there is no revelation, people cast
off restraint;
but blessed is the one who heeds
wisdom's instruction.

¹⁹ Servants cannot be corrected by mere
words;
though they understand, they will not
respond.

²⁰ Do you see someone who speaks in haste?
There is more hope for a fool than for
them.

²¹ A servant pampered from youth
will turn out to be insolent.

²² An angry person stirs up conflict,
and a hot-tempered person commits
many sins.

²³ Pride brings a person low,
but the lowly in spirit gain honor.

²⁴ The accomplices of thieves are their own
enemies;
they are put under oath and dare not
testify.

²⁵ Fear of man will prove to be a snare,
but whoever trusts in the LORD is
kept safe.

²⁶ Many seek an audience with a ruler,
but it is from the LORD that one gets
justice.

²⁷ The righteous detest the dishonest;
the wicked detest the upright.

Sayings of Agur

30 The sayings of Agur son of Jakeh —
an inspired utterance.

This man's utterance to Ithiel:

"I am weary, God,
but I can prevail.*b*
² Surely I am only a brute, not a man;
I do not have human understanding.

---

a 4 Or *who give*   *b 1* With a different word division of the Hebrew; Masoretic Text *utterance to Ithiel, / to Ithiel and Ukal:*

3 I have not learned wisdom,
  nor have I attained to the knowledge of
    the Holy One.
4 Who has gone up to heaven and come
    down?
  Whose hands have gathered up the
    wind?
  Who has wrapped up the waters in a
    cloak?
  Who has established all the ends of the
    earth?
  What is his name, and what is the name
    of his son?
  Surely you know!

5 "Every word of God is flawless;
  he is a shield to those who take refuge
    in him.
6 Do not add to his words,
  or he will rebuke you and prove you
    a liar.

7 "Two things I ask of you, LORD;
  do not refuse me before I die:
8 Keep falsehood and lies far from me;
  give me neither poverty nor riches,
  but give me only my daily bread.
9 Otherwise, I may have too much and
    disown you
  and say, 'Who is the LORD?'
  Or I may become poor and steal,
  and so dishonor the name of my God.

10 "Do not slander a servant to their master,
  or they will curse you, and you will
    pay for it.

11 "There are those who curse their fathers
  and do not bless their mothers;
12 those who are pure in their own eyes
  and yet are not cleansed of their filth;
13 those whose eyes are ever so haughty,
  whose glances are so disdainful;
14 those whose teeth are swords
  and whose jaws are set with knives
to devour the poor from the earth
  and the needy from among mankind.

15 "The leech has two daughters.
  'Give! Give!' they cry.

"There are three things that are never
    satisfied,
  four that never say, 'Enough!':
16 the grave, the barren womb,

land, which is never satisfied with
    water,
  and fire, which never says, 'Enough!'

17 "The eye that mocks a father,
  that scorns an aged mother,
will be pecked out by the ravens of the
    valley,
  will be eaten by the vultures.

18 "There are three things that are too
    amazing for me,
  four that I do not understand:
19 the way of an eagle in the sky,
  the way of a snake on a rock,
the way of a ship on the high seas,
  and the way of a man with a young
    woman.

20 "This is the way of an adulterous
    woman:
  She eats and wipes her mouth
  and says, 'I've done nothing wrong.'

21 "Under three things the earth trembles,
  under four it cannot bear up:
22 a servant who becomes king,
  a godless fool who gets plenty to eat,
23 a contemptible woman who gets married,
  and a servant who displaces her
    mistress.

24 "Four things on earth are small,
  yet they are extremely wise:
25 Ants are creatures of little strength,
  yet they store up their food in the
    summer;
26 hyraxes are creatures of little power,
  yet they make their home in
    the crags;
27 locusts have no king,
  yet they advance together in ranks;
28 a lizard can be caught with the hand,
  yet it is found in kings' palaces.

29 "There are three things that are stately in
    their stride,
  four that move with stately bearing:
30 a lion, mighty among beasts,
  who retreats before nothing;
31 a strutting rooster, a he-goat,
  and a king secure against revolt.[a]

32 "If you play the fool and exalt yourself,
  or if you plan evil,
  clap your hand over your mouth!

a 31 The meaning of the Hebrew for this phrase is uncertain.

The Proverbs 31 Wife

By Linda Montgomery

READ: Proverbs 31:10–31

I am convinced that the woman described in Proverbs 31:10 – 31 is a military wife. After all, this Proverbs 31 wife demonstrates the qualities of strength and flexibility that are necessary to function throughout years of managing a family and household in the military environment.

We see this Scriptural woman of honor described as (1) a woman of integrity (see verses 11 – 12). This wife is one who can be trusted, especially when her husband is deployed and she has responsibility for the day-to-day decisions.

We also see this virtuous woman passing on her competencies to others. She is (2) a woman of instruction (see verse 26). Military wives know their greatest teachers are those who have gone before and are willing to train them in the skills and attitudes necessary to accomplish tasks well. So the noble military wife's responsibility is to learn from senior wives and model their wise ways to the next generation.

Unit commanders know the value of a trusted military wife and rely on her to help others. She is known as (3) a woman of influence (see verses 28 – 29). It's not unusual for a military unit to honor the spouses during ceremonies. After all, without support from the home front, the mission is more difficult to accomplish on the battlefront.

The foundation of this wife's integrity, instruction and influence is her reliance on God. Her faith makes her (4) a woman of inspiration (see verses 30 – 31). Through years of military service, she maintains the strength of character that grows more beautiful with each completed assignment.

Recently I met a military wife who was attending her preschool daughter's Mother's Day program. Her husband was serving in Afghanistan — another separation for this veteran family of multiple deployments. Modern technology allowed a tender moment for this wife and her husband as he texted her the words from Proverbs 31:27: "She watches over the affairs of her household and does not eat the bread of idleness." Moments later another text came to her: "Many women do noble things, but you surpass them all" (verse 29). Scriptural encouragement penetrated the weary soul of this military wife.

May each of us strive to demonstrate integrity, instruction, influence and inspiration in our own home. The laundry may pile up, and the kids may leave the house with peanut butter still on their faces from time to time, but "a woman who fears the LORD is to be praised" (verse 30).

Charm is deceptive, and beauty is fleeting; but a woman who fears the LORD is to be praised.

PROVERBS 31:30

DEBRIEF

- In what ways does the description of the Proverbs 31 wife inspire me?
- In what ways does this wife reflect the character of God in her home? How can I do the same?

REPORT

Lord, I want to demonstrate your grace, kindness, wisdom, creativity, trust and faithfulness in my home. Guide me to patiently grow in your likeness day by day. In Jesus' name I pray. Amen.

³³ For as churning cream produces butter,
and as twisting the nose produces
blood,
so stirring up anger produces strife."

Sayings of King Lemuel

31 The sayings of King Lemuel — an inspired utterance his mother taught
him.

² Listen, my son! Listen, son of my womb!
Listen, my son, the answer to my
prayers!
³ Do not spend your strength^a on women,
your vigor on those who ruin kings.

⁴ It is not for kings, Lemuel —
it is not for kings to drink wine,
not for rulers to crave beer,
⁵ lest they drink and forget what has been
decreed,
and deprive all the oppressed of their
rights.
⁶ Let beer be for those who are perishing,
wine for those who are in anguish!
⁷ Let them drink and forget their poverty
and remember their misery no more.

⁸ Speak up for those who cannot speak for
themselves,
for the rights of all who are destitute.
⁹ Speak up and judge fairly;
defend the rights of the poor and
needy.

Epilogue:
The Wife of Noble Character

¹⁰ ^b A wife of noble character who can find?
She is worth far more than rubies.
¹¹ Her husband has full confidence in her
and lacks nothing of value.
¹² She brings him good, not harm,
all the days of her life.
¹³ She selects wool and flax
and works with eager hands.
¹⁴ She is like the merchant ships,
bringing her food from afar.

¹⁵ She gets up while it is still night;
she provides food for her family
and portions for her female servants.
¹⁶ She considers a field and buys it;
out of her earnings she plants a
vineyard.
¹⁷ She sets about her work vigorously;
her arms are strong for her tasks.
¹⁸ She sees that her trading is profitable,
and her lamp does not go out at night.
¹⁹ In her hand she holds the distaff
and grasps the spindle with her
fingers.
²⁰ She opens her arms to the poor
and extends her hands to the needy.
²¹ When it snows, she has no fear for her
household;
for all of them are clothed in scarlet.
²² She makes coverings for her bed;
she is clothed in fine linen and purple.
²³ Her husband is respected at the city gate,
where he takes his seat among the
elders of the land.
²⁴ She makes linen garments and sells them,
and supplies the merchants with
sashes.
²⁵ She is clothed with strength and dignity;
she can laugh at the days to come.
²⁶ She speaks with wisdom,
and faithful instruction is on her
tongue.
²⁷ She watches over the affairs of her
household
and does not eat the bread of idleness.
²⁸ Her children arise and call her blessed;
her husband also, and he praises her:
²⁹ "Many women do noble things,
but you surpass them all."
³⁰ Charm is deceptive, and beauty is
fleeting;
but a woman who fears the LORD is to
be praised.
³¹ Honor her for all that her hands have
done,
and let her works bring her praise at
the city gate.

---

^a 3 Or *wealth*   ^b 10 Verses 10-31 are an acrostic poem, the verses of which begin with the successive
letters of the Hebrew alphabet.

Study Helps

Study Helps

★ ★ ★

[SUBJECT INDEX]

★ ★ ★

[CONTRIBUTOR BIOGRAPHIES]

Sarah Ball

Sarah Ball is the wife of a U.S. Army chaplain and the mother of four children. She has learned about God's sovereignty through six moves in the past eight years, about God's sustaining grace during three year-long deployments, and about God's strength while juggling family, ministry and writing.

Sarah is actively involved in the Army Chapel community and is a regular leader and volunteer for both children's ministries and women's ministries (such as Protestant Women of the Chapel and Military MOPS). She has written for numerous children's magazines and educational publications but values devotional writing in particular. She is a contributing author to *Faith Deployed: Daily Encouragement for Military Wives* and *Faith Deployed ... Again: More Daily Encouragement for Military Wives*. From her earliest memory, she was blessed to be taught God's Word by missionary parents, and she considers each opportunity to share Biblical truth with other military spouses a high privilege. Her prayer for each military wife reading this Bible comes from a favorite childhood verse: "Your word is a lamp for my feet and a light on my path" (Psalm 119:105).

Rebekah Benimoff

Rebekah Benimoff is a contributing author to *Faith Deployed: Daily Encouragement for Military Wives*, *Faith Deployed ... Again: More Daily Encouragement for Military Wives*, *Faith Under Fire: An Army Chaplain's Memoir* and *Stories of Faith and Courage from the Home Front*. She is a freelance writer who contributes to several blogs, including *faithdeployed.com*, *ladiesbydesign.com* and *differentdream.com*.

She enjoys sharing lessons learned as wife to Roger, a retired U.S. Army chaplain who has post-traumatic stress disorder (PTSD), and as mommy to two boys with special issues: Tyler, who has juvenile diabetes and celiac disease, and Blaine, who has a sensory processing disorder. Rebekah is living the journey, learning to balance caring for her family's needs and self-care for the caregiver. She often speaks to wives who are caregivers of wounded veterans as well as to families of children with special needs.

Her mission: Helping families embrace the grieving process and find hope as they heal. Her motto: Prayer, prayer and more prayer! Her ministry: Sharing the hope she has in Jesus, her healer and sanity on difficult days.

Rebekah currently resides in Grand Prairie, Texas. She loves reading, writing and taking long walks in nature to breathe in the beauty of her surroundings and connect with the Lover of her soul.

Sharron Carrns

Sharron Carrns is passionate about writing and training to help people dig deep, explore and grow. For more than 20 years she has developed training to accompany both fiction and non-fiction books, church ministry resources and corporate programs. She created the Basic Training feature in this Bible. As a U.S. Army wife and mom, a small groups director and a corporate training manager, she has written leadership development materials and conducted training programs for corporations, government and non-profits. For her dedication to helping military families in the U.S. Army, she received the Helping Hands Award from General Thomas A. Schwartz and was awarded the Order of St. Joan D'Arc Medallion from the United States Armor Association.

Sharron is a contributing author to *Faith Deployed ... Again: More Daily Encouragement for Military Wives* and *Mother of Pearl*, and is cofounder of the Breathe Christian Writer's Conference. She lives with her family in Spring Lake, Michigan, where she enjoys spending time with her husband, John, her children and her granddaughter. The military has always been part of her life — through the World War II stories of her grandfather, the accounts of her father's service in Korea and the military service of her husband, daughter and son-in-law during times of war and peace-keeping in the Middle East.

Ouida DeDahlin Carter

Ouida is the last family member in her generation alive. She is a wife, mother, grandmother and great-grandmother who is actively involved in her church in Myakka City, Florida. In July 2011, she finally took a trip to France, where she visited one of the American cemeteries and traveled near the area where her brother, Recie, died 67 years earlier during World War II. Soon after, a friend put her in touch with a certified interpretive guide at the Normandy American Cemetery who filled in details about Recie's unit. The trip and information brought healing and closure. Ouida is comforted by the assurance that before long she will be in heaven, where she will see him again. She is thankful for the gift of the brother she had for a brief time in her life because he gave her so much. Recie received the Purple Heart for his bravery and sacrifice.

Jane Hampton Cook

Presidential historian and national speaker Jane Hampton Cook is a former White House webmaster to former president George W. Bush and author of eight books, including *American Phoenix*, *What Does the President Look Like?* and *What Do the First Ladies Wear?* She is also the author of *The Faith of America's First Ladies* and *Battlefields and Blessings: Stories of Faith and Courage from the Revolutionary War*. She is a coauthor with Jocelyn Green and John Croushorn of *Battlefields and Blessings: Stories of Faith and Courage from the War in Iraq & Afghanistan*. Jane is a frequent guest on *Your World with Neil Cavuto* on the Fox News Channel and is the host of a documentary on the Revolutionary War for Liberty Tree House on *gbtv.com*. She lives in Fairfax, Virginia, with her husband and two boys. For more information, visit *janecook.com*.

Bettina Dowell

Often wishing to be a godly woman who inspires other women to new heights in their own journeys, Bettina more frequently finds herself struggling with the very issues about which she writes and speaks to encourage women. Telling the simple stories of her own life (think mice in the pantry or a free cup of coffee), Bettina loves how things begin to make more sense when light is shed on them from the timeless truths of God's Word. As a military wife for more than 29 years, she especially loves the opportunity to minister to military spouses. She is a contributing author to *Faith Deployed ... Again: More Daily Encouragement for Military Wives* and *Stories of Faith and Courage from the Home Front*. She also enjoys blogging.

Though it has never been an easy job, Bettina's husband, Rob Dowell, has patiently loved and supported her for more than 30 years. They are currently exploring the new adventure of being empty nesters outside of Washington, D.C. They are blessed to have two sons, a daughter and a daughter-in-law living from one coast to another, each of whom is pursuing their own adventure with God.

Visit her at *simplestoriestimelesstruths.blogspot.com*.

Catherine Fitzgerald

Catherine Fitzgerald is the proud wife of a U.S. Marine. She is a contributing author to *Faith Deployed ... Again: More Daily Encouragement for Military Wives* and wrote the group study guides for *Faith Deployed: Daily Encouragement for Military Wives* and *Faith Deployed ... Again: More Daily Encouragement for Military Wives*. She currently lives just outside of Wilmington, North Carolina. Her husband is a CH – 53 helicopter pilot and together they have two children, Grace and Asher. She currently leads a ministry through her local church called Operation: Hope Front, which ministers to the needs of fellow military families in her area. Her family also serves in the college ministry, where she has found an endless supply of babysitters and lawn mowers for every deployment.

When she's not changing diapers, chasing her firstborn or doing ministry, she loves to cook, party plan, shop and write. Her greatest joy in military life is seeing the Gospel transform the lives of her military sisters as Scripture is applied to their daily walk.

Jocelyn Green

Jocelyn Green, the wife of a former Coast Guard officer, is an award-winning author and freelance writer. Along with several contributing writers, she is the author of *Faith Deployed: Daily Encouragement for Military Wives* and its sequel, *Faith Deployed ... Again: More Daily Encouragement for Military Wives*. She is also coauthor with Jane Hampton Cook and John Croushorn of *Battlefields and Blessings: Stories of Faith and Courage from the War in Iraq & Afghanistan* and coauthor with Karen Whiting of *Stories of Faith and Courage from the Home Front*. Her novel *Wedded to War* was inspired by a true home-front hero of the Civil War, nurse Georgeanna Woolsey.

She is the founding editor of *Wives in Bloom: The Online Magazine of Christian Military Wives Ministry* (*wivesinbloom.com*), a branch of Christian Military Fellowship. She is also a contributor to the website *startmarriageright.com*.

Jocelyn is an active member of the Evangelical Press Association, Christian Authors Network, the Advanced Writers and Speakers Association, American Christian Fiction Writers, and the Military Writers Society of America.

Jocelyn lives with her husband, Rob, and their two young children in Cedar Falls, Iowa. Visit her at *jocelyngreen.com*.

Kathy Guzzo

Kathy Guzzo is a contributing author to *Faith Deployed ... Again: More Daily Encouragement for Military Wives* and *Stories of Faith and Courage from the Home Front*. She is a regular contributor to *homefrontunited.com, faithdeployed.com* and *differentdream.com*, and she wrote the brochure "Deployment: What's a Family To Do?" During her son's first deployment, she felt God's leading to begin Hope at Home, a ministry for all women with a loved one in the military. For this ministry she writes a bi-monthly newsletter that is sent to women around the country. Kathy and her husband, Mickey, have four adult children, a daughter-in-law, a son-in-law and two grandchildren. They live in Rockford, Illinois. Since only one of their four children lives nearby, any free time they have is spent traveling to see their family. Their son served in the USMC from 2004 to 2008.

Penny Monetti

From finding a toilet in her hallway to booking a next-day flight to England to save her war-torn marriage, author and motivational speaker Penny Monetti and her husband, Lieutenant Colonel Tony Monetti, a B – 2 stealth bomber pilot, share experiences drawn from 25 years of military life from both the warrior's and the spouse's perspectives in *Called to Serve: Encouragement, Support, and Inspiration for Military Families* and *Honored to Serve: Guidance and Encouragement for Military Families in Transition.*

Penny's dynamic and humorous presentations inspire spouses nationwide to laugh, cry and be encouraged regarding the challenges of military life. She has appeared on national radio and television shows, including *Focus on the Family*, and is certified to help combat veterans and their families dealing with PTSD through the American Academy of Christian Counselors. Penny represents the voice of military families nationwide as a military advisory board member for Missouri Congresswoman and House Armed Services committee member Vicky Hartzler. Penny's biggest achievement is raising three wonderful children. Her heart is passionate for military families, especially for military spouses, and she is honored to answer the "call to serve" those selflessly serving this wonderful country. Visit her at *pennymonetti.com*.

Linda Montgomery

Linda Montgomery and her husband, Mike, serve as field missionaries with Military Ministry of Cru in Hampton Roads, Virginia. They are coauthors of the FamilyLife Bible study *Making Your Marriage Deployment Ready* and the devotional *Our Connection: Staying Close When Worlds Apart*. Linda is the founder, the managing editor and a contributing author for Military Ministry's devotional website *Excellent or Praiseworthy* (*excellentorpraiseworthy.org*). That website includes her popular *Deployment Dare*, a 40-day answer to the question "How do you do *The Love Dare* when separated by deployment?" She is a contributing author to *Faith Deployed … Again: More Daily Encouragement for Military Wives* and *Stories of Faith and Courage from the Home Front*.

Mike and Linda have two adult children and a growing number of grandchildren. The Montgomery family served around the world for 23 years until Mike's retirement as a colonel in 1995. Together they consider Psalm 89:1 to be their ministry verse: "I will sing of the LORD's great love forever; with my mouth I will make your faithfulness known through all generations."

Alane Pearce

After nearly 20 years as the wife of a U.S. Air Force member, Alane Pearce spends her time mentoring women and helping them live to their fullest potential.

Alane has written *Notes from the Margins: Healing Conversations with God* and a companion study, *Comparing Notes: A Bible Study Exploring God's Presence in Life's Trials*, about years of dealing with extreme loss and grief. She is also a contributing author to *Faith Deployed … Again: More Daily Encouragement for Military Wives* and *The One Year Life Verse Devotional*. She has also written articles for *Today's Christian Woman*, *The Busy Woman's Guide to a Balanced Life*, *Military Spouse Magazine Online*, *Faith and Family Magazine* and for several blogs.

Alane has lived in Colorado, Texas, Virginia, Hawaii and Maryland. She likes Colorado the best. She loves to hike, camp, drink good coffee and spend time with friends and family.

Alane is an author coach who helps writers become published and promoted authors. Learn more at *alanepearce.com*.

Pattie Reitz

Pattie Reitz is the proud wife of her U.S. Air Force chaplain husband, Roland, and in 2012 they celebrated 22 years of marriage and ministry together, 11 years with the military. They are the proud parents of two teenage daughters. Pattie holds a BA from Southwest Baptist University and an MSEd from Northwest Missouri State University, both in English education. She taught high school and college English for many years and now teaches composition for an external campus of Wayland Baptist University.

Pattie has volunteered in chapel ministries such as worship team and PWOC and has served as web content editor for *Wives of Faith*. Pattie's work has appeared online at *wivesoffaith.org* and *bluestarfam.org*, in the books *God Strong*, *Tour of Duty* and *Faith Deployed ... Again: More Daily Encouragement for Military Wives*, and in the devotional magazine *Open Windows*. The Reitz family currently lives in Eagle River, Alaska, where they enjoy seeing moose, bears and bald eagles.

Sheryl Shearer

Sheryl Shearer has earned degrees in music (BA, Minnesota State University – Moorhead) and theology (MATS, MDiv, Assemblies of God Theological Seminary). Along with home-schooling her four amazing daughters, she teaches piano, history and language courses at Homeschool Plus, a local homeschool co-op in Norfolk, Virginia. She also teaches piano at Music & Arts in Yorktown, Virginia. She is a licensed minister with the Assemblies of God and enjoys writing and teaching adult Bible studies and leading the kids' ministry in her local church. During nearly 20 years of marriage to Brian, a Navy chaplain, they have weathered 13 moves, most with the military. Her favorite duty stations were Germany and Kaneohe Bay, Hawaii. In her spare moments, Sheryl spends her time playing piano, reading, writing, following politics, running, watching Duke basketball and Steeler football games and hanging out with her family. She lives in Newport News, Virginia.

Ronda Sturgill

After being thrown from a horse at the age of 18, Ronda became a paraplegic. A follower of Christ for the past 30 years, she is most passionate about leading and writing transformative Bible studies. Ronda is the author of *Wives of the Warriors: Living Confidently in Christ* and the Bible studies *Desperate Housecries: Discovering Genuine Hope in God* and *Extreme Makeover: Heart Edition*. She is also a contributing author to *Faith Deployed: Daily Encouragement for Military Wives* and the *God Allows U-Turns* series. She is also a monthly columnist for *Wives In Bloom*.

Currently pursuing an MA in Curriculum and Instruction/Adult Education from Regent University, Ronda's strengths are training Christian lay leaders and teachers to teach adults in ways that promote transformative learning. With an extremely tender heart toward the poor and homeless, Ronda also serves at Target Dayton Ministries in Dayton, Ohio, as a cook, Bible study leader and literacy teacher. Her hobbies include cooking and taking photographs of beautiful flowers.

Ronda and her husband, Tim, reside in Fairborn, Ohio, where Tim serves as an Air Force chaplain at Wright Patterson AFB. They have one grown son, Toby. For more information about Ronda, visit her website at *rondasturgill.com*.

Leeana Tankersley

Leeana Tankersley is currently stationed in Bahrain with her Navy SEAL husband, Steve, and their three children. She is the author of *Found Art: Discovering Beauty in Foreign*

Places, a memoir about her time in the Middle East. She has also contributed to *Always There: Reflections for Moms on God's Presence* and *Faith Deployed ... Again: More Daily Encouragement for Military Wives*. In addition to working on her second book, Leeana is inspiring fellow gypsies at *gypsyink.com*. You can follow Leeana on Twitter @ lmtankersley.

Marshéle Carter Waddell

Marshéle Carter Waddell served around the world for 28 years with her husband, CDR (ret) Mark Waddell, a career U.S. Navy SEAL. In her first two books, *Hope for the Home Front: Winning the Emotional and Spiritual Battles of a Military Wife* and its companion Bible study, *Hope for the Home Front Bible Study*, Marshéle arms military wives with God's promises of his presence, power and protection. Together with their three children, the Waddells have endured many lengthy separations and frequent deployments. Today, her husband is a disabled combat veteran with PTSD and multiple TBIs. Her son recently returned from his second combat tour with Operation Enduring Freedom, Afghanistan, with the 3/7 Marines.

Her newest book is *Wounded Warrior, Wounded Home: Hope and Healing for Families Living with PTSD and TBI*.

Marshéle is an international speaker for military, government and women's events. She is the founder and president of Hope for the Home Front, a non-profit organization based in Fort Worth, Texas. She was awarded the Bloomberg Assistantship at the University of North Carolina at Chapel Hill and is currently pursuing her MA in Journalism-Strategic Corporate Communication.

Karen Whiting

Karen Whiting, a military wife and mother, is the author of 16 books, including *Stories of Faith and Courage from the Home Front* (coauthored with Jocelyn Green). She writes for families and girls. She loves to let creativity splash onto the page as she writes. Whiting's books include the popular series *God's Girls*, inspirational craft books for tween girls, and the devotional *The 365 Most Important Bible Passages for Women*. Her more than 500 articles and devotions have been published in more than four dozen magazines, including *Focus on the Family*, *The Lookout*, *Today's Christian Woman*, *Enrichment Journal*, *Reminisce* and *Devo-Zine*.

Karen also directed an award-winning tween and teen puppet ministry for more than a dozen years and hosted the television series *Puppets on Parade* on WLRN Miami educational television. Karen is a speaker for women's groups, retreats, schools and mother-daughter events.

She has been married to James Whiting, a retired U.S. Coast Guard officer, for more than 35 years. Whiting's oldest son, a graduate of the U.S. Air Force Academy, served in Iraq and is still on active duty. She is a mother of five and grandmother of eight. She has a heart for encouraging families to connect with, serve and treasure one another.

Rosie Williams

Army wife Rosie Williams is the Home Front Coordinator for Point Man Ministries of Kansas. She has planned four national Home Front retreats and helps to set up Home Front groups across the state of Kansas in support of wives and family members of veterans and active military families. Rosie was born and raised in Topeka, Kansas, and now lives in Tecumseh, Kansas. She is married to Steve, a Vietnam War veteran who was with the 101st Airborne Division.

She is a public speaker, a writer and a contributing author to *Faith Deployed ... Again: More Daily Encouragement for Military Wives*. Steve and Rosie's stories have appeared in *Stories of Faith and Courage from Vietnam* and *Stories of Faith and Courage from the Home Front*.

They have three sons, two daughters-in-law and two grandchildren. Rosie and Steve have worked with Point Man Ministries, a Christian organization for veterans, for the past 17 years. Rosie has a BS in Family and Child Development from Kansas State University. She has an antique booth in Topeka and enjoys going to estate and garage sales, scrapbooking, swimming and, most of all, playing with her grandkids! Visit her at *pointmankansas.org*.

FAVORITE BIBLE VERSES
FOR MILITARY WIVES

Scriptures for Comfort and Compassion

Psalm 34:17–19
Psalm 42:8
Psalm 56:8–9
Psalm 68:5
Psalm 90:14–15,17
2 Corinthians 1:3–4

Scriptures for Fear

Psalm 23:4
Psalm 27:1
Psalm 56:3–4
Psalm 112:7
Isaiah 41:10–13
Isaiah 43:1–3
Matthew 6:34
2 Timothy 1:7

Scriptures for Hope

Psalm 30:5
Psalm 33:20–22
Psalm 42:11
Psalm 121:1–2
Psalm 145:13–16
Jeremiah 29:11–13
Romans 5:3–4
2 Corinthians 1:8–11

Scriptures for Peace

Psalm 4:8
Isaiah 26:3–4
John 14:27
Romans 15:13
Philippians 4:4–7
Philippians 4:6–8
Hebrews 12:11

Scriptures for the Daily Grind

Psalm 46:10
Psalms 118:24
Psalm 139
Romans 8:28
Romans 12:12
1 Corinthians 10:13
Ephesians 6:10–18
Philippians 4:8–13
James 1:2–4
1 Peter 5:7

Scriptures for Sleepless Nights

Psalm 3:5
Psalm 4:8
Psalm 62:5
Psalm 63:6
Psalm 119:147–148
Psalm 121:3–4
Lamentations 2:19

Scriptures for Strength

Joshua 1:9
Psalm 29:11
Psalm 46:1
Psalm 73:26
Isaiah 40:31
2 Corinthians 12:9–10
Ephesians 3:16–19
Philippians 4:13

Scriptures for Trusting the Lord

Psalm 9:10
Psalm 13:5
Psalm 16:8
Psalm 27:13–14
Psalm 33:20–22
Psalm 73:28
Proverbs 3:5–6

★ ★ ★

Ten Favorite Hymns
for Military Wives

The Lord Will Provide

Though troubles around us and dangers affright,
Though friends all should fail and foes all unite;
Yet there's one thing secures us whatever betide,
The scripture assures us, the Lord will provide.

The birds without barn, without storehouse are fed,
From them let us learn to trust for our bread:
For the saints, e'er repeating, they won't be denied,
As long as 'tis written, the Lord will provide.

His call we obey like Abraham of old,
Not knowing our way but faith makes us bold;
For though we are strangers, well, we have a good guide,
Have trust in all dangers, the Lord will provide.

When Satan appears to stop up our path,
He fills us with fears, but won't lose our faith;
He cannot take from us though hard he has tried,
This heart-cheering promise, the Lord will provide.

He tells us so slyly our hope is in vain,
All the good that we seek, well, we ne'er shall obtain,
But when such suggestions our spirits have tried,
This answers all questions, the Lord will provide.

WORDS: John Newton, 1725 – 1807
MUSIC: Johann M. Haydn, 1737 – 1806

Nearer, My God, to Thee

Nearer, my God, to thee, nearer to thee!
E'en though it be a cross that raiseth me,
still all my song shall be,
nearer, my God, to thee;
nearer, my God, to thee, nearer to thee!

Though like the wanderer, the sun gone down,
darkness be over me, my rest a stone;
yet in my dreams I'd be
nearer, my God, to thee;
nearer, my God, to thee, nearer to thee!

There let the way appear, steps unto heaven;
all that thou sendest me, in mercy given;
angels to beckon me
nearer, my God, to thee;
nearer, my God, to thee, nearer to thee!

Then, with my waking thoughts bright with thy praise,
out of my stony griefs Bethel I'll raise;
so by my woes to be
nearer, my God, to thee;
nearer, my God, to thee, nearer to thee!

Or if, on joyful wing cleaving the sky,
sun, moon, and stars forgot, upward I fly,
still all my song shall be,
nearer, my God, to thee;
nearer, my God, to thee, nearer to thee!

WORDS: Sarah F. Adams, 1805 – 1848
MUSIC: Lowell Mason, 1792 – 1872

Be Still, My Soul

Be still, my soul: the Lord is on thy side.
Bear patiently the cross of grief or pain.
Leave to thy God to order and provide;
In every change, He faithful will remain.
Be still, my soul: thy best, thy heavenly Friend
Through thorny ways leads to a joyful end.

Be still, my soul: thy God doth undertake
To guide the future, as He has the past.
Thy hope, thy confidence let nothing shake;
All now mysterious shall be bright at last.
Be still, my soul: the waves and winds still know
His voice Who ruled them while He dwelt below.

Be still, my soul: when dearest friends depart,
And all is darkened in the vale of tears,
Then shalt thou better know His love, His heart,
Who comes to soothe thy sorrow and thy fears.
Be still, my soul: thy Jesus can repay
From His own fullness all He takes away.

Be still, my soul: the hour is hastening on
When we shall be forever with the Lord.
When disappointment, grief and fear are gone,
Sorrow forgot, love's purest joys restored.
Be still, my soul: when change and tears are past
All safe and blessèd we shall meet at last.

Be still, my soul: begin the song of praise
On earth, believing, to Thy Lord on high;
Acknowledge Him in all thy words and ways,
So shall He view thee with a well pleased eye.
Be still, my soul: the Sun of life divine
Through passing clouds shall but more brightly shine.

WORDS: Katharina von Schlegel, 1697 – 1768; translated from
German to English by Jane L. Borthwick, 1813 – 1897
MUSIC: Jean Sibelius, 1865 – 1957

A Mighty Fortress Is Our God

A mighty fortress is our God, a bulwark never failing;
our helper he amid the flood of mortal ills prevailing.
For still our ancient foe doth seek to work us woe;
his craft and power are great, and armed with cruel
    hate, on earth is not his equal.

Did we in our own strength confide, our striving would
    be losing,
were not the right man on our side, the man of God's
    own choosing.
Dost ask who that may be? Christ Jesus, it is he;
Lord Sabaoth, his name, from age to age the same, and
    he must win the battle.

And though this world, with devils filled, should threaten
    to undo us,
we will not fear, for God hath willed his truth to triumph
    through us.
The Prince of Darkness grim, we tremble not for him;
his rage we can endure, for lo, his doom is sure; one little
    word shall fell him.

That word above all earthly powers, no thanks to them,
    abideth;
the Spirit and the gifts are ours, thru him who with us
    sideth.
Let goods and kindred go, this mortal life also;
the body they may kill; God's truth abideth still; his
    kingdom is forever.

TEXT: Martin Luther, 1483 – 1546; translated from German to
    English by Frederick H. Hedge, 1805 – 1890
MUSIC: Martin Luther, 1483 – 1546

How Firm a Foundation

How firm a foundation, ye saints of the Lord,
is laid for your faith in his excellent word!
What more can he say than to you he hath said,
to you who for refuge to Jesus have fled?

Fear not, I am with thee, O be not dismayed,
for I am thy God and will still give thee aid;
I'll strengthen and help thee, and cause thee to stand
upheld by my righteous, omnipotent hand.

When through deep waters I call thee to go,
the rivers of woe shall not thee overflow;
for I will be with thee, thy troubles to bless,
and sanctify to thee thy deepest distress.

When through fiery trials thy pathways shall lie,
my grace, all-sufficient, shall be thy supply;
the flame shall not hurt thee; I only design
thy dross to consume, and thy gold to refine.

WORDS: John Rippon, 1751 – 1836
MUSIC: Joseph Funk, 1778 – 1862

Count Your Blessings

When upon life's billows you are tempest tossed,
When you are discouraged, thinking all is lost,
Count your many blessings, name them one by one,
And it will surprise you what the Lord hath done.

Refrain
Count your blessings, name them one by one,
Count your blessings, see what God hath done!
Count your blessings, name them one by one,
And it will surprise you what the Lord hath done.

Are you ever burdened with a load of care?
Does the cross seem heavy you are called to bear?
Count your many blessings, every doubt will fly,
And you will keep singing as the days go by.

Refrain

When you look at others with their lands and gold,
Think that Christ has promised you His wealth untold;
Count your many blessings. Wealth can never buy
Your reward in heaven, nor your home on high.

Refrain

So, amid the conflict whether great or small,
Do not be disheartened, God is over all;
Count your many blessings, angels will attend,
Help and comfort give you to your journey's end.

Refrain

WORDS: Johnson Oatman, Jr., 1856 – 1922
MUSIC: Edwin O. Excell, 1851 – 1921

Take My Life and Let It Be

Take my life, and let it be consecrated, Lord, to Thee.
Take my moments and my days; let them flow in ceaseless praise.
Take my hands, and let them move at the impulse of Thy love.
Take my feet, and let them be swift and beautiful for Thee.

Take my voice, and let me sing always, only, for my King.
Take my lips, and let them be filled with messages from Thee.
Take my silver and my gold; not a mite would I withhold.
Take my intellect, and use every power as Thou shalt choose.

Take my will, and make it Thine; it shall be no longer mine.
Take my heart, it is Thine own; it shall be Thy royal throne.
Take my love, my Lord, I pour at Thy feet its treasure store.
Take myself, and I will be ever, only, all for Thee.

WORDS: Francis R. Havergal, 1836 – 1879
MUSIC: Louis J. F. Herold, 1791 – 1833

Jesus, I My Cross Have Taken

Jesus, I my cross have taken,
All to leave and follow Thee;
Destitute, despised, forsaken,
Thou from hence my All shalt be.
Perish every fond ambition,
All I've sought or hoped or known;
Yet how rich is my condition!
God and heaven are still my own.

Let the world despise and leave me,
They have left my Savior, too.
Human hearts and looks deceive me;
Thou art not, like them, untrue.
And while Thou shalt smile upon me,
God of wisdom, love, and might,
Foes may hate and friends may shun me;
Show Thy face, and all is bright.

Man may trouble and distress me,
'Twill but drive me to Thy breast;
Life with trials hard may press me,
Heaven will bring me sweeter rest.
Oh, 'tis not in grief to harm me
While Thy love is left to me;
Oh, 'twere not in joy to charm me
Were that joy unmixed with Thee.

Haste, then, on from grace to glory,
Armed by faith and winged by prayer;
Heaven's eternal day's before thee,
God's own hand shall guide thee there.
Soon shall close the earthly mission,
Swift shall pass thy pilgrim days,
Hope soon change to glad fruition,
Faith to sight, and prayer to praise.

WORDS: Henry F. Lyte, 1793 – 1847
MUSIC: Rowland H. Prichard, 1811 – 1887

Lead On, O King Eternal

Lead on, O King eternal,
The day of march has come;
Henceforth in fields of conquest
Thy tents shall be our home.
Through days of preparation
Thy grace has made us strong;
And now, O King eternal,
We lift our battle song.

Lead on, O King eternal,
Till sin's fierce war shall cease,
And holiness shall whisper
The sweet amen of peace.
For not with swords' loud clashing,
Nor roll of stirring drums;
With deeds of love and mercy
The heavenly kingdom comes.

Lead on, O King eternal,
We follow, not with fears,
For gladness breaks like morning
Where'er Thy face appears.
Thy cross is lifted over us,
We journey in its light;
The crown awaits the conquest;
Lead on, O God of might.

WORDS: Ernest W. Shurtleff, 1862 – 1917
MUSIC: Henry T. Smart, 1813 – 1879

I Love to Tell the Story

I love to tell the story of unseen things above,
Of Jesus and His glory, of Jesus and His love.
I love to tell the story, because I know 'tis true;
It satisfies my longings as nothing else can do.

Refrain

I love to tell the story, 'twill be my theme in glory,
To tell the old, old story of Jesus and His love.

I love to tell the story; more wonderful it seems
Than all the golden fancies of all our golden dreams.
I love to tell the story, it did so much for me;
And that is just the reason I tell it now to thee.

Refrain

I love to tell the story; 'tis pleasant to repeat
What seems, each time I tell it, more wonderfully sweet.
I love to tell the story, for some have never heard
The message of salvation from God's own holy Word.

Refrain

I love to tell the story, for those who know it best
Seem hungering and thirsting to hear it like the rest.
And when, in scenes of glory, I sing the new, new song,
'Twill be the old, old story that I have loved so long.

Refrain

WORDS: A. Katherine Hankey, 1834 – 1911
MUSIC: William G. Fischer, 1835 – 1912

★ ★ ★

Basic Training

Depend on the Shepherd

"There were many times when I would tell God, 'I do not like this path, and you need to change it.' And God's love for us is so amazing that he would reply, 'I understand your anger. I feel it too about what happened to Brian. But I won't change this path. However, I will walk down it with you.'"

—Mel Birdwell in *Refined by Fire*

Read Psalm 23.
In one or two sentences, summarize the verse that most stands out to you.

Verse 4 says, "Your rod and your staff, they comfort me." A shepherd's rod is a tool of strength, power, authority and discipline. A shepherd's staff is a tool with a hook that rescues sheep that have begun to go astray or have fallen into dangerous places. How can God's rod and staff comfort you?

In Psalm 23, the author, David, declared what he would do—and would not do—because of his faith in his shepherd. Read the verses listed and write below what David declared.

1. (Verse 1) _____
2. (Verse 4) _____
3. (Verse 6) _____

Psalm 23 begins by identifying the Lord as David's shepherd. A shepherd gives sheep direction, comfort and protection. Think about the names of the Lord and the roles he has in your life and write them below.

Verse 4 declares, "I will fear no evil." You were not created to experience evil, and you have a healthy inner awareness to flee from it. But Satan twists that awareness into a powerful form of fear that is evil. What are the fears you face as a military wife? Share those fears with God and write a declaration against each of them below.

Lord, I fear _____. I declare that _____ will not rule over me.

Lord, I fear _____. I declare that _____ will not rule over me.

Lord, I fear _____. I declare that _____ will not rule over me.

SOUL ARMOR

God is good and loving, no matter what circumstances you face. Take some time to memorize Psalm 23:6, and then:

- Ask God to bring to your mind a circumstance you have faced during which he has shown his goodness and love.

- Praise God for revealing his goodness and love to you in that situation.

- Praise God because you can trust in his goodness and love in all situations.

- Share with God any areas in which you find it hard to trust in God's goodness and love, and ask him to give you peace and comfort.

- Pray Psalm 23 as your own affirmation and trust in God. Begin with, "Lord, you are my shepherd, I lack nothing. You give me rest like sheep in green pastures and comfort like the peace of quiet waters ..."

MARCHING ORDERS

Envision yourself as a lamb, always dependent on the shepherd.

★ ★ ★

Surpass Them All

"I want to be the wife who is a blessing to her family, who is praised and remembered, not for the activities or projects I checked off, but for the smiles I wore, the peace I shared, and the deep love of God I hope I instilled wherever I went. That's my prayer."

—Sara Horn in *My So-Called Life as a Proverbs 31 Wife ... and Its Surprising Results*

Read Proverbs 31:10–31.
In one or two sentences, summarize the verse that most stands out to you.

The "wife of noble character" in this passage possesses many virtues and performs many faithful tasks. Write the virtues listed in the verses below.

1. (Verse 11) _____

2. (Verse 12) _____

3. (Verse 25) _____

4. (Verse 26) _____

Verse 23 says, "Her husband is respected at the city gate." How does her role as a wife affect how others view him?

How does your talk and behavior in your role as a military wife affect how your husband is viewed by others?

Your daily life is different from that of the wife in Proverbs 31, yet you have your own virtues and tasks you perform faithfully. What are some of the virtues you, and those who know you, would say you possess?

What are some of the tasks that you perform faithfully as a military wife?

As a military wife, you may feel as if what you do behind the scenes to support your husband is not as important as his job. Look at yourself from God's perspective. What do you do that he says is important?

Look at yourself from your husband's perspective. What would he say is important? If you aren't sure, ask him, and let him know you value his encouragement.

SOUL ARMOR

Take some time to memorize Proverbs 31:30 – 31, and then:

- Praise God that he understands your life as a military wife.
- Praise God that he values you and promises to reward you (see verse 31).
- Ask God to show you how you can be a "wife of noble character."
- Ask God to give you encouragement, direction and strength in your role as a military wife.
- Ask God to help you live in such a way that your works will be valued and you will be worthy of praise (see verse 31).

MARCHING ORDERS

Wife of noble character, let your works bring you praise.

Be Battle Ready for Temptation

"Certain temptations knock more loudly on my door when my husband is away … At this point, the enemy launches psy-ops on me, that is, psychological operations. All sorts of sordid suggestions materialize in my brain matter, temptations targeted at my weak spots by an unseen, skilled archer."

—Marshéle Carter Waddell in *Hope for the Home Front:
Winning the Emotional and Spiritual Battles of a Military Wife*

Read Matthew 4:1 – 11.
In one or two sentences, summarize the verse that most stands out to you.

What is the title used for Satan in verse three?

What are some other titles and tactics that could describe Satan?

In Matthew 16:21 – 28 Jesus told his disciples he would suffer, die and rise again. Well-meaning Peter told Jesus this would never happen to Jesus. But Jesus recognized that Satan was at work in Peter, trying to convince Jesus to avoid the will of God. Have you had a time when you recognized Satan trying to convince you of "nice" lies? If so, write it down below.

In what ways could you be vulnerable to physical temptation as a military wife?

In what ways could you be vulnerable emotionally?

Jesus was tempted, yet we know he was never guilty of sin. Satan will also tempt you. If you do not give in to sin, he will attempt to make you feel guilty for merely being tempted. What can you say to him?

James 4:7 says, "Resist the devil, and he will flee from you." When have you resisted Satan and his tactics? How did your faith and what you know about God's Word help you?

SOUL ARMOR

Are you confident using the same words Jesus used in Matthew 4:10? Take some time to memorize what Jesus said in verse 10, and then:

- Praise God for Jesus' example of using God's Word when you are tempted.
- Praise God for the protection you have against allowing temptation to grow into sin.
- Confess any areas in which you have given in to sin.
- Ask the Lord to help you recognize temptation and reject it when it comes.
- Ask the Lord to be the Commander in Chief of your life, directing you as you plan your defense.

MARCHING ORDERS

Make a plan for defensive action so you will be ready when the tempter comes.

Do Not Worry

"There is so much that we can't change as military wives, but God is more than able to work through our trials and bless us when we seek to do his will. God will give us what we need to face each day if we earnestly turn to him for our strength. On the worst days, when I am tempted to panic over the future, I need to remind myself of his truth several times a day."

—Rachel Latham in *Faith Deployed ...*
Again: More Daily Encouragement for Military Wives

Read Matthew 6:25–34.
In one or two sentences, summarize the verse that most stands out to you.

Circle in your Bible the times the phrase "Do not worry" appears in Matthew 6:25–34. How many times did you find that phrase?

Why should we not worry, according to these verses?

1. (Verse 27) _____

2. (Verses 32–33) _____

3. (Verse 34) _____

In verse 33, what does Jesus tell us to be most concerned about?

Think about the past week. What have you been worried about?

Do you believe that God is trustworthy to meet your needs?

The next time you find worry in your heart, what can you do to cast it out?

SOUL ARMOR

Take some time to memorize Matthew 6:33–34, and then:

- Praise God for his past provision in your life. Name at least one specific example. Praise him for his promise to take care of you.

- Confess any areas in your life about which you consistently worry.

- Ask the Lord to help you surrender that anxiety to him. Ask him to fill you with contentment and peace instead. Ask for his help to "seek first his kingdom and his righteousness."

- Do you know someone who struggles with worry? Pray for him or her to trust God for his provision instead.

MARCHING ORDERS

Seek to live a righteous life, and let God take care of the rest.

Shout Out to Jesus

"I need a break and I need support. It seems that we're in a place of isolation. I miss my family and I miss my friends from Ft. Carson. My husband is falling apart and I have no support here. Father God, I want to give up, but I won't. Help me dig into you and let you fill the voids. There are so many."

—Rebekah Benimoff in *Faith Under Fire: An Army Chaplain's Memoir*

Read Mark 10:46 – 52.
In one or two sentences, summarize the verse that most stands out to you.

Jesus did not "fall in" with the troops to silence Bartimaeus. Read verses 49 – 52 and describe below what Jesus did and said.

Mark 10:46 – 52 reveals a great deal about the character of Jesus and his attitude toward his children. What did Bartimaeus shout to Jesus (see verses 47 – 48)?

What did Jesus say to Bartimaeus (see verse 51)?

What happened (see verse 52)?

What did Bartimaeus do after he received his sight?

Poverty was a symptom of Bartimaeus's blindness. He could have asked Jesus for money, but he instead asked for healing to solve the root of the problem. What would you ask of Jesus in your toughest times as a military wife?

Would your request get rid of the symptom or get at the root of your struggle?

Verse 48 says many rebuked Bartimaeus and told him to be quiet, but he shouted all the more. Even in circumstances that might seem impossible, would you be quiet or keep shouting to Jesus to help you? Explain your answer.

Based on what you know to be true about Jesus, what do you think his response to you would be?

SOUL ARMOR
Take some time to memorize Mark 10:47, and then:

- Ask God to help you believe that he will hear you, just as he heard Bartimaeus.
- Ask God to help you know beyond a shadow of a doubt that you are important to him.
- Praise God for a time when you know he heard you and had mercy on you.
- Praise God for his goodness and mercy.
- Praise God that he is never too busy for you and that he is not controlled by any crowd.

MARCHING ORDERS
Shout to Jesus and be confident he is listening.

Stop Doubting and Believe

"Sometimes you can't see or touch or feel the dream, or the person, or God, and you have to believe anyway. I have spent many a night in a bed by myself, married to thin air, more or less. Something inside me, though, continues … Maybe because of, not in spite of, all the craziness, I have learned the power of believing."

—Leeana Tankersley in *Found Art: Discovering Beauty in Foreign Places*

Read John 20:24 – 29.

In one or two sentences, summarize the verse that most stands out to you.

Thomas told the disciples who had seen Jesus that he would not believe them unless he had proof. What three actions did Thomas say he would have to take in order to believe (see verse 25)?

1. _____

2. _____

3. _____

In verse 27 Jesus asked Thomas to do the very three things Thomas had said he needed for proof. What was the final action Jesus asked Thomas to take (see the end of verse 27)?

Jesus showed his scars to Thomas to prove his identity and credibility. As a military wife, you may have scars because you have been through hardships. Your scars give you credibility to minister to others. How might you help others find comfort and understanding?

When have you been comforted by, and gained understanding from, another woman who shared with you what she had experienced?

Thomas doubted because he wanted to know the truth. He was open about his doubts. How open are you to sharing your doubts with God? Whom can you trust to talk with in times of doubt?

As you live through times of doubt that are followed by times of Jesus revealing himself to you, you will learn to believe without seeing. What does Jesus say about believing without seeing?

SOUL ARMOR

Take some time to memorize what Jesus said to Thomas in John 20:27, and then:

- Praise God that he loves and assures you even in your times of doubt.
- Praise God that he knows everything about you because he created you.
- Praise God that he does not condemn you for the times you struggle to believe, even while he longs for you to believe without seeing.
- Ask God to help you have peace as you learn to believe without seeing.
- Ask God to bless you and to allow you to be a blessing to others.

MARCHING ORDERS

Go in peace, and learn to believe without seeing.

The Meaning of Love

"*I* decided to make our relationship work … Only after choosing to honor our marriage commitment when the feelings of love disappeared did Christ revive our dying relationship."

—Penny Monetti in *Called to Serve:*
Encouragement, Support and Inspiration for Military Families

Read 1 Corinthians 13:1 – 13.
In one or two sentences, summarize the verse that most stands out to you.

This passage begins by describing all the things a person could do that would mean nothing without love. List some of them below.

What remains, according to verse 13? How is each of these important to you as a military wife?

Write the words used to define love listed in verses 4 – 8.

1. _____   2. _____
3. _____   4. _____
5. _____   6. _____
7. _____   8. _____
9. _____   10. _____
11. _____   12. _____
13. _____   14. _____
15. _____   16. _____

All people have both strengths and challenges because we are human. But in verse 12 we are assured that someday we will be made whole, able to see with God's perspective. How does this give you hope?

Verses 1–3 say you could speak in tongues, prophesy, move mountains, give everything to the poor, surrender your body to hardship, and more—but do all these things without love. Does it surprise you that actions of this magnitude could be done without love? Explain.

There are countless actions and activities you perform as a military wife. List some of them; next to each item, write whether or not you perform them with love.

SOUL ARMOR

Take some time to memorize 1 Corinthians 13:12, and then:

- Praise God that he has given you 1 Corinthians 13 to help you understand love.
- Praise God that he loves you perfectly, despite your imperfections.
- Ask God to help you act out of love, even when it doesn't feel good.
- Ask God to give you his love and perspective.

MARCHING ORDERS

Choose to act out of love.

★ ★ ★

Out of Reverence for the Lord

"Honoring Jim was easy when I felt he understood my feelings and sympathized with my inadequacies as a military wife. But when his work became all-consuming, when lunch dates were forgotten, and when married life became tedious, honor seemed a vague notion."

—Beatrice Fishback in *Loving Your Military Man:
A Study for Women Based on Philippians 4:8*

Read Ephesians 5:21 – 33.
In one or two sentences, summarize the verse that most stands out to you.

Verse 21 says, "Submit to one another." Why are we to do this, according to the second part of the verse?

Why does Ephesians 5:22 – 24 say wives should submit to their husbands?
1. (Verse 22) _____
2. (Verse 23) _____
3. (Verse 24) _____
What does "as you do to the Lord" mean in verse 22?

God created you as a unique person with your own gifts and personality, and he loves you. What does it mean to submit to your husband while continuing to be the person God created and loves?

In our culture the concept of submitting to your husband is unpopular. This may be because submission has been misinterpreted and abused, or because of a secular view of our "rights." Either way, what does submission mean in your marriage?

The military command says, "Mission first." To a military wife, that can sound like you are second in importance. How does putting the mission first actually make you first?

How does respecting your husband's requirement to put the mission first prevent him from being torn between you and his job?

SOUL ARMOR

Take some time to memorize Ephesians 5:21, and then:

- Praise Jesus that he loves the church and gave himself up for her to make her holy.
- Praise Jesus that he cleansed the church by the "washing with water through the word" (verse 26).
- Praise Jesus that his plan for leadership is perfect for you.
- Ask God to help you see submission from his perspective, not from your culture's perspective.
- Ask God to help both you and your husband to understand submission and to act with loving submission to one another as he has taught in his Word.

MARCHING ORDERS

Submit to your husband out of reverence for Christ.

All in the Name of Jesus

"I had to get used to the fact that as an airman's wife, I represented him—especially when interacting with others on base. This is true of us as Christians as well. Our words and actions represent Jesus to others."

—Jill Hart in *Faith Deployed: Daily Encouragement for Military Wives*

Read Colossians 3:5–17.

In one or two sentences, summarize the verse that most stands out to you.

How does God describe you in verse 12?

1. _____

2. _____

3. _____

With what should you clothe yourself, and how should you act toward others, including your husband (and yourself!)?

1. (Verse 12) _____

2. (Verse 13) _____

3. (Verse 14) _____

What does it mean to "let the peace of Christ rule in your hearts" (verse 15)?

Verses 15–17 describe the overall attitude Christians should have. Read these verses again; then write out how your attitude matches—or doesn't match—the description.

Since the beginning of our nation, our military has called on God, attempting to act "in word or deed ... in the name of the Lord Jesus" (verse 17). What does it mean to follow this Scripture as a nation?

What does it mean to act "in word or deed ... in the name of the Lord Jesus" as a military wife?

When you became a military wife, a whole new level of commitment was added to your life. Paul says you are continually being "renewed in knowledge in the image of [your] Creator" (verse 10). How does each training exercise, deployment and military function renew your knowledge of God?

According to verse 17, "whatever you do, whether in word or deed, do it all in the name of the Lord Jesus, giving thanks to God the Father through him." How can you, as a woman, live with this command as a foundation for your words and actions?

SOUL ARMOR

Take some time to memorize Colossians 3:17, and then:

- Praise God that he knows your desire to honor what is said in this verse.

- Praise God that when your words or actions fall short of honoring God, he will love you, forgive you and help you restore your commitment to him.

- Praise God for his peace that transcends all understanding.

- Ask God to help you allow the peace of Christ to rule in your heart.

- Ask God to help you be filled with love that brings perfect unity.

MARCHING ORDERS

Let everything you do and say reflect the love of the Lord Jesus.

Preventing a Fire

"When these military men and women are concerned about overwhelming issues at home, they have trouble concentrating on their jobs over there. When they cannot concentrate as well, it translates into potential accidents. When there are accidents, there is death. So if you want to do your part to save lives in Iraq, then you tell your husband that you love him, you're proud of him, and you're going to be all right. Then when he gets home safely, you can vent all you want, and even make him change a few diapers, too."

—Ellie Kay in *Heroes at Home: Help and Hope for America's Military Families*

Read James 3:1 – 12.
In one or two sentences, summarize the verse that most stands out to you.

What does verse 1 say about teachers?

What does verse 2 say about all of us?

List five things the tongue is or does, according to verses 5 – 8.

1. _____
2. _____
3. _____
4. _____
5. _____

Why do you think a passage of Scripture dealing with the tongue would start by warning teachers that they will be judged more strictly than others?

Whether you are a teacher of the Word or a student of the Word, what are you doing to make sure you have a deeper understanding of the Word?

An untamed tongue can cause dissention, fearful rumors, and even death in the military. How has someone's untamed tongue affected you or someone you know?

How can you use your tongue for good as a military wife?

How can you prevent your tongue from being used for evil as a military wife?

Verse 6 says the tongue itself is "set on fire by hell," meaning Satan uses the words we say to accomplish his plans. When have you said words you knew were not from God?

Satan knows where you are weakest and wants to provoke you to speak words "set on fire by hell." In what area do you think you are weakest? Your temper? Gossiping? Complaining? Demanding?

SOUL ARMOR

Take some time to memorize James 3:5, and then:

- Praise God that you can call on him to help you with your tongue, so that your words bring good and not evil.
- Praise God for the times when someone's words brought you good.
- Ask God to help you to never begin a sentence with, "I shouldn't say this but . . ." or to even listen to a sentence that begins with those words.
- Ask God to show you when you are about to use your tongue for evil, so that you can immediately stop speaking.
- Ask God to fill your mind and your mouth with his words.

MARCHING ORDERS

Use your tongue for good and not evil.

NIV MILITARY WIVES'
NEW TESTAMENT WITH
PSALMS & PROVERBS

EXECUTIVE EDITOR: Timothy J. Beals

GENERAL EDITOR: Jocelyn Green

MANAGING EDITOR: Amy Ballor

EDITORIAL ASSISTANCE: Natalie J. Block, Jane Haradine

THEOLOGICAL REVIEW: Andrew Sloan, M.Div., Oral Roberts University

INTERIOR AND COVER DESIGN: Jamie DeBruyn

INTERIOR TYPESETTING: Mark Sheeres, Matthew Van Zomeren, and Katherine Lloyd

GUARANTEE

NOTES

NOTES

NOTES

NOTES

NOTES

NOTES

NOTES

NOTES

NOTES